Arab Society

Class, Gender, Power, and Development

ARAB SOCIETY

Class, Gender, Power, and Development

Edited by
Nicholas S. Hopkins
Saad Eddin Ibrahim

The American University in Cairo Press

Cairo New York

Copyright © 1997, 2006 by
The American University in Cairo Press
113 Sharia Kasr el Aini, Cairo, Egypt
420 Fifth Avenue, New York 10018
www.aucpress.com

Third edition
Fifth printing with new Afterword 2006

First edition published in 1977 under the title *Arab Society in Transition*
Second edition published in 1985 under the title *Arab Society: Social Science Perspectives*

Dar el Kutub No. 7314/96
ISBN 977 424 404 4

Printed in Egypt

Contents

Preface

This book of readings has a long history. It was conceived to fill a very special need. "Arab Society" is the title of a course taught at the American University in Cairo and required of all undergraduates, as part of AUC's Core Curriculum program. The purpose of this course is to introduce university students to the major social and cultural parameters and problems of Arab society and to investigate the social bases for Arab unity. It follows courses in Arab literature and history, as well as courses in scientific thinking, philosophic thinking, and a general survey of major ideas, the "core seminar." "Arab Society" is thus in some sense the capstone course of the core curriculum sequence.

Both the editors joined the faculty of the American University in Cairo in 1975 and began teaching this course. It was quickly apparent that the reading material for the students enrolled in this course was not satisfactory. We began experimenting, in the spring of 1976, with a number of readings (journal articles, book chapters, and so on) in our sections of "Arab Society." From these experiments, the first edition, under the title of *Arab Society in Transition* was prepared, and was ready for use in the spring semester of 1978. The first edition did yeoman service for us but it finally went out of print. We elected to prepare a new edition, in part based on the first edition, but mostly containing new material. This second edition, *Arab Society: Social Science Perspectives* (1985), has lasted us for over twelve years, and now is sorely in need of replacement by more contemporary articles and selections. This time we opted to discard everything we had been using and start with a completely fresh selection. Hence this third version of our reader, which we offer under the title of *Arab Society: Class, Gender, Power, and Development.*

Once again, our choice of selections was based on student response to the articles, readability, our own sense of a coherent overall package, an effort to achieve geographic balance, a preference for recent articles that would not date too quickly, a desire to present a variety of methodological and theoretical approaches, and the need to present a large number of views from inside Arab society. This last consideration was an important one for us. We have continued to make a special effort to locate and include material written by Arab social scientists.

The task of selection in 1995–1997 was different from our first effort in 1976–1978. The various fields that make up the study of the Arab world have changed in nature and in emphasis, and it would not have been possible simply to have plugged in an up-to-date piece in the place of each discarded one. It is also true that although some issues remain current, new ones have emerged, and others have changed. Thus it proved very hard in this edition not to be overwhelmed by pieces in which gender played a central role; the concern with gender (or with women) has largely replaced a concern with family that we found in the 1970s. Two new areas that we have endeavored to include are the issue of human rights and the problems relating to environmental preservation and sustainability. Given the absorption of the media with the role of religion (Islam) in the Arab world, it is remarkable how difficult it was to find suitable selections conveying a sense of what it means to be a Muslim, of one sort or another, in the contemporary Arab world; most writing is concerned with the political threat alleged to be inherent in Islam and was not suitable for us. On the other hand, twenty years have done nothing to resolve the population problem (except that there is now less concern with migration to the oil countries, but not necessarily less migration). The Palestinian issue has seen the intifada come and go, various peace efforts move from hope to frustration, and remains as intractable as ever. The Arab world is perhaps overall slightly more prosperous, but is still in a precarious slot in the world system. Divisions between rich and poor individuals remain; divisions between and within countries bedevil the political scene; there is plenty of tension, anxiety, and anger. One consequence from our point of view is that there are still many countries in the Arab world where on-the-spot field research in the social sciences is difficult or impossible; this affects the material from which we can choose.

We have divided the material into seven sections corresponding to a fourteen-week semester. Instructors may very well prefer other arrangements. Further thoughts on our arrangement are given in the introductions to each section. In the first section we preferred to present material giving an overview of Arab society, and also a suggestion of contrasting methods. The second section then covers issues of population policy and demography, and should be used in conjunction with some of the material in the Statistical Abstract. We interpret population somewhat broadly to include living conditions. In the third section we include material on family and gender, though other related material is scattered throughout the book. The fourth section contains four selections on rural development issues in the Arab world. In the fifth section we move on to the political sociology of the Arab world, seen through various case studies. Two areas, environment and human rights, are then examined in the sixth section. And the final section incorporates material on the social role of religion. Thus we both begin and end at a fairly general level, and have more detailed studies in between.

Although this collection is designed for our students at the American University in Cairo, we feel that it should appeal to a wider scholarly and lay audience interested in learning more about the processes of social change in the Arab world. In particular we hope that it will be of use in other universities in the Arab world and in the United States. It is not intended to deal directly with current events in the Arab world, but to provide the scholarly social science background essential for an informed understanding of those events. The coverage ranges from family process to political process, from the study of religious notions at the village level to the analysis of large-scale demographic trends.

We want to offer our thanks first of all to our fellow instructors in "Arab Society," and especially those who have offered their comments and advice over the years: Dr. Soraya Altorki, Ms. Afaf al-Bassam, Dr. Donald Cole, Dr. Frank Fanselow, Dr. Jawad Fatayer, Ms. Nemat Guenena, Dr. Nazek Nosseir, Dr. Sami Omar, Dr. Malak Rouchdy, Dr. Madiha al-Safty, Dr. Saneya Saleh, Dr. Ted Swedenburg, and Dr. James Toth. Needless to say none of them bears any responsibility for the final choices.

Thanks are due to the researchers at the Ibn Khaldoun Center, especially Ms. Yvette Fayez Ishaq and Ms. Sarah El-Deeb, who prepared some of the quantitative materials and carried out the word processing of the introductory sections.

We want to thank most warmly the generations of students who have, knowingly or not, offered their criticisms of the various reading selections we were trying out on them.

Our thanks also to the staff at the American University in Cairo Press for their help in this intricate project—especially to Simon O'Rourke and Alex Dessouky, and to Mark Linz for general support. Our thanks, too, to the authors who took the time to answer individual queries.

Our thanks to those who authorized the use of materials for which they hold copyright are expressed at the bottom of the first page of each selection. However, it is not out of place to express our gratitude in general to these organizations and individuals who have been so cooperative throughout the lengthy process of constructing this book.

Statistical Abstract of the Arab World

Table 1

Population, area, and other features, by country

	Population in 1993 (millions)[1]	Area[2] ('000 km[2])	Rural population[3] (% of total)	Main telephone lines[4] (per 100 people)	Military expenditures, 1990–91[5] (as % of combined education and health expenditures)
Algeria	26.7	2,382	46	3.4	11
Bahrain	0.5	0.7	11	19.4	41
Comoros	0.5	2.2	71	0.7	–
Djibouti	0.6	23	18	1.4	–
Egypt	56.4	1,001	56	3.6	52
Iraq	19.5	438	27	3.6	271
Jordan	4.1	89	30	6.4	138
Kuwait	1.8	18	4	16.1	88
Lebanon	3.9	10	14	11.1	–
Libya	5.0	1,760	15	–	71
Mauritania	2.2	1,026	49	0.4	40
Morocco	25.9	447	53	1.9	72
Oman	2.0	212	88	7.6	293
Qatar	0.5	11	9	21.9	192
Saudi Arabia	17.4	2,150	21	8.4	151
Somalia	9.0	638	75	0.2	200
Sudan	26.6	2,506	76	0.2	44
Syria	13.7	185	49	3.9	373
Tunisia	8.7	164	44	4.1	31
UAE	1.8	84	17	29.5	44
Yemen	13.2	528	68	1.1	197
West Bank/Gaza	–	6	–	–	–
Total	240.0	13,681			

Sources:
1. *World Development Report 1995*, Tables 1 & 1a. Washington: World Bank (Oxford University Press), 1995.
2. Idem.
3. *Human Development Report 1996*, Table 8. New York: UNDP and Oxford University Press, 1996.
4. Ibid, Table 15.
5. Ibid, Table 19.

Table 2

Economic indicators, by country

	GNP 1989 (US$ billion)	GNP per capita, 1993 (US$)[1]	GNP average annual growth per capita, 1980–1993 (%)[2]	Official development assistance per capita, 1993 [3] ($ equivalent)
Algeria	53.1	1,780	-0.8	13.4
Bahrain	3.0	8,030	-2.9	–
Comoros	0.2	560	-0.4	–
Djibouti	0.3	780	–	–
Egypt	32.5	660	+2.8	40.8
Iraq	35.0	b	–	–
Jordan	5.3	1,190	–	59.7
Kuwait	33.1	19,360	-4.3	1.5
Lebanon	2.3	b	–	–
Libya	23.0	c	–	–
Mauritania	0.9	500	-0.8	153.2
Morocco	22.1	1,040	+1.2	29.0
Oman	7.8	4,850	+3.4	538.8
Qatar	4.1	15,030	-7.2	–
Saudi Arabia	90.0	–	-3.6	2.0
Somalia	1.0	a	–	–
Sudan	10.1	a	–	–
Syria	12.4	b	–	–
Tunisia	10.1	1,720	+1.2	28.9
UAE	28.4	21,430	-4.4	-4.8
Yemen	8.4	–	–	23.4
West Bank/Gaza		b	–	
Total Arab world	383.1[d]			

Sources:

1. Michael Kidron and Ronald Segal, *The New State of the World Atlas.* New York: Simon and Schuster, 1991.

2. *World Development Report 1995*, Tables 1 and 1a. Washington: World Bank (Oxford University Press), 1995.

3. Ibid., Table 19.

Notes:

[a] Somalia and Sudan are considered to be low income, i.e., less than $695 per capita.

[b] Iraq, Lebanon, Syria, and West Bank/Gaza are considered to be lower-middle income, i.e., $696 to $2,785.

[c] Libya is considered to be upper-middle income, i.e., $2,786 to $8,625.

[d] The total GNP for the Arab world is between that of Canada and Spain.

Table 3

Political systems

	Capital city	Type of government	Date of independence from colonial rule	Date of significant political change
Algeria	Algiers	Republic	1962	
Bahrain	Manama	Monarchy	1971	
Comoros	Moroni	Republic	1975	
Djibouti	Djibouti	Republic	1977	
Egypt[a,c]	Cairo	Republic	1923/36/56	1952
Iraq[c]	Baghdad	Republic	1932	1958
Jordan	Amman	Monarchy	1946	
Kuwait	Kuwait	Monarchy	1961	
Lebanon[b]	Beirut	Republic	1941/46	
Libya[c]	Tripoli	Republic	1952	1969
Mauritania	Nouakchott	Republic	1960	
Morocco	Rabat	Monarchy	1956	
Oman[c]	Muscat	Monarchy	1970	1970
Qatar	Doha	Monarchy	1971	
Saudi Arabia	Riyadh	Monarchy	1932	
Somalia	Mogadishu	Republic	1960	
Sudan	Khartoum	Republic	1956	
Syria[b]	Damascus	Republic	1941/46	
Tunisia	Tunis	Republic	1956	
UAE	Abu Dhabi	Monarchy	1971	
Yemen[c]	Sana'a	Republic	1962	1962

Notes:

[a] Egypt had internal self-government in 1923, was internationally recognized in 1936, overthrew the monarchy in 1952, and was free of foreign troops in 1956. "Independence" is a process more than an event.

[b] Lebanon and Syria were under French mandate from 1920, partly independent from 1941, and fully so from 1946, when they were already UN members.

[c] In Egypt, Iraq, Libya, and Yemen the replacement of the monarchy by a republic was a key date. In Oman the overthrow of Sa'id by Qabus marked a major change.

Arab founding members of the UN: Egypt, Iraq, Lebanon, Saudi Arabia, Syria.

Founding members of the Arab League: Egypt, Iraq, Jordan, Lebanon, Saudi Arabia, Syria, Yemen.

Table 4

Demographic indicators, by country

	Infant mortality rate per 1000 live births, 1993[1]	Total fertility rate, 1992[2]	Annual population growth rate, 1960–1993 (%)[3]	Annual population growth rate, 1993–2000 (%)[4]
Algeria	54	3.9	2.8	2.2
Bahrain	18	3.8	3.8	2.4
Comoros	88	7.1	3.2	3.6
Djibouti	114	5.8	5.9	2.1
Egypt	66	3.9	2.4	2.0
Iraq	58	5.7	3.2	2.9
Jordan	35	5.6	3.3	3.8
Kuwait	18	3.1	5.8	0.3
Lebanon	34	3.1	1.3	2.3
Libya	67	6.4	4.1	3.4
Mauritania	100	5.4	2.4	2.6
Morocco	67	3.8	2.5	1.9
Oman	29	7.2	3.9	4.0
Qatar	20	4.3	7.8	1.9
Saudi Arabia	28	6.4	4.4	3.1
Somalia	121	7.0	2.6	2.7
Sudan	77	5.7	2.7	2.7
Syria	39	5.9	3.4	3.4
Tunisia	43	3.2	2.2	1.8
UAE	18	4.2	9.5	2.1
Yemen	119	7.6	2.8	3.7

Sources:
1. *Human Development Report 1996,* Table 6.. New York: UNDP and Oxford University Press, 1996.
2. Ibid., Table 9.
3. Ibid., Table 21
4. Ibid., Table 21

Table 5

Social groups, languages, and religions

This listing approximates the situation of distinctive social categories in the Arab world, with an emphasis on those set off by language (L) or by religion (R). Some but not all are minorities in the sociological sense of the term. The percentages indicate an order of magnitude more than an exact count; where none are given the numbers are small. Arabic-speaking Sunni Muslims are generally but not always the majority.

Algeria	L:	Berbers, including Amazigh (25%).
	R:	Ibadhites
Bahrain	R:	Shi'a(70%), Sunni (30%)
Comoros	L:	Comorian Swahili (majority)
Djibouti	L:	Somali (47%), Afar (37%)
Egypt	R:	Christians (7%)
	L:	Nubians; Beja; Berber (<1%)
Iraq	L:	Kurds (20%), Turkmen, etc.
	R:	Shi'a (55%), Sunni Arab + Kurd (40%); Christians (3%)
Jordan	R:	Christians (8%)
		Social Groups: Circassians
Kuwait	R:	Shi'a(20%), Sunni (80%)
Lebanon	R:	Christians (Maronites; Greek Orthodox; Greek Catholics; Armenians) (25–30%)
		Muslims (Shi'a; Sunni; Druze; Alawites) (70–75%)
Libya	L:	Berber (5–10%)
Mauritania	L:	speakers of African languages (Wolof, Tukulor, Soninke, etc.) (30%)
Morocco	L:	Berber languages (33%)
Oman	R:	Ibadhites (75%), Sunni (25%)
	L:	South Arabian languages
Qatar	–	
Saudi Arabia	R:	Shi'a(5%)
Somalia	L:	Somali (90%), Bantu languages
Sudan	L:	Various African languages (60%)
	R:	Christians (5%) and pagans (18%); Muslims (70%)
Syria	R:	Christians, incl. Armenians (10%);
		Alawites + Druze (16%); Sunni (74%)
Tunisia	L:	Berber (<1%)
	R:	Ibadhites (<1%)
UAE	–	
Yemen	R:	Sunni (53%); Shi'a(46%); Ismaili

Historically the major concentrations of Jews in the Arab world were in North Africa (Morocco, Algeria, Tunisia, and Libya), in Iraq, and in Yemen. There were also proportionately smaller Jewish communities in Syria, Lebanon, Palestine, and Egypt. Only small groups remain.

There are recent migrants with distinctive backgrounds in the Gulf countries. Many are from the Indian subcontinent, and include Hindus and Christians as well as Muslims. There are also ethnic Persians, Baluches, Filipinos, etc.

There are Arab minorities in Turkey, Iran, Israel (16%), Chad, and Mali. In addition, there is an Arab diaspora that covers much of Europe, the Americas, Australia.

Table 6
Human Development Index (HDI) for the Arab World (1993 data)

Arab country ranking	World Ranking (out of 174)	Human Development Index (HDI)[a]	Gender-related development index (GDI)[b]	Life expectancy (years)	Adult literacy rate (%)	Real GDP (PPP $)[c] per capita	(Arab populations in millions in 1996)
High Human Development (57 countries)		0.901		73.8	97.2	14,922	(5.0)
1 Bahrain	39	0.866	0.276	71.7	84.1	15,500	(0.6)
2 United Arab Emirates	42	0.864	0.710	73.9	78.2	20,940	(1.9)
3 Qatar	50	0.839	0.700	70.6	78.5	22,910	(0.7)
4 Kuwait	51	0.836	0.719	75.0	77.4	21,630	(1.8)
Medium Human Development	(69)	0.674		67.0	80.7	3,044	(202.1)
5 Libya	59	0.792	0.633	63.4	73.7	6,125	(5.4)
6 Saudi Arabia	63	0.771	0.551	69.9	61.3	5,894	(19.4)
7 Algeria	69	0.746	0.596	67.3	58.8	5,570	(29.0)
8 Jordan	70	0.741	–	68.1	84.8	4,380	(4.4)
9 Tunisia	78	0.727	0.647	68.0	64.1	4,950	(9.2)
10 Oman	82	0.716	–	69.8	35.0	10,420	(2.3)
11 Syria	92	0.690	0.591	67.3	68.7	4,196	(15.6)
12 Lebanon	97	0.664	0.615	68.7	91.7	2,500	(3.8)
13 Egypt	106	0.610	0.545	63.9	49.8	2,200	(64.0)
14 Iraq	109	0.599	0.486	66.1	55.7	3,413	(21.4)
15 Morocco	123	0.534	0.391	63.6	41.7	3,270	(27.6)
Low Human Development	(48)	0.396		56.0	48.9	1,241	(56.6)
16 Comoros Islands	139	0.399	0.391	56.2	56.2	1,130	(0.6)
17 Yemen	142	0.366	0.311	50.4	41.1	1,600	(14.7)
18 Sudan	146	0.359	0.327	53.2	43.8	1,350	(28.9)
19 Mauritania	149	0.353	0.338	51.7	36.7	1,610	(2.3)
20 Djibouti	164	0.287	–	48.4	44.2	775	(0.6)
21 Somalia	172	0.221	–	47.2	24.9	712	(9.5)
All developing countries		0.563		61.8	68.8	2,696	
Least developed countries		0.331		51.0	46.5	898	
Industrial countries		0.909		74.3	98.3	15,136	
World averages		0.746		63.0	76.3	5,428	

Source: Human Development Report 1996, compiled from Tables 1 and 2. New York: UNDP and Oxford University Press, 1996.

Notes to Table 6 (opposite):

a The human development index (HDI) measures the average achievement in basic human capabilities, and indicates whether all people in a country lead a long and healthy life, are educated and knowledgeable, and enjoy a decent standard of living.
For details on how the index is calculated, see *Human Development Report 1996.*
The rank numbers refer to the rank of each country in the total list of 174 countries.
b The gender-related development index (GDI) measures achievement in the same basic capabilities as the HDI does, but takes note of inequality in achievement between women and men.
c Purchasing power parity.

Table 7

Highlights of the Egyptian census of 1996

Total population	
1996	61,452,382
1986	50,504,238

There were estimated to be 2,180,000 temporary migrants in 1996; there were 2,250,000 in 1986. These figures are included in the totals. There were estimated to be 720,000 permanent migrants in 1996.

Percentage of total population that is	
male	51.2
female	48.8
(954 females for every 1000 males)	
under 15 years old	35
1986	38.8
(birth rate is falling)	
Muslim	93.7 (57.6 million)
Christian	6.2 (3.8 million)
literate	61.4
1986	50.4
holding a higher education degree	7.3
1986	4.3
Rate of population growth	2.1
1986	2.8
Average family size[a]	4.6 persons
1986	4.9 persons
Percentage of buildings hooked up to potable water network	53.7
(73.5 percent of households)	
Percentage of buildings with electricity	80.3
(95.7 percent of households)	

1,957,445 (28.8 percent) of the 6,789,479 people in Cairo governorate live in informal housing. The figures are similar for other governorates.

Sources: Al-Ahram, June 3, 1997, p. 13; *Progrès Egyptien,* June 4, 1997, p. 2

a The average urban family size is 4.3 persons. The average rural family size is 5 persons.

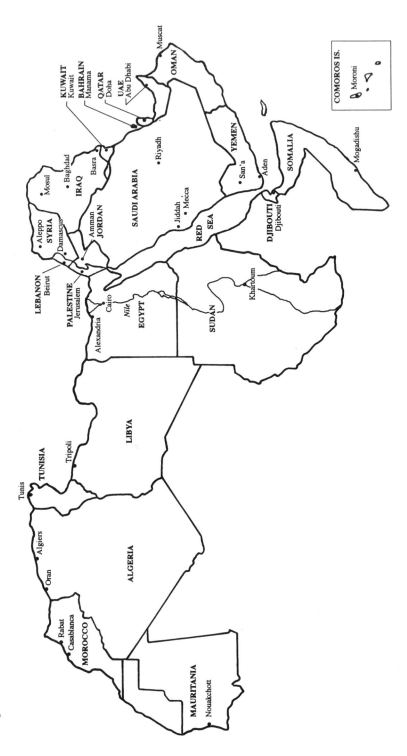

Map of the Arab World Showing Major Cities

One

Introduction

The Social Basis of Arab Unity

The "Arabs" are people who speak the Arabic language, identify themselves as "Arabs," and are nationals or residents of member countries of the League of Arab States. In the late 1990s, the Arabs numbered over 260 million—i.e., about 5 percent of the world's population.

The geographic area in which the Arabs live is a contiguous mass of about 14 million square kilometers. It extends from the shores of the Arab–Persian Gulf in the east to the coasts of Mauritania and Morocco on the Atlantic ocean in the West, and from the slopes of the Anatolian plateau and the Mediterranean Sea in the north to the Sahara desert, Equatoria, and the Indian ocean in the south. Most of the Arab region is desert and consequently has very low population densities, though there are striking concentrations of people in some of the cities and river valleys. The major economic resources of the area are oil and agriculture; the major economic activities, at least until modern times, were farming, herding, and trading.

Islam is the religion of over 90 percent of the population in this huge land mass. The land, the people, and the culture dominated by the Arabic language and by Islam have created, over several centuries, a unique entity called by the Arabs themselves the "Arab Homeland" (al-Watan al-Arabi), the "Arab world," or, as we are calling it in this volume, "Arab Society."

Being an "Arab" does not connote in itself either a particular "race" or a particular religion. Arabs come in all colors (e.g., white, brown, or black) and in many religions (Islam, Christianity, and Judaism). Arabdom and Arabism are purely cultural concepts.

The Arab world is marked by considerable geographical, social, and cultural diversity. Arab society has traditionally been viewed as a trinity of Bedouins, peasants, and urban dwellers, living together in some kind of symbiosis. Detailed studies have tended to stress the differences between these and other categories of people, differences which the social and economic politics of Arab and foreign regimes have long tended to exacerbate.

The area is divided into twenty-two different states and territories ranging in size from the city-states of the Gulf (Bahrain, Qatar, Kuwait) through the agrarian states of the Maghrib and the Fertile Crescent to the overpopulated Nile valley state of Egypt. Many of these states have long individual histories. Egypt has its pharaonic past; Tunisia follows on Carthage; Morocco goes back at least to

1

the Roman occupation of North Africa; and Iraq has roots in Sumeria, Babylonia, and Assyria. Other states are recent creations with arbitrary boundaries resulting from the colonial period, such as the desert states of Mauritania, Libya, Saudi Arabia, or Jordan. At this writing the Palestinian Authority is in a transitional phase, almost but not quite a state in the international legal sense. At present the different political regimes are divided between republics, some military in origin, and various kinds of monarchies. The diversity of the population of many of these states reflects the ebb and flow of empires, and the spread of cultures and religions in the past—thus the concentration of Berber-speakers in the Maghrib, the inclusion of Nuer, Dinka, Azande, Fur, and others in Sudan, and the combination of Christians and Druze in Lebanon.

Arabdom is neither eternal nor is it a creation of yesterday. It has been evolving over more than two millennia. At the earliest period, the "Arabs" were confined to what is known as the Arabian Peninsula, living in tribal formations, and relying for sustenance on herding, trading, and raiding. Whenever their population exceeded the carrying capacity of that peninsula, they quietly migrated to greener pastures of neighboring areas—e.g., the Fertile Crescent and the Nile Valley. It was only with the appearance of the new religion of Islam (A.D. 610) that the Arabs of the peninsula made their forceful march onto the stage of world history. Islam gave the Arab tribes an unprecedented unity, pride, and a sense of sacred mission. Within one century, the Arab Muslims managed to conquer all the leading empires of the time (Roman, Persian, and Byzantine) and to establish their own, extending from the borders of China in East Asia to the Iberian Peninsula in Western Europe. Within this vast empire, an Arab–Islamic civilization flowered, incorporating the legacies and achievements of contemporary and previous cultures and civilization. It was this inclusive outreach which facilitated the two macrosocietal processes that brought about the "Arab world," "Arab culture," "Arab homeland," or "Arab society," as we know them today. These two processes were "Islamization" and "Arabization" of most peoples of the newly created empire, outside the Arabian Peninsula.

Like all empires in history, the Arab Muslim empire decayed, disintegrated, and finally collapsed with the symbolic fall of Baghdad in A.D. 1258 to the non-Muslim, non-Arab Mongols of Central Asia. However, the fall of empires or states does not necessarily entail the perishing of societies or culture. The Arabs and their culture have continued, albeit without sovereignty or political power. In the three centuries after the fall of Baghdad there was a succession of Muslim but non-Arab contenders for the Caliphate. The most successful and long lasting of these contenders were the Ottomans, who established a great Muslim empire of their own. Much of Arabdom became part of the new Muslim Ottoman empire and remained as such from the sixteenth well into the nineteenth century.

Again the Ottoman empire began to decay and to be challenged by the new, more robust industrial powers of Europe. The latter set out to colonize whatever territories they could reach overseas. The competition for colonies among rising European commercial–industrial powers on a world scale gave rise to what became known as the age of "colonialism," which lasted well into the early twentieth century, and targeted the territories of the older empires as well. European colonialism began its encroachment on the Arab provinces of the Ottoman empire in the late eighteenth century and continued to expand for the long century of 1798 to 1918.

The intensity of colonial competition over the Arab world was due not only to the quest for markets and raw materials, but also for its many strategic advantages. The Arab homeland is geographically situated at the center of the "Old World" of Asia, Africa, and Europe; with the high grounds controlling several waterways—e.g., the Strait of Gibraltar, the Suez Canal, the Strait of Bab Al-Mandab, and the Strait of Hormoz.

The colonial period of the nineteenth and twentieth centuries affected the various parts of the Arab world differently. At the beginning of the nineteenth century, most of the Arab world was under at least nominal Ottoman domination. The Ottomans tried to reinforce their hold in Iraq, Yemen, and Libya during that century. But the Maghrib, on Western Europe's doorstep, fell under the colonial domination of France fairly early (Algeria from 1830, Tunisia in 1881, Morocco by 1912) and Egypt was absorbed into the European economic and then political sphere at the same time as a result of its cotton potential and strategic location. The British occupation of Egypt began in 1882. Sudan escaped Egyptian domination under the Mahdi (1881) only to fall under Anglo-Egyptian rule after 1898. But most of the Arabian peninsula never fell under direct European colonial rule, and the Fertile Crescent states of Iraq, Syria, and Lebanon all spent less than a generation under European rule after having remained under the Ottomans until the Allied victory in the First World War. Palestine is a special case, for it has suffered from a multiple imperialism—after the Ottomans, the British held a mandate from 1920 to 1948, and then came the Israelis. The cultural influence resulting from colonial expansion was either French or British (or both, as in Egypt), with smaller areas feeling Italian or Spanish influence. But many countries and the interior parts of most others were only marginally affected by such cultural influences.

The Arab struggle against foreign domination started in the nineteenth century—partly against the Ottomans who, though Muslims, were becoming more despotic towards the Arabs; and partly against the Europeans who were encroaching on them since the Ottomans were unable to defend the Arab world. The Arab struggles since the nineteenth century have had a dual objective: independence and pan-Arab unification. Independence for much of the Arab world was attained between the 1920s and the 1960s. Unification has been far more problematic.

The Arab world is one broad cultural area, but remains politically divided among some twenty-two Arab states, including Palestine. There are also Arab minorities in neighboring countries. This "cultural unity" has been pragmatically reconciled with the "political divisions" by the creation in 1945 of a regional organization known as the League of Arab States (LAS). The Arabs, their world, cultural unity, and political division have been evolving throughout history. Even the cultural boundaries, let alone the political borders, have continued to change. Thus in the 1970s, three new countries in sub-Saharan Africa opted to identify themselves as "Arab" and joined the LAS: Mauritania, Somalia, and Djibouti, followed in the 1990s by the Comoros Islands in the Indian ocean. Of these, only Mauritania has a historic Arabic-speaking majority.

Nevertheless, the quest for Arab political unification has not ceased. There were several attempts at political unification in the 1950s and 1960s, the most important of which was that of Egypt and Syria in February 1958 under the United Arab Republic. But it collapsed in less than four years in September 1961. In the 1980s, sub-Arab regional groupings began to form as "economic cooperation" councils—e.g., the Gulf Cooperation Council (GCC) of the oil-rich states (Saudi Arabia, Kuwait, Bahrain, Qatar, United Arab Emirates, and Oman); the Arab Cooperation Council (ACC)' made up of Egypt, Jordan, Iraq, and Yemen; and the Arab Maghrib Union (AMU), made up of Mauritania, Morocco, Algeria, Tunisia, and Libya. However, these regional subgroupings have not fared very well either. The Iraqi invasion of Kuwait in August 1990 was a traumatic event which split the Arab world and aborted one of these newly created sub-regional councils, the ACC. The latest attempt at unification was that of the two Yemens (the Arab Republic of Yemen or North Yemen, and the People's Republic of Yemen or South Yemen) in April 1990. But even here, the sailing was not as smooth as had been expected. A profound political difference between the southern and northern elites soon escalated into a full-fledged civil war in the summer of 1994, which North Yemen ultimately won, but with much destruction and deep wounds.

This reader treats the Arabs and their respective "sovereign states" as one socio-cultural area—i.e., an Arab society. There are several reasons for such treatment.[1]

First, the Arab political regimes, on the normative prescriptive level, consider their states as parts of one nation. No Arab regime in any of the twenty-two states has dared formally to go against this proclaimed national self-identification. None, in theory, equates its present legal status of a "sovereign state" with that of a "sovereign nation-state." Despite many practices to the contrary, the explicit or implicit assumption is that the present state of affairs, i.e., separation into several sovereign countries, is only "temporary." The prescribed goal, in theory again, is for these separate Arab states ultimately to unite in one "nation-state." This is not asserted today as much as it was in the 1950s and 1960s, but neither has any leader or government gone the other way to negate the prescribed norm. The belief in one Arab Nation to which all Arabs belong is still nominally observed by most regimes at present.

Second, this belief in the importance of one Arab Nation is shared by most people in all countries, classes, and subgroupings of the area extending from Iraq to Morocco. In an attitudinal survey[2] conducted in ten Arab countries (Kuwait, Qatar, Yemen, Jordan, Palestine, Lebanon, Egypt, Sudan, Tunisia, and Morocco), about 80 percent of a cross-section of the adult population identified themselves as Arabs, belonging to one Arab Nation. Of course, there were variations between countries, but in no country did the percentage of people holding this belief fall below 60 percent (e.g., Lebanon, Morocco, and Sudan); it was about 90 percent in others (e.g., Yemen, Kuwait, and Jordan). Underlying this common belief is people's perception of shared language, religion, way of life, and problems. Islam especially was considered crucial in forging the Arab Nation. The majority of those surveyed aspired to see the Arab countries unite politically, although only a minority thought that would happen in the near future.

Third, it is because of both governmental and popular belief in being parts of the same nation that several pan-Arab organizations have been created to foster closer cooperation, if not outright integration. The League of Arab States was established in 1945, and some twenty specialized agencies have sprung up over the last five decades in nearly every field of human endeavor. Countries blessed with oil wealth have found it morally obligatory and politically expedient to set up individual and collective funds to extend aid for development in "poor sister states." Many of these efforts fall short of what "ought to be" in the views of ardent Arab nationalists. Nevertheless, they have given this region of the world an appearance of a "unity" of sorts, hardly matched in any other region of the Third World. Such unity has particularly asserted itself in times of regional crisis (e.g., the Arab–Israeli wars, the 1956 Suez Crisis, the resignation of Nasser in 1967 and his death in 1970, and the 1973 Arab–Israeli [October] war). Even the 1990–91 Gulf crisis (following Iraq's invasion of Kuwait) is evidence of the passionate engagement of all Arabs in the same issue, albeit not with one voice.

Fourth, the increased volume of human movement and interaction across state lines in the last forty years has added a sociological dimension to both the pan-Arab political norms and institutional arrangements. In the 1950s and 1960s, the bulk of interstate human movement was for study and tourism. In the 1970s and 1980s, most of such movement was for work. In the 1990s the interstate movement has been for all purposes including trade and investment.

These reasons, and others, justify looking at the Arab world as one cultural and one societal unit. In this respect, it stands socioculturally at a midpoint between, say, Western Europe and North America—more culturally homogeneous than the former but less politically united than the latter. There are concentric political-cultural-legal identities for most Arabs, all of them salient and readily invocable. The broader political-cultural identity as an "Arab" is relevant when the person is outside the Arab world. The particularistic-country-legal identity (Syrian, Egyptian, Saudi, Iraqi, etc.) is mostly invoked within the Arab world itself, or when crossing sovereign state borders.

Treating the Arab world as one single cultural area and as one Arab society implies an emphasis on the broad cultural "unifiers"—e.g., language, religion, shared traditions, common history, and common aspirations. But there are as many cultural "diversifiers." Thus within the common language there are different dialects, and within the common religion there are denominations and sects. Times of Arab strength and glory are those in which the "unifiers" are invoked. Periods of weakness or decline are those in which the "diversifiers" are manipulated by indigenous or external forces to divide the Arabs. Much of Arab history can be viewed as an interplay between the unifiers and the diversifiers. The great heroes in Arab history are those who stimulated the cultural unifiers, especially in times of external challenge (e.g., Salah al-Din during the Crusades, Nasser in the immediate past). Individual and group loyalties in such times are to Islam, the Arab Nation, or the Motherland. On the other hand, the bleak · moments in Arab history are when the diversifiers get magnified out of proportion and focus the passions and behavior of individuals and groups on primordial and local loyalties—e.g., ethnicity, sect, and tribe. The concerted Arab action in the October War of 1973 was an example of the power of broad unifiers. The civil wars in Lebanon (1975–1985), Sudan (1956–1973, 1983–1996), Iraq (1964–1975, 1991–1996) and Yemen (North, 1964–1967, and between North and South in 1996) are important examples of stimulating and manipulating narrower diversifiers.

Unity and diversity are not the only keys to understanding Arab society. Other parameters could be as helpful. The interplay between forces of "continuity" and forces of "change," for example, account for some of the most heated debates in the Arab world at present. Among these are relations with the West, the so-called "New Global Order," issues of "gender," family planning, human rights, women's rights, minority rights, the role of the state, civil society, the private sector, limits of economic and sociopolitical liberalization, and democratization. Even issues of identity and religion are being confronted anew. Some of these battles were believed to have been settled several decades ago, but we have been discovering otherwise in recent years. Some of these battles were fought in the 1950s and 1960s under the banners of pan-Arab nationalism against country-based patriotism, "socialism" against "feudalism" or "capitalism," anti-Western against pro-Western.

Since the late 1970s, and especially with the Iranian Islamic Revolution in 1978, Islamic discourse has dominated much of the public debate. Pan-Islamism has emerged as a competing paradigm contending for public space with other paradigms, older and newer. Among the older is, of course, the pan-Arabism of which Egypt's Nasser was the symbol in the 1950s and 1960s. Among the newer paradigms are the so-called "New Middle East" and the "Euro-Mediterranean Partnership." While the Pan-Islamic vision for the region would incorporate the entire Arab world and at least Turkey and Iran—and possibly the new Islamic Central Asian republics—it excludes Israel and stays at a distance, not necessarily hostile, from the West.

The New Middle East vision was articulated and popularized by Israeli Prime Minister Shimon Peres and the United States; it includes Israel as well as the non-Arab states of the region, and calls for American, European, and Japanese economic partnership. This vision has evolved with the peace process to settle the protracted Arab–Israeli conflict over Palestine. Though the peace process started with Egypt's President Sadat's initiative (November 1977), the Israelis and Americans contend that without economic cooperation, any peace process is bound to falter or even be easily reversed. Three economic summits were held in 1994 (Casablanca), 1995 (Amman), and 1996 (Cairo) in which Arab and Israeli businessmen, along with counterparts from the US and Europe deliberated ways and means of bringing about this New Middle East in concrete terms. However, many outspoken Arab intellectuals have been hostile to the "New Middle East" vision, as they see in this "normalization" a weakening of Arab identity, a cultural-political legitimation of Israel, and a strategic-economic-technological hegemony of Israel over the Arab world.

The Euro-Mediterranean partnership vision of the Arab Middle East is also new, championed by the northern Mediterranean countries of France, Italy, Spain, Portugal, and Greece. It was formally enunciated in what came to be known as the Barcelona Declaration (1995). It envisaged a full economic partnership among countries bordering the Mediterranean, which include many Arab countries and Israel, but not the US. Many Arab activists are lukewarm toward it, but are not as hostile toward the Mediterranean vision as they are toward the New Middle East vision.

While more appealing to the rank-and-file Arabs, the two indigenous visions, i.e., Pan-Arabism and Pan-Islamism, have yet to develop the economic and organizational capacity which the two exogenous visions have.

We know too well that "blueprints" for the Arab Middle Eastern region rarely materialize as originally envisioned. Reality unfolds as millions of ordinary people struggle for survival, and continuously negotiate, transact, cooperate, compete, and conflict on the microlevel. While this reader attempts to draw and make sense of the big picture, it is ultimately the grassroots that seem to shape the march of Arab society.

In This Section

The three articles in this section introduce the study of the Arab world from the point of view of sociology and anthropology. Their common themes are the centrality of change, and the importance of two major institutional structures, class and the state, in understanding the Arab world. Two of the pieces take a macrosociological viewpoint; Farsoun focuses on the Arab East, the Mashriq, while Hermassi concentrates on the Arab West, the Maghrib. Altorki and Cole analyze similar questions from the point of view of a single community, 'Unayzah, in central Saudi Arabia, whose social dynamics parallel that of many other Arab communities.

Samih Farsoun argues that the class structure of the Arab world is a reflection of the economic organization of society on the one hand, and of state policy on the other. A class is a group of people who are alike in that they share the same position within the overall system (reflecting the division of labor within a social organization of production). Farsoun stresses the integration of the countries of the Mashriq into a unified system based on oil production. Thus the Arab world has a single class system, which serves to unify it. The state is simultaneously the traditional bureaucracy, the organizer of development, and the instrument of political repression. Its role is changing with the pressure for "liberalization," i.e., a market-oriented economy that aims to reduce state subsidies and thus rupture the contract between state and people. In this context, the rise of consumerism parallels the rise of individualism, and the social fabric of the Arab world appears fractured. An implicit question is whether classes in the Arab world derive more from the organization of production, distribution, and consumption, or from the competition for influence and control within the state apparatus, i.e., from economics or power.

Soraya Altorki and Donald Cole describe the changing role of the state and the shifting identity of classes in the context of a single Mashriqi community, but the implications of their argument are far-ranging. 'Unayzah has lost its political autonomy through its absorption into the Kingdom of Saudi Arabia. People are materially better off through the spread of education and salaried employment; the rapid increase in income due to the oil boom of the post-1973 period has enabled much new construction and encouraged consumption. New patterns of socializing have emerged, and the role of women continues strong. The new wealth has benefited some more than others. But there are serious questions as to the sustainability of this evolution, whether seen ecologically in the new forms of agriculture, or economically in the reliance of the people on sources of income outside their immediate control.

Abdelbaki Hermassi also analyzes the role of classes in the political competition around the state in the Maghrib. He stresses the problematic legitimacy of the regimes of the Mahgribi states, based initially on their success in the nationalist struggle for independence, but now seeking a new basis. Initially the states had a tendency to take on all tasks, to ensure identity and justice, but the states are now retreating in the name of market principles, and the poor feel abandoned. There are common forces for change: new political parties, human rights organizations, and women's movements, but also Islamism. To some extent the struggle between the Islamists and the state is a class struggle involving the elites and the middle classes on the side of the state.

Thus the three pieces in this section raise the question of the social and cultural unity of the Arab world. The challenge is to develop a common analytic language for the key processes and institutions. The material in this section, and in the book as a whole, raises the question of whether there are general social change processes, or a common class structure, in the Arab world. Are there parallel social and political processes based on similar underlying structures? How are alternative patterns—and they surely exist—explicable?

Notes

1   This argument is excerpted from Saad Eddin Ibrahim, *The New Arab Social Order* (Boulder: Westview Press, 1982), pp. 123–25.
2   Saad Eddin Ibrahim, *Trends of Arab Public Opinion Toward Arab Unity* (in Arabic) (Beirut: Center for Arab Unity Studies, 1980), pp. 75–85.

1

Class Structure and Social Change in the Arab World

Samih K. Farsoun

The study of the class structure and dynamics of the Arab world is very difficult, given the diversity of the region, and given the spotty and uneven character of relevant data. Difficult as it is to draw a picture of the contemporary class
structure and dynamics of the Arab world, it seems an almost impossible task to
attempt a projection a decade into the future. Perhaps the best approach is to
sketch out a synoptic view of major developments of social structure and state,
then attempt to draw out in terms of these changes the derivative class formations and class dynamics. This in turn will enable us to make some commentary
on the potential political directions internal to major Arab countries and in the
region as a whole.[1]

Political Economy of the Arab World

The Arab world—divided into relatively distinct regions, the Mashriq and the
Maghrib—has experienced three broad phases in its modern political economy.
In the Mashriq, the first phase was characterized by an integrated precapitalist
economy under the Ottomans.[2] The second was a period of European colonization which resulted in political, economic, and social fragmentation of the area.
The third has been the post-World War II period of politically independent and
Balkanized nation-states. Despite a period of radical political and economic
nationalism during the 1960s, the Arab world in the 1970s and 1980s experienced accelerating integration into a new Western division of labor. This new
division of labor is characterized by an international circulation of capital and
labor. The oil-rich Mashriq countries export money capital along with oil and
import labor power and vast varieties of commodities and consumer goods.[3]
While exporting money capital to the West, the oil-rich nations import labor
power from the oil-poor Arab countries, thus integrating the Mashriq as a region
into the new international division of labor.

On the other hand, the Maghrib exports labor power to Europe and imports
tourists/consumers from the north. The oil-poor Arab countries have become the

Reprinted from Hisham Sharabi, ed., *The Next Arab Decade* (Boulder: Westview Press,
1988), pp. 221–38. Reprinted by permission. Samih K. Farsoun is a professor of sociology at American University in Washington, D.C.

locus for the reproduction of major supplies of labor power for European and oil-rich Arab states. In this sense these Arab countries have emerged as labor reserves for the labor-hungry nations of Europe and the oil-rich states.[4] Labor-exporting Arab countries import monetary remittances from expatriate labor.[5] The size of worker remittances as a percentage of total exports reached 28 percent for Egypt, 43 percent for Morocco, 198 percent for Jordan, and 5,897 percent for Yemen.[6]

The process of accelerated integration into the new international division of labor has had its consequences for both the individual Arab countries and the region as a whole. The Arab Mashriq is undergoing its own division of labor in response to regional dynamics and the more powerful dynamics of its linkage to Western capital. Elements of Arab Mashriq regional integration are the already-noted movement of labor and commodities accompanied by the equally massive counterflow of monetary capital. In addition to remittances from individuals, the capital counterflow includes bilateral state-to-state aid, joint Arab institutional aid, joint Arab investment capital, and direct private investment. The flow of such massive amounts of capital has energized the economic expansion of oil-poor Arab countries. The whole Mashriq has become one "oil economy," as Roger Owen argues,[7] while the Maghrib remains divided and unintegrated economically.

Paradoxically, increasing Mashriq regional integration has been taking place simultaneously with the process of greater consolidation of individual Arab countries' national economies, yet this seemingly contradictory development is in large part due to the fact that the processes working for the greater integration of the Arab Mashriq are weak by comparison to those integrating each of the Arab countries, individually, into the international division of labor.

Accompanying the region's accelerated integration into the world economy, a decline in subsistence production and other transformations have taken place.[8] Accordingly, massive occupational shifts from agricultural to industrial and service activities have occurred.[9] The agricultural sector in the various Arab nations has been undergoing increasing transformation, which is leading to class changes in the rural areas. This is not only forcing people off the land, but is also creating new rural social relations. There is, thus, a massive exodus of surplus agricultural labor, in particular poor, unskilled, and young farmers or peasants, to the urban conglomerations and to the oil-rich states. Two specific aspects of these developments are noteworthy: one is the marginalization of Arab women from production in those areas where commercial agriculture has taken root, and the second is the proletarianization of the young male migrant. One other derivative feature is of long-term consquence. Infitah (economic liberalization) policies of oil-poor nations have led to a process of economic denationalization and the increasing reprivatization of the economy, which allows the growth of new entrepreneurs and a new bourgeoisie in both rural and urban areas.

However, the significance of the policies of infitah and reprivatization have differed in different Arab states. For example, these two policies were instituted earliest (in the early 1970s) and most extensively by Anwar al-Sadat in Egypt. In Sudan, North Yemen, Syria, and Iran, they were introduced later, in lesser scope and differently. Algeria, since Boumedienne, has become the latest of the radical nationalist states to quietly undertake a version of such policies. While Sadat announced the introduction of these policies with much political fanfare coupled with an exaggerated promise of well-being for all Egyptians, the leaders of the latter states introduced "liberalization" quietly, usually under an ideological rubric of reform. Of course, in the oil-rich countries, accelerated integration into the world economy produced a quantum leap of commercialization and the final destruction of the subsistence economy.

In the oil-poor Arab countries, and also Iraq, the previously radical nationalist regimes of the 1960s instituted extensive land reform which broke up the vast holdings of the feudal landlords and distributed some of the confiscated land to peasants and other small farmers. Their agrarian policy over the years created a new kulak class of landowners. This class, with the help of the state, increasingly rationalized its agricultural production and introduced scientific farming and rural wage labor in place of tenancy, sharecropping, and other precapitalist forms of relations of production. These developments stimulated further the rural-to-urban exodus. In oil-rich countries (but to a lesser extent in Libya than in the rest), settlement of nomads with the help of enormous state subsidies is also creating a rural landowning bourgeoisie which in Saudi Arabia is using expatriate wage labor.

Commercialization of agriculture in the Arab world has come to mean increasing dependency on state economic policy regarding infrastructure, financing, pricing, price supports, subsidies, and import policies concerning farm equipment, fertilizers, pesticides, warehousing, transport, and marketing. Thus, through the infitah policies of the 1970s, well-connected agrarian capitalists have increasingly gained the advantage over others in a process which has begun a more intensive concentration and capitalization of the countryside and a deeper structural change there. While this analytical description is general, research is needed to delineate and analyze country-specific transformations.

Arab industrial growth is very uneven[10] and generally has a weak financial base, except of course in oil-related industries in oil-rich states. Arab state industrialization is highly differentiated in both the depth and the level of industrial and technical development.[11] There seems to be a dual tendency of industrial centralization and concentration in oil-producing states and some decentralization and deconcentration in the labor-exporting oil-poor nations. Of course, Iraq and Algeria share aspects of both oil-poor and oil-rich states. Import substitution, textiles, and some high-technology and heavy industries are characteristic of the oil-poor states. The older industries, such as textile and steel (in

Egypt, for example), are stagnating. The new high-tech industries have not taken solid root, and the transition from old, declining industries to new ones is not taking place rapidly or smoothly. It is problematic socially, politically, and economically.

In general, Arab industry has a weak competitive position both in the region and internationally (except, of course, for the extractive oil industry—but not for petrochemicals). This weakness, as well as the particular structure of the regional and individual state industries, is directly related to Arab state policy in regard to finance, subsidy, import regulation, and marketing. The status of the public, mixed, and private industrial sectors in individual Arab states needs detailed study. The Arab industrial bourgeoisies are weak, much too small and insecure to make a significant impact in the present Arab political economy. The local bourgeoisies cannot compete with Western capital and must either complement Western or state capital or enter into weak areas of business. While studies on and plans for pan-Arab economic—including industrial—development abound, few concrete results have materialized.

Industrial development, largely capital-intensive, has not absorbed very large numbers of the workers who have been displaced from the rural areas. Migrant Arab labor is employed mostly in services and construction. Hardly any Arab country has more than 15 percent of its labor force in industry.[12] Displaced villagers swell the urban mass of the unemployed and the underemployed in the oil-poor Arab states. The older and declining industries of the oil-poor countries, with their more skilled and unionized workers, are likely to suffer attrition in employment and worsening working conditions. The new high-tech industries will have such a diversified and unorganized group of workers that they will add to the variation and fragmentation of the various Arab countries' working classes. This, in addition to a growing internal differentiation of the working class, will have important future social and political implications. That is, an increasingly differentiated and fragmented working class will produce new and diverse and fragmented styles of political action in the future.

In the Arab world, real estate capital has assumed major significance by absorbing large amounts of private savings, bank capital, and in some states (principally the oil-producing ones) government subsidy. This investment pattern has reflected itself in the investments that Arab entrepreneurs have been making in Western industrial countries. In the Arab world, however, real estate investment is not restricted to the new rich or the wealthy. The small savings of many a returning labor migrant also have been invested in real estate.[13] The popularization of real estate investment is caused not only by housing shortages, but in part also by the security of such investments. Furthermore, real estate holdings do not interfere with other occupations and have become an important source of income to an increasing number of families.

Rent income, small business investment income, and possibly income from wages or other labor have emerged as key sources for an increasing number of multiple-income households. This pattern, which has been accelerating since the beginning of the oil decade, clearly blurs class lines, decreases the likelihood of class consciousness and class-based politics, and increases the chances for new styles of social and political action. What form this action will take in rich oil-producing states and in oil-poor, labor-exporting countries is difficult to predict. It will derive from the increasingly fragmented nature of Arab societies.

Perhaps of greatest significance in this structural fragmentation is the reproduction in Arab Mashriq societies of petty commodity producers and distributors (including services). This is the great mass of very small-scale family enterprises and of self-employed merchants, manufacturers and artisans, repairmen, service and transport workers, and others in the rural areas.[14] Petty commodity producers and distributors form an especially large part of the "informal sector" (which includes women) or of the so-called "underground economy." Most of these petty economic activities are traditional in style of organization and social relations of work (patronage), that is, in the labor process. Such "old" petty commodity producers and distributors have been accompanied by "new" similar strata. These are modern, efficient, and competitive small- and medium-sized enterprises of entrepreneurs, designers, professionals, and subcontractors, specialized and technically very advanced or highly skilled. They operate domestically and regionally, sometimes even internationally, and may have a network of their own smaller subcontractors to whom they farm out work. The reproduction of the "old" and the emergence of the "new" petty commodity producers and services distributors have increased the internal differentiation and heterogeneity of this class as well as increased its size, contrary to conventional wisdom. The traditional sector is not declining in favor of the modern. Further, members of this latter sector often own stocks and bonds in Western stock markets, local land, or other real estate, and therefore have diversified investments and multiple incomes. Thus they increase internal differentiation and stratification, reinforcing the blurring of class lines and the social fragmentation and heterogeneity of these societies.

The reproduction and expansion, not diminution, of petty commodity producers and distributors have accompanied the development of typically state-promoted, large-scale, capital-intensive, and technologically advanced industry. This seemingly contradictory dual development is directly linked to the role of the Arab world in the international division of labor, that is, to the nature of integration of the region into the European and American economies. In short, the reproduction and expansion of precapitalist forms and relations of production and distribution simultaneously accompany distorted capitalist growth and development in the region.

These transformations of interlocked and mutually reinforcing capitalist and precapitalist forms of production and labor processes have not caused an irrevocable rupture with the social relations, ideology, and culture associated with the previous "traditional" social formation. On the contrary, they helped reproduce those traditional social relations associated with the precapitalist social structure of economic activity, social values, kinship relations, and political behavior.

Patriarchy, patronage, and the mercantile spirit became intertwined with new capitalist social relations to produce a unique amalgam which manifests itself in the behavior and values of contemporary Arab society.[15] The resultant heterogeneous and fragmented class structure and heterogeneous and fragmented social forms produce fragmented and heterogeneous social views and social action. Less energized by nationalist issues than the previous generation, this fragmented urban mass is also less likely to engage in class organization. It is more likely to engage in social and political action based on kinship or on neighborhood, street, ethnic, sectarian, or religious organizing. This will be more so in the absence of socially conscious and relatively autonomous (from the government) political parties.

Class and Social Change

Accelerated integration of the Arab world into the capitalist world system, the collection of vast and unprecedented oil revenues, and the rapid economic growth of constituent states of the region have led to significant class transformation and social change.

To begin with, we noted that the massive labor migration of waves of people over the last decade has meant, among many other things, the externalized proletarianization (transformation into wage labor) of increasing numbers of former peasants and the subsequent repatriation of a fraction of these as members of the petite bourgeoisie. An agricultural villager exits a peasant, becomes employed as a wage worker, returns home with some small savings, and often establishes himself as a petty commodity producer and/or distributor. While externally-induced proletarianization and bourgeoisification are taking place, simultaneous large-scale internal subproletarianization also is proceeding. The rural/urban population ratio has been falling rapidly, and urbanization has been progressing explosively. This double process of externalized proletarianization/bourgeoisification and internal subproletarianization in association with some industrialization is producing growing differentiation and fragmentation in the working class of the varied oil-poor Arab countries and in mixed Arab communities of the oil-rich city-states.

While some of the repatriated workers often become petty bourgeois, a smaller number make large fortunes and return to join a rapidly expanding new bourgeoisie in their respective countries. This, along with the infitah in the oil-poor nations of the Arab world, has allowed the rapid accumulation of private capital and created in the process a powerful new grande bourgeoisie. In the oil-rich peninsula, the new bourgeoisie is largely a group of middlemen, merchants, brokers, and agents of and for Western economic interests, allowed—indeed encouraged—by the state to enrich themselves practically overnight. The activities of this new class quickly spilled into investments and ventures overseas in the Western world, primarily in real estate (hotels, office buildings, shopping malls, etc.), government securities, stock and bond trading, and mercantile activity. This class has helped integrate the Arab world into Western capital. While in the oil-rich countries this class is composed of members of the ruling dynasties and their relatives, close associates, and advisors, in the oil-poor nations it is constituted from among those repatriated from the oil areas and those who capitalized on their position in or access to the state to enrich themselves quickly. Corruption and patronage have been rampant. The officer corps of the military establishments of most of the Arab states have not been immune to this. Many an officer or ex-officer or a close relative has joined the ranks of the nouveaux riches by capitalizing on their position or connections in the state.

The state policies which helped produce the new bourgeoisie and expand the petite bourgeoisie also vastly expanded the white-collar strata employed in the state bureaucracy, its ministries, its coercive apparatuses, and its social and economic agencies. In many countries of the Arab world, the state is by far the largest single employer. In addition to those in the above state bureaucracies, the public sector employees also are subject directly to the state. In Jordan, for example, just over 50 percent of the labor force is employed by the state.[16] In Syria, the figure may be higher. For many of these state bureaucrats, after-hours employment or business[17] or real estate investment provides one or more additional sources of income. Here again, among the middle strata, multiple-income households are proliferating. As among many workers, increasing numbers of the middle strata occupy more than one class position, reinforcing further the process of the blurring of class lines and of increasing social heterogeneity and fragmentation.

The regional factors that generated the social class transformations are the very same ones responsible for a group of other social phenomena. The first is the steady rise in income and the rapid rise in the standard of living for vast sectors of the population of the Arab world. This embourgeoisement is reflected visibly not only in gross economic growth rates, but also in the rapid spread of consumerism,[18] especially of imported Western goods. In turn, this has helped to homogenize the Arab consumer lifestyle, many of whose aspects are mimetic of Western styles, first in consumer goods, but increasingly in behavior. This homogenization of consumer lifestyles among Arabs is paradoxically associated with social fragmentation and the resurgence of parochial identities including ethnic, sectarian, religious, regional, tribal, and clan consciousness. It is the processes of social fragmentation and corresponding fragmentation of social forms and views which allow the reproduction and reinforcement of patriarchal and parochial consciousness despite homogenized consumerism.

The second of these new social phenomena is the reproduction and expansion of inequalities[19] in the Arab world despite the clear overall bourgeoisification and visible rise in the standard of living. R. Paul Shaw analyzes three types of inequalities in the Arab Mashriq which have grown so rapidly that the phenomenon is quite unique in history. Shaw writes:

> Previous to . . . [1973/74], the absolute differential in GDP per capita between the two groups of countries [oil-producing and labor-exporting] was only $460 . . . By 1980, it had swollen to over $5,000 per capita and the ratio of per capita incomes in oil-rich versus oil-poor countries had more than doubled to 7.3.[20]
> Between 1976 and 1981, the oil-rich countries allocated an average of $36 billion per year for the implementation of their national development plans . . . This compares with an average of $14.5 billion per year for the oil-poor countries. On a per capita basis, the oil-rich countries invested an average of $1,360 per year versus only $115 for their oil-poor counterparts.[21]

The poorer Arab countries have significant trade balance deficits, staggering foreign debts, and huge debt service, in contrast to the oil-rich countries, which have substantial surpluses deployed overseas. These inter-regional inequalities are accompanied by inter-sectoral inequalities as well. Restricting the analysis to the contrast between agriculture and industry, Shaw writes: "Agriculture . . . employs no less than 50 percent of the total Arab labor force. Yet between 1976 and 1981, it received only 8.8 percent of total development funds. In contrast, urban-based manufacturing, with only 9 percent of the total Arab labor force, was slated for approximately 20.3 percent of the total development budget."[22]

Like development expenditures, per capita income of the agricultural labor force is a small fraction of that of the personnel in urban industrial and services establishments. Differences in per capita and/or household incomes are especially severe among the oil-poor countries. For example, in Egypt and Morocco 44 percent of rural families are below official poverty lines.[23] Within rural areas, continuing severe income discrepancies still exist despite ambitious land reform programs.

> In Egypt, an initial reduction in the concentration of landholders between 1958 and 1965 gave way to a subsequent rise in concentration because (1) land distribution was limited to previous tenants and small farmers, and (2) later reforms did not distribute land rights to the growing number of landless peasants.[24]

Increasing commercialization and capitalization of agriculture may have caused an arrest of land redistribution and/or caused reconcentration in land ownership.

> According to the latest round of agricultural censuses, large farms still hold disproportionate shares of arable land. For example, in Syria, 2.5 percent of the relatively large farms (say, in excess of 50 hectares) hold 29 percent of the arable land; in Algeria, 2.2 percent hold 47 percent; in Tunisia, 4.6 percent hold 46 percent; in Morocco, 2.5 percent hold 27 percent; in Kuwait, 3.1 percent hold 37 percent; and in Lebanon, 0.2 percent hold 15 percent. In Egypt, 12 percent of the land is still held by only 0.2 percent of the farms and, with 46 percent of the total land being rented, the reign of the absentee landlord may again be visible.[25]

While income distribution data[26] for the region and the aggregate data cited above include important exceptions, there is no doubt of the extremely wide inequalities between and within oil-rich and oil-poor countries of the Arab world. These wide inequalities, along with those among the various economic sectors, have also increased substantially[27] over the "oil decade."

Inequalities in the region and within each country also contribute to the fragmentation and heterogeneity of the Arab social formation. The ability to make new wealth has been determined principally by the degree to which the middleman entrepreneur or merchant has a connection or access to the power centers of the state and not by innovative industrial or other productive development. Such patterns reinforce the patriarchal and patronage system of social relations, thus reinforcing fragmented social relations, views, and consciousness in Arab societies—that is, parochialism.

Arab intellectuals have not really addressed the above processes or derivative social/political issues. The majority of the intellectuals/activists of the 1950s and 1960s have been professionalized and absorbed into a bureaucratized apparatus, that is, institutionalized. Indeed, some of them have abandoned their socialist principles (even principles of Islamic social justice) and emerged as ideologues of the new bourgeoisified social order. These new ideologues propagate neo-liberal doctrines and a "born-again democracy" which objectively justify state postures that during the past oil decade brought about infitah policies characterized by a frantic rush for get-rich-quick schemes, by a predatory class of comprador bourgeoisie that has strongly influenced the development model of the region, and by further social fragmentation. These policies discouraged, at least in the oil-poor states, authentic attempts at socioeconomic development of the productive sectors. Instead, they reinforced service-based capitalist transformation of the region. They also linked organically the economic destiny of the region to the fate of Western economies. Thus, the status of Arab economic wellbeing is externally determined rather than domestically controlled by its own people.

The State, Class, and Political Change

Arab countries have syncretic states characterized by what James Petras calls "multiple states"—that is, three "states" in one.[28] The first is the "historic state," the traditional bureaucracy which functions as an instrument for political patronage and—as in Nasser's Egypt—the "employment agency of last resort." This "state" dispenses economic favors, positions of power, and employment. The ruling elite uses the system of patronage to consolidate its position and to gain solidarity and support from varied sectors of the population.

In the oil-rich countries, the system of patronage is a vehicle of cooptation which functions principally along kinship, clan, and tribal lines, but incorporates adjuncts, agents, friends, colleagues, handlers, and others. This historic state is subject and responsive to the political elites and their constituencies in the population. In the oil-poor countries, the "historic states" function in a similar manner, but are subject as well to claims from the leadership of the dominant political party or coalition of parties. It is this process of patronage which recruits into the top leadership kinsmen, relatives, and close members of the same clan or tribe or the same ethnic, sectarian, or class fragment, and gives the different Arab regimes the character of a narrow social base, as Hanna Batatu typically argues.[29]

This patronage system is associated with the second "state"—the "modern state"—a conglomerate of autonomous and semi-autonomous agencies and bureaucracies. This is the state of technocrats, often educated in the United States, and of the development-oriented sectors of the local bourgeoisie. It performs in the Arab nations two principal functions, the first of which is the planning, financing, and establishing of new economic enterprises and infrastructure.

The second function is the establishment, financing, and managing of the bureaucracies of the welfare state. In the oil-rich nations, the welfare state agencies serve to integrate the native into the nation-state and to legitimize the regime, especially the ruling elite. Above all, they serve to mobilize solidarity of the natives of the oil-rich states with one another and with the ruling elites against the ultimate threat of the more numerous resident migrant workers.

On the other hand, in the oil-poor countries, the welfare state programs, which include basic food subsidy, also function to defuse discontent and mobilize solidarity with the ruling elite. In Egypt, for example, the Sadat-instituted welfare program came to be known popularly as "ma'ash al-Sadat" (the Sadat pension).

The point of overlap between the "historic state" and the "modern state" is the patronage-based positions of power in the varied agencies of development and welfare. This linkage meshes effectively to legitimize the regime and mobilize support for it. In short, both modern and traditional leaderships have a vested interest in the survival and stability of the regimes of their respective states of the Arab world.

The third major "state" is the "repressive state." This is the self-contained caste that operates the repressive organs of the state which protect the ruling class, the elite, and the propertied classes. It often stands above society and above the law, and as often makes its own law. It is the proverbial stick to the welfare carrot of the Arab states. It can be as harsh as it pleases, and can violate the human and civil rights of the citizens without having to answer to anyone except its own caste leaders. Like the other bureaucracies, the "repressive state" is also an important employer of last resort and functions in its own right as a mobilizer of support and enforcer for the regime.

This syncretic "state-in-three" constitutes the contemporary state structure in the Arab world. However, the inter-penetration of the three states may lead to contradictory and conflicting processes within the state and within the society as a whole. In the short term, such contradictory processes may lead to some political instability, while for the long term they set the stage for a more profound transformation. One such example of the latter should suffice here.

The welfare programs and basic food subsidies that have been instituted by ruling elites to defuse popular discontent and to mobilize support for the regime will change over the years from being a grant of favor by the rulers to a political right of the citizen. Thus, any dismantling or severe constraint of the programs in the future will likely trigger movements of opposition against the regime. In short, unwittingly, all states of the Arab Mashriq are planting the seeds of an important political principle: that is, the citizen's political (not merely humanitarian) right to economic security.

This right may then emerge in the early twenty-first century as the central issue of domestic Arab politics. The issue may or may not be directly linked to the foreign policy of the respective states, as it already has been in Egypt. What will determine the nature of the linkage is the actual dynamics of domestic and regional politics in the final years of the twentieth century.

Two aspects of the contemporary fragmented and heterogeneous social structure of the Arab Mashriq will have a direct bearing on the future of Arab politics. The first is ideological, and the second is organizational. Leaders of the Arab regimes of both the oil-rich and the oil-poor states have come to be seen by their own compatriots as corrupt and with little legitimacy or popularity. However, with rapid embourgeoisement or, more correctly, the Arab individual's frantic rush to enrichment, especially in the Mashriq, cynicism has replaced much of the progressive (nationalist or leftist) and conservative (traditionally Islamic) ideology of the previously activist masses, groups, intellectuals, and individuals. This development may be one factor behind the rise of militant Islamic fundamentalism. The post-World War II great liberating Arab ideologies of freedom, independence, social justice, development, and citizen involvement have been replaced among the middle strata by a political culture of rampant consumerism, possessive individualism, and disenchanted political withdrawal; and among the working and poor strata, by religious revival and utopian idealism. A new security-conscious statism which imports the tools and social organization of repression has replaced the liberationist Arab nationalism with the pan-Arabism (or sub-regionalism) of repression. Social and political repression have become generalized and more intensive in most Arab societies. It is as if the patriarchal tyranny of the traditional Arab family has been generalized into a modern state-security apparatus and ideology which pervades everyday life.

Arab institutions of civil society have retained little legitimacy and efficacy. The formal mediating institutions, such as unions and parties, which previously linked the individual with the state have progressively lost their autonomy, their substance, and their legitimacy. They have become shells of their former selves and have been turned into ready tools with which the Arab states control their citizens. That is, instead of being the mechanism for mobilizing the people and acting as centers for checking the authority of the state, these mediating institutions have become a means of control of the people by the state. The fragmented social formation of Arab societies is at once a contributor to the destruction of these formal institutions of civil society and a product of their demise. Without civil society, the Arab individual is a subject, not a citizen of the state. Democracy in the sense of participation in the decisions affecting one's life and destiny is not possible without civil society.

Many an analyst has noted the impact of the new wealth in the oil decade on the demise or corruption of an indigenous Arab social revolution. The impact of *al-tharwa* (wealth) on *al-thawra* (revolution) is not merely a cliché. It is a capsule characterization of the rise of the new parasitical clans or classes that have enriched themselves on the staggering surpluses of oil revenues. As merchants, contractors, agents, technocrats, and others, they allied themselves with ruling oil dynasties or minority rulers to create a new political order and a new political culture.

This political culture articulates well with a new set of cultural mores which include the demise of the work ethic[30]; work is now hardly related to high income or success. It is one's connections or one's status which determines the patronage—the key to quick and assured wealth. The new Arab mores are characterized by rampant consumerism and conspicuous consumption; status distinction and snobbism; reinforcement of the ideology of patriarchy, hierarchy, and subordination; loss of cultural authenticity; the rise of mimetic (of the West) culture; and finally, the loss of indigenous folk culture associated with the rise of the consumption of American (and European) mass culture. Such new cultural mores are both a reflection of and a factor reinforcing the fractured character of Arab social formations. The consequences for the political culture of the Arab world have been devastating. The Arab collective sense has been atomized, and the progressive thrust has been reversed.

In the post–World War II era, the Arab struggle for political, economic, and social independence gave rise to state capitalism in several core countries. Arab state capitalism has an inner dynamic logic with a natural history that propels it from progressive social, economic, and foreign policies into counter-revolutionary ones[31]; witness the shifts from the 1960s to the 1970s and 1980s.

The structure and dynamics of Arab state capitalism are complex and demand serious detailed research. Suffice it here to say that Arab state capitalism produces not only parasitic, but also predatory, bourgeoisies and helps reproduce overdeveloped state structures and underdeveloped productive forces. The overbureaucratization, inefficiency, repression, corruption, patronage, and welfare of state capitalism in the context of general oil-related bourgeoisification have not produced wide-scale disaffection and organized opposition. Instead, this has produced "politics of resentment" laced in some states with ethnic/sectarian resentment over distribution of resources, over access to the state (which is lucrative), over discrimination, over the lack of civil and human rights, and, among some sectors, over social oppression.

Expression of resentment is fragmented, as are the social structure, social views, and social consciousness. The religious fundamentalist movement is itself fragmented and reflects its social base. Even anti-regime violence is fragmented and discontinuous.

On an individual level, the Arab states have experienced in the oil decade the rise of economic neo-liberalism, political repression, and social conservativism, whereas on a regional level, the Arab world suffered a loss of pan-Arab national identity, of independence, and of regional coordination in social, economic, or foreign policies.

Along with these changes, the terrain of struggle also has shifted away from the mobilized streets and relatively autonomous political institutions and movements into the courts and lobbies internal to the ruling dynasties or one-party regimes. Most of the Arab populace are more like political spectators than participants. This transformation is in part also responsible for the emergence of fragmented new styles of social and political action and of violence by small fragmented groups.

In conclusion, the heterogeneous and fragmented class structure makes possible a political order with higher levels of state repression. The commensurate destruction of civil society and democratic freedoms is in part a product of the greater integration of the Arab world into Western political economy. In short, dependency and repression go together in a natural union.

Conclusion

Major class transformations do not occur overnight. Ruling elites or regimes may come and go in the next decade, and class conflict within any given country, or even the Arab region, may escalate or subside, but broad class changes will move somewhat more slowly. Of course, this assumes that an overarching crisis resulting in a revolutionary takeover is not in the cards in the next decade. The structural processes of change which are in motion now will continue in the same direction, but perhaps at somewhat attenuated rates because of the decline in oil revenues and growth rates. The reasons for this, as should be clear by now, are to be found in the economic and social structure of each country separately and in the region as a whole.

Contemporary Arab economic and social structures have been set and the die has been cast, so to speak, over the last two decades, but especially since the oil boom started. Current economic policy and economic development plans of the major Arab states do not indicate the probability of any wrenching shifts from past policy. This is in part a consequence of the class character of the states in these Arab societies and of their sociopolitical role.

The states in almost every Arab country have expanded in scope, function, and power, particularly in the economic sphere, and therefore in shaping the class structure of their respective social formations. The states of the Mashriq countries have become so centralized, all-pervasive, and efficient that they have managed to neutralize all organized opposition and to mobilize the support of large sectors of their own population, who benefit, albeit differentially, from their policies. This is the case despite the fact that the regimes' social bases are narrow—in clan, ethnic group, or economic strata. This phenomenon may be encapsulated in the following conception: etatization of Arab societies and privatization of the state.

It is this seemingly self-contradictory feature—expansion of structure and function but narrowness of base—which is responsible for the pattern of coercion and co-optation so typical of contemporary Arab states. This double capability is behind the relative political stability of the regimes (and to a lesser degree the rulers) of the Arab states. My contention, then, is that even with changes in regime, the expanded role of the contemporary state in the Arab region will likely produce similar socioeconomic policies in the short and medium terms. Thus, resultant social processes, class formations, and dynamics also will be reproduced substantially unchanged in the next decade.

This projection into the future is all the more tenable because of the nature of the social structure in which this contemporary state is operating. As I have argued above, the development of capitalism in conjunction with the reproduction and expansion of petty commodity production and distribution since World War II has produced and continues to produce a heterogeneous and fractured social structure which reinforces fragmented and heterogeneous social consciousness and social-political action, and, therefore, dynamic, occasionally violent, immobilism.

These trends picked up momentum and a relentless drive in the years following the spectacular increase in oil revenues. The pace of change escalated dramatically during the "seven fat years" of the oil boom and has slowed down, but has neither reversed direction nor changed character in what currently appears to be a period of "seven lean years."

The downturn so far is not riven with severe crises. It is, however, taking place at an important socioeconomic conjuncture: vast numbers of youth coming of age for employment (in most Arab countries 50 percent of the population is under 20 years of age). The plight of vast masses of unskilled and unemployed youth in social conditions lacking hope and future is a perfect social formula for frustration, bitterness, and violence—both criminal and political. If this is coupled with severe repression, as is the case for the Palestinians under Israeli occupation in the West Bank and Gaza and for their brethren in Lebanon who face Lebanese hostility and repression, then the likelihood of political violence—individual or organized—increases dramatically. While the conditions of the Palestinians are the most dramatic, other peoples, the Egyptians for example, are not far behind. But it should be clear that among other peoples, the bases of organizing this violence and political militancy in general are more traditional (through the kin, the clan, the neighborhood, the street, the sect, the ethnic group, and so on), fragmented, and discontinuous.

In short, the economic, cultural, social, and political structures of the contemporary Arab world are the foundations of the societal and class systems not merely in 1995, but also into the twenty-first century. The logic of dependent service-based capitalism formally in articulation with precapitalist social forms and social relations will reproduce the contemporary society in the short and medium terms, but may be developing into a real crisis in the long term when oil is depleted and/or when labor is repatriated.

Broadly, then, the class structure in the next decade will be composed of a tiny grande bourgeoisie intimately integrated into Western capital and acting increasingly as an international bourgeoisie with international and diversified holdings. It is a dynamic bourgeoisie, but its dynamism rests essentially on the (rapid) accumulation of capital through service activity rather than through the exploitation of land or labor. This comprador mercantile-financial bourgeoisie (with extensive interests as well in construction and real estate holdings) is dominant and sets the parameters of Arab development, particularly in the Mashriq. Its service base does not augur well for future investment in the productive sectors of the Arab world. These are left for the states themselves, but their performance in the past decade leaves much to be desired.

The industrial bourgeoisie is the weakest segment of the bourgeoisie. Despite state capitalism, the industrial working class is and will remain very small (averaging 9 to 12 percent of the workforce throughout the Arab world), weak, and protective of privileges won over the years, especially in the face of a vast reserve army of unemployed or underemployed labor. In between exists and will continue to expand a broad and great mass of stratified petty bourgeoisie—old and new petty commodity producers and distributors (including the service professionals). Furthermore, an increasing number of these petty and middle commodity producers and distributors will continue to derive their income from varied sources, leading to the important phenomenon of multiple-income families whose class position will be unclear and whose cross-cutting interests will encourage heterogeneous and fragmented consciousness and politics. At best, one will expect populist politics of varied styles, as this broad and unproductive mass of people can hardly be organized and mobilized at the point of production. The bases of organizing such a mass will by necessity be as heterogeneous as the mass itself.

Such a fragmented and heterogeneous social structure will allow dramatic mass movements in periods of overarching crisis, not unlike that of Khomeini's Islamic revolution in Iran. In other periods, diverse, uncoordinated, fragmented, discontinuously violent opposition will emerge. Wide-scale spontaneous and potentially violent upheavals may also emerge when threats to "bread and butter" interests materialize, especially among the poorer classes of the urban centers. These will not be significantly different than the "food" or "bread" riots that took place in the past decade in Egypt, Morocco, Tunisia, Sudan, and elsewhere. Otherwise, the centralized and disciplined military of both the republics and the monarchies will in alliance with mercantile, real estate, and money capital continue to rule an Arab world characterized by structural dynamic immobilism. Political change or large-scale instability, if it is to occur, will likely be a product of factional (fragmented) conflict within the pivotal military establishment or dynasty, or else the military will intervene in the context of crisis of governance, as it did in Sudan.

In short, the Arab world, long known for volatility and political instability, will actually be increasingly transformed into a cluster of societies which will be structurally fractured but relatively stable, albeit occasionally punctuated by dramatic violence.

This relative political stability—characterized by a low level of violence—is a form of domestic balance of forces. It is, however, contingent in part upon the regional balance of power. If the latter is seriously upset, either through full-scale war (not merely a border conflict) or through a political realignment between pivotal powers in which one of the regimes is replaced and the regional balance altered significantly, then the relatively stable domestic sociopolitical structure in related (linked) states could become very volatile.

The regional balance of power, dependent as it is on both regional and domestic relations, is also directly linked to the policies and activities of the superpowers. In conclusion, it is ironic that the very same external linkages (integration) which helped generate fragmented but relatively stable social structures in the states of the region may be, in the next decade, the cause of both regional and domestic political instability and change.

Notes

1 The approach of this paper is inspired by that of a paper given by James Petras at the International Conference on Social Classes, Social Change, and Economic Development in the Mediterranean, Foundation for Mediterranean Studies, May 36, 1984 (Athens, Greece).

2 See an analysis of its last phases by I. M. Smilianskaya, "From Subsistence to Market Economy, 1850s," in Charles Issawi, ed., *The Economic History of the Middle East, 1800–1914* (Chicago: University of Chicago, 1966).

3 Estimates of the number of migrant workers in the oil-rich states of Arabia range from three to six million in a given year. These do not include the families of a substantial fraction of these workers. See J. S. Birks and C. A. Sinclair, *Arab Manpower* (New York: St. Martin's Press, 1980); and idem., *Migration and Development in the Arab World* (Geneva: International Labor Organization, 1980).

4 The Palestinian Arabs of the West Bank and Gaza are the labor reserves of both Israel and the oil-rich Arab states. See E. A. Gharaibeh, *The Economies of the West Bank and Gaza Strip* (Boulder: Westview Press, 1985).

5 Estimates for Egypt are usually $3 billion. David Ottaway of *The Washington Post* reports a remittance income for Egypt of between $6 billion and $10 billion.

6 H. Askari, "Oil and Economic Development in the Middle East," lecture, 1985 (Washington, DC). See also M. Abdul Fadil, *al-Naft wa-al-wihda al-'arabiyya* (Oil and Arab Unity) (Beirut: Centre for Arab Unity Studies, 1980), p. 57.

7 R. Owen, "The Arab Oil Economy: Present Structure and Future Prospects," in S. K. Farsoun, ed., *Arab Society: Continuity and Change* (London: Croom Helm, 1985).

8 See K. T. Ali, "Tatawwurat muqliqa li-awda' al-zira'a wa-al-ghitha' fi al-watan al-'arabi khilal al-sab'inat" (Disturbing Developments in the Conditions of Agriculture and Nutrition in the Arab Nation During the Seventies), in *Dirasat fi al-tanmiya waal-takamul al-iqtisadi al-'arabi* (Studies in Arab Economic Development and Integration) (Beirut: Centre for Arab Unity Studies, 1982), pp. 405–43.

9 See A. H. Brahimi, *Ab'ad al-indimaj al-iqtisadi al-'arabi wa-ihtimalat al-mustaqbal* (Implications of Arab Economic Integration and Expectations for the Future) (Beirut: Centre for Arab Unity Studies, 1980), especially pp. 51–125.

10 See A. H. Brahimi, *Ab'ad al-indimaj al-iqtisadi al-'arabi*; R. S. Basadah, "Al-Anmat al-'ama li-al-tanmiya al-sina'iyya fi al-watan al-'arabi, 1960-1975" (General Modes of Industrial Development in the Arab Nation, 1960–1975), in *Anmat altanmiya fi al-watan al-'arabi*, 1960–1975 (Kuwait: Al-Ma'had al-'Arabi li-al-takhtit, 1980), pp. 165–210. See also A. Bourgey et al., *Industrialisation et Changements Sociaux dans L'Orient Arabe* (Beirut: Centre d'Etudes et de Recherches sur le Moyen Orient Contemporain, 1982).

11 Ibid.

12 Lebanon has been an exception.

13 See, for example, C. B. Keely and B. Saket, "Jordanian Migrant Workers in the Arab Region: A Case Study of Consequences for Labor Supplying Countries," *Middle East Journal* 38, no. 4 (Autumn 1984): 695.

14 Statistics on this are very difficult to find. One indicator is the persistence and/or increase of artisanal and other small-scale productive and distributive establishments. For example, in Lebanon the number of establishments employing less than 10 workers increased from 7,149 in 1955 to 13,939 in 1971, while for Iraq the comparable figures are 21,733 in 1954 and 37,669 in 1976, and in East Jordan 2,140 in 1967 and 4,790 in 1977. See S. Nasr, "Les Travailleurs de L'Industrie Manufacturière au Machrek," in A. Bourgey et al., *Industrialisation et Changements Sociaux,* p. 158. Rose Musleh reports that in 1978, 92.7 percent of the industrial workforce of East Jordan was working in establishments of one to nine individuals. R. Musleh, "Al-Sina'a fi sharq al-Urdun, 1967-1979" (Industry in Transjordan, 1967-1979), *Shu'un filistiniyya* no. 99 (February 1980): 10.

15 See H. Sharabi, "The Dialectics of Patriarchy in Arab Society," in S. K. Farsoun, ed., *Arab Society.*

16 *Al-Dustur,* March 20, 1985.

17 Employment in state bureaucracies usually ends at 1 or 2 p.m.

18 Y. A. Sayigh, "Al-Taklifa al-ijtima'iyya li-al-'aidat al-naftiyya" (Social Costs of the Oil Revenues), in *Dirasat fi al-tanmiya wa-al-takamul al-iqtisadi al-'arabi,* p. 357, Keeley and Saket, "Jordanian Migrant Workers in the Arab Region"; M. Abdul-Fadil, *Al-Naft wa-al-wihda al-'arabiyya,* pp. 60-86.

19 Y. A. Sayigh, "Al-Taklifa al-ijtima'iyya," p. 364.

20 R. Paul Shaw, "The Political Economy of Inequality in the Arab World," *Arab Studies Quarterly* 6, nos. 1 and 2 (Winter and Spring, 1984): 126–27.

21 Ibid.

22 Ibid.

23 Ibid.

24 Ibid.

25 Ibid.

26 M. Abdul-Fadil, "Anmat tawzi' al-dakhil fi al-watan al-'arabi (1960–1975)" (Modes of Income Distribution in the Arab Nation [1960-1975]), in *Anmat al-tanmiya fi al-watan al-'arabi,* Part II, pp. 243–90.

27 Y. A. Sayigh, "al-Taklifa al-ijtima'iyya," p. 364.

28 J. Petras, paper delivered at the International Conference on Social Classes.

29 H. Batatu, "Political Power and Social Structure in Syria and Iraq," in S. K. Farsoun, *Arab Society.*

30 Y. A. Sayigh, "al-Taklifa al-'arabiyya."

31 S. K. Farsoun and W. Carroll, "State Capitalism and Counterrevolution: A Thesis," in B. H. Kaplan, ed., *Social Change in the Capitalist World Economy* (Beverly Hills, CA: Sage, 1978).

2

Change in Saudi Arabia: A View From "Paris of Najd"

Soraya Altorki and Donald P. Cole

In the early 1920s Amin Rihani served as an advisor to 'Abd al-'Aziz Ibn 'Abd al-Rahman Ibn Sa'ud, at that time the Imam of Najd and, later on, Saudi Arabia's first king. Rihani, a Christian Arab from Lebanon who had studied French and lived for many years in the United States, was also a celebrated poet. On one occasion during his sojourn in Arabia, he traveled by camel caravan from the then very small town of Riyadh to the oasis and market city of 'Unayzah. The caravan first passed through the district of Washm, with its settlements and farms, and then crossed a wide expanse of arid range land before arriving in the Qasim district, some 400 kilometers northwest of Riyadh.

Traversed by the Wadi ar-Rimmah and thus having a good source of underground water, Qasim had a large and diverse population of peasant farmers, Bedouin livestock raisers, artisans and craftworkers, transporters and traders, moneylenders and merchant capitalists, and religious scholars. The Bedouin lived in goat-hair tents woven by women and were nomadic. However, the majority of people in Qasim were sedentary and lived in houses constructed out of mudbrick. Most of the dwellings in Qasim's villages and the cities of 'Unayzah and Buraydah were small. However, some of the urban houses were grand edifices five or six stories high and had been built by local master craftsmen, who richly decorated them with abstract designs.

Rihani recorded the caravan's arrival ,at 'Ashwaziyah, a village in Qasim, and then continued, as follows:

> The hospitality of 'Ashwaziyah was but the beginning of days of generosity in 'Unayzah, the queen of Qasim. 'Unayzah, the fortress of freedom and the stopping place of travelers! 'Unayzah, the epitome of good taste and of literature, Paris of Najd! Yet, it is more beautiful than Paris.
> . . , for Paris has neither palm trees nor an area of golden sand dunes
> *(nafud)*. 'Unayzah is small, calm, peaceful and enchants you with its colors—like a picture painted by Manet, illustrating a story from the tales of *A Thousand and One Nights*. It is like a pearl in a plate of gold with a border of lapis lazuli. 'Unayzah is tranquility personified. It is as though

Soraya Altorki and Donald P. Cole are professors of anthropology at the American University in Cairo.

this tranquility built for itself a temple among the palm trees and decorated it with golden sand and crowned it with a wreath of tamarisk *(athal)*

'Unayzah is crowded with people, about 30,000; and its markets are like caverns *(sardab)*, because the people build bridges over them, and above the bridges are houses. The great markets are illuminated and astonish you with their shapes and colors. They remind you of America or the country of the English, and they transport you to India and to Japan. You hear the English, French, and Hindustani languages and many Arabic dialects.

'Unayzah has old families with ancient lineages and long traditions of virtuous behavior. Its fathers have toured the distant countries of east and west; and travel has made them kind and charming. . ., so that they elevate hospitality to a level where they open the doors of homes and hearts. Indeed, the stranger forgets, in this city, that he is a stranger— whether he is Muslim or infidel, whether he believes in one God or in many. Here, he feels that he is among people who are accustomed to meeting people like him. And more than that, they are people who are used to being hospitable to a guest no matter who he is.

The stranger enjoys himself very much and gratefully welcomes their invitations. "Come in for coffee!" It is an invitation similar to that of the English for tea. In both cases, the hospitality includes something more beautiful than coffee and tea. In both, there is a tendency to converse and to socialize. But the generosity of the Arab from 'Unayzah is distinct from the hospitality of the Englishman, because the head of the household serves you himself from the minute he welcomes you until the minute he bids you farewell. What beautiful generosity and gentleness, especially that these two virtues arose with a dignity that does not need pomp to reinforce it.

Rihani wrote that he spoke with 'Unayzah's amir, Ibn Sulaym, about a wide range of topics, including geography, agriculture, America, doctors, and poets. The amir was especially interested in doctors and complained that 'Unayzah did not have a dentist. Rihani told him that the best dentists were in America; and the amir responded, "Is this true? Perhaps we will travel to America to see its tall buildings and have our teeth fixed" (Rihani 1980 [1924], 2:120–25).

A Paris, a "city of light," deep in the interior of Najd, the remote, arid center of Arabia? Since Rihani was a poet, is this metaphor the creative imagination of a literary figure with little or no basis in fact? No; Rihani's view of the old 'Unayzah and its people is affirmed by others.[1] Philby, a British explorer and political agent, visited 'Unayzah in 1918 and characterized it as "one of the great cities of Arabia" and "a gem among Arabian cities." He also considered the community to be a "highly civilized and even cultured society" and praised its citizens for their "open-handed hospitality and . . . complete freedom from any kind of religious or sectarian bigotry" (Philby 1928:160–62). Moreover, Ibn Sa'ud is reported to have visited 'Unayzah and its market in 1904 and to have remarked that he hoped that his own capital of Riyadh might one day develop and become like 'Unayzah (al-Wasil 1986:112).

In 1986, when we conducted anthropological fieldwork there (Altorki and Cole 1989), 'Unayzah had a population of perhaps 70,000,[2] most of whom resided in recently acquired new housing. Much of the old mudbrick city had been abandoned and lay in ruins or was occupied by expatriate workers. The great old market had been torn down and replaced by small new shops owned and operated by men and a separate area where local women retailers sold their wares to men and women. The old city's artisan and craft production had largely disappeared, but small workshops existed for automobile repairs and a few other "industrial" activities. Some of 'Unayzah's old agriculture remained, but many of its ancient palm groves had been cut down to make way for new housing or other buildings. However, a few large and many small and medium-sized new farms had been developed in nearby areas. The distinctive ziggurat-style minaret of the city's old main mosque remained as part of the city's heritage, but its mudbrick clashed with the shining white marble of the new main mosque.

By 1986, the capital city of Riyadh, the new urban complex of Dammam, al-Khubar, and Dhahran, and the port and commercial city of Jiddah had long eclipsed 'Unayzah in size and function.[3] 'Unayzah was no longer "one of the great cities of Arabia." It lost its political autonomy as a *de facto* independent amirate as early as 1904 and a long series of subsequent economic changes transformed 'Unayzah into a small provincial town within the political economic context of the contemporary Saudi Arabian state and its oil revenue-based economy. As has often happened in many other cases of change, 'Unayzah has been, paradoxically, both a beneficiary and a victim of modernization and development.

In this article, we summarize the main changes that have unfolded in 'Unayzah or that have involved people from the community. Our goal is to illustrate important features of change in Saudi Arabia—and the Arab World in general. In this Saudi Arabian case,[4] transformation has especially involved a process of state formation since 1902 and the development of an oil revenue-based economy since about 1950. As the presentation shows, a process of substantive development that was mainly positive and that built on achievements of the past flourished during the 1950s, 60s, and early 70s, when Saudi Arabia benefited from modest amounts of oil revenue. However, the boom that resulted from high oil prices from the mid 1970s through the early 1980s brought spectacular changes that led to high standards of living but which raise questions of sustainability,[5] along with other serious concerns.

State-Building and Early Change, 1902 to around 1950

Many people believe, wrongly, that no modern change occurred in what is today Saudi Arabia until the development of its oil industry following the end of the Second World War.[6] However, a process of state formation within the territories of what is today Saudi Arabia had long existed and included efforts by the Bani Khalid at the end of the seventeenth century, by the al-Sa'ud in the eighteenth and nineteenth centuries, and by the al-Rashid and the al-Idrisi, also in the nineteenth century. Creation of the present state began under the leadership of Ibn Sa'ud with the conquest of Riyadh in 1902. 'Unayzah was peacefully incorporated by treaty into this process in 1904, when much of the rest of central Najd was brought under state control. Following a series of conquests and threats of conquest, the remainder of Najd and the regions of Ahsa', 'Asir, and Hijaz and other territories were incorporated into the new state, which was formally created in its present form as the Kingdom of Saudi Arabia in 1932. As it has developed throughout the twentieth century, this state has gradually become more and more centralized and bureaucratic in its structure and organization.

Unlike most other contemporary Arab states, the Saudi Arabian state rose from local factors and owes its emergence and continuity to its own will rather than to any foreign will or determination.[7] The role of Ibn Sa'ud and other members of the al-Sa'ud in the creation and development of the state has been highly publicized. Also important and well known was the involvement of the *muwahidun* (unitarian) religious reform movement initiated by Shaykh Muhammad Ibn 'Abd al-Wahhab in the eighteenth century. This movement provided religious ideological support and sent out preachers from among the old sedentary communities of Najd to convince people to join in the process. The movement also recruited Bedouin as *ikhwan* (brethren) who provided the main body of *mujahidun* (holy warriors) that fought for the establishment of the new state.[8]

Less well known, at least to outsiders, are the roles of merchant capitalists and other men with at least some modern secular education. Many of these men were from 'Unayzah. Wealthy traders from the city provided significant and crucial financial support to Ibn Sa'ud through contributions and interest-free loans, many of which were never paid back. Most of the first employees of the *diwan al-maliki,* "royal court," were men from 'Unayzah, who had graduated from a private school established there in 1926 by Ibn Salih, a son of the city. Moreover, a sterling example of a non-royal person in the government during its early development was 'Abd Allah Ibn Sulayman, a man from a non-tribal background in 'Unayzah.

He took a job as an assistant clerk in the new bureaucracy in the early 1920s and then worked his way up through the system until he became minister of finance with total control over the state treasury until soon after the death of Ibn Sa'ud in 1953. According to one observer,

Suleiman was the ultimate *eminence grise,* always self-effacing and keeping himself in the wings. Nevertheless, his power and influence became so monumental that I often thought of him as the uncrowned king of Arabia... At the height of his power, Suleiman was by far the most important man in the kingdom outside the royal family (Almana 1980: 192–97).

Men from 'Unayzah and other sedentary communities in Qasim also fought to defeat the *ikhwan* at the decisive battle of Sabilah in 1929 and thus contributed to the predominance of sedentary folk not active in the *muwahidun* movement in many of the higher echelons of the new state. However, the major contribution of these men was in the bureaucracy. Men from Hijaz, although not totally trusted at first because of their previous connections with the *ashraf,*[9] also manned the new bureaucracy. Such men, or their sons, have occupied major positions in almost all the ministries. However, political power in the past (and at present) has been monopolized by the al-Sa'ud—thus blocking the ascendance of non-royal personnel to the main centers of power, such as the ministries of interior and defense and the leadership of the national guard.

Rihani mentioned that 'Unayzah's "fathers have toured the distant countries of east and west." They had done so not as tourists but as traders, transporters, and workers. Poor men from the community had toiled in the digging of the Suez Canal and in the construction of the Hijaz railroad. Some of them had also worked, along with Lawrence of Arabia, to destroy that railroad as part of the Arab Revolt during the First World War. Moreover, men from 'Unayzah had long managed and operated far-flung networks of trade and transport. As late as 1930, some 40 'Unayzah-based caravans, each with between 40 and 140 camels, regularly carried goods between 'Unayzah and Kuwait, Jubayl, Riyadh, Makkah, and Madinah. At that time, the city's main merchants were also still engaged in the lucrative long-distance export trade of camels and horses to Egypt, Syria, Iraq, and India. However, the introduction of motor vehicles into Arabia and elsewhere put an end to this trade and transport by around 1940, when camel caravans for transport and the large-scale export of camels and horses ceased.

Other innovations also brought change. Mechanical pumps, for example, were first introduced into 'Unayzah in 1925 and made irrigation much less expensive and time-consuming than had been the case previously. Most important, perhaps, was the introduction of modern secular education. 'Unayzah had long had *katatib,* Islamic schools, for boys and for girls. Indeed, the old city had numerous *'ulama'* (religious scholars), and visitors in the nineteenth century reported the existence of private libraries with books on both religious and secular subjects. As previously mentioned, a scholar from the city, in 1926, opened a private school for boys, the first modern school in Najd. A decade later, in

1936, the first state schools for boys were opened in Najd—including the 'Aziziyah school in 'Unayzah. In its first year, this school had six teachers, all men from 'Unayzah, and 150 students, who were mainly sons of well-to-do local merchants.

Thus, before oil revenue transformed the economy and society in the territories of today's Saudi Arabia, cities and a strong urban tradition had long existed and were as much a part of the country as were the region's more famous nomadic Bedouin. Settled villages and farms existed, and most of the food locally consumed was produced in the country. Local, regional, and long-distance trade and transport also had a long and complex history in the country. Technological innovations were not unknown, and a basic modern educational system for boys was in place before revenue from the sale of oil began to trickle into Saudi Arabia around 1950.

Effective centralized state authority had often been absent, especially in areas outside of Hijaz. However, the contemporary state was also firmly in place before oil revenue began to be important. This state was dominated by male members of a lineage, the al-Sa'ud, from the 'Anazah tribe; but these men were not the only men involved in the state. Moreover, this state was much more complex in organization than was the case for kin-based tribes among the nomadic Bedouin and some others in the country. Tribe-based units were important in the internal organization of the *Ikhwan* (and still are important in the *Ikhwan*'s secular successor, the National Guard). However, this tribe-based organization was not (and is not) absolute; and participants in the *Ikhwan* were not there as *tribes*men but as holy warriors.[10]

Some of the bureaucrats were (and are) men of tribal descent status, but they come from sedentary communities such as 'Unayzah and almost never from among the nomadic Bedouin. Conversely, many of these men were not (and are not) from tribal backgrounds. All of these men were (and are) members of the bureaucracy primarily because of their education and, thus, their achieved qualifications to carry out modern state functions. Tribal affairs continue to be of importance to the Saudi Arabian state; however, the state has many other concerns, which have nothing to do with tribes or tribalism.

Substantive Development, 1950s to 1973–74

The need for financial assistance and technical military aid had led Ibn Sa'ud to compromise the state's autonomy as early as 1915 by the acceptance of aid from the British. In an attempt to lessen his dependence on the British, Ibn Sa'ud, in 1933, granted concessions to American companies to explore for oil. In 1938, oil in commercial quantities was discovered in Dhahran; but development of the oil industry was interrupted by the Second World War. Although not intended by Ibn Sa'ud, the country's political autonomy and economic independence was radically compromised by the development and exploitation of its vast oil resources by the American companies. Moreover, until early 1974, most of the income derived from the sale of Saudi Arabia's oil went to the companies and to the United States government in the form of American taxes paid by the companies.

Nonetheless, Saudi Arabia began to receive modest but significant revenue from its oil around 1950. By fiscal year 1969–70, Saudi Arabia's revenue from oil and all other sources reached 5.7 billion riyals,[11] a small fraction of the 368 billion riyals it was to receive at the height of the oil boom in 1981–82. However, with modest revenue from oil in the 1950s, 60s, and early 70s, a gradual and incremental process of substantive development began.

In the case of 'Unayzah, these changes triggered a large emigration of mainly young men from sharecropper, peasant, craft, and small trader backgrounds to seek waged labor opportunities in construction in Riyadh and in the building of the Riyadh-Dammam railroad and of Tapline (a major oil pipeline). Many also signed on as workers for the Arabian American Oil Company (ARAMCO) and toiled in the exploration for oil and the drilling of the massive wells that tap the world's largest proven oil reserves. Other young 'Unayzah men, usually from relatively well-to-do local backgrounds and with modern education, became salaried employees of the state as teachers and bureaucrats and worked in a wide range of small and large communities, especially in Najd and the Eastern Province. Some others also established themselves as traders in other cities.

Many of these migrants settled in the new communities where they worked—a prime example being al-Khubar.[12] Typically, these men brought wives and other family members from 'Unayzah to join them. Some of the men who signed on with ARAMCO eventually rose up through the ranks to occupy high positions in this company, which is now mainly managed by Saudi Arabian men. Others set up businesses. Among them was an 'Unayzah man who, early on, established a small company to provide transportation for ARAMCO. His company eventually became one of the largest private firms in Saudi Arabia, while he is one of the country's richest citizens. Likewise, many of those who worked as teachers and bureaucrats eventually achieved high positions in their fields. Meanwhile, Saudi Arabia's highly computerized oil industry now relies on the expertise of young Saudi Arabian engineers and computer experts, some of whom are the grandsons of men who left 'Unayzah in search of waged labor or salaried employment in the 1950s.

These men and their families and descendants do not forget that they are from 'Unayzah. They maintain strong ties with the community and contribute to its development; and some of the early migrants have retired there or plan to retire there. Of course, many of those who left in the 1950s did not stay away long but returned after accumulating modest savings. They and the majority who did not migrate saw some improvements in their community, but they also experienced its relative decline.

Among changes from this period that we consider to be positive are the following: the paving of highways and local roads and the building of the Qasim regional airport (1960s); the establishment of state offices and agencies in the city, including a directorate of agriculture (early 1950s), a branch of the agricultural bank and an agricultural research center (1960s), a public hospital (1959), the municipality (1961), a social affairs center (1962); the creation of local voluntary associations or non-governmental organizations, including a philanthropic fund (1954), a people's committee (1962), and a sports club (1960s); and a major expansion in education for both boys and girls.

We noted earlier that *katatib* had existed for girls in the old 'Unayzah. Like their brothers, girls too studied the Holy Qur'an and other religious subjects. After completing these studies, a few girls, usually with the help of male relatives, continued to expand their knowledge. For example, one elderly woman reported that her brother had owned a bookshop in al-Khubar and had often sent her books to read. According to her, "[in the old days] I read everything I could put my hands on. I particularly enjoyed reading some of the world's classics in translation." Another elderly woman said that she learned to be a teacher in one of the old *katatib* for girls by assisting her nearly blind father in his religious studies with a well-known shaykh. In the process, she had improved her knowledge of the Holy Qur'an and the Hadith.

However, modern secular education was first reserved for boys. Following the introduction of public primary education for boys in the 1930s, the first intermediate school for boys in 'Unayzah opened in 1953 and the first secondary school for boys in 1956. The first public primary school for girls did not open until 1960, when 15 such schools were opened in different Saudi Arabian cities. In 'Unayzah, 285 girls enrolled in the school's first year. In the second year, they more than doubled to a total of 680 girls. An intermediate school for girls opened in 1970 and a secondary school for girls in 1974.

With this base strongly established in the 1950s and 60s and given a high valuation of learning among people in 'Unayzah, the educational system expanded rapidly. In 1986, 'Unayzah had 24 primary schools for boys and 29 for girls, five intermediate schools for boys and six for girls, and two general secondary schools each for boys and girls. Girls schools in 1986 enrolled 5,893 pupils and had 503 teachers; boys schools had 6,503 pupils and 425 teachers. Also, all but a few of 'Unayzah's school-aged children were enrolled in schools in 1986, according to school officials and other local citizens.

What we consider to be a negative change from this period is the decline in the productive base of 'Unayzah's local economy. Craftwork and artisanry had flourished in the old 'Unayzah and were integral parts of the city's market. A wide range of specializations existed—including, among others, leather processing, sandal-making, silver- and goldsmithery, woodwork and carpentry, house-building, and well-digging. Some of these occupations were held by individual men, and sometimes women, who chose to work on their own; but much of 'Unayzah's craft production was organized as domestic labor by family units and involved the participation of both men and women. With the import of cheap manufactured goods from both Western and Eastern industrial capitalist economies, the local craft production was undermined. By the mid-1970s, only a few sandal-makers and a smattering of other craftworkers continued to ply their trades.

Agriculture, the other main productive base of the economy, was also transformed. Some mechanization of farming was introduced. In the early 1960s, 'Unayzah had more than 500 mechanical irrigation pumps, about ten tractors, and some 20 threshing machines. The community had about 300 farms, of which about a fifth were new. Most of the new farms were larger than the old ones and produced new fruit and vegetable crops, in addition to the traditional dates, wheat, millet, alfalfa, squash, eggplant, and some spices. Reciprocal labor parties, which had involved male and female neighbors, became rare. Wage labor, which had always existed in 'Unayzah's agriculture and included both men and women, increased in scale. However, despite some marked advances in agricultural production during this period, farming began to be marginalized in the local economy. Those who worked on the farms were usually the very poor—especially women. The better educated and more ambitious youth (all males) obtained salaried employment, opened small businesses, or migrated for better opportunities elsewhere. Moreover, large areas of the old agriculture were destroyed to make way for new urban development.

Meanwhile, more and more of the food consumed in 'Unayzah was imported from abroad, as was also the case for consumer durables. The import of these items was no longer managed by 'Unayzah merchants and transporters, as had been the case in the past when local men directly organized all of 'Unayzah's imports of coffee, tea, cardamom, sugar, pepper, rice, cloth, and kerosene and its exports of dates, wheat, and ghee to other Arabian cities and of camels and horses to other countries. The town's new consumer items were increasingly imported by large commercial establishments in Riyadh and other cities. Thus, the trading dimension of 'Unayzah's market declined along with its craft and artisanry dimension. During this period, the market also lost its role as a major social center for men, who previously had regularly visited the market to meet friends and to exchange news about political, social, and other issues of common interest.

The Boom and Afterward, 1974 to 1986

In conjunction with the Sixth of October/Tenth of Ramadan War in 1973 against the Jewish state, Saudi Arabia and other oil producers declared a boycott on the sale of petroleum to numerous countries that supported Israel. As a result of this action, the Organization of Petroleum Exporting Countries (OPEC) was able to quadruple the world price of oil to about 12 U.S. dollars per barrel by early 1974. Subsequently, the price of oil soared to around 40 dollars. However, the price began to fall in 1982 and plummeted to about 13 dollars by the end of the 1980s. Since then, the price of oil has recovered slightly and, except for a short period associated with the Iraq–Kuwait conflict, has hovered between about 14 and 17 dollars a barrel. Oil has thus once again become a cheap commodity—at least in terms of constant dollars for production at the well-head.

As Saudi Arabia's revenue increased, the state's expenditures also increased—from 6 billion riyals in 1969–70 to a high of 283 billion riyals in 1981–82. Revenue fell by more than 22 percent in the following fiscal year, and expenditures dropped by 6 percent. With decline in both revenue and expenditures, a general slowing down of the economy started. In 1985–86, the Saudi Arabian state incurred its first budget deficit—of 50 billion riyals on expenditures of 181.5 billion riyals (Kingdom of Saudi Arabia 1984; 1987). Ten years later, as this article is written, the state is heavily in debt—largely a result of expenditures incurred to pay the United States for its Desert Shield and Desert Storm operations against Iraq in 1990 and 1991.

During the period of high oil prices (1974–82), Saudi Arabia embarked upon massive development programs and projects. These changes ignited what Saudi Arabians call the *tufra* ("boom" or "mutation"), which spread throughout the country from its main cities to the most remote villages and Bedouin camps.[13] The construction sector mushroomed, as the state rushed to build new highways, ports, airports, and other physical infrastructure and as families rushed to build new housing with generous subsidized loans from the state. New agriculture, also heavily subsidized by the state, expanded rapidly. Two huge industrial cities were created at Yanbu' on the Red Sea and Jubayl on the Arab Gulf. Large amounts of money were also spent on the expansion of social services, especially education and health care but also welfare programs for the needy. Along with these changes, masses of other Arab and foreign workers and professionals poured into the country and, according to Sirageldin, Sherbiny, and Serageldin (1984:32), represented an estimated 31 percent of the population and 53 percent of the labor force in 1980.

In 'Unayzah, one main manifestation of the *tufra* was the development of new agriculture, with major financial support through loans extended by the state's agricultural bank. Modest support for local agriculture had begun in 1965. However, the bank's lending capacity increased significantly in 1975–76, and between 1982 and 1986 the bank extended more than 1,500 loans to local farm-owners for a total of more than 230 million riyals. These loans were all interest-free, and many were subject to 50 percent discounts of the principal. They supported the purchase of imported irrigation and other farm equipment, the development of hothouse and chicken and egg farms, and other aspects of farm development.

The new agricultural development, initiated at the national level to ensure food security, has had spectacular results in the 'Unayzah area. Old farms in the Wadi ar-Rimmah have been modernized; and much of the nearby desert blooms with vast new fields of wheat, large and small orchards of fruit trees, and many new vegetable farms. All of the new desert agriculture is watered by supermodern irrigation systems, including central pivots and drip irrigation. A fish farm with seven artificial lakes was created in the desert near 'Unayzah; and several technologically sophisticated and computerized greenhouses produce huge amounts of vegetables year round for sale in large, modern supermarkets in Riyadh, Dammam, and Kuwait. The wheat grown near 'Unayzah has contributed to Saudi Arabia becoming self-sufficient in and a net exporter of this basic food crop. In 'Unayzah itself, the local market is often flooded with locally grown produce that exceeds local demand.

Yet, the success of the new agriculture is challenged by questions of ecological sustainability. Underground water within the Wadi ar-Rimmah is renewable from occasional rainfall. However, wells within the wadi are increasingly sunk to lower levels, indicating that water is being used more quickly than it is replenished. Water for irrigation in the desert outside the wadi comes from extremely expensive wells sunk to depths of 800 to 1,000 meters. These wells tap nonrenewable sources of water that formed in previous geological ages. The quantity of this ancient water is debated; but, like Saudi Arabia's oil, it cannot last forever. Moreover, the financial costs of this water extraction are almost never factored into cost-benefit analyses of the new agriculture.

The economic sustainability of the new agriculture is another challenge. The cost of producing a kilogram of wheat in Saudi Arabia was much higher than the world market price for wheat at the time of our fieldwork in 1986. Accordingly, the state purchased wheat from producers at the highly subsidized price of 3.5 riyals per kilo. Given its budget deficit in fiscal year 1985–86, the state lowered its price to 2 riyals in 1987—which produced howls of protest from farm-owners. Many of these began to switch to production of barley for use as fodder, which continued to have high subsidies as an indirect payment to the country's largely sedentarized Bedouin livestock raisers. Also, failure to develop modern processing and distribution systems has compromised 'Unayzah's production achievements, as huge amounts of fresh vegetables and fruits often go unsold in the local market and have to be destroyed.

Much of the new agriculture developed in other parts of Qasim and elsewhere in Saudi Arabia involved participation by members of the royal family and other super-rich urban business people who took advantage of the state's subsidies and engaged in this development for profit motives. None of the super-rich have been involved in 'Unayzah's new agriculture. Indeed, some of the new farms were developed by local men from lower and middle income levels and by the region's Bedouin; however, others are owned by relatively well-to-do local merchants, contractors, high-ranking bureaucrats, and the like. Some of these men have previous backgrounds in agriculture, while others do not.

Our guesstimate is that about 1,500 'Unayzah men have invested in developing a new farm or in significantly modernizing and expanding old ones. Most have hoped for easy profits; and, for some, a new farm has been seen more as a social investment than an economic one. This is especially the case for *basatin,* "gardens," located near the city. At best, many of the *basatin* barely covered their costs in 1986; but owners were content to enjoy social gatherings there with friends and family in modest chalets or around small swimming pools on the farms.

Since the *tufra,* both new and old agriculture in 'Unayzah has engaged local people almost exclusively as owner-managers. Manual labor on farms is no longer provided by local people, with a few minor exceptions when 'Unayzah women occasionally cut alfalfa or perform a few other farm chores. Thus, all farmworkers in 1986 were recruited from abroad, especially from Egypt but also from Pakistan, India, Afghanistan, the Philippines, and even several from Holland and the United States. According to our guesstimate, these expatriate farmworkers numbered about 3,300 men. By contrast, in 1974 just before the *tufra* began to have an impact, 'Unayzah's agriculture employed no full-time expatriates whatsoever.[14]

Another local manifestation of the *tufra* has been the construction of what is essentially a new city outside the perimeters of the old city, although the main market and the main mosque continue to be located within the area of the old 'Unayzah. The state's contribution to the new urban development has been enormous, as it financed all the required infrastructure—including well-paved streets and modern sewerage, water, electrical, and telephone networks. The state also provided financial assistance to individuals to construct new housing; and thus between 1973 and 1986 the real estate development fund extended some 4,800 interest-free loans of up to 300,000 riyals each to local citizens.

The building of the new 'Unayzah triggered spectacular increases in land prices, and some local real estate developers, contractors, and home furnishers made small fortunes. The construction also required the importation of a vast labor force from abroad, and for a while 'Unayzah was thronged with mainly unskilled expatriate laborers from Egypt, Pakistan, and other countries. Since most of the construction had been completed by the time of our research in 1986, these laborers were no longer a significant part of the scene in 'Unayzah. However, our guesstimate is that about 1,000 expatriate workers continued to be employed in construction and some other small "industrial" enterprises in the city.

By 1986, all but a handful of 'Unayzah people lived in new residences. The new houses are spacious and most have two and sometimes three floors, with men's reception rooms on the ground floor and women's reception rooms and the family living quarters on the upper floor or floors. Unlike the situation in parts of Riyadh, Jiddah, and some other Saudi Arabian cities, 'Unayzah has no palaces or exorbitantly luxurious villas. However, the new housing is fully equipped with modern conveniences, including air conditioning, and is usually well-furnished with a combination of Western and Arab styles. People say they are comfortable in the new housing, but many told us that much of it had been built in a rush by unskilled workers and, therefore, was quickly in need of repairs. Moreover, the costs of maintaining the new housing are high, especially after the state removed subsidies on electricity, water, sewerage, and telephones.

The local people acquired new housing but lost their old neighborhoods. These had been close-knit units in the old 'Unayzah, where extended families usually lived together and where women easily visited each other and maintained strong ties of cooperation and neighborliness. Also, both rich and poor had lived side by side in the old neighborhoods and together shared a common social world that was strongly focused on the neighborhood mosque. By contrast, the new urban areas are more stratified by income levels and also have a dispersed settlement pattern where houses are physically isolated from each other. Women, forbidden to drive automobiles in Saudi Arabia, are especially isolated in their new homes, as are elderly men who are unable to drive. Moreover, the new housing has contributed to a weakening of the extended family, since many younger people—with the help of state-sponsored loans—have been able to establish neolocal residences.

The *tufra* brought many other changes to 'Unayzah. Most of Saudi Arabia's private banks and major currency exchange houses (one of them founded by a man from 'Unayzah) opened branches in the city or expanded activities there. Small and moderate-scale commercial establishments mushroomed to sell imported irrigation and farm equipment, household appliances and furnishings, cars and pick-up trucks, and so on. The market expanded and began a brisk business in sales of a wide variety of cheap imported cloth and consumer durables— especially to the many expatriates who thronged the central market area on the Thursday–Friday weekend. Grocery stores, butcheries, bakeries, and moderate-sized supermarkets proliferated. The number of gold and jewelry shops increased. All of these commercial establishments are owned by local men and, in some cases, women, who are themselves active in the business. Some establishments engage sons of the owners in sales and other activities; but many only employ expatriate men, especially from Pakistan. According to our guesstimate, the market and commercial establishments engaged about 2,500 local men and women and employed about 3,600 expatriate men in 1986.

'Unayzah's private voluntary organizations also increased during the *tufra.*

A new philanthropic society was created in 1975 to help the needy and handi-
capped, to foster the development of cultural activities, and to maintain and
strengthen the society. Although supported by the state, up to 80 percent of the
society's financial resources came from *zakat* (alms) paid by individuals. In
1986, the society provided support to about 250 needy families, along with
assistance for a poor man to pay the *mahr* (dower) to get married and for a poor
woman to repay the *mahr* in case of a divorce initiated by her. It also provided
assistance for medical treatment not available in public hospitals and for meeting the payment of *diyah* (bloodwealth) in the case of deaths due to automobile
accidents. Moreover, the society was in the process of developing a nursing and
physical therapy center for both men and women and was eager to provide assistance to people who wished to pursue a career in technical occupations.

Meanwhile, two other voluntary associations flourished in 'Unayzah at the
time of our fieldwork. The Ibn Salih Center, founded to honor the memory of
'Unayzah's first modern school teacher, had impressive facilities and a wide
array of planned cultural, sports, and local development programs. A Committee
for the Beautification and Cleanliness of the City of 'Unayzah raised funds
through a small voluntary local tax on salaries and other contributions to plant
trees along major streets, build fountains and monuments in squares, develop
parks and recreational areas, and preserve 'Unayzah's architectural heritage
through restoration of old buildings and reconstruction of the main gates of the
old walled city.

All three of the associations enjoyed the strong support of local men and
women and of emigrants from the community. Many 'Unayzah people proudly
pointed to the associations and to many other voluntary initiatives by local individuals to improve the community as their own attempts to complement the
development efforts of the state. Indeed, they often said, "The government has
not done a little"—to imply that the state had done much but could not be
expected to provide everything needed for the creation of a fully developed
modern society.

Social Change

Rihani praised the hospitality of the people of 'Unayzah, who opened "the
doors of homes and hearts" to engage in conversation and social interaction. According to 'Unayzah's librarian, a man who largely ignored the
tufra, 'Unayzah's men all but abandoned their coffee hearths during the
tufra to run after business deals. However, by 1986, with the *tufra* over or
coming to a close, local men dedicated themselves, once again, to an active
social life of evenings, and often weekends, in the company of other men.
Like other Saudi Arabian communities, 'Unayzah maintains strong gender
segregation; Cole, the male anthropologist in our joint research, regularly

interacted as a participant observer in a comprehensive range of social settings that engage men.

These settings include groups composed of three or four generations of an extended family and others composed of peers and friends. Examples of the latter are a group of elderly men who share a common interest in farming and who meet every Thursday evening; a group of young and middle-aged employees of the agricultural directorate, bank, and research center who have a social gathering once a month; various groups of five to ten men of various ages who are members of a *da'ira* (circle) that meet daily or weekly on a rotating basis in the homes of the participants; and ad hoc groupings of friends that spend an evening or sometimes all day on Friday at a *bustan* or in the *barr* (wilderness) outside of town in the sand dunes. In addition, various men in 'Unayzah maintain open reception rooms, where all and sundry pass by to exchange greetings and to hear and pass on news of interest to the community.

Copious amounts of coffee and tea are consumed in all these gatherings and sometimes a meal is shared. In many cases, the men, young and old, dedicate themselves with passion to playing *balawt* (French, "*belote*"), a card game; but the art of conversation is highly developed. A taboo against talk about local women is strictly maintained, and open discussion of Saudi Arabia's internal politics almost never occurs. Yet, the men display keen interest in international politics and foreign cultural practices, often discuss business deals, and argue the pros and cons of investment in, say, foreign currency speculation. They exchange information about the techniques and practices of modern agriculture, complain about marketing problems for their farm produce, and discuss the difficulties of recruiting, training, and keeping expatriate laborers.

Very often the discourse of young and old recounts 'Unayzah's past glory and suggests a feeling of loss and, also, apprehension about the future. Younger men also speak generally about changing relations within the family—what working wives do with their salaries, how a husband feels when his wife's salary is higher than his own, the pros and cons of the nuclear family as compared to the extended family, the number of children a modern couple should have, and so on.

Women's socializing—as participated in and observed by Altorki, the female anthropologist in this study—is equally active in 'Unayzah, although women are much more constricted than men in their ability to move about the city to visit, because of their dependence on men to drive them from place to place. Thus to a large degree, women's visitations are focused among neighbors in the new areas where they now live and where women have particularly made a conscious effort to create and maintain ties among new neighbors. Following the construction of the new city as part of the *tufra,* women have initiated new friendship networks that regularly involve social gatherings that rotate weekly or biweekly among the homes of women in a network. These gatherings, which take place in the mornings, involve 15 or so women who live in walking distance of each other and are usually composed of older and unemployed women. Gatherings that include employed women usually take place in the afternoons but before sunset. The afternoon gatherings tend to include more younger women and unmarried girls who are still in school.

Topics of conversation vary somewhat by age and educational levels, but as is also the case among the men, interaction is egalitarian. Richer and poorer members of the group participate equally in animated conversations; and all are served by the hostess and her daughters, even when domestic servants exist. Often, the women discuss and evaluate new alternatives that confront women in almost all fields of behavior. They consider the importance and value of literacy for women; exchange information about employment and investment opportunities for women; argue about the ideal number of children a woman should bear; complain about the problems of recruiting, training, and keeping expatriate domestic servants; analyze the reasons for a divorce and the likelihood of whether a new marriage will be successful or not; discuss the achievements and problems of their children and other acquaintances; and so on. Like some of the men, older women express nostalgia for the old 'Unayzah with its tight-knit neighborhoods, strong extended families, and unquestioned respect for older members of the community.

The young in 'Unayzah still express deference to their elders; but the educated young men and women often prefer styles of behavior and dress that differ from those of the older generation; and many of them have new occupations where both men and women receive earned income. As mentioned, the young especially want to live as nuclear families, a phenomenon that often brings pain to a son's mother. Although the tendency is towards neolocal residence at marriage and thus the creation of a new nuclear family, the extended family continues to cast a strong shadow over the new household, which is unlikely to declare complete independence or break off as an autonomous unit separate from the web of family and kin ties.

Even as nuclear family households become more common, women strongly reaffirm ties to their natal families by regular visits and often by spending a whole day, usually Friday, at the homes of their mothers and fathers. Meanwhile, clan dinners that, along with affines, bring together men and women who share a common ancestral name have become regular occurrences that take place about once a month. Although the men and women sit and eat separately, the ties of family and kinship are maintained, as young and old meet and reaffirm ties of solidarity. Also, economic and education-based class barriers are muted, as literate and illiterate and rich and poor interact together as the common descendants of so-and-so. Meanwhile, clans increasingly research their genealogies and produce elaborate trees that in many cases now include the names of women and not only those of men, as was the case previously. Such groups also now form bank trusts from contributions from all the kindred to provide support for any relative in time of need.

Yet, a young wife wants to be free from the strict control of her mother-in-law and to have significant social interaction with her husband. As an individual, a young man also seeks a wife with a similar educational background and expects to share decisions with her. At the same time, however, he does not wish to lose his prerogatives as a man—to spend long evenings with his friends, to go on a vacation by himself or with friends, and to provide and control the household budget.

Except for the positions of amir and *'alim* (religious scholar) and work that involved travel, women in the old 'Unayzah engaged in the same occupations as did the men. A gendered division of labor existed, whereby—for example—men climbed palm trees to harvest dates but women processed the dates, and men planted wheat but women participated in the harvest and winnowed it. Very often men and women worked together as teams—to process leather, to draw water from wells by camel power and to irrigate fields, and so on. Although waged labor existed in the old 'Unayzah, most men and women worked as members of their domestic units and were not paid in cash but consumed what they jointly produced and/or what they could afford to buy from the sale of their products.

With development and the *tufra,* the economy in 'Unayzah has become totally monetized, and new occupations now engage the majority of 'Unayzah men and women. Economic change has not meant that women are strictly confined to the home and to housework and child-rearing. Indeed, 'Unayzah women continue to be active in the labor force outside the home; and, as in the past, they have jobs that often are not that different from those of their brothers and husbands. In public education, for example, 'Unayzah women, in 1986, held 876 out of 1,090 salaried positions (80 percent) as teachers and administrative and other personnel in girls' schools. An additional 350 local women daily commuted to work in girls' education in the nearby city of Buraydah and to villages in the region. They also worked as salaried employees in kindergartens, hospitals, clinics, health units, and the social affairs center. Still others worked as journalists, as managers and tellers in a bank for women, and as librarians and assistants in the women's library. Several 'Unayzah women were moneylenders; a significant number were owners or partners in business enterprises; and a few had achieved considerable success as self-employed tailors and dressmakers. Meanwhile, about 150 'Unayzah women managed and staffed their own shops in the central market.

These data challenge the widely held but mistaken belief that Saudi Arabian women do not work outside the home because of tradition. They clearly did so in the "traditional" past, and many work outside the home today. One motive for some who work as employees today is a chance to get out of the house and to pursue a career for individual social rewards. For many others, the income earned is a main motive that not only helps pay the bills but provides a woman with greater security in her relationship with her husband and in case of divorce. The importance of a woman's earned income to the household budget is seen indirectly when a young husband says, as is often the case, that his wife spends what she earns to buy clothes for herself and her children and to help pay for extraordinary household expenses, such as a year's supply of dates. The husband insists that he pays for the maintenance of his family in accord with an Islamic injunction to that effect. However, the "extras" his wife provides are of significant importance to the well-being of the household and, in most cases, improve the wife's status vis-à-vis her husband.

Women from wealthy families in 'Unayzah, it must also be mentioned, have worked as teachers out of a strong sense of community duty, even when it meant arduous travel across long and rough desert tracks to impart knowledge to youngsters in a remote village. Other high-status 'Unayzah women have likewise trained and worked as nurses so as to help abolish local cultural values against work in health care and nursing. Meanwhile, working outside the home is an "ordinary" fact of life for most 'Unayzah women today. Fathers usually support their daughters in this regard and insist that their right to work be included in their marriage contracts. And daughters almost always formally recognize the support of their fathers by giving him the money of their first month's salary. The only religiously sanctioned cultural restriction to a woman working outside the home is that she work in a gender segregated setting. However, a strong non-cultural barrier to women working outside the home in 1986 was a lack of job opportunities.

Educated 'Unayzah men, like their sisters and wives, also staff public education in the city and in nearby communities. However, local men have more opportunities for government employment, since most Saudi Arabian government offices are staffed exclusively by men. Before the *tufra,* many government positions that required technical expertise were staffed by professionals from other Arab countries. However, by 1986, young Saudi Arabians with university degrees or other appropriate higher education had replaced almost all other Arab professionals in government service in 'Unayzah. Thus, our guesstimate is that government employment in the city engaged about 3,000 Saudi Arabians and about 500 expatriates.

Almost all of the Saudi Arabians were people from 'Unayzah, while an additional 1,000 or so local residents were employed in similar work in Buraydah and other nearby villages and towns. The 500 or so expatriates were mainly employed in secondary schools, teacher training colleges, nursing and other higher technical institutes, a college of the Qasim branch of King Sa'ud University, and as doctors and dentists. However, with increasing numbers of appropriately qualified local men and women available, dependence on expatriate professionals was in decline.

The above presentation supports the conclusion that the wide majority of 'Unayzah's people have become middle class in terms of educational levels and types of occupation. They predominate in education and civil service positions and increasingly in professional work. They are also the owner-managers of farms, shops in the market and other commercial establishments, and of the city's few "industrial" enterprises. Most local citizens in 1986 enjoyed what they considered to be middle levels of income, while the locally rich were only moderately well-to-do when compared with the rich and super-rich of Riyadh, Jiddah, and Gulf coast cities such as al-Khubar. The locally poor, or those with limited incomes, were mainly Bedouin who had recently settled in the city or its suburbs; but Bedouin youth were rapidly acquiring modern general and technical education and were beginning their ascent into the middle class alongside their sedentary urban *(hadar)* compatriots.

The other poor in the community were expatriate laborers—perhaps 3,300 farm workers, 1,000 construction and "industrial" workers, 1,000 domestic servants, and 300 street sweepers and janitors. Many of the farm workers lived in relatively poor conditions on remote farms, while most of the others (except for the domestic servants who lived in the homes of their employers) crowded into the semi-ruins of housing in the old city. In addition to these workers, about 3,600 other expatriates were employees in the market and commercial establishments. They had higher salaries and usually higher educational levels than the laborers, tended to live in old but moderately good housing, and formed a kind of lower middle class. Meanwhile, the 500 expatriate professionals mentioned above were the elite among 'Unayzah's expatriates and enjoyed relatively high incomes and good physical standards of living.

Taken together, expatriates in 'Unayzah accounted for more than half of the actively engaged labor force in the community, according to our guesstimate in 1986. These people were clearly *in* the society but not *of* it. Among themselves, they were divided by nationality, class, and religion and thus did not act together as a group. Although some had accumulated long years of residence in 'Unayzah, turnover was high. Many of the expatriates worked for a couple of years, accumulated what to them were significant savings, and returned to their home countries. Thus, expatriate workers were generally seen as a problem by most local people. They were difficult to recruit; and most had to be trained locally—even Egyptian farmworkers from the Nile Valley lacked knowledge of and experience with modern desert agriculture and had to be trained almost from scratch. By the time they were properly trained, they tended to leave—often to be replaced by unskilled relatives or friends from their home villages.

Although seen as a problem, most local employers nonetheless found expatriates to be a cheap source of labor that was relatively docile and easy to control by termination of contract (and usually expulsion from the country) in cases of conflict or labor disputes. Expatriate farmworkers and other manual laborers faced no local competition for their jobs, since none of the local population wanted to engage in hard manual labor, as many of their grandfathers and grandmothers had done in the old 'Unayzah. However, expatriate employees in shops and commercial establishments did face potential competition from local people, at least according to our projections.

As educated young men and young women from 'Unayzah increasingly filled the locally available positions in government and education, their younger brothers and sisters were faced with unemployment, migration to other less desirable communities where good government jobs were still available, or acceptance of employment in local private sector commercial establishments. Yet, their employment in the local private sector was constricted by a combination of low salaries, employers' attitudes that Saudi Arabian employees are much harder to manage and control than the easily dismissed and usually docile expatriates, and a local social value that discourages local people from accepting employment from local people considered to be social equals or, in some cases, inferiors. Nonetheless, the younger generation of local people, faced with high costs of living and the economic slow-down after the end of the boom, were lowering their expectations and reluctantly beginning to accept second-choice employment in the local private sector.

Concluding Remarks

As anthropologists, one of our main goals in this presentation has been to de-essentialize discourse about Saudi Arabia. All too often, Saudi Arabia is stereotyped as composed of Bedouin and tribes, as being a super-rich oil producer, as having a powerful and conservative strain of Islamic belief and practice, as afflicted with high levels of corruption among political and business elites, as dependent on expatriate labor and expertise, and as having an authoritarian form of monarchical government. All of these elements exist within the social formation that is Saudi Arabia; but none of these elements alone or taken together represent the totality of the system that is contemporary Saudi Arabia.

Moreover, the structure and process of events that have unfolded in the country throughout the twentieth century have their Saudi Arabian specificities but are not unique as forms of development and transformation. Space does not permit a comparative presentation to prove this point; but we hold that a social scientific understanding of the country's transformation requires that Saudi Arabia not be exoticized or treated as a special case without parallel in other parts of the Arab World or elsewhere. Concomitantly, lessons learned from Saudi Arabia's experience with change and development can be applied to the experience of other countries and regions, and vice versa.

In early 1987 we sat together in Jiddah to reflect about what we had seen and heard in 'Unayzah and to write up our data. We often marveled at the pride and strength that emanated from the discourses of old and young and of men and women. Aside from occasional references to 'Abd al-'Aziz Ibn Sa'ud, we had heard almost nothing about the more recent kings or other members of the royal family. They and other super-rich urban business people, one might conclude, were irrelevant to the local community or perhaps were so involved in the global culture of international business and of foreign capitals and luxurious resorts that they had little in common with the "ordinary" people of provincial 'Unayzah, even if it had once been described as "Paris of Najd." Yet, the state loomed large in the development of the community and its economy.

People appreciated the contributions of the state to their local development; but they also stressed their own contributions and refused to be passive recipients of state handouts. Nonetheless, they eagerly took advantage of whatever was offered and often asserted that whatever revenue came from the sale of oil was, in fact, their money and not just the property of the state or of the royal family. We heard whispered references to the 1979 takeover of the Holy Ka'aba in Makkah by Muslims who spoke the old *muwahidun* language of austere self-reliance and the equality of believers. We knew others who eagerly researched the history of Qasim and Najd to counter the hegemonic view of the kingdom's history as presented in school textbooks. Others quietly expressed concern for what they saw as the excesses of the *tufra* and the squandering of vast sums of money, whether well-intentioned or not. Should one conclude that these muted voices were a sign of protest, of opposition?

We were astonished, along with the local people, at how the desert had bloomed with the new agriculture. Yet, we and they wondered about its future, given the water problem and the high economic subsidy the state could no longer afford. Was wheat grown in the country but dependent on imported labor, machines, and their spare parts really a contribution to national food security? Equally or more troubling was the future that awaited 'Unayzah's educated younger generations. Would they accept no jobs or not very good jobs without questioning the system that provides great wealth to some but only trickles of benefits to young men and women who are the descendants of what Rihani called "old families with ancient lineages and long traditions of virtuous behavior?" For how long can the state system, which once eagerly recruited and depended on the educated men of 'Unayzah and other old cities of Najd and Hijaz, block the active and regular political participation of the masses that the state itself helped to educate?

The peoples who live within the vast territories of Saudi Arabia have experienced and participated in two processes of change, each of which has been of transformational—even revolutionary—proportions. These are the creation of the contemporary state, which began almost 100 years ago, and the development of an oil-revenue based national economy about 50 years ago. Both of these "revolutions" have produced excesses, a phenomenon that is not uncommon in any substantive transformation. Yet, they are part of the history of the contemporary society and thus structure the future development of that society. The future, of course, is unknown; but further transformation seems likely. The high leadership of the state in the mid 1990s is aged, ailing, and tied more to the old society than to that of the present. The overwhelming importance of oil revenue in the national economy is also declining.

Thus, the peoples of Saudi Arabia, especially the rapidly growing and educated younger generations of men and women, face the challenge of restructuring the state system to allow for constructive political participation by all citizens without compromising the territorial unity forged by the contemporary state and without destroying its many achievements. Meanwhile, the peoples of Saudi Arabia, young and old, face the challenge of changed economic conditions that require adjustments in living standards, while the younger generations replace expatriate workers and professionals in the national labor force. The excesses and high expectations of the *tufra* are already part of the past; and adjustments to changed economic conditions and the replacement of the expatriate labor force are underway. Hopefully, at least from our point of view, the state will transcend its rigidity and foster, or at least allow, the creation of a political economy that is inclusive and thus strong in its capacity to guarantee the political and economic well-being of the national society in all of its multiple and complex dimensions—including 'Unayzah, the old "fortress of freedom . . . , the epitome of good taste and of literature, Paris of Najd!"

Notes

1   For a detailed description of 'Unayzah in 1878, see Doughty (1979 [1888], 2:357–485). For more recent works that address the past and, also, contemporary changes in 'Unayzah, see Sharif (1970), al-Misallam (1985), al-Wasil (1986), and as-Salman (1989).

2   The national census conducted in 1974 was classified and thus not available to us. We estimated that the city had about 50,000 inhabitants in 1986; but local officials usually gave a figure of 70,000 for the population at that time.

3   Unayzah is not unique in this regard. Other old cities which have declined in *relative* size and importance are 'Unayzah's old rival, Buraydah, and Ha'il, Hufuf, and at-Ta'if. Makkah and Madinah, of course, remain as enduring holy cities of Islam. An old city that has recently gained in importance is Abha, while small towns that have rapidly expanded include, among others, Khamis Mushayt, Yanbu', Jubayl, and Tabuk.

4   One community, of course, cannot be taken as typical or representative of the country as a whole. However, 'Unayzah is a part of Saudi Arabia and shares much with numerous other communities that exist between the extreme poles of the country's now almost non-existent nomadic Bedouin and the cosmopolitan elites of, say, Jiddah or Riyadh.

5   "Sustainability" refers to the capacity of a process to maintain itself indefinitely. Thus, *sustainable* economic growth is a process that will continue for a significantly long period of time. *Sustainability* from the perspective of the ecology implies that environmental resources will not be depleted but will be maintained for the use of future generations.

6   For an example of this point of view, see Sirageldin, Sherbiny, and Serageldin (1984). Other strong stereotypes that distort the complex and changing realities of Saudi Arabia are Sweet's characterization of Najd as a "Bedouin zone" where exchange occurred through raiding rather than markets (1965), Ibrahim's assertion that the highest sociopolitical form ever achieved was the tribe and that the country's modern institutions and infrastructure had to be built "from scratch" by migrants from outside Saudi Arabia (1982:104, 151), and Safran's claim that Arabia previously existed in "a state of nature" (1985:21).

7   Most contemporary Arab states were formerly provinces of the Ottoman *dawla* (state) and were also entities in the British, French, or Italian empires. Saudi Arabia, as presently constituted, was not an Ottoman province. However, some parts of the country were variously included in the Ottoman system—but more in theory than in practice, except for the cities of Hijaz and, on some occasions, Ahsa'. None of the territories of Saudi Arabia were ever colonized. For a discussion of these issues, see Salame (1980:35–41).

8   See Habib (1978), Kishk (1981), and al-Hamad (1986) for discussions of the roles of the *muwahidun*, the *ikhwan*, and others in the creation of the contemporary state.

9   Descendants of the Prophet, the *ashraf* formed a "nobility" in the Hijaz. The Sharif of Makkah and other Hijazi officials were usually appointed by the Ottoman state from among the Hashemite "nobles," or *ashraf*, in the area.

10   See Cole and Altorki (1992) for a discussion of tribal and non-tribal sociopolitical organization in pre-oil Arabia.

11   One U.S. dollar was equivalent to about 3.65 Saudi riyals at the time of our research.

12   Significant numbers of 'Unayzah migrants from this and earlier periods have settled in Jiddah, Riyadh, Bahrain, Kuwait, and Zubayr in Iraq.

13   The *tufra* in Saudi Arabia coincided with the *infitah*, or open door economic policy, in Egypt. Indeed, the two processes had strong links, including the labor migration of millions of Egyptians to Saudi Arabia and other Arab oil-producing countries. Remittances sent back by these workers and professionals provided a main source of financial capital for private initiatives in Egypt associated with the *infitah*.

14   Some non-local men were engaged as casual laborers on farms, most of them from Yemen or Hadramawt (see al-Wasil 1986:80).

Bibliography

Almana, Mohammed. 1980. *Arabia United: A Portrait of Ibn Saud*. London: Hutchinson Benham.

Altorki, Soraya, and Donald P. Cole. 1989. *Arabian Oasis City: The Transformation of 'Unayzah*. Austin: University of Texas Press.

Cole, Donald P., and Soraya Altorki. 1992. "Was Arabia Tribal? A Reinterpretation of the Pre-Oil Society." *Journal of Asian and Middle Eastern Studies* 25 (4):71–87.

Doughty, Charles M. 1979. *Travels in Arabia Deserta*. New York: Dover Publications. (First published 1888.)

Habib, John S. 1978. *Ibn Sa'ud's Warriors of Islam: The Ikhwan of Najd and Their Role in the Creation of the Sa'udi Kingdom, 1910–1930*. Leiden: E. J. Brill.

al-Hamad, Turki. 1986. "Tawhid al-jazira al-'arabiya: dawr al-'idyulujiyah wa-l-tanzim fi tahtim al-bunya al-'ijtima'iya al-'iqtisadiya al-mu'ayyiqa li-l-wahda," *al-Mustaqbal al-'Arabi* 93:27–40.

Ibrahim, Saad Eddin. 1982. *The New Arab Social Order: A Study of the Social Impact of Oil Wealth*. Boulder: Westview Press.

Kingdom of Saudi Arabia. 1984. *Achievements of the Development Plans 1390–1404 (1970–1984): Facts and Figures*. Riyadh: Ministry of Planning.

———. 1987. *Annual Report 1406 (1986)*. Riyadh: Saudi Arabian Monetary Agency.

Kishk, Muhammad Jalal. 1981. *As-Sa'udiyun wa-l-hal al-islami: masdar shar'iya li-l-nizam al-sa'udi*. Cairo: al-Matba'a al-Fanniyah (1984 edition).

al-Misallam, Ibrahim. 1985. *al-'Uqaylat*. Riyadh: Dar al-Asasalah li-l-Thaqafah wa-l-Nashr wa-l-'Alam.

Philby, Harry St. John. 1928. *Arabia of the Wahhabis*. London: Constable and Company.

Rihani, Amin. 1980. *Muluk al-'arab*. Beirut: al-Muassasah al-'Arabiya li-l-Dirasat wa-l-Nashr. (First published in 1924.)

Safran, Nadav. 1980. *Saudi Arabia: The Ceaseless Quest for Security*. Cambridge, MA: Harvard University Press.

Salame, Ghassan. 1980. *Al-Siyasa al-kharijiya al-sa'udiya mundu 'amm 1945*. Beirut: M'ahad al-Inma' al-'Arabi.

as-Salman, M. A. 1989. *'Unayzah*. Riyadh: Matba'a Jami'at al-Malik Sa'ud.

Sharif, 'Abd ar-Rahman Sadiq. 1970. *Mantiqat 'Unayzah: Dirasah 'Iqilimiyah*. Cairo: Matba'at an-Nahdah al-'Arabiya.

Sirageldin, Ismail A., Naiem A.Sherbiny, and Ismail M. Serageldin. 1984. *Saudis in Transition: The Challenge of A Changing Labor Market*. Oxford: Oxford University Press.

Sweet, Louise E. 1965. "Camel Raiding of North Arabian Bedouin: A Mechanism of Ecological Adaptation." *American Anthropologist* 67:1132–50.

al-Wasil, 'Abd ar-Rahman bin 'Abd Allah. 1986. "al-'Umran al-rifi fi mantiqat 'Unayzah" Masters thesis, Imam Muhammad Ibn Sa'ud University, Saudi Arabia.

3

State, Legitimacy, and Democratization in the Maghreb

Abdelbaki Hermassi

Is the Arab state condemned to remain a diminished state, permanently suffering from a legitimacy deficit? Does the absence of sufficient legitimacy result from a recurrent structural lack of moral justification, from a political experience of non-correspondence between the political entity and the community of which it is a member?

Historically the Arab state has had to find its justification in its being linked to the Islamic ecumenical grouping; once decolonization got under way, the ecumenical grouping of Islam shrank simply to a religious community. It is now the Arab corpus that is the main unit of reference and identification; it is with reference to the Arab whole that the public interest is seen and the general will defined. Abdallah Laroui notes that the state organization is merely "the transitional instrument that has to be used to bring into being a human type that alone is judged to be worthy of the legitimate ambition of the Arabs. Like the nostalgia for the caliphate (which it replaces), the utopia of the union does instead of a theory of the lawful state; in this very way it prevents a serious grasp of the real state."[1]

Even with the strengthening of the state apparatus and territorial sovereignties, in the absence of a theory of the state, the modern Arab state lacks legitimacy. Salafism and unionism deny states any possibility of legitimatization because they see in them the main obstacle to the achieving of a wider entity, one that would better satisfy hearts and spirits—in a word, a charismatic community. The same goes for modern ideologies; both liberalism and Marxism tend to present existing states not as legitimate in their own right, but as instruments of a class or of a constellation of classes pursuing immediate material interests. At the very moment when the state is becoming stronger in material terms, it cannot win the loyalty of its citizens because of an ideological heritage that is both negative and impossible to circumvent.

This kind of approach to the question of state legitimacy, while generally valid for the whole Arab world, must nonetheless take account of a certain num-

From Ellis Goldberg et al, eds., *Rules and Rights in the Middle East: Democracy, Law, and Society* (Seattle: University of Washington Press, 1993), pp. 102–117. Reprinted by permission. Abdelbaki Hermassi is Professor of Sociology at the University of Tunis and currently Minister of Culture of Tunisia.

ber of regional specificities. The particular cases of the Maghreb states are notable, if only because there the twin sources of state delegitimatization spring mainly from Berberism and Islamism.

State capabilities also affect the bases of legitimacy. How able the state is to carry out certain duties and offer well-defined services expected by its inhabitants will, beyond any shadow of a doubt, affect the state's legitimacy, just as it will that of the regime and that of its government. In answering people's needs to identify with a group or a community, the state creates a basis for what we may call external legitimacy. But there is also an internal legitimacy of the regime, ensuring peace, protecting members from outside and domestic dangers, and maintaining at least a minimum of welfare and a certain standard of living.

Where the state fails to perform these tasks, one can find all sorts of reactions—the dissatisfied may protest to attract the attention of the authorities, or they may transfer their loyalty to revolutionary movements or to ethnic groups. They may sink into cynicism or alienation, interspersed from time to time with riots, terrorist acts, or other expressions of discontent.[2]

The Maghreb state has always tried to define its legitimacy in black-and-white terms: one indivisible nation, Arab language, Islamic faith. Such a position almost by definition excludes the expression of conflicting interests or the affirming of ethnic or religious diversity. Thus, instead of laying down general values susceptible of normative and situational adaptation, the call for legitimacy tends to stiffen into a rigid formula, unable to accommodate differences.

We may claim at the outset the impossibility of legitimizing the Maghreb state through the Islamist or Arab utopia. These competing conceptions of political order would deprive the state of any form of loyalty and leave it only the language of force. "The local State equips, teaches, employs and organizes . . . but these achievements do not bring it loyalty or create a consensus around it, particularly since its propaganda endlessly repeats that the State only represents a stage along the road to the great unitary Arab State."[3] These utopias would convey an ideology at odds with the tasks the state performs in its existing boundaries.

When assessing state-building in the Maghreb, it is important to draw a distinction between the Maghreb states—which are widely accepted as frameworks of political reference—and the Maghreb regimes—which are going through a fairly severe legitimacy crisis. This distinction may help account for both the conflicts and the resistance that the government's action (or inaction) provokes and the true limits of the various levels of anti-establishment activity.

The Maghreb of the last fifty years has enshrined nationalism as the dominant ideology. It was nationalism that enabled it to withstand the long night of colonialism; it was the triumph of nationalism that led it to build up the state system and set in place ambitious projects of economic development. Unlike the

Arab East, where the ideology of Pan-Arab unity triumphed, it was the idea of a territorially limited national state and nationalism that emerged triumphant. This happened in the 1930s, when the national elites succeeded in downgrading Salafi reformism and elbowing out the supporters of liberalism and socialism. Moreover, none of the political parties that embraced the national movement presented a Pan-Arab platform. The (1958) Tangiers Congress, meeting with the dominant theme of the unity of the Greater Arab Maghreb, merely consecrated the independent territorial state, a position already enjoyed by Morocco and Tunisia, and one that had to be won for Algeria.

It is not that the nationalists let slip opportunities for mobilizing religious feeling or activating the sense of Arab solidarity. The striking fact remains, however, that these issues were subordinated to one major cause—that of serving the political communities that were taking shape in Tunisia and Morocco and Algeria, which were seen almost as nations in themselves. We shall have the chance to see that the ambiguity between local nationalism and wider Arab nationalism persisted. But the fact remains that Maghrebis have an attitude to the national state that is not constitutively negative. The idea, widespread in the Arab East, of a state that is nothing but the artificial creation of a colonialism that splintered up entities into states, is one that does not correspond to the experience of most Maghrebis. Even though the regimes in power have had to face a series of crises reflecting the painful birth of civil society, the idea of a national state has not been directly challenged.

Why were Maghrebi states more broadly accepted than those in the Arab East? Among the reasons are a history of relatively powerful political centers (this tradition was greatly strengthened by the colonial impact), the fact that the Maghreb was profoundly Islamized but not completely Arabized, and the Maghreb's geopolitical position, including its role as a cultural boundary. The result of all this has been that the Islamic (or, if one prefers, the Arab–Muslim) connotation is more likely to prevail over ideological and militant Arabism. It is in the light of these influences that one starts to understand how lasting, distinct political entities, based on a deep sense of collective identity, have historically taken shape.

And what has become of the regimes at the end of over a quarter century of independent existence? First, we must understand that everything, or nearly everything—the legacy from the past, the rapid erosion of traditional society— has helped place the state at the center of the processes of national integration and socioeconomic development. What the people expected from independence and independent government was that it give access to everything the colonial system had withheld—security, jobs, social mobility, and dignity. The converging of these expectations with the demands of state-building constituted the substance of the national project as it presented itself over the last few decades. Ideally, the formula strove towards the taking over of society by the state. As it was not possible to count on the spontaneous functioning of social forces to realize so ambitious a project, the idea was that the society had to be transformed. Whether it was a plausible reason or an excuse, this postulate allowed the existing social institutions to be neutralized and replaced by more or less corporate structures for the purpose of providing a framework of society within the state apparatus.

The degree to which the state could take over rested on a whole series of considerations: the class structure, the degree of social and political mobilization, and, particularly, each state's predisposition. Morocco was from the outset liberal; Algeria enlisted the state in a vast project of industrialization; and Tunisia vacillated (as it still does) between bureaucratic and liberal capitalism.

But despite differences of approach, the enlisting of the state produced results that were everywhere dramatically visible. Since independence, the infrastructure of each state has doubled or tripled; societies have been profoundly shaken and transformed to the point of becoming unrecognizable under the weight of a series of development plants; a new class of private and state entrepreneurs has been born; a broad, replenished working class is starting to test its strength.

Yet popular support for the state's ambitious project could not last forever. Disenchantment with development policies became obvious in the late 1970s, as increasingly did the fact that the political formula and the very program of the national liberation movement seemed to have exhausted their potential.

It is true that in the past signs of discontent had always existed, but the government of the first years of independence enjoyed a considerable margin of maneuver. People were ready to have faith and accept measures of austerity and hardship in the hope of a better future, if not for themselves then for their children. It was only when certain outcomes of the development policy, such as the widening of old gaps and the creation of new disparities, started to become visible that discontent took on crisis proportions and that the national consensus was challenged.

In society, the crisis has taken the form of an increasingly marked intolerance of inequality. This intolerance first showed itself in the working-class union milieu, where there was a record number of strikes, both legal and illegal. Worse still was the bursting in on the political scene of the rejects, those whom growth has excluded. Class consciousness and corporate-based and sector-based interests have become more pronounced, to the detriment of national unity. Above and beyond the objective disparities between income brackets, what has made awareness of the gaps between the various social categories more acute has been the behavior of the nouveaux riches. From Ibn Khaldun to Veblen it has been clear that the nouveaux riches display luxury and novelty, leading to social disintegration. Ostentatious consumption produces hostility and envy in the popular classes and despair among the young, particularly the students. With the proliferation of educational degrees, the student masses have lost all hope of achieving a status similar to that which preceding generations of graduates attained.

Increasingly, success and mobility are seen as linked to favoritism, patronage, and regionalism rather than to hard work and competence. The politicians themselves, to paraphrase Max Weber, do little to dispel the impression that they live *from* rather than *for* politics. The result is that Maghreb states are far from the takeover of society by the state that was seen as the start of independence. Indeed, these states are far closer to the privatizing of the state. Certainly, the "state" never really drowned the "private," even in its most authoritarian phases. What is distinctive about the present situation is, on the one hand, the attempt by pressure groups to monopolize the state and, on the other, the appearance of resistance and protest that can no longer be accommodated within the existing framework.

What people now call national disenchantment does not exclusively concern class conflicts; the challenges of the left and unions to specific politics are aimed at the social and political arrangements themselves. The essential preoccupation of the leading elites has been with economic and social development—"how to catch up with the West." In the past, the opposition attacked the means, the state-centered framework, rather than the ultimate ends. In contrast, the new opposition has been concerned with considerations of identity and justice, the state-centered framework, and is almost indifferent to the problems of development and efficiency.

In the past there was a more or less explicit social pact by which citizens abdicated their political rights in favor of the government which, in turn, guaranteed them social rights. It was in the name of this pact that the people granted a quarter of a century of obedience to the political slogan of the day: "One man, one party, one plan." The 1970s and 1980s were years of social and cultural clashes. By the 1990s the state was showing increasing signs of withdrawal and disengagement; it is the whole political system that will be convulsed.

After years when the number of strikes increased dramatically among the workers, a cycle of riots began: urban riots in Morocco in 1981 and Tunisia in 1984 [see the article by Lahmar in this volume], and the Algerian explosion of October 1988. In most cases, these came in reaction to the state's retreat from certain sectors of social life as a result of adjustments ordered by the International Monetary Fund. There was thus a weakening of the distributive capacity of the state, hurting the lower classes. At the same time, these adjustments led to a closer association between the rulers and the nouveaux riches.

The protest is, in part, against the class nature of the state and the dwindling of its scope. But there is also protest against the state's cultural policy and its identification with the worldly nouveaux riches. The reaction to the cultural orientation of the state can be seen in the reemergence of a Berber cultural claim, very well described (as regards Algeria) by Mohamed Harbi.

Harbi tells how the Kabyle cadres, when independence dawned, felt great bitterness at being excluded from political power, while other groups, even those less committed on the battlefield, benefited from the fruits of Kabyle action. The successive presidents of Algeria were aware of these Kabyle reservations, but they believed they could overcome them [by] treating Kabylia in an economically and socially preferential way. At the same time, haunted by the fear of any Kabyle separatism, they prevented all demonstrations of Berber identity. Supported by the desire to assert the authority of the state and to create a uniform society, Arabization was originally thought of as a social control operation. The aim of state leaders was less the solution of the cultural question than the orchestration of the voice of the people, but their policies served to show all the erring ways of the state as primary employer and sole cultural entrepreneur.

Administrative Arabization, with its daily harassments in the courts, in traffic checks, and in schools, provoked tensions and bad feelings. A tendency to reject the Arabic language, hitherto unknown in Kabylia, gradually grew up. The signs of cultural unrest continued to increase. In Paris in 1967 the Berber Academy was born, which took up all the excesses and ideological simplifications of Arab Islamism. In 1973 the Algerian government took another step towards cultural repression by abolishing the chair in Berber held by the writer Mouloud Mammeri. Assertion of cultural identity left the university benches and went out into the street. It was shown by exclusive use of Berber and French in a number of cafés, hotels, and restaurants and even in some administrations in Algiers (the Popular Communal Assembly and Wylaya). Everything became a pretext for refusing the arbitrary decisions of the state. Under the cover of sport, the J.S.K. Tizi-Ouzou football club served as a rallying point and attracted increasingly anti-authority crowds. In May 1977 at Algiers stadium, in the presence of President Boumedienne, the cultural demand became explicit.

> The explosion of Tizi-Ouzou in 1980 was aimed at the absolutist state and posed the problem of democracy and the right to be different for all Algerians. A form of national integration that denied diversity compromised the unity of Algeria, a unity that no Kabyle questions today.[4]

Even on an economic level, the national state saw itself deprived of its monopoly. It was the entrepreneurs and the business people in the private sector and especially the informal sector who were going to gain in status at the expense of the cadres and the educated elites. This phenomenon is well described by Moncef Bouchrara, talking about what he calls the rampant industrialization in Tunisia.

The vast majority of entrepreneurs in the informal sector and even the big entrepreneurs have not finished their schooling (that is, they are mainly monolingual in Arabic). Nevertheless, they have shown an extraordinary spirit of enterprise. But this enterprise is only partly based on individual initiatives, ingenuity, and motivation. It depends, too, on the mobilization and strategies of traditional basic groups such as family, clan, village, and regional communities. (For example, the political and institutional role of private entrepreneurs: Makhtar Zarrouk, Abdelwaheb Ben Ayed, Haj Soula, and the emergence of Sfax, the areas of the Cap Bon, and Sidi Bou Zid.) It is an "ethno-entrepreneurial class."

This ethno-entrepreneurial class, from Sfax, Djerba, Metouia, and Khiari, is founded on cultural resources. Today, three-quarters of the commercial and industrial businesses created in Tunis belong to people who come from the south of Tunisia—from Sfax to Djerba, including Metouia and Matmata. This class's activities reach to Europe, as migrants create enterprises across networks of economic specialization and ethnic solidarity. For the last ten years, across the Maghreb, it [this class] has been at the forefront of economic growth. It has given birth to thousands of illegal and unauthorized markets. Trabendo, Souk Libya, and 'la Rue Zarkoun' are just so many places of exchange and negotiation, just so many means for people to organize *things* at a societal level that they cannot do at the state level.

The crisis of authoritarian legitimacy, along with the difficulties of the state in taking a central position on the socioeconomic level, foretells a certain autonomization of civil societies. In this respect, we can see three vectors of change.

First and foremost is the formation of political parties, even if these parties continue to experience difficulties in building up a social basis of their own in order to get away from their club status and have a real say on the political scene. Then there are the human rights organizations. More numerous and more active in the Maghreb than in the Mashreq, these groups make up a growing opposition. Even when used by the powers that be, they show a sensitivity to the law and serve as an embryo of public opinion. Finally, there are the women. Excluded from society and from power in certain Arab countries, suffering under the weight of discriminatory legislation in most Arab states, everywhere subject to what Stuart Mill called the despotism of custom, Arab women have been the rejects of social development. In several Arab countries, they have demonstrated their disagreement when discriminatory legislation has been adopted. In addition to defending statutory interests, the Arab women's protest has the value of an example to society as a whole. She is asking for her autonomy, in fact. In practice, it not a question of knowing—as certain people would have it—whether religion or the law grants these rights to women, but of knowing what women think and do with the rights that are granted.

It is, however, essential to note here that the emergence of a civil society and the birth of free public opinion continue to meet serious obstacles. What can be confirmed is that different elements in society see themselves less and less in terms of the vertical, monolithic organization of the party-state. The state is trying to disengage itself from society, without giving up its political monopoly.

Maghreb states have readjusted their economic politics in response to national and international pressures. But they believed they could do this without turning the local political configuration upside down. Economic liberalization *(infitah)* could be accompanied by the maintenance of political hegemony: what Clifford Geertz calls authoritarian liberalism, or the emergence of a combination between "this Smithian idea of how to get rich and this Hobbesian idea of how to rule."[5]

It is in this context that we should situate the rise in power of the Islamist movement. Islamism was inconceivable as long as the national state still operated, in fact and in belief, as a welfare state. It was only when the population felt abandoned to bare market principles, and when the party-states reacted to the advances of the civil society and to the erosion of their authority by a reinforcement of their monopoly, that Islamism erupted onto the scene. It was with the dismantling of the national union, the Tunisian General Workers' Union (UGTT—Union Générale des Travailleurs Tunisiens) in 1978, which represented the most important social counterpower, that the Tunisian regime signed its defeat; in Algeria, it was the riots of 1988 and the murderous scale of repression that consecrated the end of populism and the beginning of political anomie.[6]

The Islamist movement presented itself as the appointed beneficiary and sole legitimate inheritor, bringing the legitimacy crisis to its paroxysm. One has to acknowledge the skill of this movement in exploiting the two themes to which the Maghreb population was very sensitive, namely, justice and identity. It is because the political parties did not identify this kind of concern that they did not capture the aspirations of the people. The IMF-induced reforms carried out by the government provoked serious resistance; the move from a distributive economy to an economy regulated by the price system and competition inevitably creates apprehension.

Throughout the Maghreb, those who were excluded from economic growth and those who lost out in the structural adjustment found a voice in the Islamist associations, which set out to improve conditions of daily life: employment, housing, transport. Weaving social protest with a moral and religious discourse denouncing inequality and injustice, corruption and complacency, the Islamists quickly became the leading opposition. They knew the language that transforms the humiliating daily battle to find food into a general struggle against a political regime held up as responsible for the frustrations of every moment.

With the exhaustion of official nationalism as well as the left-wing ideologies, Islam rapidly became a pole for mobilization; an instrument of training, a field for political autonomization, cultural possibilities, and economic development. Does the Islamist component carry demands for fundamental modification of the political system?

This is François Burgat's thesis; he sees a new wave of nationalism in contemporary Islamism. Doubtless, he argues, Islamist mobilization is owing in part to the weakening of the regimes in place. Doubtless it also contains an "extremist" section. But Islamism is really pursuing in a more global way the exploitation of an old nationalist dynamism.[7]

It restores to the dominated the possibility of expressing themselves in their own language. By enabling them to act and express themselves politically in the categories of their culture, it restores historical continuity to the collective imagination, which the colonial parenthesis had interrupted. This lexical and syntactic break with Western political terminology is deeply felt by the countries of the North. The response of the French right reminds us of its reaction towards those known as *fellaghas*; as for the left, stuck in their literal attachment to the symbols of secularism, it is will suffering from the possibility

> that one day someone might dare to write a piece of history in a different vocabulary to the one it has forged. But in fact, the birth of a new Islamist political generation is no less or more hostile to France and no less or more incapable of adopting democratic behavior than these fellaghas, whom it supports today, were in their time.[8]

However, the image of Islamism that is most often taken up by those in power and in the media is that of accumulated frustrations, a sign of dead ends rather than a medium of transformation. This interpretation is almost perfectly illustrated in the writings of Gilles Kepel. The democratic aspirations of young people, in this view, have been blocked by those who have grabbed power and wealth since independence, and who are today attempting to pass on privilege to their children. Those children have been educated in Europe, in the United States, or in Western educational institutions on the spot, while the majority only has the right to monolingual education, putting it at a disadvantage on the labor market, which in turn feeds frustration even more.

> During the last fifteen years, this democratic frustration among the young has mainly been expressed through the only channel open to it: the reislamization movements. . . . [T]hese movements have sought to fill the function left vacant by oulamas that have been weakened or taken into the public service. Expressing themselves "in the name of God," interpreting as they please the sacred texts that are all their militants (the literate ones) read, they denounced in the same breath the "impiety of those in power and the social injustice suffered by a younger generation denied a future."[9]

Kepel argues that reislamization "from the top," the conquest of the state following the example of the Khomeinist strategy, began to run out of steam in the

1980s. The new movements of reislamization "from the bottom" had no revolutionary ambition. Instead, they offered palliatives to the shortcomings of the state in all the social domains (education, health, youth training, unemployment, etc.). They sought to create a sort of countersociety around the network of mosques that obeyed the commands of the sacred texts to the letter in daily life. These "from the bottom" movements, unlike their predecessors, were endowed with a real popular base and profited both from the leniency of the established authorities, who saw them as a distraction from the radical and political forms of reislamization, and from considerable subsidies, particularly from Saudi Arabia and Kuwait.

Thus there is a countersociety that can be tolerated up to a certain point, but that invariably, at one time or another, poses the question of its access to the political system and that more often than not is blocked. Cornered in this impasse are the youth who have been tempted by violent solutions or the search for distractions, even temporary ones, such as the recent support (1990–91) for the adventure of the Iraqi regime. Unless the West manages to find solutions to the structural economic problems of the Middle East, "the political language of revolutionary Islam," says Kepel, "will inevitably become the bellicose speech of a South looking for revenge."[10]

How can one deal with Islam? The failure of the Maghreb regimes in terms of satisfying material needs and offering hope to the urban youth does not necessarily put them on a collision course with the Islamists. What I and Remy Leveau, among others, are arguing is for inclusion of the Islamists in a more democratic setting. A democratic state and Islamists could have distinct and complementary functional roles.

Leveau suggests a parallel between the role played by the Islamists in the contemporary Maghreb and Arab societies and the role of the communist parties in Europe in the 1930s; the two movements effectively offer those who have been disappointed by economic growth and modernization a "somewhere else." This alternative allows them to dream, while at the same time accepting compromises that will reinforce the system for the time being, allowing the states to make a certain number of concessions to the latest challengers.

Leveau writes,

> If the Islamist movements still appear in the collective imagination as a
> sort of counterstate, a more realistic perception should attempt to analyze
> what their role could be in a more democratic setup. The sudden changes
> that have taken place in the Maghreb since the removal of Bourguiba in
> November 1987 allow us, perhaps for the first time, to envisage democ-
> ratization as a realistic strategy for the state apparatus to consolidate its
> power while running fewer risks than in maintaining a facade of abso-
> lutism that puts it at a disadvantage in the competition with the Islamists.
> This supposes on the one hand that the Islamist movements are granted

recognition and that in return they agree to participate in an institutional interaction that will legitimize the state and whose objective will in fact be protection against the seizure of power. For this, the various participants have to trust one another, especially in the transition phase, and the Islamist leaders, if they are not thinking of taking all the power for the moment by submitting themselves to the decisions of universal suffrage, as is foreseeable, have to have the hope of participating in an institutional setup where they have some influence.[11]

I have quoted this text in full, because it is a text that, while presenting the political problem confronting the Maghreb and the Arab world, also includes and the apriorisms and constraints that prevent easy or rapid solutions. Given the accumulated vulnerabilities of states in pursuit of legitimacy, is it possible for them to concede a "forum function" of defending those excluded from growth to their Islamist challengers? And are the Islamists, who have for so long claimed to be the exclusive representatives of the community, capable of coming out of anti-establishment activity and agreeing to be one party among many? All the signs indicate that the process of learning democracy will be long and difficult.

In reality, political openness has started badly. Since the early 1980s, the regimes began to envisage or to introduce a multiparty system not as an end in itself, but rather as the price of a certain disengagement of the state from society and as a compensation for getting the different social partners to accept economic reforms. Even in the Algerian experience—where the regime invested the most in the democratic wager—from the outset, the experience was an opening manipulated by Chadli's team, which wanted to remain in power, and by part of the FLN, which wanted to participate in a new government dominated by the Islamists. In fact, the stake in the October 1988 crisis and the ensuing "openness" was not initially the setting up of a transition to democracy. This after all was not what workers and young rioters were demanding. As Abdelkader Djeghloul saw so clearly, Chadli's team sought the "eviction of the old guard," whether populist or FLN, which represented an obstacle to liberal economic reforms. By winning the "Indian wrestling," in some way they played the sorcerer's apprentice: they did indeed liberate forces over which they had less and less control.[12]

Elsewhere, political liberalization took place on a basis of antagonism between the most acculturated elites and the Islamist counterelites, an antagonism that took the form of a real cultural schism. If the elites as a whole became hostile to those in power, it remains that both the elites and the middle classes saw in the rise of Islamism a serious threat to their status, their vision of the world, and their way of life. This growing split was noticed in the universities, in the union struggles, and in the great debates about subjects as diverse as the status of women, the Gulf crisis, and the nature of civil society. Gradually the competition between the two poles became an almost limitless struggle for hegemony rather than an accommodation within a democratic setting.

In fact, all the camps have hegemonic ideas and have difficulty imagining sharing power with their rivals. One side "inhibits" the political system as a whole by trying to impose religious formulations on contemporary problems. By reducing all the things that don't work in society to their religious dimension—their nonconformity to divine prescriptions—the Islamists doom to failure the efforts of all those—political parties, intellectuals—who would undertake to bring partial solutions to the problems being faced. It is this disqualification, whether real or potential, of the government and above all of the cosmopolitan intelligentsia that finally forces the latter to favor an alliance with the government. This alliance does not, of course, acknowledge itself as such, since it is made paradoxically in the name of defending civil society.

It is this very logic that led the urban elites and the middle classes to prefer the authoritarian solution to the risks of democratization. Rarely, writes Jean Daniel, speaking of Algeria, has a bid for power against a democratic process delighted so many democrats.[13] Rarely has action against Islamism reassured so many Muslims. Rarely has such a large number of civilians felt themselves so protected by a military putsch. As soon as the cancellation of the second round of the general elections in Algeria was announced (January 1992), the Tunisians, the Moroccans, the Egyptians, and in Algeria the women and the Kabyles, like all those who regretted having abstained in the first round and thereby having played into the hands of the Islamic Salvation Front, breathed again. France as well. Both the internal antagonisms and the pressures of the problems posed mean that democracy is not for this time. It is to be feared that the traumas caused by the delays and frustrations may discredit the authorities and reinstate the traditional divorce between the state and society. Because one political formula is dead and a new formula is taking a long time to appear, it is not time for instant recipes and results. Rather, it is time for reflection on the means, the ways, and the cost of transition.

Notes

1   Abdallah Laroui, *Islam et modernité* (Paris, La Découverte, 1987), p. 44.
2   John H. Herz, "Legitimacy, Can we retrieve it?" *Comparative Politics*, April 1978, pp. 317–43.
3   Abdallah Laroui, *Mafhoum al-Dawla* (Casablanca: Arab Cultural Center, 1981), p. 169.
4   Mohamed Harbi, "Nationalisme algérien et identité berbère," *Peuples Méditerranéens*, April–June 1980, pp. 31–38. [Tizi-Ouzou is the main city in the Berber-speaking Kabyle area of Algeria.]
5   Comment in plenary session, in *Daedalus*, winter 1989, p. 238.

6   Abdelkader Djeghloul, "L'Algérie en état d'anomie politique," *Le Monde Diplomatique*, March 1990.

7   François Burgat, "Des fellaghas aux intégristes," *Le Monde*, 3 June 1991. [The *fellagha*s or "bandits" were guerillas fighting for Tunisian independence from the French.]

8   Burgat, "Des fellaghas aux intégristes," p. 2.

9   Gilles Kepel, "Impasses arabes," *Le Monde*, 7 March 1991.

10 Kepel, "Impasses arabes."

11 Remy Leveau, "Eléments de reflexion sur l'Etat au Maghreb," in *Changements politiques au Maghreb*, ed., Michel Camau (Paris, CNRS, 1991), pp. 269–80.

12 Djeghloul, "L'Algérie en état d'anomie politique."

13 Jean Daniel, in *Le nouvel observateur*, one week after the coup of January 1992.

Two

Introduction

Population and Demography

When our first edition appeared in 1977, the Arab world had a population of less than 150 million. Twenty years later, with this third edition, the Arab world has an estimated population of 266 million. The 266 million Arabs are distributed among twenty-two Arab countries[1] with a total area of nearly 14 million square kilometers. These additional 116 million Arabs were born in a world drastically changed from that of their parents, both within the Arab homeland and outside. This sizable population represents the human base of the greater Arab society.

First, Arab population is characterized at present by a rapid tempo of natural growth. Until the mid-nineteenth century, Arab population was fairly stable in size with little fluctuation in either direction.[2] It was estimated at that time to be around 50 million. Then Arab population began a slow upward growth. From the middle of the twentieth century, when the total population was around 90 million, the growth picked up speed, and the Arab world had one of the fastest growing populations in the world. However, recent data indicate that the major sizable countries of Egypt, Morocco, Algeria, and Tunisia are slowing down their rate of population growth. Thus, while the rate was around 3.0 percent annually, in the third quarter of the century, now it is down to 2.5 percent (see Table 1 in the Statistical Abstract). Still even at this declining growth rate, the Arab population could double in 28 years—i.e., to become 500 million by the year 2024.

There are demographic differences within the Arab world. In terms of natural increase (the difference between births and deaths every year), the growth rate was lowest in Qatar (1.6 percent) and Tunisia (1.7 percent). Most other Arab countries have hovered around 2.5 percent annually. In some exceptional cases the annual natural growth rate has been as high as 3.9 percent (e.g., the Palestinians and Omanis). But aside from this natural increase, there has been another source of population growth—net migration, i.e., the difference between in-migration and out-migration. This applies especially in the case of some Arab oil-producing countries such as Bahrain, Kuwait, Qatar, Libya, Saudi Arabia, and the United Arab Emirates. This source of population increase, however, is not as important in the 1990s as it was in the 1970s–1980s. Overall, the rapid natural increase in the Arab world has been due to declining mortality in general, and that of infant mortality in particular. The infant mortality rate in the Arab world has steadily declined from nearly 200 per thousand in 1950 to about 60 in 1996.

Second, the majority of Arabs are young. The young age groups, including those under 15 years of age, account for over 42 percent, and those under 20 are 52 percent of the total. The equivalent percentage worldwide is 32 percent; in more advanced countries it is 20 percent—less than half of that of the Arab world. This fact has several social and economic ramifications. For one thing, it implies a continued trend of rapid increase for the next two decades. But with so many children in the population, the "dependency ratio" in the Arab world is very high.[3] This tends to overtax the few productive elements of the population, and it burdens the states which must provide education, health, and other services for many children who are not of a productive age. Related to this is the low participation rate in the Arab labor force, which is around 30 percent of the total population. This is primarily due to the high percentage of children below productive age. But it is also due to the fact that most adult Arab women do not participate in gainfully productive employment outside the household—either because of tradition or because of lack of skills and literacy. The overall low rate of economic participation of Arab population means that 30 percent are carrying the burden of supporting 70 percent of the population. To appreciate the negative repercussions of this fact for socioeconomic development we may compare the situation in the Arab world on this point with that in the first world (U.S. and Western Europe) where the participation rate is 60 percent. In former Soviet Bloc countries this rate was as high as 65 percent.

Third, the characteristics of Arab population reflect overall lower sociohuman capabilities. Many people are illiterate, in poor health, and have low levels of technical skills. Nearly half of the adult population (primarily women) are not gainfully employed; the men who are employed tend to have low productivity.

The literacy rate in the Arab world around 1995 was no more than 45 percent of the population above ten years of age. It is true that the Arab countries have nearly tripled the percentage of literates in thirty-five years (18 percent in 1960 compared to 45 percent in 1995); and it is true that the Arabs are better in this respect than most of the Third World. But it is also true that the majority of Arabs are still illiterates, while in developed countries the illiterates are less than 3 percent. The Arab countries display a wide range of variation in education as well as other socioeconomic indicators. In Somalia and Sudan the literacy rate in 1995 was as low as 28 percent; while in Bahrain, Lebanon, and Jordan it was as high as 80 percent. Between these two extremes, most other Arab countries had literacy rates between 30 percent and 75 percent. Thus Egypt's was 48 percent, Algeria's 57 percent, Syria's 64 percent, and Tunisia's 65 percent. It is worth noting that the wealth of an Arab country is not always the most important factor in producing a high or low literacy rate. For example Jordan with a modest per capita income ($1,400) had a literacy rate of 80 percent—compared with 53 percent in the United Arab Emirates, the wealthiest in terms of income per capita ($21,500). The quality of population, therefore, is a

.function of the social policies in a given country more than being a function of wealth alone.

In terms of health, the life expectancy in the Arab world was around 63 years in 1996, compared to 64 worldwide and 77 in the U.S. and Western Europe. The Arab average has improved by 18 years since 1960 when it was 45. This improvement is indicated by the reduction of infant mortality from 150 to 60 per thousand during that period. This was helped by growing health services, and improved public health, notably due to a cleaner water supply and expanded sewage systems. Thus while there was only one physician for every three thousand Arabs in 1960, there was one for every 700 in 1995—compared to one for every 130 persons in the U.S. and Europe.

Thus while there is steady improvement, most Arabs are still illiterate and their health conditions leave much to be desired. This impacts, in turn, on productivity. It has been estimated that an Arab industrial worker produces only one-fifth of what his counterpart in the U.S. and Europe produces. An Arab farmer produces less than one-tenth of what his counterpart does in those countries.

Fourth, Arab populations tend to be unevenly distributed on the land, both among Arab countries and within each country. In 1996, the Gulf states of Bahrain and Qatar, as well as Comoros and Djibouti, for example, have less than 700,000 inhabitants each, while Egypt has 64 million. The density per square kilometer varies sharply from three persons in Libya to as many as 1,000 in Bahrain. One reason for this is that over 85 percent of the Arab world is barren desert. Thus in Egypt the non-desert areas of the Nile Valley and the Delta have a density of over 1,200 inhabitants per square kilometer, while the desert areas (over 95 percent of total territory) have a density of one.

This distinction between the two types of density explains why despite the territorial vastness of the Arab world (nearly 14 million square kilometers) which means an arithmetic density of no more than 20 persons per square kilometer, the real density of inhabited land (less than 2 million square kilometers) is more than six times as many, or 133 persons per square kilometer in 1996. Most Arab cities and villages seem crowded, even overcrowded. So much is this the case that an aerial map of the Arab world would show it as separate patches of settlement—like greenery in an otherwise empty landscape. The 64 million Egyptians are clustered in the Nile Delta and Valley, equal to about 4 percent of Egypt's territory, and about 90 percent of the Kuwaiti population are concentrated in one city—less than 10 percent of the territory. This pattern implies mounting pressures on the limited non-desert areas of the Arab world.

Such pressures, along with a multitude of other socioeconomic and political factors, have triggered three types of migrations. The first is a stream of rural-urban migration within each country—leading to a rapid urbanization in the Arab world. This has been going on at various speeds in different Arab countries for the past one hundred years. The second type is inter-Arab migration—

i.e., across Arab country borders, especially from poor non-oil-producing states to oil-rich countries. This oil-induced migration is more recent; it reached its peak around 1980. The third type is international migration—Arabs streaming out of the Arab world to study, work, or reside in Europe, the Americas, and Australia. In the mid-1990s an estimated three to five million Arabs were living in Western Europe, especially France which has many legal as well as illegal North African migrants. In fact, Arab-Muslim expatriates in France and the rest of Europe are becoming increasingly a domestic political issue, giving rise to some racist tendencies. There has also been migration into the Arab world—by Europeans under "settler colonialism," and by Asians seeking employment in the oil countries.

The pattern of voluntary migration has been doubled by involuntary migration. There have been major flows of political refugees, beginning with the Palestinian refugees from the establishment of Israel, and including nowadays refugees from various wars and disputes, notably in Sudan, in Iraq, and in Lebanon. In Sudan there are also many people displaced by drought and unsettled conditions in the rural areas (see the article by Abdel Ghaffar Ahmed in Section Six). Many of these refugees of all kinds end up in urban areas.

Fifth, the rapid urbanization of Arab population, resulting from the first type of migration, carries with it serious socioeconomic problems. The inflow of rural migrants to Arab cities is much faster than the pace at which those migrants are incorporated into modern economic sectors. As a result, most Arab cities are crowded with thousands of unemployed and underemployed people. More than fifteen Arab cities have already passed the one million mark (by the mid-1990s), and Greater Cairo has already passed the ten-million mark. Since most Arab cities are old and preindustrial in their physical layouts, serious problems of deterioration or even total collapse create a situation approaching an urban crisis. One case in point is Egypt's slum or informal areas, often referred to in the Egyptian media as "manatiq 'ashwaiya" (literally, "random areas"). These have spontaneously sprung up around major and middle size cities. They are overcrowded, destitute, and with hardly any services (see the article by Tekçe et al. in Section Four). In the mid-1990s these slum areas were estimated to house nearly 12 million Egyptians. These slum areas have become infested by vice, violence, organized crime, and religious extremism. One such area, Munira al-Gharbiya, was the scene of a six-week armed confrontation between state security forces and Islamic militants in 1992. Munira al-Gharbiya had sprung up on the edges of Giza's district of Imbaba in the 1970s and 1980s.[4] In 1992, it had nearly one million inhabitants, with no health, education, recreation, or police services. What exists in and around Egypt's urban areas also exists in basically the same manner in several Arab countries of similar sociodemographic evolution—e.g., Algeria, Morocco, Tunisia, Syria, Jordan, and Lebanon.

Sixth, the size, composition, and distribution of population in the Arab world bear directly and indirectly on overall socioeconomic development. In this respect there are three basic configurations. Though in some sense quite different in appearance, all three impede development. The first configuration is overpopulation and over urbanization as seen in Egypt, Algeria, Tunisia and Morocco, as just described. Here there are more people, born faster than the economy grows, and more rural-urban migration than the cities can accommodate. The second configuration is one of underpopulation and overurbanization, as in Iraq, Sudan, and Saudi Arabia. Here the economies, though growing, have a limit on their expansion due to shortages of population and mismanagement of resources. The impediment to economic development in some of these countries is further compounded by the flight of the few farmers from rural areas where they are badly needed to till arable land, to urban areas where they are neither needed nor can be readily integrated into modern sectors of the economy. The third configuration, that of the small Gulf states, resembles the second in many respects. But due to their small original demographic base, and with huge oil revenues and ambitious development plans, the Gulf states have been heavily importing expatriate labor. The percentage of non-native labor in some of these countries (e.g., the United Arab Emirates) is more than 70 percent of the labor force, and more than 50 percent of total population in the mid-1990s. Between half and two-thirds of these expatriates are from non-Arab countries, mostly from South and South East Asia. This huge influx of non-Arabs threatens the national and cultural identity of the Gulf states. Thus while expatriates are carrying out an important economic role, their continued economic presence may have far-reaching cultural, ethnic, and political repercussions.

The varied and seemingly contradictory demographic scene in the Arab world can best be understood in the light of its transitional nature—from a "traditional" equilibrium (high birth rate and high death rate) to a "modern" equilibrium (low birth rate and low death rate). The "transitional" phase (declining death rate while the birth rate remains high) did not start in all parts of the Arab world at the same time. Countries of the northern tier (e.g., Egypt, Lebanon, Morocco, Algeria) initiated their "demographic transition" some fifty to a hundred years earlier than countries of the southern tier of the Arab world (e.g., Sudan, Saudi Arabia, and the Gulf states). Meanwhile various political and economic transitions also started at different times in these countries. This explains why some Arab countries are suffering from "overpopulation," and others from "underpopulation," and why the urbanization and migration issues assume differential seriousness in various Arab countries.

Some of the above generalizations are best refined by empirical data which are presented in the following set of tables and charts. The articles in this section further show the inner dynamics of the Arab demographic transition. More Arab women in more Arab countries are attending to family planning. More governments are beginning to recognize that it is "quality," not sheer numbers of population, which makes the difference in sustainable development. Thus while it may seem that the Arab world as a whole reached the peak of natural growth sometime in the 1980s, there is still a long way before fertility rates decline in all Arab countries, especially in the southern tier.

The overall picture is thus one where the growth rate remains high as infant mortality declines but birth rates remain high. Providing adequate health, education, and jobs for this growing problem is a public administration struggle. The Arab world is roughly half urban, and the proportion is increasing.

In This Section

Philippe Fargues provides a cautiously optimistic interpretation of the current demographic situation of the Arab world. He shows that population growth rates are declining, while of course the population itself continues to rise. This slowing of the growth rate is linked to knowledge, and in particular to the spread of knowledge among ordinary people. But the implications of this are that there will be increased demand for education, health, and jobs; hence the notion of rupture. Fargues is particularly interested in the impact of broader patterns of evolution on relations between the genders and between the generations. He argues that the long-term trends are towards more equality between the genders, and also to an equalization of educational levels between the generations after a period in which the young and the old "knew" very different things.

Saad Eddin Ibrahim's article traces the changing attitudes towards birth control and family planning among different categories of the Egyptian population. The spread of family planning ideas is shown to be hampered more by institutional and political factors in Egyptian society than by the attitudes and feelings of the women themselves. Ibrahim stresses the pronatalist attitudes of certain trends in Egyptian society, such as the Islamicists and the socialists, but argues that civil society (voluntary) organizations work for the opposite viewpoint. Many of his arguments are supported by interviews and survey data.

Christine Eickelman explores some of the social and cultural reasons for a high birth rate in Oman. She agrees with Fargues that in the oil-producing countries of the Gulf, female literacy does not lead to a lower birth rate, as it does elsewhere in the Arab world, and that the easy availability of social services removes the economic pressures to control family size. To this she adds the perception that, for a woman, giving birth plays a key role in the establishment and maintenance of social networks, since the act triggers off cycles of visiting. It should be noted that in general the changes Eickelman describes in the Omani community of al-Hamra parallel those analyzed by Altorki and Cole in their detailed discussion of 'Unayzah.

Barbara Ibrahim and her colleagues examine the delicate issue of women's autonomy in Egypt. They ask to what extent women are able to make the decisions that affect their own lives, and conclude that this is limited. This being so, the ability of women to share in the process of implementing a population policy of slowed growth by opting to have fewer children is also limited. One implication of this study is that decisions about family size in Egypt must involve the father/husband as well as the mother/wife.

The quality of any human population is intimately linked to its living conditions. In the book from which the passage on the urban community of Manshiet Nasser was drawn, Belgin Tekçe and her colleagues were concerned with the environmental factors that affected child health, indeed the physical survival of the newborn and the children. Communities like Manshiet Nasser, part of greater Cairo, have relatively high rates of infant and child mortality, taken as an indicator of the general level of human welfare. Tekçe et al. set out to identify the reasons for this. Thus in the passage included here they examine the social organization and living conditions found in this community—historical origins of the community, family structure and values, a form of local self-government, and the occupational structure, as well as the ways in which the community fits into the Egyptian institutional pattern of property rights, provision of services, and politics.

Notes

1 Including Palestine. See Tables 1 and 4 in the Statistical Abstract. The population estimate assumes the 1993 population of 240 million, plus 2.5 percent a year for four years.

2 Most Arab countries began to conduct regular population censuses only in the last three decades, although Egypt did so as early as 1897.

3 The dependency ratio is the ratio of persons in the dependent ages (under 15 and over 64 years) to those in the economically productive ages in a population.

4 On Munira al-Gharbiya, see Linda Oldham, Haguer el-Hadidi, and Hussein Tamaa, "Informal communities in Cairo: the Basis of a Typology" in *Cairo Papers in Social Science*, vol. 10, no. 4 (Winter 1987).

4

From Demographic Explosion to Social Rupture

Philippe Fargues

Experts and politicians seem to agree that the demographic structures of the Arab countries have reached a critical point. They acknowledge that rapid population growth seriously constrains a country's economy and, consequently, its social and political possibilities. In the relationship between consumption, savings, and investment, demographic imbalance imposes an inordinate weight on consumption, thus encumbering development. If a state appears incapable of mobilizing for internal savings or external aid, it can only resort to unacceptable repressive measures to cope with the inevitable demands for bread, jobs, and housing. "Demographic folly has contributed to the rapid dereliction of the world and its values," wrote Rachid Mimouni in a recent essay. "One can ask oneself if it isn't the origin of all of Algeria's ills."[1]

Paradoxically, it is at the moment when contrary tendencies are becoming apparent in the region's demographic trends that this simplistic and fatalistic vision has become accepted wisdom. Present Arab population structures carry in them the end of the demographic "explosion." In the Maghreb, for instance, the number of children reaching school age each year has already stopped growing, but the proportion of that group actually attending, or seeking to attend, school continues to increase. This rising demand—not rising numbers—is the source of today's crisis.

The economy is not the only thing that the region's changing demographic profile has destabilized. The slowing rates of demographic growth are increasingly tied to a revolution in knowledge and its systems of transmission, under a new consciousness that is inconsistent with traditional values. Domestication of technical knowledge by an elite had initially opened the way to population growth: with the development of medicine, material production and communications, mortality rates fell dramatically. The decline in birth rates will largely be in response to the diffusion of public education—appropriation at a mass level of general knowledge, no longer privately in family circles but publicly in

From *Middle East Report* 190 (1994), pp. 6–10. Reprinted by permission of MERIP/Middle East Reports, 1500 Massachusetts Ave., NW, #119, Washington, D.C., 20005. Translated from the French by Bryce Giddens and Joe Stork. Philippe Fargues, a demographer, is director of the Centre d'Etudes et de Documentation Economiques, Juridiques et Sociales (CEDEJ), Cairo.

schools. Against the hierarchies of generation and gender which still structure power, in the family and globally, young people now surpass the qualifications of their elders, and women are on the way to overtaking men. The demographic explosion has run its course, and today cedes place to the social rupture.

Demography or Democracy

Just two or three decades ago in the Maghreb, and less than one decade ago in the Mashreq, large families were the rule.[2] The reproductive life of an average couple included the births of seven to nine children. Less than one generation later, at the beginning of the 1990s, young adults construct families which, once complete, will be less than half the size of those in which they grew up. The decline in the Maghreb recalls the experience a quarter of a century ago in southern Europe, from Catholic Italy and Spain to Orthodox Greece and, by its magnitude, that of the Asian "dragons." But both of these sets of societies emerged against completely different backdrops: burgeoning secularization in Mediterranean Europe and industrial take-off in East Asia. A similar point of transition is occurring in Arab countries, but there the revitalization of Islam and persistent underdevelopment create an appearance of contradictory conditions.

In all the Mediterranean Arab countries, the rate of population growth has actually started to decline. Egypt, in 1986, recorded some 1,928,000 births; five years later, in 1991, the number had diminished by 10 percent to 1,754,000 births. In Tunisia births dropped from 235,000 in 1986 to 205,000 in 1990, and in Algeria from 845,000 in 1985 to 739,000 in 1989.

The measurable effects of the stabilization of births takes time. Medical and health institutions, which deal with newborns, are the first to feel the effects. One must only wait six years—the beginning of the 1990s in the Maghreb and Egypt—for the primary schools to show the benefit. And it will be 20–25 years later—around the year 2010—that demographic pressures on labor and housing markets will ease.

But in each of these domains, the stabilization of actual population growth does not signify a leveling of demand. Consider neo-natal and infant health: the reduced number of infants per family is accompanied, here as elsewhere, by concern for improved care, and one knows the path that must be followed to provide health care equitably. In education, groups that do not have access will increasingly demand it. In Morocco, for example, there were 4 million children of primary school age (6–11 years) in 1990. The number will be about the same in the year 2000. If school attendance stays at 53 percent, where it is today, the number of students will remain at about 2.1 million. But if schooling is made universal, 4 million places will have to be found. The 90 percent increase will originate not from demography but from the democratization of schooling. In countries where access to mass education is almost universal—Iraq, Jordan,

Lebanon, Syria and the Gulf principalities in the Mashreq, and Algeria and Tunisia in the Maghreb—the school systems have already reached a plateau. It will be more of the same in years to come—jobs to create or houses to build. Additional future costs will be less and less attributable to the increase in numbers, and more and more to rising aspirations. Of the diverse phenomena which have converged to produce the present congestion of Arab urban labor markets, the rates of natural increase and rural-urban migration have undoubtedly been the most visible. But rural exodus, in the massive form that it took in the 1960s and 1970s, is becoming part of the past for the whole of the Arab world, with the exception perhaps of Sudan, where civil war and repeated droughts continue to push peasants into the streets of Khartoum. Spatial mobility has everywhere else taken the dominant form of movement between cities, with no effect on overall urban employment.[3] Demographic growth will continue to exert increasing pressure until the no-growth generations reach young adulthood, between 2005 in Tunisia and 2020 in Syria. In the interval, the Arab countries will face very different situations, as the differential birthrates of the 1970s and 1980s make themselves felt.

The group aged 20–24 gives an approximate idea of the potential demand for first jobs. Tunisia will experience only 30 percent growth in this category, whereas Syria will pay dearly for the delay in mastering its birthrate by an increase four or five times greater. Between these two extremes, Algeria, Egypt, and Morocco will have to respond to a growth of around 50 percent in potential demand for first-time employment in the course of the coming 30 years.

The active population does not comprise only new arrivals on the job market, but all those who have already entered it over the last 40 years. Its total number will thus continue to grow until the time when the age groups which exit (60–64 years) surpass the number of those who enter (20–24 years). This moment is not far away in Tunisia (2015) but it is well beyond the horizon in Egypt (2025) and even further off in Syria. In the interim, the jobs to be created each year will range from 40 percent above the 1990 level for Tunisia to 125 percent for Syria.

Employment does not depend on demography alone. Two tendencies modulate its evolution, with contrary effects. Increasing schooling levels and professional qualifications tend to moderate the growth of the active population by delaying entry into the job market. Conversely, the appearance of women on the urban job market (in Lebanon, Tunisia, and Egypt, for example) tends to accelerate that growth. If demographic projection can quickly give us an order of magnitude for future male employment, it tells us nothing about female employment. If, in the year 2025, women were to reach the level of economic activity of men, total demand for employment would rise by 70 percent in Tunisia and by close to 300 percent in Syria. Population growth would play a modest role in this scenario.

Roughly 60 years pass between the birth of a person and his or her exit from the labor market. Job markets will be subject to demographic pressure to the extent that the generations trying to enter it outnumber those leaving it: this will continue for another quarter or half a century, depending on the country. But over the course of this period, social factors that slow demographic growth—education and changes in the status of women—will themselves increasingly determine the rise in demand for jobs and the like.

Disparities

In family matters, as in others, innovation starts with deviation: the replacement of large families by small ones has proceeded gradually, affecting certain strata of society without touching others. Located midway in this process, Arab populations are today more heterogeneous than they were in the past and probably more than they will be in the future. The average Arab couple, who today produce four children, are no more "normal" than the family with seven or more children, or the family with just two or three.

During this transitional phase, almost all identifiable distinctions within the population reflect different levels of fertility. Geography sketches the most visible lines of difference. In the countryside, fertility remains almost unchanged, whereas city dwellers have, in one short generation, made a leap that took a century in Europe. Average fertility is now scarcely greater than the norm in Europe—2.3 children per woman in Morocco and Tunisia, 3.0 in Algeria, in 1992.

Partially obscuring the town-country differential are other, regional differences. Contact with modernity, or with the outside world, has centered on the metropolitan regions and the areas opening on the Mediterranean. In Algeria in 1988, for example, women still gave birth to more than six children in the south but fewer than four in the north. Lebanon, despite its small size, likewise harbors strong regional contrasts: from Beirut (2.3 children per woman) to the north (4.3), two different stages of demographic transition coexist. The gradient everywhere orients itself from the interior toward the coast—in Morocco, Tunisia, or even in Egypt, where the average family numbers only 3.6 children in Port Said but 8.2 in Fayoum. The cultural models confronted by migrants reinforce this geography of demographic transition, as Youssef Courbage shows in his discussion of Egypt and Morocco.[4]

Economic cleavages also leave their demographic traces. The reduction in family size for a long time was an affair of the well-to-do. For the poor, children remained the ultimate wealth. Today in the towns—those of the Maghreb in any case—the difficulties of material life have raised new barriers to high fertility. Destitution appears to be dissociating from prolific reproduction.

The greater or lesser fall in birthrates, its rapidity or its slowness, its diffusion throughout the society or its confinement to certain groups—all are responses to diverse causes. Politics is one: in the Arab countries where public action in favor of limiting births is the most vigorous and longstanding, fertility is the lowest. But the campaigns to popularize contraception were most efficient where segments of the population had already begun to practice it, often with difficulty. Egypt and Tunisia in 1964, and Morocco in 1966, were the first to adopt official population programs. These countries saw their fertility rates decline ten years ahead of Algeria and 15 years ahead of Syria, Jordan and Iraq. At the beginning of the 1970s, Algerian President Houari Boumedienne declared that "our [birth control] pill is development"—in order to affirm the priority of developing the productive apparatus over restructuring the family. After 1982, President Chadli Benjedid attempted a complete reversal—indeed the most neo-Malthusian campaign in the Maghreb. But the fertility rate had not waited for him: three or four years earlier it had begun its decline.

Demography responds to political economy as much as it does to the overt politics of population policy. Classical theory tells us that children progressively lose their role as producers, i.e., their economic utility, and come to represent a cost in strictly material terms. In diverse parts of the world, and notably in the Arab region, one observes today, in contradiction to the model, some demographic transitions that are accelerated by economic crisis and nondevelopment, and others that are curbed by wealth.

Among the Arab countries, the greatest material differences are between underdeveloped economies endowed with relatively diversified productive sectors, and economies organized completely around plentiful petroleum rents. In countries without oil wealth, families confront, without state support, the costs of raising children and the need to mobilize their workforce—including women—in order to assure adequate family incomes. These are the countries where fertility rates have dropped. The oil countries, by contrast, have encouraged fertility rates to remain at the highest possible levels. The state assumes many costs of child-rearing, and imports workers to preempt the entry of women into the national labor market. These states have effectively suspended all evolution in fertility, deactivating factors that motivate demographic change—female education, most notably—at the precise moment when the need for them starts to manifest itself.

Tunisia and Morocco illustrate the first type of experience; Saudi Arabia, the Gulf states and perhaps Libya typify the second. Algeria and Iraq, despite their wealth in hydrocarbons, are too populous for the state to assist families substantially. In Algeria, the collapse in oil and gas receipts in the mid-1980s coincided with falling birth rates. Similarly, Egypt lived a period of rentier reproduction at the beginning of Sadat's *infitah*. One can partially transpose the rentier explanation with the fertility record of the occupied Palestinian territories: dissociating procreation from its costs, Palestinian and international solidarity

(UNRWA) permits families to raise numerous children independent of their own resources, in synergy with the political will to mobilize the "demographic weapon."

Gender Convergence

More than state policies and economic systems, it is transformations in society and in the status of women that are at work in the gradual spread of the small-family model.[5] Continued progress in the schooling of girls over the last quarter-century is the most significant of these transformations in all the Arab countries. If average fertility is still high in Syria and already low in Tunisia, one observes a correlation with levels of female illiteracy and schooling. In Tunisia and Morocco, and for some time now in Lebanon, women who have attended high school or university have no more children today than do Europeans.

The opening of a public space long reserved for boys—i.e., the school—has been a powerful motor for demographic transition. It is toward the age of 7 that one emerges from illiteracy, at age 11 that one enters high school, and at age 15 that one becomes part of one of three strata distinguished here: illiterate, primary education, and secondary education or higher. The average age of procreativity is around 30. The students of 1993 will be the mothers of 2008. Current school attendance figures suggest that in 15 years the educational level of these women will be much higher than that of mothers today. Consider a census of the population where a generation is designated not by its date of birth but by that of its thirtieth birthday. In Algeria, for instance, illiterate women will be only a small minority among those of child-bearing age. Thus the structures of today's population carry within them a future decline in fertility.

The admission of women into the professions and formal labor markets is the second component of differential fertility. The Arab countries, like most of the Muslim world, have surprisingly low rates of urban female workforce participation—from 5 percent in the Arabian Peninsula to hardly more than 25 percent in Tunisia, while the world average is around 50 percent. Are women absent from the world of work, or simply from the statistics compiled by men? (It is men, not their wives, who generally reply to census questions, thus attesting to the fact that, at least in the minds of the men, women do not or must not work.) The rate of female workforce activity is in perfect negative correlation with average fertility.

There is nothing exceptional about this. In all societies, domestic responsibilities which weigh upon women increase with the size of the family and, past a certain point, impede them from practicing a profession or occupation outside the home. Another mechanism, more specific to Arab societies, also seems to be operating. It appears that a large proportion, sometimes a majority, of Arab women working outside the home before marriage leave their jobs upon getting married—even before they have children. Husbands, not children, seem to be responsible for removing women from the job market. The correlation is thus not one of high fertility and the invisibility of women in the urban workforce, but between these two phenomena and a third: the strength and relevance of the patriarchal family. The erosion of this structure has allowed a diversification of women's roles by reducing their domestic responsibilities (a decrease in children) and facilitating an increase of their activity outside the home. The demographic transition thus accompanies the erosion of a masculine monopoly on public space, not only in schools but also in the job market.

The convergence in the status of men and women is not limited to the different gender mix in public space, if one judges by the revelations that the statistics contain. In the recent past, marriage adhered to certain rules which formed a coherent system. A man married a young woman or girl an average of ten years his junior, belonging to an age cohort more numerous than his own. The resulting excess of marriageable women was reabsorbed by remarriages, more frequent for men than for women, whether by polygamy or by second marriages. The inequality of ages underlay in some ways the inequality of rights. Polygamy, which seems not to have been very frequent in the Arab world, has diminished everywhere: according to country, it only represents between 2 and 10 percent of marriages (in Tunisia, it is prohibited). Divorce, according to Egyptian and Algerian statistics, has greatly declined since the first part of this century, when it terminated more than one third of marriages. The age differential of married couples (a form of male domination) has declined in proportion to the disappearance of these regulators, polygamy and repudiation. In most Arab countries, the difference now no longer exceeds five years.

Access to education reveals yet another dimension of the statutory convergence of the sexes. The Arab generations born at the beginning of the century remained primarily illiterate. Schools, therefore, did not introduce inequality between the sexes. Reserved for the children of the elite, not surprisingly they attracted more boys than girls. Among the masses, boys as well as girls never entered them. The later diffusion of education benefited only boys at first, constructing a new type of gender inequality. The entrance of women into schools toward the middle of the century progressed at first less rapidly than did the longer duration of studies for the boys. The gender gap increased up to the generation born between 1950–60, the most unequal of all. The modernizing pressures to increase girls' enrollment were worldwide, transmitted chiefly through international organizations such as UNESCO. In Algeria, for example, thanks to the progress in primary education in the early post-independence period, young women today are no more illiterate than the men they are going to marry. Inequality between the sexes created by educational institutions today affects the generation between 40 and 60 years old—the age of power.

Double Hierarchy

Just as gender hierarchy is losing little by little, the hierarchy of generations, the foundation which gave a triple advantage to the man—age, education, and economic activity—is likewise offset by the diffusion of education. This is particularly acute in the Arab world, where the phase in which mortality declines lasted a bit longer than elsewhere—almost a century in Egypt, for example. People born around 1960 grew up in the largest families: more than those of the past, which had been thinned out by child mortality, and more than those of the future, which were and will be limited by birth control. Reaching adult age, this generation has confronted a situation of relative scarcity in work, housing, and even marriage. The weight of young adults (20–29 years) in the population is greater than it has ever been—and will ever be.

The second result of the decline in mortality has been to compel the generations to live together for an ever-longer period of time. Today, one still lives with one's father at an age where, in the past, one would have already succeeded him. In a distribution of family roles still strongly imprinted with patriarchal rules the father conserves family authority for a longer time. In Algeria, for example, the number of married men responsible for families but living under the authority of their fathers has grown considerably in the 1970s. Demographic shifts have thus set the stage for horizontal competition among peers and vertical competition among generations.

This conflict is playing itself out in a period of rapid and large-scale diffusion of formal education. The relationship of the literacy rate of sons to fathers gives a good indication of the generational disparity in knowledge. The equality of generations will be re-established when the fathers themselves have all become literate—around the year 2030. Because schooling has spread quickly and on a base of preponderant illiteracy, it is in Algeria and Tunisia that the conflictual potential is strongest. Everywhere the generational dissociation of knowledge and power is too strong not to have some disruptive impact on the political systems.

The patriarchal order of the family has been seriously shaken, and with it the neopatriarchal order of the entire society.[6] On this canvas there is a contest which, in the name of religion, extolls the restoration of a distinction between the sexes, one codified by *shari'a* but frustrated by social evolution. One may think of the competition among peers and the generational conflict which accompany the transition from one state (the widespread illiteracy of yesterday) to another (the universal education of tomorrow) as reinforcing this contestation. When they become adults, the young generations will no longer face the same pressures from their brothers, because birth rates will have declined. When the students of today are themselves fathers, the dissociation of knowledge and power will have become blurred.

In its extreme form, this demographic disequilibrium will have lasted only one generation. It takes on the character of a crisis because, short-lived as it may be in the broad time-frame of demographic evolution, the imbalance of these existing population structures is nevertheless sufficiently strong to provoke disorder in the much more immediate time-frame of politics.

Notes

1 Rachid Mimouni, *De la Barbarie en général et de l 'intégrisme en particulier* (Paris: Les Préaux Clercs, 1992).

2 Philippe Fargues, "Un siecle de transition démograhique en Afrique méditerranéenne: 1885–1985," *Population* 2 (1986), pp. 205–32.

3 Rohert Escallier and Pierre Signoles, *Changement économique, social et culturel et modifications des chomps migratoires internes dans le monde arabe,* 2 vols. (Tours: URBAMA, 1992).

4 Youssef Courbage, "Demographic Change in the Arab World: The Impact of Migration, Education and Taxes in Egypt and Morocco," in *Middle East Report* 190 (vol. 24, no. 5), Sept.–Oct. 1994, pp. 19–22.

5 Carla Makhlouf Obermeyer, "Islam, Women and Politics: The Demography of Arab Countries," *Population and Development Review* 18, 1 (1992).

6 Hisham Sharabi, *Neopatriarchy: A Theory of Distorted Change in Arab Society* (New York: Oxford University Press, 1988).

5

State, Women, and Civil Society: An Evaluation of Egypt's Population Policy

Saad Eddin Ibrahim

The international debate on population policy has for a number of years fostered opposing camps—one promoting the provision of family planning services and another backing overall socioeconomic development as favored strategies for population growth reduction (Dixon-Mueller, 1993). But the fortunes of a population policy may be no better or worse than other public policies in a given country at a given time. What contributes to the overall competence of the state in formulating and implementing public policies? Which groups in society reinforce policy objectives and which act as 'saboteurs'? To address these questions, this paper examines Egypt's population policy over three decades to locate where, how, and why it may have succeeded or failed. We do so by assessing the different roles of a number of relevant actors operating in the public space bearing on human reproduction.

Egypt's demographers and social scientists noted the country's population problem as early as the mid-1930s: an exponential population growth at rates outstripping the country's capabilities to expand its resource base. Yet it was only in 1960 that the Egyptian state would formally adopt a population policy, and a vague one at that, to slow the rate of population growth and speed up the rate of economic development. While the growth of real income per capita may have kept pace, financing Egypt's economic development has led to a heavy external and internal public debt. The persistent high rate of population growth is often cited as the culprit, and the population policy is judged to have fallen markedly short of its objectives.

While population policy in theory concerns mortality, fertility, and migration, in Egypt the policy focus has been predominantly on fertility reduction (NPC, 1994). Population policy (like all public policies) is formulated at the upper echelon of the state. The middle and lower echelons oversee its implementation by targeting families, with the objective of reducing births and

From *Family, Gender, and Population in the Middle East: Policies in Context,* ed. Carla Makhlouf Obermeyer. (Cairo: The American University in Cairo Press, 1995), pp. 57–79. Reprinted by permission. Saad Eddin Ibrahim is professor of sociology at the American University in Cairo and Director of the the Ibn Khaldoun Center for Development Studies in Cairo.

achieving longer spacing between them. Whether or not these echelons have been equally committed to the policy, and whether the institutional channels and the proper inputs have been adequately provided by the state are one set of variables to be evaluated.

However, as important as state-related variables are, those bearing on the targeted group of individuals are even more critical. The intimate decisions of men and women are made within families and a community of peers, neighbors, and friends. Increasingly, and especially in Egypt's urban areas, formal and semi-formal associational networks have become powerful intermediaries in shaping, sifting, and sorting an individual's world view bearing on reproductive behavior. In other words, the state's messages and actions pass through many filters before they affect individuals' attitudes and behavior. Those layers of non-state actors are what we loosely refer to as 'civil society.' They include some obvious actors, such as religious leaders, and other less obvious groups such as politically mobilized professional unions. An evaluation of Egypt's policy performance thus necessitates an assessment of the degree of concordance or discordance among civil formations and protest formations like the Islamic activists and between those groups and the state's population policy.

Egypt's Population Policy: The Rumblings of the 1930s and the Timid Encounter in the 1950s

In 1932, Abbas Ammar, a social geographer at Cairo University, and Wendel Cleland, a professor at the American University in Cairo (Cleland, 1936; Darwish, 1989; Mahran speech, 1994; Abdel Hakim, 1994), triggered the first alarm bells over Egypt's population problem. By then, trend statistics were available, as Egypt had conducted at least four consecutive ten-year censuses since 1897. If estimates of the country's population by Napoleon's experts of the French expedition a century earlier (1798–1801) were accurate at around four million, then Egypt must have doubled its population in one hundred years—to about nine million. By 1932 the country was already approaching one half of the second doubling, to about fifteen million in less than thirty-five years. In 1937, a conference of Egyptian physicians called publicly for national programs to curb population growth.

Only a few non-governmental organizations and small groups of Egyptian scholars and intellectuals took the warning seriously.[1] They began studying and advocating the need for something to be done. Among their proposals was a reform of the conditions of the Egyptian peasant in rural areas, and even—a daring suggestion—a redistributive measure to reduce the flagrant concentration of land ownership. This was an early, if vague, awareness of a link between the population problem and socioeconomic development. These early rumblings did not result in a formal population policy as such. But they led the government to establish a special "Peasant Affairs Department" (Maslahat al-Fallah) in the mid-1930s, which would quickly evolve into the Ministry of Social Affairs in 1939. World War II and nationalist aspirations pushed the population problem to the margins of Egypt's public space until well into the 1950s.

Once the 1952 Revolutionary Free Officers established themselves at the helm of government, they began to look seriously into Egypt's socioeconomic problems. In 1953, two Permanent Supreme Councils were established, one to promote production, the second to promote services. A National Committee for Population Affairs (NCPA) was formed to address population. The current debate on the best approach for coping with rapid population increase was ignited in the NCPA. The majority opinion, backed by the Free Officers, was that equitable socioeconomic development was bound to curb population growth in time. The minority opinion held that Egypt should not wait until the fruits of such development made their impact on demographic trends, because the growth rate itself could derail economic growth (NPC, 1994).

Some observers at the time suspected that Nasser, himself a father of five children, felt that bigger population gave Egypt much greater weight in Arab, Middle Eastern, and international affairs. Some of his public statements seem to substantiate this suspicion (*Al-Ahram,* 1955). However, Nasser would change his views on the matter several years later.

An Objective Without a Policy in the 1960s and a Policy Without Objectives in the 1970s

Nine years after Nasser came to power, he articulated his general vision and proposed an agenda for the country in a famous document titled "The National Charter." It was widely representative of the views of all major social forces at the time. Of interest to us is an unequivocal statement asserting that "high growth rates represent the most dangerous obstacle that hinders efforts to raise the standard of living of the Egyptian people" (Egypt's National Charter, 1961). Since then, every Egyptian government has reiterated this assertion.

However, it took four more years after the issuing of the charter before the assertion was operationalized in a concrete objective. In 1965, the Egyptian government declared its first population target objective, "aiming at reducing the crude birth rate by one per thousand per annum" (NPC, 1994). It also declared its support for family planning efforts, pledging to prepare a network of family planning service delivery outlets. However, because the government was preoccupied at the time with pressing economic and military concerns, it invested little other than rhetoric during this period. The 1967 military defeat in the third Arab–Israeli war engulfed the country even further in other concerns. Nevertheless, the mobilization of one million Egyptian soldiers along the Suez

Canal for the following seven years helped to achieve the government's objective of slowing down the rate of population growth. It was an achievement by default, however, and not the result of a policy.

Shortly after the 1973 October war and demobilization of troops, the first true national population policy was formulated, with a ten-year implementation plan (1973–82). Both the policy and the plan were couched in the most general of terms. They emphasized the links between population growth and socioeconomic development, and reiterated the majority opinion of the NCPA of exactly twenty years earlier. The policy took as an article of faith that "demand for family planning services hinges critically on the level and nature of development efforts" (NPC, 1994). This would include the expediting of several factors in advance of explicit demographic variables including: raising the standard of living; mechanizing agriculture and industry; upgrading education; improving the status of women; extending coverage of social security programs; reducing infant and child mortality; adopting relevant information, education, and communication programs; and upgrading family planning services.

This list of "desirables," however commendable, got the population practitioners nowhere. However, in a policy re-articulation in 1975, four dimensions of Egypt's population problem were clearly identified: rapid growth, spatial maldistribution, low level characteristics (indicators of development), and uneven structure (NPC, 1994). Though noted by many observers for decades, the dimension of spatial maldistribution appears for the first time in an official document as a policy concern. It would continue to be so in the following policy statements. A definite advance over previous governmental documents, the 1973–75 National Population Policy still lacked measurable targets and resource commitments equal to the magnitude of the task (NPC, 1994).

The 1980s and 1990s: Clarifying Policy and Consolidating Implementation

A second national population policy was issued by the Egyptian government in 1980. It was titled "National Strategy Framework for Population, Human Resource Development, and the Family Planning Program" (NPC, 1994). In this and related documents, we see for the first time clear objectives or targets, and definite measures for their achievement according to a specified time-schedule. One target was to reduce the crude birth rate by 20 per thousand by the year 2000—i.e., one per thousand per year from 1980 on. A mark of this commitment was the holding of the National Population Conference in 1984, and the establishment of the National Population Council (NPC) shortly afterward to replace a succession of lower-level governmental bodies. The president himself headed the NPC board in its early years, and in 1986, the NPC formulated the third national population plan. It was far more advanced than previous plans in its clarity of targets and programmatic implementability, and in fact, many of the objectives of the third plan were achieved on time or even before the set dates.

Reflecting the lessons learned from more than three decades, the plan put greater emphasis on "free choice" of citizens to control or plan their families, and their right to migrate internally or externally. All the fashionable principles and development catch phrases are to be found in the plan document—for example, grass-roots participation, empowerment of women, education for all, environmental concerns, and a decisive role for the NGOs. Equally significant is the fact that the third population plan was integrated in the National Five-Year Plan of 1987/88–1991/92 for the first time ever. This meant, among other things, a parliamentary debate enacting it into law, and specific allocation of budgetary resources for its implementation.

It is significant that on October 14, 1993, a new cabinet position, the minister of state for population and family welfare, was created.[2] This represents considerable elevation from the first governmental body dealing with population in 1953, when it was merely the National Committee for Population Affairs. The evolving symbolism reflects the increasing importance of the issue at hand in the priorities of the Egyptian state. Perhaps of even greater policy importance was the presidential decree naming the new prime minister, also in October 1993. Seven national priorities were charged by President Mubarak for attention from the new government. For the first time ever, the population problem was among them. Thus, in symbolism and substance, and at the highest state level, population has become a paramount policy issue in the 1990s.

Evaluating Egypt's Policy

Egypt's population policy entails, in theory, more than family planning. In the mid-1970s, two other goals were formulated: a more balanced distribution of population over the territory, with the aim of reducing the high density of some urban areas; and enhancing the overall status of the population—including women's status—through national development.

Success in reaching these two goals has been limited. According to both the Population Plan and the National Five-Year Plan 1987/88–1991/92 for Socioeconomic Development, Egypt was to build some twenty new cities in desert and border governorates between 1987 and 1992. But despite the large public and private investments that were made in these projects, they have not attracted more than 7 percent of the targeted population. The highly dense governorates have grown even more between the 1976 and 1986 censuses. The four border governorates of the New Valley, Matruh, the Red Sea, and Sinai have remained with nearly the same thin density.

Egypt has made some progress on other indicators of socioeconomic development. In the health area, there has been marked improvement, as indicated by the fall in the infant mortality rate from about three hundred to about sixty of every thousand live births between the 1960s and 1990s. Between 1960 and 1990, the number of those who obtain safe drinking water rose from 50 to 90 percent, calorie intake increased from 90 to 127 percent of the daily human requirements, adult literacy rose from 30 to about 50 percent, primary and secondary school enrollment rose from 55 to 89 percent of those eligible, and the per capita share of GDP (adjusted for purchasing power) increased from $500 to $1,934 (UNDP, 1992: table 4). But such changes cannot be attributed to Egypt's population policy as such. Indeed, despite the formulation of other goals, slowing down the rate of growth has been the primary focus of Egypt's policy, and the distribution of birth control methods in family planning clinics has continued to be the principal method of implementation.

Available statistics suggest that Egypt's success in reducing fertility has been mixed. There has been an increase in the age at marriage. During a quarter of a century, the percentage of women sixteen years of age and older who were never married rose from 12 per thousand to 20 per thousand. Egypt's Demographic and Health Survey (EDHS) data for 1988 and 1992 indicate that the medium age at first marriage has increased by about 2.5 years during the last quarter of a century. There has also been a rise in the percentage of women using contraceptives. The percentage of women reporting contraceptive use has risen from about 25 percent in 1980 to slightly over 47 percent among currently married women. The biggest net increase between 1988 and 1992 was in Lower Egypt (11.3 percent), followed by Upper Egypt (9.3 percent), and the urban governorates (3.1 percent). But total fertility remains high at 3.9 children per woman (DHS, 1993), despite increasing levels of female education and rising standards of living. To understand the factors behind this limited success, we need to consider the processes underlying the official policies, as well as the impact of these policies on their intended audience.

A Small-Scale Survey

With these objectives in mind, a survey was conducted of nearly seven hundred individuals who in one way or another are 'stake holders' in family planning programs and fertility reduction. The sample included senior national decision-makers, top and middle executives on the governmental level, family planning service providers, local community leaders, and women aged 15–49 who are the potential users of family planning services.[3] Communities included in this survey were purposely selected from among low-income urban neighborhoods in the capitals of nine governorates, as well as village communities in nearby rural areas. The nine governorates included three in Upper Egypt, three in Lower

Table 1
The population issue in the consciousness of Egypt's relevant actors

	Percentage who		
	Spontaneously mention the issue	Mention after probing	Deny the issue after probing
Senior national executives (n=22)	18.2	27.3	54.5
Middle executives (n=45)	24.4	26.7	48.9
Family planning practitioners (n=54)	40.7	11.1	48.2
Physicians (n=36)	25.0	8.3	66.7
Social workers (n=18)	72.2	16.7	11.1
Community leaders (n=72)	34.7	19.5	45.8
Civic (n=36)	58.3	30.6	11.1
Religious (n=36)	11.1	8.3	80.6
Women 15–49 (n=503)	14.1	48.7	37.2
Total (n=696)	19.1	40.7	40.2

Source: Ibn Khaldoun Survey Data (1993)

Egypt, one remote region, and two urban governorates. The doctors, social workers, and community leaders, both religious and civic, were drawn from the same neighborhoods as the larger sample of women (a breakdown of the number of respondents in each category is shown in Table 1). The subsample of women was drawn from current clients at sampled family planning clinics, and one or more of their female neighbors. The fact that this was a relatively small sample of convenience suggests that the findings from this survey should be seen as indicative and informative, rather than as representative of Egypt as a whole.

Evaluating Major Policy Actors:
The Presidency and Top-Level Decision-Makers

It took President Nasser (1952–70) nearly ten years in office before recognizing the serious impact of Egypt's rapid population growth, which is first mentioned in the National Charter only in 1961. President Sadat (1970–81) hardly paid any attention to the problem. In fact, Sadat acted as a negative role model by arranging one of his daughters' marriages before she reached the legal age of sixteen. President Mubarak (1981–present) spent four years in office before he paid serious attention to the issue. Mubarak agreed to chair the newly created NPC in its first three years (1985–88), but his interest seemed to have waned when he delegated the chairmanship to the prime minister, who convened the NPC executive board only once, though holding periodic consultations with the NPC's secretary general. In the last three years, however, President Mubarak has taken a direct and renewed interest in the population issue.

Why did both Nasser and Mubarak come to believe well into their presidencies that population issues deserved greater attention? In Nasser's case, it appears that radical fervor and single-minded belief in his economic reforms became tempered over time by the intractable nature of poverty in the country. Similarly, Mubarak appears to have concluded that his policies of economic liberalization were not going to lift Egypt's fortunes on their own. Both men were faced with the stark demographic reality that population growth was swallowing up gains on the socioeconomic front.

According to a top presidential aide, Mubarak has taken more interest in the population issue since 1991. The informant attributed this to several factors: the implementation of the IMF agreement for economic reform in the spring of 1991; the repeated attention given to population issues by high-level foreign visitors, especially Western aid donors; and the International Conference on Population and Development (ICPD) hosted in Cairo (September 1994). This growing presidential interest has recently been reflected on several occasions, the last of which were the establishment of the Ministry of State for Population and Family Welfare in October 1993 and the president's address to the parliament on November 11, 1993 (Al-Musawwar, 1993; Al-Ahram, 1993).[4]

However, Mubarak has yet to devote a public speech to population as one of the country's pressing economic and political issues. Population policy is usually mentioned in the context of broader policy statements and along with many other issues. While there is presidential recognition of the importance of Egypt's population problem, it is not perceived as warranting top attention. Moreover, the presidential perception of the issue has narrowly focused on family planning, as an element best handled by technocrats, especially MDs. Only recently, in late 1993 and early 1994, the president began to make proclamations about a "national strategic project," referring to efforts to develop and settle Sinai and the Red Sea governorates.[5]

The interviews with top executives also suggest a mixed degree of commitment to a strong population policy. For the purpose of this paper, twenty-two cabinet level executives were interviewed—eighteen ministers and four governors.[6] The interview typically started by asking about Egypt's major problems and/or challenges at present and in the near future. No specific mention was made of the population issue by the interviewer (a former cabinet-level official himself). The results of these interviews are summarized in Table 1. Only four out of the twenty-two officials (18 percent) spontaneously mentioned the population question on their list of major problems/challenges. None of the four listed it in first or second place. Two mentioned it as third and tenth. The top executive who had the longest list of problems (fourteen) mentioned population as number thirteen. Problems which had primacy, or were more frequently mentioned, included economic, political, social, and religious problems. Extremism and terrorism were equally high on the executives' lists. Governmental inefficiency, lack of coordination, and shortage of state resources were also mentioned. Aside from the four who mentioned it spontaneously, our interviewer probed with the question of whether the respondent would include population as a "problem." Out of the eighteen, only six conceded that it was; another eight thought overall development would take care of it; and four said population was merely an excuse for other state failures!

These testimonies were unexpected, given that Egypt's current population plan has assigned specific roles to many of the state institutions over which these top executives preside. The Five-Year Plan specifically mentions at least nine ministries responsible for programs and activities bearing on the three policy objectives. All pertinent ministers (current or former) were among our sample of top executives. Such a weak commitment to the state's population policy by a decisive majority of Egyptian decision-makers immediately below the president may well help to explain why so few of the objectives have been achieved. Even those who either mentioned the population problem on their own or conceded its existence felt no direct responsibility for policy implementation. Their view was that only the NPC, Ministry of Health, and Ministry of Social Affairs were responsible for implementation. Given Egypt's political culture, we expect that the president's recent forceful statements on population and the international attention on Egypt surrounding the UN Population Conference will have a marked effect on the views of cabinet level decision-makers.

The Implementers: Middle Executives, Physicians, and Social Workers

Forty-five high-level executives were interviewed in nine governorates; each had direct responsibility for some aspect of population policy implementation. In each governorate, they included the directors general of health, social affairs, education, and information and the senior representative of the NPC. Our interviewers used the same format as with the cabinet members—that is, a general question asking about Egypt's major problems, followed by questions on the importance of the population issue and their views on the effectiveness of various societal actors in addressing the population problem. Their responses are also summarized in Table 1.

Only eleven executives (out of the forty-five) put the population problem on their list (that is, 25 percent), and these included seven of the NPC senior representatives. When they were probed, twelve more of them agreed, bringing the total to twenty-three, or 51 percent. One NPC representative in Upper Egypt did not mention population spontaneously, and denied it was a significant problem even when the interviewer specifically probed him about the population issue. When told in effect that population is the raison d'être of his work, he responded that it was "just a job."

Among the 49 percent of respondents at this high technocratic level who did not mention population on their problem-list, the most frequently mentioned problems, in order, were the following: unemployment, absence of democracy, terrorism, poor public educational system, backwardness of women, corruption in high circles, the growing gap between government and the people, weak sense of belonging among people (especially youth), poverty, governmental neglect of Upper Egypt and urban slum areas, weakness of social and religious values, and loss of credibility and confidence in the state and its media.

It is striking that directors general of health, social affairs, and education in six out of the nine governorates did not include population in their problem-list. When probed about it, they persisted in denying its seriousness. Many of them thought the main problem was one of underdevelopment and spatial distribution. Our research team interviewing at this level concluded that a majority of the leading state technocrats, in all nine governorates, is not supportive of the population policy, and that many of them are outright hostile toward it. They may comply with directives from their respective ministries in Cairo, but they do not really accept or support the policy. At any rate, as we saw earlier, the higher-level executives did not display any better profile on the issue.

The next level of public workers interviewed were doctors and social workers in the local family planning units, including maternal and child health clinics. Some fifty-four respondents in this category were interviewed: two-thirds MDs and one-third social workers. These field practitioners are the ones having direct contact with women who are the potential end-users of family planning. Ten to twenty years younger than their superiors discussed above, the field practitioners nonetheless display fairly similar attitudes.

On the first, open question about Egypt's problems and challenges, only 41 percent of the field practitioners mentioned population in their problem-list, as shown in Table 1. However, separating MDs from social workers reveals a more disturbing pattern. Fully three-quarters of the thirty-six MDs practicing family planning did not mention population as a problem, whereas among social workers, three-quarters did so. Aside from the tension that this asymmetry may create among practitioners of different professions in the same work place, it suggests a variable 'world-view,' possibly resulting from early college training. The interviewers also observed that many of the young male doctors were bearded, and nine of the seventeen female doctors were veiled, which suggests a religious orientation among these young physicians. This was further substantiated by content analysis of the problem-lists of young doctors. "Corruption" and "lack of religious values" were among the most frequently mentioned problems. Another problem (hardly encountered in the lists of higher state functionaries) was that of "Western conspiracies" to keep Muslims weak. Other problems were similar to those mentioned by other groups—unemployment, inflation, illiteracy, social injustice, lack of competent leadership, and heavy-handed bureaucracy.

With the second round of questions specifically probing the population issue, very few of those who had not mentioned it initially would consider it as a serious problem. Only six more respondents added it to their problem-lists—three MDs and three social workers, to bring their percentages to 33 percent and 89 percent respectively. In other words, some 67 percent of the MDs, whose work is to inform and help women with family-planning decisions, persisted in rejecting the notion that population is a problem in Egypt today.

The research team also observed some markedly overt hostility among field practitioners toward the government and its population policy. When asked to evaluate the role of the state in dealing with the population issue, more than 60 percent of the respondents in this category ranked its performance as weak or very weak. The other 40 percent gave the state a less harsh evaluation, but none ranked it as good or very good. The practitioners were more positive in their evaluation of the role of NGOs; misgivings expressed about NGOs were either because of the foreign connections of some or because they yield to governmental restrictions. This overall profile of state criticism and ambivalence toward the goals of the program in which they are key service providers suggests several possible explanations. One is that doctors' education has emphasized technical training at the expense of broader societal problems and issues. Another possibility is that some public-sector physicians have been influenced by the anti-state and anti-Western ideology of Islamist political groups, who are known to be active within Egypt's medical profession.

Community Leaders: Civic and Religious

As part of our sample, we targeted religious and civic community leaders—seventy-two respondents, evenly divided (thirty-six of each). Respondents were selected from middle- and low-income areas, in or near localities where a family planning service existed.

In our category of religious community leaders were the imams (preachers) of state and non-governmental mosques (eighteen in each sub-category). Only four out of the thirty-six imams mentioned population in their problem-list. When the other thirty-two imams were probed specifically about population, another three added it to their problem-lists, in all seven out of thirty-six, or 19.4 percent. These seven were imams of governmental mosques, or state employees. The other twenty-nine Imams (80.6 percent) were adamant in denying that a population problem exists in this country—or any Islamic country for that matter. For them, it is all "Western propaganda." While the government imams would not preach openly against family planning, they were as unequivocal as their non-governmental counterparts in condemning "birth control" *(tahdid al-nasl)*, a phrase our interviewers and our questionnaires did not use. But for most imams, "family planning" *(tanzim al-usra)* was synonymous with "birth control," which is tampering with God's will.

The non-governmental imams were overtly against the government policies in general and that of population in particular. They all indicated that they preach in mosques and advise in private against "birth control" of any kind. When asked what large families with limited means or mothers with poor health and four or five children should do, about 75 percent of all imams said "there will always be divine providence" and other "compassionate Muslims" to help. The other 25 percent would counsel such parents to "persevere and be patient."

In addition to religious leaders, thirty-six notables (well-regarded officers of at least one active NGO) from the communities surveyed were targeted for interviewing. Actually, eighteen of those interviewed (50 percent) had multiple membership in NGOs, all of them in urban communities.

Table 2 compares the responses of religious and civic leaders on a number of pertinent issues. More than 58 percent of the civic leaders readily mentioned population in their initial problem-list, compared to only 11 percent of the religious leaders. As a matter of fact, with the exception of family planning social workers, the civic leaders were more concerned about the population problem in Egypt than any other category among the nearly six hundred respondents. Even among those who had not spontaneously mentioned it in their problem-list (30 percent), many readily added it under probing, to bring their total to 81 percent, compared to 19 percent of the religious leaders.

With these civic leaders, there was more than recognition of and concern about the population problem. As shown in Table 2, the proportion among them who have something positive to say about governmental efforts is greater (53 percent) than among their religious counterparts (6 percent); it is also greater

Table 2

Comparison of religious and civic community leaders on population issues (percentage; n=36)

	Civic leaders	Religious leaders
Government efforts on population issues		
Positive ranking	53.1	6.2
Negative ranking	46.9	93.8
NGOs' efforts on population issues		
Positive ranking	71.9	12.5
Negative ranking	29.1	68.8
No response	0.0	18.7
Citizens' cooperation on population issues		
Positive ranking	56.3	31.3
Negative ranking	43.7	37.5
No response	0.0	31.3

Source: Ibn Khaldoun Survey Data (1993)

than among government service providers of family planning (40 percent; see Table 1 under family planning practitioners). When it came to evaluating NGOs, civic leaders were even more positive (72 percent). While there may be biased responses by civic leaders toward like-minded NGOs, we observe that on this score both religious leaders and grumbling MD practitioners tended to be more positive in evaluating NGOs' efforts compared to those of the government. NGOs were evaluated as more efficient and less corrupt. Equally significant is the fact that civic leaders seem to be generally more positive (56 percent) in their perception of citizens' cooperation in dealing with the population problem. With the religious leaders, the question must have been perplexing. "Citizens' cooperation" for some of them must have been understood as defying the government population policy. Disregarding the seven imams who were supportive of that policy, we observed a negative evaluation (38 percent) or simply no answer to a question on citizens' cooperation.

We found several areas in which community leaders, both civic and religious, seem to hold common views, even if for different reasons. Many criticized the state for the ambiguity and weakness of its public policy on population and education. The next most common opinion with regard to population was a demand for "more forceful spatial redistribution." Many civic leaders, however, complained that the state has so far failed in obtaining a definitive opinion from authoritative religious sources "legitimating" family planning. The civic leaders feel that much of the government effort, regardless of efficacy, is undermined by conflicting signals about the religious legitimacy of family planning.[7] One other misgiving many civic leaders expressed was over the government's undue restriction of and interferences with the efforts of NGOs. They feel on the whole that these organizations do a good job in the field of family planning, and would do much better if they were not over-regulated by the state.

In sum, our research team found that of all the categories encountered in the course of their field work, the community civic leaders are the most concerned about the population issue. While critical, they are not hostile toward the state, and are appreciative of some of its efforts. Likewise, while wishing for a more positive response from fellow citizens in their respective communities, they maintain a higher level of confidence in people's cooperation. It may be appropriate to recall that it was civic leaders and NGOs who issued the earliest warning about Egypt's population problem some sixty years ago, a full thirty years before the state would take serious note of the issue. It was also Egypt's NGOs that took concrete action nineteen years before the first state-sponsored family planning service was set up. That long tradition among Egypt's NGOs is highly regarded in the community, but needs greater recognition at official national levels.

Women's Views of Population Issues

Since the early 1960s, women of reproductive age (15–49) have been the primary target of the family planning policy of the state. Here we take a closer look at those who are the ultimate measure of success or failure—the women who make reproductive choices.

We interviewed over five hundred women in their reproductive years, from nine of Egypt's twenty-six governorates (four in Upper Egypt, four in Lower Egypt, and a border governorate). They all had children, and their age distribution approximated that of the national population (34 percent from fifteen to thirty; 49 percent from thirty to forty-five; and 17 percent from forty-five to forty-nine). The sample was somewhat tilted in favor of rural women and urban women in poorer and lower middle-class areas.

As Table 3 indicates, nearly all the women in our sample know about family planning methods, both modern and traditional, which is consistent with the results of recent surveys. Radio and television were mentioned by almost all women (92 percent) as sources of this knowledge, followed by relatives and neighbors (55 percent), and family planning centers and health clinics (24 percent), while other sources of information were mentioned by fewer women in the sample (15 percent). As shown in section C of Table 3, television and radio (which in Egypt are state-controlled media) are highly regarded by most of those exposed to them; however, as many as 15 percent of our sample considered the media messages on population and family planning useless or "sheer propaganda."

Exposure to family planning knowledge obviously affects women's attitudes—93 percent of them expressed supportive attitudes. A somewhat lower proportion have ever used a family planning method (85 percent), and an even lower proportion are regular users (about 40 percent). Those who once used but stopped to have more children are 27 percent. As many as 20 percent stopped because of religious, moral, or health reasons, or husband's disapproval or other family-related reasons. There was occasional dissonance between expressed attitudes and actual family planning practices. Some of the women who were favorable to family planning did not practice it. And some who thought negatively of family planning, for religious or moral reasons, are nevertheless practicing it. The two groups of dissonant cases were a minority of about 21 percent in our sample. As with other groups in our survey, we started the women's interviews with two open questions about personal or family concerns and Egypt's problems nowadays. More than the other groups, women's problem-lists were replete with the immediate and concrete—on both the personal and national levels.

Of significance to our analysis is where the population issue figures in their problem-lists. Some 14 percent of the women mentioned it spontaneously with-

Table 3

Selective indicators of knowledge, views, and practices of reproductive women (n=503)

Indicator	%
A Knowledge of family planning methods (FPM)	
Modern methods only	76.7
Traditional methods only	2.0
Both modern and traditional methods	21.3
B Sources of knowledge of family planning methods mentioned[a]	
Radio and/or television	92.4
Relatives and neighbors	55.3
Family planning centers	12.9
Health clinics	11.9
Newspapers and magazines	7.4
Rural social workers	4.6
Lectures, conferences, and seminars	3.2
C Opinions of T.V. and radio family planning information	
Very informative	70.8
A constant reminder of proper use	12.2
Useless propaganda	15.1
Unexposed to it	2.9
D Attitudes toward family planning	
Definitely supportive	93.2
Definitely opposed	6.8
E Ever practiced family planning	
Yes	82.9
No	6.8
F Reasons for not practicing family planning at present (n=301)	
Husband or family disapprove	51.0
Religiously or morally repugnant	31.0
Fear of side effects	9.0
Other reasons	9.0
G Frequency ranking of current personal and/or family concerns[a]	
Limited income and high cost of living	71.0
Educating the children	44.3
Unemployment of a family member	38.0
Crowded or substandard housing	29.2
Raising too many children	24.8
Rising health and medication cost	20.3
H Frequency ranking of Egypt's problems[a]	
Inflation and low incomes	38.4
Housing	35.6
Terrorism	31.8
Unemployment	20.0
Too many people	13.8
Declining morality	10.5
Corruption	9.0

Source: Survey Data Files, Ibn Khaldoun Center, 1993

[a] Totals are more than 100 percent because categories are not exclusive. The figures indicate the percentage of women in the sample who mentioned each item.

out probing. Many of them stated it in simple terms—for example, "too many people crowding everything." When probed with the standard question ("What about population, which some think of as a problem?"), 63 percent readily agreed. This suggests that women, being immediately responsible for bearing and raising children, may more easily appreciate the burdens of high population.

State, Civil Society, and Women:
Convergence or Divergence of Interests?

National decision-makers responsible for Egypt's population policy have often formulated sweeping and well-intentioned programs to serve the policy objectives—including those bearing on women's education, training, employment, and public participation. But the overall coordinator of the policy (the Ministry of Population) has no real control over other organs of the state that implement those programs, not to mention the society at large. We have seen from this field study how little interest or commitment was shown by most cabinet-level decision-makers, technocratic executives, and MD field practitioners toward family planning. While this is only one component in Egypt's larger population policy, clearly it is the most important from the state's viewpoint.

Likewise, intra-governmental rivalries have undermined the effective implementation of much of Egypt's population policy. For years, there has been a three-way conflict among the Ministry of Population (and its predecessors), the Ministry of Health, and the Ministry of Social Affairs. The intensity of the conflict frustrated President Mubarak to the point of removing himself from the chairmanship of the NPC executive board, and delegating the job to his prime minister. The power struggles at the top are often devolved to the governorate level or all the way down to the field units. We saw how divergent were the views of MDs (mostly with the Ministry of Health) and the social workers, who are mostly with the Ministry of Social Affairs or the NPC.

Moreover, because the implementation of Egypt's population policy is multi-level and multi-sectoral, the plethora of agencies and activities[8] makes it difficult to determine where true accountability for results rests within the system. The problem has been compounded by recent efforts to decentralize responsibility for population targets. Thus a new layer of governmental actors—the governors and local officials—is added into the picture.

The more serious cleavage in Egypt today, which undermines many public policies, and especially that of population, is a three-way conflict among the state, civil society, and the militant religious groups. We saw how divergent, for example, were the views of community civic and religious leaders. All three actors are fighting for a share of Egypt's public space. Both the state with its centralized hierarchic traditions and the religious groups with their absolutist dogma want full control of that space, and with it full control of the intention and reproductive behavior of women. For their part, organs of civil society are valiantly trying to expand their minute share of Egypt's public space.

Each of the three actors has its own, albeit unequal, arsenal of communication weapons to deploy in this conflict. The state has the powerful official media, institutional and financial resources, some four thousand mother and child health clinics, and twenty thousand government mosques. However, its fighting forces are not in the best shape: having been demoralized by bureaucratic inertia, they may comply with orders but with little enthusiasm. The Islamic activists have at least one opposition paper *(al-Sha'b)*, forty thousand non-governmental mosques, and activists to distribute hundreds of thousands of cassette-tapes, with messages often attacking family planning programs as external plots against Muslims. Their fighting forces are single-minded zealots who have managed in some cases to penetrate the state agencies, at least as we have seen at the field practitioner level. Civil society has some twenty thousand trade and professional unions, political parties, PVOs and NGOs, cooperatives, youth clubs, and business associations. Only a fraction are directly involved in family planning per se, though most are generally committed to empowerment and freedom of choice for all, including women. But civil society is outgunned by the state through over-regulation and by the Islamic activists through powerful local organization. However, in the specific battle of family planning, civil society has become an uneasy ally of the state, and is credited for effective family planning services. Unfortunately, the state's insistence on over-control has kept the potentials of civil society substantially unrealized to date.

Another potential threat to the policy, however, comes from other actors: MD field practitioners in some of the state family planning and maternal health centers, and religious community leaders. Implicitly or explicitly, these two groups are presently quite hostile to state policies in general and to the population policy in particular. Their pro-natalist attitude is a function of a radical Islamic ideology that has been spreading among young, educated Egyptians, especially in medical schools where they are not exposed to any social science training. Curiously enough, a similar radical socialist ideology was in vogue from the mid-1960s to the mid-1970s, and was equally pro-natalist. It was that ideology which propagated overall development and social equity as a substitute for family planning and contraception services. Different as they are on many other societal issues, and doggedly competing in Egypt's public space, the two radical ideologies see eye-to-eye on the population issue. They were partly responsible for setting back Egypt's population policy after a promising start (1961–66).

With this state of affairs in Egypt in recent years, it is perhaps surprising that the country has moved to a contraceptive prevalence rate of 47 percent. Part of this progress must be attributed not so much to official harmony of effort, but to the individual decisions reached by women and couples far from the political struggles.

Conclusion

Despite the zigzagging and ambiguity, Egypt's population policy seems to be taking shape and proceeding on a well-defined track. A review of Egypt's long history of public concern over population issues reveals a number of important lessons.

First, starting in the early 1930s, it took three full decades of warnings from Egypt's civil society and non-governmental organizations before the Egyptian state issued its first public declaration on the population problem in the early 1960s. In the interim, the country's population had already doubled. Even the delayed state response was hampered for over two additional decades by competing paradigms of what to do about the problem, by oscillating commitments of the top leadership, and by conflicting bureaucracies over how it was to be done and who was to do it. In the interim, Egypt's population doubled again. Out of the three decades of state concern, only the first and the last five years witnessed a forceful joint action by the state and civil society in pursuing the primary objective of the policy—the reduction of the growth rate.

While still short of the performance of the first five years, the results of the last five years are quite impressive. But they are potentially threatened by a number of factors and counter forces. The renewed presidential commitment to the three-pronged population policy (reduction of growth rate, spatial redistribution, and upgrading population characteristics) is not matched by many cabinet members, or top and middle state executives. The pro-natalist attitudes of radical Islamic activists, presently in vogue especially among young MDs, are consistent with deep-seated traditional values and reproductive norms in rural and poorer urban areas. Nevertheless, and powerful as they are, such counterforces to the state population policy are not in full monopoly of Egypt's public space. The state has several actual and potential allies. Part of the state bureaucracy and nearly all civil society organizations are committed to Egypt's population policy. Because of raised consciousness, health reasons, or socioeconomic pressures, most of Egypt's women have become positively disposed to family planning, and nearly one half are current users. Approximately another one-fourth are willing or eager to try it if proper conditions are created—e.g., husband and family approval, easier access, and quality medical care or assurances against side-effects.

The battle over the future of the country's population policy—indeed over Egypt's destiny—is contingent on a forceful commitment to educating and empowering women, achieving sustained commitment at the highest level of decision-making, and increasing the margin of freedom of Egypt's civil society organizations.

Notes

1   Notable among these were three Egyptian NGOs: al-Nahda (Renaissance), al-Ruwwad (Pioneers), and the Egyptian Feminist Union. For details, see Darwish, 1989:74–85.

2   In Egypt, power is highly centralized and concentrated in the executive branch of the state. Egyptians have learned to take their clues of the relative importance of policies, issues, events, and persons from a number of political symbols. The designation of a governmental organization as a 'committee,' a 'commission,' a 'council,' or a 'ministry,' carries with it progressive prestige and importance. Dr. Maher Mahran, who had been the Secretary General of the National Population Council since 1986, was appointed as the first minister of state for population and family welfare.

3   Absent from these target groups are husbands and male heads of households, to whom very little attention has been given by official policy.

4   On these and other recent occasions, the president placed population as number four on a six-point national agenda for the remainder of the 1990s.

5   See briefing on a series of presidential meetings with the Cabinet and the ruling National Democratic Party (NDP) (*Al-Ahram*, 1994).

6   Some have since left their positions in a recent cabinet reshuffle (October 14, 1993).

7   This view is in fact incorrect, as the religious authorities of al-Azhar have, as early as the 1930s, promulgated fatwas (official opinions) affirming the acceptability of family planning.

8   For example, the third policy objective of population redistribution is the responsibility of five ministries: the Ministry of Reconstruction and New Settlements, the Ministry of Defense, the Ministry of Tourism, the Ministry of Land Reclamation, and the Ministry of Industry. Each of them is to generate plans, programs, projects, and activities to lure people away from the overcrowded Nile Valley and Delta toward new communities in the desert and border governorates (the Red Sea, Sinai, Matruh, and the New Valley). Likewise, the Ministry of Manpower and Training is in charge of reducing unemployment among men and increasing paid employment for women, through targeted training and retraining. Along with upgrading education and health, this task is to contribute to the policy objective of improving population characteristics.

References

Abdel Hakim, M. S. 1994. An interview on the genesis of Egypt's population policy. Ibn Khaldoun Center, Cairo, January 11, 1994.

Al-Ahram. 1955. July 24.

Al-Ahram. 1993. Interview with President Mubarak, November 12.

Al-Ahram. 1994. December 27, December 29, January 6.

Al-Musawwar. 1993. Interview with President Mubarak, September 24.

Cleland, W. 1936. *The Population Problem in Egypt: A Study of Population Trends and*

Conditions in Modern Egypt. Lancaster, Penn.: Science Press.

Darwish, Y. 1989. *Mu'tamar al-tanzimat al-ahliya al-'arabiya*. In the proceedings of the Conference on Arab Non-governmental Organizations held in Cairo, October 31–November 3, 1989.

DHS. 1988. *Egypt Demographic and Health Survey, 1988*. Cairo: National Population Council.

DHS. 1993. *Egypt Demographic and Health Survey, 1992*. Cairo: National Population Council.

Dixon-Mueller, R. 1993. *Population Policy and Women's Rights: Transforming Reproductive Choice*. Westport, Conn. and London: Praeger.

Egypt's National Charter. 1961. Cairo: Department of Information.

Mahran, M. 1994. "Egypt's Population Policy: Past, Present, and Future." Presentation at Ibn Khaldoun Center, Cairo, January 6, 1994.

National Population Council (NPC). 1994. *Egypt National Report on Population*. Draft submitted to the International Conference on Population and Development, 1994. Cairo: National Population Council.

United Nations Development Programme (UNDP). 1992. *The Human Development Report*. New York: Oxford University Press.

World Bank. 1993. *World Development Report*. Washington, D.C. and New York: Oxford University Press.

6

Fertility and Social Change in Oman: Women's Perspectives

Christine Eickelman

Women in Oman play highly active roles in sustaining the social position of their households and *hayyans* (family clusters). Their perceptions of status and prestige are closely linked to women's reproductive roles. Omani women, many of whom appear to the outside observer to be passive recipients of current economic and social transformations, use high birth rates and, more specifically, postpartum visiting as conscious personal strategies for reaffirming family and household social status and for enhancing their status in other areas.

On a general level, an analysis of the role women play in making fertility decisions and in managing postpartum visiting networks reveals how women whom both Western and Muslim observers consider highly "traditional" complement the strategies used by men to acquire social prestige, and how they contribute to the social transformations of their communities by adapting older attitudes to changing contexts. At a more specific level, this analysis suggests the conditions under which effective population strategies, which inherently involve women—and even "empower" them—might be developed in the Arabian Peninsula.

Oman's population has been growing at an estimated 3.8 percent a year, one of the highest rates in the world. The annual birth rates of other Arabian Peninsula countries—namely, Kuwait, Saudi Arabia, and Yemen—have been equally high, and demographers expect the population of the entire peninsula to double by the year 2000.[1] Population experts and some Omanis regard the pattern of high birth rates as unbeneficial for individual Omanis and for Omani society. Presently, however, it seems that Oman's oil wealth can provide a cushion against economic and social problems—such as unemployment, pollution, the depletion of food, and water resources, overburdened government programs, and social unrest—that the country will face if the population continues to grow at its current rate.[2]

From *Middle East Journal* 47 (4):652–66 (1993). Reprinted by permission. Christine Eickelman is a visiting scholar in the Department of Anthropology at Dartmouth College and the author of *Women and Community in Oman* (New York and London: New York University Press, 1984). She wishes to thank Jeanne Bergman, Dale F. Eickelman, Deborah Hodges, and James Piscatori for comments on an earlier version of this article.

Since the 1970s, demographers-and historians have argued that women and men in premodern European societies and contemporary Third World countries could avail themselves of reproductive control through such "direct" practices as abortion, birth control, infanticide, and child abandonment and through "indirect" ones, such as late marriage and abstinence from sexual relations until a child is weaned.[3] Similar arguments about women assuming active roles in Arabian Peninsula societies are obscured by the often polemical literature concerning women's roles in Muslim societies: Until recently, demographers attributed continuing high birth rates in Middle Eastern countries to the persistence of a fertility pattern no longer curbed by a high infant and child mortality rate; some even characterized the incidence of high birth rates as a general characteristic of Islamic societies—assumptions that impute to women passive and subordinate cultural and social roles.[4]

The reluctance of political authorities in Arabian Peninsula societies to allow the open discussion of population strategies has discouraged research in this area. Baquer al-Najjar, a Bahraini sociologist, recently commented that "population policy" in the Gulf states continues to be restricted to the regulation and control of the non-citizen population. State authorities prohibit public discussion of strategies to influence decisions on family size—sometimes citing religious reasons—perhaps because they believe that a large citizen population can be translated into political strength.[5]

The Impact of Time

The interval between this author's two research visits to Oman is significant because the changes that occurred during this period dispel any assumption of fixed and enduring "traditional" practices. The first visit to al-Hamra, a provincial capital and oasis in the northern Omani interior and major town of the Abriyin tribe, was undertaken in 1979-1980, less than a decade after the beginning of Oman's economic development. The original goal of the field visit was to explore women's changing understandings of family, privacy, propriety, education, work, children, and status.[6] The second visit took place in the spring of 1988. In the interval, the population of the oasis more than doubled from 2,510 people in 1980 to about 6,000 people by 1988.[7]

Between the first and second field visits, Oman's oil economy physically transformed the northern interior of the country. In al-Hamra in 1979–1980, almost everyone lived in mud-brick houses in the older quarters. In 1988, many of these mud-brick houses stood empty and dilapidated, abandoned by households that had moved to new cement-block houses with piped water and electricity and located along a newly paved road that circled the oasis. Other houses had been built on land several kilometers from town. A bank, a garage, government offices, a house for the governor and his family, two large schools—

one for boys and one for girls—and shops of Indian tailors stood alongside the road leading out of the oasis. Amid great clouds of dust, Indian technicians were installing al-Hamra's first telephone lines.

The transformations were not just physical. The effects of formal schooling for women had begun to influence daily routines. Books and magazines were visible in many of the guest rooms where women visited and drank coffee with one another. Women sometimes jotted housekeeping memos in small note-books. Two young women from al-Hamra worked in the local girls' school, one as a teacher and the other as a secretary. Eight women in the community, including a married woman with a child, were studying in the capital area of Muscat-Mutrah and planning to return as teachers to al-Hamra. Another woman spoke with pride of a granddaughter who was studying Islamic sciences at Sultan Qaboos University, which admitted its first students in 1988. Others extolled medicine as a good career for a woman.

Women in 1988 discussed fertility and birth in significantly different ways than they had in 1979–1980. During the earlier period, women often disguised their concerns and anxieties about fertility-related issues by discussing them in a joking manner. By 1988, topics such as the value of girls as compared to boys, sterility, and family size stirred active debate among women.[8] The most surprising aspect of these conversations were the statements by several women that they wanted as many as 20 children. Young children were everywhere, and many women had given birth to four or five children in eight years.[9]

The emphasis on large families was illustrated vividly through an account of a 1987 incident in al-Hamra. Two brothers, who for years had lived together with their wives and children in a single household—not an uncommon practice in Oman—were obliged to form separate households because their wives had quarreled.[10] The loss in prestige that accompanies a public quarrel was clear in the scornful tones used by women who spoke about the quarrel. It occurred because one of the sisters-in-law, who had three healthy sons, desperately wanted another child. Her sister-in-law had given birth six times in the preceding eight years.

The more prolific sister-in-law was pleased at having borne so many children in such a short time. "I am thin and ugly," the woman smiled, "because of all the children." She lifted her youngest son onto her lap and said abruptly, "I want more." When asked, "Why more? You now have six," she replied, "We want twenty. Why? I don't know." After a pause, she added, "My husband wants children, so I want them. Why? I don't know." She shrugged. There were many other women who claimed to be willing to give birth for as long as possible, or, if they were beyond childbearing age, who encouraged younger women in a joint household or extended family to continue having children.

On another occasion, a mother-in-law became furious when her daughter-in-law, who had just given birth to a fourth child, was asked if there were women in al-Hamra who said "enough" after four, five, or six births and used some form of birth control. The older woman exclaimed, "We Omanis have twenty children." "Why do you say this?" this author asked. "You know how I love children, but I would never want twenty. Twenty children cannot be good for any woman! In America a woman chooses to have two, three, or four children, and then she stops." Dismissing this reply with a wave of her hand, the mother-in-law retorted, "We are like animals." Clearly, however, she did not perceive of herself as an "animal"; rather, this was how women from al-Hamra thought foreigners—Americans or expatriate Egyptian schoolteachers (who have few children)—perceive Omani women who give birth frequently.

The daughter-in-law then spoke in a low, intense voice. "What do you use in America? Needles? Pills?" Before her question could be answered, several guests entered the room, and everyone settled down to drink coffee. The mother-in-law, who had heard her daughter-in-law's question, addressed the guests in an uncharacteristically loud and mocking voice while pointing her finger at this author: "This woman says that in America women take medicine so that they only have two children!" The guests began to laugh and to jeer at the idea of controlling births.[11]

The question regarding why women want so many children inadvertently exposed an important source of disagreement between the mother-in-law and daughter-in-law. In Inner Oman, mothers-in-law and daughters-in-law are not expected to quarrel, and open disagreement is rare. It was easy to understand the young woman's point of view, partially revealed by her hurried question on birth control. It was the older woman's emphasis on the importance of a long period of fecundity that was puzzling. The day before, the same mother-in-law had complained that the antics of her grandchildren often made her lose her temper. Also perplexing was the guests' jeering at women who wished to regulate their fertility. In 1988, many women in al-Hamra and elsewhere in Oman, often young and with some education, resisted the idea of regulating births.

Concepts of Fertility

Omanis perceive children as signs of social strength. Children fill emotional needs and care for aging parents in later life. People need sons to work outside the community and help them cope with an increasingly complex world. People need daughters to build and maintain social ties within the community. The "value of the child," a demographic term, helps explain why people have four, five, or six children.[12] This explanation is not adequate, however, for understanding why many Omani women desire to prolong their years of fecundity.

Muslim populations have known of and used birth control at various times in the past, notwithstanding resistance to the idea in some contemporary Muslim societies.[13] Changes in fertility patterns reflect a micro-level response to social and economic transformations in the wider society. Islamic beliefs and values, given present and past variations, are not responsible for the high birth rates prevalent today in many parts of the Middle East. These high birth rates are relatively recent rather than a continuation of age-old fertility patterns. Demographers, however, do not fully understand the reasons behind the changes.[14]

Many women in Oman find it difficult to understand discussions of fertility that focus on individual pregnancies, "choice," and birth control. For Omani women, the act of giving birth to a live child is as significant a social event as raising a child. In the late 1970s, when women were asked the number of children they had, they often responded with the number of times they had given birth to a live child, even though many of the children had died shortly after birth. Postpartum visiting takes place even if an infant dies a few hours after birth. (In the late 1970s, such deaths were still commonplace.) The parents mourn the infant only when they are alone. In front of guests, the death of the child is not mentioned.

The Omani concept of fertility encompasses giving birth *regularly* to a live child, which is acknowledged in the community by postpartum visiting, and nurturing the child and the mother-child relationship, which has its own set of rewards. *Regularly* is stressed because regular sequences of births are valued most of all. It is common to hear women ask a mother with a child not old enough to walk whether she is again pregnant. Women often say that they pity mothers who give birth only two or three times.

The birth of a first child is a rite of passage that transforms a woman into a social adult. She may then visit households that are neither kin nor close neighbors in the community. Infertile women or women who never marry participate much less intensively in visiting networks, and they start visiting at a later age. They cannot reciprocate postpartum visits, which places them at a considerable social disadvantage because births are the most frequent reason for formal visiting. These visits are essential to recognition as a full social person.[15]

The relation between birth and hospitality is firmly embedded in the taken-for-granted, practical routines of daily activities for women in Oman. Giving birth and providing hospitality go hand in hand somewhat similarly to the roles of "wife and mother" in some segments of Western society. Indeed, the Western role of "wife and mother" does not apply in Oman. The role of wife belongs to the private world of family life, never disclosed to outsiders, while the role of mother is one that a woman can display in public.

The way Omanis present themselves in photographs demonstrates these cultural differences. In al-Hamra it is impossible to take a family snapshot that includes a husband and a wife surrounded by their children. This is not because the nuclear family is not a familiar concept; indeed, a significant percentage of households in al-Hamra are nuclear. Rather, it is unthinkable for a woman to be photographed next to her husband because it would imply her private role as wife. Husband and wife never visit in the community as a couple, and men and women go to great lengths to avoid being in the same room when a non-family member is present. Occasions when husband, wife, and children interact together are not shared with non-family members of either gender.

In contrast, women display their public roles as mothers with ease in the community and to strangers. In al-Hamra women willingly allow themselves to be photographed with a child and often place themselves next to coffeepots or trays of fruit, which is to suggest hospitality to anyone viewing the photograph.[16] In this respect, they are presenting themselves in the two roles that usually go hand in hand as mothers and as persons who receive guests generously and participate in visiting networks.

Family Clusters and Visiting Networks

The concept of family clusters is crucial to understanding social life and networking throughout Oman. The term is applied to a wide range of paternal and maternal kin who live in several households—in the past often clustered together but now spatially dispersed—and perceive themselves as bound by obligations of mutual support, including the sharing of information that is not revealed to others. Family clusters are linked to one another through kinship, marriage, and patron–client ties, and, until the 1970s, most political and economic activities were built upon them.[17] These interrelated family clusters were, and are, the basis of tribes.

Until the mid-twentieth century, virtually all aspects of people's lives in Inner Oman revolved around the framework of tribal politics. A tribal elite monopolized economic and political resources as well as religious learning. Everyone else depended almost totally on the tribal elite for protection. Oman's post-1970 economic growth, however, lessened the control of the tribal leaders over economic opportunities. After the economic and political improvements that followed Oman's 1970 coup d'état, many men from al-Hamra who had been obliged to seek wage labor in neighboring countries to feed their families returned home. Many found jobs as drivers and guards in the rapidly expanding state bureaucracy; others joined the army and the police. A few households moved to the capital area, but the lack of affordable housing, together with the strength of extended family ties, kept most families in al-Hamra, with men returning to their homes in the oasis on weekends.

For people who do not belong to the tribal elite, social mobility in post-1970 Oman has meant obtaining a government job and sustaining the image of their family clusters as large, cohesive, economically autonomous, educated, and hospitable. Until the 1970s transformation, only the tribal elite could successfully present themselves as possessing these qualities. Wealth, education, and extensive extra-tribal political contacts continue to give the tribal elite a competitive edge, but this advantage is rapidly narrowing. Social competition now occurs in two mutually interactive arenas: the local community, where many more women than men live full-time, and the cosmopolitan, urban setting of the capital area, where many men work and where some households now have moved from the oases of the interior. People need local ties, however, to present themselves to their best advantage in the capital area, just as some use the status acquired in the capital to manipulate and improve their standing in their oasis of origin. Households that have moved to the capital area return regularly to al-Hamra to maintain their land and houses, to oversee small local businesses, and to sustain their extended family ties and those of their visiting networks. In spite of the better medical care available in the capital area, women who live there often return to al-Hamra to give birth (unless they anticipate a difficult pregnancy) or return there immediately afterward. Most women return to the oasis regularly to participate in postpartum visiting networks.

The need for women to network has increased, and hospitality has become more elaborate as the tribal elite competes with other upwardly mobile family clusters and as men increasingly work outside the oasis.[18] The large guest rooms for women in the newly constructed cement block houses in al-Hamra indicate the value placed upon women's visiting networks. In one household that this author visited in 1988, men used an old mud-brick guest room adjacent to the new, concrete block house for their visiting. Its bare simplicity stood in sharp contrast to the women's luxurious setting. An older woman from the tribal elite described how full the house had been at a recent wedding: "Fifty cars were parked outside." Weddings, which were generally restricted to the family cluster in the late 1970s, are now public occasions for large-scale hospitality.

Postpartum Visiting

Postpartum visiting occurs in a climate of intensive social competition, image-building of family clusters, and testing of the social order. The *murabbiya* (postpartum visiting period) extends over several weeks, and women representing all households of the community and the surrounding countryside are obliged to visit at least once. During *murabbiya*, guests are received by the new mother's mother-in-law and other married women who live in her household. Other close female relatives who live in the oasis attend the *murabbiya* for several hours daily. No other occasions except mournings—not even weddings—bring so many people together for so long.

When a woman is about to begin labor, she does not speak of it to anyone outside her household. Birth is a private occasion, assisted only by close relatives and a midwife.[19] Once the child is born, however, the news spreads quickly throughout the community, and a *murabbiya* ensues.[20] The new mother lies on a steel cot at the head of a room and receives visitors from morning until sunset. A woman who is descended from a *khadima* (slave) is hired for the occasion to serve guests and help with housework during the entire period.

As stated earlier, an infant need only live a few hours for the full cycle of postpartum visiting to take place. The sex of the infant and the number of times a woman has given birth do not affect the public aspects of postpartum visiting in any significant way. There are, however, differences in what households do in private. For a first-born son, members of a family cluster may collect money to buy an animal as a gift for the child.

Men claim to have nothing to do with the *murabbiya* and other birth-related activities although this is not wholly truthful. Men from the household in which a birth has taken place buy the food, incense, and perfume used in offering hospitality, and they stay away from their homes until women visitors have left. The use of pickup trucks and automobiles has complicated the choreography of gender separation. Although women in Oman are permitted to drive, few women in the interior do so, and most households have only one vehicle. Thus, men are enlisted to drive women to visits and sometimes there are problems of coordination and "getting the car." In practice, maintenance of the strictly segregated men's and women's visiting networks requires careful coordination on the part of both men and women.

Between this author's visits in 1979-1980 and 1988, the public aspects of the *murabbiya* changed. During the earlier period, guests rarely saw newborn infants because they were left in a side room. By 1988, women began to use plastic bathtubs as cribs, and mothers would keep their newborn infants, no longer swaddled, close to them so that they could tend to the infant's needs as they received guests. The guests, however, would not speak of the birth or the child, and they would leave gifts unobtrusively at the entrance to the guest room. These gifts, often coffee beans or fruit, usually consisted of items that could be served to subsequent guests. The gifts were never items for the mother or for the newborn child.

In general, postpartum visits are not oriented toward children, and younger children are kept away from the guests. If a toddler is known to be difficult— and from a young child's perspective, a *murabbiya* is a period of great tension— he or she may be sent to a relative's house for its duration. Women often complain about the "problems" young children cause for guests. For example, children sometimes play with the guests' sandals, which are left at the entrance of the guest room, often misplacing them; the children would sometimes have temper tantrums, and, in general, grow restless. Women arrange for child-care prior to visits unless the visit is within their own family cluster.

One aspect of the *murabbiya* involves items—such as clothes, perfumes, pots and pans—that many women sell to guests during postpartum visits. These objects are placed on shelves around the room, and guests can ask to see them, although they are under no obligation to buy. Women of the tribal elite cannot sell items because of their social position, but in 1988, a client was observed selling items in the household of her patron, a member of the tribal elite. The young elite woman who had given birth recorded each transaction in a small notebook for her client because the woman was illiterate. At another time, in the same household, another client used a room adjacent to where the guests sat to perform medicinal branding, a traditional form of medicine still practiced in the Arabian Peninsula.

Conversations during a *murabbiya* remain polite and neutral. A new machine embroidery stitch for pantaloons, a visit to the recently opened Qaboos University in the capital area, even some mild joking or teasing about who is pregnant are typical topics of conversation. Most visits to households outside one's own family cluster last no longer than 30 minutes. If all the women present know one another well, the atmosphere is more casual and relaxed. If, however, there are wide discrepancies in the social position of the women present, or there are disagreements between the family clusters of the visitors and the host, then guests remain silent unless spoken to.

The number and range of persons a *murabbiya* attracts reflect a family's social standing. The size of the room where visitors are received, the quality of the rug, the food and perfumes offered, the size and composition of the clusters of guests, the number of women of slave descent serving guests, and the presence of clients offering a variety of services are all factors considered when attempting to present the household as a generous one, and one accustomed to receiving and pleasing guests. Other factors—seating arrangements, greeting etiquette, and the demeanor of the hosting women and their guests—can change rapidly. Women who are smooth conversationalists lapse into silence or offer monosyllabic responses to direct questions when women from the tribal elite enter a guest room. Some women, in formal deference to such guests, will also move immediately to the least prestigious seats in the room. Likewise, coffee, fruit, and perfume may be served in a relaxed manner for some guests, while it may be a rushed affair with others.

The length and frequency of visits are also indicators of status, so the matter-of-fact exchange of information on visiting patterns during the visits provides an almost direct means of challenging social claims.[21] For example, during one visit a woman of the tribal elite was asked whether she often visited the wife of the *wali* (governor).[22] She replied that she did not know the governor's wife and changed the subject. Yet, later in the privacy of the car on the way home, she added, "You know at the mourning for X"—she named a well-known older woman of the tribal elite—"the governor's wife only came once!" The single visit was a bitter insult, suggesting that the governor's family perceived the tribal elite as no more than clients.

Although the tribal notables and the governor appeared to have cordial relations at official functions, the women's formal networking suggested underlying tensions.[23]

Similarly, women seeking to enhance their claims to higher social ranking—such as women of slave descent or clients of the Abriyin tribe whose husbands or brothers have become officers in the police, army, or security services—avoid visits that place them at a social disadvantage. Even if their men are accorded respect at formal gatherings for state and religious holidays, earlier understandings of their client status prevail at women's gatherings, and thus they seek to avoid them.

The women of the tribal leadership now indirectly compete with other family clusters to attract large numbers of guests. The physical dispersal of housing away from the original mud-brick village has not only blurred spatial representations of status, but it has also made frequent visits to acknowledge respect and status much more difficult than when most members of the community lived less than a 20-minute walk from the extremes of the oasis. The need for women living in al-Hamra to arrange for transport as well as child-care sometimes cuts the number of visitors well below what hosts may be expecting.[24] Visiting obligations are numerous, and women regularly combine two or three formal visits in one afternoon. These sets of visits, however, must consist of the same level of formality; for example, formal visits to non-kin households are not mixed with those to one's own family cluster or informal gatherings of neighbors. *Murabbiya* visits can, however, be combined with those to offer condolences after a death. Typically, women visit in small groups of twos or threes, usually neighbors, sisters, or mother and daughter.

Before committing to a visit, some women may need a day to weigh their options. Which women in the household should participate in a visit? Younger women tend to visit more often for births and older women for mournings, but there are many exceptions. How long should they stay? Lengths of visits are more difficult to control because women are increasingly dependent on male drivers. Who else can they visit on the same day? Will a delay of three or four days be interpreted unfavorably? Should they come at all? Are people whom they wish to avoid likely to visit on certain days?

As discussed earlier, women who have moved to the capital area often return to al-Hamra to give birth or for postpartum visiting. Women from elsewhere in Oman also return to their towns and villages of origin. One woman from Salala—the capital of Oman's southern Dhufar region—seven months pregnant with a fifth child, said she was returning to Salala for six months. A co-wife, herself two months pregnant, was to follow in a few weeks. The eyes of both women shone as they talked of Salala postpartum visiting, insisting that nothing compared to it in the capital area or elsewhere in Oman.

The Limits of Directed Change

In Oman, issues such as decreasing natural resources do not motivate individuals to make better personal choices regarding family size, especially when medical care, education, and social services are perceived as cost-free. In addition, there are no indications that married couples actively discuss the options open to them and their social implications. Yet, Oman and other countries of the Arabian Peninsula cannot afford to wait for fertility rates to stabilize on their own. Oman has no official family-planning policy, but, unlike Saudi Arabia, which bans the sale of contraceptives,[25] modern birth control is available in pharmacies in the capital area and from private doctors, some of whom reputedly encourage women to space their births. Oman's official religious spokespersons—including Shaykh Ahmad bin Hamad al-Khalili, Oman's mufti—have not taken a clear stand on family planning, although many do speak out on the role of women in society.

From an outsider's perspective, Omani women appear to be in a quandary not unlike that of women in Sudan and East Africa, where government efforts to prohibit female circumcision have been widely ignored and even denounced by women who fear that abandoning the practice would deprive them of marriage and prevent them from becoming responsible adults.[26] In the Omani case, the conundrum is more subtle: the degree to which many women are able to participate actively in the process of social transformations remains tied to prolonging their period of fertility.

To perceive women's postpartum networking as merely a reflection of status is to simplify the meaning Omani men and women attach to formal visiting. Face-to-face interaction continues to be the most valued way of obtaining "reliable" information in Oman, yet communities are rapidly losing their physical closeness. People are no longer as able to maintain extensive and active face-to-face ties. Men and women need to "divide up the labor" of social obligations in order to collect and disseminate information among themselves and to keep up with constantly changing versions of social relations within their expanding communities.

Because of the importance attached to postpartum visitation, any Omani government effort to encourage decreased fertility is not likely to be successful. In fact, cumbersome bureaucracies and an insensitivity toward religious and cultural values have plagued many Third World population-control programs.[27] A program that stresses a lifestyle for women that is perceived as Western is also unlikely to succeed. In Malaysia, for example, the government's population program backfired because it privileged the mother-child relationship, reflecting the Western family model, while ignoring the central role of the Muslim father's conjugal and paternity rights.[28] In Egypt, in contrast, the government's National Population Council claims that family size decreased from 7 children in the

1970s to 4.3 children in 1991. It attributed the reduction to media appeals, including the use of popular soap operas.[29]

In Oman, it is doubtful that the media is sufficient to change attitudes toward fertility. Women and men place little trust in the media, and there is no precedent for applying its messages to their immediate concerns. Although official pronouncements call for formal obedience to the sultan in all matters, in practice, the government rarely interferes in the private aspects of people's lives. Government measures in the past, including the placement of limits on the amount that men could pay in *sadaq* (bride wealth) for marriage, are widely ignored.

In Muslim countries such as Morocco, family-planning programs utilize, with some success, workers who visit households to explain birth control options and distribute contraceptives. Again, it is doubtful that a similar program could be implemented in Oman given the unwillingness of Omanis to interfere in the private affairs of other family clusters and the close link between women's reproductive roles and perceptions of status and prestige. The concern for privacy is not unique to Oman. Population experts have discovered that in Botswana, Kenya, and Zimbabwe, regions of Africa with some of the highest fertility rates in the world, fertility declined rapidly when contraceptives became available in private pharmacies rather than in public clinics.[30] The highest demand for contraception came from women who wanted to defer pregnancy for a variety of reasons and who valued a distribution system that afforded them privacy.

More important than discussions on how to implement birth control policies, however, are efforts to "objectify" issues related to family planning. One of the consequences of modern education is broader discussion of decisions affecting family matters. A strength of Persian Gulf society has been the spatial representation of social relations in oasis societies and the use of visiting networks as means of conveying information. Population programs must take account of the "division of social labor" that takes place in Omani society. Such programs will need to reorient people toward a transformed lifestyle, where networking is no longer dependent on women giving birth. New social occasions for visiting in urbanized Gulf society include departure and arrival from a long voyage, moving into a new house, and children's birthday parties, a recent innovation adopted by capital-area Omanis and Omanis overseas. Breaking the pattern of multiple births quickly and effectively in Oman requires a program that sensitizes people to the subtle relation between fertility and other aspects of culture and prompts them to articulate issues related to fertility, potency, and family planning.

Notes

1   The natural annual rate of increase is the surplus of births over deaths in a population without regard to migration. For Kuwait the rate is 3.0, for Saudi Arabia 3.4, and for Yemen 3.5. See *World Population Data Sheet* (Washington, D.C.: Population

Reference Bureau, 1991). Oman's first census was planned for early 1993. The 1991 estimate used by the Population Reference Bureau is 1.6 million. This includes non-citizen foreigners, who constitute roughly 21 percent of the country's population, a low proportion in comparison with other Persian Gulf states. For planning purposes, the Omani government uses a figure of 2 million. See the Sultanate of Oman, Development Council, Technical Secretariat, *Statistical Yearbook*, 1988 (Muscat: Development Secretariat, 1989).

2   See Paul Kennedy, "Preparing for the 21st Century," *New York Review of Books*, February 11, 1993, pp. 41–42, and Michael Teitelbaum, "The Population Threat," *Foreign Affairs* 71, no. 5 (1992–93) .

3   See Stephen Polgar, "Population History and Population Policies from an Anthropological Perspective," *Current Anthropology* 13 (1972); Susan Scrimshaw, "Infant Mortality and Behavior in The Regulation of Family Size," in Nick Eberstadt, ed., *Fertility Decline in The Less Developed Countries* (New York: Praeger Publishers, 1981), pp. 295–318; Robert A. LeVine and Susan Scrimshaw., "Effects of Culture on Fertility: Anthropological Contributions," in Rodolfo A. Bulatao et al., eds., *Determinants of Fertility in Developing Countries*, vol. 2 (New York and London: Academic Press, 1983), pp. 245–46; Angus McLaren, *Reproductive Rituals: The Perception of Fertility in England from the Sixteenth to the Nineteenth Century* (London and New York: Methuen, 1984); and John Boswell, *The Kindness of Strangers: The Abandonment of Children in Western Europe from Late Antiquity to the Renaissance* (New York: Pantheon Books, 1988).

4   For example, see the comments on the "Islamic family" in John C. Caldwell, "Fertility in Africa," in Nick Eberstadt, ed., *Fertility Decline in the Less Developed Countries* (New York: Praeger Publishers, 1981), pp. 112–13. On the "Asian family," see Mead Cain, *Women's Status and Fertility in Developing Countries: Son Preference and Economic Security*, Working Paper no. 682 (Washingon, D.C.: World Bank, 1984). For a discussion of the problems that population experts face in assessing the status of women in the Third World, see Karen Oppenheim Mason, *The Status of Woman: A Review of its Relationships to Fertility and Mortality* (New York: Rockefeller Foundation, Population Science Division, 1984).

5   Baquer al-Najjar, personal communication, July 1989.

6   Christine Eickelman, *Women and Community in Oman* (New York and London: New York University Press, 1984).

7   Dale F. Eickelman, "Counting and Surveying an 'Inner' Omani Community: Hamra al-Abriyin," in E.G.H. Joffe and C.R. Pennel, eds., *Tribe and State: Essays in Honour of David Montgomery Hart* (Wisbech, UK: MENAS Press, 1991), p. 258.

8   This author's presence in Oman virtually compelled discussion of family practices because of her somewhat anomalous role as an Arabic-speaking wife and mother, accompanied during her first field visit by her husband and an adopted daughter, who was then two years old and whose features clearly did not resemble hers. On her second visit in 1988, she was accompanied by a second adopted daughter. Omanis are

reluctant to raise children whose families they do not know. In questioning the author about her choices, women discussed their perspectives through examples of their own practices and those of neighbors.

9 The birth rate in Oman prior to the 1970s is not reliably known. Using field notes from al-Hamra, this author estimates that, prior to 1970, a fertile woman could reasonably hope to raise three or four children to adulthood. Many only had one or two children survive; a few had eight or nine who survived. At least 40 percent of the children born to women in the interior of Oman died before reaching adulthood. See UNICEF, *Beliefs and Practices Related to Health, Nutrition and Child Rearing in Two Communities of Oman*, pt. 3 (Abu Dhabi: UNICEF, Gulf Area Office, 1973), p. 52. This child mortality rate is comparable to those found by anthropologists working in the Middle East in the 1930s and 1940s. See Hamad Ammar, *Growing Up in an Egyptian Village* (London: Routledge and Kegan Paul, 1954), p. 112, and Karen Seger, ed., *Portrait of a Palestinian Village: The Photographs of Hilma Granqvist* (London: Third World Center for Research and Publishing, 1981), p. 56.

Oman's population grew rapidly in the 1970s. A 1977–79 United Nations survey of 11 towns reported that women gave birth to an average of 5.5 children, although the survey indicated that the true figure was probably closer to 7 or 8 children. See United Nations Economic Commission for Western Asia, *The Population Situation in the ECWA Region: Oman* (Beirut, 1981), pp. 9–16. A high fertility rate was also reported in a 1977 survey of Oman's coastal Khabura region. See J.S. Birks and Clive Sinclair, *Aspects of the Demography of the Sultanate of Oman* (Durham, UK: University of Durham, International Migration Project, 1977), pp. 39–47. The World Population Data Sheet (1991) gives as 7.2 Oman's "total fertility rate," an estimate of the average number of children a woman will have throughout her childbearing years (assuming that age-specific birth rates remain constant).

10 In 1980, 22.8 percent of al-Hamra households contained more than one married couple. See D. Eickelman, "Counting and Surveying," p. 269.

11 Omani women occasionally said in 1979–1980 that four children were enough, although no one actually said how they controlled their fertility.

12 Demographers have considered the rewards of fertility mainly from the perspective of the child. See, for example, the introduction to Rodolfo A. Bulatao et al., eds., *Determinants of Fertility in Developing Countries*, vol. I (New York and London: Academic Press, 1983), pp. 1–26. Their framework for the study of fertility data includes the supply of children, the demand for children, and fertility regulation. For a summary of how demographers assess the costs and benefits of children, see John D. Kasarda, John O. G. Billy, and Kirsten Walsh, *Status Enhancement and Fertility Regulation Responses to Social Mobility and Education Opportunities* (Orlando, FL: Academic Press, 1986), pp. 134–44.

13 See, for example, Basim F. Musallam, *Sex and Society in Islam: Birth Control before the Nineteenth Century* (London and New York: Cambridge University Press, 1983), Avner Giladi, "Some Observations on Infanticide in Medieval Muslim Society,"

International Journal of Middle East Studies 22, no. 2 (May 1990); and Alan Duben and Cem Behar, *Istanbul Households: Marriage, Family and Fertility, 1880–1940* (Cambridge and New York: Cambridge University Press, 1990). Musallam provides evidence that birth control and contraceptives were known and used in Egypt and Syria in the middle and late Middle Ages. Giladi argues that infanticide, although rejected by Islamic law, was practiced in medieval Muslim society if other means, such as coitus interruptus and abortion, failed. Duben and Behar report a dramatic decline in childbearing years for women living in Istanbul in 1900. This decline was not simply a characteristic of the Westernized strata. Family size decreased as Istanbul society became child-oriented and people made connections between child-rearing, education, and social reform.

14 See Eberstadt's "Introduction," in *Fertility Decline*, p. 12. Anthropologists too have paid little attention to the high fertility rates now prevalent in the Middle East. See, for example, Soraya Altorki and Donald P. Cole, *Arabian Oasis City: The Transformation of Unayzah* (Austin: University of Texas Press, 1989). Indeed, given the importance of fertility in the lives of most Middle Eastern women, it is surprising how little anthropological work has been done on how women of the region perceive pregnancy, delivery, the postpartum period, and child-care and how these fertility-related activities and roles are rewarded within the family and the community. There is also a dearth of work on the importance for men of having children and the perception of male virility. These are usually taken for granted as part of regional understandings of "honor." Some accounts of child delivery in Middle Eastern countries include Soheir Morsy, "Childbirth in an Egyptian Village," in Margarita Artschwager Kay, ed., *Anthropology of Human Birth* (Philadelphia, PA: F.A. Davis, 1982), pp. 47–74, and Ammar, *Growing Up*, pp. 87–106. For Yemen, see Susan Dorsky, *Women of Amran: A Middle Eastern Ethnographic Study* (Salt Lake City: University of Utah Press, 1986), pp. 153–70. For Turkey. see Carol Delaney, *The Seed and The Soil: Gender and Cosmology in Turkish Village Society* (Berkeley and Los Angeles: University of California Press, 1991), pp. 25–72. For Oman, see UNICEF, *Beliefs and Practices*, pp. 53–67. For a discussion of the social impact of the postpartum confinement period among Muslim women of Mandarin China, see Barbara L.K. Pillsbury, "'Doing the Month': Confinement and Convalescence of Chinese Women after Childbirth," in Margarita Artschwager Kay, ed., *Anthropology of Human Birth* (Philadelphia, PA: F.A. Davis, 1982), pp. 119–46. Recently, anthropologists have collected stories to portray how Middle Eastern women construct their lives and the lives of those near them. Some of the stories provide a wealth of information on women' s attitudes toward fertility and birth. See Erika Friedl's *Women of Deh Koh: Lives in an Iranian Village* (Washington and London: Smithsonian Institution Press, 1989), pp. 12–25, 47–65, and Lila Abu-Lughod's *Writing Women's Worlds: Bedouin Stories* (Berkeley and Los Angeles: University of California Press, 1993), pp. 127–65.

15 Fertility even affects informal coffee-drinking among close neighbors, who avoid

gathering in the households of childless women. In 1979–1980, one neighbor in al-Hamra, a respected midwife who had never given birth, drank coffee daily in the households of immediate neighbors. Her own house, however, was never used as an informal gathering place.

16 For two examples of women who present themselves in this manner, see the photograph in C. Eickelman, *Women and Community,* p. 158, and the lead photograph of "Growing Up in the Gulf," *Middle East,* August 1985, p. 45.

17 See Christine Eickelman, "Women and Politics in an Arabian Oasis," in Farhad Kazemi and R. D. McChesney, eds., *A Way Prepared: Essays on Islamic Culture in Honor of Richard Bayly Winder* (New York and London: New York University Press, 1988), pp. 199–215.

18 The dramatic increase in *qat* parties in the Yemen Arab Republic during the 1970s is an example of the need to represent spatially, through the ritual of qat chewing, transformations in the social order. The chewing of qat, a mild, tobacco-like narcotic, was once reserved for special occasions, but is now practiced regularly. Migrant labor is transforming social categories, and Yemenis use the qat chewing network both to manipulate their status in their local communities and obtain information about others. See Shelagh Weir, *Qat in Yemen: Consumption and Social Change* (n.p.: British Museum Publications Limited, 1980), pp. 109–67.

19 In 1988, most women in al-Hamra gave birth in their own homes, going to hospitals only in case of anticipated difficulties. A 1973 UNICEF survey of Omani health practices found that many women in Nizwa, the largest oasis of the northern interior, preferred to give birth alone and then to call a relative or neighbor to cut the umbilical cord. Six percent of the women interviewed in Nizwa delivered one or more of their children by themselves, including cutting the cord. See UNICEF, *Beliefs and Practices,* p. 56.

20 In many parts of the Middle East, there is a confinement period after a woman gives birth. The length of the postpartum visiting period varies regionally from 2 weeks to 40 days.

21 A woman from the tribal elite once proffered simple guidelines for visiting obligations for a birth or a mourning: daily visits to households which are part of one's own family cluster, "occasional" visits to a neighbor's household, and once only to households of descendants of slaves. In practice, however, the decision as to how little or how much to visit is not so simple.

22 In Oman, governors are usually not from the provinces they administer.

23 For an excellent account of the complementarity of men's "official" visiting networks and the "informal" ones of women, see Nancy Tapper, "Gender and Religion in a Turkish Town: A Comparison of Two Types of Formal Women's Gathering," in P. Holden, ed., *Women's Religious Experience* (London: Croom Helm, 1983), pp. 71–88. For an analysis of visiting rituals and the ambiguous power relationships between guests and hosts, see Aida Sami Kanafani, *Aesthetics and Ritual in the United Arab Emirates: The Anthropology of Food and Personal Adornment among Arabian Women* (Beirut: American University of Beirut Press, 1983).

24 For a discussion of the transportation problems Saudi women face today, see Altorki and Cole, *Arabian Oasis City*, pp. 216–18.

25 See Robert J. Lapham, "Population Policies in the Middle East and North Africa," *Middle East Studies Association Bulletin* 11, no. 2 (May 1977), p. 13.

26 See Scilla McLean and Stella Efua Graham, eds., *Female Circumcision, Excision, and Infibulation: Facts and Proposals for Change*, Report no. 47, 2nd rev. ed. (London: Minority Rights Group, 1985).

27 See, for example, "India to Shake Up Birth-Control Bureaucracy," *New York Times*, March 14, 1990, p. A9.

28 See Aihwa Ong, "State versus Islam: Malay Families, Women's Bodies, and the Body Politic in Malaysia," *American Ethnologist* 17, no. 2 (May 1990), p. 266.

29 See "Egyptians Use Soap Operas to Preach Birth Control," *Valley News* (Upper Connecticut River Valley), May 23, 1991. p. 14.

30 See "Why Africans Want Fewer Babies," *The Economist*, January 9, 1993, p. 74.

7

Women's Autonomy and the Limits of Population Policy in Egypt

Barbara Ibrahim, Laila Nawar, and Cynthia B. Lloyd

Introduction

The international dialogue over what constitutes appropriate population policy hinges on concepts whose universal applicability across cultures and social settings has not been closely examined. Older policies calling for "fertility control" have been criticized for neglecting the welfare of the individual. More recent policy formulations emphasize the need for voluntary family planning services and respect for individual rights. But concepts referring to "choice," "rights," and "personal autonomy" may be especially problematic when they are employed according to purely Western understandings. It is important to analyze whether these terms have similar relevance for understanding the behavior of women and men in non-Western societies such as those of the Arab world.

This article attempts to refine an understanding of personal autonomy as it applies to the lives of women—particularly married women—in contemporary Egypt. In doing so we consider the cultural dimensions of gender relations as they were traditionally understood and as they are currently being modified by the social and economic realities of everyday life. The article draws on recent household survey data in order to compare what we can learn about Egyptian women's autonomy with some of the assumptions underlying population programs in Egypt.

Population policy in Egypt, in its pursuit of lower levels of population growth and fertility, has been primarily targeted at women as clients through the national family planning program. Women have been looked to as agents of change and leaders of the demographic transition. Radio and television spots urge women to make use of the clinics providing mostly female family planning methods. This is despite the fact that, within the traditional Egyptian family, men are expected to have most of the decision-making authority and women are

Barbara Ibrahim, a sociologist, is senior representative for West Asia and North Africa at the Population Council in Cairo. Laila Nawar is an advisor to the Population Council in Cairo. Cynthia Lloyd is senior associate and deputy director of the Population Council in New York.

assumed to have relatively little personal autonomy. To be effective, population policy must be based on a realistic view of family dynamics and women's role within it. Are Egyptian policy makers expecting too much of women and neglecting the role of men and of negotiation within marriage?

It is clear from a number of studies and observations that the Egyptian family is indeed changing in response to a variety of influences, both external and indigenous. At the same time that education, economic transformation, and modern communications bring new ideas into the smallest village, a trend toward religious conservatism sends contradictory messages rejecting change and calling for a return to more traditional social arrangements. In the midst of these counterpressures, women and men continue to pursue their daily lives, making whatever adaptations they see as desirable or necessary to meet their basic needs and fulfill their aspirations.

While facts about women's fertility and their practice of family planning abound, until very recently much less attention had been paid in demographic and economic surveys to the actual extent of women's personal autonomy. Fortunately, several recent surveys—the 1991 study on the role of Egyptian women in the family, or ROWIF (CAPMAS 1991),[1] and the Egyptian Demographic and Health Survey (DHS, 1988; 1992)—have devoted considerable attention to these issues, and these data provide the basis for an assessment of women's autonomy and gender roles within the family in contemporary Egypt.

We begin with some background on Egyptian women's marriage patterns and household living arrangements. This is followed by a discussion of the concept of autonomy and its various dimensions. Subsequent sections explore several aspects of women's autonomy, starting with early life influences on the development of autonomy and proceeding to more contemporary assessments of women's gender awareness and views on autonomy, their role in family decision-making and more overt manifestations of autonomous behavior (in particular, participation in the formal labor force). The final section looks at generational differences in autonomy and includes a discussion of possible implications for the fertility preferences and behavior of Egyptian women. Throughout the article, the focus is on currently married women, since we are interested in how autonomy is expressed within marriage and since Egyptian family planning programs are exclusively addressed to married individuals.

The Setting: Marriage Patterns and Household Living Arrangements

According to the 1992 Demographic and Health Survey, women can expect to spend 71 percent of their reproductive years (ages 15–49) married. During the peak childbearing years between ages 25 and 34, 90 percent of Egyptian women are currently married (El-Zanaty et al., 1993). Probably because of declines in mortality and delays in the initiation of marriage, there has been a small increase in the percentage of ever-married women who still remain in their first marriage at the end of their reproductive years (73 to 77 percent). The most notable change in marriage patterns is a decline in the proportion of women remarrying; of women aged 40–49 whose first marriage had ended due to divorce or widowhood, the proportion who remarry declined from 48 to 38 percent between 1980 and 1988.

Among all households that include married women, the nuclear family (consisting of any combination of husband, wife, and unmarried children) represents the dominant feature among Egyptian household types (84 percent). The enlarged nuclear family type and the extended family type comprise the remaining 16 percent of all households. The enlarged nuclear household (including either dependent parents, brother, or sister) is an adaptation of the nuclear type whereas the extended family household is more complex in structure, often encompassing several nuclear units. Only 4 percent of households that included married women are identified by DHS surveys as female headed, with the majority of nuclear-type households containing two generations and the majority of other household types containing three generations. Even in rural areas, over three quarters of households are nuclear. This reflects the increasing tendency across all of contemporary Egypt for couples to live apart from other family members. The dominance and increasing prevalence of the nuclear household type justifies our primary focus on the marriage relationship in studying various aspects of women's autonomy.

The Concept of Autonomy

The concept of personal autonomy is multifaceted, encompassing elements of individual temperament, past experience, and social conditioning. Autonomy is likewise displayed in a variety of contexts, ranging from decision-making within the family to personal independence of judgment and action. In recognition of this complexity, our study looks at a number of component elements of autonomy that appear to have relevance in the lives of Egyptian women. The following working definition of autonomy guided this study: personal autonomy is the ability to think and act independently of others to achieve one's goals or intentions.

Expressions of autonomy go beyond simple traits of personality or personal preference. Autonomy is conditioned by the fact that all human behavior is embedded in economic and institutional systems, social norms and personal interconnections. Therefore, the extent to which any individual achieves personal autonomy is highly relative to his or her social context. In all societies, gender is one of the important dimensions of social differentiation, but many other factors such as age, income, ethnicity, and religion can be factors as well. Indeed, we will see that the importance of gender as a determinant of levels of autonomy in Egypt is conditioned by the relative importance of these other factors.

When looking at autonomy in terms of gender, a further complication arises in that the very definitions of appropriate behavior for men and women proscribe or encourage autonomy (Unger and Crawford 1992). For example, psychological theories often highlight the centrality of interpersonal connections in women's lives, contrasting the concept of affiliation (female) with the concept of autonomy, which is characterized as male (Berlin and Johnson 1989). Furthermore, in nearly all cultures, women are socialized to publicly express lower levels of autonomy than men even when their actual behavior suggests otherwise.

To add a further level of complexity, cultures differ in the extent to which autonomy is valued and sought as a social "good." Contemporary western societies may equate autonomy with power, independence, and privacy, all of which are highly valued. Non-western societies, including Egypt, often place higher value on social interdependence and the support and status achieved from belonging to a group. Even in these settings, however, there is tacit recognition that the ability to carry out one's intentions is desirable, though it may be expressed in terms of "influence" as opposed to autonomy.

The Extent of Women's Autonomy

For all of the above considerations, it is important to give close attention to the particular social and cultural context in which women's personal autonomy is expressed. To do so in the Egyptian context, we have broken down the concept of autonomy into several component parts. These include factors relating to early life experiences that may shape an adult woman's sense of controlling outcomes; those having to do with independence of opinion and gender awareness; factors reflecting ability to act independently, and those relating to negotiated decision-making within the family. One aspect of the ability to act independently, namely whether or not a woman works outside the home, is given special consideration.

In interpreting our findings, note must be taken of the fact that the survey data consist of self-reports of women interviewed by strangers in a society not accustomed to voicing individual opinions. Other studies in Egypt suggest that survey respondents tend to report agreement with the expected cultural norms of their society, even when those norms are at odds with actual behavior. For example, women may tell an interviewer that it is a husband's right to stop his wife from working and later in the survey report that they actually work despite husbands' strong objections (Tessler et al. 1985). This awareness makes us cautious about drawing firm conclusions regarding behavior from opinion questions. At the same time it strengthens our conviction that when women do state views that deviate from the expected norm, these in fact represent important information about diversity among women and changing attitudes in present-day Egypt.

Early Familial Influences on Autonomy
One important dimension of autonomy is personal mastery or efficacy, the sense of being able to control the outcome of events in one's everyday life. Research findings suggest that mastery is acquired early in life as a result of childhood and teenage experience. Our data allow us to examine two areas of experience for young girls: leaving school, and the selection of a marriage partner.

A large proportion of Egyptian women are illiterate and never attended school. For those women who started school, however, but were obliged to drop out before college, the survey shows "family objections" are the most frequently mentioned reason for dropping out (30 percent). Another 20 percent left school in order to get married and 20 percent left because of the "difficulty" of school (CAPMAS 1991). If reasons for dropping out are compared by the age of the respondent, however, it is apparent that "family objections" are less important now than in the past. While 44 percent of women over age 40 left school due to family pressures, that proportion is only 16 percent for women less than 30. For this younger age group, marriage and the difficulty of school are more frequently mentioned as reasons that led them to end their formal education. To the extent that family objections appear to be declining from earlier high levels, one might conjecture that girls are gaining more say in the decision to continue or leave school. However, leaving school in order to marry is gaining in importance as girls remain in school longer.

Indeed, marriage is the first nearly universal life event for which we have information about women's autonomy, and this concerns the choice of spouse and whether or not the spouse is a relative. Traditionally in Egypt, contact between unmarried men and women is restricted, and family members initiate marriage arrangements on behalf of both partners. In practice, the girl's involvement in choosing her spouse can range from a forced match to one in which she selects a man unknown to other members of the family. These are extremes, however, and most Egyptian marriages involve some pre-selection of suitable partners by family members with the girl giving her consent in the final choice.

The survey data show that a majority of currently married Egyptian women were not primarily responsible for selecting the man they married (see Table 1). Regardless of education level, age at marriage or household type, most Egyptian women form marriages based on a choice made by relatives, rather than making an independent decision of their own. However, both the age at which a woman marries and her education level affect the likelihood that she will have

7. Ibrahim B. Tables

Table 1
Marriage arrangements of Egyptian women by selected characteristics

Variable	Marriage arranged by self (percentage)	Married to relative (percentage)	Sample size n[a]	%
Current age				
<30	32	31	459	29.1
30–39	26	27	498	31.5
40–49	18	28	325	20.6
50+	10	28	297	18.8
Age at marriage				
<16	11	35	335	21.1
16–19	18	33	591	37.3
20–24	31	25	460	29.0
25–29	40	15	162	10.2
30+	31	17	36	0.2
Education years				
None	16	33	1,005	63.6
<6[b]	22	26	137	8.7
6–9	28	27	155	9.8
10+	46	15	282	17.9
Total	23	29	1,579	100.0

Source: CAPMAS, 1991.
[a] The sample size for individual categories is sometimes less than the total because of missing values on a particular variable. In the case of household type, the sample size is the number of households rather than the number of women.
[b] Includes some women with informal education.

a stronger voice in the decision. For the 21 percent of women who married below the age of 16 (which in Egypt is the legal minimum age of marriage for girls), the likelihood is one in ten of choosing the husband. For women who married over the age of 25 on the other hand, the likelihood reaches 40 percent. The group of women most likely to have chosen their husbands are those with 10 or more years of schooling (46 percent). This is consistent with the fact that those women had more opportunity for contact with young men beyond the family network and had also achieved higher status from their advanced education.

Women's Views on Autonomy and Awareness of Gender Issues
Married women were asked whether or not it is important for a woman to seek her husband's approval on every matter or decision. Since this kind of question should be answered in the affirmative according to customary norms in Egypt, it provides a good indicator of movement away from those normative expectations. Overall, only 10 percent said that it was not always important to seek the

Table 2
Attitudes toward personal autonomy among married women
(percentage answering 'yes')

Variable	Woman should always seek husband's approval	I know about women's rights	Work is important for women's personal fulfillment[a]	Sample size n[b]	%
Current age					
<30	94	19	22	459	29.1
30–39	88	26	26	498	31.5
40–49	86	21	27	325	20.6
50+	91	18	21	297	18.8
Household type					
Nuclear	89	24	26	1,078	72.7
Enlarged nuclear	93	27	27	120	8.1
Extended	95	8	15	284	19.2
Education (years)					
None	94	8	16	1,005	63.6
<6[c]	90	23	29	137	8.7
6–9	83	41	38	155	9.8
10+	81	59	45	282	17.9
Total	90	21	24	1,579	100.0

Source: CAPMAS, 1991.
[a] Percentage of women who gave at least one out of the following answers: to acquire social status, to acquire self-confidence, to gain economic independence.
[b] See note a in Table 1.
[c] Includes some women with informal education.

husband's approval (see Table 2). The percentage rises with greater education, employment, and standard of living, but in all cases, the overwhelming majority of women felt the need to seek their husbands' approval.

For women who said approval is not always necessary, a further question was asked about what areas they could act in without seeking the husband's approval. Again, only a small percentage of women felt that they could act without approval. In some issues like visiting family or friends, urban residence had a strong positive influence on women's sense of independence and tended to neutralize the effects of education levels; that is, urban women are relatively more autonomous when it comes to visiting, even if they are not well educated. In fact, illiterate urban women are more likely than highly educated women overall to say they can go visiting without seeking their husbands' approval (48 percent compared to 41 percent). By contrast, the proportion of rural women in all education categories who say they can visit without approval is negligible.

Even though a small percentage of Egyptian women actually participate in the labor force, all women express opinions about the reasons women should work. The majority believe that the legitimate reasons for working are connected to economic necessity and helping the family financially. And, in fact, a majority of women who are working for an income state that they do so out of economic necessity. Given this overall context, it is interesting to look at the proportion of women who believe that work is primarily an avenue to greater personal independence.

In the survey, women were asked to choose one or two reasons for the importance or value of work for women. Twenty-four percent mentioned answers that can be categorized as reflecting a degree of autonomy: "to acquire social status," "to acquire self-confidence," or "to gain economic independence." (The more typical answers included "financial need," "family's wish," "husband's wish" or "to raise the economic standard of the family.") Education was strongly associated with attitudes about the importance of work: only 16 percent of illiterate women mentioned reasons for work linked to autonomy, while 45 percent of those with secondary level education and above did so. As was the case for other aspects of autonomy, education is strongly associated with the expression of more personal rather than family-oriented interests.

Married women were asked whether or not they "were aware of women's rights within personal status and political laws." Only 21 percent answered "yes." As would be expected, knowledge of women's rights was strongly associated with higher education levels and with increased socioeconomic status. This is one of the few dimensions of potential autonomy (at least of attitude or awareness) in which there is considerable variation among women in the sample.

Autonomous Behavior

The preceding discussion focused on aspects of women's knowledge and opinions. We now turn to some areas in which personal autonomy may be expressed through actual behavior. These include data on whether and to what degree married women were able to act independently in matters of leisure, civic participation, and health-seeking behavior.

We expected to find variation, for example, in the types of women who participate in cultural, social or political associations in Egypt. There is a long tradition of volunteerism in the country and over 10,000 local and national associations. Even rural women in theory have access to membership in their local community development association. In fact, among this sample of women, participation in any type of association is extremely rare (less than 1 percent among women with less than 9 years of education). Even among women with high school education or beyond, the percent participating was only 18 percent. Of all women reporting membership, 92 percentage are urban residents. It appears that the efforts to involve rural women in community associations have had limited success, at least in the case of married women. One must be cautious in concluding that this pattern reflects low personal autonomy, however, since an alternative interpretation is that women find outlets for community involvement through more informal social networks, as has been noted in some ethnographic studies in Egypt (Rugh, 1979). If membership is similarly low for men, it may be that civic participation is a dimension of autonomy with greater relevance in western contexts.

The survey also contained questions relating to women's self-care and ability to go out of the house for leisure activities. Less than half of the women reported positive answers. In all cases, illiterate women were least likely to report that they took specific measures to care for themselves. This probably reflects two factors: less knowledge about proper care (exercise and diet, for example) and less access to resources to spend on their own care. This presumption is borne out by the data on medical checkups. Illiterate women are half as likely as those with some education below secondary level to have regular medical checkups, even though they are as likely to state that caring for their own health is as important as caring for that of other family members.

Work and Autonomy
It can be reasonably assumed that, if women are working in the labor force, they have indeed achieved a fair measure of personal autonomy within the Egyptian context. Even when the work itself requires little skill and is poorly paid, it allows women to leave the confines of the household and acquire some resources that they potentially control. Ethnographic research on Cairo communities suggests that when women work for wages their status is elevated within the family, resulting in privileged treatment and a greater say in financial matters (Hoodfar, 1988; Ibrahim, 1982). Thus, an analysis of women's labor force participation or work for cash may provide important information regarding patterns of personal autonomy.

Regardless of the definition of work used, however, we found that relatively few married women report themselves as currently working. Even the broadest measures of women's participation in the labor force, which include questions about informal income-generating activity (in the 1991 ROWIF survey), or assistance with work to family members or non-members (DHS, 1992), show no more than 19 to 20 percent of currently married women of reproductive age working. During the peak childbearing years under 30, only 12 percent of currently married women are working, again using the broadest definitions. That percentage more than doubles to 26 percent for the age group in their 30s, which is the period of the life cycle when women experience their peak childrearing responsibilities.

The type of work captured by these surveys is mostly formal labor force participation, which usually involves an employer/employee relationship and takes women outside their homes. Over 50 percent of working women in the ROWIF sample, even in rural areas, are government employees. A majority of workers are in white collar clerical jobs in both rural and urban areas. Among the very few women in the labor force in rural areas, less than 20 percent work in farming. A demanding six-day work week is typical, with rural working women often reporting working seven days a week. This situation suggests that the meaning of work for many women and the implications of having a personal income may be closer to drudgery than independence or autonomy.

The preceding discussion of various dimensions of personal autonomy suggests two overall conclusions. One is that the range of autonomous opinion and behavior among Egyptian women is fairly narrow. A majority of women in all categories express low autonomy in absolute terms, and also in relation to what could be expected from women from many other parts of the world. At the same time, within the low overall levels of autonomy we have uncovered significant variation in independent thinking and behavior among women. The higher levels of personal autonomy sometimes expressed by younger women, and by those with more education and exposure to the labor force, clearly suggest the direction of probable future trends in Egypt. The next section shifts attention to aspects of autonomy that are expressed in interactions within the family.

Women's Influence in Family Decision-Making
Within contemporary Egyptian families, as has traditionally been the case, the majority of married women report that their husbands decide important family matters. However, joint decisions of husbands and wives are more likely to occur when wives are working or highly educated, reside in urban areas, and live in nuclear families (see Table 3). The possibility of making joint decisions is suggestive of the ability to influence desired outcomes through negotiation— by our definitions an important dimension of autonomy.

In cases where differences of opinion arise between husband and wife, the majority say they finally agree or choose to accept the husband's opinion. However, working women, more educated women, and, to a lesser extent, women in nuclear households are much less willing to accept their husband's opinion in the case of disagreements and are more likely to try to convince husbands of their opinion or attempt to reconcile the two views (see Table 4). On the other hand, it is rare for wives to insist on their own opinion, at least in their reports to survey interviewers.

Are there some areas where women believe they should have the greater say? With specific reference to decisions about family size a majority of married women (62 percent) say that in their marriage it is a joint decision.

In fact, the greatest expressions of personal influence, particularly among nonworking women, illiterate women, and rural women, come in relationship to those aspects of family life most related to children and marriage (see Table 4). Women are clearly articulating more assertiveness in those areas traditionally defined as appropriate spheres of concern for women. For example, roughly two-thirds of nonworking women do not think that the husband should have the

Table 3
Gender roles in decision-making (percentage)

Variable	Who makes decisions in important family matters[a]			Who has the say in determining family size		
	Wife	Husband	Both	Wife	Husband	Both
Current age						
< 30	2	72	25[b]	9	21	67
30–39	4	61	34	14	20	62
40–49	7	64	29	18	16	60
50+	10	60	30	18	19	58
Residence						
Urban	7	52	40	18	16	63
Rural	1	86	12	8	25	61
Household type						
Nuclear	6	60	33	15	19	63
Enlarged nuclear	4	71	25	18	23	55
Extended	3	77	19	9	21	64
Education (years)						
None	6	72	21	13	22	59
<6[c]	5	57	37	21	16	60
6–9	8	52	40	20	15	63
10+	2	47	51	12	12	75
Work status						
Working	5	51	43	15	15	67
Not working	5	67	27	14	20	61
Total	5	65	30	14	19	62

Source: CAPMAS, 1991.
[a] For example, travel, buying, and selling.
[b] Percentages may not add up to 100 because other possible answers with very low response rates were disregarded.
[c] Includes some women with informal education.

last word on having another child, or on children's education and marriage plans. Three-quarters feel this way about decisions involving the use of family planning. This does not mean that women believe they should have full independence in these areas, just that their husband's views should not hold ultimate sway. Women concede greater control to their husbands in areas such as the household budget and with respect to lending and borrowing.

Women's Autonomy and Family Outcomes

We have previously defined autonomy as the ability to think and act independently of others to achieve one's intentions. Having assessed the autonomy of married women in Egypt both in terms of its scope and its variation among women, we now pose the question of whether and how this ability or lack thereof affects outcomes within the home, including fertility decision-making.

Childbearing and Domestic Tasks
Roughly half of all married women report that both parents are responsible for raising the children and 40 percent say it is primarily the mother's responsibility. There is very little difference in these responses across groups. When it comes to helping with children's studies, however, 67 percent of married women rely on teachers or others to help, reflecting the high proportion of illiterate women in our sample. The percentage of women, sometimes alone and sometimes with the help of the husband, who help children with studies increases dramatically with education. Not surprisingly, while 82 percent of illiterate women rely on others to help their children study, only 21 percent of women with a high school education do so. Forty-five percent of working women are involved in helping their child study while only 15 percent of nonworking women are involved. Despite their longer work hours, working women are much less likely to delegate this responsibility to others.

When gender roles are strictly segregated, as in Egypt, it is interesting to examine how male roles adapt to changing role configurations for women. Some earlier research in working class areas of Cairo suggested that men are resistant to taking over domestic responsibilities when their wives work, although younger men are more willing than those in older age groups (Ibrahim, 1980). The ROWIF survey data indicate that women with greater autonomy are more able to get their husbands to help with the housework. However, even among the most educated women, 59 percent of husbands do not help at all as compared with 87 percent for the least educated women. While 14 percent of husbands help sometimes, a larger percent of husbands help at least sometimes when women work (33 percent), when they live in nuclear households (23 percent), or when they have better living conditions (roughly 25 percent). When husbands help it is most likely to be for shopping, but this is in fact a traditional male responsibility since it involves contact outside the home. Help is rarely provided in cleaning, cooking, and washing, although here husbands of working wives do sometimes help out.

Reproductive Intentions and Fertility Decision-Making
Because of the division of household tasks, married women clearly bear a particularly heavy burden during their childbearing and rearing years. The implications of this for differences between husbands and wives in fertility preferences are apparent. While the data do not actually provide information on husband's fertility preferences directly, it is possible to compare the expressed fertility preferences and achieved fertility of married women according to how they handle disagreements with their husbands. When women report their hus-

Table 4
Gender roles and family decision-making (percentage answering 'yes')

Variable	In disagreements, wife should speak up	Wife respects husband more if he listens and accepts her opinion	Wife's view should carry same weight as husband's	Visits to relatives	Household budget	Lending and borrowing	Having another child	Children's education	Children's marriage plans	Use of family planning	Sample size[a]
				Husbands should not have last word on							
Residence											
Urban	61	65	50	47	57	52	78	80	76	87	3,998
Rural	32	39	32	25	28	29	57	52	49	63	4,215
Education level											
None	31	38	30	25	31	30	58	54	51	65	4,100
Primary	50	55	43	36	44	42	70	70	65	79	2,614
Secondary	79	78	65	58	65	57	86	91	88	93	1,069
Higher	86	86	76	76	83	73	95	97	95	97	424
Standard of Living Index[b]											
Low	28	35	30	22	26	28	54	48	45	59	3,294
Medium	50	55	41	36	45	43	71	71	68	81	2,907
High	73	74	61	59	67	58	85	88	86	93	1,725
Income-earning status											
Earning income	70	72	62	60	72	61	83	87	84	89	984
No earnings	44	50	39	33	39	38	66	64	61	74	6,566
Total	46	51	41	36	42	40	68	66	62	75	8,214

Source: DHS, 1988.

a Total sample sizes vary because of varying non-response rates under different categories.

b Standard of Living Index: quality of flooring (wood, tiles, marble, waxed plastic=1), kitchen inside house (yes=1), toilet facilities (modern=2, traditional with or without tank=1, other=0), drinking-water tap inside home (yes=1), hot-water heater (yes=1), car or video player (yes=2), color television (yes=1).

Table 5
Family decision-making on reproductive intentions and behavior

	What do you do if you and your husband disagree?		
	Insist on or try to convince him of my views	Reconcile the two views or try to involve some relatives	Comply with husband's views
Mean desired number of children for ages			
<30	2.3	2.2	2.4
30–39	2.3	2.5	2.5
40–49	2.2	2.2	2.4
50+	1.9	2.5	2.5
Completed fertility			
45–54	3.1	4.8	6.7
55+	3.9	6.4	7.5

Source: CAPMAS, 1991.

bands as the dominant decision makers, expressed fertility preferences are somewhat higher at all ages, but the differences are small for younger women currently in their reproductive years.

On the other hand, actual achieved fertility levels are dramatically lower among women who insist on their own views (see Table 5). The fertility of women aged 45–54 who reported complying with husband's views was 3.6 children higher than those who insisted on their own view or tried to convince their husband of their views. The fertility levels of women who work toward reconciliation were roughly halfway between the other two groups. Autonomy appears clearly linked to women's ability to achieve their fertility goals.

Implications of Women's Autonomy for Future Fertility Behavior
Despite relatively low levels of autonomy overall, Egyptian women have shown a growing interest in controlling their fertility, as reflected in the 1992 data from the DHS showing 47 percent of currently married women using contraception (El-Zanaty et al., 1993). As has been indicated in the previous discussion, this is the area of family decision-making where women are most likely to play a role. Fertility preferences are low, even among the least autonomous women and, when other relevant factors are adjusted for, there is no systematic variation by autonomy level. However, among the youngest women, greater autonomy appears to be more likely than in the past to be expressed in terms of lower fertility. Thus, further improvements in women's education and economic conditions, as well as increased urbanization and women's labor force participation—factors that support a more independent role for women—are likely to contribute to some further declines in fertility preferences.

Despite relatively low expressed family size desires, achieved fertility is

Table 6
Aspirations for daughters (percentage of currently married women, age 15–49)

	Approve of daughters working	Suitable age of marriage >20	Daughter should have no more than two children
Current age			
<30	82	22	53
30–39	81	29	57
40–49	76	27	52
Residence			
Urban	86	42	66
Rural	76	10	43
Education level			
None	74	11	44
Primary	86	27	60
Secondary	88	57	71
Higher	90	80	72
Work status			
Working for cash	89	58	71
Not working[a]	79	22	52
Total	80	25	54

Source: DHS, 1988.
[a]Excluding women assisting in family work.

high among women past the end of their childbearing years (see Table 5). While the gap between actual fertility and fertility preferences remains wide among all groups, more autonomous women who have completed their fertility appear to bear fewer children on average than women scoring lower on autonomy, even after other relevant factors have been controlled for statistically. Thus, we can posit that the future importance of growing autonomy for women, particularly in fertility decision-making, is likely to be expressed in terms of a reduction in the level of unwanted fertility, as actual fertility falls closer to desired levels.

The Next Generation

With regard to longer-term implications, however, even currently married women with few of the characteristics associated with autonomy have aspirations for their daughters which imply dramatic changes in women's roles as they relate to work and fertility (see Table 6). Survey questions asked about married women's aspirations for their daughters, specifically whether they would approve of their daughter working, and at what age their daughters should marry and how many children they should have. Eighty percent of women approve of the idea of their daughter working, and the percentages remain high even among the least autonomous women, as measured by work status or education. For example, 79 percent of nonworking women approve of the idea of their daughter working. Fifty-four percent of all currently married women think that their daughters should have not more than two children, and the percentage remains surprisingly high even among the most traditional groups. For example, 44 percent of women with no education express a preference of no more than two children for their daughters.

On the other hand, the large majority (75 percent) of women expect their daughters to marry by the age of 20. The preferences for daughters' marriage over the age of 20 show the largest variation by education, with only 11 percent of illiterate women thinking their daughter should marry over the age of 20 as compared to 80 percent of the most highly educated group. As marriage age has an important link with educational attainment and the selection of a spouse, it would appear likely that women who prefer their daughters to marry young may be less likely to realize their other aspirations for their daughters, in terms of both fertility and work, because these daughters will not be in a position to think and act independently.

Conclusion

Overall, Egyptian women are remarkably consistent in expressing dependence on their spouses with respect to family decision-making and extraordinarily committed to their families in terms of the amount of domestic responsibility they assume. Their overall levels of autonomy as measured in the survey are quite low. However, within that characterization lies a much more complex reality in which women within families do have a strong voice in particular decisions of most relevance to them, such as family planning and childrearing.

Furthermore, they are able to gain stronger influence within the family and greater personal independence with more education, when they make a greater economic contribution to the family and when they live in a more urban or modern environment. The waning of extended family living arrangements is also supportive of those trends. Indeed, it appears that Egyptian women's scope for increased autonomy of thought and action is potentially quite broad. However, the realization of the potential for change depends heavily on parents and other relatives, who continue to make early critical decisions on their daughters' behalf in terms of schooling and choice of mate. The data on parental aspirations for daughters are encouraging, but these aspirations have a greater chance of being turned into reality when daughters' marriages are delayed—a much more likely event if the daughter has an educated mother.

Levels of autonomy among married women are positively associated with age, education, urban residence, and more affluent living conditions. However, even among the least advantaged groups, many women express an assertive role in family decision-making within traditional domains. On the other hand, and even among the most advantaged groups, most women continue to seek their husbands' approval and show limited knowledge of gender issues or involvement in activities outside the family. Over time, women's scope for autonomy within marriage can be expected to grow as the economy continues to modernize and levels of education for women improve. Women's autonomy is linked to slightly lower family size preferences but, more significantly, to an increased ability to achieve their family size goals. Indeed, these changes, among others, have most certainly played a role in the rapid increase in contraceptive prevalence in Egypt in recent years.

To return to the question posed at the outset: should policy planners assume that women have autonomy in matters of fertility and family planning? The answer is a qualified no; therefore more attention should be given to patterns of negotiation between husbands and wives, and male preferences need to be more fully studied and addressed. Other implications of our findings for the population policy field are clear: women's autonomy is associated with success in achieving desired reductions in family size, but autonomy remains low, hampered by women's poor educational achievement and restricted access to paid work. Investments in female education, employment, and programs to reduce underage marriage need to be given higher priority, alongside the current emphasis on providing family planning services.

Notes

This article is a condensed and revised version of the monograph "Women's Autonomy and Gender Roles in the Egyptian Family" which appeared in Carla Makhlouf Obermeyer (ed.), *Family, Gender and Population in the Middle East: Policies in Context* (Cairo: The American University in Cairo Press, 1995).

1   The Egyptian Central Agency for Public Mobilization and Statistics (CAPMAS) conducted a survey in three governorates in 1991 titled "The Characteristics of the Households and the Role of Egyptian Women in the Family." A total of 1,992 ever married women were selected, representing large urban, middle urban, and rural communities. This article is based on the information provided by the 1,592 currently married women in the sample

References

Berlin, Sharon and Craig G. Johnson. 1989. "Women and Autonomy: Using Structural Analysis of Social Behavior to Find Autonomy within Connections," *Psychiatry* 52: 79–95.

CAPMAS. 1983. *Labor Force Sample Survey Report.* Cairo: Central Agency for Public Mobilization and Statistics.

———. 1991. *The Characteristics of the Household and the Role of Egyptian Women in the Family.* Cairo: Central Agency for Public Mobilization and Statistics.

Doan Miles, Rebecca and Leila Bisharat. 1990. "Female Autonomy and Child Nutritional Status: The Extended Family Residential Unit Amman, Jordan," *Social Science and Medicine* (31) 7: 783–89.

Dyson, Tim and Mick Moore. 1983. "Kinship Structure, Female Autonomy, and Demographic Behavior in India," *Population and Development Review* 9 (1): 35–60.

DHS. 1988. *Egypt Demographic and Health Survey 1988.* Cairo: National Population Council.

———. 1992. *Egypt Demographic and Health Survey 1992.* Cairo: National Population Council.

FAO. 1993. *Gender Disaggregated Data and Statistics on Human Resources in the Middle East.* Unpublished paper. Food and Agriculture Organization of the United Nations.

Hoodfar, Homa. 1988. "Household Budgeting and Financial Management in a Lower-Income Cairo Neighborhood," in Daisy Dwyer and Judith Bruce (eds.), *A Home Divided: Women and Income in the Third World.* Stanford: Stanford University Press.

Ibrahim, Barbara. 1980. "Social Change and the Industrial Experience: Women as Production Workers in Urban Egypt," Ph.D. dissertation, Indiana University.

———. 1982. "Family Strategies: A Perspective on Women's Entry to the Labor Force in Egypt," *International Journal of Sociology of the Family,* December.

Mason, Karen Oppenheim. 1984. *The Status of Women: A Review of its Relationships to Fertility and Mortality.* The Rockefeller Foundation, New York.

Naguib, Nora Guhl and Cynthia B. Lloyd. 1994. "Gender Inequalities and Demographic Behavior: The Case of Egypt," presented at the Population Council meeting on Family, Gender, and Population Policy: International Debates and Middle Eastern Realities, Cairo, February 1994.

Oppong, Christine. 1993. "Women's Roles, Opportunity Costs, and Fertility," in *Determinants of Fertility in Developing Countries.* Edited by R.A. Bulatao and R.D. Lee et al. New York: Academic Press.

Rugh, Andrea. 1979. "Coping with Poverty in a Cairo Community," *Cairo Papers in Social Science,* vol. 2, monograph 1. Cairo: The American University in Cairo Press.

Singerman, Diane and Homa Hoodfar. Forthcoming. "Development, Social Change and Gender in Cairo: A View from the Household," Indiana University Press.

Tessler, Mark, Monte Palmer, Tawfik Farah, and Barbara Ibrahim. 1985. *The Evaluation and Application of Survey Research in the Arab World.* Boulder and London: Westview Press.

United Nations. 1987. *Fertility Behavior in the Context of Development,* New York.

Unger, Rhoda and Mary Crawford. 1992. *Women and Gender: A Feminist Psychology.* New York: McGraw-Hill, Inc.

Youssef, Nadia H. 1982. "The Interrelationship between the Division of Labor in the Household, Women's Roles and their Impact on Fertility," in *Women's Roles and Population Trends in the Third World.* Edited by R. Anker, M. Buvinic and N. H. Youssef. London: Croom Helm.

8

Manshiet Nasser: A Cairo Neighborhood

Belgin Tekçe, Linda Oldham, and Frederic C. Shorter

Setting

Manshiet Nasser is situated on the rocky slopes of the Muqattam range of hills which forms an eastern physical boundary to the city of Cairo. Behind and beyond the hills lies the Eastern Desert. The settlement occupies land that has been quarried for limestone for centuries, and some parts of the quarry continue to be actively mined today. It faces the northern section of the vast Mamluk burial quarters, and beyond them it looks at the oldest and one of the most densely populated quarters of the city, the Gamaliya, including the historic bazaar and the al-Azhar quarters. Manshiet Nasser is separated from the medieval core of the city, only two kilometers away, by the cemetery areas. A newly built highway delineates where Manshiet Nasser ends and the cemeteries begin. There is also a single track rail line along this boundary of the settlement. Topography dictates the roughly rectangular shape of the settlement; the community is wedged between the cemetery on one side and the rugged cliffs rising above the settlement on the other. The total area of occupation is approximately 1.5 square kilometers.

A large community of garbage collectors, the Zabbaleen, occupies the top of the Muqattam hills, overlooking Manshiet Nasser. Members of this community collect household garbage in Cairo, transport it up the hill, sort, recycle, and sell its useful components. Many of the Zabbaleen travel down through Manshiet Nasser with their donkey carts early in the morning on their way to collect garbage, and return with loaded carts in the afternoon. They use land for animals, sorting yards, and storage, with a lower human settlement density than in Manshiet Nasser. The Zabbaleen are mostly Christians, while the neighboring residents of Manshiet Nasser below are predominantly Muslim. The pace of expansion is so rapid that the Zabbaleen community, which could be seen only

From *A Place to Live: Families and Child Health in a Cairo Neighborhood* (Cairo: The American University in Cairo Press, 1994), pp. 20–43, 53–61. Reprinted by permission. Belgin Tekçe is Professor of Sociology at Bogaziçi University in Istanbul, Turkey; Linda Oldham is an anthropologist and consultant, formerly resident in Cairo; and Frederic C. Shorter is an economic demographer currently working in Turkey. He formerly headed the Population Council office in Cairo.

at a distance in 1980, has now merged with Manshiet Nasser. At the boundaries, there is now a spillover of house renting, cross-overs for utilization of social services, and commercial intercourse—all on a limited scale but indicative of social blending as well.

The garbage collectors serving Manshiet Nasser know its layout well. Their route map for the settlement, drawn in the early 1980s when they were preparing to offer collection services, is shown in Figure 1. Today, their donkey carts, and sometimes narrow vehicles, pass along the lanes shown in the map. The twenty-one routes, distinguished by different shadings of the lanes that lead upward to the interior, approximately define the areal extent of the settlement. When the present research was initiated, the expertise of these people helped us to map and divide the settlement into nine zones where the buildings and dwelling units were listed.

On the northeastern heights, Manshiet Nasser abuts another smaller settlement, Duweiqa, with no more delineation of the boundary than an internal roadway. Duweiqa is built on public land surrounding a large municipal dump. A heavy haze of smoke hangs over the Duweiqa settlement most of the time. This settlement contains multi-story government housing designed for evacuees from collapsed buildings in central Cairo, along with some privately constructed homes similar to those of Manshiet Nasser. There are also some flimsy structures, including tents, erected by families of nomadic origin.

While the hillside where Manshiet Nasser is located is public land and the inhabitants are legally squatters, the precariousness which this implies is not reflected in the physical structures of the settlement today. Most of the buildings are multi-storied, particularly at the older and lower elevations of the settlement, and are largely made of brick and reinforced concrete. There is nothing furtive or transient about the physical appearance of the individual houses which identifies them as illegal or temporary; it is only the relationship among buildings in terms of absence of air shafts and setbacks, and lengthy blocks without side streets, that suggests that this is not an officially planned community. Clearly the residents do not perceive eviction as an imminent danger.

The main entry to Manshiet Nasser is an unpaved road from the main highway about halfway along the length of the settlement. It crosses the rail track and becomes a road passing alongside the track inside the settlement. The first dwellings of the settlement were built near this entrance. There are other less important entries, each one sloping up from the highway and crossing over the railway to the dirt road that parallels the rail line on the Manshiet Nasser side of the tracks. We call this the 'spine road' of the settlement. A second road parallels the spine road inside Manshiet Nasser. This one is densely built up on both sides and has many commercial establishments. Lateral roads and lanes lead irregularly from the main interior road up into the slopes.

Manshiet Nasser has become a large, bustling community of houses, shops,

Figure 1. Garbage route map for Manshiet Nasser

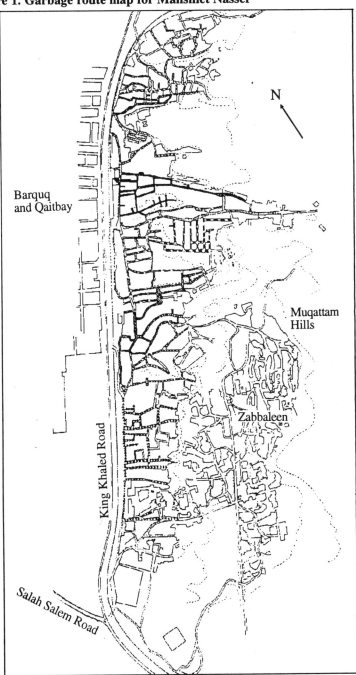

and workshops, all co-existing without any pre-planned land-use configuration. In 1984, it accommodated over 64,000 residents and more than two thousand commercial and industrial establishments ranging from tiny grocery shops to aluminum foundries. It had a residential density of more than forty thousand persons per square kilometer, and was continuing to grow in density. About one-third of the population lives within two hundred meters of the spine road, where density is highest.

Neither Manshiet Nasser, nor any of the neighboring communities on the hilltops to the east or the flatlands and slopes to the north, existed prior to 1960. The settlement was founded in the early 1960s when a number of low income families living elsewhere in Cairo were evicted by urban building projects and needed a place to go. Prior to their move, the northern slopes of Muqattam were inhabited chiefly by fugitives from the law and by quarry guards. The area was barren rock graced by neither a water supply nor vegetation. The history of the Manshia, as residents refer to their community, is thus the history of a group, mostly quite poor, who managed to carve their living space out of an inhospitable environment. How they managed to establish a viable community on their own and made it grow is in itself a story worth knowing.

History of the Settlement

Origins

The nucleus of the Manshia community was formed by a group of families that was evicted from a self-help settlement located not far from the present site in a subdistrict of the Gamaliya. This community had grown near the historic bazaar area around the time of the Second World War. It was settled initially by migrants from Upper Egypt, predominantly from Qena and Sohag Governorates. A number of the migrants specialized in recycling low grade steel that they recovered from used oil drums. Over the years, people in this community developed a brisk trade in recovered steel. Others established warehouses on the site, and began to sell used building materials such as wood and bricks. The community of houses and warehouses that they constructed, mostly out of recovered steel sheeting, was called the 'sheet metal hamlet' ('Ezbat al-Safih). It was known throughout the city as a center for recycling and cheap supplies for the building trades. Construction workers, both skilled and unskilled, living in Upper Egypt or elsewhere in Cairo, came to join them, seeking a place to live, to work, and to hire themselves out for jobs in the city.

The growth of the 'Ezba was one reflection of the profound changes that were occurring in the life of Cairo around the war years. The population of the city had increased strikingly during and immediately following the Second World War, as it did in cities all over the Arab world (Abu-Lughod, 1971:171–80; Issawi, 1982:102). Quartering of troops and shipping blockades raised demand sharply for locally produced goods. One elderly resident of

Manshiet Nasser tells of working for the British army while he was living in the cemetery grounds, coincident with the founding of the 'Ezbat al-Safih settlement. Recycling of every useful material flourished, and the 'Ezba was built on this new industry.

Municipal authorities had warned the 'Ezba that construction of permanent shelters would not be tolerated at this location. An oft-recounted bit of the oral history of the settlement is the story of residents who hid permanent construction inside the temporary steel sheet walls to fool the authorities. By and large, however, the community was left undisturbed for many years. In about 1960, the Governorate of Cairo announced that it needed the land occupied by the 'Ezba to build a school and a hospital. Community leaders, including the one who functions as an *'umda* (local mayor or headman)[1] for the settlement, demanded that alternative living space be provided before eviction occurred. There ensued long negotiations which appear to have taken place over many months. The government was represented in these discussions by deputies of the National Assembly from the district in which 'Ezbat al-Safih was located. The authorities finally agreed that as 'compensation' they would arrange for tacit permission to be granted to the community to resettle on public land on the Muqattam hills. The elderly residents say the settlement was named Manshiet Nasser in honor of Egypt's president to help ensure continuing land tenure.

The designated place was in close proximity to the older parts of Cairo, but the land was then of little value. It was a rugged, inhospitable site with sharply diverging elevations, lacking all infrastructure, but the people agreed. The leaders were able to organize the move so that it could be carried out in a staggered way. Water was obtained from taps in mosques across the road in the cemetery of Qaitbay. Lighting was by kerosene lamps. The government provided three water taps along the main street of the community within a few months of the initial move.

Land Development

The original settlers were concerned about security primarily because they did not have title to the land. They were also worried about the reputation of Muqattam as a refuge of criminals. They huddled together at the lower reaches of the hillside, building their houses on plots of land which were usually about 100 square meters, and their warehouses on larger plots. Some of the early settlers, however, staked claims to larger plots located farther up the hill, behind the initial cordon of houses, which were sold to newcomers later on.[2]

The leaders of 'Ezbat al-Safih, by then firmly established as the leaders of the new community, organized the division of land along the spine road near the main entrance. The divisions were made in a way which grouped people from the same areas of origin together. This arrangement was strengthened by families helping relatives and co-villagers to find space and settle near themselves.

Settlers recount a pattern of relatively rapid growth in the early years. Apparently every attempt was made to entice co-villagers and Cairenes of common origin from Upper Egypt to move to the settlement in the interests of mutual support and security. Once the front line of the settlement had been established, and perhaps even as it was being formed, a new pattern of land subdivision began to develop on the middle reaches of the steep hillsides. Families who came after the initial settlers would claim about two to three hundred square meters of land, build a home on approximately one hundred square meters and subsequently sell the rest to newcomers, usually relatives or people from their home villages. While the size of the plots may have been justified initially by hopes to build on all of the space, it turned out instead to be an effective mechanism for selecting one's neighbors. Plots were sold relatively inexpensively or sometimes simply given to relatives and co-villagers who could be depended upon for support in times of trouble and for cooperation in general.

Land continued to be freely available on the heights of the hillsides, beyond the settled area, for many years. At the lower levels, however, an informal but well-regulated system of validating claims on plots in the settled area came into existence. Persons would stake a new claim or purchase one from an earlier claimant. The land would not be considered definitively theirs unless they built on it within a reasonable period of time. In the interim between claiming and building, tenure was in question to a varying extent depending on the relationship of the claimant to the community as a whole, and to any other claimant in particular, and the location of the land itself.

The strongest claim to a plot was that of somebody already resident in the community who had no land or building. Such a claim was almost incontestable, and if contested the community would support the resident's claim against all others. The oral record of land transactions tells of a number of cases of persons who had claimed more than one piece of land, but were forced by social pressure to give up the second claim to persons who had no plot based on a sense of equity. It also tells of a case in the 1980s when the response to claim-jumping was murder.

The strength of a claim to land was somewhat weaker if a homeowner in the Manshia took the plot in order to build for children. Such a claim could be overridden by a family in greater immediate need, especially if the project was construction on behalf of a daughter; she is expected to take a husband who will provide housing for the couple after marriage. If a claimant was from outside the community and did not plan to take up residence soon after making a claim, that person would have difficulty sustaining the claim. The best course would be to erect a flimsy room on the plot and live there until permanent construction was started. Without the physical presence of the owner or, as a weaker choice, the immediate proximity of a close relative to act as a representative, the chances of being able to build would be low.

While the initial occupation of the settlement went forward without anyone needing to pay for land, free land is no longer available. A market in land and buildings has emerged, because the supply is now limited relative to families wanting to settle in the community.[3] The residents are very much aware that they do not officially own the land. Therefore carefully worded bills of sale are written describing the money paid for a piece of land as money given to the original holder to 'leave it' to the buyer and not as the purchase price. In the case of built space, the building is described as personal property and the land as government owned.[4]

Sociopolitical Organization
The growth of this community has been greatly influenced by the remarkable degree of internal sociopolitical order and cohesion it manifested from its early days. The community instituted a system of local governance and conflict resolution managed by a traditional headman *('umda)* and supported by a council of elders, known as the 'Arab Council' *(maglis 'Arab)*. This institution derives its model from the Bedouin system of governance, in which disputes are resolved within a hierarchical framework with the arbiter being the person or persons who constitute the link, at one level up, between the two parties. In the Bedouin model, a dispute between two brothers is resolved by their father, between cousins by their grandfathers, between more distant relations by the tribal elders, and between tribes by a council of elders. This model of conflict resolution was well-known to the elders of 'Ezbat al-Safih and subsequently Manshiet Nasser, as many of them, including the leader of the council, originate from areas in Upper Egypt which have been strongly influenced by Arab traditions. Not themselves of Bedouin origin, they nonetheless succeeded in adapting this system in such a way that a highly flexible system of community governance emerged.

The council consists of a leader *('umda)* and members who represent the areas of the country with the largest numbers of residents in the community. These are typically older men who have authority within their own particular segments of the community and who are known to the other segments. The residents who come from areas of the country with smaller numbers of residents may be associated with one of the larger groups, and their leaders are called to participate in deliberations when cases involving them are being discussed.

The council has functioned to contain and resolve disputes between individuals and families living within the area as well to represent community interests in relations with other communities and with public authorities. It has met nearly every day to resolve problems and disputes arising from diverse aspects of daily life in the community, ranging from family disagreements to disputes about land and housing, and commercial conflicts. In serious cases where formal authorities such as the police have to be involved, various cooperative arrangements are worked out, and conflict resolved as far as possible by the community itself. These typically allow the council to reach some resolution of the dispute between the parties before formal procedures such as arrest are undertaken. Institutionalization of community interests within this type of a quasi-tribal framework has been important in enabling the community to manage the growth of the settlement in a relatively orderly manner and in obtaining modest amounts of resources from the official bureaucracy for the settlement. In the beginning the community's first concern was to minimize the attention of official administrative circles to the Manshia. Local dispute resolution and problem solving mechanisms made it possible to maintain a low profile.

As the community grew so did the need to adjudicate more and more conflicts. The need to interact with official bodies and to represent community interests also grew. Then came negotiations to increase urban services to the community. The penetration by government authority grew and the strength of the Arab Council ebbed, receiving a serious blow when the 'umda himself died in 1989. The sociopolitical framework has been steadily revised until a new structure could be said to have emerged by the early 1990s.

Economic History

The families who were involved in recovering and recycling sheet metal in 'Ezbat al-Safih continued to practice their trade in the workshops which they established in the Manshia. As the settlement grew in size and the threat of eviction receded, skilled workmen employed in workshops of the nearby bazaar area, making shoes, carpets and many other items, began to take advantage of the available land and open their own enterprises in the area behind the first settlers. The demand for construction workers grew as people moved into the settlement, making this an attractive location for reinforced concrete workers, masons, painters, electricians, plumbers, and carpenters serving both the settlement and the nearby neighborhoods of Cairo. By the early 1970s, coffee shops near the main interior road of the settlement were serving as recruiting stations where labor contractors would come from greater Cairo looking for skilled workers and day laborers. Up until the present, construction workers' coffee shops continue to be the key contact points for the construction labor market in Cairo (Assaad, 1990b:20–22).

In the middle 1970s, international prices for copper rose so steeply that the traditional practice of providing a new bride with copper household utensils could not be sustained, and aluminum was substituted for copper on a wide scale. This change was facilitated by the establishment of a new aluminum smeltery in Upper Egypt (at Nag' Hammadi) using electric power from the recently completed Aswan High Dam. The old aluminum foundries which had depended on recycled and imported raw aluminum prior to the establishment of the Nag' Hammadi plant began to expand their production, and small workshops producing finished aluminum goods increased rapidly. The foundries constituted more and more of a nuisance in the densely populated Gamaliya area of Cairo where they were clustered. At about the time that the population at Manshiet Nasser was beginning to feel secure from eviction, municipal authorities began exerting heavy pressure on foundry owners to move out of the city center. Manshiet Nasser was an obvious alternative location, close to markets but with ample empty land and a low level of official attention. First one and then several foundries were established at the southern end of Manshiet Nasser, drawing in their wake many small aluminum workshops. As had been the case with the workshops founded during the early years, Manshiet Nasser offered land cheap enough for skilled workers to open their own establishments, and many of these workers-turned-entrepreneurs moved into the community as residents.

Just as the aluminum foundries and workshops had been sources of air pollution, noise, and unregulated work practices in the Gamaliya, so they became the same on an even larger scale in the Manshia. One indicator that the Manshia has become an officially recognized quarter is that the municipal authorities are once again in 1990 pressuring the foundries to move.

Portrait of Physical Growth in the 1980s

How Housing is Built and Tenanted

A considerable stock of housing has been generated in Manshiet Nasser since the settlement began in the 1960s. The era of tin shacks and small independent structures is long past. Recently, buildings of up to nine stories have appeared, showing that built space is reaching a high level of density. These buildings represent particularly substantial investments given the extremely irregular topography and steep slopes that characterize the location. Establishment of a surface sufficiently flat for building usually requires laborious leveling with hand tools and sometimes dynamite. Although land prices have been increasing steadily, it was still true in 1984 that the cost of leveling land for building often exceeded the cost of access to the land itself.[5] To make streets as settlement proceeds, the residents share the costs of leveling roads. In many cases they also share costs of cutting stairways into the hillsides for pedestrian traffic.

To finance construction, families show a remarkable ability to keep current household expenditures at a bare minimum in order to save every piaster. For loans, they draw not only upon their immediate family circle, but on more distant relatives and friends as well. Investment in housing is a very high priority for Egyptian families; to own a building which can house one's own family and those of one's children is the ambition of the great majority of Egyptian families.

When the self-help construction of a building gets under way, there are important inputs from the owner-builders themselves. They educate themselves in all aspects of construction and the building trades so that they will know how to finance, manage, and supervise every detail of the process. The owner-builder consults friends and kin who have themselves recently constructed or added to their homes concerning reliable tradesman, daily rates, relative advantages of payment by day or by piece, costs of materials, suppliers, alternate means of transport of materials, and various means of cutting corners. In short, the prospective builder turns himself into a serious contractor who devotes himself and family members unsparingly to the task. From the beginning, he usually lives in the community, as a previous renter or with friends, or he is building a better house to replace his present one, or for sons or daughters.

'Self-help' means that the owner-builder manages the construction process. If he is a construction worker by trade, or has relatives who are, the women and girls of the family will carry water for making mortar and wetting bricks. Recently, however, even men who are not in the construction trades, and occasionally women as well, are seen doing building maintenance or making improvements, saving on expenses by working themselves.

When the money is available to begin construction, an owner-builder takes time off from his work and together with his wife works closely with groups of skilled workmen, organizing and coordinating different stages of the construction. The owner-builder and his wife purchase all the materials, supervise workers, carry water (a construction input), and provide cigarettes, tea, and sometimes food for the workers. They may also help as support labor doing unskilled work such as carrying sand, bricks, and mortar. By building in stages, a room or a floor at a time, owners match the pace of construction with their ability to mobilize financial resources and their need for space. Buildings often take years to be completely finished.[6]

As soon as independent dwelling units are habitable—finishing work comes later—they are occupied by the owner's family or the newly marrying family members, or the units are rented. Shop rentals are also part of the economics of financing the cost of building. Space is seldom left empty. We found a vacancy rate for dwelling units of only 5 percent.[7]

The building stock is constantly expanded or improved as resources are accumulated. Since the first houses were built in the 1960s, construction has shifted from structures made solely of brick and cut rock to buildings framed with reinforced concrete and then filled with brick walls. There is a structural (not zoning) limit on height of two, at most three, floors, when the building is supported solely by brick or cut rock walls. Older buildings are razed and rebuilt with a reinforced concrete frame, reusing the original materials to fill in the walls. When floors are added, their design usually provides additional complete dwelling units rather than extra room space for existing units.

The tenants also participate in ongoing construction by providing demand

Table 1
Physical characteristics of dwelling units

Living space	Mean
Rooms per unit (excluding toilet or separate kitchen	1.85
By room size	Percent
One room	47
Two rooms	30
Three or more	23
All sizes	100
Facilities	
Separate kitchen (own use)	29
Own toilet	30

Sample size N=1,118

for new units, renegotiating old rental agreements to pay for improvements, and also by engaging directly in improvements themselves with the permission of the owners. Most tenants prefer, wherever possible, to improve their units rather than move. A new rental normally requires a substantial up-front payment which is only partially offset by asking for a share in the 'key money' that the new tenant in one's old place will pay. These initial payments have risen rapidly with the inflation in housing costs and make a move very expensive indeed. Staying rather than moving is also preferred because access to valued goods

Table 2
Owners and renters of dwelling units

Occupant of dwelling unit	Percent
Owner (part or sole)	29
Renter from non-relative	54
Renter from relative	9
Rent-free from relative	8
Where the owner of the dwelling unit lives	
Owner lives in own unit (owner-occupied)	29
Elsewhere in the same building	52
Elsewhere in settlement	10
Outside Manshiet Nasser	9
How owner acquired the dwelling unit	
Built	66
Bought	25
Inherited	9

Sample size N=1,118

Table 3
Land use in the settlement

Plot use	Number of structures
Residential structures	
Exclusively residential	3,770
Structures that include shop space for	
commercial and manufacturing establishments	
(includes 2,093 shops and workshops)[a]	1,230
Structures committed exclusively to commercial and	
manufacturing use (266 establishments)[a]	159
Structures for social services	
Mosques	19
Schools	2
Health centers[b]	1
Vacant plots	87
Under construction (use not yet defined)	212

Source: Building survey, 1983.

a. The number of establishments given in parentheses totals 2,359. They are enterprises not plots, since there can be more than one shop or workshop in a building that occupies a single plot. The total number of establishments is subclassified into 1,504 shops and 855 workshops.

b. The health unit belongs to the Ministry of Health. It is located in a multi-story public housing structure that was built early in Manshiet Nasser's history for evacuees from other quarters of Cairo.

and services, as well as ambiance and affective relationships, are tied to social networks which may take years to develop, and moves generally compromise them.

The case of one family illustrates the resourceful ways in which tenant families try to improve their housing space. A young couple with three children had been living in a single-room dwelling with a shared toilet in the building for LE9.5 per month. After several years, a room across the hall became vacant. At that time, the family renegotiated the rental agreement with the owner to rent the other room, to be allowed to enclose the portion of the corridor between the two, and to build a toilet within part of this newly created private space. In return, they agreed to bear all the costs of the improvement and to increase the rent payment to LE20 per month. A new official rent contract was drawn up with these provisions and the work carried out. By then the family consisted of 6 individuals, but they now had two rooms, hall space, and a private toilet.

By the mid-1980s, a stock of approximately 14,000 dwelling units had been built. They were physically configured as shown in Table 1. The dwellings are organized most often in multi-floor buildings (60 percent), which is the trend as the settlement becomes more and more densely built. Another important configuration is a group of typically four to eight units (often single rooms) built around a small courtyard, sharing toilet facilities and a water tap, if any. This configuration (30 percent in 1984) remains only at the middle and higher (newly built) elevations and is declining in importance. Single dwelling units built as separate buildings have always been few; we found only 10 percent of this type. Many represent the first stage of housing capital accumulation and will be superseded later by larger multi-unit buildings.

Built space in the settlement is now bought, sold, and rented. However, title registration, building permits, regular enforcement of codes, and prior planning of physical layouts by the city are lacking. After two and a half decades of growth, Manshiet Nasser is no longer a settlement purely of self-help owners (Table 2). Our data show that 54 percent of the dwelling units were occupied by renters in the strictest sense of the term. If we add the families 'renting' from relatives, the figure is higher. Despite the high prevalence of renting, this is not an absentee-landlord community. Most owners of flats live in the same building or close by; they watch over their property carefully.

Rental is often a long-term arrangement that is the near equivalent of sale under the rent control laws. The owner retains control of shared space such as hallways, roof, and courtyard, and he controls all structural modifications. With the existing tenancy arrangements, all extensions of infrastructure involve complex negotiation and cooperation between tenants and owners. Rights of tenants, under rent control laws, are to a large extent observed, unless the parties make verbal agreements keeping open the possibility of subsequent renegotiation. A government-appointed housing committee, established under the rent control law, visits the settlement to review rents charged by owners and to set ceilings. Theoretically, renters can also obtain redress in the courts. This is expensive and takes a long time, so it does not happen often. However, a few cases have had a salutary effect by setting patterns for resolution of disputes outside the courts.

Manshiet Nasser occupies a space of 1.5 square kilometers predominantly for residential use, though a significant amount of space is also used for commercial and industrial purposes (Table 3). The different uses of land are intermingled spatially and often occur in the same buildings, with residences above and commercial shops or workshops below. As we shall see in our discussion of economic production below, Manshiet Nasser is an attractive location for small enterprises. It has become an extension of the workshop areas historically located in a nearby quarter, the Gamaliya, which houses the old bazaar and many small businesses.

Regularization of Tenure

This flourishing community of homes, shops, and workshops is in most respects legally invisible, though numerous links exist with public authorities for some services, and even for the application of rent control regulations. The granting of freehold tenure has been on the agenda since the late 1970s. This means that the costs of infrastructure (water, sewerage, roads, public buildings) installed under an upgrading program were to be distributed over the square meters of built land, with owners asked to purchase their land from the government at a price sufficient to pay for these installations. However, as of 1990 there had been no progress on this front. Officially this is because the city government wants to resolve land tenure issues citywide all in one action, rather than dealing with the communities included in upgrading programs one by one. Unofficially, the situation is that in the past thirteen years no one has ever been able to agree who can make the decisions about pricing of land in areas whose tenure is not recognized by the government, nor the mechanisms which will be used for legalizing. This whole issue is rife with rumors, ploys from the government, and counterploys from communities.

According to the conventional wisdom of urban area upgrading worldwide, the granting of secure legal titles to people who have in fact settled, but without permission, is supposed to galvanize their energies, causing them to convert from temporary to permanent housing, make home improvements, and become good citizens. The communities, once legalized, are also supposed to become more effective at establishing community institutions to solve problems that in their nature require joint, not individual solutions.[8]

The paradigm doesn't fit the upgrading sequence for Manshiet Nasser or other communities brought under upgrading projects during the late 1970s and 1980s in Cairo. People invested in permanent housing long before the upgrading projects were planned. The people could preempt the sequence because the government was not willing to raze the homes of residents unless they were severe nuisances. Thus, in such communities as Manshiet Nasser the settlement could reach a sufficient size of permanently housed residents to assure their security of tenure *de facto*, without need of the upgrading feature of freehold titles.

The community has also proceeded without benefit of legal tenure to face some of the problems that require joint action; for example, the Arab Council brought 'law and order' relative to land claims and was able to settle family disputes and deal with some types of crime.

The most serious challenges, however, have arisen at the intersection of the community and Cairo's urban services, water and sewerage in particular. While housing can be built by individuals and small groups, whether legal or not, services from the city agencies that supply water, connect sewers, remove solid waste (garbage) from dumps, and pave roads, require recognition and cooperation from the official establishments. The question is, how does a community acquire these basic urban services when it exists actually, but does not exist in

Table 4
Service connections

Service	Connected to dwelling unit	Elsewhere in building or courtyard
Electricity	90	na
Municipal sewer[a]	18	33
Municipal water tap	11	14

Sample size N=1,118

a. The survey did not assess whether the connection was working or not. We observed many that were blocked or improperly connected.

the legal framework surrounding the activities of the responsible government agencies? The answer in Egypt is that there is a polity and a long tradition of communities reaching into and mobilizing one or another government institution on their behalf. It has never been easy for people from the lower classes to do so, but they do have connections and networks through relatives and friends located at different levels of the vast bureaucracy. Often some help is obtained, and occasionally it is substantial, depending upon political and bargaining factors. Financial feasibility and the internal workings of each service organization differ, so each has to be approached uniquely.[9]

Organizing the Infrastructure
The general situation in the mid-1980s was one of serious deficiencies in all urban services for the Manshia except two: electricity was connected throughout most of the settlement and a solid-waste (garbage) collection system for households was in place. All roads within the settlement area were unpaved and most were very narrow, frequently ending as blind alleys. The surfaces were uneven and gradients steep. For water connections and sewerage, the situation was also poor (Table 4).

The hilly topography and rock structure of the terrain raise the cost of placing pipes and pumps or siphons, which is a special problem in the Manshia not faced in most other settlements of Cairo. However, electric extensions could develop quickly, partly because the cost is lower and collection of rates follows immediately. When illegal wires were strung, the end-users paid the owners at meter points. While this is illegal, and providers of electricity to neighbors risk confiscation of their electricity meters, this is temporary. The Electricity Authority provides meters to residents on demand, insisting only that owners meet the initial cost. The authority has a reputation for supplying services whether people have established a legal right of occupancy or not, whereas some of the other utility organizations have been much less forthcoming.

Sanitation and water are particularly important in this study because of their influence on health and illness. For women and young girls, who must carry fresh water in and waste water out, these facilities make a great deal of difference. Costs are also raised when water is bought and waste must be removed by the householders. Manshiet Nasser's adaptation to the realities that had to be faced, and its progress toward better solutions will be discussed next. First, we take up sanitation, beginning with solid waste; then the system for disposal of human waste and gray water. After that, we shall turn to the question of water requirements and how they are met in the Manshia.

During its first twenty years of existence, the Manshia had no household solid waste collection service. Street surfaces, vacant lots, and railway lines and other peripheral areas of the community were clogged with garbage placed there by residents who literally had no alternative. Children played in these areas, and residents had to pick their way around dumps when moving in and out of the community. In 1980, with the mediation of a private Egyptian organization, Environmental Quality International, a plan was agreed whereby the garbage collectors who live in the Zabbaleen settlement collect the household solid wastes of neighboring Manshiet Nasser on a regular basis in return for a monthly fee per household.[10] For one year the District Sanitation Department paid; thereafter the householders paid.

This venture became the occasion for the Zabbaleen to found their own private institution *(gama'iyya)* to take over management of the routes and fee collection. Ten years later, in 1991, the system continues to function well. The monthly fee has increased from LE0.25 to LE1.25 (now applying to groups of households in each building). The technology originally was donkey carts, but that too has changed. Small motorized vehicles that can negotiate the alleys now work alongside the reliable, even if dilapidated, donkey carts.

The collection service improved the cleanliness of the environment and increased the awareness and commitment of the people to community sanitation. People appreciate the cleanliness and through social pressure have reduced the number of households throwing their garbage on dumps to a small number. Garbage continues to accumulate along the railway line, but it is dumped mainly by the market, shops, and workshops. Although the garbage collectors offer their service to these establishments for a fee, the temptation to dump rather than pay is there. Residents complain and the municipality periodically sends in trucks and crews to clear away the garbage on the community's perimeter.

Cairo had grown far beyond the capacity of its infrastructure by the time of the Second World War. The situation became progressively worse as the population more than doubled from its pre-war size up to the early 1970s. During the 1970s, massive foreign financial assistance became available, and a general strategy was adopted to solve accumulated problems of roads, water and sewerage. First, a large network of roads, flyovers, and bridges was quickly built.

Simultaneously, projects were initiated to dramatically increase the pumping capacity of the water and sewer networks and the length and size of their trunk lines. The new installations would carry the overloads already existing, and at a later stage the local networks themselves would be repaired and extended. According to this strategy, communities like Manshiet Nasser were last in line.

Fortunately, and despite many obstacles, there was one tenuous factor on Manshiet Nasser's side. A World Bank upgrading project for Egypt (see below) selected the community for special attention during the late 1970s. Through this exception to the general strategy, funding was made available to the government to install a local network within the settlement of sewers and water pipes. As we tell the story below, it took more than a decade and the project was neither completed nor up to engineering standards, but in the end there were some benefits for the community.

The principal technology for disposing of human waste in Manshiet Nasser is private pits cut out of the limestone rock in front of or alongside each building. These are rock vaults, not soak pits, so gray water (waste water) is introduced sparingly. The pits are emptied periodically. In 1984 this was done either by tanker vehicles with a pumping capacity or by laborers who carried the wastes out of the pits using buckets hung on shoulder poles. In both procedures, the sludge was carried only short distances before being dumped into empty spaces.

Since then, with increasing density and the development of small businesses in the settlement who offer cleaning as a service, a donkey cart system for pumping out the sludge is now used almost universally. By 1990 the service was available on call for an average fee per cleaning of LE80, depending on terrain and size of the pit. Disposal is still on dumps, but at a further distance.

Many of the pits are connected to the sewage collection network, but we found many of these connections were not working properly in the mid-1980s. By 1990, the situation had improved after a decision by the parliament that the sewer organization should serve settlements being upgraded under programs funded by the World Bank or USAID. They responded by making an additional effort to extend the Manshiet Nasser network, but refused to make the individual connections, saying that these had not been specifically authorized. In consequence, many owners connected on their own, without official supervision. This may be a reason for the extensive leakage of sewage which spills onto the lower levels of the settlement, complicated by frequent breakages in the substandard mains. Spillage constitutes a serious risk of infection to anyone who lives on these streets, particularly children, who play in the roadways.

Without a second survey, we cannot specify the proportion of buildings now connected, but there has been an improvement over 1984 (see Table 4). Wherever there is piped water, there is now likely to be a sewer main as well. Earlier there was little coordination between the two systems except along the spine road at the bottom of the settlement. Many of the Manshia's water problems are connected with the sewer problem. One cannot use water in significant amounts unless there is a practical way to get rid of it afterwards.

Women in households lacking sewer connections typically dispose of domestic waste water, other than toilet wastes, by scattering it across the street surface. Neighbors insist that women do not dump their water at a single point, but sprinkle it around in the vicinity of the front door, to minimize the formation of ruts on street surfaces. Where the amount of water is limited, this is effective because evaporation is fast. As housing densities have increased, however, open ground has diminished, and the quantity of waste water which must be disposed of has increased, reducing the convenience of this system.

Obtaining sufficient water for drinking and other domestic uses is a major preoccupation of households in most self-help communities in Cairo. Communities established on the agricultural perimeters of Cairo use a variety of water sources when they cannot get municipal water: tubewells, canals, and the Nile itself. Manshiet Nasser, however, was built on the slopes of waterless hills, so all water for the community enters through municipal mains. Households lacking connections with the water system mostly obtain their water from other households which have connections, though some take from public taps.

Water mains were installed first along the lower reaches of the settlement. While this would have been quickly followed in most communities by a proliferation of self-help water connections, there was not enough water pressure to carry the water up the hillsides of Manshiet Nasser. At the time of the survey, one-quarter of the households of the settlement had piped water inside their dwelling units or elsewhere in their buildings (see Table 4). Even for these households, the city-wide problem of irregular and insufficient pumping pressure meant frequent cuts or no water at all. On an individual basis, some of the more affluent residents have installed private household pumps that lift water to tanks placed on the roof. This helps some people, but empties the mains and induces others to follow suit in a self-defeating competition.

Household members, particularly women, allocate considerable time and often money to the acquisition of water. Most households have intricate arrangements to ensure an adequate water supply. They use more than one source: their own taps, taps of households which sell water, public taps (whose water is carried by women of the household or by someone else for a fee), and delivery carts. Even for those with piped water, low pressure and cuts in service are frequent enough that households need to supplement from other sources and to store water. The most prevalent alternative to one's own tap is the tap of someone else. Public taps play only a minor direct role in supplying domestic water, though they are used by delivery carts as a source.

From dawn to dusk there are long lines of women and young girls patiently waiting their turn to draw water in front of buildings along the main street. One woman recounted breastfeeding the child of a woman whose own milk supply had failed, as an act of kindness and charity, but also, as she laughingly reported, 'It is convenient and good insurance to have access to her water tap.'

It is mostly the women and young girls who provide their households with water. Training in water-carrying is an important part of preparation for womanhood. Mothers start their daughters at an early age, teaching them to carry water in a small metal container (*bastilla banati*—girl's container) balanced on their heads. When one or more teenage daughters or daughters-in-law are available to carry water, the mother phases herself out of water carrying. Whenever possible, pregnant and lactating women are exempted from water carrying, but in young families without others to help or that cannot afford to pay someone to carry or deliver water, these women also have to carry.

Everyone has to have a water carrying system. Women and young girls may help fetch water for male relatives living alone, elderly kin, or families of young men to whom they are engaged. Women may carry water for payment for men living alone. Occasionally men carry water. About 6 percent of the households that carry their water mentioned male members as carriers. They were mostly single men living together, or men whose wives were away. Where the wife or mother is present, husbands and sons rarely carry water.

Every home, whether it has a tap or not, stores water in an array of pots, tins, and barrels. The most common container is the barrel (*barmil*), the larger size of which holds three hundred liters. Over 40 percent of the households had at least one such barrel and one household had seven. Total storage capacity is highly variable, averaging 270 liters per household. Considering the small size of most dwelling units in this settlement (see Table 1), water storage consumes a good deal of living space.

Water is also a high cost input to household life in Manshiet Nasser. The energy and time of women and girls is a cost even if undervalued, containers cost money, and the living space allocated to storage is a cost. Finally, there are current expenses to pay for water. The magnitude of the time and energy cost is broadly suggested by the fact that 64 percent of households carry all of their water, and another 17 percent carry at least some of it. Only about a quarter of households obtain water without carrying, by taking it from taps in their own homes or buildings, or from donkey cart vendors. The dependence upon carrying where the terrain is difficult and there are long lines at taps reflects the tight income constraints under which people live.

That was the situation in the mid-1980s. The basic patterns remain, but two important improvements were seen by the early 1990s. First, a pumping station with a large storage tank has been built at the Citadel end of the settlement on the highest point. This was part of the agenda of the World Bank project, so long delayed in implementation. The mains have been extended and feed the system below. It seems that this system is working well. It does not serve the entire settlement, because some areas are at too high an elevation or pipes were not placed for the local area. We estimate, without benefit of a survey, that more than half of the households now have piped water. Some parts of the settlement, however, still have no running water at all, not even standpipes.

The second important improvement is the development of a more standard-ized and economical system of private water delivery. Now there are small vehi-cles plying the narrow streets selling water in standard containers. They are everywhere, supplementing the supply from small tank trucks pulled by don-keys. With water cuts still frequent, and many homes without water, these sys-tems of home delivery are vital. Water continues to be carried and hosed from dwelling to dwelling, but not to the extent of earlier years. The water is sold in returnable containers,[11] each with fifty liters of water. A deposit is paid and the containers are rotated when a filled one is purchased. The price is LE0.35 at the higher elevations and LE0.15 lower down. This is small-scale private business filling a major gap not tended by the public services. It is headquartered on the spine road at the bottom where water supply is best.

The present system is more cost-effective for the residents than the choices available in 1984. At that time, we found that households that were buying water spent an average of LE4.20 per month It is now cheaper, in real terms, and there are fewer women and girls carrying water. On the assumption that households must replenish their supply of stored water on a five-day cycle, the monthly cost for those who cannot refill from taps in their own buildings is about LE8.10 per month in 1990.[12] The international value of the Egyptian pound has meanwhile decreased to one-third what it was at the earlier date.

The World Bank 'Up-Grading' Project

International lending and aid agencies came to Egypt in the mid-1970s on a wave of international studies—mostly in Latin America—of so-called squatter or informal urban settlement, each with suggestions about what should be done to channel and build upon the inherent energy of the new settlements. The World Bank joined with the Egyptian government to pursue what came to be known as the Egypt Urban Development Project, funded and technically advised by the Bank. This project included components for the upgrading of Manshiet Nasser's physical infrastructure, and provision of health, educational and social facilities. The plan was to regularize tenure by selling the land to building owners at a square-meter price sufficient to cover the costs of the infrastructure. Regularization of tenure has not been achieved, but some of the physical aims were partially or wholly realized.[13]

The project commenced in 1977, but then had to be stretched out, finally ending with its official closure in 1985. We saw some of the sewerage and water distribution systems in place at the time of our survey. The pumping station, school, and social buildings were completed later by Egyptian organizations that followed through after the project had been officially closed.

While all this was going on, there was a public debate and many meetings on whether 'informal' settlements should be bulldozed or assisted. In practice, the bulldozer approach was rarely used, and only when small numbers of squatters settled in defiance of other building plans. Public money for housing typically went to build housing for public employees, or for people evicted when public space was needed, or whose houses had collapsed—needy groups. Some public housing was built in Duweiqa, next to Manshiet Nasser, to house families who were relocated.

The World Bank project was relevant to this debate because it tried to show that public money could also be used to support the self-help community building process. This approach is demonstrably cheaper than public housing and it responds directly to demand. The idea that tenure could be regularized with title deeds in exchange for assessments on improvements never worked out. It is a moot point whether a system of assessments could ever have been agreed that would speed up the extension of infrastructure which is what the residents want. They are not worried about eviction. Yet it is obvious that capital projects such as pumping stations and trunk lines for sewers and water can only be organized under a public authority, which takes money and time; the complaint is that it takes too much time.

Portrait of Social Conditions in the 1980s

Who Lives Here: Regional and Local Origins
This particular settlement has a strong infusion of Upper Egyptian backgrounds, which is the origin of much of Cairo's outborn population. The Manshia's household heads were born mainly in Asyut, Sohag, and Qena in Upper Egypt. Fayoum, which is an hour's drive to the southwest of Cairo, was also the birthplace for many residents. Nevertheless, the majority of household heads (61 percent) moved to Manshiet Nasser from Cairo, some of them as native-born Cairenes and others as second-stage migrants from Upper Egypt.

First-generation Upper Egyptians are still the dominant group among property owners in the Manshia. Their lifestyles, political alliances, and ideas have dominated the life of the settlement since the outset. However, this generation is becoming elderly, and many of the founding residents, including the *'umda* himself, have died. As the children of the Manshia themselves have matured, the customs and values that they have learned at the social intersections of the settlement and the city have become stronger factors. The hold of provincial custom is likely to be loosened, and that very special Cairo distillate, expressed as the *baladi* living style, may weaken; at the very least it will be modified.

To be *baladi* is to identify oneself as having a lifestyle that preserves many of the values concerning dress, honor, marriage, honesty, and extended family relationships of Upper Egyptian life (seldom are these people Delta migrants). The women are conspicuous by their wearing of ankle-length black wraps, the *milaya-laff* or the *abaya*, with adequate display of contour and movement to be attractive. *Baladi* is an urban, not rural, lifestyle. Such families live mostly in nuclear households, men rule, but women are strong, and the airs of the 'modernized' middle and upper urban classes are eschewed. A person can be accepted from the higher classes as *baladi* if they hold to the same personal standards and acknowledge their own solidarity with this sub-cultural group, but this is exceptional (el-Messiri, 1978:522–40).

The current stream of in-migrants is households predominantly formed by young couples, two-thirds of whom had moved to the community from elsewhere in Cairo. Some had already started their families (a little less than half of the couples), probably while living briefly as newlyweds in their parental homes; others came to the community as couples without children, presumably with plans to start their families in Manshiet Nasser.

While three-quarters of the migrant households were young families, the other quarter was an assortment of generally non-family households. They were formed mostly of males, workers and students, and came largely from outside Cairo, i.e., they were truly new migrants to Cairo and settled first in Manshiet Nasser, typically renting one-room dwelling units.

Social Networks

In the city, as in the countryside, individuals and households are connected to other individuals and households, as well as to institutions, by a web of personal relationships. For newcomers to the Manshia, the organizing principles of these relationships are initially those of kinship or place of origin, which may include friends made in other Cairo neighborhoods. Over time these networks expand to include neighbors and colleagues, such as co-workers of men or women who travel outside the settlement, in an ever expanding web.

For women more than men, but even for men, residential proximity is important in the formation of networks. They retain relationships, especially those of kin, that pre-existed in distant parts of the city, but travel is necessary and not always convenient. The spatial configuration of urban life consequently forces atrophy of some networks and the development of others. As time has passed and the community has matured, however, there has been a major increase in the reach and complexity of networks for both men and women.

Social networks of the Manshia mediate access to many kinds of resources, including material goods and services, information, and emotional support. Individuals rely on networks of reciprocal exchange to find employment, ensure job security, obtain interest free loans of cash, buy or build housing, and facilitate routine tasks by borrowing food, clothing, labor, and small household items.

These networks also constitute the context within which beliefs, attitudes, and practices, including ones which foster child health, are formulated and changed. Exchanges promote security, cooperation, and trust among community residents. Reciprocity is implicit and weaves bonds of trust supported by kinship, common origin, neighborliness or collegiality.

Networks are used by Manshia residents to gain entry to public distribution systems in health, education, and subsidized goods. Such networks enable otherwise powerless people to manipulate state redistribution systems for their own benefit. These personalized systems also enable residents to gain control over preferential market transactions which are rife in the market economy.[14]

Women's Networks

Myriad tiny grocery stores dot the streets of the settlement, and they have become the sites for social interaction among women. Public taps are at a distance and women mostly buy from water trucks anyway. Laundry is done inside the houses. Women rarely if ever visit the homes of non-relatives, though men do. Thus, an important part of daily social life for the women centers around the grocery shops. Each grocery has a regular clientele that never goes elsewhere unless an urgent need for an out-of-stock item requires it. Relationships at the grocery are cemented by credit, which usually is extended only to the end of day, and rarely beyond another day or two.

The grocery shops are a socially acceptable setting for women meeting one another, gossiping, exchanging advice, and establishing or extending a social network. The grocery visits are so important that women typically spread their purchases over the morning hours when men are at work, thereby maximizing the time that can be spent with other women at the store without incurring criticism.

Our observations in small groceries over a period of many weeks showed that a wide range of information is exchanged in these conversations: identification of who is a reliable borrower of household items and who is not, opinions on potential marriage partners for children, illnesses and referrals to physicians, means of protection from supernatural or natural risks to mother and child during the first days after a child's birth, and many others. News about events in the homes of near neighbors who are not personally visited comes to women in this way, keeping them well informed about their immediate neighborhood.

The savings group (*gama'iyya*) is a common urban form of informal association, which is not kin-based. While men are increasingly entering into these associations, women are the main organizers and participants. Their commitment to the group overrides any reluctance on the part of their husbands to part with the money which must be contributed periodically. On a rotating basis a designated participant receives the whole fund for some purpose; e.g., key money, furniture or home appliances, marriage or funeral expenses, or schooling. The organizer is a respected woman sought out by the others to form the group, hold the cash, and decide the frequency of rotation, contributions, and who shall be next to receive the fund, all this with consultation among participants. The fund is recreated monthly, or on some other schedule, by everyone making their payment.

The *gama'iyya* not only serves a saving function for members, but is perceived by women as a prior commitment to each other to provide support in time of future need, a need which may or may not be financial. The savings group may be established to last a long time, or only for a short period, and women may be members of more than one concurrently. For many women in the community, participation in such savings groups is an important experience in the movement toward a truly urban form of social relations.

Men's Networks

Men also try assiduously to strengthen and widen their networks of social relations. Migrants to the Manshia from Upper Egypt, whether directly or via Cairo, have often obtained their first jobs in the city through kin or regional links, and the same applies for their housing. For example, jobs in the Cairo Bus Authority are particularly accessible to men from Esna in Upper Egypt. Those from Araba in Sohag have extensive links to certain building trades: exterior plastering, house painting, and concrete contracting. Migrants from Fayoum, on the other hand, tend to be unskilled construction workers. These experiences are the initial ones as men build their own networks, many of the elements being employment-based. By marrying one or more sons or daughters to spouses who are from their village of origin, and by placing others in a range of different occupations, both public and private, networks are maintained and expanded.

Today the Manshia resident who needs to borrow money or collect information on how to economize while building a home, who is coping with breach of contract by a business partner, who is considering prospective suitors for his daughter or employment for his sons, or who is simply gossiping to track events, interacts at least as much with co-workers as with neighbors and relatives. His social network is likely to extend far beyond the borders of the Manshia, into many quarters of the city. Place of origin has lost some of its salience though by no means all. By now, the majority of the population of the Manshia is Cairo-born, and patterns of interaction are becoming similar to those of the older urban neighborhoods.

The Arab Council which governed the settlement for many years was itself the epitome of extensive networks. Its most important function was to transform the original settlement from one with very particularistic orientations, and weld it into a community where interaction, in the final analysis, is based on common interests rather than on common origin.

Table 5
Resident working population of Manshiet Nasser,
by sex and location of work (age ten and above)
(percentage)

Location of work	Males	Females	Both sexes
In settlement	20	48	22
In Cairo	65	49	64
Itinerant	9	2[a]	8
Outside Cairo	4	1[a]	4
All	100	100	100
Sample N	1,359	102	1,461

a. The itinerant females are two peddlers, one of whom is a girl of 11 who helps her father. The only female working outside Cairo is a young woman who helps her brother peddling clothes.

Economic Production in the Settlement

The self-help communities of Cairo are suitable settings for enterprises that can organize themselves to produce efficiently without much relationship to the official state apparatus or the so-called formal sector of the economy. Many such communities have small-scale production and repair workshops, but few show the diversity, vigor, and size that characterizes the small-scale commercial-industrial complex in Manshiet Nasser.

Growing up as a logical extension of the commercial-industrial establishment of the traditional bazaar area in Gamaliya, the Manshia was able to capitalize on the social and economic infrastructure supporting production in the bazaar while being a less expensive area with more space available to the individual workshop. As in the older location, enterprises in Manshiet Nasser tend to specialize in one step in a manufacturing process or trading, then pass the product to others, often nearby, to continue adding value. By the mid-1980s, many industrial and commercial workers who had learned their skills in Manshiet Nasser had spun off to establish their own workshops in nearby communities such as Duweiqa, for exactly the reasons that the proprietors of Manshiet Nasser shops had spun off from those in Gamaliya.

Thus, in keeping with its informality of building and residential arrangements, the Manshia is also part of the ubiquitous informal economy of Cairo. By 'informal' we mean the way in which enterprises conduct their business, having only a limited relationship to laws and institutions that attempt to license and regulate production, set labor standards or organize labor, and collect taxes or fix prices (Castells and Portes, 1989). The activities of these enterprises are not necessarily illegal (although they sometimes are), but are structured to make profits and earn compensation for labor efficiently in an economic environment that offers little appropriate formal support.

The market demand that makes the Manshia's enterprises profitable comes from two sources. First there is the inter-enterprise demand, just discussed, which takes products ultimately to the larger markets of Cairo. Second, a community of this size generates demands of its own for commercial, service, and construction activities to take care of the needs of residents. Where public infrastructure is lacking, small scale private enterprises tend to substitute for the state in providing services in the form of water vending, pit cleaning, garbage collection, and transportation. There is also an abundance of small groceries; in Manshiet Nasser, the average grocery store serves a clientele of about fifty households, functioning as a communication center for the women in particular. Construction is a continuous and integral part of life, so that skilled building tradesmen and shops for construction materials are particularly numerous.

Labor and Entrepreneurial Inputs

The industrial structure of the Manshia goes on growing as workshops expand their businesses and skilled workers branch out on their own. In 1984, the settlement had over two thousand economic establishments ranging from tiny refreshment stands to foundries, some of them with considerable capital investment relative to their small scale. Thus, there was about one economic establishment for every six residential dwelling units. While diminishing land availability is inhibiting construction of new buildings for commercial and industrial use, this area is so well located that building owners find it profitable to build new floors for residential living in order to free lower floors for use as workshops. In this way, the number of manufacturing establishments continues to grow.

The presence of numerous workshops in or close to residential buildings compromises the quality of the living and working environment in the settlement. Their production activities spill out into the alleys, obstructing circulation of people and vehicles and generating noise, smoke, and fumes. While the workshops provide an economic base for some residents, they also burden the community with industrial pollution in a physical setting which already suffers from poor sewerage and other problems.

A substantial share of the labor input comes from outside the settlement. However, the presence of this active and diversified economic base means that residents of the community itself find some of their own employment within the area. Twenty percent of Manshiet Nasser's employed males work regularly within the settlement area (Table 5). Considering the ratio of six households to one enterprise, this means that local residents are providing a significant proportion of the labor themselves.

Since the construction trades are an important part of employment for the Manshia's men, one finds many of them at the local hiring halls every day. These are not actually hiring halls in the Western tradition, but coffee shops located near entrances of the community. There, the market is 'made.' Rates and terms are set and men are engaged by employers or clients who need skilled or unskilled workers by the day or for short periods of time. Ragui Assaad (1990a; 1990b) tells us that the men in one such coffee shop function very much like a guild of old, having a structured system of leaders and participation of their 'members.' They are quite successful at accommodating themselves to the realities of wide fluctuations in demand for labor. They have shared norms and practices about apprenticeship, skill classification, and control of entry into the trade that support their own interests.

Some of the enterprises are 'on the street' rather than in buildings as workshops or trading stores. Women work as self-employed or family workers as grocers and greengrocers and as peddlers selling food, bread, drinks, cloth and clothing items, or notions direct to consumers. Most of what they sell· is obtained from wholesale sources, but some of their products are home produced, particularly food and some clothing items. The number of such enterprises is not large, but our survey of what women do as part of family support systems showed that 3 to 4 percent of women work in the settlement, many of them in this type of activity.

Workshops of the Manshia that make carpets, clothes pins, shoes, and wires also employ young women as workers. However, except for a limited range of enterprises the community's local economy does not offer many opportunities for female labor. Jobs are primarily a male affair within the settlement. Male labor is drawn from outside as well as inside the community.

In some instances, small capitalist enterprises of the settlement use subcontracting to employ women residents for work that they can do at home; e.g., packaging spices and dried edible seeds, stringing beads, assembling upholstery tacks, painting military medals, and assembling earrings, headbands, and plastic slippers. Women accept this type of work because they do not have the education and skills to compete profitably elsewhere, and because it can be interspersed with regular household tasks and does not separate them from their children. Furthermore, being a home subcontractor involves no expenses for transport or for appropriate clothing to work outside. Since the overall participation of women in cash earning activities, whether at home or in shops, is low in the Manshia, it seems that home-based subcontracting is not a major form of economic production in the community. It is low paid. Women themselves generally negotiate the agreements and determine how the cash income will be used.

Inter-Industry Relations with Metropolitan Cairo
The location of production enterprises, once highly concentrated near the spine

road and at the northern end of the settlement, has now spread throughout the settlement area, entering almost every street or alley way. These workshops supply products to the major historic market locations of Cairo, in 'Ataba and al-Husayn, in the form of brass and alabaster items, gold work, carpets, handmade braiding, spools for thread, shoes, aluminum wares, plastic goods, traditional furniture, and many other items. Some are for final sale by the entrepreneurs who are based both in Manshiet Nasser and elsewhere with an outlet in the city, or are for inter-industry sale, moving along a chain of linked stages of production that add value until the final sale point is reached. Customers are also attracted to Manshiet Nasser from elsewhere in Cairo, for example for car repairs and painting.

A number of the manufacturing establishments also export to Arab countries and the Sudan, using commercial networks strengthened by the contacts of a continuous flow of Egyptian workers and businessmen among the Arab countries. One enterprise was discovered during the study which subcontracts to a Swiss factory. Thus, it is shown once more how the Manshia is by no means a community separate and unto itself. Although its inner ways are intensely interesting, it is also part of greater Cairo and the world to which Cairo belongs.

Notes

1 He is not an *'umda* in the legal sense, since the term refers to village headmen who are appointed by the central government, an office that never existed in urban places. The powers of an *'umda* have been circumscribed considerably since the 1952 revolution. They used to be chosen from among the most influential people in the village community and performed a variety of administrative tasks including resolution of local disputes. In terms of his leadership position and function in this urban community the leader of Manshiet Nasser was considered to be an *'umda* in the old village style.

2 There have been cases of persons who took quite substantial portions of land, a thousand square meters or more, both at the outset and subsequently. Some of these lands are only now being subdivided and sold at high prices. The general pattern of land development, however, was quite different from that seen in some other rapidly growing self-help areas. In these other places, middlemen staked claims to substantial tracts of publicly owned land, and then subdivided and sold off plots for construction. This type of large-scale land speculation was not seen in Manshiet Nasser, although profits on the increase of land values have certainly been made.

3 It is difficult to untangle the land tenure situation from oral accounts due to community insecurity regarding its legal status. Even today there is some insecurity about tenure, so that people are anxious to present what they think is the best picture of the way in which they acquired their land although they are unsure of what that might be. Some who did actually pay insist that they took their land without paying for it, in the belief that the law against trading in government land applies to the buyer as

well as the seller. Some argue the opposite with the hope of reducing charges for tenure in case there is regularization of status.

4 The title transfer document for buildings states: 'I, [name], hereby sell my house built on land owned by the government to [name].'

5 In the case of one plot purchased in about 1980, for instance, sixty square meters of land were purchased for LE700. Subsequent expenditures to level the ground reached LE2,000, and thus the final investment was LE45 per square meter. To some extent these costs are balanced by having to invest little in building foundations since the rock is solid enough to support high buildings with little concrete and steel as compared to that needed on agricultural land.

6 John Turner (1967) characterizes as "progressive development," the process whereby "families build their housing and their community in stages as their resources permit, the more important elements first." Houses and communities are lived in while they are built and modified as resources accumulate and the needs of the family cycle change. He contrasts this with the "instant development" model which officially requires that minimum standard structures and community installations be in place prior to occupancy. Furthermore, little modification is allowed; people should move to another community when their needs change.

7 The owner's standard of habitability was accepted. If the official housing standards were applied most of these units would be classified as under construction (not finished) rather than as vacant.

8 A favorable attitude toward upgrading of existing settlements came into vogue among international assistance agencies and some governments in the 1970s, following a long period when demolition was seen as the answer to undesirable housing. For the rationale of this policy change, see Gilbert (1986) and an influential contribution to the attendant controversy by Turner (1967, 1968).

9 For a rich exposition of how networks of family, neighbors, and mid-level political processes function in Cairo on behalf of important needs that families have, see Diane Singerman, *Avenues of Participation: Family, Politics, and Networks in Urban Quarters of Cairo* (American University in Cairo Press, 1997).

10 EQI undertook the project to demonstrate an affordable and sustainable approach to Cairo's garbage problems (EQI, 1982). It did so on behalf of the Governorate of Cairo. The experience gained has strengthened the institutions and organizational capacity of the Zabbaleen garbage collectors themselves. They now have a variety of systems for gathering garbage which they use as inputs for their recycling businesses.

11 The plastic containers are shaped like the steel containers for petrol that were known as 'Jerry cans' during the Second World War. In Cairo, the plastic ones are called *jerkins*.

12 Average storage of 270 liters would need 5.4 *jerkins* (fifty liters) six times per month for an average cost of LE0.25 x 5.4 x 6 = LE8.10 per month.

13 Hoda Sakr's Ph.D. dissertation (1990) provides the best documentation of the World

Bank project and insight into how it was managed.
14 For an early application of Polanyi's typology of exchange systems (reciprocity, redistribution, and market exchange) to an urban setting, see Lomnitz's (1974) study of life in a squatter settlement in Mexico City. A recent study of how the urban poor use social networks to manipulate the system in relation to daily needs and housing in a large city on the Turkish Mediterranean coast is by Duben (1991). For other neighborhoods of Cairo, see the articulate and detailed study of the heart of old Cairo by Singerman (1989: Chapter 3), as well as the valuable studies of Nadim (1977) and Hoodfar (1988: Chapter 9).\

Bibliography

Abu-Lughod, Janet. 1971. *Cairo: 1001 Years of the City Victorious*. Princeton: Princeton University Press.

Assaad, Ragui. 1990a. "Structured Labor Markets: The Case of the Construction Sector in Egypt." Ph.D. dissertation, Cornell University, Ithaca, New York.

Assaad, Ragui. 1990b. "Informal Labor Markets: The Case of the Construction Sector in Egypt." Paper presented at the 1990 annual conference of the Middle East Studies Association. New Orleans.

Castells, Manuel and Alejandro Portes. 1989. "World Underneath: The Origins, Dynamics, and Effects of the Informal Economy," *The Informal Economy: Studies in Advanced and Less Developed Countries*, A. Portes, M. Castells, and L.A. Benton (eds). Baltimore and London: Johns Hopkins University Press. pp. 11–37.

Duben, Alan. 1991. "The Rationality of an Informal Economy: The Provision of Housing in Southern Turkey," *Structural Change in Turkish Society*, ed. M. Kiray. Indiana University Turkish Studies No. 10.

Environmental Quality International (EQI). 1982. 'Completion of the Manshiet Nasser Pilot Solid Waste Route Extension Program,' Final Report presented to the Governorate of Cairo, November.

Gilbert, A. 1987. "The Housing of the Urban Poor," *Cities, Poverty, and Development*, A. Gilbert and J. Gugler (eds). Oxford: Oxford University Press. pp. 81–115.

Hoodfar, Homa. 1988. "Survival Strategies in Low-Income Neighbourhoods of Cairo, Egypt," Ph.D. dissertation, University of Kent, United Kingdom.

Issawi, C. 1982. *An Economic History of the Middle East and North Africa*. New York: Columbia University Press.

Lomnitz, L. 1974. "The Social and Economic Organization of a Mexican Shantytown," *Anthropological Perspectives on Latin American Urbanization*, W. Cornelius and F. Trueblood (eds). Latin American Urban Research, vol 4. Beverly Hills: Sage Publications. pp. 135–55.

Nadim, Nawal el-Messiri. 1977. 'Family Relationships in a Harah in Cairo,' *Arab Society in Transition: A Reader*, Saad Eddin Ibrahim and Nicholas S. Hopkins (eds). Cairo:

The American University in Cairo Press, pp 107–120. Republished in *Arab Society: Social Science Perspectives*, Hopkins and Ibrahim (eds). Cairo: The American University in Cairo Press, 1985, pp. 212–22.

Sakr, Hoda. 1990. "Underlying Collegial Relationships Controlling Project Implementation: Case Study of Egypt." Ph.D. dissertation in Urban and Regional Planning, Massachusetts Institute of Technology.

Singerman, Diane. 1997. *Avenues of Participation: Family, Politics and Networks in Urban Quarters of Cairo*. Cairo: American University in Cairo Press.

Turner, John F.C. 1967. "Barriers and Channels for Housing Development in Modernizing Countries," *Journal of the American Institute of Planners* 33: 167–81.

Turner, John F.C. 1968. "Uncontrolled Urban Settlement: Problems and Policies," *The City in Newly Developing Countries*, G. Breese (ed). Englewood Cliffs, NJ: Prentice Hall. pp. 507–534.

Three

Introduction

Family and Gender

The most durable of all social institutions is the family. The family is a socially sanctioned arrangement regulating the bond between men, women, and their offspring. It provides for sexual satisfaction, procreation, and early care and socialization of children. Yet this does not mean the family as an institution is unchanging. Like other social institutions, the family is a product of the environmental and structural forces of society. These forces are as powerful as any moral or spiritual vision in shaping social institutions such as the family. These forces have ample chance to work because individuals are always moving through the family cycle as they age and find themselves in different places in the wider system. The articles in this section analyze some of these social forces as they bear on the Arab family and on gender issues in diverse localities.

One of the greatest shifts in the social science literature on the Arab world over the last twenty years is the burgeoning of material on gender. Discussion of gender has largely taken the place of the earlier writings on the family, though of course the stress and the content are different. This substitution is partly a function of the legitimate quest of Arab women social scientists to correct an earlier gender imbalance in scholarship. But correcting scholarly imbalance in writing about gender is one thing and correcting injustice in reality between males and females is another. One of the silent revolutions in the twentieth century has been the quest for gender equality. While this gender revolution has its roots in the industrially advanced Western countries, it was bound to spread to various parts of the globe, including the Arab world, where it is something of an uphill battle.

Gender is the social construction of the biological differences that divide human beings into two categories. Stressing the social aspect of this construction implies that the differences we see between men and women, or the differences that people report and talk about, are contingent aspects of culture rather than inherent in the biology. One of the ways in which women and men differ is in their understanding of the distinction between men and women. Cross-gender misunderstandings notwithstanding, women and men combine to form a single society.

The Vision of a Muslim Family

The Arab family has undergone major changes in its formation, structure, and functions over the last fourteen centuries. Islam introduced radical changes into the pattern of family life and characteristics of pre-Islamic Arabia, generally by supporting women's rights. The family was recognized as a basic pillar in the community of believers, the umma. A man's religiosity was not complete until he was married. Marriage itself became a contractual arrangement sanctioned by God and the community. Consent of both parties to the marriage was made more explicit; adult women had an equal right of choice. If the woman was under age, it was her guardian's duty to confirm the compatibility of the male suitor on behalf of the young girl. The mahr or sadaq became explicitly the right of the woman and not that of her father or male kin. Women were entitled to a share in the inheritance defined as half that of the brother. They equally were entitled to own property and have their own business.

Islam, through the Qur'an and the Sunna (sayings of the Prophet Muhammad), stipulates the rights and obligations of husband, wife, and children. The interrelatedness of the three roles is reflected in their complementarity: the obligations of each role are automatically the rights of the other two roles. Thus the husband's obligations include providing for the family, discipline of the children, and fidelity to his wife. The wife's obligations include obedience, respect, and fidelity to her husband in addition to care for children and the household. Children receive nourishment, clothing, shelter, protection, and education from their parents. They are expected to obey, respect, show compassion, and take care of their parents in old age.

The rights and obligations of marriage are also stipulated. Polygamy is permitted, but restricted and organized. The adult male is allowed to marry up to four wives, but stringent conditions are attached to this privilege, e.g., material ability to support and moral ability to treat all wives fairly and equally. Dissolving marriage by divorce remains very much in the hands of the husband. It is obvious that Islam meant to make divorce, in the words of the Prophet, "the most hateful privilege granted by God." Thus Islam stipulates remedial steps before allowing divorce. Meanwhile, a woman could theoretically have an equal right to divorce, if she stipulates that in the marriage contract at the outset. This practice is called having the 'isma in the wife's hand. However, many women do not know about this option, and many hesitate to use it even when they are informed about it.

Divorce places certain obligations on both men and women. The husband has to pay his divorced wife a delayed installment of the mahr, an alimony, and has to support all the children living with their mother, including those born within ten months of the divorce. The divorced wife is obliged to remain unmarried for a period of about three months to ensure there is no pregnancy from the divorced husband, and to take good care of the children in her custody until they no longer need a mother's care.

Marriage and the family as envisioned by Islam may not be the most egalitarian pattern by the standards of the twentieth or the twenty-first century. But more than a millennium ago, the vision was no doubt far more progressive than what had prevailed immediately before Islam. Whatever its shortcomings, even this vision was not adhered to in spirit for very long.

The Reality of the Arab Family: Patriarchy

If Islam's vision of marriage and family was ever adhered to, such adherence was probably only during the lives of the Prophet Muhammad and the Guided Caliphs during the first century of Islam (the seventh century C.E.). After that a widening gap between vision and reality began to emerge. The form and the ritual, to be sure, have persisted, while the spirit of relative equality and the rights and status of women have gradually eroded. Between the ninth and the nineteenth centuries, the traditional Arab family displayed many of the features generally found in other complex traditional societies. This is not to suggest that Islam's impact on the family diminished, but rather that a synthesis of pre-Islamic, Islamic, and post-Islamic elements evolved.

What emerged was essentially a partriarchal extended family ritualistically governed by Islamic dicta, but actually functioning according to other current social forces at work. Power and authority in this traditional Arab family were distributed along two axes—age and sex. As a rule, males had more power than females, and older members had more power than younger members of the household. Men had all the rights stipulated for them by Islam but they often ignored many of the obligations. Women were compelled to observe all the obligations but were rarely allowed to exercise the rights articulated in the vision. Men abused some of their rights—especially with regard to divorce and polygamy. While most married males were monogamous, those who were polygamous rarely observed the conditions regulating the privilege of marrying more than one wife. While a minority resorted to divorce, those who did rarely attempted the remedial steps built into the vision.

The external solidarity of the traditional Arab family was forged by strict authority, hierarchy, dependency, and repression. These characteristics, to be sure, were common to other social institutions in Arab society and were so deeply internalized as to be taken for granted by family members. In this sense the family embodied and sustained the structure of traditional Arab society.

The internalization of traditional family values, norms, and rules of conduct relied on physical and/or psychological punishment. To behave properly meant to learn to suppress individual impulses. Since individuals had to take the clues of proper behavior from traditional authority and heritage, and since they were not allowed to choose or judge outside that framework, independent thinking and analytical ability remained undeveloped, if not deliberately stunted. Indeed, the socialization process over-emphasized rote learning and memorizing.

Discussion of sex in the traditional family was forbidden, veiled in silence and secrecy. In theory sex was strictly confined to marriage, and a great premium was placed on sexual honor. Girls learned very early in life that such honor, symbolized by virginity, was a matter of life or death. Any shame brought by the slightest violation of sexual honor was a collective shame for the entire kinship group. Violent reaction, therefore, was merciless and collectively sanctioned. Men, however, had more liberties, not only to talk to each other about sex, but occasionally—if discretely—to practice it out of wedlock.

These features, offered here as generalizations, should not suggest that a uniformity without exception existed all over the Arab world. Nor should it leave the reader with a bleak image of the traditional Arab family. We should not judge it by today's "modern" standards. Members of the traditional Arab family in those centuries had no other frame of reference. Furthermore, the extended patriarchal family provided its members with a multitude of advantages. They never had to face the world alone; they were socially and economically secure. Even the strict sexual codes had corresponding arrangements to ensure their observance, e.g., early marriage and minimizing interaction between unmarried people of opposite sexes.

The traditional Arab family, as outlined above, hardly exists in Arab society today. Along with other social institutions, the Arab family has been undergoing steady transformation for the past century and a half, as part of the broader process of social change. The changes first occurred in those parts of the Arab world, such as Egypt and the Levant, that were contacted and penetrated by the West in the early nineteenth century. Even here, the family was the social institution that held out longest in resisting change. This is reflected in the attitudes toward modern education for girls, which was avoided for at least half a century after it was granted to males. However, women's education has now been present in some Arab countries for over a century. Already by the 1970s in countries like Egypt, Iraq, Tunisia, and Syria, as much as 40 percent of the enrollment in the public education systems was female. On the university level, the percentage in Egypt and Iraq exceeded 30 percent. Other Arab countries, especially of the southern tier, have been moving in the same direction.

These impressive educational attainments did not result in an automatic entry by women into gainful employment. This has been hard to accomplish, not for lack of desire or ability on the part of women, but as a result of deeply rooted traditional values. Thus, despite their rising percentage in schools, women's participation in the labor force has lagged markedly behind. In Egypt, Tunisia, and Iraq in 1995 such participation was around 15 percent, and rising, especially in public and governmental sectors. The law in Algeria, Tunisia, Egypt, Syria, Iraq, Jordan, and Yemen treats women equally in employment as far as state jobs are concerned. Political rights, i.e., voting and running for public office, have also been granted in most of these countries. However, women, and for that matter most men, have not taken full advantage of such civil and political rights.

The changing conditions of women in Arab society have affected the whole contemporary family institution. In urban areas, marriage is becoming less arranged and more based on individual "romantic" selection—though parental approval and blessing are still eagerly sought. The urban family itself is becoming an "Arab" version of the nuclear family. Like its Western counterpart it consists of husband, wife, and children, but with the provision that the children are expected to live with their parents until they get married if they work in the same community. In rural and desert communities, the extended family is more common than in the cities.

The contemporary urban family is reluctantly, but steadily, moving in the direction of egalitarianism. With more and more wives working and financially contributing to the household, they are increasingly gaining implicit, and sometimes explicit, rights in areas formerly considered a man's preserve. In the public sphere, the wife may still appear to concede all decision-making to the husband, but in the private sphere decisions are increasingly shared (see the article by Fargues in Section Two).

To appreciate the magnitude of the changes in the urban family, we must remember that the urban population in the Arab world today represents about 50 percent of the total. These changes, however, are neither uniform across social classes, nor do they mean that several persistent features of the traditional Arab family have been eliminated. While women are gaining more rights, they also feel an acute sense of frustration. Women are still expected to carry out many of the obligations of the traditional roles along with whatever modern roles they may be occupying. Arab women may have as much work to do outside the home as the man, but they are still expected to take primary responsibility for all domestic chores, childbearing, and child raising. They are still expected to abstain from interaction with men outside the kinship group. While there may be a measure of freedom of choice in selecting one's mate, the pressure to conform to family wishes is still tremendous.

Thus the Arab family today is neither totally traditional nor totally modern in the Western sense; it is in a state of transition, in structure, functions, and values. Women epitomize this transition. But a state of transition is one of flux and incongruency. Such a state may be moving toward a new equilibrium, but until that happens, individuals are torn by internal conflicts, competing obligations, and contradictory expectations. There are great imbalances between duties and rights, aspirations and attainments, espoused values and actual behavior. In Arab society today, women and to a lesser extent youth, are at the very heart of these imbalances. They, more than any other group in society, pay the physical, emotional, and social price of transition. By focusing on them we may see the dilemma, the pain, and the unfolding drama, not only of the Arab family but of the entire Arab society as well.

The contemporary Arab family is in a state of transition, in another sense—
it is caught between the vision of Islam and the uneven pattern of change in the
environmental and structural forces in the Arab world. For in the name of Islam,
some emerging movements are trying to reverse women's educational, occupational, and political gains. There are persistent attempts to "re-veil" women in
more than the literal sense of modesty. There is still a need to free men, women,
and family life from the oppressive patterns of the past or its resurrection so that
the creative forces inherent in them can be released to the benefit of the development of Arab society.

The selections which follow illustrate the spectrum of the drama engulfing
the Arab family as it copes with the process of change in the wider society or in
the world at large. These selections do not exhaust all that can be noted in the
changing Arab family. Among these, for example, is the increasing "feminization" of the Arab family as a result of male migration to urban areas in the same
country, neighboring Arab countries, or to the West. The men often leave their
wives and children behind temporarily or for extended periods of time, so that
the wives find themselves increasingly in charge of many things previously
attended to by men. While finding this pattern stressful at least initially, many
Arab women have developed a sense of efficacy, autonomy, and independence.
In the early 1990s, as many husbands returned home and tried to recoup their
traditional power in the family, gender conflicts erupted.

Although the broader changes in the Arab world have favored the nuclear
family, the extended family still plays a role outside the household. This is visible in the preference for related nuclear family households to reside near one
another, and to maintain fairly intense contact. In cities like Cairo, a typical pattern at present is to build a multi-story or multi-apartment building with various
married kin, each occupying their independent apartment. This novel combination gives the adults many of the positive features of modern nuclear family and
gives the children many of the positive features of the traditional extended family. Relatives live as neighbors, but in economically independent households.

Other changes not sufficiently treated in the following selections are issues
raised during the International Conference of Population and Development
(ICPD) hosted in Cairo in 1994, and the fourth World Conference on Women,
hosted in Beijing in 1995. Some of these issues became polemical and were
passionately debated in the Arab world. Among them were female circumcision or female genital mutilation (FGM),[1] equality and women's freedom of
choice of a husband, family size, education, work, and a divorce. Curiously
enough, conservative forces from outside the Arab world—such as the
Vatican—tried to strike alliances with like-minded forces in the Arab world and
Muslim worlds to shape the international agenda on these and other related
issues. Governments in the region and in these international conferences
attempted to compromise. Thus instead of asserting outright gender "equality"

in political, civil, and economic matters (e.g., inheritance), the concept of "equity" was adopted.

Arab women in several Arab countries have fought a "trench war" for political and civil equality. Three examples here may suffice. First is that of Egyptian women who won the right to vote and run for political office in 1956. But their numbers in elected councils remained less than 3 percent. Twenty years later, and with the backing of the then First Lady of Egypt, Mrs. Jihan Sadat, a law was passed stipulating the election of a minimum of 30 women deputies to the People's Assembly. The Egyptian constitution had stipulated similar provision for peasants and workers in the early 1960s (a minimum of 50 percent of the seats must go to these two categories). While these provisions have repeatedly been criticized, especially since the mid-1970s, they were never contested in court. In contrast, the 1978 provision reserving 30 seats for women was vehemently challenged by some men who succeeded in obtaining a constitutional court ruling canceling it in 1986. The number of women elected declined.

The second example is from Saudi Arabia, where both sexes are yet to have any political rights at all. Yet men have many civil and socioeconomic rights which Saudi women do not yet have, among which is the right to drive a car. During the Gulf crisis of 1990–91, the Iraqi invasion of Kuwait compelled neighboring Saudi Arabia to seek defensive-preventive military help. Among the countries heeding the Saudi plea was the United States, whose armed forces do not discriminate on a gender basis. Observing hundreds of American female soldiers driving all types of vehicles on their country's soil, a group of Saudi women dared to break the ban on their own driving through a public show. They were immediately arrested, those working were dismissed from their jobs, and all were banned from traveling abroad for at least three years.

The third example is from Kuwait. When Saddam Hussein's Iraqi military forces invaded Kuwait on August 2, 1990, about one half of the Kuwaiti population was already vacationing abroad. The other half steadfastly resisted the occupation. Kuwaiti women in their own country were reported to have been the most gallant in the resistance. Their refusal to leave the country encouraged male relatives to stay as well, and prompted others to secretly make their way back into the country, to join the resistance. Kuwaiti women were arrested, tortured, raped, and killed. In the absence of a Kuwaiti state, women were the ones who organized much of the civilian daily life under occupation. From the food cooperatives and mosques, Kuwaiti women distributed food, clothes, medical, educational, informational, and other social services. Kuwaiti men inside and outside the country were both impressed and full of gratitude to the women. Many demanded that upon liberating the country, Kuwaiti women must be granted full civil and political rights. Kuwait was ultimately liberated (February 1991), and two parliamentary elections were held, in 1992 and 1996. Kuwaiti women still do not have the right of equal political participation. Many Kuwaiti men seem to have forgotten their own promises of political equality to their women, or simply forgot the much-hailed sacrifices of these women during occupation (see the article by Longva in Section Five).

In This Section

The articles in this section deal in various ways with the issues of gender, male–female relations, family and kinship. Seteney Shami and Lucine Taminian start by reminding us of the importance of children in Arab society. They focus on the social organization of child care in an Amman slum area inhabited by Palestinians who are integrated into Jordanian society. They show the importance of a wide set of relations among families in raising children, as different adults take on responsibility for children at different times. The children themselves often also form the link between different households, and so inspire relations outside their own households. That adults do not always agree on how to raise children is another story. The authors report that although the men earn the money, it is managed on a day-to-day basis by the women, and thus note that among this group of urban poor, women have considerable authority in household management.

Using the extended example of the Moroccan migrant worker, Haddou, David McMurray examines a different set of family relations, and this time from a male point of view. Haddou's effort to establish and maintain his family relations from a distance highlights not only gender but also the differences in generation and in social class. The sincere and difficult strivings of Haddou contrast with the image of the male as effortlessly dominant.

On the basis of fieldwork in a small Moroccan working class town, Susan Davis examines the changing relations between adolescent boys and girls. As in much of the rest of the Arab world, public norms discourage most forms of contact between unrelated boys and girls. Yet, not surprisingly, the young people find a way. The focus of Davis's article is on the feelings and strategies of the adolescents in this town as they contemplate the various paths of schooling, work, and marriage, and seek ways to place themselves in society. Marriage is important to the girls and their families, perhaps more so than to the boys; there is a double standard in evaluating behavior.

Suad Joseph shifts the gender focus from boy–girl to brother–sister. Using material from the heterogeneous Beirut working-class neighborhood known as Camp Trad, part of the larger area of Borj Hammoud, Joseph examines the contexts in which male superiority (patriarchy) is reaffirmed. The "love" that should exist between a brother and a sister is only part of a wider complex of ideas that includes the power of the male over the female. Joseph builds her analysis around three levels: the psychodynamic, the social structural, and the cultural. Norms exist at the cultural level, are enacted with respect to the particular social structural setting of the individual family (for instance, the presence or absence of a strong father), and result in a pattern of interpersonal relations among cross-siblings in which the individuals are substantially involved with one another (what Joseph calls "connectivity").

The article by Rhoda Kanaaneh represents a form of experimental writing in anthropology. The author places herself very much in the text, and uses her own position as a research tool to unlock the meaning of the folk tale that is at the heart of the piece. The analysis is a form of deconstruction, seeking the hidden implications of the tale. The issue is what it means to be female, and by implication, male, in contemporary Arab society, specifically in Palestine. Gender identity and national identity crosscut each other. As in Joseph's argument, the creation of the female self is understood as an outcome of its encounter with the male self. Kanaaneh underlines the passivity of the female; women's resistance to this pattern is the alternative way of creating a sense of self.

Notes

1   In the Arab world, FGM is found in the Nile valley countries of Egypt and Sudan, and in the Horn of Africa (Djibouti and Somalia). In Egypt it is practised by both Muslims and Christians, with a frequency rate of 95 percent or more acording to a 1995 survey. With the possible exception of the southern Arabian peninsula, it is unknown in the rest of the Arab world.

9

Children of Amman: Childhood and Child Care in Squatter Areas of Amman, Jordan

Seteney Shami and Lucine Taminian

The experience of childhood is as yet understudied in the Middle East. By focusing upon the social environment of children in a squatter area of Amman, this essay addresses some of the aspects that determine the quality of life for children, particularly the impact of the household and kin-group on the one hand, and the residential community on the other.

Within the household, the position and role of women and their ability to make decisions concerning their childbearing and child-rearing behavior varies in accordance with the household structure and composition. This in turn depends upon the stage of the household in the developmental cycle. The household structure also determines the amount of help upon which a childbearing woman can depend. The kin-group and community are also a resource in that reciprocal relations between households provide help and information concerning reproduction and child care. Besides this, the community sets the general expectations for behavior, especially as it affects childbearing and child rearing. However, these expectations are articulated differently in individual households. Although differences in income and education do affect child care and may explain some variations, in this community, household and kin-group structure plays the determining role.

The Setting of the Study

The Wadi is a squatter slum area in the heart of Amman. Its inhabitants are mainly Palestinian refugees who, for a variety of reasons, were unable or unwilling to live in refugee camps. The area was first settled after 1948, but more than half the families moved in after 1967. A 1980 survey of the area shows a community composed of 284 households, with the average size of a household being 6.58 and a density of 3.54 persons per room. The average

From Elizabeth Warnock Fernea, ed., *Children in the Muslim Middle East* (Austin: University of Texas Press, 1995), pp. 68–76. Reprinted by permission. Seteney Shami is a Jordanian anthropologist working at the Cairo office of the Population Council. She formerly taught at Yarmouk University. Lucine Taminian, also from Jordan, is a graduate student in anthropology at the University of Michigan, Ann Arbor, Michigan.

income for the household was 90 Jordanian dinars per month, earned by one or possibly two members of the household. (At the time of the research [1985], 1 Jordanian dinar equaled approximately 3 U.S. dollars. Since then the dinar has been devalued to equal about 1.4 U.S. dollars.) Work was mostly in small-scale workshops, the construction industry, and low-level government employment (Urban Development Department 1980). Services such as water, electricity, and sewage were extended only gradually into the community after 1969 and the area is still largely dependent upon services provided in the camp by the United Nations Relief and Works Agency, such as schools and clinics. (The UNRWA was created to deal with the Palestinian refugee problem. It administers refugee camps and distributes aid as well as providing primary health care, schooling, and technical training for registered refugees.)

Socially the Wadi is a stable community with a small amount of in- and out-migration (Urban Development Department 1980). The most important networks are based on kinship and extend to the adjacent neighborhoods, into the refugee camp, and beyond. In addition, the Wadi and its inhabitants, similar to squatter areas elsewhere in the world, are fully integrated economically and politically into the urban dynamics of the city (Lomnitz 1977, Perlman 1976, Velez-Ibanez 1983). The network of relationships within the Wadi are thus determined by kinship and secondarily by physical proximity. To a certain extent, the Wadi during the daytime is an extension of the domestic sphere of the courtyard. It is a world of women and children while men spend their days at work and then sit in coffeehouses or shops owned by their friends up on the main street. On Fridays and holidays, men and children stroll in the alleys while women are restricted to their houses.

Physically the Wadi is subdivided into two major parts by the road which bisects it roughly from southeast to northwest. The heavy traffic on the road deters easy communication between the two parts and prevents children from going back and forth. Another defining feature of the settlement is the wide ditch (the seil) that runs through it carrying wastewater from the refugee camp up the hill. Winter rains cause the seil to flood, sometimes forcing the people living alongside it to evacuate their houses for some days. In particularly bad winters, children have been drowned in the seil.

Communal areas consist of a rocky area or a few trees by the seil providing a space for women to sit together over their embroidery. A communal clothesline by the side of the road serves the nearby households. The steep sides of the Wadi and the seil are a favorite playground where the children find wooden boxes, rusty tins, and wires to create toys. The seil is also where wastewater is thrown out, rubbish is burnt, and a few households keep goats and sheep during the daytime.

During our eighteen months of fieldwork in the Wadi we came to know twenty-one households intimately. Of these households, at the beginning of the study, ten were single-family households (SFH: father-mother-children), two were extended-family households (EFH: father-mother-children-parent or sibling(s) of father), seven were multiple-family households (MFH: two or more simple or extended families), and two were what we came to call multiple-household dwellings (MHD) (see Shami and Taminian 1990).

Households and Mutual Aid Units

The authority to make decisions in the household is first of all divided between men and women. The recognized head of the household is the father as long as he is still working and in good health. The working sons, especially those who are married, also have a measure of authority in the household. However, the domain of male authority is that which determines the general contours of the life of the household: the income, the place of residence, the relationship with other heads of households within the kinship group. Within these constraints the women make the intricate decisions: how the income is spent, the living conditions, and the daily interaction with kinsfolk. Thus while men may set the general policy of the family for marriage and childbearing, it is the women who will make such expectations succeed or fail. A father may express the desire to have his son marry his brother's daughter, but it is the mother who will either arrange the marriage or, instead, arrange for the son to marry his brother's daughter. As for child care, it is women who decide upon nutrition and general care and treatment for illness. Men's role in child care is restricted to major emergencies and to a few hours in the evening when the children are already fed and are expected to look clean and be obedient.

The authority within the women's domain usually falls to the oldest woman, the mother or the mother-in-law, unless she is too old or inactive; however, other women in the household also have some share in this authority. The older unmarried daughters eventually share in their mother's authority vis-à-vis the other children, even vis-à-vis the father/husband (see Shami 1985). The other contender for authority is the daughter-in-law.

A daughter-in-law gains status and thus authority in the family, and among her husband's kin in general, through the financial resources she controls, the number of her children, and the quality of her relationship with her husband. A woman's financial resources consist of her portion of the bride-price, mostly in the form of gold jewelry or money presented to her by her own family, and especially her brothers, on special occasions, and the spending money given to her by her husband. However, such resources do not always guarantee status. In some cases, especially in MFH, there is pressure on the daughter-in-law to sell her gold to help the family through some crisis or another. In such cases, if her own family does not come to her support, the young wife may find herself quite powerless. Others, with the help of their families, may use their resources to help the husband buy or rent a separate dwelling and thus gain independence from their in-laws.

Most men in the Wadi turn over their entire wages, except for a small amount of "cigarette money," to their wives or to their mothers. This money is an indication of a woman's authority in the household and the measure of her control over it. It also means that it is up to the woman to make the money last the month and to provide for the food, the necessities, and the emergencies.

Running a large household on a small amount of money is a time-consuming and difficult matter. Women in different households have to rely upon each other for help in housework, shopping, and child care; for aid in financial emergencies; and for information on where the cheapest vegetables or the cheapest doctors are to be found. Households that reciprocate daily in such matters may be said to form "mutual aid units." Such units are generally based on kinship, yet they are formed selectively. That is, not all households related by kinship will form one unit. Rather, from all the possible combinations, one or two units will emerge. The prevalent pattern is that units tend to be formed between sisters-in-law, between husband's sister and brother's wife. These mutual aid units are formed and maintained by women, irrespective of the quality of the relationship between the male heads of these households.

Reciprocity within the units flows from women to women and children to children. In addition there are adult-child relations as in child care and in the services that children perform for women, such as shopping and running errands and carrying messages. Thus children play as important a role in the maintenance and perpetuation of these units as the women.

Childbearing

Children are seen as necessary in consolidating a marriage as well as in ensuring the continuity of a family. The general expectations concerning childbearing are conveyed by the kin group of the husband and of the wife, as well as by the community at large. A woman fulfills these expectations by having four to five children, at least two being males, at a fairly rapid pace. Having thus proven her ability in bearing children through her fertility and general good health, a woman gains security and status in her husband's household.

Factors encouraging continued childbearing vary according to the woman's status in the household. In a single-family household a woman has enough independence to make her own decisions for she can withstand pressure from kin and community. However, in a multifamily household or an extended-family household she has to deal with direct pressure and competition from other members of the household. If her decision-making powers are limited, then she may seek to gain authority within the household by having a large number of children and, at the same time, urge her husband to set up an independent household.

Child Rearing

In an EFH or MFH, the mother-in-law plays a major role in child care, and especially during the first few years of her daughter-in-law's presence in the household. Since the mother-in-law runs the household and controls the financial resources, she decides on what the children will be fed and how they will be treated for illness and whether a doctor is necessary or not. Much of the conflict between mother and daughter-in-law stems from the attempts of the latter to make her own decisions concerning her children.

The larger the household the less control a mother has over her children. Even a woman who has authority in the household cannot, and does not, control the behavior of all the members of the household. Thus the older children, the aunts, and the uncles all feed, play with, and discipline the younger members of the household. All members of the household express their opinions on child health and the treatment of illness and all are listened to.

A mother cannot set rules for her children that run contrary to the rhythm of life in the household. Some of the younger women, and especially those with a high level of education (beyond secondary school), do express their dissatisfaction with the behavior of the children in their household and criticize their mother-in-law's lack of discipline. However, they do little to enforce their own ideas. This is true also of daughters-in-law who work outside the household and, by having their own income, are to some measure independent and have authority within the household. However, they cannot afford to be too critical since their living in the same house means that they depend completely on their in-laws for child care.

Case Study: Um Farid al-Saadi

For two and a half years after her marriage, Um Farid lived with her mother-in-law, a paternal aunt of hers. During that time her mother-in-law was in full charge of running the house. She let Um Farid do the "unimportant" tasks of cleaning and washing. Um Farid did not mind this because she felt that it was her mother-in-law's house in the first place. Um Farid did not want to challenge her authority by interfering or doing the important tasks.

Um Farid believed that her mother-in-law was far more knowledgeable than she in matters concerning child care. So when her first baby was born she let her mother-in-law make all the decisions concerning his health and feeding. Her mother-in-law decided that Um Farid should only breast-feed Farid and give him no supplementary food. Um Farid stopped breast-feeding Farid when she got pregnant again. He was three months old and Um Farid wanted to give him baby milk formula. But her mother-in-law insisted that Farid should have only solid food. When he was sick her mother-in-law treated him by massaging him with olive oil. When he was teething she rubbed his gums with her fingers to make the teeth come out faster, and this caused an infection, but he was not taken to the doctor till his mouth became inflamed. Um Farid never doubted the wisdom of her mother-in-law's knowledge, yet she mentions that Farid was more often sick than any of her later babies, one of whom was born shortly before her mother-in-law's death and two after her death.

Um Farid's mother-in-law's death was sudden and Um Farid found herself in a very difficult situation: she had to run the house, take care of her children, and take care of the visitors who came from outside the country for the funeral and stayed with her for weeks. All of a sudden Um Farid found herself in a position of decision making, a position she had never had before. She believed that she could not run her house nor take care of her children by herself. Her husband was not sympathetic; he always reminded her of his mother's efficiency in running the house.

It was at this time that Um Farid sought the help of her neighbors, and Karima, who was ten at the time, began to help Um Farid with shopping and taking care of the children. Once Um Farid got the help she needed she began to calm down and regain confidence. She rearranged the furniture completely, got rid of her mother-in-law's clothes and bed, and thus gained control of her house. Um Farid's new independence caused great changes in her relationship with her husband's kin group. However, in terms of children she continued to follow her mother-in-law's practices in general. Although she does take the children to the doctor more often, she only does so when they are seriously ill. As the number of Um Farid's children increased, she came to rely more and more upon Karima in all aspects including child care.

Young Girls as Child-Rearers

Young girls play a major role in child rearing. This may start at an extremely young age with a four-year-old girl being told to carry her baby sibling and sit with him in the sun. This task is not confined only to little girls, but is part of the role preschool children of both sexes play in these households. Little boys and girls run errands, are sent to borrow money from relatives, and are called in from playing in the street to hold the baby and give it its bottle. Children may also perform these services for neighbors and relatives who live close by.

Once the child enters school his or her tasks decrease somewhat, except for the eldest girl, who will start playing an active role in housework around the age of eight. She will also be left alone in charge of all her brothers and sisters when the mother has to go out. However, the significant role of a girl in child rearing begins at the age of fourteen or so, especially if she leaves school around this age. Thus the extent to which a young girl incorporates housework and child rearing into her life depends on many factors such as her age, her birth order among her siblings, and whether she has left school.

During adolescence, the young girl's chores and errands are transformed into active responsibilities. The eldest daughter assumes these tasks first, unless she is still at school while a younger sister has left school. These tasks include baking bread, preparing certain meals, and the almost daily chore of washing clothes. The mother may gradually hand over these tasks to her daughter completely but often retains control of cooking the main meal, which requires her special touch.

A child born at this time to the mother often becomes this young girl's charge. This is especially true if the mother experiences some kind of crisis at, or soon after, the arrival of the newly born. Elder children are regarded as more valuable than the newly born, whose survival is, after all, still a matter of doubt. A mother's crisis is often the reason to start bottle-feeding the baby and leaving its care to the elder sister.

But even without a crisis, the mother's busy life and daily absences from home (for shopping etc.) are reason enough for the child to be gradually "adopted" by the older sister. A situation may even develop where each one of the adolescent daughters in the household is in charge of a younger sibling. While the eldest sister will eventually be in charge of supervising the meals, baths, and studies of all her younger siblings, her role in child rearing is the total bonding with one infant. The child grows up to call its elder sister "mother," sometimes "my young mother" as opposed to "my old mother." The "young mother" is responsible for feeding, bathing, clothing the child, and even for taking it to the doctor when sick. In addition, the child sleeps next to its young mother at night. The child is later subjected to much teasing and questioning about whom he loves more: his young mother or his old mother. At the same time, the child experiences a great deal more love and care than his old mother alone can afford to give him.

Conclusion

The children of the Wadi lead active lives. Since the alleys are too narrow for cars, children are granted a great deal of mobility and even infants crawl in and out of courtyards as they will. Thus children move constantly back and forth between their house and other households in the community. This movement is not random but structured by kinship and mutual-aid relationships maintained by the mother. Children eat, sleep, and play freely in these mutual-aid households and are often given money to go out and buy what they wish from the several small shops scattered throughout the Wadi. Moreover, children accompany their mothers everywhere. Tiny babies are taken to weddings where they are handed from one person to another the whole evening. Whenever a mother leaves the house—whether to do shopping, to go visiting, or to see the doctor—

she takes at least one of her children with her as a sign that she is a married woman going on a necessary errand. Unmarried girls will take their younger siblings for much the same reason of chaperoning. Little boys often are conscious of this role and carry it out very seriously.

In this way, the children of the Wadi grow up in a rich and varied environment of social relations. They are full members of the intertwined social units within which they fulfill certain functions. In terms of communications, children are the prime carriers of messages and gossip and have the advantage of providing the adults with the possibility of denial if necessary. They also cement reciprocal obligations since they are the object of requests for help and, when a little older, the providers of help. With these activities, children establish their own relations with other children and with adults outside their immediate family. They also play an important economic role in the home by peddling home-made goods, investigating the best prices in the vegetable market, and enabling the mother to maximize scarce resources (Shami and Taminian 1990). In addition, children are obviously the means for the reproduction of these social units. Children secure the continuity of marriage and family ties. Through children, mothers obtain security in their youth and status in their prime. Through children, fathers obtain status in their youth and security when elderly. Children are both objects and actors in the complex, and often competitive, relationships embodied in kinship and community. Equally, they are sources of amusement, affection, and pride. Just as the children of the Wadi often hold center stage in the lives of their families, so the centrality of children should be recognized in the ethnographic text.

Acknowledgments

This study was made possible by a grant from the International Development Research Center of Canada. The anthropological study conducted in 1984–1985 was one component of the Amman Follow-up Health and Population Assessment project, codirected by Dr. Leila Bisharat and Dr. Seteney Shami and conducted under the auspices of the Urban Development Department— Municipality of Amman.

References

Laslett, Peter. 1972–1978. Household and Family in Past Time. London: Cambridge University Press.

Lomnitz, L. 1977. Networks and Marginality: Life in a Mexican Shantytown. New York: Academic Press.

Perlman, J. 1976. The Myth of Marginality: Urban Poverty and Politics in Rio de Janeiro. Berkeley: University of California Press.

Shami, Seteney. 1985. "Maternal Practices in Child Care in an Urban Area." A paper presented to the Workshop on Girls in the Middle East and North Africa, UNICEF, Amman (March).

Shami, Seteney, and Lucine Taminian. 1990. "Women's Participation in the Jordanian Labor Force: A Comparison of Urban and Rural Patterns." In S. Shami et al., Women in Arab Society: Work Patterns and Gender Relations in Egypt, Jordan, and Sudan (London: Berg/Unesco), pp. 1–86.

Urban Development Department. 1980. Summary Table of Comprehensive Social-Physical Survey. Amman.

Velez-Ibanez, Carlos. 1983. Rituals of Marginality: Politics, Process, and Cultural Change in Urban Central Mexico. Berkeley: University of California Press.

10

Haddou: A Moroccan Migrant Worker

David McMurray

David McMurray's portrait of Haddou, a Moroccan migrant, presents us with yet another facet of the new Middle East: Arab labor migration to Western Europe. The presence of ever greater numbers of Arab workers in the European economy is a sign of the internationalization of labor (as is the presence of Mexicans and Hispanics in the United States) and the globalization of the world economy. The sources of this migration are complex; its consequences for the future of relations between Europe and the Middle East are considerable.

As in the United States, where World War II hastened the dissolution of the black peasantry in the South and led to the massive civil rights movement of the 1960s, the end of the war brought momentous changes for North Africa. One result, to be schematic, was the independence movement of the 1950s and 1960s. A second was a large-scale peasant migration to the cities not just of North Africa but increasingly of Western Europe as well.

As part of the latter trend Haddou, a Moroccan Berber from the region around Nador, left his home in northern Morocco in the 1960s and voluntarily expatriated himself to seek work. By this time migrants from North Africa had already established a beachhead for themselves in Western Europe, where they did jobs that no Europeans would do anymore. Initially, migration was a seasonal phenomenon. But by the late 1970s and 1980s it had led to the emergence of large permanent communities of migrants—with an increasingly problematic insertion into European society. The rhythms of Haddou's life largely follow this script, though not without complications.

On one level, Haddou's biography can be read as a story of economic success. We can trace his ascent from his early low-paying jobs as a young man in northern Morocco to positions of growing income and security in France and Germany. By careful planning and much hard work, he had achieved his original goal: to construct an imposing home in which he could live in his old age, surrounded by his married sons and their families.

Yet this reading contrasts with Haddou's own sense of his life. Despite a measure of worldly success he has not, for all that, achieved happiness. His

From Edmund Burke, ed., *Struggle and Survival in the Modern Middle East* (Berkeley: University of California Press, 1993), pp. 377–93. Reprinted by permission. David McMurray teaches anthropology at Oregon State University, Corvallis, Oregon.

years of hard work and voluntary deprivation have gone for naught, and he finds himself in his fifties alienated from his family, his authority not respected. As far as his children (whom he sees only one month out of a year) are concerned, his primary role is to bankroll their desires for the latest consumer items. Even his eldest son, Driss, who now also works in Europe, is a disappointment to him. Instead of sending monthly remittances to the family, as the Moroccan family-centered ethos requires, Driss spends his income on himself and his Dutch girl-friend.

By the mid-1980s, when this essay was written, Haddou was no longer content with an annual migration to his village of origin. The years of deprivation and loneliness had taken their toll, his estrangement from his children had chilled his welcome. He had begun to establish himself and his wife, Thraithmas, in Dusseldorf. While it is unclear what he eventually decided, one possibility was that he would gradually sever his ties with Morocco and make his home in Germany. If so, he would join the increasing numbers of Turks, West Africans, Yugoslavs, and other recent migrants who have put down roots in the new multiethnic Europe. —*Ed.*

Haddou sat on the bed, thumbing through his passport. It was full of entry and exit stamps from his many trips between his family in Morocco and his job in Dusseldorf, Germany. As the pages flipped he stopped again to look at the visa he had received from the German government just that afternoon. He had to smile, for this newest visa guaranteed him a court hearing before any deportation measures could be taken against him. It made him feel relaxed. He did not need to fear every time the boss yelled at him or every time the border guards interrogated him. He had had very few close calls over the years, but you could never be too careful. He thought of that time when while riding his bicycle to work the cops stopped him, claiming he had run a red light. They said to him, "Hey, where do you think you are, Turkey? Here in Germany we obey the law. Do that again and you'll be riding that bike back in Istanbul!" Haddou was upset that they assumed he was a Turk. It further irritated him that they assumed he disobeyed the law when in fact he bent over backwards to keep his nose clean. With the new visa he would not have to jump every time a police car passed him.

He looked up at the railway calendar on the opposite wall next to his television set. He could not make out the date exactly, for now, at fifty, his eyes were going bad. He put it up mainly for decoration anyway. The calendars were free, given out at the train yard where he worked. He often thought of getting glasses but did not, because he suspected that the railway company might consider him unfit to continue working. His job consisted essentially of copying down the numbers of each boxcar on each train as it came into Dusseldorf. So if he was having trouble seeing and they found out about it, well . . . .

Haddou's thoughts always drifted back to Morocco whenever he found himself alone in his railroad company apartment. Thinking about the visa this time set him to remembering what his life had been like before he started migrating to Europe.

As far back as Haddou could remember he had worked. Everyone did. Everyone except his oldest brother, that is. Haddou's father determined that his four younger sons would work and pool their wages so that the eldest would be able to attend school in Fez. Even Haddou's father pitched in. He supplemented the produce from their small farm with wages earned in Algeria. Every year in early May Haddou's father left for Oran province in Algeria to work the harvest on the farms of the French *colons* (settlers). He would then hurry back to harvest his own barley crop the month after.

Haddou's first job was as a ticket taker on the local bus route between Kariat Arkman, a small town near his *char*, or lineage settlement, and Villa Nador, the Spanish provincial capital of the whole region. He got the job during the great drought of 1944–45, when he was only seven years old. Prior to that he had worked on the family farm, watching the goats or helping with the planting and harvesting. The drought proved to be so bad, however, that his father was forced to sell the goats—and that was after the goats had eaten what little of the barley actually sprouted that year.

The whole of northern Morocco was under Spanish protectorate control from 1912 until 1956, the year of Moroccan independence. Villa Nador sprang up in the late 1920s as the easternmost Spanish administrative center. Nador paled, however, in comparison with Melilla, a purely Spanish city less than fifteen miles from Nador on a peninsula jutting out into the Mediterranean. Melilla had been a Spanish garrison and trading center on the coast since the end of the fifteenth century. It exerted a stronger influence than Nador over the surrounding countryside by providing menial jobs for the local Moroccans and by consuming much of the surplus produced on farms in the area. Eventually Haddou found a job running produce into the Spanish city. Every morning throughout the early 1950s he loaded up a donkey cart with eggs or vegetables or fruit—depending on the season—and delivered them to the Melilla market.

When in his late teens, Haddou finally landed a good paying job working in Kariat Arkman in an automobile upholstery shop. Since the business was owned by a Spaniard and all of the customers were Spaniards, when the Spanish population in the region began to decline after independence, so, unfortunately, did the business. Before it closed, however, Haddou managed to save enough money to get married. That same year he and a friend from the shop decided to emigrate to Europe to look for work.

Haddou got up from his bed to make himself a cup of tea. He had a one-burner hot plate and three little teacups. While he was measuring out the tea leaves into the pot, he thought back to his first job in Europe and the very beginnings of his " dream house" idea, as he called it.

Haddou had started as an unskilled construction worker on a job in the outskirts of Paris. He lived in a shack on the site to save money. Many other North Africans lived there also. They guarded the site during the night in exchange for their room. That is how Haddou met the big bosses. Every Saturday evening after work had finished, the architect, contractor, and their cronies returned to the job site. Haddou would open the gate to let them in, after which they would enter his guard hut and pull out the cards and liquor and proceed to play poker until early in the morning. Haddou's job was to wash their cars and then wait outside and stand guard in case of trouble. Since he was a Muslim, they reasoned, he did not want to go out on the town or to play or drink with them. He could thus be trusted to stay nearby, sober and alert. He could also be trusted to guard their liquor stash during the week. They did not have to worry about his taking a nip behind their backs. They did not see the need to pay him extra for his special duties either.

One Saturday night as Haddou sat in the dark, the cars all clean and shiny, the architect came out to stretch. Haddou seized this opportunity to request once more that the architect sketch out a floor plan for Haddou's dream house. He did not know what he wanted exactly from the architect, he just knew that the man was very well educated and very talented and that whatever he designed Haddou would be proud to build. This time the architect obliged Haddou. He quickly sketched on a scrap of paper the rough design and dimensions of a floor plan.

Haddou carried that scrap with him for years, unfolding it every time he thought of his future dream house. He slowly managed to save enough from his wages to put a down payment on a small plot of land on the edge of the city of Nador. That was in the late 1960s. By 1975 he had saved enough to start construction of the house. His land no longer stood on the edge of the city. Nador had grown so much in the interim through migrants relocating their families in the city that Haddou was now starting out to build his house on one of the nicest streets in Nador.

Haddou took his architect's design to a local draftsman to be filled in. He then hired a construction foreman to round up a crew and get started. They came from the region of Ouarzazate in southern Morocco, just like most of the other construction workers in Nador. Haddou liked them because they worked hard for little money and without complaint. They had migrated in search of work just like himself.

The house rose slowly over the next decade. Each year Haddou saved enough to pay for a few months of work. The first year they laid the foundation. The second year they raised the support pillars and laid the first floor. The third year, as soon as the ground-level garage was enclosed, Haddou moved his young family in. He wanted them to start attending the city schools as soon as possible—even if that meant setting up house in the garage. He did this because his vision of the family's future included good schools and then good jobs for all of his boys. He had grown up in the countryside without benefit of education and did not want that to happen to his children.

The dream house actually contained four apartments of five rooms each, two apartments to a floor, each the mirror image of the other. When they grew up, Haddou figured, each of his boys and their respective families would get an apartment. As the house was being built, he occasionally reflected on how similar it looked to all of the other buildings in the neighborhood. This was odd because the French architect had never been to Nador and thus did not know what the houses looked like there. What Haddou found out later was that the majority of draftsmen in Nador were unlicensed and more or less trained by each other. Therefore the same three or four blueprints were reproduced with slight variation by most of them. Haddou's architect's design had been quietly but efficiently reworked by the local draftsman to conform to Nador standards.

All of this reminiscing was making Haddou homesick again. He finished his tea, put the passport back in his pocket, and reached for his coat. By the time he stepped outside his apartment in the company's housing complex it was almost dark. He walked to the phone booth on the corner, entered, closed the door, and dialed the number he had dialed countless times before. Hassan, his second son, heard the ring and picked up the phone at the other end in Nador, Morocco. "Is your mother there?"

Haddou always asked first about his wife, Thraithmas. He was crazy about her, as devoted to her now as he had been at the time of their marriage. In 1958 she had begged him not to go to work in Europe. He assured her that he would return regularly. Unfortunately, he had had to wait a long time before his first vacation. His eldest son, Driss, was already over two years old by the time Haddou initially saw him. Even now, after thirty years of marriage, Haddou and Thraithmas has spent less than three years total in each other's company.

In the beginning of his sojourn in Europe Haddou kept in touch with his family in Morocco by means of professional runners whose job it was to transfer money and messages back to Morocco. As the migrant communities grew in Europe, runners were replaced by migrants, and Haddou came to depend on fellow workers from his tribal region to help keep up contact with his family. The migrants took turns relaying greetings and gifts back and forth for each other's respective families. Those who could write sometimes used the mail, but many complained that their letters never arrived or had been opened before arrival. Moreover, the petty bureaucrats in the post office in Nador often forced the migrants' families to buy "lottery tickets" or pay some other form of bribe before receiving their letters from overseas. The postal workers, who made very little money working for the state, were jealous of the uneducated migrants and their relatively large European salaries.

They thus seized the opportunity provided by their positions to profit from the migrants.

The migrants' other option was to arrange to make a long-distance telephone call from one public telephone to another. This often proved difficult, however, for international connections took a long time in the early days, reception was bad, and the whole province had to use the same little office in Nador, which created long lines.

The first big change in means of communication came with the spread of the tape recorder, particularly the cassette recorder. The actual voices of the migrants could now be relayed to the families instead of just their secondhand salutations. A minute or minute-and-a-half conversation cost as little as the stamps on the package.

By the mid-1980s, the private telephone had become the communication medium of choice. The wait for phone installation sometimes lasted three or four years, but the freedom it provided from theft, censorship, waiting in line, and general worry was worth it. Most importantly—from Haddou's point of view—the telephone reinstated the migrant as master of the house, whether he was there or not. Migrants in Haddou's position, that is, those who moved their families into the city from the country while they continued working in Europe, customarily demanded that their wives remain in the house during the migrants' absence. Worrying about the well-being and fidelity of the women back home occupied a good share of the migrants' time. Haddou was no different. Once they installed the phone in his house in Nador, however, Haddou could call any time of the day or night to find out if his wife was there. During any given week he called at least three times, always at a different hour and on a different day so as not to establish a pattern. That way no one in the house could plan their activities around his phone calls. He also kept the phone dial in Nador locked so no one could call out but could only receive calls. He could thus monitor and manage the activities of his whole family thousands of miles away. In effect, Haddou transformed the telephone into a technology trap.

Haddou also controlled the household by controlling its purse strings. He sent a monthly stipend through the Moroccan Banque populaire. The bank had established branches throughout Europe and gave the migrants a fair exchange rate to make it easier for them to send money home. The bank had to do something, because most migrants did not trust the banking system. Migrants traditionally brought the biggest share of their earnings home with them at vacation time. Money changers in the Nador market or in the nearby Spanish port town of Melilla then bought the migrants' European currency and sold them Moroccan dirhams. Haddou and the others who worked abroad did this because they feared that the government might some day confiscate their earnings if they deposited them all in Morocco. Besides, the migrants did not want Moroccan officials to know how much they earned so that they could avoid paying

Moroccan taxes. They still brought the lion's share of their earnings home this way. Now, however, Haddou also transferred about fifteen hundred dirhams (approximately two hundred dollars) a month to his account in Nador. His son, Hassan, would write a check on the account for the family. Haddou would then telephone instructions as to how the money was to be spent.

Yet try as he might to enforce his will upon them, Haddou's family found ways to subvert his authority during his absence. Even his loving wife, Thraithmas, dipped into the family's monthly stipend. For example, every week or two Thraithmas's mother came to visit. She would stay for a few days and then return home with a little money and some tea, sugar, or meat given to her by her daughter. The mother gladly accepted the food paid for by her daughter because she was dependent on a pitifully small pension from the Spanish government given in recognition of her husband's death during the Spanish civil war. Over seventy years old and beginning to stiffen up, she was also glad of the chance to forgo the hour's walk needed to reach the weekly market nearest her country home.

Hassan, who was in charge of the accounts, skimmed the most. He exaggerated the extent of his school and clothing expenses regularly. Occasionally he pocketed money earmarked for bills and then spent the money in cafés and on other forms of entertainment enjoyed by the richer boys on the block. Even little Murad, Haddou's youngest son, pocketed the change from the daily shopping trips it was his duty to perform. The whole family habitually ran up credit at various stores, which Haddou then had to pay off during his vacation.

These problems with the children began early and at the top for Haddou. Driss, the eldest, disappointed him first by not passing his baccalaureat (high school graduation exam) and then by becoming a migrant. Haddou had always intended that he alone would migrate so that none of the others would have to leave home. Unfortunately, when Driss was visiting his maternal uncle, a migrant in Lille, the Socialist government of France declared an amnesty for all foreigners working without papers. Driss's uncle quickly talked his boss into hiring Driss so that he could apply for papers and a visa. The plan worked, and Driss got a job in a warehouse in northern France. But that was only half of the problem, according to Haddou. What was worse, Driss begged off contributing to the household budget from his own salary by claiming that the European cost of living ate up all of his savings. Yet Haddou knew only too well that Driss's major expense happened to be his weekly trips and gifts to a certain Dutch girlfriend Driss had met while she was on vacation in France.

The family's insubordination troubled Haddou constantly. He felt he had worked all of his life just to provide for them and yet they were not appreciative. All they ever asked for was more money; all they ever complained about was their "small" family stipend. He had poured his savings into a piece of property and then built a four-apartment building on it, all for them. He had never asked for anything more than to be allowed to retire back in Nador on a comfortable German pension, to live surrounded by his children and their families, all under one roof in a building of his own creation. Was that too much to ask? Now, however, his eldest son wanted to quit his job in France and move in with his girlfriend in Holland. Since his second son had failed the baccalaureat, he would not be able to go to university or find a decent job in Morocco. Maybe the two youngest sons would mature and prosper, though they seemed no more likely to fulfill their father's dream than the older brothers.

The frustrations of being an absent head of household preoccupied Haddou as he walked back from the phone booth to his apartment. Haddou partly blamed himself for the family's failure. He had not been there to raise the children properly and knew he could not make up in one month for eleven months of absence. He also suspected that his children did not entirely respect him, for he, like many other migrants, had never lived in the city and thus had few of the social graces typical of the nonmigrant fathers of his children's friends. What was worse, Haddou had none of the contacts needed to ease his children's access into good schools and jobs. Years of giving and receiving favors and of sitting in cafés with men of influence were needed to develop a network of acquaintances. Haddou had spent his adult life out of the country, which meant that his circle of acquaintances was strictly limited to men he had known before he migrated. He was thus in the unenviable position of having an income and house commensurate with a high status but none of the personal prestige needed to get others to do his bidding. The children, he sensed, resented him for this.

On the other hand, Haddou knew how to work for something he wanted, and the children did not. They expected it all to be laid out before them. They disdained manual labor and assumed, instead, that only white-collar jobs were respectable. Take last winter when the sewer pipe backed up. Haddou jumped right in and dug up the pipe while the boys disappeared. They were embarrassed to have the neighbors see their father digging in the dirt. Yet what did they think their father did all year to earn money that kept them from having to work? He deserved their respect if only for that.

At least Haddou's daughters were loyal. Fatima, the older one, had last year married without complaint a successful migrant working in Holland. The man had approached Haddou requesting that Fatima live abroad as his second wife while his first stayed in Nador with their children. People in the neighborhood were aghast that Haddou consented to give his daughter away as a second wife. They said that showed what a country bumpkin he was. A good city family would never stoop so low. But Haddou defended his actions by claiming that the man was from his tribal region, earned an excellent income, owned a nice house in Nador, and was a migrant—in short, he was just like Haddou himself and therefore a good match for his daughter.

Haddou's other daughter, Malika, never gave him cause for concern. Her high school grades were impressive; she did particularly well in French. Yet she also helped her mother with the cooking and cleaning in the house and even found time to take sewing classes from a seamstress a few blocks away. In Haddou's eyes, Malika was the model daughter. He daydreamed on occasion of keeping her unmarried and at home so that she could tend to his needs in his old age. He justified this by saying it would be a pity to separate Malika from her mother, because they were so close. Unlike the others, Malika never asked him to raise the monthly stipend.

Haddou could not help smiling as he closed the door to his apartment and took off his coat. It was Malika, after all, who had said he looked like Charles Bronson and that he should stop working and start making movies. Bronson's mustache was smaller and his eyes not as round as Haddou's, but otherwise he had to agree with her: the resemblance was striking. Maybe he would buy a VCR this time to take back with him on his upcoming vacation to Nador. That way the whole family could watch Bronson movies together.

Haddou chose to take his vacation and return to Nador during the month of December. The winters were cold in Germany, and he no longer wanted to compete for space with the hundreds of thousands of Moroccan migrants who returned in July and August. He disliked the crowded Spanish highways and the crush at the boat docks and the Moroccan border caused by the summertime returnees. It had grown so bad in recent years that some migrants now wasted a week of their vacation time just getting home. Once back in Nador, the streets became jammed with the migrants' Mercedes. Every summer weekend, one procession after another of honking cars followed by fireworks displays created a ruckus, all due to the dozens of weddings taking place simultaneously. This was caused by the migrants' families back home, who found brides for the unmarried male migrants and arranged for their weddings to coincide with their vacations. The locals, too, preferred to marry in the summer, hence the noise and confusion of that season.

The changed nature of the wedding celebration also added to the mayhem. Prior to the influx of peasants and migrants into Nador (in 1960 Nador's population was seventeen thousand; in 1985 it was eighty-five thousand) weddings took place within the confines of the village and kin group. However, the tremendous growth of the city, the creation of neighborhoods full of strangers, and the dramatic rise in family income following labor migration to Europe led to the development of open, lavish matrimonial displays. The families of newlyweds used fireworks, Mercedes-Benz cortèges, and professional, electronic orchestras to compete with each other and to make a big splash in front of the neighbors and relatives.

Haddou personally disliked the lavish displays because the only marriage he had been responsible for, that of his elder daughter, Fatima, was a secret affair carried out quietly behind closed doors and windows, due to the shame attached to his daughter's becoming a second wife. He justified his displeasure at large public weddings in more sweeping and general terms though by citing the wastefulness of such extravagance. Why should he, a hardworking father with dependents, squander his savings on celebrations meant to impress strangers? On the other hand, he did not mind competing with his neighbors when it came to building a big house or decorating its facade. That kind of social competition required no face-to-face interaction or mastery of urban etiquette. Making sure his children were reasonably well dressed and had imported electronic toys to play with on the street was another form of social display of which Haddou approved, for as a migrant he was in a position to purchase cheaply such foreign articles. Haddou, like all the other Moroccan migrants, always brought home presents for the whole family. In his family the boys normally received shirts and pants, while Thraithmas and Malika got scarves and dresses. The boys proudly wore their German clothes—when they fit—but the women tended to leave theirs in the closet, since the clothes Haddou picked out were often too ugly or too risqué (sleeveless, for example) to be worn in Nador.

Haddou also brought back items from Germany for the house. Like many Moroccans, Haddou considered foreign-made goods to be superior to domestic products. In fact, so strong was the allure of commodities from industrial Europe that Haddou carried back items as small as faucets and door handles made in Germany, not to mention tea glasses, pots and pans, and tablecloths. Driss, the son with the self-professed high living costs, tended to buy cheap presents for the family from Spain, Taiwan, or Hong Kong when he returned, and then to claim that they were really made in Germany or France.

One year Haddou brought back a Mercedes-Benz for a colonel in the Moroccan air force. He met Haddou on the train to Rabat. They started talking, and the man ended up contracting with Haddou to purchase a car in Germany and then drive it back to Rabat for him. The colonel, in turn, saw to it that Haddou met no resistance from Moroccan officials. Thus protected, Haddou seized the opportunity to load the car down with items for his own household, including a television, a sewing machine, folding chairs, and bundles of towels. No one asked him for bribes on that trip.

Haddou set about brewing another pot of tea. He realized as he thought about his own vacation that he had to make a decision soon on whether to bring Thraithmas to Dusseldorf that year. Since the mid-1980s, when Murad became ten and could be left in the care of his brothers and sisters, Haddou had begun to bring Thraithmas to Germany to stay with him for a month each year. When it was time for his mother to go, Hassan would wake up while it was still dark, go down to the taxicab stand, and bring a car right up to the front door. Thraithmas would heavily veil herself and then quickly step out of the house and into the car. She and Hassan would then take the taxi to the Oujda International Airport long before anyone in the neighborhood awoke. Once in

Dusseldorf, Thraithmas would change out of her Moroccan dress and into Western clothing. Haddou insisted on that. He remembered too well when she first arrived in Germany wearing her jallaba. All eyes were upon her, staring at her as if she were a freak. When she wore her Western clothes, no one paid attention. Luckily for Haddou, unlike her mother, Thraithmas had never tattooed her face with the markings of her natal region, so nothing about her attracted the Germans' curiosity.

Haddou deeply appreciated her visits. She brought with her delicacies from Morocco: almonds, prepared barley dishes, pickled lemons, olive oil, fresh mint. She also made his favorite food, limsimen, a fried bread of many layers made by folding the dough again and again. More than anything else, Thraithmas's visits broke the monotony of Haddou's existence in Dusseldorf. Without her, his routine consisted of waking early, making tea on the small hot plate, riding his bicycle down to the rail yard, and then working as long as they needed him. He would ride home after finishing, change his clothes, and go out to buy a little food for supper. He then watched television for a while or flipped through a magazine before going to bed. The weekends were mainly reserved for washing clothes and straightening up his room.

The only excitement of the week occurred on Saturday afternoons, at which time Haddou liked to walk down to a certain tearoom in a nicer neighborhood where German women gathered. There he would sit for a few hours, listening to their conversations. Sometimes when the place was full, women even sat at his table. They would start to ask him about his homeland or about his religion. Haddou enjoyed these little exchanges very much because they were practically his only informal contacts with the locals. During the rest of the week he talked to Germans only as a worker talks to a boss or as a customer talks to a storekeeper. The women at the tearoom were the only Germans who showed Haddou any consideration.

With Thraithmas around, Haddou had no need for the Germans. What is more, when he woke up in the morning she had his tea ready. When he got home at night she was cooking his supper. During the day while Haddou was working, Thraithmas would often go across the hall and sit in the apartment of the railway widow who lived there. They watched television together and communicated through gestures. That was enough. They just enjoyed each other's presence. When Haddou returned at night or on weekends, he and Thraithmas sometimes went shopping in one of the big discount department stores. She doubly enjoyed these outings because she, like other relatively wealthy migrants' wives, was not allowed to go out shopping in Nador. By going out with Haddou in Dusseldorf she could also buy more tasteful clothes for the family back home—at least clothes that fit. She also enjoyed buying inexpensive perfumes, soaps, and candies to place around the house in Nador on special occasions and to give to guests when they visited.

Perhaps more than anything, Haddou appreciated Thraithmas's visits because they provided him with a sense of stability and worth. Her calm and respectful manner toward him, her familiar way of speaking, her correct behavior, all reminded him that he belonged, as a proud believer and father of a family, to an Islamic community with a set of values and way of living totally distinct from his present European surroundings. He had not always felt this way. During those early years in Paris no one had been overly concerned with strictly maintaining the religious practices and precepts of their Islamic homeland. They were too busy working. Besides, there was only one mosque in all of Paris.

Sometime during the 1970s a mosque opened in Haddou's quarter of Dusseldorf. It began as a room where Muslims could gather and pray. An Egyptian led the prayers. Haddou visited the mosque once or twice, but he did not know the other men. They seemed too serious anyway and were too interested in trying to run his life. One day while Haddou was in the train yard recording the boxcar numbers of the most recent train to arrive, a Turkish worker from the mosque approached him and asked him to join an Islamic group then forming. They wanted to petition the boss for the right to stop work during prayer times. Some companies in France had even set aside rooms to be used as mosques—right inside the factories. Maybe the Germans could be persuaded to do the same thing.

Haddou refused to have anything to do with the man or his group and their objectives. He said he was in Europe to earn money, not to pray. God had given him two hands and a strong back to use to provide for himself and his family. Who was going to put food on the table back in Nador if he decided to spend all day at the mosque? In any case, he did not need a bunch of bearded migrants telling him what was and was not Islamic.

And look at the way the religiously militant migrants were greeted back home! The cops at the Moroccan customs bureau treated them like criminals. They knew who the troublemakers were because the government spied on the migrants in Europe. The consulates and the Moroccan migrants' associations were full of spies who kept track of everyone. When the migrants got to the Moroccan border, the customs agents went through all their possessions, looking for religious tracts. They even began confiscating the migrants' audio and video cassettes. Supposedly the militants smuggled the sermons of subversive preachers into the country on these tapes.

Locals in Nador also complained of the way the bearded migrants came home and preached to them about the "true" Islam. The locals viewed them as hicks from the countryside who had spent most of their adult lives in Christian Europe. Now they were coming back every vacation to Islamic Morocco and had the gall to preach to the people who had never abandoned their country and its religion.

Haddou had to admit, however, that it was the risk of being fired from his job and then deported from Germany that weighed most heavily on him and kept him from getting involved with the group. The Germans used any excuse to get rid of foreigners. Even with his new visa he did not entirely trust them, so he was going to continue to make sure he never arrived late for work or left early. If they wanted him to work night shifts outside in the train yard in the middle of winter, he would still be there. He would even continue to have his paycheck deposited directly into his account so that the bank could automatically pay his rent and utilities bills. That way he would never miss a payment and give the Germans a reason for firing him.

Haddou had to admit that he respected the Germans as well as feared them. They worked hard, built good products, and kept their streets and parks clean— more than he could say for the Moroccans. The Germans were also honest with you. If you asked them a question, they would tell you the answer. If a Moroccan knew, he would never tell; if he did not know, he would make something up. On the other hand, unlike the Moroccans, the Germans were morally bankrupt. The family meant nothing to them. Old people were all sent off to live alone in homes for the aged. Daughters and wives went about scantily clad, even drinking and talking to strangers if they so desired. The men were too weak to keep their families in line. What was worst, they were all racists, young and old. It was best to steer clear of them, for nothing good ever came from mixing. The Germans knew nothing of the proper Islamic way of life. Haddou knew this through one of his friends who had married a German woman. At first the man had been enthralled with his new wife and her Christian way of life. He danced and drank and even began to eat pork. Soon, however, their marriage deteriorated, and he rediscovered his Islamic heritage. Nonetheless, she refused to maintain an Islamic household. The couple ended up with two kitchens in the house: one for her pork and alcohol dishes and the other for him, free of impurities. The man now spent most of his free time at the mosque in the company of other strict believers.

"Why don't you just go home?" Haddou thought to himself on many occasions. That is what the racists wanted too. Haddou's answer was always the same: "To do what?" Most Moroccan men's answer to this would be to set up a shop and sell something. But Haddou felt himself to be unsuited to the life of a small merchant. They were not involved in productive activity anyway, just buying and selling what others had made. In any case, he needed contacts to make a good profit. Otherwise no one would buy from him, and the Moroccan bureaucracy would slowly bleed him to death without a patron to protect him. Even if he wanted to make some kind of productive investment, the banks were not safe, laws were not enforced, and, besides, in what kind of manufacturing could he invest in Morocco that could possibly compete with foreign manufactures? The government favored imported goods by keeping import tariffs low. What was worse, the Moroccan consumer was convinced that quality came only from abroad. The only domestic products worth buying consisted mainly of foods and traditional clothing. If he chose to produce them, who would buy his modern shoes, for example, when they could purchase imported Italian shoes? Or who would buy his Moroccan-made shampoo when they could buy it from France or Spain? Even dinner plates imported from Taiwan were preferable to those produced locally. The Moroccan government made matters worse by throwing their support behind commercial activities producing for export. In the region of Nador that meant growing citrus fruit for Europe. But citrus grew locally only on irrigated land, and most of the good, irrigated land had been bought up long ago by wealthy men with contacts. They had been told of the planned irrigation system before everyone else and had bought the land at a cheaper price in order to take advantage of the development. Today that land was too expensive to buy. Equally vexing was the fact that many of the prices for crops grown on unirrigated land were controlled by middlemen and the government in such a restrictive manner that they barely repaid the farmers' investments—and then only during good years. No subsidies existed to carry the farmers during the bad years, which in recent times had far outnumbered the good.

Given these conditions back home, Haddou never could understand why so many Europeans expected the migrants just to pick up and leave. They acted as if the migrants had come uninvited. On the contrary, he and the millions of other migrants from around the world were in Europe because the European governments, factories, and shop owners originally asked them to come work. The first time Haddou went back on vacation during the early 1960s, his boss gave him hundreds of work contracts to hand out to people in the Moroccan countryside who might want to join him in Europe, so eager was the boss to expand his migrant labor force. No, migrants did not originally knock down the door; it was opened for them. Unlike the better organized and more demanding European workers, migrants could be made to work harder and longer or to do dirtier and more dangerous jobs, thus providing greater profits for their European employers. As Haddou saw it, the real dilemma was that Moroccans were dependent on Europe no matter what they did. They could stay home and—if they were lucky enough to find a job at all—produce goods for export to Europe, work on assembling and distributing products legally imported from Europe, illegally smuggle products in from Europe, or, like himself, they could just pick up and go to work right in Europe. Directly, or indirectly, in Morocco or abroad, they were all working for the Europeans.

Being a migrant in the modern world is serious business. Moroccans like Haddou know this well, for he and close to a million of his compatriots have left their families and homeland in Morocco in order to earn a wage a thousand miles away in the countries of Europe. They have had to learn how to navigate through the Moroccan bureaucracy, which selectively issues or withholds necessary papers and passports, as well as how to master the complex European system of visa and residency requirements, which determines how long—or even whether—they can stay. Along the way they have been victimized by an array of corrupt Moroccan and European officials.

The migrants' vulnerability increased during the 1970s and 1980s. On the Moroccan side, their allegiance to the state has come under suspicion, particularly with the growing influence of Islamic revivalists in the migrant community. On the European side, the growing power of right-wing groups places a further burden on the migrants, who now find themselves threatened physically by racist thugs and legally hemmed in by restrictive legislation.

Yet it would be a mistake to see Haddou and migrants like him as merely pawns, pushed about by political and economic forces out of their control, for in spite of official harassment, forbiddingly long distances, and minimal time spent with their families, migrants continue to invest their own sacrifices with meaning by committing themselves to the betterment of the lives of their dependents. As the career of Haddou reveals, however, the male migrant's vision of what constitutes a good life, a good family, or even a good father is often at odds with the perceptions of others close to him. It may be difficult to agree with the way Haddou managed his familial affairs and relations, but it is not difficult to respect his ability to sustain, in the face of what amounted to almost lifelong hardship and privation, his commitment to what he valued most: the construction and maintenance of an economically stable and emotionally nurturing household.

A Note on Sources

My wife, Joan Cross, and I spent most of 1986 and 1987 living in Nador studying the impact of migration on the region, which is how we came to know Haddou and his family, whose stories, of course, provided the sources for this article. For obvious reasons, we have not given his real name. Fulbright, Social Science Research Council, and American Institute of Maghrib Studies dissertation grants made our stay possible.

Suggestions for Further Reading

The study of international migration is an industry in itself so I will mention only a few of the more theoretical works on this general topic. Michael Piore's *Birds of Passage: Migrant Labor and Industrial Societies* (Cambridge: Cambridge University Press, 1979) still stands as one of the best mainstream neoclassical studies of the field. Alejandro Portes and John Walton's *Labor, Class and the International System* (New York: Academic Press, 1981) is a good Marxist study. Stephen Castles, Heather Booth, and Tina Wallace have written a more militantly committed, though no less theoretical, work entitled *Here for Good: Western Europe's New Ethnic Minorities* (London: Pluto Press, 1984). On the Moroccan context, most important for this article is David Seddon, *Moroccan Peasants: A Century of Change in the Eastern Rif, 1870–1970* (Folkestone: Dawson, 1981), which is one of the best sources of information in English on the history and development of the region of Nador, as well as on the early years of migration from that region. Most Moroccan researchers write on the subject of migration either in Arabic or French, the two national languages of Morocco. One important work in French is Tahar Ben Jelloun's account of the sexual frustrations of migrants. See his *La plus haute des solitudes* (Paris: Seuil, 1979). Several Moroccan novels concerning various migration experiences have been translated into English. Some of the most interesting come from the collaboration of Paul Bowles and Mohammed Mrabet, notably their *Love with a Few Hairs* (London: Arena/Anchor Books, 1986 [1967]), which chronicles the life of a migrant to Tangier from the eastern Rif. Bowles has also translated Mohamed Choukri's *For Bread Alone* (London: Grafton Books, 1987), the autobiography of another Rifi from Nador province who was forced to migrate to Tangier. See also Driss Chraibi, *The Simple Past* (Washington D.C.: Three Continents Press, 1989). Finally, Ali Ghanem's *A Wife For My Son,* trans. G. Koziolas (London: Zed Press, 1984) describes in depth the familial stresses and strains accompanying an emigrant's attempt to work in Europe while maintaining a family in Algeria. It has recently been made into a film.

11

Changing Gender Relations in a Moroccan Town

Susan Schaefer Davis

The topic of this article is especially well suited for a discussion of old boundaries and new frontiers for women in Arab society. The current state of gender
relations between young people in a Moroccan town is itself a dynamic between
old boundaries and new frontiers, especially in terms of acceptable behavior for
females.[1] More generally, anthropologists have recently become interested in
systems of meaning in different societies; an entire issue of one journal was
devoted, tellingly, to several scholars exploring "how systems of meaning are
currently contested and maintained in Middle Eastern contexts."[2] The focus on
changing gender relations illustrates aspects of both contest and maintenance.
Moroccan sociologist Fatima Mernissi commented on changing gender relations in urban areas that appeared in data she gathered in the early 1970s:

> In rural Morocco the access of young men to young women is subject to
> strict and apparently efficient control. In urban centers, access seems to
> be much less restricted. Young people meet each other frequently enough
> to fall in love and want to get married. . . . I believe that sexual segrega-
> tion, one of the main pillars of Islam's social control over sexuality, is
> breaking down.[3]

The data presented here, gathered in a semi-rural area in the early 1980s,
support her general point and illustrate that changing relations are not limited to
urban areas. In what follows I will describe the old boundaries in terms of traditional norms and behaviors, and the new frontiers as reflected in changing
ideals and behaviors concerning relations between the sexes, especially prior to
marriage. The basis for these changes will be seen in several broader areas of
the society.

The Research Site

To understand the implications of these data,[4] it is important to know something
about the setting in which they were collected. The research site is the semi-

From Judith E. Tucker, ed., *Arab Women* (Bloomington: Indiana University Press, 1993),
pp. 208–223. Reprinted by permission. Susan S. Davis, an anthropologist, is an independent scholar and consultant based in Haverford, Pennsylvania.

rural community of Zawiya, a town of eleven thousand on the edge of a rich
agricultural plain in north central Morocco near Meknes; the town is described
more fully in my monograph *Patience and Power* (1983a). While earlier generations were raised in villages of fifty to seventy-five households in which subsistence was based mainly on agriculture and herding, many people lost their
land during French colonization (1912–56). The economy is now more diverse,
with people working in agriculture mainly as day laborers, or in commerce,
transport, or trades like construction; a few men work in Europe. Although very
few of the parental generation attended school, today virtually all children
attend the town's primary school and many go on to secondary school in nearby "Kabar," a market town of about forty-five thousand. Until the early 1980s,
all administrative services such as government offices, banks, and police were
located in Kabar. This, in addition to the lack of running water and the unpaved
streets, gives Zawiya the feel of a village despite its size. In fact, this semi-rural
aspect of Zawiya makes it an ideal site to study change in gender relations. It is
very different from the atypical westernized upper-class areas in the cities, and
also from isolated rural communities which have experienced more limited
change. Zawiya's proximity to both a larger community and to roads and rail-
roads linking it to large cities, as well as the easy access to television, expose
local youth to change while they are living in a traditional town. This situation
is common in Morocco, where small towns are growing rapidly, and is probably found throughout the Middle East.

Traditional Gender Relations in Zawiya

Norms. Especially with regard to female behavior, the norms[5] concerning gender
relations both before and after marriage were very restrictive, and in general fit
the western stereotype related to the secluded Muslim woman. Marriages were
arranged by parents, and the spouses may never have seen each other if they were
not relatives, since females past puberty were not to speak to unrelated males.
Older girls and women were to veil if they must go out before the public eye, but
preferably they were to remain inside their homes, only leaving "to marry and to
be buried," as one old woman said. A further restriction on females was that
proof of chastity was required as part of the marriage ceremony. The test of virginity was practiced, in which hymeneal blood was displayed to wedding guests.
If there was no blood on the marital linens, the marriage contract could be
declared void and the bride sent away in sackcloth. All of these prescriptions for
females served as a strong deterrent to interacting or forming relationships with
unrelated men. In this regard, it should be noted that the term "sexuality" concerns a wider range of behavior in this Moroccan context than it would in the
West. In a culture that traditionally has discouraged unrelated males and females
from speaking to each other, most cross-sex interaction takes on a sexual tone.

Behavior. In attempting to move beyond traditional norms and discuss behavior, one encounters an obstacle: obtaining valid data on past heterosexual interaction is even more difficult than assessing it for a current group. Two types of data were especially useful. For the first I interviewed a long-time resident about "deviant" behavior in each of the approximately fifty families we worked with intensively in 1982, including accusations of crimes, illegitimate pregnancies, abortions, incidents of drinking (alcohol is forbidden in Islam) and drug use. Because the informant was young, the information only went back about fifteen years. She described eighteen cases of breaking sexual norms for the younger generation and ten in the parental generation. These included cases of young women being found alone with young men (suggesting intimacy), and also of girls becoming pregnant while unmarried.

My second approach was to ask an older woman for case histories of sexual behavior that violated norms in the nearby village where she had grown up. These data went back about forty years and showed that even then the norms were violated. In a village of about fifty households, the informant reported eight cases of illicit sexual activity, three for single women, four for married women, and one for a divorcee. Further, these were publicly known incidents; one expects there were others. This informant also reported the harsh local reaction to such cases: women were sent to jail, were banished from the village, or had their heads shaved. The only fatality was a man shot and killed by an aggrieved husband. An interesting note is that some of these "shamed" women have reformed and are currently materially well-off, accepted members of the community.

Although norms in the past proscribed heterosexual interaction outside the family, the data make it clear that, as is universally true, the norms were not always followed. However, ethnographic observation over the last twenty years suggests that deviation from norms was more limited in the past, and also that there has recently been some change in the norms themselves. For more details, we must examine the current situation.

Gender Relations in Zawiya Today

Norms. During our research in 1982, the restrictive traditional norms were still cited with general approval by most informants in Zawiya. It was shameful for an unrelated boy and girl to be seen talking together, girls should not be outside the household unnecessarily, and parents were still involved in arranging marriages. The display of hymeneal blood to prove virginity was still a part of marriage ceremonies. This quote from a young woman of eighteen shows that she recognizes the weight of these restrictions on her behavior: "A girl only stays home—that's all. It gets a little dark and she can't go out; she's not allowed to go out. She mustn't go to the movies . . . she shouldn't go out at night . . . she shouldn't do anything! As for the boy, it's no problem for him." We found direct evidence suggesting that females find their role limited when we asked Moroccan adolescents to "draw a person." Sixty percent of girls drew a male first, which is often interpreted as meaning the drawer prefers that role.[6]

However, there was also evidence that some of these norms are changing. One area of change is a decrease in the idea that females should not be seen by unrelated males, which can be inferred by changing behaviors. Girls do spend more time outside the home than they did in the past, mainly because a much larger number attend school. Veiling has decreased greatly in the past decade, so that while older adolescent girls always veiled in the past, now none do. This has also affected married women, so that currently only about one-third of them veil in Zawiya, while all did in the 1960s. We interpret these behaviors as reflecting changing social norms, because there was no comment on how certain persons were violating this or that norm by their behavior.

Another indication of changing norms is found in young people's responses to our questions about marriage. When we asked thirty-eight boys and fifty-three girls if they thought their parents, themselves, or both should choose their future spouse, 29 percent of the boys and 26 percent of the girls said they wanted to choose for themselves. This answer was related to their ages and their level of education, so that older adolescents were significantly more likely (at the .05 level) to want to choose for themselves, as were those with a higher level of education (at the .01 level of significance). Choosing one's own spouse necessitates some level of contact between the sexes, and this was indicated in these young people's answers to "What are the characteristics of an ideal spouse?" Although the majority of answers focused on characteristics that could be judged by one's parents—that a woman should be beautiful "in body and in mind," or that a man should have a good job—many responses were different. These noted the need for a good relationship, suggesting a desire to know the spouse before marriage in order to evaluate him/her. Sixteen percent of males and 33 percent of females defined the ideal spouse in terms involving their relationship, such as, "I have to like her—to agree with her," and "He should be good; he should have a good personality, and we should respect each other and be honest with each other, not insulting each other." These responses suggest that the traditional norm rejecting any relationship between unmarried boys and girls is being questioned, at least by some.

Behavior. When we move beyond norms and examine current practices, we find stronger indications of increased heterosexual interaction. This interaction appears to have increased in both the amount and the variety of different activities involving young men and women. We will first examine the different activities of young couples, and then discuss the frequency of interaction.

My taped interviews with young people are a valuable source of information about their own views on this topic. They include discussions of how young women think about developing relationships with boys, or the characteristics of a "platonic" as opposed to a "love" relationship, and of the usual stages in a developing relationship.

When I asked a girl of fourteen with a primary school education, "What's important to you these days? What do you often talk about with your friend, so that I can see what interests you? I want to know what you have on your mind, what preoccupies you most," she replied:

> F. What interests us [on some occasions, people use the "royal we," as here] is to see how girls date so that we learn too. We do want to start dating. However, if we do now, we won't know what to do. For example, they [boys] may say a word to us that we wouldn't know. We're still learning step by step.
> S. So what do you want to learn?
> F. I want to learn to hold a discussion, how to become shrewd.
> S. Who is going to teach you? How do you expect to learn? Do you want to date and learn gradually, or does your friend show you, or other girls who are knowledgeable, or what?
> F. No. She [the friend] watches girls from her own family and from my family and we teach each other. I learn from my relatives in cities; I do learn from them . . . I learned from my sister when she was still a girl. She was shrewd.
> S. Soumia?
> F. Yes. She on the other hand learned from her [older] sister and her sister's friends. To learn well, we teach each other.
> S. Did you discuss things with your sister before she got married or did you ask questions?
> F. No, I was just watching. . . . If I had asked her, it wouldn't have been appropriate. I would have looked bad.
> S. What do you mean you wouldn't look good? Why?
> F. She wouldn't like me. She would say "You are starting to learn at this age?" I have to be older so that becoming shrewd will help me accept what a boy would tell me. At the same time, one's parents won't fear for her. For example, we're too young and our parents worry about us. . . .
> S. Your girlfriend teaches you. Are you going to talk to boys to learn also?
> F. Little by little. You start first with young ones. You don't discuss with older ones. If you are young, you select your age so that you get trained. Once you learn from young boys, then you move to older ones.

Although most young women didn't begin to meet with boys until the age of fifteen or sixteen, this fourteen-year-old indicates that there is considerable attention to forming relationships before then. Her statement that she could not openly ask her sister about interactions with boys is an indication that the norms against interaction are still strong, even if belied by behavior.

Quite early on I learned that there are nuances in relationships between the sexes, so that two Arabic terms for friend (male), *sadiq* and *sahib,* have distinctly different meanings for girls. A *sadiq* is a platonic friend, usually someone you do schoolwork with, though uneducated girls sometimes said they considered a friend of their older brothers who regularly visited their homes as a *sadiq.* If a girl has a *sahib,* on the other hand, he is what we would call a boyfriend. Horriya, a young woman of sixteen in secondary school, described a dilemma she faced when a *sadiq* wanted to become a *sahib:*

> H. One day a boy told me "Come here; I want to talk to you." He's a neighbor of ours who lives up there. . . . Well, I did not suspect anything because I used to go and have him help me with schoolwork. I didn't expect him to tell me anything. So I went to his house. He helped me with my homework and then said to me, "I want to talk to you." I said, "What do you want to tell me?" He replied, "I want to talk to you and I want us to become friends."

She told him she had to think about it, and after talking it over with her best friend she decided not to accept his offer, and wrote him a letter saying so. Her explanation of why she made that decision shows the difference between the two types of friend, and also that to "talk" and to "laugh" with boys have different meanings.

> H. I don't want to be anybody's [girl]friend. I decided, and it is the right thing. I must really not talk to anybody. . . . It wouldn't be nice for me because everybody will know about it. It looks bad. That's why I want him to be like all our other neighbors' kids. We will laugh and all that. I don't want him to tell me that kind of talk. . . .
> S. This is what I don't understand—the difference between talking and laughing.
> H. The other guy [the sahib] will carry on, telling you "I like you, I love you, etc.," but with the other guys [sadiqs] we only talk about school, and we tell jokes. . . . What I like are talks about studies, jokes. I don't like anybody telling me "I like you" and then taking advantage of me as they usually do of others.

Thus one "laughs" or kids around with a platonic friend or sadiq and "talks" more seriously about romantic topics with a boyfriend or sahib. Horriya's account also suggests that norms are against the latter relationship when she says she turned her neighbor down partly because "it looks bad"; she wants to maintain a certain image of herself.[7]

A young woman in her twenties comments on "talking" in a way suggesting that while it was disapproved of in the past, the norms are changing.

S. Let's go back to the girl talking to the boy near the well. [You feel] this is the right thing to do, right? Why?

A. Listen, Susan, there is absolutely no girl on earth who would reach the age of twenty or twenty-four—the age of being asked for in marriage—without having felt the need at least to smile, talk and laugh with a boy, or even desire one in her own family. [Cousin marriage is approved.]

S. You are talking about this time now; before it wasn't so?

A. This time, not in the past.

If a girl decides she wants to pursue a relationship with a sahib or boyfriend, it will progress along a fairly regular course from casual meetings to an intimate relationship. Besides walking to school, the most likely settings for girls and boys to meet initially are the seven taps where the community of eleven thousand obtain their water. Girls between ten and twenty are the main water carriers, and they gather at the tap waiting their turn, while young men between roughly fourteen and twenty lounge against the walls of the surrounding houses, talking and watching the girls. Carrying all the water for a large family is an exhausting task, and a girl may carry 30 five-liter containers to her house in several relays. The whole process, including waiting, may take three hours a day. Given all this, I expected girls to despise fetching water, but few complained and several were even enthusiastic. Only when I understood the role of the water taps as meeting places was I able to explain this attitude. A boy who finds a particular girl attractive may ask her for a drink of water, toss a joke or compliment her way, or try to talk with her on her way home.

Once a couple has become acquainted in this way, if they decide to see more of each other they will arrange to meet in dark or isolated corners while the girl is running evening errands, buying mint for tea, or fetching the bread for her family. During these meetings they will talk about their feelings for each other and perhaps kiss. This phase may last several months before moving to the next stage.

If the couple desire a more intimate relationship, they arrange to meet outside town in a place where their activities will not be so easily observed. This may be the nearby town of Kabar, where they can walk together and window shop; the girl may suggest that the boy buy her a gift, which she will treasure as a souvenir. They may go to a shop to be photographed together, but both sexes are often wary of this because a photo provides concrete evidence of the relationship that may be used by a jilted lover. They may go to an empty house which the boy has arranged to borrow, or to the fields adjoining Zawiya; there they may engage in heavy petting, but the girl will attempt to preserve her virginity. Being discovered alone together, even just talking, is very shameful because it implies greater intimacy, so girls feel quite anxious when they agree to such meetings.

In fact, some girls do lose their virginity in these more isolated settings, although many couples use interfemoral intercourse or very shallow penetration and withdrawal before ejaculation to preserve the hymen. In the cases of lost virginity that I heard about, it was said that the male was drunk and had lost control of his behavior. It is interesting that no one ever reported a couple "getting carried away," but rather always cited an external cause, drunkenness, for the lack of control.[8]

A final indication of the commonness of heterosexual relationships was in the answers of my clinical informants to the question "How many girls your age have boyfriends?" (Early on I tried asking girls directly if they had a boyfriend, but since all denied it adamantly—again attesting to norms condemning such interactions—I used the more indirect question.) Of six girls between eleven and fifteen, one said no primary school girls (grades one through five, ages seven to fifteen) had boyfriends (but older girls did), while others answered "few" and one "many," often giving examples in their own classes. The change in estimates, which seems congruent with behavioral reality, comes around age sixteen. One sixteen-year-old who was not in school said "few" girls her age had boyfriends, while another who attended school said that although *she* had no boyfriends, "98 to 100 percent of girls do." Of the six girls seventeen and over, one said about 60 percent had boyfriends, and the rest said "all" or "nearly all" had boyfriends.

Thus while norms and practice did not and do not totally coincide, it appears that the proportion of young people involved in heterosexual relationships before marriage today is greater than in the past. It also seems that while couples in the past might have met in the field outside town, today's youth have a wider variety of options available. What are the reasons for the desired, and *de facto*, increase in these relationships? The answers are to be found in the wider society.

Causes and Consequences of Changing Gender Relations

Causes of Change. Several factors are responsible for the increase in heterosexual relationships, all related to the change from village to town life within the span of one or two generations. The majority of parents and grandparents in Zawiya grew up in small, kin-based villages that were much more isolated, by both distance and technology, from the modern world than Zawiya. Zawiya's size and heterogeneity, its integration in a national wage economy which encourages public education, and its effective integration into a nation-state all have the effect of making it more possible for boys and girls to spend time together. While young people most likely had the same desires in the past, getting together was more difficult in a village setting.

The greatest consequence of Zawiya's larger size is the attenuation of social control over heterosexual behavior. The town offers many settings in which the sexes can mix, either without being censured or without being observed. These settings include school, work place, and neighborhoods away from one's household. A girl can use the excuse of running an errand to meet a boy, and because of the large and varied population, she is unlikely to be seen with him by kin or family friends. Girls both went out less and were likely to be recognized and reported in small villages in the past. More adventuresome youths can even meet in larger cities because of Zawiya's access to transportation. Few of these possibilities existed for their parents.

Other reasons for change are at base economic, resulting from the fact that Zawiya is no longer a subsistence-based agricultural village, but rather tied into the national and international economy. This means that girls may now work in salaried jobs outside the household, and in some cases require education for these jobs. Another factor is worldwide inflation and national underemployment, which has led to what I call a "marriage crisis" for some young women. Finally, better transportation networks have been built, largely to move agricultural and mining products but resulting in greater general mobility.

In the past very few girls were educated, either because of lack of schools or of women's jobs requiring education, but this has changed for today's adolescents. Public schooling was not generally available until after independence in 1956, when it became a national priority; Zawiya opened its primary school in the 1960s. We see evidence of this lack of schooling in the parents of the adolescents we worked with: only two of a hundred parents had completed the five years of primary school. Even after schooling became available, parents educated sons more often than daughters for two main reasons. Girls were more helpful than their brothers, and thus were often kept home to do chores. Second, although schooling was free it required the purchase of books and clothing, and many families found even this minimal expense difficult to meet. When resources were limited, sons were educated because they were expected to use their education in white-collar jobs to contribute to the support of the family. Few women held such jobs in the early 1960s (and certainly not earlier, in villages), so parents did not see a similar payoff in educating girls.

By the early 1980s, educated young women were beginning to hold white-collar jobs, and many girls now aspire to them. Thus today virtually all children try to complete primary school. When we asked over a hundred adolescents what they hoped for in the future, about forty percent of boys and girls wanted to be teachers[9]; half of the Zawiya teachers are females. The school settings (which are not segregated by sex), especially the secondary schools outside the town, provide an opportunity for boys and girls to meet and talk unobserved by their parents. Uneducated girls also have opportunities to meet boys at work; those who work as agricultural day laborers are in settings away from their home villages (transported in trucks up to sixty kilometers) in groups that include males.

Another economically based factor is the "marriage crisis" for young women who are currently between about twenty-five and thirty-five. In the past, virtually all women in Zawiya were (or had been) married, but this is no longer true. The diversified economy that allows young men to have jobs and earn money independently of their families also ties them into the world economy, including inflation and the recent worldwide recession. This, in addition to local economic conditions, has led to a high rate of unemployment and made it harder for young men to amass a bride price and to maintain a new household. In support of this, anecdotal data indicate that currently young men living on family farms in the nearby countryside marry five to ten years earlier than their town cousins, since they can live and work with their families. When town men finally accumulate the money to marry, it appears they will skip their own generation and marry younger women. If the process were continuous, it would just mean that men married younger women, but this is not the case. This problem began in the early 1970s, and the women who were of marriageable age then were skipped over when their cohort finally married, because of cultural ideals encouraging both young brides (around twenty now) and beauty. A perhaps less conscious reason that men skip their own cohort is because those women have had ample time to develop their own personalities and are probably less malleable to a husband's taste. This marriage crisis causes some young women to fear that they will not marry, and they take action to maximize their chances, including increased interaction with males.

Change in the composition and functioning of the local political unit is an additional influence on changing heterosexual behavior. In the parental generation, people lived in isolated communities that were nominally under outside control, but they virtually ran their own affairs through a popularly selected council of village elders. These elders were also relatives, and their judgments were taken very seriously. In the past, infractions of sexual norms were first dealt with by the girl's parents or the father's male kin. If they did not put a stop to her behavior, the community elders would speak to the family and take action themselves if necessary. Punishments were common and often harsh, as described above. Today's situation is very different. People in Zawiya live within easy reach of a central government. Local officials are mainly people appointed from outside the area, and they are less involved in enforcing norms than in the past. People may still refer behavior that breaches norms to the authorities, but these authorities are less personally interested in the cases, less efficient (there may be long trials) and less harsh in meting out punishment. This means that another deterrent to heterosexual behavior, like the stronger social control of smaller communities, does not function as well today as it did in the past.

Consequences of Changing Gender Relations. What are the effects of this increase in heterosexual interaction? We see consequences in several areas including the physical, the affective, and the normative. In physical terms, there does not appear to be the epidemic of teenage pregnancies that is found in the

United States. This is due to several factors, including the fact that girls attempt to protect their virginity by avoiding full penetration. If a girl should become pregnant, she may resort to a traditional or modern form of abortion, although neither is strictly legal. Another physical consequence can be the loss of virginity, so that a girl would fail to produce hymeneal blood on her wedding night; this might cause severe social problems, like the cancellation of the marriage contract. However, this physical effect is seldom manifested. Beginning at least as early as the time of Harun ar-Rashid in the ninth century, chicken blood was used as a substitute in the bridal chamber, and this and other substitutes are currently in use.

The effect of increased heterosexual interaction on young people's feelings toward each other is rather ironically ambivalent. On the one hand, we have described how an increasing number of young people wish to choose their own spouse, and hope for a relationship of mutual affection and understanding. In this sense, they place higher affectional expectations on marriage than did most of their parents, who saw marriage more in terms of economic cooperation in raising a family. In the past, women's needs for affection were met by children and by other females, not to any large extent by husbands.[10] At this point I do not have data from young couples describing whether and how these expectations are met; this is an important area for further research.

However, I do have data on how young people currently feel about their interactions with the opposite sex before marriage, and these feelings are deeply ambivalent. Both sexes want to get together, and have romantic ideals about potential relationships. Once in a relationship, however, males distrust any girl who would let herself be dishonored by participating, and females fear young men will "love them and leave them," based on the experience of their peers. Hence these relationships operate on a profound "double standard." Further, if people hear about a relationship, a girl's chances for a good marriage might be decreased. These themes came up again and again in different sections of the interviews with clinical informants.

A young man in his twenties with quite a bit of education responded to a question about what love meant to him in a way that combined romantic ideals with the expectation of some problems—over which he expected to triumph.

> To love a girl is to give her, or to advise her, to help her, to take care of her, to show her the wrong things and the right ones. Not let her do the worst things but only the best and to be perfect. To tell her to ignore what people say to her because it s all lies and meant only to destroy her. . . . If that girl for instance is a good person, and she is working when people learn that I am going to marry her, they'll start gossiping about her. They will start telling me how bad she is, that she is not serious, she talks to many boys [i.e., goes out with them] and that I should reconsider and try to find another girl. . . . But the people don't really know what kind

of relationship I have with her. I take what they say as lies because they may be just taking revenge for whatever misunderstanding they may have had with her, or something of that nature. But I do what I like.

In another conversation, he presented a less idealistic view of relations between the sexes. I had asked him how a poor man could get expensive medicine for his dying wife (the Heinz dilemma used by Kohlberg, 1984). He said that it would be very hard for the man to get money, but much easier for a woman, who could use

> sex, for instance. And I know so many women who do that, and not even to buy medicine for their husbands, but only to buy a fancy dress to wear for a party or to buy a jellaba [long robe] or to buy new shoes or what have you.

The following edited excerpt from a taped interview gives a feeling for the young women's concerns. I had asked Amina, a single woman with a primary school education, to describe something that happened to her that was not right or was unfair:

> It concerns this matter of marriage. There's a boy—you trust him and he trusts you. He tells you "I care for you. If I don't see you, I'll go crazy; if you're away from me for only half a day, it feels like a year to me." And at that time the boy has feelings. He cares for you. Truly. Powerfully. But he doesn't have any money, and you just keep sacrificing yourself for him, talking to him, laughing with him. And you lose your value—and your family's. Okay, people see you together, but you say "They don't matter to me. Because even if I'm standing with him, he'll marry me, God willing."
>
> And finally, he doesn't marry you—how do you feel? It feels like a calamity, like a "psychological complex."[11] You feel angry at home, and you're always upset, because you don't trust anyone, even your parents. Since you sacrificed yourself for that boy, even in public you talked to him . . . and in the end he marries someone else; how do you imagine you would feel? You will remember your times together and what you went through in the past. You see how things happen. That a boy gives you his word of honor and later doesn't keep it is not right. That is what doesn't allow the girl who's become mature and responsible to trust a boy. She doesn't trust boys—never.

This excerpt reveals the common fear of being exploited by males in a relationship. It appears that males are mainly interested in the immediate sexual relationship, while females focus more on the long-term outcome, which they hope will be marriage. One wonders whether girls might say the goal is marriage because they do not want to admit enjoying sex, yet nearly all do want to marry, and being caught with someone who's "just for fun" may well decrease one's chances. It is interesting that girls in Zawiya do not see increased hetero-sexual interaction as part of a movement to greater general freedom, but as a means of attaining the traditional goal of marriage.

The different goals of males and females in relationships raises another interesting point. When my husband and I examined our data on heterosexual interaction, we found that most of the female data focus on relationships, while those for males focus more specifically on sexual behavior. This is interesting with regard to Carol Gilligan's recent work on the "different voices" she per-ceives in research on moral development. Although she says the different voic-es are "characterized not by gender but by theme," she notes that the association of one voice with women "is an empirical observation" although "this associa-tion is not absolute."[12] She identifies an ethic of care and an ethic of justice, the former more often associated with females and the latter with males in her research. "The logic underlying an ethic of care is a psychological logic of rela-tionships, which contrasts with the formal logic of fairness that informs the jus-tice approach."[13] "Instead of attachment [for females], individual achievement rivets the male imagination."[14] The greater concern of Zawiya girls with rela-tionships, while boys are more interested in the specific activity (might it be seen as achievement?), is suggestive of different orientations by gender in Morocco. Recall also that twice as many girls as boys (33 percent vs. 16 per-cent) said they wanted a good relationship with their future spouse. However, this area requires much more systematic investigation; it will be pursued in future work, including the analysis of a set of "describe yourself" interviews developed in collaboration with Gilligan.

A final effect of increased heterosexual interaction is that Zawiya is begin-ning to experience some change in norms. As we saw above, heterosexual behavior is still usually viewed negatively, but this is less so than in the past. This is visible in two main areas. First, while all the factors which allow an increase in heterosexual interaction have put some pressure on the traditional restrictive norms, the "marriage crisis" described above is the primary factor, and it has mothers wondering how to maximize their daughters' chances of mar-riage. Edited excerpts from an interview with a mother of three teenagers high-light these concerns.

> S. Is there another issue that shows this [generation] gap?
> M. There are hundreds of issues. . . . Do you think our parents could mention marriage to us? If the word marriage was uttered in the street [about me], I would throw stones and hit our neighbors [who said it]. . . . Now talk to her [the daughter is sixteen] about marriage, and she won't object; she'll like it. . . . A neighbor girl argued that because girls like her-

self just stay home, nobody cares about them. . . . [She said] "A great
many girls leave here and bring back a man, while we are staying home
and nobody is checking us out." . . . She does not go out . . . always staying home, always covering her head. [Other] girls go out, they wear
modern clothes . . . so they bring home husbands and we don't bring anything.

Many girls want to get married. . . . [One] told me "If I could find a
husband, I'd buy him with money. He wouldn't have to give anything
[i.e., bride price]. . . . All he needs to do is to come and propose marriage
to me. I'll buy clothes for him, do everything he needs, and go with
him."

While this mother is partially disparaging of girls' current interest in marriage, her concern with it is telling. I heard the themes she raised on many occasions: girls who stay at home (the traditional norm) don't get married, while
those who go out and are "seen" do. I had in fact noticed this during 1982, and
by 1984, mothers and daughters were discussing it. While I know of no specific examples, other people mentioned girls' families offering to pay the bride
price to ensure their daughters' marriage. Thus the motivation for girls to marry
is very strong, and is encouraging the decline of the norm of female seclusion
and isolation from males.

A second indication of changing norms is found in a recent change in marriage
ceremonies. In the past, couples were legally married about a year before their
families held a large party, at which evidence of virginity was displayed and after
which the couple cohabited. Recently, some couples have stopped having the
large party, and instead have a smaller family celebration at the time the marriage
contract is signed. They note that this is inspired by economy; the large parties are
costly and they prefer to spend the money furnishing a home. While this is certainly true, another characteristic of the smaller parties is that there is no test of
virginity, then or later. Couples may cohabit immediately, since they are legally
married, or they may wait. I suggest that this ceremonial change is a covert recognition that the norm of virginity for brides is declining. Instead of omitting the display of virginity from the usual ceremony (which is sometimes done), this new
ceremony avoids a focus of attention on the omission, and is also economical.

I have examined how the Moroccan system of meaning with regard to heterosexual interaction is both contested and maintained. This was done by presenting an intensive view over time of both the norms designed to maintain traditional sex-segregated behavior and the activities that are challenging these
norms. The current "marriage crisis" for some young women shows this
sequence can also be reversed, providing an example of the pursuit of a traditional goal (marriage) leading to a movement away from traditional norms (little or no contact between the sexes before marriage).

Another motivation for more heterosexual interaction before marriage is the increasing expectation of affectional support from a spouse, whom one should thus know. Yet rather than leading to a supportive relationship, the effect of increased interaction is to give couples more realistic bases for their expectations than the romantic fantasies of secluded adolescents. At this point in Zawiya, increased interaction usually leads to distrust by females and disgust by males, hardly bases for a close relationship after marriage. I agree with Mernissi that the "direct confrontation between men and women brought up in sexually antagonistic traditions is likely to be, in this transitional period, loaded with tensions and fears on both sides."[15]

By the early 1980s, many growing semi-rural towns shared with Zawiya the larger population, greater educational and employment opportunities for females, and less immediate political control than in the past. In these conditions, we would expect heterosexual interactions to be changing in a similar way. One might note that even in a quite different and supposedly less antagonistic tradition, the attempts of many American couples to be "closer" are fraught with tensions.[16] However, in my experience Moroccan women have been very resourceful in dealing with problems, and their various responses to the current situation will be followed with interest. Currently, the young women of Zawiya appear to be learning to maneuver themselves skillfully between the old boundaries and the new frontiers.

Notes

1   The research on which this paper is based was supported by grants from the National Institute of Mental Health and the William T. Grant Foundation. I would like to thank Professors Beatrice Whiting and Douglas A. Davis for helpful comments on an earlier version of this paper.

2   Dale F. Eickelman, "Introduction: Self and Community in Middle Eastern Societies," *Anthropological Quarterly,* 1985, 58:135–40.

3   Fatima Mernissi, *Beyond the Veil: Male–Female Dynamics in a Modern Muslim Society,* Cambridge, Mass.: Schenkman, 1975, p. 58.

4   These data were collected in 1982 and 1984 by myself and my husband, Douglas A. Davis, as part of research for the Harvard Adolescence Project directed by John and Beatrice Whiting and Irven DeVore. The data were collected from a sample of fifty families who had lived in the same neighborhood of Zawiya for at least ten years, including well-off, middle-class, and poor families (all in local terms). The data used here include self-reports from over one hundred youths aged ten to twenty-two, plus a psychological test "Draw a Person" on gender role preference taken by sixty adolescents. In addition, we conducted open-ended interviews with about twenty-five young people and a few parents; some of these were taped and provide an exceptionally rich source of data on how they feel about the current changes in heterosexual interaction and what it means to be male or female in Morocco today. We also

obtained data in casual conversations about and observations of young people interacting. Direct questions on sensitive topics are difficult in any culture, and Zawiya
was no exception. However, my work in the town over twenty years allowed me to
develop sensitivity to local concerns, a basis for trust with many people, and to
observe changes over time myself.

5   By norms, I mean what people state to be proper behavior rather than what they do.
The traditional norms described here are based on statements of the parental generation in the neighborhood of Zawiya in which we worked. They refer to how people
should have behaved in the past; actual behavior is analyzed below.

6   Susan Schaefer Davis, "Sexual Maturation, Cultural Constraint, and the Concept of
the Self," paper presented at the Annual Meeting of the American Anthropological
Association in Chicago, November 16–20, 1983.

7   It is interesting that apparently norms in the U.S. are just the reverse; boyfriends are
approved, but boys as friends are often discouraged, as reported in a first-person
account by a twelve-year-old (Spiro 1985).

8   This is interesting with regard to Frayser's (1986) finding that many American
teenagers do not use birth control because they prefer to feel their sexual activity is
a result of being "swept away" rather than premeditated.

9   Susan Schaefer Davis and Douglas A. Davis, "Adolescence in a Moroccan Town,"
in the series *Adolescents in a Changing World,* New Brunswick, N.J.: Rutgers
University Press, 1989.

10 Susan Schaefer Davis, *Patience and Power: Women's Lives in a Moroccan Village,*
Cambridge, Mass.: Schenkman, 1983.

11 The recent use of this term by Zawiya residents is striking, and suggests that western psychological concepts are entering Moroccan discourse along with the emotional consequences of "westernization."

12 Carol Gilligan, *In a Different Voice: Psychological Theory and Women's
Development,* Cambridge, Mass.: Harvard University Press, 1983, p. 2.

13 Ibid., p. 73.

14 Ibid., p. 163.

15 Mernissi, p. 104.

16 Lillian B. Rubin, *Worlds of Pain: Life in the Working-Class Family,* New York: Basic
Books, 1976; *Intimate Strangers: Men and Women Together,* New York: Harper and
Row, 1983.

References

Davis, Susan Schaefer. 1983a. *Patience and Power: Women's Lives in a Moroccan
Village.* Cambridge, Mass.: Schenkman.
————. 1983b. "Sexual Maturation, Cultural Constraint, and the Concept of the Self."
Paper presented at the Annual Meeting of the American Anthropological Association
in Chicago, November 16–20.

Davis, Susan Schaefer, and Douglas A. Davis. 1989. *Adolescence in a Moroccan Town.* In the series *Adolescents in a Changing World.* New Brunswick, N.J.: Rutgers University Press.

Eickelman, Dale F. 1985. "Introduction: Self and Community in Middle Eastern Societies." *Anthropological Quarterly* 58:135–40.

Frayser, Suzanne. 1986. "Sex and the American Teenager." Paper presented at the Annual Meeting of the Society for Cross-Cultural Research in San Diego, February 14–16.

Gilligan, Carol. 1982. *In a Different Voice: Psychological Theory and Women's Development.* Cambridge, Mass.: Harvard University Press.

Kohlberg, Lawrence. 1984. *The Psychology of Moral Development.* New York: Harper and Row.

Mernissi, Fatima. 1975. *Beyond the Veil: Male–Female Dynamics in a Modern Muslim Society.* Cambridge, Mass.: Schenkman.

Rubin, Lillian B. 1976. *Worlds of Pain: Life in the Working-Class Family.* New York: Basic Books.

———. 1983. *Intimate Strangers: Men and Women Together.* New York: Harper and Row.

Spiro, Jaala. 1985. "Just Friends." *Ms.* September: 87–88.

12

Brother/Sister Relationships: Connectivity, Love, and Power in the Reproduction of Patriarchy in Lebanon

Suad Joseph

The Yusifs[1] were a working-class family living in the urban neighborhood of Camp Trad, Borj Hammoud, a part of the Greater Beirut area of Lebanon. Abu Hanna,[2] the Lebanese Maronite father, was a man who, even on the rare occasions when he was angry, spoke with the soft slow lull of someone who had just awoken from a deep sleep. Um Hanna, the mother and Palestinian Catholic, graced an abundant figure and a shy yet welcoming smile.[3] A caring family with five boys and two girls, the Yusifs were respected as peace-loving, honorable folks by their neighbors. I lived next door to the Yusifs from 1971 to 1973 and came to know them well over the course of a decade.[4] When I first met them, I sensed a harmony. There never seemed to be a raised voice. I developed close relationships with all the members of the family, taking on the role of sister with the parents and aunt with the younger children.[5]

I was particularly close to the oldest son, Hanna. With soft wavy brown hair and roguish brown eyes that seemed always poised to make an assertion, Hanna, at 19, was seen as a highly attractive marriage choice. Very conscious of his grooming and masculine self-presentation, he ritually combed his hair with a comb kept in his back pocket. His medium build and height seemed to expand as he walked with firm yet graceful movements that appeared thought-out. There were few college students in this street, and Hanna was already in the 11th grade in 1972. A politically active bridge-builder with friends across ethnic and religious groups, Hanna was viewed as peace-loving and conscientious.

I was shocked, therefore, one sunny afternoon to hear Hanna shouting at his sister Flaur and slapping her across her face. Flaur, at 12, was the oldest daughter and the third oldest child. She seemed to have an opinion on most things, was never shy to speak her mind, and welcomed guests with boisterous laughter and dancing light brown eyes that invited visitors to wonder what she was up to. With a lively sense of humor and good-natured mischief about her, neighbors thought of her as a live wire, despite the fact that she did not conform to Lebanese ideals of feminine beauty.

From *American Ethnologist* 21 (1):50–73 (1994). Reprinted by permission. Suad Joseph is Professor of Anthropology at the University of California, Davis.

Hanna played father to Flaur, even though she helped care for the younger siblings who looked to her for mothering. Hanna repeatedly instructed Flaur to comb her hair, dress attractively, and carry herself with grace. In a local culture in which self-grooming occupied young women, Flaur seemed to pay no attention to her clothing, hair, body, or comportment. Her curls fluttered around her face, her clothes were often wrinkled and worn, and hugging her you could feel a few pre-adolescent rolls adorning her hips and waist. This irritated Hanna considerably. His ire at her peaked, though, whenever he caught her lingering on the street corner near their apartment building gossiping with other girls. He would forcefully escort her upstairs to their apartment, slap her, and demand that she behave with dignity. No doubt the charge in their relationship came in part because Flaur was entering puberty as Hanna was reaching manhood.

Perhaps because of my special relationship with the family, I was stunned at Hanna's behavior. Flaur sometimes ran crying into my apartment. A few times I heard Flaur screaming, and I ran across the hall. Um Hanna watched. No one, myself included, questioned my right to intervene.

Hanna took it as his right and responsibility to mold and discipline his sister.[6] Neither Um Hanna nor Flaur appeared to appeal to Abu Hanna about Hanna's behavior. Flaur's 17-year-old brother, Farid, might have protected her, but he deferred to Hanna. Family members, including Flaur, agreed that Hanna was acting within his brotherly role.

Hanna regarded me as an older sister, consulting me on personal, social, and political matters. I had accepted that role and so felt comfortable speaking to him about his behavior. When we talked, he said he knew what the world was like and she did not. It was his brotherly responsibility to train Flaur to be a lady. I suggested he might teach rather than beat her. He responded, with a smile in his eyes, that Flaur could not understand words and he did not hurt her. With authority, he added, he did it *"minshanha, minshan mistakbilha"* ("for her, for her future").

When I discussed Hanna's behavior with Um Hanna, she found the matter amusing. I was surprised. She claimed that Hanna was doing his brotherly duty. She continued that Hanna cared deeply about Flaur. Besides, she added, Flaur provoked Hanna and brought his violence upon herself. Maybe, she chuckled, Flaur even liked it.

Flaur, for her part, seemed not unmindful of her own power over Hanna. While she admired her brother, she teased him about his constant grooming or the romantic interests of neighborhood women in him. She was aware that her behavior would provoke Hanna. There was a willful element to her behavior that I thought was either an attempt to assert her own identity or to involve her brother intimately in her life.

On one occasion when Um Hanna, Flaur, and I were discussing Hanna's behavior, Um Hanna repeated, in Flaur's presence, that Flaur invited and enjoyed Hanna's aggression. With a mischievous smile in her eyes, Flaur laughed and agreed. She added, with bravado, "It doesn't even hurt when Hanna hits me." On another occasion, she indicated that she would like a husband like Hanna.

When I returned to Camp Trad in 1978 during the Civil War,[7] I stayed for a couple of days with the Yusifs. Flaur was married and had a one-year-old baby. While taller, more voluptuous, and womanly, she still seemed a bit disheveled. Her husband was quiet, thin, and pale to the point of seeming unhealthy. Um Hanna asked me what I thought of Flaur's husband. I responded that I thought he was *'akil* (well-mannered). Um Hanna continued that, prior to her marriage, Flaur had lost weight and had become quite pretty. In the pocket-size wedding picture she showed me, Flaur did look beautiful and like a perfect size eight. She had had a number of suitors, Um Hanna, went on, and could have gotten a better looking man. She asserted, *"Win Hanna wa win hada"* ("Where is Hanna and where is this one")—implying that the best match for Flaur would have been someone like Hanna.

The relationship between Hanna and Flaur is a prime example of the connective love/power dynamic between brothers and sisters in these Arab families. That dynamic was critical to Hanna's empowerment and masculinization and Flaur's domestication and feminization. Hanna was teaching Flaur to accept male power in the name of love. His family supported his learning that loving his sister meant taking charge of her and that he could discipline her if his action was understood to be in her interest. Flaur was reinforced in learning that the love of a male could include that male's violent control and that to receive this love involved submission to control. She was learning that her brother was a loving protector and controlling power in her life.

Hanna was additionally teaching Flaur how to present her feminine sexuality. She was learning to become a sexual person for her brother. Given Abu Hanna's absence and the interest that Hanna took in her, her brother was the most involved male sexual figure during her puberty. By feminizing Flaur, Hanna was masculinizing himself. Hanna also was using his culturally acceptable control over his sister to challenge his father's authority in the family. By taking charge of his sister, with blessings of his mother and siblings, he highlighted his father's failures as head of the household. Hanna was learning to become a patriarch by becoming the man of the house in relation to his sister, mother, and younger siblings. Hanna and Flaur's relationship socialized each into the links between gender, sexuality, love, and power. Their mutual dependency was underwritten by patriarchal connectivity inscribed as love. Their relationship reveals psychodynamic, social structural, and cultural processes through which the brother/sister relationship contributes to the reproduction of Arab patriarchy—a role that scholars of the Arab world have yet to unravel.

Brother/Sister Relationships: The Arab Context

While brother/sister relationships have received anthropological attention in the literature on a number of societies,[8] relatively little of the work on Arab societies has considered the centrality of brother/sister relationships to the reproduction of family life and patriarchy. This lacuna comes in part from the relative lack of studies problematizing the internal dynamics of Arab family life. With the "Arab family" becoming increasingly the center of controversy in the literature and popular culture of the Middle East, new efforts have been made to more closely scrutinize familial issues on both Arab and national bases.[9] Most of the research on family in the Arab world, stressing the cultural ideals of patriarchy, patrilineality, patrilocality, and patrilineal endogamy, has focused on relationships among males, however.[10] Scholars have paid less attention to brother/sister or other key male/female relationships. Research on Lebanon also offers insights into family life but does not address the brother/sister relationship in detail.[11]

The little work that does exist on brother/sister relationships in the Arab World tends to regard it as either romantic or patriarchal, focusing respectively on "love" or "power." Scholars who focus on "love" aspects of the relationship are often attuned to psychodynamics but usually do not link them with social structural and cultural process. Scholars identifying the "power" aspects of the relationship tend to be interested not in brother/sister relationships per se but in family structure and culture. These scholars often neglect psychodynamics or inadequately connect them to social structural and cultural processes. Few studies effectively link psychodynamic, social structural, and cultural processes. Most, therefore, do not recognize the connectivity that charges the love/power dynamics underpinning the central role played by the brother/sister relationship in the reproduction of Arab patriarchy.

The Romantic View

In a functionalist vein, the romantic view represents the brother/sister relationship as a kind of safety valve—a relationship of love and mutuality in a presumed cold and authoritarian family system. The approach differentiates the brother/sister relationship from the father/daughter and other familial relationships as the only safe cross-gender relationship in otherwise relatively gender-segregated societies. Given patrilineal endogamy and a family culture in which a woman continues to belong to her natal kin group and her male kin continue to be responsible for her throughout her life, the romantic view valorizes the link to a brother as the woman's lifeline.

One of the best representatives of this romantic view of brother/sister relationships is folklorist Hassan El-Shamy. El-Shamy (1979) contends that the brother/sister relationship and its derivative, the ego/maternal uncle relationship, are characterized by a mutual loving not found in other family relationships. All other family relationships (parent/child, spouse, brother/brother, sister/sister, ego/paternal uncle, brother/sister's husband, sister/brother's wife), he claims, are organized around hostility. He asserts (1981:319) that there are incestuous tendencies underlying the Arab brother/sister relationship, which are unrecognized and untreated in the Arabic psychiatric literature. Basing his analysis on variations of a folktale found in most Arab countries (1979),[12] analysis of selected Egyptian fiction (1976), and a review of some Arab psychiatric literature (1981), he posits a "Brother–Sister Syndrome." This syndrome, is "responsible for the development of a distinctive culture and personality pattern characteristic of the Arab, which transcends religious, regional, and social class differences" and "plays a decisive role in the formation, development, and maintenance of family structure and all other related organizations" (El-Shamy 1979:1). El-Shamy, while recognizing significant psychodynamics of the brother/sister relationship, sees little of the hierarchy and so does not link the relationship to Arab patriarchy.

El-Shamy is not alone in casting the cross-sibling relationship in romantic terms, however.[13] Hilma Granqvist, in her classic early studies of Palestinian peasants, contends that for the Palestinian *fellahin* (peasants) of the 1930s the love between sisters and brothers was "more beautiful than the love between wife and husband, because not founded on passion" (1935:II:254). Granqvist notes that when a woman married, her brother offered himself as her "camel" to carry her burdens (1935:II:252).[14] The brother was more responsible for a woman than her husband. "The husband is only a garment which a woman puts on or throws off again, or she herself can be 'thrown off' by her husband, but the brother is the one, who is always there" (Granqvist 1935:II:253). If a married woman committed a shameful act, the father or brother, not the husband, was responsible (1935:II:253). The man's responsibility for his sister had eternal consequences, according to one of Granqvist's informants who asserted: "This is my sister. To-morrow in eternity [i.e., at the Judgment Day] she will make me responsible, but not my children and my wife" (l935:II:254).[15] Although the power between brothers and sisters seems apparent here, Granqvist makes little of it, focusing on the implied love.

Michael Meeker (1976:388) offers an intriguing comparison of Turkish and Arab brother/sister and husband/wife relationships.[16] He contends that among Arabs the disgrace of a woman must be responded to by "those who 'love,'" while among the Turks it must be responded to by "those who 'control.'" Given that among both the Arabs and the Turks, the brother/sister relationship is one of love and the husband/wife relationship is one of control, then among the Arabs the brother must respond to a sister's disgrace, whereas among the Turks it is the husband. Meeker, however, does not discuss the connection between love and responsibility. The brother's responsibility of response invests him in controlling the sister's behavior so that he would not have to respond. Responsibility translates into power; love and power become intertwined.

The romantic view of the brother/sister relationship is at times reproduced by scholars in the important attempt to represent Arab persons by respecting their voices. In a portrayal of Egyptian feminist Huda Sha'rawi, Leila Ahmed comments that Sha'rawi's love for her brother was the deepest and most intense of her life.[17] Ahmed quotes Sha'rawi as asserting that when her brother died in her late 30s, "'all my hopes died,' and but for a sense of duty toward her children, 'I would not have survived him by an instant'" (Ahmed 1989:161). Offering significant insights into her life, Ahmed views Sha'rawi's relationship with her brother through Sha'rawi's lens of love, even in transactions that also could be interpreted as displays of power. For example, after a period of estrangement, Sha'rawi separated from her husband. According to Sha'rawi's report, her brother refused to proceed with his own marriage until she returned to her husband. Ahmed observes, "Not wanting to stand in the way of her brother's happiness, she agreed to a reconciliation" (1989:172). One could read love/power dynamics here also—the brother using his happiness to control his sister.

The Patriarchal View
Most of the literature on the honor/shame complex focuses on social structural and cultural rather than psychodynamic processes. The scholars interested in psychodynamic aspects of honor/shame rarely apply their analyses systematically to brother/sister relationships and tend to focus on non-Arab Mediterranean societies (Gilmore 1987). Scholars who recognize the hierarchy in the brother/sister relationship tend to be interested in the social structure and culture of the Arab family rather than in psychodynamics or the brother/sister relationship per se.

In this patriarchal view, the brother/sister relationship, as an extension of the father/daughter relationship, is an instrument of the honor/shame complex thought by many scholars to predominate in Mediterranean family culture.[18] Women, through their modesty, are supposed to uphold family honor. Should they bring shame onto the family, their closest male patrilineal relatives must restore family honor by disciplining them or the other culprits involved. Usually the task belongs to fathers or brothers, but also might be undertaken by paternal uncles or male cousins.

Most scholars tend not to discriminate conditions under which one or another of the patrilineal males responds. We might wonder whether Arabs differentiate. For example, a Jordanian adage appears to gloss male patrilineal relatives: "'Deficiency harks back to [patrilineal] origins' but the mare belongs to the rider [husband]'" (Antoun 1968:692).[19] Yet assertions specifying responsibility can also be found. Alois Musil notes that for the Rwala Bedouins:

The person whom the married woman can most inconvenience is her own brother; hence the proverb: "the brother of a married woman is far removed from any good done by her, but very close to any evil she may be guilty of." [Musil 1928:494]

In this view, the father and brother are also responsible for the protection and well-being of the daughter/sister. The father/brother are entrusted with control and protection of the daughter/sister throughout their lives. The brother, then, as a representative of the patrilineal line, exerts patriarchal authority to protect and control the sister in order to maintain family honor.[20] Recognizing the power brothers exert over sisters, scholars adopting this view link the brother/sister relationship with the reproduction of patriarchy. But they tend not to differentiate it from a woman's relationship with her father or her close patrilineal relatives, thereby missing the complexity of the love/power dynamics between brothers and sisters.

Privileging social structural and cultural processes and conflating brother/sister relationships with others patrilineally distorts the brother/sister relationship. We must unravel the historically and culturally specific dynamics and analyze the co-determinancy of psychodynamic, social structural, and cultural processes.

Connectivity, Love, and Power in the Reproduction of Patriarchy in Lebanon: Psychodynamic, Social Structural, and Cultural Processes

It would be an easy error to assume that if one privileges psychodynamic events in brother/sister relationships, their mutual love is foregrounded and that if one privileges social structural and cultural events, their disparate power is foregrounded. I argue that the patriarchal connectivity of brothers and sisters in love/nurturance and power/violence dynamics was expressed psychodynamically, social structurally, and culturally. It was the interlinking of connectivity, love, and power, throughout, that gave the brother/sister relationship its centrality in the reproduction of Arab patriarchy.

Classical Middle Eastern patriarchy is probably best understood in terms of those pastoral societies in which kinship was coterminous with society and was the key force in organizing politics, economics, religion, and other social processes. The dominance of male elders over kin groups translated into dominance over society. The emergence of state structures transformed classical patriarchy, as state leaders competed with kinship leaders for control over individuals and groups often by co-oping kin structures, kin morality, and kin idioms into the state, leading to state patriarchal forms. In many contemporary Middle Eastern societies, kin groups continue to offer effective resistance to state control over their membership. Contemporary patriarchy in the Arab Middle East, therefore, takes many forms. Minimally, then, I will use patriarchy here to mean the dominance of males over females and elders over juniors (males and females) and the mobilization of kinship structures, morality, and idioms to institutionalize and legitimate these forms of power. By power, I mean the capacity to direct the behavior of others, even against their will.

Contemporary Arab patriarchy takes many forms leading to variability in brother/sister relationships based on state, class, religion, ethnic, rural/urban, and other differences.[21] I have chosen, nevertheless, to refer to the phenomenon I am analyzing as "Arab" because of the national, ethnic, and religious heterogeneity of the population of Camp Trad (see below). In using the term "Arab" to refer to the patterns described here, I am signaling the recent origins of the residents of the neighborhood and their heterogeneity.[22] Camp Trad was mostly working class and was, therefore, relatively homogeneous in class terms. As the material below indicates, however, I observed many of the same patterns in other social classes in Lebanon.[23] The national, ethnic, and religious mixture of families, their relative recency in Lebanon and/or Camp Trad, and the observations of similar patterns in other social classes in Lebanon would suggest that the general patterns described were not unique to this urban situation. The meaning of any institution or social practice must be understood in its historically and culturally specific context, however. The implications of the patterns described here for brother/sister relationships in other Arab countries or classes would need to be tested empirically.

Psychodynamic Processes: Connectivity and Love in Patriarchy in Lebanon
I use connectivity to mean psychodynamic processes by which one person comes to see him/herself as part of another. Boundaries between persons are relatively fluid so that each needs the other to complete the sense of selfhood. One's sense of self is intimately linked with the self of another such that the security, identity, integrity, dignity, and self-worth of one is tied to the actions of the other. Connective persons are not separate or autonomous. They are open to and require the involvement of others in shaping their emotions, desires, attitudes, and identities. Like Catherine Keller (1986:9, 114), I use connective, rather than connected, to indicate an activity or intention rather than a state of being.[24]

The concept of connectivity is useful in characterizing the social production of relational selves with diffuse boundaries who require continuous interaction with significant others for a sense of completion. Defined as such, it is a non-culturally specific concept. I use connectivity to depart from Western-centric notions of relationality that are associated with judgments of dysfunctionality. The leading theorist of dysfunctional notions of relationality, Salvador Minuchin (1978), offered the concept of enmeshment to describe constructs of self that resonated with my observations in Camp Trad. His insights, though powerful, are limited by his Western-based assumptions that individuation, autonomy, and separateness are psychodynamically necessary for healthy maturation. This judgment emerges from evaluations of persons in Western, industrialized, market, and contract-based societies organized around the expectation of mobile and autonomous selves. Minuchin's family systems theory is also limited by its functionalism and his neglect of patriarchy (Luepnitz 1988:57).

Rather, I employ connectivity in the context of a culture in which the family was valued over and above the person or society and in which "individuation," "autonomy," "separateness," and "boundedness" as understood in the American psychotherapeutic literature were less valued than bonding with and commitment to family.[25] It is in the context of the primacy of the family over the person and society that the love/power dynamics of the brother/sister relationship made sense and contributed to the reproduction of Arab patriarchy.[26] This is not to say, however, that there were no individuated, autonomous, separate, bounded selves in Camp Trad. Rather, I argue that such bounded selfhood was relatively unsupported, while connective selfhood was both supported and valorized.

In Camp Trad, brothers and sisters were expected to love one another. I use "love" here to mean deep "feelings" of caring. Current research has significantly contributed to culturally sensitizing emotion words (Abu-Lughod 1986; Lutz 1988; Rosaldo 1984). While I do not employ a literary usage of "love" as does Lila Abu-Lughod in her important work, I agree with her that emotion words can signal culturally significant values that "contribute to the representations of the self, representations that are tied to morality, which in turn is ultimately tied to politics in its broadest sense" (1986:34). Meanings of emotion words must be understood in the context of local cultures, the value systems they signal, and the culturally specific notions of selfhood that they represent.

Connective relationships could be loving or hostile. Connective relationships were considered loving when persons anticipated each other's needs, attended to and acted in each other's interests, and took on each other's concerns, pains, and joys as theirs. In Camp Trad, love was understood as an enactment of connective relationships. Brothers and sisters were called upon to develop such loving relationships. Their senses of self, identity, and future called for their mutual involvement with each other. They saw themselves reflected in each other's eyes and lives. A brother was responsible for his sister's behavior. A sister was expected to embrace a brother's wishes as her own. The boundaries between them were fluid. They were to read each other, anticipate needs, and fulfill expectations unasked. Figuring out what was his, what was hers, were not central preoccupations. They were to share, care, and commit to each other.

Connectivity was poignant among Camp Trad brothers and sisters because the expectation of love and nurturance was coupled with gendered dominance

supported by familial structure and culture. Through the brother/sister relationship, men learned that loving women entailed controlling them and women
learned that loving men entailed submitting to them. Sisters also had some
power over brothers. Women had numerous avenues for involving their brothers in their lives. Because a woman's behavior immediately reflected on her
brothers' honor, dignity, and sense of self, she could enhance or detract from her
brothers' status by her actions and potentially compel her brothers into action.
Connectivity was a double-ended hook joining the lives of brothers and sisters.

As a result, the brother/sister relationship became a critical vehicle for the
socialization of males and females into culturally appropriate gender roles, thus
helping to reproduce patriarchy. That is, I am arguing that, in Camp Trad, contrary to much of Western psychodynamic theory, which places almost exclusive
stress on the parent/child relationship for modeling of appropriate gender roles,
sibling relationships were also significant vehicles of gender socialization.
Cross siblings used their relationships to learn and practice socially acceptable
notions of masculinity and femininity, dominance and submission, and commitment to patrilineal kinship structures, morality, and idioms—processes mediated through connectivity.

Social Structural Processes: Family, Marriage, and Inheritance
A number of features of Arab family social structure contributed to the dependence of Camp Trad women on their brothers. First, women were considered to
belong to their natal families even after marriage. Their natal families were ultimately responsible for their behavior and well-being—and in the long course of
lives, such responsibility fell most heavily on brothers.

Second, Muslim men could marry up to four wives, and divorce, although
uncommon in practice, was primarily a male privilege. Legally Muslim men
could divorce their wives easily and/or marry additional wives. Thus, a Muslim
marriage left women structurally vulnerable. For the same reasons, reliance on
a father could be problematic.[27] Muslim fathers could become involved with the
children of other wives and even abandon children by previous marriages. Full
siblings, however, shared the same set of family ties. Because of the structural
possibility of abandonment by the father, the brother/sister relationship also
could be a locus of contestation between sons and fathers about control over the
family. Brothers could use their rights over their sisters to challenge the authority of their fathers, thus preparing to become patriarchs in their own right.

Third, the cultural ideal of marriage between the children of brothers
(FaBroSo/Da marriage), according to most scholars,[28] bolsters both patrilineality and patriarchy—that is, reinforces the natal kin ties of both men and women.
For men, FaBroSo/Da marriages meant that their sisters could marry the men
they considered their closest allies after their own brothers and the ones most
bound to protect their sisters. For sisters it meant that their brothers could marry

the women closest to being their own sisters. And each could marry the person closest to the role of their cross-siblings.[29] Endogamy also meant brothers and sisters could live near each other, facilitating the fulfillment of the cultural expectation that brothers remain responsible for sisters throughout their lives.

Regardless of whether siblings married relatives, there seemed to be an edge in their relationships with each other's spouses. Structural strains in marriages could develop from the continued claims of brothers and sisters on each other's love and loyalty. Men and women expected their spouses to live up to their idealized images of their cross-siblings and often negatively compared their spouses to these images. El-Shamy found that Arabic folktales depict the sister's relationship with the brother's wife as one of jealousy and hostility (1979:43), while the brother's relationship with the sister's husband is depicted as mainly neutral, though at times "potentially negative" (1979:59).

Siblings could offer protections to each other's children, even against parental authority. The brother as *khal* (maternal uncle) played an important structural role as nurturer of his sister's children. El Shamy (1979:79), quoting an Arab adage, "*'al-khal walid'* (i.e., the maternal uncle is a father [literally, 'birth-giver'])," argues that the affection of the *khal* for his sister's children was an expression of brother/sister love.[30] Similarly, the sister as *'amta* (paternal aunt) was seen as nurturer. This role of the *'amta* was reflected in the popular Lebanese saying: "*al 'ammi bit 'imm matrah al um*" ("the father's sister can take the place of the mother").

Structural tensions from competing obligations could constrain the brother/sister relationship. Aging parents expected to be cared for by sons, even though in reality many were cared for by daughters. Men's obligations to their families of procreation increased as their families matured. Thus, a man's duties to his sister were always competing with claims on him by his parents, wife, and children. As a result, brothers often could not fulfill their sisters' or the culture's expectations.[31] Women were also structurally caught between competing loyalties. Husbands demanded loyalty from their wives. Children expected the undivided involvement of their mothers. Women often felt torn between families of origin and of procreation as they matured.

For sisters, another social structural source of limitations developed from the asymmetrical expectations engendered early on. Brothers were socialized to receive more than to give service to sisters. Throughout their growing years, sisters did for brothers much more than brothers did for sisters. As adults, brothers expected the same. Women at times felt frustrated by the asymmetry.

Tensions were also built into the structure of inheritance. Many women left their patrimony with their brothers as insurance against future need. This could lead to tensions with husbands who wanted to claim their wives' inheritance. Additionally, a woman's children, as they matured, might lay claims on their mother's inheritance.

The issue addressed implicitly by these observations is the preservation of patriarchy in the context of a segmentary patrilineal system. In such systems, the boundary of the kin unit could change in keeping with what was contested. Depending upon where the line was drawn around the family at a particular time, preservation of patriarchy might require opposition to siblings' spouses (in FaBroSo/Da marriages, the cousin) and at other times alliance. While these were Muslim patterns, the values surrounding them permeated Camp Trad culture across religious lines. In the Camp Trad cultural ideal, the structure of family, marriage, and inheritance reinforced sisters' dependence on brothers and brothers' responsibility for sisters despite these variable conditions.[32]

Cultural Processes: Honor and Shame
For both brothers and sisters in Camp Trad, connective identities and mutual love were linked to family honor. The ideal of brother/sister relationships in Camp Trad was based on a cultural promise: A brother will protect his sister; a sister will uphold her family's honor. Men saw themselves as their sisters' protectors.[33] Invested in their sisters' behavior, their sense of their own dignity and honor was tied to their sisters' comportment. They were permitted by their parents and the culture to see sisters as extensions of themselves and thus to be molded to fit their sense of self. This included the cultural sanction to discipline their sisters when their behavior was considered improper.

Sisters identified with their brothers as their security. A woman without a brother was seen as somewhat naked in the world. A brother's achievements opened opportunities for their sisters, just as their failures closed doors. Sisters understood that to receive the protection and support of brothers, they had to address their brothers' expectations.[34] They were socialized to accept their brothers' authority over their lives and to see it in their own interests to accept that authority. Even when they might have disagreed with their brothers, sisters acknowledged their brothers' "rights" over them as a central vehicle for maintaining family honor.

Thus, connectivity was an underlying psychodynamic process supporting the enactment of the cultural practices entailed in maintaining family honor. It is, I argue, because their connectivity encouraged brothers and sisters to view love and power as parts of the same dynamic that their relationship was so critical an instrument of the reproduction of Arab patriarchy. It is also because love and power were experienced as part of the same dynamic that these patriarchal relations had such a hold on the members of Arab families. That is, patriarchy seated in love may be much harder to unseat than patriarchy in which loving and nurturance are not so explicitly mandated and supported.[35]

My data are presented around three sets of processes. After describing the local community, I will first discuss psychodynamic processes in brother/sister relationships focusing on the love and power dimensions of connectivity.

Second, I analyze social structural processes of family, marriage, and inheritance, drawing out the implications for cross-sibling mutual dependence and responsibility. Finally, I consider how cultural processes, working through notions of honor and shame, link brothers' and sisters' senses of self. The processes I discuss below did not characterize all brother/sister relationships at all times in Camp Trad. Yet, they constituted such a significant pattern of relationality in discourse and in practice that one could see, and I demonstrate, a fundamental intertwining of connectivity, love, and power in psychodynamic, and social structural, and cultural processes.

Borj Hammoud is an urban working-class municipality in the Greater Beirut area. In the early 1970s, almost all of the religious sects and ethnic groups of both Lebanon and the neighboring Arab countries were represented in Borj Hammoud. About 40 percent of the population were Lebanese Shi'a. Forty percent were Armenian Orthodox, Armenian Catholic, or Armenian Protestant. The remaining 20 percent were Maronite, Roman Catholic, Greek Orthodox, Greek Catholic, Arab Protestant, Syrian Orthodox, Syrian Catholic, Sunni, Druze, or 'Alawite.[36] The population included Lebanese, Syrians, Palestinians, Greeks, Jordanians, and Egyptians.

My fieldwork in the Camp Trad neighborhood of Borj Hammoud just prior to the outbreak of the civil war in 1975 captured a unique moment of modern Lebanese history. It was a period of change, escalating tensions, and potential (Barakat 1977; Salibi 1976). Camp Trad experienced an unprecedented high degree of heterogeneous relationships among peoples of different religious sects, ethnic groups, and nationalities. Its residents, primarily Arab, included members of all of the communities mentioned above. Many shared patterns of family life developed across religious, ethnic, and national lines (Joseph 1982,1983).

Most of the families in Camp Trad were recent migrants to the area.[37] A Lebanese Maronite agricultural area at the turn of the century, the neighborhood became gradually urbanized, particularly in the 1940s with the influx of Armenian refugees. Palestinians entered the area after the creation of Israel in 1948. Syrians and rural Lebanese began settling in the 1950s for economic opportunities or to escape political insecurities. In the early 1970s, few household heads had been born in Camp Trad or Borj Hammoud. Almost all the residents had come from rural backgrounds, where extended family ties remained vital. Some, like the Palestinians and Armenians, were cut off from their places of origin; while others, like the Lebanese, Syrians, Jordanians, and Egyptians, had access to natal family and village ties. A number of the residents had managed to reconstitute parts of their extended families within Camp Trad and Borj Hammoud. Sociologically, there were many household forms: nuclear families, joint, extended, duo-focal, single-parent, single individual. Yet, culturally, Arab family ideals of patrilineality, patriarchy, and patrilocality were relatively strong for most residents.

In the early 1970s, when I began fieldwork, Lebanon was in the midst of economic, political, and social crises. Banking, trade, and tourism were being undermined by the Arab-Israeli conflict fought on Lebanese soil. Inflation, unemployment and underemployment, and worker strikes fueled the sense of economic crisis. Rapid urbanization had left the infrastructure of Greater Beirut ill-equipped to respond to the mass demand for basic services. A "ring of poverty" circled Beirut.

The Lebanese state system was being challenged from within and without. Lebanon had become the primary site for attacks by Israel against the Palestinians and vice versa. Political minorities, such as the Shi'a, were organizing to demand equitable representation in government. Bribery and brokerage became necessary for most political transactions (Joseph 1990). Stalemated, the minimalist Lebanese state could not provide the services and protection citizens wanted (Barakat 1977; Haley and Snider 1979; Joseph 1978; Odeh 1985).

In this economic, political, and social pressure cooker, individuals were thrown onto their families for help finding jobs, financial assistance, political protection, and emotional support (Joseph 1982). Family had always been central to social, economic, and political life in Lebanon. Ruling elites recruited following and distributed services to their clientele on the basis of kinship (Khalaf 1968). Non-elite individuals relied on their families for brokerage and protection in a state that was perceived as untrustworthy and inefficient.[38] While it was not new for individuals to rely on their families, such dependence was precarious, because the same pressures were limiting the avenues through which family members lived out their obligations. So, while individuals needed, turned to, and believed in their families as the repositories of their identities and securities, family members found it increasingly difficult to carry out familial obligations.

The conditions of the early 1970s in urban Lebanon, therefore, in many ways were undermining the foundations of patriarchy. It was a struggle for brothers and sisters to live out the roles and responsibilities for which they were socialized. Under these pressures, it is remarkable that brother/sister relationships remained powerful. It is only by linking psychodynamic, social structural, and cultural processes that we can understand the ongoing struggle to live out brother/sister relationships even under conditions undermining the family system which gave them meaning.

Psychodynamics of Connectivity

Connectivity as Love
In Camp Trad, connectivity was taken to be an expression of love. Brothers and sisters were taught to bond with each other and see themselves mirrored in each other. Brothers saw their identities and sense of self wrapped up with their sisters' attributes and behavior. Sisters saw their dignity and security tied to their

brothers' character and fortunes. Brothers and sisters were expected to love and look out for each other through adulthood.[39] Parents and other relatives encouraged brothers and sisters to idealize and romanticize each other. They supported their using each other as standards for judging potential spouses. I had a sense that something precious was undermined by the marriage of either.[40] Um Hanna's (above) concern that Flaur's husband was not as handsome as Flaur's brother was, in cultural terms, an acceptable criticism of Flaur's husband. Idealization of the brothers and sisters was expressed through sayings that children learned. *"Al ikt hanuni"* ("The sister is sympathetic") was a frequently repeated saying in Camp Trad. Sisters referred to their brothers as *"akh al hanun," "al 'atuf," "al 'aziz," "al habib,"* and *"al ghali,"* ("the brother is sympathetic," "sensitive," "dear," "beloved," and "priceless"). The idealization of cross-siblings continued after marriage. Brothers and sisters named their children after each other at times. Nimr Zahr, a 73-year-old Lebanese Shi'i from Kfar Dunin in Southern Lebanon, had a sister who had died when she was about 20. Five years later, when he had his own first born child, a girl, he named her after the deceased sister. His second son was named after the wife's brother.

Sonia Fraij was a 35-year-old Lebanese Maronite married to 36-year-old Greek Orthodox bus driver's aide. Two of her brothers lived next door to her. She had named her oldest son after the younger of these two brothers and her youngest son after her youngest brother, who was living in Australia. A strong-willed and outspoken woman, she continually praised her brothers, described them lovingly, and compared them favorably to her husband. In interviews she subtly, in his presence, put her husband down in relation to her brothers. The older brother traveled frequently. The younger, John, a strikingly handsome 26-year-old, was a chronically unemployed construction worker. Sonia had a loving relationship with John. As his apartment was right across the hall from hers, he spent much of his leisure time with her in one of their apartments. John spoke in the most affectionate terms of Sonia, gazed on her lovingly, and seemed to hang on her words. The expressions of devotion were among the most pronounced in the neighborhood. They were together all the time. She both served him and took charge of his life in some ways: she cooked for him, washed his clothes, went shopping with him, received her house visitors with him, and at times took him with her when she paid some of her formal calls. In some ways, John acted as a husband in the absence of her husband, who worked long hours. Having a brother nearby whom she loved, served, and to some degree managed, and who also protected her, empowered her.

A number of neighborhood women seemed to compare their husbands to their brothers. Yasmin Unis, a 47-year-old Lebanese Shi'i, married for love, and yet said her brothers *"binawru hiyyati"* ("light up my life"). Her sense of identity came from her natal family. She and her children referred to her brothers repeatedly when speaking of themselves. Her marriage was relatively stable, yet she spoke of her husband as *maskin* ("poor, humble"), a mixed compliment and criticism.

I found this idealization/romanticization of brother/sister relationships in other social classes in Lebanon, particularly the Beirut middle classes. Among the families I observed, married and unmarried brothers and sisters talked of each other affectionately. Middle-class brothers and sisters went together to parties, movies, theaters, and other social occasions. They danced together, escorted each other in cohort group events, traveled together, and often walked arm in arm in the streets. Brothers, by accompanying their sisters, might have been giving them access to activities they might not have had otherwise. In playing the dual role of sister's protector and partner, they contributed to the romanticization of the relationship.

Unmarried women often devoted themselves to their brothers and their brothers' children. Unmarried men often relied on their sisters to provide emotional support and household service. Unmarried adults usually lived with their natal families, so unmarried brothers and sisters often became each other's primary caretakers.[41] In one case, a married Maronite woman with no children had raised her brother's two children while he was working in West Africa with his wife. The children called their aunt, "Mama" and her husband, "Baba" (father). While there is little research on sexuality in brother/sister relationships in Arab societies, my own fieldwork indicates that the brother/sister relationship was sexually charged.[42] Boys and girls in Camp Trad practiced sexual presentation with each other in socially approved ways. They seemed to groom themselves as much, if not more, for each other as for other opposite-gender individuals. Brothers paid attention to and commented on sisters' clothing, hair styling, and makeup. Sisters sought their brothers' approval for their self-presentations, as well as offering their own evaluations of their brothers' presentation. Brothers defined their sexuality in part by asserting control over and lavishing attention on sisters. Sisters defined their sexuality in part by acceding to their brothers and/or by affording resistance.

Among a number of middle-class Beiruti families, also, I noticed that brothers and sisters were very involved in each other's attire and comportment. Brothers in these families often participated in purchasing their sisters' wardrobes. Sisters, while not having similar control over the brothers, often, nevertheless, significantly influenced their style by their evaluations.

On festive occasions, when Camp Trad young people dressed up and could engage in sexual play-acting, brothers and sisters seemed particularly involved with each other. Few families had much in the way of fancy attire. Going to church on Sunday or the mosque on Fridays, visiting neighbors and family on Christian and Muslim holidays, and attending weddings and funerals were among the few occasions on which Camp Trad youth could parade themselves. On these occasions, brothers and sisters often escorted each other or went in the company of their families. On such occasions, they usually spent more time in the company of each other than with nonfamily individuals. Brothers and sisters, as well as the rest of the family, were on display to each other and seemed to take great interest in the opportunity for expression that such occasions provided.

I noticed in other parts of Beirut and surrounding suburbs that festive occasions were similarly occasions for constructing sexualities. Here too, brothers and sisters seemed to use each other for role playing. For example, in family gatherings, brothers and sisters danced with each other from a young age. On one occasion, I observed two preadolescent, middle-class siblings (children of a Syrian Christian mother and an Italian father) dancing together in their home in a suburb of Beirut during a festive gathering. The boy was advancing toward his younger sister. With roars of approval and great laughter the men and the women in the room (all Arab, except the father) shouted, *"bi hajim, bi hajim"* ("he attacks, he attacks"). The little boy, appearing somewhat confused, accelerated the behavior. The little girl, seemingly as confused, was ignored and continued dancing. Such occasions were prime times for learning culturally appropriate sexual behavior.

The romanticization/sexualization of the brother/sister relationship appeared to have had concrete expression at times. There was one half-sibling marriage reported by Camp Trad informants.[43] Sa'da Hamid was a 55-year-old Lebanese Shi'i from Bint Jbeil in Southern Lebanon. Both her parents had been married twice. She reported a marriage between her sister by her mother and her full brother—that is, the couple shared a mother, but had different fathers. In 1972, Sa'da's brother, 82, and his wife/half-sister, 78, were living in their village of birth.[44] In a more ambiguous case, Yasmin Unis, a Lebanese Shi'i reported a marriage between her step siblings who did not share a parent.

Connectivity as Power
Romanticization and sexualization differentiated the brother/sister relationship from other familial cross-gender relationships. The relationship was differentiated, also, in terms of its role in gender socialization. Training for relationships of power organized around gender, brothers and sisters were used in the family system and used each other to learn culturally appropriate hierarchal masculine and feminine roles and identities. Additionally, young males emerging into their manhood might compete with their fathers for control over the family, using relationships with their sisters as a base of power—at times with the cooperation of their sisters and mothers.

Brothers and sisters learned early on that love and power were parts of the same dynamic. Love meant acceptance of the power asymmetry and culturally approved assertions of the asymmetry were taken as expressions of love. Parents taught daughters that loving their brothers included serving them and taught brothers that loving their sisters included some control over them. Families may have preferred brothers to fathers as sisters' protectors because their secondary positions relative to fathers would burden them with less responsibility should violence occur.[45] Little girls practiced modesty, seductiveness, and serving authoritative males with their brothers, thereby learning how to be feminine. Brothers practiced sexual assertion, receiving feminine nurturances, and protecting and taking charge of the life and sexuality of females. Although connective love/power dynamics were enacted in parent/child and other family relationships, the mutual gender socialization distinguished the brother/sister relationships.[46]

Young men also distinguished themselves from their fathers in relation to sisters by being physically present in the house. Fathers were often absent, working long hours six days a week. Brothers usually did not work if they were still in school and spent much of their nonschool time at home. When they did work, they often spent more time at home or around the neighborhood than their fathers. Married brothers could play their cultural roles toward their sisters more effectively if they lived in proximity to their sisters. A remarkable number of Camp Trad adults indicated that they did have siblings in other parts of Borj Hammoud or neighboring districts. Those whose cross-siblings lived further away, still expressed similar attitudes toward their siblings.

For young males living with their families, adolescence was the period to shape their manhood. Taking charge of the lives of their sisters and, at times, those of their mothers and younger brothers, was an avenue of empowerment for some males. Mothers often deferred to their older sons' control over younger children.[47] Some fathers deferred to their sons, while others resisted. The degree of power the brothers took, then, was affected by how much power the father asserted. The more controlling the fathers, the less power the brothers could assert. In the case of the Dawuds, a Palestinian Catholic family (discussed below), the eldest son exerted considerable authority, including defying his parents to help his sister marry the man she loved. In the case of the Rafik family, Abu Mufid,[48] a Syrian Sunni, exerted patriarchal control to such a degree that the oldest son could assert little.

Differences in the brother's view and the sister's view of their relationship or in their reading their own and each other's needs could create spaces for resistance.[49] Yet, when resistance occurred, the challenge most often was not to the basic premises (love/power) of the brother/sister relationship. Rather, it usually centered on whether the sibling was acting on those premises properly, or it was understood as miscommunication or was explained away as flukes of character. Flaur's persistence in her behavior, despite Hanna's response, might be seen as resistance, except for the fact that she did not challenge his right to have authority over her or that he loved her and that she loved him. Instead, she and her family brushed it off as the consequence of her feistiness.

Structure of Family, Marriage, and Inheritance

Family and Marriage

Some of my informants stated a preference for non-kin marriage. The cultural norm of marriage between relatives, however, was still valued as an ideal by most of my Muslim informants.[50] While expressed as an ideal less frequently by Christians, endogamy was nevertheless practiced among them as well. Sa'da Hamid, the Lebanese Shi'i whose brother and half-sister had married (above), was herself married to her father's brother's son. Five of her seven married children were married to relatives, including two sons who had married two sisters. Two other sons had not married relatives, but their wives were related to each other. All but one of her children lived in Borj Hammoud and were very involved in each other's lives. Four of Sa'ada's siblings had married relatives and two of them (a brother and sister) lived in Camp Trad.

Brothers and sisters were involved also with each other's children. The father's brother (*'am*) was viewed as a formal authority often feared second only to the father, but the *khal* (maternal uncle) was seen to be affectionate, loving, warm, and playful. He could become a substitute father in the absence of the father. The *khal* could also shelter the sister's children from their father. In one incident, a young Camp Trad Maronite man had a heated dispute with his father after which the son took refuge in the home of his *khal*. The children of the *khal*, both sons and daughters, were also sources of emotional support and compassion—at times, in contrast to the children of the father's siblings. In the cultural ideal, a similar relationship was expressed with the mother's sister (*khalta*) and her children. The sister, as the *'amta* (paternal aunt),was expected to be affectionate to her brother's children. A common saying in Camp Trad depicted this relationship: *"ya 'amti ya ikt bayyi hamm min ummi 'aliyyi"* ("my aunt, my father's sister, worries for me more than my mother"). At the same time, as a member of the patriline, the *'amta* also occupied a position of authority vis-à-vis her brother's children. Hanan, a Lebanese Shi'i, lived two stories below her brother's daughter, Dalal. Visiting each other daily, more than they each visited anyone else, Hanan helped Dalal by watching the three children (the oldest of which was four), shopping for her, and cooking with her.

Inheritance

Inheritance and property issues impacted the brother/sister as well as the husband/brother-in-law relationship.[51] Women often did not take their inheritances from their natal families. Leaving their inheritance with their brothers could offer them insurance should they need protection from their families of origin.[52] A woman's attitude toward inheritance could change as she and her family of procreation matured. She might want the inheritance to help support her children. As her sons grew older, she might rely more on them than on her brothers.[53] Husbands and brothers could compete over a woman's inheritance.[54]

Najat, a 32-year-old Lebanese Sunni married to a 41-year-old Lebanese Sunni (son of a Tunisian Sunni) had three brothers between 26 and 36 years old. Najat's siblings (married, divorced, and single) all lived with their mother in nearby Sin il Fil except for a married sister in Aley. Her father had died earlier in 1972, shortly before my interview. Najat claimed that she had refused to take any inheritance from her father's property. She had left it with her brothers. As she said, "My brothers' and mine are the same. It will always be there for me."

Family Culture: Honor and Shame

Ideally, brothers continued to be responsible for their sisters' behavior and welfare throughout their lives, even after marriage,[55] although practices were often contradictory in the 1970s. Should a woman commit a shameful act or be compromised in any way, her brothers shared responsibility with her father in disciplining or avenging her.[56] The range and limits of brotherly responsibility for protecting and controlling adult sisters can be seen in the following example. The whole neighborhood street became involved in this dramatic enactment of the brothers' roles as protectors of their sisters' and families' honor. The key actors included the Dawuds, a Palestinian Catholic family; Amira Antun, a recently widowed Lebanese Chaldean Catholic of Syrian origins; Amira's son Edward and brother Francis; Abu Mufid, a Syrian Sunni discussed above; and Abu Mufid's brother's son, Adnan.

The Dawuds were a close family. The parents and sisters were bonded in devout admiration of their sons/brothers. They saw the sons/brothers, especially the oldest, Antoine, as heroes (*abtal*).[57] The parents and sisters outdid each other in superlatives describing Antoine. They emphasized his strength and courage. Active in the Fateh wing of the Palestine Liberation Organization, Antoine was frequently armed, which no doubt added to the family's sense of his fearsomeness.

Antoine had helped his sister Antoinette elope against their parent's opposition. Antoine was 19 when Antoinette (18) decided she wanted to marry their mother's father's sister's son. Their parents opposed the marriage because Fadi was poor. Antoine was interested in marrying Fadi's sister. Overriding his parents, Antoine had helped his sister elope with the intention that Fadi would then assist in arranging his marriage to his sister. Later, Antoine decided that Fadi's sister was too demanding and did not marry her. Antoinette's marriage was still intact, however. Antoine and Antoinette had a close relationship, and she continued to think of him as her protector.[58]

Antoine and his brothers appeared to derive pleasure and personal pride from the beauty and comportment of their sisters. The sisters also felt their security and dignity were linked to their brother's involvement with them. The Dawud sisters boasted continually about their brothers. Twenty-one-year-old Therese often said that if she could only find a man like her brothers, she would marry instantly.

In spring of 1973, Adnan, a young Sunni, had eyes on an unidentified young woman living on the street. Neighbors thought it was Therese. In a manner considered inappropriate, Adnan drove repeatedly in front of her house. He sped his car screeching through the street. Given the narrow streets and the fact that small children usually played outside unsupervised, neighbors complained. Adding to this concern was the fact that while intermarriages did occur in the neighborhood, they were usually arranged in a more discrete manner. It was a breach of etiquette for courting to take place in this manner, particularly given the intersectarian character of the relationship. Therese's brothers (Antoine 24, Jacque 19, and Michel 14) discussed the matter with several male friends living on the street, including Edward Antun (the 20-year-old son of Amira Antun), Rafik Abdullah (18-year-old son of a Maronite divorced woman from her Shi'i husband), and Hanna and Farid Yusif (Hanna's 17-year-old brother). They decided to stop Adnan.

One afternoon late in March, Adnan sped through the street several times. Michel Dawud and Edward Antun were at home. At his next pass, they stopped his car and told him they did not want him to drive through the street because there were children playing. Adnan had a friend with him. He replied that he was free to come and go as he wished, and furthermore, that they were not to speak with him but could speak with his friend. The friend had a long knife and made "teasing" or "threatening" looks at the young men. Michel Dawud became irritated and hit Adnan's friend in the face. Adnan sped away.

The commotion attracted the attention of a number of residents. Rafik Abdullah was home ill but came down to the street in his pajamas. Farid Yusif was coming down the stairs from his apartment and went to join his friends. Abu Antoine (Therese and Michel's father) had overheard the conversation and had come to try to make peace. 'Adil and Zaynab, close Shi'a friends of Amira Antun (Edward's mother), stepped out as well. Within a few minutes, over 50 people had gathered in the street, and many stood on their balconies or rooftops watching.

Adnan, in the meantime, had collected his friends and relatives from the predominately Shi'i neighborhood of Nab'a. They returned to the street in two cars. At an apparently prearranged whistle, the two cars drove through the narrow street at top speed aiming right at the crowd. Most of the people jumped out of the way, but Edward Antun was slightly injured. A car parked at the end of the street blocked Adnan's escape. Neighbors began beating the cars and breaking the windows. Within a few minutes, though, the two cars sped away.

It was early evening by this time, and I heard the commotion at my end of the street. I had been helping Um Hanna who was ill. I went down the street to find members of practically every household talking excitedly. Um Antoine was arguing with Zaynab. Um Antoine shrieked, "This is the fault of the Muslims. The Muslims are coming to get us!" Zaynab, a Shi'i, shouted, "Don't make this sectarian!" Hanna Yusif told me that his brother Farid had noticed that one of the two cars had been that of Mufid (the son of the Syrian Sunni, Abu Mufid) and that he thought he had seen Mufid with them, but he could not be sure.

Edward Antun was rushed to the hospital by 'Adil, Zaynab's husband and Amira Antun's good friend. Amira became hysterical, tearing at her clothes and screaming uncontrollably. Amira was a 41-year-old mother of ten children ranging in age from 5 to 22. Her husband had died in 1971, just as I was beginning my fieldwork. She had six sons (her four oldest children were all male), including a married son, but she turned to her second oldest brother, Francis, as a father-substitute for her children. Francis, 34, married with no children, owned a pinball arcade two short blocks away from Amira's apartment.

When Edward was injured, Amira's neighbors gathered around her, particularly her good friends, Zaynab[59] and 'Adil. Amira had excellent friends in the neighborhood; however, the primacy of the brother was apparent. Francis was informed of the incident and came quickly. When he arrived on the street, the crowds parted to let him through. I vividly remember the hushed silence as he approached his sister and embraced her. There was a stirring sense among the neighbors that Amira was now in the care of the most honorable of protectors— her brother. The silence among the neighbors added to the drama and the authoritative voice with which he spoke. He turned to the people and demanded to know what had happened to his nephew. As her brother stood there next to her, there seemed to be a feeling that now justice would be done.

Abu Antoine sent for his son, Antoine. The tension noticeably increased as Antoine arrived almost immediately with a motorcade of armed Palestinian guerrillas dressed in civilian clothes. The neighbors now felt bold and invincible. The presence of Therese's brother Antoine, backed by the Palestinian guerrillas, and Amira's brother Francis, along with practically all the men of the neighborhood, enhanced the incredible sense of neighborhood solidarity.[60]

The crowd gathered around to tell the story of the incident. Some of the young men of the neighborhood had run after the car. Later, a couple of the culprits were found in a shop near Francis's pinball machine store. Francis was among the neighborhood men who found them. They beat the culprits and called the police. The families of the Shi'a young men were mistakenly told that one of their sons had been killed. Several cars from the Shi'i neighborhood of Nab'a, filled with men and guns, came immediately to Camp Trad. The Nab'a families arrived just as the police pulled in, so they drove away. The one person who was still in custody was taken to the police station. Within minutes, a phone call came from a *za'im* (political leader), and he was released.

Adnan's paternal uncle (FaBro), Abu Mufid, deflated the conflict. He lived on the same street as the Dawuds and was highly respected. Abu Mufid told me that he thought his nephew was a bit wild, and he would rather not have gotten involved. He felt he had no choice but to intervene for the sake of neighborly good will and to protect his own name. Arranging a meeting between Adnan and the Dawuds and Antuns, Abu Mufid forced his nephew to apologize.

The incident provoked a neighborhood crisis. Across religious, ethnic, and national lines, neighborhood people supported the brothers' actions. It was uniformly discussed in terms of the brothers protecting the honor of their sisters and families. Men and women seemed to agree that the incident was primarily about honor, not religion. Therese and her parents extravagantly praised Michel and Antoine, while Amira heaped praise on her son Edward and brother Francis. The men were described as abtal ("heroes"). The neighborhood men, in general, appeared to take great pride in their manly display of solidarity. And the women glowed in admiration of the men. In the immediate days after the incident, there was a noticeable swagger in the walk of the men directly involved. Displays of boasting by both men and women created a sense of possession— they owned this street. Brothers had protected their sisters and men had protected their women—the ultimate social boundary of the community. The community was reminded of the importance sisters had in their brothers' lives. For all the participants, the incident reinforced the cultural belief that brothers were the foundation of sisters' security. The culture had been supremely upheld in a most honorable manner.

Arab Brothers and Sisters: Connectivity, Love, and Power in the Reproduction of Patriarchy

Granqvist (1935:II:252–56) reports a story about brother/sister relations cited among Palestinian fellahin. She indicates that fellahin women, given a choice as to whom they would prefer to free from military service (which was equated with death), would choose to free their brothers rather than their husbands or sons.[61] The reasoning reported was: "A husband may [always] be had; a son can [also] be born; but a beloved brother, from where shall he come back [when he is once dead]?" (Granqvist 1935:II:253).[62] This is a story about brother/sister love for Granqvist (1935:II:254). But it is also about the centrality of the brother/sister relationship to the reproduction of patrilineality and patriarchy. Arab sisters, committed to preserving their patrilineages, invested in their brothers— for it was only through their brothers that they insured the continuity of their patrilines and security.[63]

In Camp Trad, the brother/sister relationship was central to the reproduction of patriarchy. It contributed to socializing young males and females into appropriate gender roles. Young females learned feminine roles by submitting to brothers. Young males learned to be patriarchs by practicing first on their sisters and younger brothers. Brothers could also use their relationships with their sisters to contest their fathers' authority and attempt to build a sphere of influence from which they would mature as patriarchs.

The sister paid a price for the protection of the brother. She served the brother, to some degree shaped herself into his image, at times put her brother before her husband. Sisters had some power in this relationship because their conduct directly affected their brothers' and families' standing. The tensions around the issues of honor, protection, and control at times led to violence.

At the same time, the brother/sister relationship was one of love. Brothers and sisters reported deep caring and concern for each other. They were expected by others and expected themselves to protect and nurture each other for all their lives. Brother/sister love was romanticized. Their masculinity and femininity were defined and practiced in a connective relationship that was often sexually charged.

Complexity is missing in much of the literature. As my analysis suggests, the brother/sister relationship was a connective relationship built on the duality of love and power expressed psychodynamically, social structurally, and culturally. It was second only to the mother/son relation in evoking love, and yet it was premised on a power asymmetry—the subordination of the sister to the brother. The intense involvement of brothers and sisters in each other's lives invested each in their natal family and its reproduction. Life-long connectivity organized around love and power gave the brother/sister relationship a forceful role in the reproduction of Arab patriarchy. By the early 1970s, Camp Trad brothers and sisters were living with external stresses that made achievement of cultural prescriptions concerning their relationships more difficult. The instability of family life; the economic, political, and social uncertainty; and the limitations of the Lebanese state in providing services and protections thrust people onto their families for support at a time when it was increasingly difficult for family members to help each other. It is striking that, under these conditions, men and women, nevertheless, still made the effort to embrace their cross-siblings and the patriarchy and patrilineality their siblingship supported.

Notes

Acknowledgments. The article was developed in part under a fellowship from the University of California, Davis, Humanities Institute and benefited from the generous support of the director and staff. I would like to thank the following colleagues for comments on this article in its various stages of development: Etel Adnan, Simone Fattal, Smadar Lavie, Barbara Metcalf, G. William Skinner, Carol A. Smith, Cynthia Brantley, Carole Joffe, Anna Kuhn, Kari Lokke, Lyn Roller, Stephanie Shields, Juliana Schiesari, and the 1989–90 University of California, Davis, Humanities Institute Fellows.

1 Names of all Camp Trad residents have been changed.

2 Abu Hanna means "father of Hanna." Adults with children were referred to by the name of their oldest male child. Thus, Hanna's mother was called "Um Hanna," the "mother of Hanna."

3 It was not uncommon among urban working classes in Lebanon for women to be overweight during and after their childbearing years.

4 Field work was carried out from 1971–73 under an NIMH predoctoral research grant. Briefer follow-up research was undertaken in 1974, 1976, 1978, 1980, and 1993. Unless otherwise indicated, the argument in this article refers to the period just prior to the outbreak of the Lebanese civil war in 1975.

5 The dynamics of these families resonated with me. Having been born in a village not far from Camp Trad and raised as an Arab American, my relationships with these families and my analysis in this article have been shaped and informed partly by my own family experiences.

6 Corporal punishment for perceived misdeeds was not specifically a cross-sex pattern among Camp Trad families. It was considered socially acceptable for parents to discipline children and older siblings to discipline younger ones in this manner regardless of sex.

7 Civil war erupted in Lebanon in 1975, two years after I completed the initial fieldwork, and continues to this writing.

8 See Malinowski 1913, Radcliffe-Brown 1924 , Firth 1936, Burridge 1959, Schneider and Gough 1961, Mabuchi 1964, Weiner 1976, Kelly 1977, and Marshall 1983.

9 See Barakat 1985, Fernea 1985, and Sharabi 1988 for pan-Arab discussions and comparisons. For specific national studies see Al-Haj 1987, Altorki 1986, Davis and Davis 1989, Eickleman 1984, Hatem 1987, Munson 1984, and Rugh 1984.

10 The debates that concern the FaBroDa/So marriage have spanned several decades. Scholars have evoked functionalist, structuralist, ecological, political–economic, and psychodynamic theories. See Murphy and Kasdan 1959, Patai 1960, Ripinsky 1968, Barth 1954, Khuri 1970 and McCabe 1983.

11 See Prothero 1961, Fuller 1961, Williams 1968, Khalaf 1968 and 1971, Farsoun 1970, Prothero and Diab 1974, Alamuddin and Star 1980, and Joseph 1982.

12 The folktale has many renditions recorded in different Arab countries. Briefly, the main themes are as follows: A woman gave birth to a boy and girl. The mother died when the children were little, but before dying entrusted the care of the brother to the sister. The sister lovingly raised the brother and gave him all the inheritance when he reached manhood. He chose a wife with the guidance of the sister and they all lived together. The sister-in-law attempted to drive a wedge between the brother and sister. Finally she induced the sister to eat a "pregnancy egg," to make her appear pregnant and told the brother to see what his sister had done. The brother, assuming the sister had had an illicit affair, took her to a deserted place intending to kill her. Unable to kill her, he abandoned her there. The local people, upon hearing the sister's story, built her a palace. One day the sister sneezed two pigeons out her nostrils. The

pigeons flew to the brother's house, proclaiming to the wife, who tried to shoo them away, that this was the home of their *khal* (mother's brother). The brother, upon hearing the pigeons, followed them to the spot where he had left his sister. Arriving at the palace, he was greeted by his sister dressed as a man. He asked about the story of the .pigeons and was told the whole story by the "man." The brother asserted that no one would know that story except his sister and asked to be taken to her to ask her forgiveness. At this, the sister revealed herself, and she and the brother embraced and cried. The brother renounced his wife and lived with the sister, begetting boys and girls.

13 Some of the literature on the Arab world reports more ambivalence in brother/sister relationships. Davis and Davis (1989:81) found considerable variation among brother/sister relationships in the Moroccan town of Zawiya. Sisters were both affectionate toward their brothers as well as resentful of the control they exercised. In the Moroccan village of Sidi Embarek, Davis (1983:132) found that sibling rivalry was greater among brothers and sisters than among sisters.

14 The brother said: "She has her father's house. Nobody can tread on the hem of her garment [i.e., insult her]. May it be as thou wishest. Our beard is on thy sack. We are thy camels [i.e., we bear all thy burdens and sorrows]." ("ilha dar abuha ma hada byidar yuhbut 'a tarafha marhababic ilhana 'ala cisic ihna jmalic") (Granqvist 1935:11:252).

15 (*"Hadi saqiqti bukra bithasibni fi-l-ahre walakin uladi u mararhi la"*) (Granqvist 1935:11:254).

16 Parallels to this romantic view of brother/sister relationships have been reported for other cultures of the Mediterranean. Literature on the ancient Mediterranean, particularly ancient Egypt and Rome, seems to indicate that intimate relationships between brothers and sisters ranged from love, to incest, to marriage (Hopkins 1980; Middleton 1962; Patai 1960; Slotkin 1947). While fascinating, interpreting this literature in relation to the contemporary period would need to be done carefully to avoid assumptions of cultural continuities. Research on the contemporary Mediterranean also reveals some parallels. Lloyd and Margaret Fallers (1976:250–58) contend that the brother/sister relationship in Edremit, Turkey, has "an almost romantic quality" and is, for many brothers and sisters, the "most intense cross-sex relationship they will ever experience." Ian Whitaker (1976:198) claims that among the Ghegs, sheepherding Albanians, a woman's dearest relation is with her brother.

17 Andrea Rugh (1984:97) maintains that, in Egypt, sisters are socialized to love their brothers and to focus on the affective aspects of the relationship. Brothers, while affectionate to sisters, are taught to focus on the jural duties of the brother to the sister. Hatem (1987) seems to indicate more ambivalence in Egyptian brother/sister relationships but does not discuss the relationship in detail.

18 Perhaps no subject related to gender and family in the Mediterranean and the Middle East has received more anthropological attention than the relationship between honor and shame. Explanations have ranged from culture (Campbell 1964; Peristiany 1966; Pitt-Rivers 1977), to ecology and political economy (Schneider 1971; Schneider and

Schneider 1976), to psychodynamics (Gilmore 1987). See Jowkar (1986) for a feminist critical review of the honor/shame literature.

19 Granqvist (1935:11:255) quotes El-Barghuthi's study of judicial courts among Bedouins of Palestine in 1922 as reporting: "'The good of a woman belongs to her husband and her evil to her family.'" Williams (1968:83) reports a similar attitude in the Lebanese Sunni village of Haouch el Harimi.

20 See Fuller 1966, Cohen 1965, Abou-Zeid 1966, Marx 1967, Antoun 1968, Pitt-Rivers 1977, and Altorki 1986.

21 The hierarchy in brother/sister relationships was also affected by family demographics such as the number of children in the family and currently in the household, residential proximity of adult siblings, gender and age orders, the presence or absence of one or both parents, the presence of extended family members in the household or in the neighborhood, and previous marriages of either parent or concurrent marriages of the father. Such demographic variables impact the living out of cultural norms and condition the practices associated with the brother/sister relationship. In general though, older brothers almost always had culturally sanctioned power over younger sisters (and brothers). Older sisters usually had control over younger brothers (and sisters) until the boys came into puberty, at which point brothers increasingly gained power over sisters. While it is not in the scope of this article to account for all the variations in brother/sister love/power dynamics related to family size, birth order, life cycle, and other aspects of family demographics, it is important to note that despite the resultant variable practices, the cultural prescriptions of brothers' dominance over sisters and mutual love between them was generally accepted and upheld among the families I observed.

22 Most of the dynamics I describe here were found in families across religious sects. Arab Christians and Muslims shared basic patrilineal and patriarchal values about family life. Christians did not articulate a cultural norm of patrilineal parallel cousin marriage. They, like Muslims, practiced close bilateral kin marriage, however. Christians and Muslims shared beliefs concerning the primacy of family loyalty, duty, and honor. They, alike, supported the creation of connective social personas. And they shared similar beliefs about brother/sister relationships. Many of these dynamics appeared in Camp Trad Armenian families as well. Because of their special history in Lebanon, however, I will not discuss them, except when it seems particularly useful to do so.

23 The scholarly research I cite indicating similar patterns in other Arab countries needs to be contextualized historically, socially, and culturally. That requires a fuller treatment of the subject than I can undertake here.

24 Catherine Keller opposes the concept of connective selfhood to separative selfhood (1986:9). For her the concept of connective selfhood is a liberatory concept indicating a self that is relational and autonomous. I use the concept more broadly to indicate a self that is relational, but whose experience and expressions vary with different political economies.

25 See Joseph (1993) for a further discussion of the notion of connectivity and its rela-
    tionship to Arab patriarchy and the limitations of family systems theory. Few schol-
    ars of the Arab world have researched the process of connectivity. Many have dis-
    cussed the immersion of the individual in the family, however (Barakat 1985; Rugh
    1984; Sharabi 1988). Some authors have applied the related concept of enmeshment
    to Egyptian families. See Paige (1984) for an application of the concept of enmesh-
    ment to Egyptian families.

26 While it is not the subject of this article, I would argue these Arab families support-
    ed connective relationships among their members in general.

27 El-Shamy (1979:79) argues that because of the possibility of polygyny, Arab children
    identified with their mothers more strongly than their fathers and with their mothers'
    family more than their father's.

28 Patai (1960) argues that this marriage rule preserves property in the patrilineal line.
    Murphy and Kasdan (1959) argue that parallel-cousin marriage allows for a gnatic
    segmentation and structural opposition at the nuclear family level. Khuri (1970)
    argues that the rule mitigates the effect of marriage on patrilineality—that is, ensures
    that marriage will not undermine patrilineal solidarity. El-Shamy (1979:60) points
    out that despite the formal anticipation of political and marital alliance between patri-
    lineal cousins, the relations between cousins and the siblings of their spouses in
    FaBro/So/Da marriages remains hostile as compared to the brother/sister relation-
    ship.

29 McCabe (1983:58) found in the Southern Lebanese village of Bayt al-'asir unmar-
    ried, opposite-sex first cousins displayed an intimacy very similar to that of cross-
    siblings. Her findings conflicted with those of Fuad Khuri's (1970) for two suburbs
    of Beirut.

30 Donald Cole observes that the most affectionate relationship across generations
    among the Al Murrah Bedouin of Saudi Arabia are between young people and their
    mothers' brothers and sisters. While he does not discuss the brother/sister relation-
    ship, per se, he notes that the coldness and indifference with which a man greets his
    wife after a period of absence sharply contrasts with the lavish warmth he offers to
    his mother, father's and mother's sisters, and his own sisters (1975:73–75).

31 This structural limitation reinforced a woman's ultimate dependence on her own
    sons, if she had any. Structurally, in some ways, a woman was encouraged to look to
    her sons to fulfill what her father, brothers, and husbands did not. This partly explains
    the great intensity of the mother/son relationship, perhaps the only cross-sex family
    relationship that overshadowed the brother/sister in the cultural stress on love.

32 Granqvist (1935:II:255) reports cases of Palestinian fellahin women risking their
    relationship with their husbands rather than risking being cut off from their natal
    families. Altorki (1986:78) reports similar cases among contemporary elite Saudi
    women.

33 Granqvist (1935:II:254) reports that Palestinian village men in the 1930s felt more
    responsible for wives and children. I would not make a similar claim for the Camp

Trad men. However it was clear that they did feel a strong responsibility for their sisters.

34 Fuller (1966:52) observes that Sunni village women in Buarij realized that to gain the protection of fathers and brothers, they had to conduct themselves with propriety.

35 I am indebted to Judith Walkowitz for pointing out the need to emphasize this point.

36 There has been no formal census in Lebanon since 1932. These percentages were estimated from interviews with local officials and residents.

37 Many families had lived in Lebanon and/or Camp Trad less than a year while few had lived there more than two generations.

38 Prothero and Diab (1974:71) report that the approximately 500 formally organized family associations in Lebanon outnumbered all other nongovernmental welfare agencies recorded in the Ministry of Interior and Ministry of Social Affairs combined. See also Khalaf (1971).

39 Prothero's (1961:94) study of rural and urban child rearing among Lebanese of different religious sects reveals that about half of the mothers reported that their children got along well with each other, while a fourth reported open hostility among siblings. Prothero does not specify gender in his report.

40 Fallers and Fallers (1976:258) similarly observe that marriage in Edremit, Turkey, breaks the highly charged brother/sister bond. The affection between brothers and sisters is so charged that the Fallers comment, "It is little wonder that marriage partners must be chosen by others and that they take so long 'to get to know each other'" (1976:258).

41 This, like many of the patterns described here, was also characteristic of non-Arabs in the neighborhood. In one Armenian Catholic family, an unmarried, adult 35-year-old woman lived with her married 43-year-old brother and his family. She stayed at home, helping with their 78-year-old mother and his four children.

42 El-Shamy (1981:319) claims that there are incestuous tendencies underlying the Arab brother/sister relationship. I cannot confirm such a tendency from my research. The distinction between gender and sexuality and the cultural specificity of these constructs warrants mention. If sexuality signals notions of the erotic and gender signals notions of masculinity and femininity and both are culturally constructed, as I believe they are, then evaluations of what constitutes a sexually charged relationship would have to be culturally specific. I believe it is important to raise this issue. Treating the subject of incest in the detail that it requires, however, necessitates more research than is available and more space than I have here.

43 For analysis of brother/sister marriages in the ancient Middle East see Hopkins 1980, Middleton 1962, and Slotkin 1947.

44 An Armenian resident of this street also reported that her mother had been adopted and raised by her father's family. She did not consider her parents to be "real" siblings, although she acknowledged that they had a special relationship.

45 I am indebted to Richard Antoun for this insight.

46 Gender socialization was affected by sibling birth order and changed through stages

of the siblings' lives. Older boys and girls often took care of younger siblings and became second parents. It was more common for girls to take on mothering roles than for boys to take on fathering roles. As boys came into puberty, however, they usually took power over sisters, regardless of age ranking, or experience of having been parented by sisters.

47 Judith Williams (1968:39) observes in the Sunni Lebanese village of Haouch el Harimi that households with sons were more disciplined than houses that were predominately female. In the absence of fathers, brothers became an effective authority.

48 For a discussion of Abu Mufid as an entrepreneur see Joseph 1990.

49 I am indebted to Joseph Massoud for this insight.

50 Prothero and Diab's (1974:65) survey of Sunni family patterns in Lebanon, Syria, and Jordan revealed that, while the trend away from endogamy was strongest in Beirut and Tripoli, the preference for marriage among relatives was still very much in evidence throughout the region. Williams (1968:100) found that a surprising two-thirds of the youth interviewed in the Lebanese Sunni village of Haouch el Harimi preferred cousin marriage. It was the preferred marriage form in the Sunni village of Buarij (Fuller:1966:65). Alamuddin and Starr (1980:75) report that about one-third of Druze marriages recorded in the Beirut courts from 1931–74 were clan endogamous, while Khuri (1970:598) found that 27 percent of the marriages among Muslims in two Beirut suburbs, Chiah and Ghobeiri, to be endogamous and among these the FaBroSo/Da marriage accounted for 38 percent.

51 In Lebanon, inheritance was governed by religious courts. A fuller discussion of the impact of inheritance on brother/sister relationships, which is beyond the scope of this article, would need to account for the constraints imposed by these courts.

52 Granqvist (1935:11:256) reports that Palestinian fellahin women were explicit in asserting that they kept their inheritances with their fathers and brothers so that they would have rights to return to their natal households should they need to do so.

53 While this needs to be the subject of a separate discussion, it is worth noting here that women often felt that their security lay with their brothers until they had sons and their sons became mature adults. Some women then refocused their energies and demands for support on their sons.

54 Altorki (1986:158) indicates that elite women of Jiddah are increasingly claiming their inheritance over the objection of male relatives.

55 Similar arguments are made by Antoun (1968:691), Rosenfeld (1960:67), and Gulick (1955:119).

56 Incidents of brothers or fathers killing their sisters or daughters in crimes of honor are reported in much of the literature (Antoun 1968:694; El-Shamy 1979:8; Rugh 1984:85).

57 Batal (*abtal,* pl.) means brave man, hero, champion. It is used to refer to folk heroes and macho men. Locally, it was one of the strongest compliments one could pay to a man.

58 Granqvist contends that Palestinian men who used their sisters to exchange for wives

had even more responsibility for those sisters than they might otherwise have had (1935:11:252). Rugh (1984:116) contends that some of the advantages of close kin marriage, in the absence of appropriate close kin, can be achieved by sibling marriages between unrelated families—that is, unrelated men exchanging their sisters as wives.

59 See Joseph (1977) for a discussion of Zaynab and her friendship with Amira.

60 While most of the Armenians would later indicate to me that they supported the actions of the brothers, many remained indoors.

61 An interesting parallel in the ancient Middle East is found in Herodotus. Herodotus (1972:250) reports a story that is supposed to have occurred in about 520 B.C. during the rise to power of Darius, king of Persia. According to the story, Intaphrenes, one of six Persians who supported King Darius in an uprising against Magus, was disrespectful to Darius. Fearing a conspiracy, Darius had him and all his near relations arrested. Intaphrenes' wife pleaded with the king to save her family. Eventually moved by the woman's pleas, King Darius offered her the choice of saving the life of only one member of her family. Her decision to save her brother surprised him, and he asked her for an explanation. She replied that she could find another husband and have another son, but she could never have another brother. Impressed with her reasoning, Darius gave her her brother and her eldest son. I am indebted to Lyn Roller for pointing out this story to me and to Nicholas A. Hopkins for pointing out a parallel story in Sophocles' Theban play, *Antigone*. Similar stories are also found in other Mediterranean cultures.

62 *"Ij-joz mawjud, il-walad mawlud il-ah il-'aziz min wen yi'ud?"* (Granqvist 1935:11:253).

63 A similar reading can be taken from a story about the noted early Egyptian feminist Huda Sha'rawi's relationship with her brother. Ahmed (1989:162) explains that Sha'rawi, while loving her brother, was dismayed that he was preferred to her. Her father's widow explained that she was a girl, and not the only girl, and her brother was a boy and the only boy. It would be his responsibility to perpetuate the name of the father. Ahmed reports that Sha'rawi was temporarily assuaged by this and loved her brother the more for it.

References

Abou-Zeid, Ahmed. 1966. *Honour and Shame among the Bedouins of Egypt.* In *Honour and Shame.* J. G. Peristiany, ed. Pp. 243–260. Chicago: University of Chicago Press.

Abu-Lughod, Lila. 1986. *Veiled Sentiments: Honor and Poetry in a Bedouin Society.* Berkeley: University of California Press.

Ahmed, Leila. 1989. *Between Two Worlds: The Formation of a Turn-of-the-Century Egyptian Feminist.* In *Life/Lines. Theorizing Women's Autobiography.* Bella Brodzki and Celeste Schenck, eds. Pp. 154–74. Ithaca: Cornell University Press.

Alamuddin, Nura S., and Paul D. Starr. 1980. *Crucial Bonds: Marriage among the Lebanese Druze.* Delmar, NY: Caravan Books.

Altorki, Soraya. 1986. *Women in Saudi Arabia: Ideology and Behavior among the Elite.* New York: Columbia University Press.

Al-Haj, Majid. 1987. *Social Change and Family Processes: Arab Communities in Shefar-A'm.* Boulder, CO: Westview Press

Antoun, Richard T. 1968. "On the Modesty of Women in Arab Muslim Villages: A Study in the Accomodation of Traditions." *American Anthropologist* 70:671–697.

Barakat, Halim. 1977. *Lebanon in Strife: Student Preludes to the Civil War.* Austin: University of Texas Press.

———. 1985. "The Arab Family and the Challenge of Social Transformation." In *Women and Family in the Middle East: New Voices of Change.* Elizabeth Wernock Fernea, ed. Pp. 27–48. Austin: University of Austin Press.

Barth, Frederick. 1954. "Father's Brother's Daughter Marriage in Kurdistan." *Southwest Journal of Anthropology* 10:164–71.

Burridge, Kenelm O. L. 1959. "Siblings in Tangu." *Oceanis* 30: 128–54.

Cambell, David. 1964. *Honour, Family, and Patronage: A Study of Institutions and Moral Values in a Greek Mountain Community.* Oxford: Clarendon Press.

Cohen, Abner. 1965. *Arab Border-Villages in Israel: A Study of Continuity and Change in Social Organization.* Manchester: Manchester University Press.

Cole, Donald Powell. 1975. *Nomads of the Nomads: The Al Murrah Bedouin of the Empty Quarter.* Arlington Heights, IL: Harlan Davidson, Inc.

Davis, Susan Schaefer. 1983. *Patience and Power: Women's Live's in a Moroccan Village.* Cambridge: Schenkman.

Davis, Susan Schaefer and Douglas A. Davis. 1989. *Adolescence in a Moroccan Town: Making Social Sense.* New Brunswick, NJ: Rutgers University Press.

Eickelman, Christine. 1984. *Women and Community in Oman.* New York: New York University Press.

El-Shamy, Hasan. 1976. "The Traditional Structure of Sentiments in Mahfouz's Trilogy: A Behavioristic Text Analysis." *Al-Arabiyya* 9:53–74.

———. 1979. "Brother and Sister Type 872: A Cognitive Behavioristic Analysis of a Middle Eastern Oikotype." *Folklore Monograph Series,* 8. Bloomington, IN: Folklore Publications Group.

———. 1981. "The Brother-Sister Syndrome in Arab Family Life, Socio-Cultural Factors in Arab Psychiatry: A Critical Review." *International Journal of Sociology of the Family* 2:313–23.

Fallers, Lloyd A. and Margaret C. 1976. "Sex Roles in Edremit." In *Mediterranean Family Structures.* J.G. Peristiany, ed. Pp. 243–71. London: Cambridge University Press.

Farsoun, Samih. 1970. "Family Structure and Society in Modern Lebanon." In *Peoples and Cultures in the Middle East.* Louise Sweet, ed. Pp. 257–307. Garden City, NY: The Natural History Press.

Fernea, Elizabeth Warnock. 1985. *Women and the Family in the Middle East: New Voices of Change.* Austin: University of Texas Press.

Firth, Raymond. 1 936. *We, the Tikopia: A Sociological Study of Kinship in Primitive Polynesia.* London: Allen & Unwin.

Fuller, Ann. 1966. *Buarij: Portrait of a Lebanese Muslim Village.* Cambridge: Center for Middle East Studies, Harvard University Press.

Gilmore, David G., ed. 1987. *Honor and Shame and the Unity of the Mediterranean.* Washington, DC: American Anthropological Association.

Granqvist, Hilma. 1935. *Marriage Conditions in a Palestinian Village.* Helsingfors: Societas Scientiarum Fennica, Commentationes Humanarum Literarum 6:8.

Gulick, John. 1955. *Social Structure and Cultural Change in a Lebanese Village.* New York: Viking Fund Publications in Anthropology.

Haley, P. Edward, and Lewis W. Snider, eds. 1979. *Lebanon in Crisis: Participants and Issues.* Syracuse, NY: Syracuse University Press.

Hatem, Mervat. 1987. "Toward the Study of the Psychodynamics of Mothering and Gender in Egyptian Families." *International Journal of Middle East Studies* 19:287–306.

Herodotus. 1972. *The Histories.* Aubrey De Selincourt, trans. Revised by A. R. Burn. New York: Penguin Books Ltd.

Hopkins, Keith. 1980. "Brother–Sister Marriage in Roman Egypt." In *Comparative Studies in Society and History.* 22:3:303–59.

Joseph, Suad. 1977. "Zaynab: An Urban Working-Class Lebanese Woman." In *Middle Eastern Muslim Women Speak.* Elizabeth Warnock Fernea and Basima Qattan Bezirgan, eds. Pp. 359–71.Austin: University of Texas Press.

———. 1978. "Muslim–Christian Conflict in Lebanon: A Perspective in the Evolution of Sectarianism." In *Muslim–Christian Conflicts: Economic, Political, and Social Origins.* Suad Joseph and Barbara L. K. Pillsbury, eds. Pp. 62–97. Boulder, CO: Westview Press.

———. 1982. "The Family as Security and Bondage: A Political Strategy of the Lebanese Urban Working Class." In *Towards a Political Economy of Urbanization in Third World Countries.* Helen Safa, ed. Pp. 151–71 New Delhi: Oxford University Press.

———. 1983. "Working Class Women's Networks in a Sectarian State: A Political Paradox." *American Ethnologist* 10:1–22

———. 1990. "Working the Law: A Lebanese Working Class Case." In *The Politics of Law in the Middle East.* Daisy Dwyer, ed. Pp. 143–59. Hadley, MA: J. F. Bergin.

———. 1993. "Connectivity and Patriarchy Among Urban Working Class Arab Families in Lebanon." *Ethos* 21:452–84.

Jowkar, Forouz. 1986. "Honor and Shame: A Feminist View from Within." *Feminist Issues* 6:1:45–63.

Keller, Catherine. 1986. *From a Broken Web: Separation, Sexism, and Self.* Boston: Beacon Press.

Kelly, Raymond C. 1977. *Etoro Social Structure: A Study in Structural Contradiction.* Ann Arbor: University of Michigan Press.

Khalaf, Samir. 1968. "Primordial Ties and Politics in Lebanon." *Middle Eastern Studies* 4:243–69.

———. 1971. "Family Associations in Lebanon." *Journal of Comparative Family Studies* 2:235–50.

Khuri, Fuad. 1970. "Parallel Cousin Marriage Reconsidered: A Middle Eastern Practice That Nullifies the Effects of Marriage on the Intensity of Family Relationships." *Man* 5:597–618.

Luepnitz, Deborah Anna. 1988. *The Family Interpreted: Feminist Theory in Clinical Practice.* New York: Basic Books.

Lutz, Catherine A. 1988. *Unnatural Emotions: Everyday Sentiments on a Micronesian Atoll and Their Challenge to Western Theory.* Chicago: University of Chicago Press.

Mabuchi, Toichi. 1964. "Spiritual Predominance of the Sister." In *Ryukyuan Culture and Society: A Survey.* Allen H. Smith, ed. Tenth Pacific Science Congress Series. Honolulu: University of Hawaii Press.

Malinowski, Bronislaw. 1913. *The Family Among the Australian Aborigines: A Sociological Study.* London: University of London Press.

Marshall, Mac, ed. 1983. *Siblingship in Oceania: Studies in the Meaning of Kin Relations.* Lanham, MD: University Press of America.

Marx, Emanuel. 1967. *Bedouin of the Negev.* New York: Frederick A. Praeger.

McCabe, Justine. 1983. "FBD Marriage: Further Support for the Westermarck Hypothesis of the Incest Taboo?" *American Anthropologist* 85:50–69.

Meeker, Michael E. 1976. "Meaning and Society in the Near East: Examples from the Black Sea Turks and the Levantine Arabs." *International Journal of Middle Eastern Studies* 7:383–422.

Middleton, Russell. 1962. "Brother–Sister and Father–Daughter Marriage in Ancient Egypt." *American Sociological Review* 27:603–611.

Minuchin, Salvador, Bernice L. Rosman, and Lester Baker. 1978. *Psychosomatic Families: Anorexia Nervosa in Context.* Cambridge: Harvard University Press.

Munson, Henry, Jr. 1984. *The House of Si Abd Allah: The Oral History of a Moroccan Family.* New Haven, CT: Yale University Press.

Murphy, Robert F. and Leonard Kasdan. 1959. "The Structure of Parallel Cousin Marriage." *American Anthropologist* 61:17–29.

Musil, Alois. 1928. *The Manners and Customs of the Rwala Bedouins.* New York: American Geographical Society.

Odeh, B.J. 1985. *Lebanon: Dynamics of Conflict.* London: Zed Books, Ltd.

Paige, Karen Ericksen. 1984. "Gender, Family Systems and Theories of State Formation." Paper presented at Middle East Studies Association Meetings, San Francisco.

Patai, Raphael. 1960. *Family, Love and the Bible.* London: McGibbon & Kee.

Peristiany, J. G. 1966. *Honor and Shame: The Values of Mediterranean Society.* Chicago: University of Chicago Press.

Pitt-Rivers, Julian. 1977. *The Fate of Shechem or the Politics of Sex: Essays in the*

Anthropology of the Mediterranean. London: Cambridge University Press.

Prothero, Edwin Terry. 1961. *Child Rearing in the Lebanon.* Cambridge: Harvard University Press.

Prothero, Edwin Terry, and Lutfy Najih Diab. 1974. *Changing Family Patterns in the Arab East.* Beirut: American University of Beirut Press.

Radcliffe-Brown, A. R. 1924. "The Mother's Brother in South Africa." *South African Journal of Science.* 21:542–55.

Ripinsky, M. M. 1968. "Middle Eastern Kinship as an Expression of a Culture-Environment System." *Muslim World* 58: 225–41.

Rosaldo, Michelle. 1984. "Toward an Anthropology of Self and Feeling." In *Culture Theory: Essays on Mind, Self and Emotion.* Richard Shweder and Robert LeVine, eds. Cambridge: Cambridge University Press.

Rosenfeld, Henry. 1960. "On Determinants of the Status of Arab Village Women." *Man* 60:66–70.

Rugh, Andrea B. 1984. *Family in Contemporary Egypt.* Syracuse, NY: Syracuse University Press.

Salibi, Kamal. 1976. *Cross Roads to Civil War: Lebanon 1958–1976.* Delmar, NY: Caravan.

Sharabi, Hisham. 1988. *Neopatriarchy: A Theory of Distorted Change in Arab Society.* New York: Oxford University Press.

Schneider, David M., and Kathleen Gough, eds. 1961. *Matrilineal Kinship.* Berkeley: University of California Press.

Schneider, Jane. 1971. *Of Vigilance and Virgins: Honour, Shame and Access to Resources in the Mediterranean Societies. Ethnology* 10:1–24.

Schneider, Jane and Peter Schneider. 1976. *Culture and Political Economy in Western Sicily.* New York: Academic Press.

Slotkin, J. S. 1947. "On the Possible Lack of Incest Regulations in Old Iran." *American Anthropologist* 49:612–17.

Weiner, Annette B. 1976. *Women of Value, Men of Renown: New Perspectives in Trobriand Exchange.* Austin: University of Texas Press.

Williams, Judith. 1968. *The Youth of Haouch El Harimi: A Lebanese Village.* Cambridge: Harvard University Press.

Whitaker, Ian. 1976. "Familial Roles in the Extended Patrilineal Kin-Group in Northern Albania." In *Mediterannean Family Structures.* J. G. Peristiany, ed. Pp. 195–203. London: Cambridge University Press.

13

We'll Talk Later

Rhoda Kanaaneh

All through my essay runs a tale, a folktale from back home. It's told by my aunt and registered by her brother. In this folktale, in how it got to me here, lies a story about who I am.

As an elderly Palestinian woman, illiterate, housewife, bearer of 20 children, mother of 11 survivors, as an asexual mature female, my aunt, like her mother and her mother's mother before her, tells tales. As she speaks, her grandchildren sit around and listen. She upholds an old tradition among Palestinian women, one of struggle to present their knowledge through oral art.

As a Palestinian man, educated, professor, head of a household of four, my uncle writes down my aunt's words and publishes them in a book. As copies of his book are sold, my uncle upholds a newer Palestinian (mostly men's) tradition of struggle to protect their culture from "modern" colonial occupation.

This story is about me because I am a woman and I am Palestinian. Like my uncle, I am concerned about a group of people, Palestinians, and our right to life, to art, to land, to speak. Like my aunt, I am female and I am concerned about a group within a group, Palestinian women, and our right to life, to art, to land, to speak. This is a concern that many uncles might not share or might see as secondary to the first concern. Unlike my aunt, I am from a younger generation. She speaks from her knowledge of coping. I speak from my knowledge that coping is not enough. So I take my aunt's tale and retell it.

When my uncle asks me why, I say I too want to preserve our cultural traditions, but I want those traditions to be traditions of hope and triumph, not submission. Uncle, your book is entitled Speak Bird, Speak Again. Well, let me speak. We'll talk later.

But I am afraid to say what I say, not because of uncle's angry glares or shaking finger, for I have been accustomed to that all my life. But because of my reader. More likely than not, you are not a Palestinian woman. Are you situated close to ideas about an outpost of Western Democracy and Civilization, that shining star in the midst of darkness—Israel? Well, once I went to a "Women in Black" demonstration in Boston, of Palestinian and Jewish women protesting Israeli military occupation of the West Bank and Gaza Strip. There were counterdemon-

From *Cultural Anthropology* 10 (1):125–35 (1995). Reprinted by permission. Rhoda Kanaaneh is a graduate student in anthropology at Columbia University.

strators holding up signs: "Arabs mutilate their women's genitals"; "Muslims sell their women for gold"; "Arabs oppress their women." Then there were signs of the logical conclusion: "Stop the Arabs from taking over," and cries of "Massacre the Arabs." Are you going to use my words to deny my people our right to speak?

More likely than not, you are saying no, saying that those people I saw are extremists, that I have become paranoid. Well, wait a minute. I have more questions for you. More likely than not, you are from the what is called the "West." You see my tale as part of the discourse on women in that area called the "Middle East." A woman, Marnia Lazreg, whose tales are often seen in this way, has said, "I discovered . . . a continuity between the traditional social science mode of comprehending North African and Middle Eastern societies, rooted as they are in French colonial epistemology, and academic women's treatment from these societies" (Lazreg 1990:327). Well, don't. Don't make any assumptions about my tale being part of the "Islamic world." Imagine if I studied you as part of the "Christian world." Did you know that many Palestinians are secular Muslims, that there are a lot of Christians and Druze? What does this mean? This alone should not mean anything at all. Don't give religion any overriding explanatory power. Don't subsume me and my words under a religion that has been written up by so many as a static, monolithic, essentially flawed entity. Give me my right to history. Sorry, no veils, seclusion, or clitoridectomy in this tale. I refuse to warp my tale to "fill the blanks in the geographical distribution made available . . . by US feminist liberalism" (Lazreg 1990:327). Audre Lorde, an African American woman, writes to Mary Daly, a European American woman, on the latter's appropriation of African women's history:

> Mary, I ask that you be aware of how this serves the destructive forces of racism and separation between women—the assumption that the herstory and myth of white women is the legitimate and sole herstory and myth of all women to call upon for power and background, and that non-white women and our herstories are noteworthy only as decorations, or examples of female victimization. [Lorde 1983:96]

So when you read my tale, don't say, "Oh yes, all women are oppressed." Listen to what I am saying instead. And we'll talk later. And to any Palestinian women who read my tale in this form, I do not speak for you. Speak for yourself. And we'll talk later. *Once upon a time there was a king who had no children except an only daughter. One day his wife laid her head down and died, and he went searching for a new wife. They spoke of this woman and that, but none pleased him. No one seemed more beautiful in his eyes, so the story goes, than his own daughter, and he had no wish to marry another. When he came into the house, she would call him "Father," but he would answer, "Don't call me 'Father'! Call me 'Cousin.'" "But father, O legitimately begotten son! I'm*

your daughter!" "It's no use," he insisted, "I've made up my mind."
I am the daughter of a king. He owns the house I live in and rules it. No one else is around. My mother is out of the picture—the story kills her softly but quickly. I have no siblings to protect or attack me. I, the daughter, stay in the house.

I hear a message: girl, beware of being "beautiful," of sending out signals of your sexuality. You will certainly arouse the most "unnatural" desires in others. And "it's no use"; once aroused, they are impossible to stop. Girl, being beautiful is a curse. It only brings upon you feelings of confusion, shame, guilt, "unnaturalness." You can do nothing about it once it starts. You arouse desires, but you cannot have any yourself.

Everyone tells me my sexuality is insatiable, indiscriminate. I have no resistance. How vulnerable and open to "persuasion" I am! I cry for mercy—but my cries are nothing in the face of my "beauty." I am "beauty." Can I be "not beautiful"? It doesn't matter, because beauty is "in his eyes."

I have no control over arousing desires. My body is dangerous. Since the beginning of the Intifada in the Israeli-occupied territories, my cousin Salwa, who lives in Ramallah in the West Bank, has been threatened by numerous Palestinian men on the street whom she did not personally know. They told her to stay at home and to dress more "modestly" because there are Israeli soldiers in town. Palestinian men, old women, children can go out, but not girls. Their beauty is a threat to the entire community.

Love is a powerful man desiring a passive woman. Anything else is outside the realm of love. So even when women desire each other, give pleasure to each other's bodies and genitals, that is not perceived as love or sex. It is not a threat, it does not exist.

You can arouse desires but you cannot speak of your own—his desire necessitates you to have none. She is passive. Any indication of her activity is perceived as a threat to everyone. A Lebanese woman, Layla Ba'labaki, once wrote a short story entitled "A Space Ship of Tenderness to the Moon." In it, the narrator says about her husband: "When he was near me, standing like a massive tower at a rocket-firing station, . . . my heart throbbed and I muttered to him that I adored his naked body. . . . He opened his arms and leaned over me. . . . I rushed into his embrace, mumbling crazily: 'I love you, I love you, I love you . . .'" (Ba'labaki 1983:279). Although the subject position that the narrator creates for herself might not be objectionable in its content, in its desire for man, it is nonetheless highly objectionable because it is she who creates it. This writer was accused by the state of Lebanon (in 1964) of intending to arouse sexual desire and of harming public morality. If the narrator were male and had said the same things about a woman as Ba'labaki says of herself—which happens quite frequently in Arabic literature—then it is not perceived as a threat to morality. In the introduction to his book, my uncle observes that "a woman must show no public interest in the subject of sex" (Muhawi and Kanaana 1989:27). You have no desire. You are simply desired.

One day he sent for the cadi and asked him, "A tree that I've cared for, feeding and watering it—is it legally mine, or can someone else claim it?" "No one else can claim it," replied the cadi. "It is rightfully yours."

I am a tree nourished by an owner who then claims me, rubs up against me, humps me, marries me. Owner feeds and waters me; thus he is responsible, rightful, legitimate in claiming "I." "I" owes her owner life, existence itself. So "I" loses itself.

The machine of religion can be made by its owners to produce anything, even trees. Don't tell me anything about "Islam." It doesn't matter. Cadis can say anything they want. Owners can make cadis say anything they want. "I," on the other hand, can say nothing. Owner is not at all concerned with my claims—but with those of other owners, cadis, men. "I" just stand open, vulnerable, ever-ready.

No sooner had the cadi left than the father went out and brought his daughter jewelry and a wedding dress. He was preparing to take her for his wife.

The girl put on the new clothes and the gold and sat in the house.

Owner says "I" is beautiful/open, and to prove it owner gives "I" some things that sparkle and glitter, and she naturally takes them, places them on her branches and trunk. Now "I" sparkles and glitters—in a silent display of "I"'s consent and owner's wealth and power.

All girls love fancy dresses and gold. During a wedding, relatives of the groom dress the bride in gold jewelry and fancy clothes, and give her expensive gifts, in a public ceremony. These gifts are a bride's first material possession after years of "selfless" daughterhood. The bride sits upon a seat, four or five folded mattresses high. They sing: "Ten jackets we have brought for the beloved ones in order to appease her." The bride is appeased. Then the groom enters and lifts the bridal veil. Long ago, the groom used to present his bride with coins until she allowed him to approach her and consummate the marriage. Today, girls are too worldly for that. But they still say: "He who has money can have the king's daughter for his bride."

He thinks he can buy me because I am by nature poor. Every man can become an owner of "I" if he has wealth. The female self is a commodity. "I" is open to anyone, and "bridewealth" is proof.

Her father came home in the evening. When she realized that he was absolutely intent on taking her, she went to a sackcloth maker and said, "Take as much money as you want, but make me a tight-fitting sackcloth that will cover my whole body, except my nostrils, mouth, and eyes. And I want it ready by tomorrow morning."

"Fine," he said. "I'll do it."

When it was finished the girl went and brought it home. She put it in a shed in front of the house and locked the door.

"Father" is intent on taking "I" away. "Daughter" has lost all control of her "self." She thus wishes to escape from this "I," from this body, to tightly cover and hide it. She wishes to be "beautiful" no longer. She has heard your warning, Aunty. The only way to escape her subjectivity is to make her body, her femininity disappear. "I" experiences the body as a source of ill. Control of femininity is impossible. Denial of femininity is the only way out. So ironically, in the face of danger of losing her "self," "daughter" tries to lose it completely. The price for exiting the realm of desirability, "beauty," is very high.

She then put on the bridal clothes and jewelry again and lounged about the house. Her father came home in the evening.

"Father!" she called to him.

"Don't call me 'Father'!" he said. "Call me 'Cousin.'"

"All right, Cousin!" she replied. "But wait until I come back from the outhouse." (All respect to the audience!)

"But you might run away."

"No, I won't," she answered. "But just to make sure, tie a rope to my wrist, and every once in a while pull your end of it and you'll discover I'm still there."

There was a big stone in the lower part of the house, and on her way out she tied her end of the rope to it, together with the bracelets. She then went out to the shed, put on her tight sack, and, invoking the help of Allah, ventured out into the night.

This is the first wish that "daughter" fulfills in the tale. Because a wish is a crime for her, the only way she can fulfill it is through deception. "Father" leaves her no other alternative. The cadi does not/cannot see her. She has no family or mother. No one can help her, and her "self" is lost too. Lying is the sole option.

Maybe that is why there are so many proverbs such as "A ghoul's proverbial cunning is not equal to that of women"; "When woman was created, the devil was delighted"; "Women's tricks have defeated the tricks of the ghouls."

In order to escape, daughter must accede to father's desire, must play his game: "All right, Cousin!" She must surrender her desires to him: "tie a rope to my wrist." Thank god for the outhouse, literally called in Arabic "the house of excrement." It is the only place where father cannot enter with daughter. It is the only place that daughter can be alone/with her self.

A neighbor, ex-classmate, and friend of mine from my village in the Galilee dropped out of school when we were in seventh grade. She now works in a small garment-subcontracting factory in a neighboring village for less than two dollars an hour. She works about ten hours a day, six days a week. She tells me she hates the job, but her family needs the money. Her boss will not let the workers (all female) talk on the factory floor. She tells me of how wonderful it is when she is excused to go to the bathroom, where she can talk, rest, and be out of the boss's sight. This woman's name is Shuruq, which means "sunrise." She too can find her self in "the house of excrement."

And thank god for jewelry. Female identity has been so tightly tied to these ornaments that in the eyes of most people they become her. The tinkle of the bracelets is an automatic indication of her presence. In the eyes of father there is no place for separation between daughter and bracelets. But this daughter is able to make that separation. She has not been blinded by the sparkle of the gold. She must pay yet another price for fleeing: any economic security those bracelets might have provided her. In order for her to escape father, daughter must give up her self, her femininity, and her possessions—the gold.

My aunt, her mother, and her mother's mother before her, all tell this tale.This is a story about their self-knowledge. They know that their identities are in danger of violation by men, and they speak of the dark nooks and crannies where that danger can be manipulated.

Daughter ventures out into the night. She leaves everything behind—but she really had nothing to leave. The night is dangerous, but father is even more frightening. She has nothing to lose and some sort of "I" to gain.

Meanwhile, the father tugged at the rope every few moments and, hearing the tinkle of the bracelets, would say to himself, "She's still here." He waited and waited until the middle of the night, and then he said, "By Allah, I've got no choice but to go check on her." When he found the rope tied to the stone, with the bracelets dangling from it, he prepared his horse, disguised himself, mounted, and went out to look for her.

By running away, daughter displays a desire of her own and a resistance to father's. This moves father to act with the aim of bringing back daughter, status quo. The display of resistance does not change his desire and does not make him aware of daughter's desire. The display gives him no insight into his self or daughter's. He is impenetrable.

She had already been gone awhile, and by the time he left the house she was well outside of the city. He followed after her, searching. When he caught up with her, she saw and recognized him, and clung to the trunk of a tree. Not recognizing her, but thinking she was a man, he asked, "Didn't you see a girl with such and such features pass this way?"

"Oh uncle, Allah save you!" answered the maiden. "Please leave me to my misery. I can barely see in front of me."

He left her and went away. Seeing him take one path, she took another.

Father owns many things including a horse. Daughter does not. Naturally his possessions give him an advantage, and he easily catches up with daughter. But her disguise is better than his. Perhaps she is more cunning. Perhaps she has more at stake. She clings to the trunk of a tree. Daughter begins to claim a new self— a masculine and freakish one. Masculine, so as to escape the perils of femininity. And freakish (a "defective male"), so as to avoid having to live up to the standards of manhood, to desire women, or engage with other men as equals. Daughter's only wish comes true when she claims this new semi-androgynous self. A woman can only desire as a man.

She kept on traveling, sleeping here and waking up there, until she came to a
city. Hunger driving her, she took shelter by the wall of a king's palace.
The king's slave girl came out with a platter to dump out leftover food.
Sackcloth fell on the scraps and set to eating. When the slave saw her, she rushed
back inside.

"O mistress!" she called out, "There's a weird sight outside—the strangest
looking man, and he's eating the leftovers."

"Go call him in and let him come here!" commanded the mistress.

"Come in and see my mistress," said the slave. "They want to have a look at
you."

"What's the situation with you, uncle?" they asked, when she came inside.
"Are you human or jinn?"

"By Allah, uncle," she replied, "I'm human, and the choicest of the race. But
Allah has created me the way I am."

"What skill do you have?" they asked. "What can you do?"

"By Allah, I don't have any skills in particular," she answered. "I can stay in
the kitchen, peeling onions and passing things over when needed."

They put her to work in the kitchen, and soon everyone was saying, "Here
comes Sackcloth! There goes Sackcloth!" How happy they were to have
Sackcloth around, and she stayed in the kitchen under the protection of the cook.

Daughter's freakishness attracts much needed attention. She is saved by a
slave. The king's household takes pity upon this hungry soul; he is human after
all. Again she becomes a dependent, now on the king's household. She works in
the kitchen, probably just like she did at her father's house, but here, as a man, it
is seen as a "skill" that she practices in exchange for her livelihood. Here she is
not completely taken for granted/erased; they are "happy" to have her around.
She does not have the responsibilities, obligations, burdens, losses (nor the gains)
of either sex. Her disguise takes the place of her female body. She becomes
"Sackcloth" rather than "daughter." And only in this way is she seen coming and
going without being possessed.

One day there was a wedding in the city, and the king's household was invit-
ed. In the evening, they were preparing to go have a look at the spectacle.

"Hey, Sackcloth!" they called out. "Don't you want to come with us and have
a look at the wedding?"

"No, Allah help me!" she exclaimed. "I can't go look at weddings or anything
else like that. You go and I wish you Godspeed, but I can't go."

The king's household and the slaves went to the wedding, and no one was left
at home except Sackcloth. Waiting till they were well on their way, she took off
her sackcloth and set out for the festivities, all made up and wearing the wed-
ding dress she had brought with her. All the women were dancing in turn, and
when her turn came, she took the handkerchiefs and danced and danced until
she had had her fill of dancing. She then dropped the handkerchiefs and left, and

*no one knew where she came from or where she went. Returning home she put
on her sackcloth, squatted alongside the walls of the palace, and went to sleep.*
During most of the wedding, men and women traditionally celebrate separately. Each sex has its own space, set of wedding songs, dances, and styles of
performance. As "Sackcloth" she cannot participate in the spectacle. She cannot
join the women, because she is a man. And she cannot join the men, because she
is defective and disgusting.

> A standard description of a wedding might sound like this: the women
> stand in a circle, singing and clapping while one of them dances in the
> middle, a colorful handkerchief in each hand. All eyes áre on her, and she
> shows off her dancing ability, her beauty and her clothes. After dancing
> awhile, she passes the handkerchiefs to another woman, who then takes
> her turn. [Muhawi and Kanaana 1989:128]

My aunt's tale tells of a wedding that has a slight twist. The women pass the
handkerchief to her and she dances all she wants. "I" expresses and fulfills a
desire by temporarily taking on a new identity, reclaiming female identity. But
the twist is that "no one knew where she came from or where she went." She is
not a normal female; she is mysterious, belongs to no one, but also can be given
to no one. When she displays her beauty or clothes among these women, it is hers
and not her father's. The other women cannot place her. She dances as a woman,
not as a daughter.

During this short period of time, she comes back in touch with her body, her
femaleness, but now it is hers. She is no longer alienated from it by father/owner.
But when she has her fill of dancing, she drops the handkerchief and leaves. She
returns to the palace and puts on her sackcloth again. She can only claim her femininity for a short while. If she is female for too long, she is in danger of being
identified and then claimed by others.

When the slaves got back from the celebration, they started badgering her.

*"What! Are you sleeping here?" They taunted, "May you never rise! If only
you'd come to the wedding, you would've seen the girl who danced and danced
and then left without anybody knowing where she went."*

*That happened the first night, and the second night the same thing happened
again. When the king's wife came home, she went to see her son.*

*"Dear son," she said, "if only we could get that girl, the one who comes to
the wedding and leaves without anybody knowing where she comes from or
where she goes—I'd ask for her hand."*

Because she is an unclaimed female who cannot be pinned down (metaphorically and literally), she attracts a lot of attention. Everybody at the wedding
notices her, wonders about her, wants to know more about her, to possess her.
When she claims this unrestricted yet unprotected female identity the second

time, she even attracts the king's wife's attention. She wishes to claim her for her son. A woman cannot continue to be unclaimed. And she is considered a good catch, a valuable acquisition, worthy of marrying a king's son simply because she can be claimed so fully.

"Let me wear women's clothes, mother," he suggested, "and take me with you to the women's side. If anyone should ask, say to them, 'This is my sister's daughter. She's here visiting us, and I brought her with me to see the celebrations.'"

"Fine," she agreed.

Putting women's clothes on him, she took him with them. Sackcloth, meanwhile, gave them enough time to get there, then took off her coat of sackcloth, and followed. She went in, danced until she had had her fill, and then slipped away. No one recognized her or knew where she came from or where she went. Returning home, she put on her sackcloth and went to sleep.

The following day the king's son said to the others, "You go to the wedding," and he hid outside the door of the house where the celebration was taking place. Sackcloth came again, went inside and danced, and then pulled herself together and slipped away. No sooner had she left than he followed her, keeping a safe distance until she reached home. No sooner did she get there than she went in, put on her coat of sackcloth, and squatted by the palace wall and went to sleep.

"What!" he said to himself, "She dwells in my own house and pretends to be some kind of freak!" He did not say anything to anyone.

The king's son is naturally interested. He sets out to *crack* the mystery, to *pin* this woman down. First he goes to see her. He disguises himself as a woman so that he can enter their space without disrupting or altering it.

Unlike her father, whom she is able to recognize and escape from, the prince has a disguise that she does not detect. He is more cunning than her and father. He is a real big owner. The next night, again undetected, he follows her to see "where she comes from and where she goes." He discovers her identity and now proceeds to claim it. By allowing her identity to be known, she loses it. Her femininity is discovered and she becomes a possession once again. The prince is further disturbed by the fact that this mystery existed under his own roof, that he did not have full knowledge/possession of everyone in his home.

The next morning he said to the slaves who bring up his meals, "I don't want any of you to bring my food up today. I want Sackcloth to serve my dinner, and I want him to share it with me."

"O master, for the sake of Allah!" she protested, "I can't do it. I'm so disgusting, how could you want to have dinner with me?"

"You must bring up my dinner so that we can eat together," he replied. The servants prepared dinner, served it onto a platter, and gave it to Sackcloth. She carried it, pretending to limp, until she was halfway up the stairs, then she made as if her foot had slipped and dropped the whole platter.

"Please, mother!" she pleaded. "Didn't I tell you I can't carry anything?"

"You must keep bringing platters and dropping them," the son of the king insisted, "until you manage to come up here on your own."
With the second platter she came up to the landing and at the top of the stairs, slipped, and dropped it. "This isn't going to get you anywhere," said the son of the king. "Do not for one moment hope to be excused."

The prince requests that she *serve* him in place of his slaves, and then eat with him. She does not know that he has discovered her identity, yet she strongly resists. She begs and pleads with him to let her go, first with words and then with actions. She insists that she is disgusting. She does not want to be desired. And to resist the orders of the king's son is no small offense. After all, he is the biggest owner of them all. She senses danger in proximity to him, in fulfilling his personal desires. She senses that the prince has taken a liking to her, but she is not falling for that gold and dresses thing again.

Yet, just like with her father, her protests are of no use. The prince's desires are unmovable, unaffected by hers. Now that a man desires her, she begins to lose her power to desire, her identity, once more. My uncle interprets this part of the tale as follows: "Her dancing in public . . . is a declaration of . . . her readiness to accept a mate" (Muhawi and Kanaana 1989:145). When Sackcloth allows herself to be sexualized, her act is immediately interpreted as a signal of readiness to be taken. The sackcloth coat was merely a cocoon out of which a fully mature, beautiful creature comes. But what if she, in fact, wanted to simply be a female "self"? What if she wanted to belong, to be loved, to be close, to be protected—without being taken? In my uncle's mind, in the king's son's mind, there is no room for her intent. Her protests have no impact whatsoever. When she says no, it really means yes. She is slowly raped of her self again.

With the third platter she limped and limped, leaning here and there, until she reached the top and served him his dinner.
"Come sit here with me," said the prince, closing the door. "Let's eat this dinner together."
"Please, master!" she protested, "Just look at my condition. Surely it will disgust you."
"No. Do sit down! I would like to have dinner with you."
They sat down to eat together, and the prince pulled out a knife and reached for the coat of sackcloth.
"You must take this thing off!" he said. "How long have we been searching, wondering who the girl was that came to the wedding. And all this time you've been living under my own roof!"
He made her remove her sackcloth coat,

Her identity is fading away, quickly dissolving in the hands of the king's son. She enters, and he closes the door behind her. She serves him. He pulls out a knife and takes off her clothes. She is now nude. Her sackcloth disguise is gone. In its place, before the prince's eyes, is a display: the surface of her skin, the hair on her body, the spaces between her parts are turned into a new disguise. Her nudity is a new form of dress; it covers an identity that is now lost forever. This new disguise can never be discarded; she can never be naked (not nude) again. From now on she will always be seen/see her "self" as belonging, but also as a belonging.

and called his mother. They sent for the cadi and wrote up their marriage contract.

"For forty days," the public crier announced, "no one is to eat or drink except at the house of the king."

They held wedding celebrations and gave her to him for a wife.

Instantaneously, they *gave* her to him. Now everyone who sees her knows "where she comes from and where she goes." In this wedding, she no longer takes the handkerchief and freely passes it. There is no longer anything mysterious about her participation. Now she will be displayed as a sparkling bride to the people, as a nude to the husband, and as nothing to herself.

And this is my tale, I've told it; and in your hands I leave it.

Aunty, you tell me there is danger. I say you are so right. You tell me there are ways of escaping. I say, yes, I could escape. You tell me it is hopeless because they will always find me and take me back. I say no! I refuse. If I am to be caught, then I will not run away. What is missing in your tale, Aunty, is that I must learn a language with which I can "speak." A language with which I can find my family "self." Language too has its dark nooks and crannies. I am now searching for those spaces in your tale and in everything around me. I am speaking now. We'll talk later.

References

Ba'labaki, Layla. 1983. "A Space Ship of Tenderness to the Moon." In *Middle Eastern Muslim Women Speak*. Elizabeth Fernea and Basima Qattan Bezirgan, eds. Pp. 274–79. Austin: University of Texas Press.

Lazreg, Mamia. 1990. "Feminism and Difference: The Perils of Writing as a Woman on Women in Algeria." In *Conflicts in Feminism*. Marianne Hirsch and Evelyn Fox Keller, eds. Pp. 326–48. New York: Routledge Press.

Lorde, Audre. 1983. "An Open Letter to Mary Daly." In *This Bridge Called My Back: Writing by Radical Women of Color*. Cherrie Moraga and Gloria Anzaldua, eds. Pp. 94–97. New York: Kitchen Table Press.

Muhawi, Ibrahim, and Sharif Kanaana. 1989. *Speak Bird, Speak Again*. Berkeley: University of California Press.

Four

Introduction

Development

The concept of "development" has been in vogue since the end of Second World War in 1945, with the general meaning of deliberate change toward a goal. It has replaced older terms, such as "progress," "advancement," "awakening," "reawakening," and "renaissance." Meanwhile, others preferred to speak of the global spread of capitalism in various forms. For nearly two decades after 1945, the term "development" was used as synonymous with that of "growth," "modernization," "industrialization," and even "westernization." At the time, "development" was thought of in basically economic terms and the industrialized West presented itself to the newly independent countries, including the Arab world, as a model to be emulated and followed. A competing model, that of the Soviet Union and the Eastern Bloc, equally presented itself as a closer and more realistic example for the new states in Asia, Africa, and Latin America. This competition among "development" models was an integral part of the ideological conflict of the Cold War between the capitalist, liberal, and democratic West and the socialist, centrally planned, and populist East.

At the time, the Arab world was caught up in this Cold War and also had one of its own, an "Arab Cold War," between those who drew closer to the Soviet model (e.g., Egypt, Algeria, Syria, Iraq) and those who remained traditionally closer to the Western model (e.g., Lebanon, Jordan, the Gulf states, Saudi Arabia, and Morocco). At any rate, all Arab countries emphasized education, attempted industrialization and provision of social services, built a modern infrastructure, and became, to various degrees, "capitalist." Most Arab countries were fairly successful in implementing their development plans in the first years following their independence. However, later problems began to appear, accumulate, and in some cases reach crisis levels. In this respect, the Arab world was not unique—many countries in the Third World were to suffer from similar problems, setbacks, and crises. The optimism of the 1960s gave way to pessimism.

By the 1990s the concept of development was rethought. The word "sustainable" was added. Thus "sustainable development" came to mean a continuous process of collective (societal) self-improvement, without jeopardizing the opportunities of future generations to do the same. This definition takes into account the ability of people in self-help and self-improvement, which are directly tied to their "nutrition," "health," and "education." Income, "gross

275

national product" (GNP), or "gross domestic product" (GDP) per capita had dominated the measurement of development in previous decades. They were reflected in the sheer economic or material well-being of a country. With the concept of "sustainable development," the emphasis is equally on the other non-material human dimensions—mainly nutrition, health, and education. In 1990, the United Nations Development Program began to issue an annual world report reflecting this more comprehensive understanding of the process: the Human Development Report. This approach is designed to show, for each country, not how well the rich are doing, but how well the poor are doing.

The Human Development Index (HDI) measures the average achievement of a country in basic human capabilities. The HDI indicates whether people lead a long and healthy life, are educated and knowledgeable, and enjoy a decent standard of living. It is based on literacy rates, life expectancy, nutrition, and a measure of income called purchasing power parity, where income is related to what it can buy in a given society. The HDI examines the average condition of all people in a country; distributional inequalities for various groups of society have to be calculated separately. The Gender-related Development Index measures achievement in the same basic capabilities as the HDI, but takes note of inequality in achievement between women and men. The GDI is thus the HDI adjusted downwards for gender inequality.

The Human Development Report figures are adjusted, refined, and made comparable worldwide for 174 countries, on available data for 1993.[1]

Table 6 in the Statistical Abstract shows where the twenty-one Arab countries (not including, for the moment, Palestine) are located in terms of sustainable human development vis-à-vis each other, and compared to the rest of the world. It will be observed that some of the figures in the table may differ from previous figures in other tables in this reader.

The small Gulf state of Bahrain ranked the highest of all Arab countries on the HDI, and ranked 39 among all 174 countries worldwide in 1993. Bahrain had a score of 0.866 out of a maximum possible score of 1.000 on the HDI. In 1993, Canada ranked first worldwide, with a score of 0.951 (followed by the U.S., Japan, the Netherlands, and Norway). Accordingly, Canada may not be the "richest," but is the "most developed." All four countries following Canada on the HDI have higher income or GDP per capita. By the same token, all three Arab countries following Bahrain have higher GDP per capita. The reason for Bahrain's highest Arab HDI ranking is its higher adult literacy (more than 84 percent) than the other three in the first group.

Only four Arab countries have made it into the ranks of the high human development group (57 countries). They have less than 2 percent of the total Arab population. More of the Arab countries (11 out of 21) are located in the medium range of HDI. This group of medium development includes also the biggest Arab countries in terms of population (202 million people, or 76 percent of the total Arab population). There were 6 Arab countries located among the least developed 48 countries worldwide. These were the Comoros Islands, Yemen, Sudan, Mauritania, Djibouti, and Somalia. Together, these least developed Arab countries make up more than one-fifth of all Arab population (about 57 million). Three of the least developed have had protracted civil armed conflicts (Yemen, Sudan, and Somalia) in the last two decades. The other three have had frequent civil strife (Comoros, Mauritania, and Djibouti).

The last remark signifies the importance of sociopolitical stability for sustainable human development. One of the obstacles to development in several Arab countries has been their inability not only to manage material resources but also to manage social and ethnic diversity peacefully. Many of the ruling Arab elites, especially from the military, thought of modern state-building in a corporate uniform fashion, and used authoritarian styles of governance to bring it about. But more often than not, this orientation backfired and derailed state-building and development alike. Among the hard lessons of postindependence is the ability to work with existing socioeconomic formations (e.g., tribes, ethnic communities, social classes) in the quest for amelioration. Some of the selections in this section display the tenacious persistence of socioeconomic formations. Sustainable development, we learn, must be "nurtured," not "forced" or "decreed."

The HDI measures deal with end products and not with the human social systems that produce the results. Much social science, including the pieces included here, focuses more on the impact of social change on the patterns of relations between human beings, and on the ways in which changes at this level promote or impede improvement in the basic measures. The following articles give an idea of urban living conditions and then address the question of rural development in the Arab world, especially under conditions of technological and broader institutional change.

In This Section

The overview of development in the Arab world only tells part of the story. Development is also a drama, and sometimes a trauma, for those involved. In this section, we concentrate on the issue of rural and agricultural development in the Arab world, as seen through a collection of case studies which can be analyzed according to a common framework.

In most parts of the Arab world, the capitalist transformation of agriculture began very early. Egypt was generally first, but the countries of the Fertile Crescent, especially Iraq and Syria, and of the Maghrib, were not far behind. Other countries, notably Yemen and Saudi Arabia (see Altorki and Cole above), did not follow the evolution described here.

The first wave of change to hit the premodern, precapitalist base took place through the introduction of machinery including irrigation pumps and tractors, and through the institution of new land tenure laws allowing for private landownership. This pattern tended to increase the patterns of inequality in the countryside, and to accentuate social tension. Thus, beginning in 1952 there was a shift toward socialist forms of organization in agriculture. These forms included agrarian reform, land redistribution, and the creation of cooperatives, and they retained or increased the use of agricultural machinery. This shift was particularly evident in Egypt, Iraq, Syria, Tunisia, and Algeria. There were partial parallels in some other countries. After the brief socialist interlude, capitalist forms reappeared in Arab agriculture. Prominent here are the international financial institutions such as the World Bank, reflecting the conventional wisdom that free-market reforms are the way toward a prosperous future. In agriculture, this means a dismantling of the state structures that subsidized and otherwise controlled agriculture, a focus on exports, and the enhancement of markets not only in labor and produce, which always existed, but also in land. The issue, particularly in Egypt, is whether the small capitalist farmer can survive the new phase of capitalist accumulation.

These three phases are described by Nicholas Hopkins for Egypt, by Suleyman Khalaf for Syria, and Mouldi Lahmar for Tunisia. The emergence of the "cotton shaikhs" in Syria, for instance, is paralleled by that of the "olive shaikhs" in southern Tunisia, and both are examples of the first wave of capitalism. In Egypt, the state became a silent partner of each farmer under socialism, but is now withdrawing credit availability. The case studies of Khalaf and Lahmar show that each of these phases brought with it a particular form of local politics and leadership, often involving, as in Egypt, patterns of social differentiation and the emergence of patron-client relations.

These three phases can be analyzed through six categories. (1) There is a long-term trend away from collective forms of land tenure and toward individual, and somewhat more secure, forms. (2) There is a trend away from reliance on family labor and labor exchange with neighbors and toward the use of hired labor. (3) Animal power is giving way to machine power, with human labor a constant. (4) Crops that used to be largely consumed by their producers are now marketed, whether through the state or privately. (5) Farmers used to provide their own capital, for instance, by keeping seed from one year to the next, but now usually rely on crop loans for operating funds. (6) Irrigation systems used to be primarily local, self-built and self-managed, and are increasingly large in scale and state-run. These factors are analyzed in detail in Hopkins's article and are alluded to elsewhere.

The exception to this pattern is Yemen. Shelagh Weir describes the capitalist response of farmers in a highland area to new opportunities, particularly the cultivation of the semi-narcotic *qat,* which is increasingly popular in urban Yemen. Qat is a tree whose leaves Yemenis chew to alter their consciousness and facilitate certain types of social relations.[2] Weir analyzes the place of qat in this regional agriculture, and shows how the increased income from qat has motivated people to build roads and otherwise improve their material conditions of existence. Qat is often regarded as undesirable by developers and moralizers, but Weir argues that its effect on the growers has often been positive.

Nicholas Hopkins' approach tackles all of Egypt rather than one specific community. He shows the factors and processes of change in the social organization of Egyptian agriculture, and argues for recognizing the continuing value of the small farmers in Egypt. The trend toward a capitalist agriculture is now enhanced by efforts to reduce the level of support by the government for small farmers.

Suleyman Khalaf analyzes the social history of a farming community in northern Syria, showing how an elite family managed to retain its place by astute strategies throughout the many changes in the Syrian development philosophy. The family prospered under early capitalism, suffered during the brief socialist period, and then re-established itself through education.

Mouldi Lahmar compares two communites, in one of which a demonstration against a government decision occurred in 1984 while in the other it did not. His goal is to see what elements of the social organization can be used to explain this contrast. Basically his answer is that in Bir Ali the traditional, tribal leadership survived and was able to contain the unrest, while in el-Hencha the traditional hierarchy has been replaced by the elements of a class structure (the working class girls in the factory, students from the local school) whose political actions were stimulated by the decision to raise prices. The traditional leadership survived in Bir Ali because of a favorable land tenure situation which prevented colonial takeover of landownership. In the 1980s this traditional leadership dominated the local branches of the dominant party in Tunisia, the Partie Socialiste Destourien, or PSD.

Overall, agriculture has often been neglected in the Arab world, while population is growing, thus posing the issue of food security. By the mid-1990s, only 30 percent of the Arab world's workforce was in agriculture, compared with 45 percent in services.[3] The question of how to organize agriculture so that it provides a decent living to the maximum number of people while still remaining highly productive remains urgent. An examination of these studies suggests some of the issues involved. Whether we focus on measures like the HDI or the patterns of interpersonal relations at the local level, improving the quality of life of all the people in the Arab world must be a top priority.

Notes

1   See the *Human Development Report 1996* (New York: UNDP and Oxford University Press, 1996), Tables 1 and 2.

2   *Catha edulis* or *qat* is indigenous to East Africa, and was probably introduced into Yemen in the fourteenth century C.E. The qat tree is easily cultivated and resistant to most pests and diseases. The active ingredients in the fresh leaves are alkaloids which stimulate the central nervous system. The three stages of influence on the chewer are a) alertness and awareness, b) introspective contentment, and c) listlessness and depression. Chewing qat depresses the appetite and interferes with sleep. Chewing qat is also a social act which expresses Yemeni identity. (See D. Varisco, "On the Meaning of Chewing: The Significance of Qat in the YAR," in *International Journal of Middle East Studies* 18 (1986):1–13).

3   *Will Arab Workers Prosper or be Left Out in the Twenty-First Century?* (Washington: World Bank, 1995).

14

Economic Aspects of the Qat Industry in North-West Yemen

Shelagh Weir

There is considerable concern in official circles and among development economists at the great expansion in qat cultivation which took place in the Yemen Arab Republic (YAR) during the 1970s. This expansion was in response to the substantial national increase in qat consumption and the inflation in qat prices which took place during the same period. Before the civil war of 1962–70 only a relatively affluent, mainly urban, minority were regular, frequent qat consumers, but during the 1970s qat consumption spread throughout the population and for the first time became a majority practice. In the early 1970s the average price of a bunch *(rubta)* of qat was about 4 rials (YR) (less than $1). By 1979/80 increased demand had pushed up the price of a rubta to an average of YR45 ($10). Most consumers were by then buying between three and eight bunches a week and many were buying much more. The increase in qat consumption and qat prices was clearly linked to the substantial rise in disposable incomes, due mainly to the great influx of cash remittances from the vast numbers of Yemenis who took up temporary employment in Saudi Arabia from the early 1970s. A large proportion of the money repatriated by these migrant laborers was being spent on qat.

Many officials believe that the huge national expenditure on qat and the high proportion of prime agricultural land devoted to its cultivation are retarding Yemen's economic development by diverting cash from productive investment, and by obstructing the officially promulgated aim of working towards greater national self-sufficiency in food production. In the author's view, these and various other assumptions which have been made about the negative effects of both the consumption and production of qat require greater scrutiny and debate than they have yet received. But so far the debate has been hindered by the dearth of information on all aspects of qat. In particular, very little is known about the structure of its production, or of the effects on regional economies of the expansion in its cultivation and the influx of high revenues from its sales. This article

From B. R. Pridham, ed., *Economy, Society, and Culture in Contemporary Yemen* (London: Croom Helm, 1985), pp. 64–82. Reprinted by permission. Shelagh Weir is Curator for Middle East Ethnography at the British Museum, Museum of Mankind, London.

is intended as a contribution to this area of knowledge. Drawing on information collected during 14 months' fieldwork in a qat-trading community in Razih, a highland province in north-west Yemen, the article will (a) outline the salient features of the local qat industry and (b) describe some of the positive economic effects qat production has had in the area. It will show that qat has helped to promote and sustain agriculture, and has stimulated and helped to finance certain technological innovations and infrastructural developments.

The community to be discussed lives on the highest slopes of a steep mountain, which will be called by the fictitious name of al-Jabal. It lies at an altitude of about 2,100 m on the western edge of the Yemeni highlands close to the international border with Saudi Arabia. Below the mountain to the west stretches the hot dry Tihama plain which borders the Red Sea; to the east extend the rugged mountains of the highland massif; and about 50 km as the crow flies beyond this craggy terrain lies the high flat central plateau of Yemen and the walled town of Sa'da.

The population of al-Jabal is about 4,500, of whom some 900 live in the largest settlement on the mountain known as the *madina* (town) of al-Jabal. The madina consists of about 70 multi-storeyed stone houses clustered along a ridge near the summit of the mountain, and has at its center a large open market-place with the main mosque of al-Jabal on its edge, both surrounded by dozens of small shops. The madina is the economic, social, religious and political center of al-Jabal. The remainder of the population lives in over. 30 small scattered hamlets perched on rocky outcrops overlooking the terraces. Until the late 1970s, when al-Jabal was first linked to the outside world by motor tracks, all travel and transportation was on foot or on donkey and camel-back along the myriad of narrow tortuous paths which wind through the mountains.

The community of al-Jabal constitutes a political unit or *qabila* (tribe) which is internally administered and externally represented by a *shaikh* and tribal elders. Al-Jabal together with a mountain to its north, occupied by a tribe of about 1,000 people, comprise the main qat-producing areas of Razih. Because of its geographical location and altitude, the upper slopes of al-Jabal are blessed with relatively high rainfall (an estimated annual average of 700–1,000 mm) and— equally important for agricultural production—the mountain is frequently bathed in humid mists which reduce evaporation from the soil. It is therefore exceptionally green and fertile compared with either the Tihama or the mountains further east which receive far less rain. The mountain is so steep that agriculture would be impossible without terracing and, above an altitude of about 1,300 m (corresponding to the zone of maximum rainfall), the slopes are clothed in row upon row of beautifully constructed stone-walled terraces. Only the most precipitous slopes are unterraced and these are one important source of fodder for domestic animals. A minority of households keep one or two cattle and three or four sheep. Domestic livestock production has always been limited by the scarcity of fodder and the lack of land suitable for grazing on the steep mountain-sides. All fodder is collected by hand by the women and brought to the animals in the settlements.

In addition to qat, the main crops cultivated in al-Jabal are coffee, banana, summer sorghum, and winter wheat and barley. There is also some interplanting of legumes, and there are a few scattered fruit trees—peach and papaya on the upper slopes and lime and citron further down. All crops except banana are exclusively rain-fed or irrigated by surface run-off water. Most banana is grown in dense plantations in narrow clefts and steep valleys containing small permanent springs which allow some controlled irrigation of the terraces.

Al-Jabal is situated in a strategic position between the Tihama and the highlands on a major trade route between the two regions which passes through the mountainous province of Razih and eventually connects with the central plateau north of Sa'da. The market of al-Jabal is therefore important not only for the exchange of local produce, but also as an entrepôt for cash-crops exported from the western highlands to the coast and abroad (skins and coffee), for foreign commodities imported at the Red Sea ports, and for grain and fruits traded west from the eastern highlands and plateau regions. Today it is the largest and most vigorous of a network of weekly markets spanning southern Razih and the adjacent Tihama.

On account of its strategic position and resources, al-Jabal has always had a diverse economy based on a combination of subsistence and commercial agriculture, small-scale domestic livestock production, commerce and petty trading, and the provision of transportation services. All these activities remain part of the local economy but their scale and relative importance have changed. The major factors for economic change have been the out-migration of local men to work in Saudi Arabia and their cash remittances; and the greatly increased financial returns on qat. As al-Jabal is situated close to the Saudi border, migration for work is not considered a long-term undertaking; men return quite frequently and many spend only part of the year abroad in order to save capital for specific projects. Much of the money earned abroad is channeled to older men in the form of bride-prices, or is spent on establishing shops or other enterprises, or on home improvements such as household cisterns. In April 1977 over 30 percent of adult men (over the age of 15) were temporarily employed in Saudi Arabia, mainly as unskilled construction workers. From December 1979 to January 1980, when the author's second census was conducted, only 10 percent were working abroad. This reduction must be partly accounted for by the increased opportunities for employment locally, especially in the qat industry and in the burgeoning commercial and transportation sectors.

The population density of al-Jabal is very high: between 100 and 200 persons/sq. km in relation to the entire mountain, and over 750/sq. km in relation to the intensively cultivated upper slopes where all the settlements are concentrated. This very high population density is closely related to the agricultural productivity of the mountain and to its commercial importance. People were attracted to relatively prosperous areas of Yemen such as al-Jabal during famines and at times of political unrest elsewhere in the country.

Because of the size of the population in relation to cultivable land, there is great pressure on land, holdings are relatively small, and a large minority of households over 30 percent own only one small terrace or no land at all. (In al-Jabal landownership is not a condition for full *qabili* (tribal) status as elsewhere in tribal Yemen.) Terraces vary in size and shape, but most fall within the range of 0.02–0.1 ha in area. The average size of a terrace is about 0.05 ha. Most households with agricultural terraces own between 0.15 and 0.5 ha of land. Anything more than this amount is considered a very large land-holding by local standards. Perhaps 5 percent of households own as much as 1 ha of terraced land. (Unterraced fodder land is also privately owned.) Because of the scarcity of land, and the high proportion devoted to the cultivation of cash-crops, al-Jabal imports much of its grain and other food requirements, and this was probably always the case, to some extent, in the past.

The qat industry was of much less importance in al-Jabal before the civil war [of the 1960s] than during the 1970s. Only a few families were involved in qat trading, and a far smaller proportion of the terraces was given over to its cultivation. Some of the qat produced then was for local consumption mainly by the wealthier members of the community, as the phenomenon was not then as widespread in al-Jabal or the surrounding areas as it is today. The rest was exported mainly to Sa'da, over two full days' travel from al-Jabal by donkey, where it was consumed by government officials stationed there or by members of the local urban elite.

In early 1977 (when the author first arrived in al-Jabal) qat was already the major crop in terms of the revenues it attracted and it was planted on approximately 15 percent of the terraces. By 1980 the area planted with qat had roughly doubled and qat occupied about 30 percent of the cultivable land on the upper slopes of the mountain.

By 1980 a very large proportion of the local workforce was involved in some capacity in the qat industry. Most people who owned terraces which received sufficient rain to support qat were growing at least some trees, and many men were intermittently employed to hoe and plow between the trees, and to apply fertilizer and insecticides Some smallholders choose not to market their qat themselves and instead sell it on the tree to qat traders, and many men were involved in the qat trade as pickers, packers and transporters. This work is also intermittent as qat is sold only when it is ready for harvesting, and new marketable leaves are produced only after rainfall. However, al-Jabal often gets rain throughout the year, including the winter months which are dry in most of Yemen; people expect to harvest their qat three times a year from each tree, and even four times if the earth is worked and fertilized frequently and there is abundant rainfall. People also harvest their qat at different times. There was therefore some work available in the qat industry throughout the year, though mostly in the periods immediately following heavy or prolonged rainfall.

Qat is traded by small-scale, family-based enterprises consisting of brothers or a father and his sons working in partnership for a share of the profits. Extra personnel are hired on an ad hoc basis as and when the extra labor is needed; these workers are often also relatives. During the qat-harvesting period in early 1980 about 15 percent of the adult men of al-Jabal were working in such family trading units, and many more were employed to pick and pack qat when family labor was insufficient. Some qat trading units owned their own donkeys or motor vehicles and took their own qat directly to market, but the majority hired transportation—almost entirely from local men.

This does not exhaust the categories of people involved one way or another in the local qat industry. In addition to landowners, agricultural laborers, qat traders and their employees and qat transporters, a number of people supply essential materials to the qat trade. The most important of these materials are banana stems. The people of al-Jabal pack their qat for market in sections of banana stem which are stiff and moist and therefore help to keep the qat leaves fresh and protect them from damage during transportation to market. The stems are carried from the plantations to the al-Jabal market, or directly to the homes of the qat traders, on donkey-back or, when the slopes are too steep for donkeys, on the backs or heads of men or women. Sometimes the carriers are the owners of the banana plants who want to make the maximum profit and so undertake the arduous task of carrying the extremely heavy stems to cut out transportation expenses. The income from selling banana stems is far in excess of that formerly earned by selling the fruit.

With the rise in the price of qat and the expansion of cultivation, theft became a major problem. A thief could pick and make off with thousands of rials' worth of qat at night in a matter of minutes. After the completion of a motor track from the Tihama to the top of al-Jabal in 1979, local traders began importing wire-mesh fencing, and most of those who owned qat terrace in vulnerable positions (especially those adjacent to the track) enclosed them with this fencing. It also became essential to guard the qat as the time for harvesting drew near; galvanized iron sheets, which were already being imported in substantial quantities to build shops, were also used to construct guard huts on the terraces. The same material was also used extensively to build huts for packing qat for market, since many traders did not have room in their houses for this purpose. It can be seen that the expansion of the qat industry generated work and income for a wide range of people in the local population.

It is impossible to be precise about the manner in which revenues from qat are distributed because of the great variability of inputs on the part of landowners and traders, and the fluctuations in the price of qat in the market-place. However, Figure 1 gives a rough indication of the way the cake is divided.

As Figure 1 illustrates, the main beneficiaries from qat revenues are the landowners and traders. According to figures collected by the author during the early 1980 qat-harvesting season, the greater proportion of gross revenues—between 50 and 70 percent—went to the trader, but the greater net profits were made by the landowner as his expenses were lower. However, this calculation does not take into account any capital expenditure on land. It is likely that these proportions vary considerably in the long term, as there are considerable fluctuations in market prices from one harvest to the next, depending on the quantity of qat produced in other areas and when it is marketed.

Figure 1
YAR: The Distribution of Qat Revenues

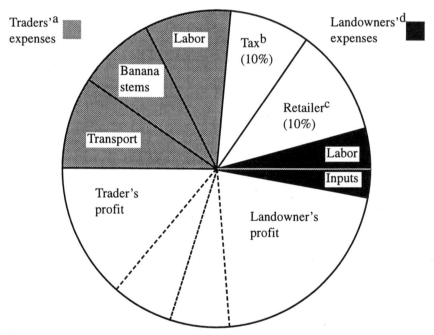

Notes

a. The fixed cost of a hut in which to pack qat and electricity costs for night work are not included.

b. The tax can be levied on production, but is more often extracted at the market.

c. Apart from taxes, this is the main part of qat revenues which remain outside the producing area.

d. Capital outlay on land and fixed costs such as fencing and guard hut are not taken into consideration.

Although qat growers and traders are among the wealthiest members of the community, the expansion of the qat industry has not resulted in their accumulating large land-holdings (as happened in the past in the coffee trade), nor has the qat trade become the monopoly of a few big merchants (as also happened with coffee). One of the effects of the high financial yields from qat has been to increase the investment value of land. This factor, combined with the great increase in general prosperity and cash incomes, has resulted in widespread reluctance to sell land and less need to do so. (During famines in the past much land was sold just to buy food.) Little land therefore comes up for sale and when it does the prices are enormous. Eight terraces of small and medium size sold between 1979 and 1981 fetched from $4,000 to $25,000, or the equivalent of between $200,000 and $600,000 a hectare. No one, however wealthy, is in a position to accumulate land at such prices even were it readily available.

Gerholm speculated that the qat trade in Haraz, also in the western highlands of Yemen, might become dominated by big merchants after the development of modern transportation facilities. For then, he reasoned, Harazi qat, which was only sold locally in the mid 1970s when he was there, could be sold in more distant markets and would fetch higher prices. As transportation expenses would be high, those with substantial capital to risk would monopolize the trade.[1] However, there is no sign of this happening in al-Jabal.

Qat trading in al-Jabal certainly favors those with substantial capital to risk but this is not mainly because of the high cost of transportation. It is not necessary to own a vehicle to be a qat trader as space in vehicles owned by others can be hired. But even if a trader owns his own truck, the cost of buying the qat from the landowner soon exceeds the cost of buying and running a vehicle. It is in qat transactions that the greatest capital investment is made and the greatest financial risk taken. For qat is bought on the tree and the price is negotiated and the money paid before the trader takes the qat to market; and although the amount agreed is based on the most recent prices fetched in the market, prices can plummet if there is a sudden glut.

The key factors which determine the character of the qat trade and which act as constraints on the development of large-scale capitalist enterprises dominated by big merchants are the high perishability of the product and the impossibility of predicting the state of the market. Qat must be sold within one or two days of picking or its leaves wilt and its value can drop to well below the price paid on the tree. The main aim of the trader is therefore to sell his consignment as quickly as possible after he arrives at the market and at a price which will yield him a profit. Until he has reached the market, however, he cannot forecast whether high prices fetched recently will be maintained or whether, as happens, other traders will also have rushed their qat to market to benefit from them, causing them to fall because of the resultant excess of supply. If the trader arrived with several truckloads of qat at such a time, not only would he be in danger of being unable to sell his qat before it wilted, but he would also contribute to the drop in prices by swelling supplies still further. In such circumstances where reliable and up-to-date information is so hard to acquire, trading could be revolutionized by the introduction of a telephone network. Fundamental changes would also come about were refrigerated trucks available

It will be evident that the best strategy for a trader aiming at an unpredictable market with a highly perishable product in which he has invested considerable capital is to buy and market it in relatively small quantities. He is thus less vulnerable to a single gigantic loss. This is the strategy employed. The maximum quantity of qat which is normally marketed by a single trading unit on each occasion is one truckload. In some cases qat sufficient to fill more than one truck is bought in one purchase but this is picked, packed and sent to market in separate smaller consignments on different days. Such large purchases are, however, the exception. The author never encountered any speculation in qat, a custom which could also theoretically lead to monopolization of the qat trade by big merchants. To her knowledge, all qat is bought when ready for harvesting, when both buyer and seller can see the quantity and quality of new leaves the trees have produced, and when they both have as good an idea as possible of the price the qat is likely to fetch two days or so later when it reaches the market.

There are thus major disincentives facing any trader who might have the capital and inclination to expand the size and scale of his enterprise. Therefore, although trading units vary in size according to the quantity of qat being prepared for market on a particular day, they never exceed a maximum of about six or seven persons as this is roughly the number of people necessary for picking and packing a single truck-size consignment in a day.

The profits to be made from qat cultivation are so great that there is no difficulty in understanding why landowners were planting the crop wherever they could in the late 1970s. In al-Jabal qat is traded in packages called *gurufs* which contain a number of branches of qat tied in small bunches and packed in sections of banana stem. Yields and sales are always discussed in terms of *gurufs*. One guruf is roughly equivalent to two bunches or rubtas of qat—one rubta being the quantity of qat most individuals consume in any one day.

In al-Jabal approximately 3,500 qat trees are planted to the hectare, yielding about 2,000 *gurufs* of qat at each harvest. In a year when the average price of a rubta of qat in the market is, say, YR50 (which was the case in 1980), the market value of the qat from 1 ha of land, if it yielded two harvests, would be YR400,000 (approx. $90,000) and if it yielded three harvests (which is common), YR600,000 (approx. $130,000). If we relate these figures to a typical individual land-holding of 0.2 ha and assume it is planted entirely with qat, the market value of the qat on that land in 1980 would have been about YR80,000 (approx. $17,000) if it yielded two harvests, and YR120,000 ($26,000) if it yielded three harvests. These figures give some indication of the enormous revenues from qat in a year when al-Jabal received good rainfall and the price of qat remained high. In years of low rainfall, however, it may not be possible to harvest the qat more than once, although the crop which is harvested might fetch a higher price in the market because of the shortage of supply. It should be remembered that the above figures do not represent the gross income to the landowner but the total cash revenues generated from specific areas of land—these being distributed among the various categories of person involved in the qat industry as indicated in Figure 1. If we assume the landowner's gross income is about 30 percent of the total price his qat fetches in the market, then his gross income on 0.2 ha of qat land in 1980 would have been approximately $5,000–7,800. Of this about 85 percent is net profit. These notional figures conform with data collected by the author on the actual incomes of several landowners for the year 1979/80. The net profits of a landowner can of course be much greater, perhaps twice as much, if he markets the qat himself, but then the financial risks are also greater.

What effects are the high revenues from qat sales and the expansion of qat cultivation having on cropping patterns and on agriculture in general in al-Jabal? One of the major criticisms leveled at qat is that it is supplanting coffee in those areas where both trees are cultivated. Qat and coffee thrive in the same ecological conditions, but qat is the hardier crop and can survive short frosts and prolonged droughts better than coffee. Although both trees are planted on the same mountain-sides, and are often interspersed on the same terraces, qat can often be found cultivated at a higher altitude than would be possible for coffee. Because of the widespread assumption that coffee trees are being uprooted throughout Yemen to make way for qat, it is important to emphasize that there was no evidence of this happening in al-Jabal. In areas where coffee is being replaced by qat on the terraces, it is probable either that the coffee is planted in marginal ecological conditions and harvests were poor, or that the higher labor-input required by coffee makes it economically prohibitive to continue cultivating it—especially for those farmers with limited family labor upon which to draw. There is a need for close studies of the local social and economic environment in each of the areas where coffee production has recently been reduced in order to elucidate the particular factors involved in each case.

In al-Jabal there are still important incentives for cultivating coffee although they are probably more social than economic. Coffee is still a lucrative cash-crop, even though the international trade in Yemeni coffee has greatly declined, because the demand within Yemen and Saudi Arabia has increased and prices have risen. In February 1980 coffee beans were selling in the local Jabali market for SR25 ($7.5) a kilo (Saudi rials are the main local currency), and the coffee husks from which Yemenis brew a popular national beverage *(qishr)* were fetching SR25 for a measure of about 2 liters. Coffee is therefore still an important cash-crop in al-Jabal, and a proportion is exported from the area. However, the profits on coffee for the landowner are several times less than those on qat, so it cannot continue to be cultivated entirely for financial reasons.

There are several reasons why coffee remains an important crop in al-Jabal despite the competition from qat. The Jabalis have always had a diverse economy, and most men derive their incomes from cultivating a range of crops and engaging in more than one occupation. It is therefore possible that they are conscious of the prudence of agricultural and economic diversification: their survival and that of their community has depended on it for centuries, punctuated by frequent droughts and political upheavals which disrupted trade. They are also aware that the demand for qat and high qat prices are linked to high incomes and could therefore easily decline if the demand for Yemeni labor in Saudi Arabia decreased (as it already showed signs of doing in 1980). Even though the local demand for coffee might also decline in such circumstances, it would be difficult for a Yemeni to imagine a radical reduction in coffee consumption—whereas the spread of qat consumption is very recent and every adult can recall when it was an almost exclusively urban phenomenon. There would probably have to be a major long-term slump in coffee consumption, both locally and nationally, before Jabalis would uproot a tree which takes six years from planting to bear fruit.

A further incentive to coffee cultivation is its prestige value, both as a crop and as a drink. When strangers arrive in al-Jabal the local people point out their terraces of coffee and qat, bursting with pride at the greenery. Coffee is an important expression of hospitality towards a guest, and is a form of 'conspicuous display' of wealth and generosity when it is brewed from the bean *(safi)* rather than the cheaper husk *(qishr)*. Coffee is also of considerable importance in formal presentations. Government officials are sometimes presented with bags of beans when they visit al-Jabal, sacks of coffee are given as political tribute to local tribal leaders and coffee is a standard present to take to one's host when visiting outside the area.

The expansion of qat cultivation in al-Jabal has not, therefore, been at the expense of coffee; it has been entirely at the expense of grain. It must be emphasized that this change in cropping ratios does not represent, at the local level, a fundamental shift away from subsistence agriculture. Agricultural economists estimate that it takes between 1 and 2 ha of well-watered land to yield grain sufficient to support one six-person family. Thus it is clear that few households in al-Jabal (which at present average 6.6 persons) have the potential to be self-supporting in grain production. Unless the community was once much smaller than today, it must always have had to import most of its grain requirements from the surrounding areas.

The people of al-Jabal have probably always grown as many cash-crops (banana, coffee, qat) as they could market or consume themselves, and grown grain on the rest of the terraces to minimize what they had to buy in. Grain, specifically the main crop of summer sorghum, was grown as much for its value as fodder and fuel as for its food value. The leaves of sorghum are stripped shortly before the grain is harvested and they are fed to sheep and cattle. After the grain harvest the long stalk is cut in half and the top half is fed to cattle while the lower half is uprooted and used as fuel in domestic ovens. Until the late 1970s sorghum was a vital resource in al-Jabal because of the limited fodder sources near the settlements, and because of the enormous distances women had to climb up and down the mountain to collect firewood. The nearest source of fuel is 1,500 m below the settlements, and fetching wood was by far the most arduous and time-consuming task women performed.

Recent changes have reduced the value of sorghum leaves and stalks as sources of fodder and fuel. Since the completion of a motor track between the Tihama and the summit of al-Jabal in 1979, wood has been trucked up the mountain from the coast and women no longer have to collect it on foot. In addition, domestic livestock production within the community of al-Jabal has decreased partly as a consequence of the rise in prosperity. Although meat consumption has greatly increased, most meat is imported on the hoof from the Tihama. Cattle were (and to a lesser extent still are) kept for their products more than for their meat; this is now less necessary as dried milk and tinned butter are available in the local market. The new conditions have therefore undermined the incentive to keep animals. Animals were always a high-risk investment: there are many diseases endemic in Yemen, and it has become increasingly expensive to provide shelter.

Wheat and barley were always crops of secondary importance to sorghum—they were cultivated in order to utilize the sorghum terraces productively during the winter months but were probably not vital to the livelihood of most landowners. Now the cost of labor has increased to such an extent that the production of these grains is hardly worthwhile and sorghum terraces are often left bare during the winter.

The high cost of labor is the major disincentive to any grain production, not only in al-Jabal but throughout Yemen. In 1980 the average daily wage in al-Jabal for an unskilled worker (such as would be employed to plow and hoe) was SR60–100 ($18–30), depending on season, and only a little less in non-qat-growing areas of Yemen. Sorghum, especially, requires a high work-input; each terrace needs to be plowed or hoed several times both before and after sowing, and there is manuring, thinning and replanting of shoots, weeding and finally harvesting to be done (although the latter task is largely the work of unpaid female family members). A landowner with small capital reserves, no animals and insufficient family labor obviously has little incentive to grow sorghum and every reason to prefer qat, which has low labor requirements compared with all other crops and a high market value, and is therefore much more profitable.

The reduction in sorghum cultivation and the virtual demise of wheat and barley in al-Jabal are not therefore to be attributed entirely to the expansion in qat production. All three crops are of less economic importance than before, for reasons unconnected with the competition from qat on the terraces and in the market-place.

It is possible, furthermore, that qat may actually be helping to sustain what grain production is still taking place in al-Jabal. Many of those who are still growing sorghum are able to afford the high wages for labor because they also grow qat. Qat revenues may therefore be helping to finance grain production. Or to put it another way, those who are cultivating qat are making more than enough money to finance even today's soaring levels of consumption and can therefore afford to maintain a terrace or two of sorghum. A financial incentive to do so is the very high price of locally produced clarified butter *(saman)*. Cattle are no longer important for subsistence but have become an important cash-crop in the new affluent conditions.

Qat is certainly helping to sustain the production of banana in al-Jabal. There is every reason to believe that the Jabalis would have stopped growing banana after the construction of the motor track from the Tihama, when imported (Del Monte) bananas flooded the local markets. Most Jabali banana is grown in deep clefts and steep narrow valleys watered by small permanent springs, and requires regular irrigation. These areas are especially vulnerable to the torrents of water which cascade down the steep mountain-sides after heavy rain and banana terraces therefore require considerable maintenance and repair. These factors make banana a very labor-intensive crop and expensive to cultivate. Banana is also relatively perishable and has none of the compensatory prestige or monetary value of qat and coffee. However, the ecological chance that makes al-Jabal suitable for the cultivation of both qat and banana has probably saved the latter from extinction as a local crop. This is because of the vital importance of banana stems as packaging materials for qat. In 1980 banana stems were being sold in the local Jabali market for between SR50 and SR200 ($15–60) each, depending on size. By then the fruit had become so unimportant that the stems were often cut down before the bananas had grown.

Qat production has had some important beneficial effects not only on agriculture in al-Jabal, but also on the agriculture of the surrounding mountains and the adjacent areas of the Tihama. These areas are ecologically unsuitable for the cultivation of qat or coffee, but they can and do support grain, vegetables and fruit. It is from these areas that the people of al-Jabal and its neighboring qat-producing mountain buy a significant proportion of their food. Even though imported wheat is cheaper than Yemeni grain, many people prefer the latter for its flavor and color, and for making traditional dishes such as sorghum porridge *('asid)*. (There is also an element of prestige in serving sorghum bread and porridge to guests, which may be another factor sustaining Jabali sorghum production.) There are a number of highly valued vegetables and fruits produced locally for which there is no competition from imports: fenugreek *(hulba)*, the beans and leaves of which are both important components of the local diet, parsley *(hilf)*, leek tops, spring onions, white radishes, various legumes, peaches, apricots, limes and lemons. In addition, large quantities of grapes and pomegranates are traded into al-Jabal from the central plateau area to the east. In short, the wealthy qat-producing communities of the western highlands provide an important market for produce from a wide area.

In many areas of Yemen manpower shortages due to the out-migration of men to work in Saudi Arabia, combined with the consequent high cost of labor at home, have caused a serious decline in agriculture. Many fields and terraces have been abandoned because the revenues from the crops which can be grown on them are insufficient for family requirements and to subsidize expensive maintenance. This often has an irrevocably disastrous effect on agriculture—especially in areas of terraced cultivation. Terraces are inundated by the torrential summer rains, the retaining walls collapse and precious soils are swept down the mountain-sides. It is difficult to imagine that such terraces could ever be reconstructed. This kind of erosion has not taken place in al-Jabal nor in much of the surrounding area. The terraces of al-Jabal are beautifully maintained and have not been allowed to fall into disrepair because their owners have powerful incentives to maintain them and the means to do so.

In addition to its beneficial effects on agriculture, the qat industry has also played a part in the improvement and development of certain important local facilities. The vital importance of trade in al-Jabal, and particularly of the qat trade, provided a powerful stimulus for a major self-help development project which had fundamental repercussions on all sectors of the local economy and everyday life—the construction of the motor track from the Tihama to the settled area at the top of the mountain. At the time this ambitious plan was initiated, in 1978, a government/Local Development Association-sponsored track was under construction which was intended to link the plateau region north of Sa'da in the east with the Tihama below al-Jabal in the west, passing through the mountainous province of Razih. However, work on the eastern section had stopped at the border of Razih, a day's walk from al-Jabal, and work on the Tihama section, which had started at about the same time, had taken the track only as far as the lower slopes of al-Jabal before it also ceased. The people of al-Jabal were extremely impatient for a motor link with the outside world and were frustrated at the lack of progress with the official tracks. They therefore decided to try to complete the track from the Tihama themselves. This would give them access to the Red Sea ports of Yemen and Saudi Arabia, with which they conducted much of their trade; of particular importance would be improved access to the major qat market of Hodaida.

The construction of the track up the mountain from the Tihama was a difficult and expensive undertaking because of the extremely steep and rocky terrain and the high cost of hiring a bulldozer and driver—SR200 ($60) an hour. The work was financed by collecting money from each adult male in the tribe according to traditional tribal custom whereby each man is obliged, as a formal condition of tribal membership, to contribute financially to certain communal enterprises defined in customary law. These occur mostly in the politico-legal domain—for example, inter-tribal litigation or blood-money payments. It was therefore of great interest to see these centuries-old mechanisms being activated for this modern purpose.

The work on the track proceeded slowly, with frequent hold-ups because of disputes over the route it should take and shortages of funds. Each time the money ran out, often every few days, another collection was made. Finally, after about 18 months, the track reached the settlements at the top of al-Jabal. The construction of this track at local initiative and expense must be counted a tremendous logistical, organizational and financial achievement. By Western standards the track is very unsafe, but it works—vehicles can, albeit with difficulty, get up and down it—and the local people are delighted with it despite its perils. They also have a vested interest in its maintenance as they built it—they do not regard this as the responsibility of a distant government bureaucracy. Whenever there are landfalls on the track, subscriptions are levied from the tribe to pay for their removal.

After the track was completed, the people of al-Jabal negotiated a financial deal with the neighboring qat-producting tribe to allow this tribe to build a feeder track into its territory from the upper section of the al-Jabal track. The shaikhs of al-Jabal argued quite reasonably that their community should receive some financial compensation for their enormous financial investment in getting the track up the mountain in the first place. The completion of the al-Jabal track provided the impetus for a flurry of road-building on the part of the other Razih tribes, and within two or three years the whole territory was covered by a network of narrow feeder tracks serving all the major settlements. The track from Sa'da finally reached al-Jabal in 1981 to complete the east-west link through the mountains.

The establishment of a motor link with the Tihama, which was both motivated and financed to a significant extent by the qat industry, had important effects on the local economy. It boosted the qat industry itself by providing the traders with quicker and easier access to the major qat market of Hodaida at a time when national demand for qat was high and prices were rising. (The gradual approach of the track from the east also affected qat trading as it reduced the distance the crop had to be transported on donkey-back, and made the qat market of Sa'da increasingly accessible.) The advent of motor transport also resulted in a dramatic increase in commercial activity generally, and a wide range of foodstuffs and other commodities could now be imported more cheaply. Large heavy equipment, which it had previously been impossible to import, could also be hauled up the mountain.

Dozens of Jabali men invested qat profits and money earned in Saudi Arabia in building shops. These were constructed from sheets of galvanized iron, which could now be imported more easily and cheaply than when they were carried up the mountain on camel-back. Between 1977 and 1980 the market nearly doubled in size: in 1977 it had contained about 70 businesses (already a great increase on the early 1970s); by 1980 there were 130. Many of these were open every day, not only on the two main market-days. (It should be noted here that there is no stigma attached to petty trading in al-Jabal as there is elsewhere in Yemen, and the majority of the shopkeepers are Jabalis of 'tribal' status.) Possibly a number of these shops were uneconomic and will be reduced to a more realistic number after any substantial fall in the qat and remittance income which is helping finance them, and in accordance with the more modest consumption levels which would result from a widespread reduction in disposable incomes. It should be emphasized, however, that—at a period when men from many other parts of Yemen were staying long periods abroad, or were seeking employment and constructing new lives in the towns—the men of al-Jabal still felt they had a major social and economic stake in their own community. The ownership of a shop in the market has, after all, important social as well as financial consequences, for it is a place to spend the day and converse with a constant flow of people, and a base for establishing a wide range of relationships. The importance of these less commonly acknowledged aspects of shopkeeping and commerce for the community of al-Jabal can be gauged from the fact that in 1980 about half the adult male population was engaged in some aspect of trade or the provision of services based in the market-place.

The advent of motor transport meant that the days of donkey and camel transport were more or less over, except for short hauls, but the men of al-Jabal transferred to motor vehicles with enthusiasm and confidence. By 1981 no fewer than 20 percent of adult men owned motor vehicles—mainly four-wheel-drive Toyota pick-ups—and a high proportion were employed in transporting people and commodities up and down the mountain and to other parts of Yemen. The increase in financial prosperity and improved transportation facilities engendered a number of improvements in the quality of life of the people of al-Jabal—which is not to deny that many problems were also created. A number of the commodities and foodstuffs which became more easily and cheaply available, or which were imported for the first time, made life easier, more comfortable and more healthy—for example, mattresses, blankets, clothing, cooking utensils, buckets and fresh fruit. A number of large generators were imported by local men and within a few months every settlement was electrified. During the day-time some of these generators were used to run flour mills. Motorized flour mills had been introduced in some settlements in the 1950s, but now every family had easy access to one and the laborious grinding of grain on stone handmills, a female task, became a thing of the past. The most radical changes, especially for women, were the importation of firewood by truck, and the construction of household cisterns. The two most arduous female chores were thus alleviated at a stroke. Women no longer had to climb down the mountain to fetch firewood, and the storage of water near their homes greatly reduced the quantity of water they had to carry up from springs way below the settlements. Cisterns are a good example of an expensive capital investment made at a period of relative affluence which should continue to benefit the community if the present economic boom comes to an end.

The economic conditions which obtained in Yemen during the second half of the 1970s were almost certainly temporary; the unprecedented affluence experienced by most Yemenis was only a fleeting moment of plenty, and may by now be nearly over. The demand for Yemeni labor from Saudi Arabia has already greatly diminished with the mass importation of cheaper labor from East Asia. Yemen can therefore expect to be thrown back increasingly on its own resources, the most valuable of which are its land and its hardworking people. Unless some alternative valuable export commodity is found to replace its labor (which is unlikely unless oil is discovered), Yemenis may be faced with a great reduction in the material standards they have recently acquired, and may have to try to subsist once again, as they did for centuries, on the land. Sadly, in many areas this will no longer be possible as the fields and terraces have been destroyed by the elements and the communities which tended them have been depleted. In qat-producing areas, however, it will be seen that the crop has performed a kind of holding operation—it has kept alive the agricultural potential and kept the people on the land, tied socially and economically to their small rural communities. In a sense the revenues from qat which flow into areas such as al-Jabal, and thence into the surrounding regions, are equivalent in their effects to the agricultural subsidies which many Third World governments make to rural districts to keep agriculture viable, and to prevent the rural–urban population drift which is familiar throughout the developing world.

Acknowledgements

The fieldwork on which this article is based was conducted on behalf of the Trustees of the British Museum, to whom I am grateful for special leave of absence. The periods spent in Razih were March to October 1977 and October 1979 to June 1980. Further information was provided by Ahmad Muhammad Jibran when he visited London from Razih in 1981; I should like to thank him for all his help both here and in al-Jabal. My gratitude to Ahmad and to all the other Jabalis who helped me will be expressed more fully and effectively when the main results of my research are published. My thanks also go to Dr. Cynthia Myntti for her help in the field in 1977, and to Dr. J .S. Birks for his painstaking and helpful comments on the first draft of this article, although he bears no responsibility for any remaining deficiencies.

Notes

1   Tomas Gerholm, *Market, Mosque and Mafraj* (University of Stockholm, Stockholm, 1977), p. 56.

15

Small Farmer Households and Agricultural Sustainability in Egypt

Nicholas S. Hopkins

This article argues that any concern for the sustainability of Egyptian agriculture has to bear in mind the central role of small farmers (Springborg 1990). A socially sustainable agriculture should be one which is built around the dynamism, energy, and ingenuity of the small farmers. The need is to combine a system of production through the small farm household with an increasingly free and open market. At the same time, it is important to be clear-minded about the present and probable future role of these small farmers. To stress the role of small farmers is to underline the importance of the family and the household as key organizational units in agriculture and rural life. The household is not only important as a managerial unit, but also as the institution in which the reproduction of the society occurs. The household is the link between the labor process in agriculture on the one hand and family and social continuity on the other. That this has political implications was already sensed by Sayed Marei (1957: 243) when he wrote that: "A peasant who owns the land he cultivates (self-supporting) is considered a sound basis for a democratic society."

But if a society of self-sufficient small farmers is suited to democracy, are these farmers also productive and efficient? It can be argued that the present structure of Egyptian agriculture, dominated by small farms, has maintained consistently high yield-levels, despite bureaucratic handicaps. The economist Simon Commander (1987: 227–229), after considering evidence from a survey in 1984, argued that "No consistent trend in terms of productivity was found to exist across farm size class," though larger farms often had higher crop values per unit of land reflecting their stronger position in the market. He infers that if larger farmers have higher yields it is because they have better land, presumably because they have invested more in it, and suggests that small farmers do better with their relatively poorer factor endowments than larger farmers do with theirs (Commander 1987: 176).

Small farmers in Egypt make good use of mechanization, for irrigation,

Reprinted from *Sustainable Agriculture in Egypt,* edited by Mohamed A. Faris and Mohmood Hasan Khan (Boulder: Lynne Rienner Publishers, 1993), pp. 185–95, with permission of the publisher. Copyright © 1993 by Lynne Rienner Publishers, Inc. Nicholas S. Hopkins is Professor of Anthropology at the American University in Cairo.

plowing, threshing, transport, and other tasks. They are integrated into complex labor markets. Practically every household either hires in labor, or has members who hire themselves out for wages to farmers, construction contractors, and so forth. The small farmer household is overwhelmingly committed to the market: all farmers sell at least some of their crops, and all householders buy at least some of what they consume. Probably the small farmers are at somewhat of a disadvantage in some of these dealings because each one acts as an independent unit rather than combining with comparable farmers to seek "economies of scale." Thus small farmers are linked vertically to machine owners, labor contractors, and market middlemen, rather than horizontally to each other.

The Egyptian village is not a tabula rasa on to which one can impress whatever one's ideology prefers. In a village are individuals seeking to achieve their goals, incorporated into family structures and organized in households; these households in turn are part of the village structure. The choices that individuals make are structured in ways that make sense to them. There is nothing inevitable about the present structure, but for the moment it guides their choices. Some of this structure, and some of these choices, can best be understood with reference to the national economy of Egypt and the integration of that economy and polity into an international division of labor—the world market. Yet these choices are not made by hypothetical economic men and women, responding to economic and financial incentives in disregard of social values and cultural concerns. Rather, they represent the outcome of people operating in an institutional (social and cultural) context.

These farmers are active in seeking their goals—such as raising income to allow for family continuity—while remaining responsive to the state's plans for agriculture through the cooperative and village bank systems. Farm households follow mixed strategies, including not only farming but also local day-labor, labor migration, education, government employment, ownership and rental of machinery, and trade. The role of women differs by region and class, and is changing under diverse outside influences. The household is the basic economic unit, the locus of exchange deriving from the gender-based division of labor; households are then related to one another in communities (reflecting community values and processes) and through the market (buying and selling labor and other commodities). Some patterns of cooperation at the local level, such as the de facto (informal) irrigation-water user associations that all farmers adhere to, are also significant.

The Farm Household

I distinguish between the house (*manzil* or *maskan*), the household *(bayt)*, and the family (*usra* or *aila*). The household is an economic unit based on people who in various ways live, produce, and consume together. Through its individual members it may have rights to certain assets—land, animals, jobs, income. The household is almost invariably built on relations of family or kinship, but the ideology of kinship should be distinguished from the economic unit. The economic unit contains within it the basic division of labor, based on gender and age. The gender-based division of labor is structurally more significant than the age differences. In fact, the gender-based division of labor operates primarily at the household level, where it is reinforced by conventional understanding of what the roles involve. This means that in most cases husbands and wives do not have to negotiate what their roles are, but can simply adopt the model provided by the culture. This model can be shattered by new patterns, such as those brought home by migrants returning from countries where different but prestigious models prevail (Abaza 1987).

Households in rural Egypt are built predominantly around a nuclear family, parents and children, to whom may be added a surviving older-generation parent or other relative. Husbands with two wives can be included here as well. This could be called the nuclear family *(usra)* household. Some households are based on an extended family *(aila)* household, typically when the sons marry and remain within the same household, or when two or more married brothers continue to form a single household. Thus a practical definition of an extended family household is one that contains two or more married couples. One of the understandings of a family, especially in the rural setting, is that it has continuity from one generation to another, and the extended family household is certainly seen as a realization of this model.

Egyptian census figures appear to be based on the notion of the family *(usra)* rather than the household *(bayt)*. My impression is that censustakers and others count each married couple as a separate family regardless of the living and working arrangements. One of the consequences of this is that figures of the size of households we have compiled from our own work are larger than the official government figures for the size of family. One can generalize that the typical household size in rural Egypt is around seven persons (Hopkins et al. 1980: 3–37). This has clear implications for the ability of the household to provide its own labor. The average family size is lower: the 1976 census estimated the average size of a rural family in Upper Egypt at 5.0 persons and in Lower Egypt at 5.6 persons. This difference can be taken as illustrative of the size difference between "household" and "family," and also of the contrast between Upper and Lower Egypt.

The Role of the State

Although currently the state in Egypt is seeking to withdraw from some involvement in "civil society," for a generation it was not so silent a partner in agriculture, working through the network of cooperatives and village banks. It provided much of the infrastructure, including irrigation, credit, inputs, and market and storage facilities; guaranteed and enforced the land tenure laws; sponsored the cooperatives; and located the country within the international market situation by seeking market outlets for agricultural products. However, Adams (1986) argues that the state's role has been to manage and control rather than to seek development. In this sense the major push for development has come from the efforts of individual farmers of all sizes. The state's intervention has often been structural and distant, such as through redoing the engineering of irrigation, and not in the details of local social organization.

At present there is a trend to restrict the role of the state, particularly by privatizing the supply of inputs (including credit) and the marketing of crops. How this reduction of the role of the state will work out at local level is not yet known. In mid-1992 a revised land tenure bill was passed in parliament. Although details of its implementation are not yet clear, it signals the state's withdrawal from its guarantee of tenure rights in rented land. This clearly has the intention of fostering land consolidation, thus eliminating many small farmers, or at least reducing the size of their holdings (Springborg 1991).

Land Tenure

The general picture is one of individual land tenure; transfers of title take place through inheritance and the market. The operative farm unit is the holding, defined for the last generation as: land owned plus land legally "rented in" minus land legally "rented out." Most often, the part that was "rented in" occupied between one-third and one-half of the holding. After the 1961 land reform, this holding was recorded at the cooperative and was the basis for dealings between the cooperative and the landholder. There is also substantial unofficial rental, at a much higher price, reflecting market conditions. This is not recorded officially.

Most holdings are small; the national average is around 2.5 feddans. There are also medium and large holdings, although the very largest—with thousands of feddans—were expropriated in various ways in the 1952 and 1961 land reforms. After 1969, the maximum holding in principle was 50 feddans, but a few landholders farmed several hundred feddans. There are many "landless" in the rural areas. Though some work as laborers, not all are involved in the agrarian structure: many—civil servants, merchants, commuting factory workers— have other occupations.

Differentiated access to land has long been a major feature of the political economy of rural Egypt. I detect a slight trend towards a new concentration of landownership, especially in the new lands, but it is less significant than the concentration of ownership of agricultural machinery, or the ability of the larger farmers to take advantage of new market opportunities. Any trend towards concentration of landownership is still inhibited by the agrarian reform rules that limited the size of holdings. For the time being, the predominant pattern in Egyptian agriculture is one of many small farmers. The relatively few larger ones are often better able to use their land intensively because of their greater access to capital and markets.

Technology and Capital

Egyptian agriculture is fairly heavily mechanized. Many tasks are done with tractors, but others, such as planting, weeding, and harvesting, are still largely carried out by hand. We are not looking at mechanized crops, or even farms, but at mechanized tasks. Tractors are used to plow the land, haul wagons, run threshing machines, and some other tasks. Pumps are used to lift water for irrigation.

There is little difference in the use of mechanization between large and small farmers; the difference is in the ownership of the machinery. In a 1982 sample (Hopkins et al. 1982), 90 percent told us they used tractors for plowing, 85 percent for threshing, and 15 percent for transport from field to village; 62 percent used irrigation pumps. But hardly any reported using machines for harvesting, planting, or weeding.

Few farmers own their own machines, especially tractors; instead they rely on the rental market. Tractors available for rental typically—in 90 percent of cases—belong to large farmers. The cooperative provides very few tractors— one or two per village; sometimes none at all. The market for rental machines in each village tends to be highly concentrated: the proportion of farmers who reported using the main renter—that is, the biggest—in each of ten villages averaged 37.3 percent, with a range of 13 percent to 53 percent. People generally say they use machinery "to save time and effort"; those few (18 percent) who preferred animal and human power argued that it resulted in higher quality production. We found a positive correlation between the use of machinery and hired labor, suggesting that those who hire machinery also hire labor. However, hired labor is very common everywhere. Somewhat paradoxically, when people talk about saving time and effort, they partly mean the time and effort spent supervising labor, which is greater under nonmechanized conditions.

No account of Egyptian agriculture is complete without reference to the role of animals. Almost all farm households try to keep a milk animal and perhaps draft animals (Hopkins et al. 1980; Zimmermann 1982). Caring for the animals in the stalls (including milk and the preparation of dairy products) is usually a woman's chore. Women also have sole responsibility for fowl and rabbits in the house. Chickens raised for meat or eggs on an industrial scale are usually tended by men (Saunders and Mehenna 1986). Men raise berseem, which is often cut and taken to the animals in their stall; men also take charge of buying and selling animals.

Labor Process

The labor process is fragmented. The analytical starting point is the commodity-producing household operating in the context of the village or other rural community and in conjunction with the state. The head of a rural household is primarily a manager, linked to other households through exchanges and hiring of labor, rental of machinery and land, and other relationships. Mechanization has contributed to the creation of a labor market by breaking up the household labor process, by fragmenting it so that households must have recourse to hired labor. Each task in the sequence of growing a crop requires a different combination of machinery, money, labor, water, etc., and farmers typically grow four or five different crops.

In our 1982 sample (Hopkins et al. 1982), farming was listed as main occupation by 81 percent of the group; 10.5 percent followed nonagricultural occupations; and the remainder were widows, pensioners, etc. (See also Radwan and Lee 1986; Commander 1987.) There is almost never an exact correspondence between household composition and the labor requirements of the farm unit. Nowadays, one of the most common features of agriculture, in Europe and North America as well as Egypt, is the part-time farmer. Some household heads work outside agriculture; in other cases, one man works on the farm while others work elsewhere, and income is to some degree shared. In the villages near Bilbeis, for instance, many men work in the Tenth of Ramadan, about 40 km away (Hopkins and Hamdy 1990).

The decentralization of the hiring of labor by the household minimizes the need for hierarchical control of the labor process. The small size and shifting composition of work groups favor the ability of the household head to make small adjustments and decisions. One of the tasks of the household head is to manage the labor input in agriculture: either that labor is from the household and subject to discipline in terms of family values and norms, or it is hired labor, subject to community values and norms. For the most part the number hired and managed by each unit is small: control of labor is thus intensive. Only the household head follows the crop through the year (crop cycle), though others do much of the physical work. With this division of labor comes a concentration of knowledge and hence something of a deskilling of farming.

Labor migration has always been an important household strategy in rural Egypt (Hopkins et al. 1982; Adams 1991; Brink 1991; Nada 1991). The new element is that people are migrating outside Egypt, which makes them subject to radically different conditions and values (often conservative in social terms). The larger amount of money people can thus earn means that this is not just a survival strategy but a chance to make a quantum leap upwards in material terms. The return of such migrants also provides another symbol of the involvement of Egyptian villages in the world economy and culture. There is no question that the money brought back and sent back by migrants has contributed to an improvement of living standards in the countryside, most visibly through an upgrading of housing, but also through the financing of nonfarm entrepreneurial activities.

Women work at home, care for animals, organize consumption. In the Delta they also trade at local markets and work in the fields—either family fields or, occasionally, for wages (Zimmermann 1982; Saunders and Mehenna 1986; Abaza 1987; Toth 1991). In Upper Egypt, since women do not work outside the house, and so not in agriculture, it places more strain on the men to accomplish all the tasks and generate the streams of income necessary (Hopkins 1991a). Where women work for wages, as in the Delta, they are typically paid about 60 percent of the male wage, and are restricted to certain jobs. Thus it is not clear that women and men are interchangeable. Some employers (near Bilbeis) report finding that women are preferable because they are more "obedient." Working on one's own farm is more common, and from one village in Minufiyya it was reported that a woman's farming skill is taken into account when deciding on a marriage (Glavanis and Glavanis 1983).

The Labor Market
In the labor market, there is limited interchangeability between men and women, adults and young, because they are usually assigned to different tasks. The big farmers set the wage scale: among the techniques used to lower the general wage level is the ploy of hiring work gangs from neighboring villages where there may be more of a labor surplus. There is a complex wage structure: different tasks are paid in different ways. The control of labor is diffused, and the decentralized control of labor is reinforced by the fact that the worker must constantly be rehired. Often the farmer hiring labor does so through a contractor. This simplifies his task and the task of labor discipline devolves onto the labor contractor. Even those who are de facto permanent workers say (as do their employers) that they are not permanent.

Going to Market

Since the household is the basic production unit, it also takes charge of the marketing. Some crops are sold to the government, such as cotton, lentils, and soybeans. Others are sold to private merchants, such as some cereals, fruits, and vegetables. The cereal crops and some other secondary products (straw for fodder, stalks for fuel) are sold separately. Fruits and vegetables are usually sold to agents of the big dealers in the Cairo and Alexandria markets, though some go to dealers from Asyut and other towns, or are sold directly to consumers. In many cases the merchant or agent is the farmer's fellow villager. Farmers attempt to deal with and control this situation, but its complexity is often beyond them. Individual small farmers do not pull much weight in this market situation: they are "price takers."

In general, the farmer deals with a different set of merchants and a different procedure for each crop. He is usually paid for the crop sometime after delivery, usually after the agent or merchant has resold the crop. This adds to the complexity. Merchants and their agents will sometimes make an advance to the farmer, financing the crop. This amounts to dealers maintaining control over farmers through indebtedness. Farmers who can remain free of this system and sell their crop at harvest to the highest bidder generally do better. Farmers are likely to retain part of their cereal crops for their own use. In fact, a majority of farmers in our study said they did not sell any of their wheat, berseem, or corn. This probably reflects their success at growing only the amount that they expect to consume. In other words, this situation does not indicate a "subsistence" orientation, but rather its opposite. They will grow a food crop for home use only if that is cheaper than buying it.

Village Politics

The village in Egypt is still a basic administrative structure, with institutions and processes. Villages are becoming more urbanized, but many also preserve vigorous local institutions of self-government that act as a screen between the designs of the state and the life of their residents. This self-government is based on the local power of the village elite. The village is also the locus where the relationships among households are worked out. Here is where the landless and the landholders relate to one another, where the large farmers set the pattern which the small only aspire to, and so on. Thus it is at the level of the village that first of all one can discern the class situations, the social contexts in which class roles are learned and acted out. The classes themselves are an outcome of the mode of production. From a national perspective, elements are absent from the village, such as the bourgeoisie, the truly large and capitalist farmers who reside in the cities, and the elite of the state bureaucracy. Thus the class structure in the village cannot be analyzed in isolation from that of the nation.

Changing Relationships

At present in the villages, patron-client relations, linking the rich and prestigious to the poor and anonymous, are more evident than class relations (Hopkins 1987: 157–77; Hopkins 1991a). A pattern of class relations was apparently emerging at the time of Gamal Abdel Nasser, but it seems that it went into remission in the early 1970s. The relationship between households is often unequal. These differences are both real (material) and symbolic. Among the symbolic differences are various signs of deference (gifts of cigarettes, evening gatherings, and directionality of hospitality). But the social organization of agriculture, insofar as the hiring of labor and machines takes place between households, reinforces unequal relations between them. In sum, the patron-client relations mark the inter-household relations.

In the community are set the values by which economic activity is regulated. There is a sense of fairness, of right and wrong. Negotiations over power (wages) are not only carried out face to face, but through community processes, such as the intermittent debate on what is fair, what is going on elsewhere in Egypt, what is necessary, and so on. The same applies to questions such as women's proper role. The settlement of disputes is also a community process; so is popular religion. The spread of education represents in part the ability of communities to organize themselves to seek new resources: frequently new schools are built with contributions from villagers, especially the rich. This is perhaps an extension of the continuing pattern of support for mosques and other religious foundations.

Another level of integration that is important for the sustainability of Egyptian agriculture, and the small farmer within it, is the region. Villages, unequal in the opportunities that they offer, often specialize. For instance, in Tukh Markaz in Qalyubiyya governorate, the village of Ammar specializes in apricots; the village of Deir in strawberries; and the villages around Kafr Mansour in citrus and citrus marketing. Namul features eggplants; Imyay the manufacture of crates for transporting fruits and vegetables; and another cluster of villages manufactures charcoal for the Cairo market. Other villages in the region grow berseem for sale to villages whose land is devoted to one of the other crops. Similar patterns could doubtless be found in many other areas (Hopkins 1987: 30–33). These factors should be kept in mind when thinking about the market relationships of the small farmers.

The Future of Rural Life

One has to visualize the Egyptian small farmer not as a peasant but a petty capitalist who is active simultaneously in the labor market, the machine rental market, and of course in the purchase of inputs and sale of outputs. The difference between the large and small farmer is thus one of degree: they do not represent, for instance, different "modes of production." One might wonder whether the basic smallholder pattern that has dominated in Egypt since the agrarian reforms of the 1952–1961 period will endure much longer. What will be the shape of Egyptian agriculture, the countryside, or the farm household, in the twenty-first century? As members of the farm household get more and more involved in education, off-farm employment, labor migration, and the like, the match between the household and the labor requirements of the farm will be less evident. There are also pressures to eliminate fully the role of the state in marketing and input-provision, which would undercut the cooperative's function for the last generation. And there is pressure to extend the market in land.

Given the general structure of Egyptian society, there is no reason to fear that the household and the family will soon disappear, despite these pressures. But these institutions could certainly change their functions. The last forty years have shown the value of the small farmer household—the household of petty commodity producers—in providing a thread of continuity in rural Egypt. Agrarian reform—which directed Egyptian agriculture away from a structure based on large estates—proved to be successful in creating the structures which now seem likely to change under the pressure of "structural adjustment" and the market principle.

Should Egyptian policy continue to support the small farmer and the corresponding family household pattern of social organization? Will the pattern continue, whether supported or not? If the goal is a sustainable agriculture—that is, growth with balance, without using up tomorrow's resources today—then what role does the family household have to play? Can we assume that the family-based farm is more conducive to a sustainable agriculture than is the large-scale, fully capitalist one? Before such choices or decisions can be made, adequate social and cultural understanding of the current functions and structure of the household is needed. A failure to understand rural social organization can lead to policies that destroy the fabric of rural life—as has happened in Iran (Hooglund 1982), Iraq (Batatu 1978), Algeria (Marouf 1981; Chaulet 1987), and other countries. And the destruction of rural life can lead to accelerated migration of rural people to urban areas, and a rootless urban class that can provide the social basis for a new regime. Not only agricultural sustainability but political stability may be at stake.

References

Abaza, Mona. "The Changing Image of Women in Rural Egypt," in *Cairo Papers in Social Science.* 1987, 10 (3).

Adams, Richard H. *Development and Social Change in Rural Egypt.* Syracuse: Syracuse University Press, 1986.

———. *The Effects of International Remittances on Poverty, Inequality, and Development in Rural Egypt.* Washington, D.C.: International Food Policy Research Institute, 1991.

Batatu, Hanna. *The Old Social Classes and the Revolutionary Movements of Iraq.* Princeton: Princeton University Press, 1978.

Brink, Judy H. "The Effect of Emigration of Husbands on the Status of Their Wives: An Egyptian Case," International Journal of Middle East Studies, 1991, 23 (2): 201–211.

Chaulet, Claudine. *La Terre, Les Frères, Et L'Argent.* Algiers: Office des Publications Universitaires,1987.

Commander, Simon. *The State and Agricultural Development in Egypt Since 1975.* London: Ithaca Press, 1987.

Glavanis, Kathy R.G., and Pandeli Glavanis. "The Sociology of Agrarian Relations in the Middle East: The Persistence of Household Production," *Current Sociology,* 1983, 31 (2): 1–109.

Hooglund, Eric. *Land and Revolution in Iran: 1960–1980.* Austin: University of Texas Press, 1982.

Hopkins, Nicholas S. et al. "Animal Husbandry and the Household Economy in Two Egyptian Villages," *Report to Catholic Relief Services,* Cairo, 1980.

Hopkins, Nicholas S. *Agrarian Transformation in Egypt.* Boulder: Westview, 1987.

———. "Women, Work, and Wages in Two Arab Villages," *Eastern Anthropologist,* 1991, 44(2): 103–23.

———. "Clan and Class in Two Arab Villages," in *Peasants and Politics in the Modern Middle East.* Edited by Farhad Kazemi and John Waterbury. Miami: Florida International University Press, 1991a, 252–76.

Hopkins, Nicholas S., Sohair Mehenna, and Bahgat Abdelmaksoud. "The State of Agricultural Mechanization in Egypt. Results of a Survey: 1982." Report to the Ministry of Agriculture, Cairo,1982.

Hopkins, Nicholas S., and Iman Hamdy. "Social Issues in Agricultural Mechanization." Report to the GTZ, Cairo, 1990.

Marei, Sayed. *Agrarian Reform in Egypt.* Cairo: Imprimerie de l'Institut Français d'Archeologie Orientale, 1957.

Marouf, Nadir. *Terroirs Et Villages Algériens.* Algiers: Office des Publications Universitaires,1981.

Nada, Atef Hanna. "Impact of Temporary International Migration on Rural Egypt," *Cairo Papers in Social Science,* 1991, 14 (3).

Radwan, Samir, and Eddy Lee. *Agrarian Change in Egypt: An Anatomy of Rural Poverty.* London: Croom Helm, 1986.

Saunders, Lucie W., and Sohair Mehenna. "Village Entrepreneurs: An Egyptian Case," *Ethnology,* 1986, 25 (1): 75–88.

Springborg, Robert. "Rolling Back Egypt's Agrarian Reform," *Middle East Report* No. 166, 1990, 38: 28–30.

———. "State-Society Relations in Egypt: The Debate Over Owner-Tenant Relations," *Middle East Journal,* 1991, 45 (2): 232–49.

Toth, James. "Pride, Purdah, or Paychecks: What Maintains the Gender Division of Labor in Rural Egypt?" *International Journal of Middle East Studies,* 1991, 23 (2): 213–36.

Zimmermann, Sonja D. *The Woman of Kafr el Bahr.* Leiden: Research Center for Women and Development, 1982.

16

Shaykhs, Peasants, and Party Comrades: Political Change in Northern Syria

Sulayman N. Khalaf

In his fine study, *The Politics of Stratification,* Bujra delineates the effects of political change on local populations as basically following two directions.[1] Either the traditionally wealthy groups are able to make greater use of new opportunities and thus continue their position of dominance, or else the poorer groups improve their economic and political conditions, thereby forcing the formerly privileged to lose their traditional high positions.

The ethnographic material from north rural Syria presented here will show that the effects of economic and political change on local groups and/or classes in a given society need not necessarily follow either the above two patterns.[2] Processes of change are characterized by complexity, specificity and variation, so much so that it is difficult to view their overall effects on local groups in terms of strict either/or directions. Research on the topic of social/political change suggests the appearance of middle-range variations where major groups in a given community can actually experience both gains and losses.[3] The analytical description of economic and political change during the last four decades in the north Syrian Euphrates village of Hawi al-Hawa will show how the members of its dominant family, the al-Meshrif, first emerged as economic entrepreneurs and innovators, then after becoming victims of political change through the Ba'th party, were in fact able to rebound from adversity, to adapt and ultimately succeed in maintaining a dominant, albeit modified, position in local society.

We should begin by considering the broad socio-economic forces which lead to the birth and development of the village and the rise of al-Meshrif as the village's only landowning shaykhly family. We can then turn to the subsequent national politico-economic transformations which the Ba'th party brought about in rural Syria, and to the new structure and patterns of political leadership generated in this particular village.

Translated from Riccardo Bocco, Ronald Jaubert, and Françoise Métral, eds., *Steppes d'Arabies—Etats, pasteurs, agriculteurs, et commerçants: le devenir des zones sèches* (Paris, PUF, 1993), pp. 178–94. Reprinted by permission. Sulayman N. Khalaf is Associate Professor of Anthropology at the United Arab Emirates University, Al Ain.

The Village of Hawi al-Hawa

The rapid development of capitalist agriculture during the late 1940s and 1950s in the Jazira/Euphrates region was followed in 1963 by socialist transformations introduced by the Ba'th as the ruling party in the country. Over the last three decades the Ba'th has restructured Syrian society according to socialist populist lines combined with the development of a capitalist sector.[4] The interplay of national and regional socio-economic and political forces, represented in this study by landed shaykhs, peasants and party comrades, can also be observed at the local village level. Thus the village of Hawi al-Hawa (located on the eastern bank of the Euphrates river ten kilometers west of Al-Raqqa town, with a population of about 1,500) will be analyzed as a small-scale arena in which changing patterns of local political leadership in the Jazira–Euphrates region may be traced in some detail. The village of Hawi al-Hawa forms an historically constructed social field. We can follow the political actions, trends and strategies of individual actors and their family groups as they move in and out of the village while pursuing their economic and political goals. By taking the village as a case study we may examine the dynamics of politico-economic change in contemporary rural Syria.

Economic Transformations in the Region

Capitalist penetration in the Jazira/Euphrates region began in the late 1940s when the merchants and agricultural operators of Aleppo and other urban centers introduced their money and modern agricultural machines to the Euphrates valley. These entrepreneurs helped not only in the development of the region and its integration within the larger national economy, but were also instrumental in generating broad socio-economic conditions which began undermining traditional forms of social and political relationships characteristic of tribal and/or semi-sedentary communities in the steppes and the valley. By the mid-1950s land-owning tribal chiefs, through their association with outside agricultural operators and *khanjiyya* (city merchants), had emerged as a new social class, nicknamed locally *shuyukh al-qutun*, the "cotton shaykhs." The members of this emerging social class were gradually able to mediate between their local communities and the larger national system, thus perpetuating their domination in their local communities.

The historical interplay of changing socio-economic and political conditions during the 1950s ultimately led to the rise of the Ba'th party on Syria's political stage.[5] The Ba'th socialist revolution of 1963 brought about major changes in rural Syria. Consequently, the agrarian base of the emerging traditional "cotton shaykhs" came to be seriously weakened, and the influential mediating roles which they had manipulated to their advantage during the 1950s were contested or eliminated. This was particularly true during the short period of what is labeled as the neo-Ba'th, from 1966 to 1970.[6]

The Birth of Hawa al-Hawa and the Rise of al-Meshrif

Members of the al-Meshrif family did not view themselves as shaykhs of their own *'ashira* (subtribe) before the 1950s; however, it was known that the family was relatively well-off and enjoyed an influential leading position within the *'ashira* of al-Musa al-Dahir, of the larger 'Afadla. The family's position within local society was reflected in the marriages with shaykhly families of different *'ashira* within the larger 'Afadla that Hajj Ibrahim had arranged for four of his sons before his death in 1949. It was also reflected in the fact that in the mid-50s they began *daqq al-qahwa* (pounding coffee beans) in their house, thus signaling it out as an open *madafa* (social club) for all men of their small local community.

Before 1950 the al-Meshrif families (Hajj Ibrahim and his five sons) were involved in both sheep herding and farming in the steppe area of Tell al-Samin along the Balikh river on the land of Daham al-Hatchem ibn Muhaid. Hajj Ibrahim was very successful in sheep raising and when he died in 1949 at Tell al-Samin he left a sizable fortune. In 1950 the al-Meshrif family bought the land of Hawi al-Hawa from an Aleppan absentee landlord for 100,000 Syrian lira, the total holding being around 400 hectares. Hajj Hamad's house was built, and then in 1951–52 a larger family house with a *madafa* (guest house) was constructed. When they moved into this new house animals were slaughtered for a party to which shaykhs of the tribe, kinsmen and eminent men were invited.

Al-Meshrif began cultivating the land to grow wheat and cotton in 1950, initially on a small scale. Gradually they brought their relatives from various other places (such as al-Balikh, Tell al-Samin, al-Salhabiyyah and al-Kassrat) to settle in the new village and work the land as sharecropping *fellahin* (peasants). During the 1950s the early settlers in the village were mostly kinsmen of al-Meshrif from al-Dahir lineage. However, the gradual expansion of the al-Meshrif's agricultural enterprise led them to recruit more *fellahin* from outside their close kin group. In 1954–55 they purchased two tractors and other modern agricultural machinery. By 1960 the al-Meshrif family were cultivating all the land of the village. During the late 1950s a large group of the Jhamat lineage, from the larger *'ashira* of al-Musa al-Dahir who were settled in the village of Ruwayyan were invited to settle in Hawi al-Hawa. They constituted about 30 peasant families, or about 20 percent of the village population. Later on another 15 families or so from Abu Saraya (non-'Afadla tribal peasants) were settled in the village. Thus by the late 1950s al-Meshrif had about 80 sharecropping peasant families settled in their village to work the land.

Production relations within the village were representative of the wider region. As *mallak/muzari'* (landowner/agricultural operator), the al-Meshrif family was responsible for providing everything needed for cotton production: the land, seeds, water pumps, fuel, canal construction and maintenance, plowing, supervision, and so forth. The *fellah*'s share of the total annual produce of his cultivated plot was around 25 percent where he and his family provided labor only. In situations where the *fellah* himself supplied fertilizer, his share increased to 33 percent of the total produce. If hired labor was needed to pick the crop, the *fellah* was also responsible for this extra cost. Usually the *fellahin* sustained their simple livelihood by borrowing from al-Meshrif throughout the year. In cases where the peasants borrowed far beyond the total value of their expected share, their debts would be transferred to the accounts of the following years, thus generating a structure of peasant dependence on the landlord.

During the 1950s the government did not intervene much in agriculture. Economic relations between the *mallak/ 'muzari'* and the *fellahin* were based on individual personal agreements, in that there were no written contracts protecting a tenure for the *fellahin*. As Hajj Khalaf described, "Before, the *fellahin* were afraid of the landlord, and therefore they worked hard. If a man did not work well, there would be no work for him the following year."[7] Production relations not only in Hawi al-Hawa but throughout the Euphrates region at large were characterized by exploitation of the *fellah* and his domination by the *mallak/muzari'*. As described by one *fellah,* conditions in the 1950s "were poverty. We were only able to earn enough food to survive and it was not secured without hardship."[8]

The marketing of cotton and other cash crops like wheat and barley was done through the *khanjiyya* of Aleppo. These were brokers, merchants and money-lenders all in one. They supplied the landed agricultural operators of the Euphrates valley with loans on the agreement that a given *muzari'* took his crop to be sold for a small commission in the *khan* of his particular *khanji*.

The economic activities in which the enterprising al-Meshrif were involved reflect the dynamic interdependence of the steppe, valley, and the city. Their rising prosperity was not confined to cotton agriculture in the valley but was also the result of other economic enterprises located in the steppes of the Jazira, such as sheep raising, dry farming of cereal winter crops (wheat and barley), and the rental of property in town. Many of the share-cropping peasant families who were settled in the village owned parcels of rain-fed land in the steppes at different locations northwest of Hawi al-Hawa. Since the early 1950s the owners of such small parcels of rain-fed land usually rented them to outside agricultural operators while they themselves lived as peasants in the villages. Sometimes local entrepreneurs like al-Meshrif rented such parcels of land from their poorer kinsmen for cultivating winter cereal crops. Many peasant families were able to keep a few sheep and goats in the steppes, to supplement their livelihood, which now had come to depend essentially on cotton farming.

Leadership and Domination

The rapid expansion of capitalist agriculture in the Euphrates-Jazira region generated a series of new interconnected consequences. Firstly, it produced new socio-economic "formations" which were associated with the emergence of a combined system of *iqta'* (feudal) and agrarian capitalism. Such capitalism involved the consolidation of large areas of land in the hands of a small class of landowners of shaykhly origin, who, as rising entrepreneurs, employed their tribesmen from the steppes as sedentarized share-cropping peasants. The rapid development of the village of Hawi al-Hawa exemplifies this phenomenon. Throughout the villages scattered in the Euphrates valley labor relations of capitalist agriculture superseded but also built upon kinship ideology.

Associated with this system was greater inequality in land ownership and wealth. Al-Meshrif, for example, established themselves in their new village/farm as a distinct local elite, and emerged as the undisputed political leaders in their village community, while in contrast, the material conditions of the peasant remained underdeveloped. The second consequence was the emergence of a new outlook. The increasing association of tribal shaykhs, now agricultural entrepreneurs, with city merchants helped to widen the gap in attitudes and values between them and their fellow peasant tribesmen. Al-Meshrif's emulation of the merchants and urban elite in the purchase of property in al-Raqqa town, the education of their school-age boys, the intensification of endogamous marriage patterns as well as their increasing association in exchanges of visits and hospitality with other shaikhly families or city merchants are expressive of the new outlook and social re-orientation of the "cotton shaykhs" as an emerging social class.

The third consequence concerned the breakdown of traditional ties of economic obligation. As tribal shaykhs became large landlords in a developing capitalist economy, they were freed from their traditional ties of economic responsibility to their tribesmen. Prior to the agricultural revolution of the early 1950s, semi-sedentary tribal communities, like the 'Afdala, gave support to the house of the shaykh by means of a "gift economy." By the mid-1950s the shaykhs and sub-shaykhs, who had in part depended on the *mashyakhiyya* gifts for the upkeep of their *madafas*, became economically independent, as their position came to rest on different bases from that of their tribesmen. Fellow tribesmen became dependent peasants.

Fourthly, the cotton shaykhs of the 'Afadla and the wider region adopted new styles and strategies that were compatible with their rising economic-political position in society. They began driving Cadillacs and Chevrolets and also employing house servants and coffee makers. They built many large *madafas*, each large enough for 60 to 100 men. The expansion as well as the elaborate size and design of the *madafa* as "strategies of accumulating capital of honor and prestige"[9] took exaggerated forms. While the *madafa* was a traditional social institution among tribesmen, the capitalization on this social institution by the new cotton shaykhs became a conscious and elaborate strategy for achieving greater consensus for their political domination.[10] The shaykhs' behavior in the national election of 1961 further illustrates the change in style of their domination and their quest for political power. Rather than relying basically on tribal loyalties or a distinct ideological election platform, significant portions of the votes were bought by cash.

The fifth consequence concerns the duties of the leader and the development of distinct patterns of leisure and life style marking off the "cotton shaykhs" as a distinct social class characterized by economic power, political influence and leisure. In the case of Hajj Khalaf of Hawi al-Hawa, we see that around the late 1950s he entrusted the financial management of the family's agricultural business to his capable son Mahmud. The supervisory responsibilities over the *fellahins'* labor in the fields was assigned to Hajj Hamad, while Hajj 'Assaf supervised the family's sheep herd in the steppes. While Hajj Khalaf supervised from a distance, as the village's leading headman, he withdrew quite early into a life of leisure, socializing with his bourgeois equals from the town and shaykhs of the region.

His son Mahmud was appointed *mukhtar* (village mayor) in 1955, while he was still in his late teens. Mahmud was the first of the family to receive modern school education, to the end of primary level. In his capacity as *mukhtar,* Mahmud performed the role of official representative of the local government as well as of the village community. Prior to the Ba'th revolution, whenever government officials came to the village, they arrived in the *madafa* and often conducted their affairs in the presence of *al-Mukhtar* Mahmud. He not only mediated in the resolution of petty problems and conflicts in the village, but also carried the stamp necessary for the official register of birth, marriages, etc., in the village. He was also required to accompany the police during the arrest or interrogation of villagers. In his socializing and leisure, *al-Mukhtar* Mahmud found friends among the young men of al-Meshlab, the paramount wealthy shaykhly families of the 'Afadla. In the early 1960s he bought a large American car (Oldsmobile) and immediately hired a chauffeur. Such were the commodities of success and social distinction characteristic of the dominant class.

The Ba'th and Party Comrades

Three decades of Ba'th socialist rule have, in the words of Hinnesbusch, left "durable consequences" in the fabric of contemporary Syrian society. In the following section we will look at how these consequences have been mirrored at the local level in the case of al-Meshrif of Hawi al-Hawa.

The political development of the Ba'th party in Syria has oscillated between what political anthropologists term "mobilization" and "reconciliatory" strategies of government.[11] Confrontationist socialist moves were made against tribal shaykhs and large landowners in the Euphrates region in 1966, during the Neo-Ba'th's shift towards more radical policies. The implementation of land reform measures in the Jazira and Euphrates dispossessed or at least weakened the newly emerged class of mercantile landlords. Populist socialist policies touched the material base of cotton shaykhs and wealthy lineage heads and politically marginalized them from meaningful participation in the political process. For some shaykhly families the downfall of their position was dramatic. Former large landowners like the Hawaidis and the Albu Hbal of the 'Afadla were left with small parcels of land, while others in neighboring areas, such as the Muhaid families of the bedouin Fed'an in the steppes of the Jazira, were left with nothing.[12] Once, in the *madafa* of the late Shaykh Faisal al-Huwaidi, I heard Shaykh Faisal himself while playing cards with other men describe the shaykhs' condition as, "*Bi-hal-ayyam falhit-na li'b al-waraq*" ("Nowadays, playing cards has become our cultivation," i.e., meaningless occupation).[13] Bitter statements of this kind reveal the shaykhs' realistic perception of their marginal role in society under the Neo-Ba'th. It also reflects the ironical nature of the situation in which they found themselves. On the one hand wider national transformations had rendered them powerless while, on the other hand, their own perception of their shaykhly position continued to force them as it were, to maintain the *madafa* as a politico-social institution even when it had been effectively emptied of its former role.

Events which struck at agrarian local leaders further illustrate the mobilizational politics of the Neo-Ba'th during the late 1960s and their effect on the landowning tribal shaykhs. In the al-Raqqa region, for example, tribal chiefs and others who were suspected of being a potential threat to the system were arrested, interrogated and on occasions jailed, including Shaykh Faisal al-Huwaidi of the larger 'Afadla as well as Hajj Khalaf al-Meshrif of Hawi al-Hawa. As a result of such rapid and drastic changes aimed at shaykhly landlords, most if not all of the chiefs of bedouin tribes in Syria, including the Muhaid shaykhly families of the Fed 'an, who were among the largest landlords in the steppes of Jazira, left the country from the late 1960s; most now live in Saudi Arabia. Many members of the shaykhly class viewed their downfall as a result of the coming of *ahl al-ittihadat* (the Unionists), i.e., the Peasants' Union, Workers' Union, Women's Union, etc.

These national and regional transformations under what Hinnebusch terms the Ba'th's "authoritarian populism," were mirrored once again at the village level.[14] After the coming of the Ba'th the village of Hawi al-Hawa went through fundamental change and socio-political polarization. The state appropriated about two thirds of al-Meshrif's land to be distributed later among 69 village peasants, and in 1966 a Peasants' Cooperative was founded. Since then conflict and competition have existed within the village community. The Meshrif of the al-Dahir *'ashira*, were extremely dissatisfied with the appropriation and division of land by the government. At the same time, the members of the larger al-Dahir clan, of which the Meshrif were the single most important family and lineage, were in competition with the other non–al-Dahir groups in the village over the control and running of the *al-jam'iyya* (Cooperative) and the *al-naqaba* (Collective). However, by virtue of their greater numbers, and most importantly, their close organizational ties with the Ba'th Party structure, the non–al-Dahir groups were able to take control of the affairs of the Cooperative, including the elected executive council. They also gained a monopoly over the political organization of the village Peasants' Collective. Similarly, there was political polarization involving the whole community, which was mirrored in the spatial location of the two main conflicting blocks within the village. The dislocation which occurred in the fabric of village life was profound. Unlike the past, leadership in the village became fragmented, paralleling the same process in the social, political and economic structures of the village community.[15]

The peasants of Hawi al-Hawa and other villages along the Euphrates, on the other hand, gained from the reform process and their political position as the largest class in society was given new strength. Changes occurred in the ownership of land, relations of production and political participation throughout rural Syria, all of which improved the life of the *fellahin*.[16]

Evolution of the Ba'th

Under the neo-Ba'th, the national economy came to stagnate and it proved difficult to absorb the socially and politically mobilized peasants into productive employment. The Neo-Ba'th populists' methods alienated large segments of the population. The crisis was resolved by the rise of the more moderate wing within the Ba'th Party.[17]

The Asad leadership, in its quest to rebuild "domestic unity," to preserve the party and to achieve stable development, abandoned radical mobilization politics and the banner of social struggle which had characterized their predecessors. It opened the door to different social groups and economic sectors, as it no longer discriminated against the effective political participation of youth from rural families of the feudal/agrarian capitalists.[18] It was within this context that many of the young men of the Meshrif families, while still pursuing their education, realized the importance of joining the Ba'th Party if they were to achieve significant political careers and/or advancement through professional education. Al-Meshrif's investment in the education of their youth ultimately proved to be a greater asset.

Land reform measures, state control over the production and marketing of crops, the lack of family planning, as well as the practice of the Islamic law of inheritance all combined to reduce not only land holdings for individual al-Meshrif families but also their overall material well-being. However, in light of the Ba'th shift towards more conciliatory national politics, or to borrow Hinnebusch's term, the Ba'th "post-populist evolution,"[19] al-Meshrif's early start toward giving their youth the best modern education available provided them in turn with future advantages, empowering them, as it were, to maintain for their families a privileged class position within both village and regional contexts. This fact remained true even in the face of state socialist policies carried out against landed families during the late 1960s. Education in modern societies, as Bourdieu and Boltanski argue, "fulfills not only functions of reproducing skilled labor power (technical production) but also functions of reproducing the positions of the agents and their groups within the social structure (social reproduction)."[20]

As late as 1991 the majority, if not all, of those from Hawi al-Hawa village who hold university degrees and have modern professional careers such as doctors, dentists, engineers, lawyers, and teachers have come from the al-Meshrif families and/or lineage. Moreover, by the mid-1970s the leading roles of political leadership of the village and beyond it at the regional level went to the educated youth of al-Meshrif. Education, as effective cultural capital in the hands of such youth, equipped them for success within a context of changing national politics and economy.

As a result of education, familiarity with urban life, and membership in the ruling party in the country, the youth of al-Meshrif have since the mid-1970s emerged as active, capable, and articulate leaders replacing, on the one hand the former traditionalist figures of Hajj Khalaf and *al-mukhtar* Mahmud and, on the other, overshadowing the non-Meshrif members of the executive council of the Peasants' Cooperative, the body which had played an active though short-lived political role in the village during the late 1960s and early 1970s.

The educated *shabab* (young men) aged between 25 and 45 years represent a new type of leadership. In their self perception and in their articulation of social and political roles they have traversed changing terrains hardly recognizable to many of their fellow villagers. In their development as local leaders, they have acquired a repertoire of experience enabling them to adjust and cope with seemingly incompatible situations and complex social and political problems.

The case of the late Hussain al-'Assaf al-Meshrif (the *mukhtar*'s first cousin) illustrates this new type of leader. Hussain studied the Quran in the village, went to al-Raqqa town for his elementary and preparatory schooling, then spent his years of secondary education in Aleppo. He participated there in student Union activities, affiliated himself to the student ranks of the Ba'th Party, and became president of the Students' Union in his school. He went on to study law at Damascus University, where he became president of the Students' Union, confirmed his position as an active Ba'th, and established useful political ties in the capital. He then returned to al-Raqqa to complete his professional training as a lawyer, and became a member of the lawyers' syndicate. Later he became an attorney for the Peasants' Union in the al-Raqqa governorate, a position which his family did not expect him to occupy, as it was the Peasant Unionists who had only recently threatened his family, al-Meshrif. In the late 1970s he was appointed as the director of a large government *mu'assasa* (establishment) for the supply of construction material in the governorate. In 1984 Hussain was elected a member of the Council of Local Administration in the al-Raqqa region. He was simultaneously performing multiple roles and duties: lawyer, administrative official, *hizbi 'amil* (active party member), family man with two children, and a member of family and tribe.

Comrade Hussain's tragic death in 1986 in a car accident at the age of 39 brought a sad end to a very promising career in the al-Raqqa region. The large attendance at his village funeral, including the governor, top party officials, party comrades, tribal shayks, and villagers, testified to his rising position in the region.

The case of *ustadh* 'Umar Abdullah al-Meshrif (a second cousin of Hussain) also illustrates the village's emerging comrade-type of leader. 'Umar is now in his mid-forties and works in al-Raqqa town as a primary school education inspector. However, before his move to town he occupied an important position in village social life and in the development of its primary and preparatory schools. With limited family income derived from the rent of land inherited in the steppes, his family managed to support his secondary school education in spite of his father's early death in 1959. From 1970 until 1983 he was both a teacher and director of the village elementary and preparatory schools. He married his cousin, Hussain's sister in 1973. He joined the Party in the same year and graduated to *'uduw 'amil* (active member) in 1977. He also volunteered his services as religious shaykh when in 1978 a village mosque was built by Hajj Khalaf and his relatives, and became the *khatib* (sermon giver) of Friday prayers. In the late 1970s he participated for some years as an instructor in the summer camps which were organized along the Syrian coast for the Ba'th political socialization of young students. During the last two decades in his village community Omar has played a number of seemingly incompatible leadership roles and activities, continually adjusting and coping with diverse demands and life pursuits.

In a similar way the case of Faris al-'Assaf, Hussain's younger brother, illustrates well how education provides future success and adaptation in social and political life. Through his personal influence and connections, Hussain secured for his brother Faris a government scholarship from Aleppo University to study auto-engineering in Romania. Faris himself joined the *hizb* (Party) before he departed to Romania in 1987, a move which allowed him to play an active political role among the Syrian students there. Being articulate and self-confident, he eventually came to assume a leadership position in the Romanian branch of the

Syrian Students' National Union. Faris then secured for himself a scholarship to do graduate studies in Moscow. He continued his active political role there, and in January 1990 he returned to Syria to a teaching position at Aleppo University. During his years in Moscow, Faris was able to secure scholarships or university admission for five students from the al-Meshrif family, including two of his brothers. These five failed to achieve admission to national universities in Syria.

The well-educated party-members of the Meshrif family, like Hussain and his cousin 'Umar as well as others, have in their various capacities and strategies played a significant role in bringing about modern changes to their village of Hawi al-Hawa far earlier than other villages in the region. Elementary and preparatory schools, an asphalt road, electricity and a reservoir for drinking water supplies have become conspicuous aspects of a rapidly modernizing village life since the late 1970s. Hussain was instrumental in bringing the village of Hawi al-Hawa and its neighboring village of al-Khatuniyya, both of which are close to al-Raqqa town, under the al-Raqqa municipality, a move designed to secure future benefits to the village in terms of land zoning, building houses, sanitation, etc. The head of the village *baladiyya* (municipal administration) is Ibrahim al-'Abd al-Meshrif, a first cousin of Hussain. Being an educated man and a party comrade, since the mid-1980s he has been emerging as one of the most vocal political figures in the village community.

As for the village Peasants' Cooperative, this too has undergone change in both its function and the character of its executive council. In the mid-1980s the Peasants' Cooperative assumed functions related to sheep raising in addition to its services for agricultural peasants, thus expanding and diversifying its membership. The Cooperative also gradually came to lose its mobilizational political role and became an organization to aid the peasants in farming. These functional re-orientations were accompanied by political changes as well. Since the mid-1980s four of the five executive council members have been from the *'ashira* of al-Dahir, including two from the al-Meshrif families. Along with the evolution of Ba'th national politics towards greater reconciliation and accommodation, the village community at large came to witness a gradual erosion of the political tension which it had experienced during the late 1960s and early 1970s. This was mainly due to the fact that al-Meshrif, as the former dominant elite, have come to adapt to the Ba'th politic-economic order over the last three decades, and to succeed in maintaining a relatively privileged position in local society, not least as many of their own educated professional men have entered this system as active participants and leaders.

Conclusion

This account suggests a number of general observations concerning political and economic change in rural north Syria. First, rural elite families have been able to survive and maintain a relatively privileged position in their societies. The account given here of al-Meshrif represents a good case in point. This reflects the fact that Ba'th rule over the last three decades has aimed at implementing certain leveling reforms, not at producing radical structural transformation in society.[21] Numerous studies conducted over the last two decades on the topics of stratification, rural elites, and leadership offer parallels to this generalization.[22] For example, Leveau in his article on the rural elite in Morocco informs us that political and economic privilege has often remained with the same extended families despite great historical changes occurring over the last century.[23]

Second, land reform and the establishment of state cooperative socialist institutions did limit the control previously exercised by landlords, agricultural operators and merchants. These same measures aided the Ba'th in the expansion and consolidation of its power base as it won peasants to the party, and replaced the former structure of peasants' dependence on landlords with one of dependence on multiple Ba'th-controlled state organizations. As also noted by Hinnesbusch, the consequence of Ba'th rule on both landowning shaykhs and peasants has, from the viewpoint of the village, created a more open social structure.[24]

Third, the establishment of peasant cooperatives and populist political institutions has not only intensified the integration of village and state at multiple levels but also generated political conflicts within village life.

Finally, the evolution of Ba'th politics at the national level led to the party adopting less populist and less radical means to maintain itself. This enabled educated members of families such as al-Meshrif to rise to prominence as local party comrades, in a position to offer access to government and to bring benefits to their families and village communities. The regime uses these men to extend modern services to the village, thus supporting their local influence, while at the same time reinforcing support for the regime among the rural communities. Consequently, the process of "village urbanization"[25] has come to be associated with the Ba'th as well as with the mediating roles performed by these local party comrades.

Notes

1 Bujra, 1971.
2 This paper is based on ethnographic material gathered in the al-Raqqa region of northeast Syria, specifically on the al-Meshrif family in their village of Hawi al-Hawa. Fieldwork research was begun in the early seventies and formed the basis of my Ph.D. dissertation (1981). However, recent data on the topic of political change covering the last decade is incorporated and synthesised in the paper here.
3 See, for example, contributions in C. A. O. Van Nieuwenhuijze, ed., (1977) and in

Richard Antoun and Harik, eds., (1972). See also other relevant studies by Emrys Peters (1963, 1972) on Lebanon and Fuad Khuri on Lebanon (1975) and Bahrain (1980), Michael Gilsenan (1977, 1981) on Lebanon, Robert Fernea (1971) on Southern Iraq, Philip Salzman (1974) on tribal chiefs and politics of encapsulation in the Middle East, Tomas Gerholm (1977) on North Yemen, Jacqueline Ismael (1982) on Kuwait, Jill Crystal (1990) on Kuwait and Qatar, Annika Rabo (1986) and Raymond Hinnebusch (1990) on Syria, and Soraya Altorki and Donald Cole (1989) on Saudi Arabia.

4   See Hinnebusch, 1990.
5   Seale, 1965; Al-Asad, 1973; Hinnebusch, 1989, 1990.
6   Khalaf, 1981; Rabo, 1986; Hinnebusch, 1990.
7   Khalaf, 1981, p. 245.
8   Khalaf, 1981, p. 362.
9   Bourdieu, 1977, p. 179.
10 Khalaf, forthcoming.
11 Apter, 1963.
12 Khalaf, forthcoming.
13 Khalaf, 1981, p. 210.
14 Hinnebusch, 1990.
15 Khalaf, 1981.
16 Salame, 1987; Hinnebusch, 1977, 1990.
17 Sadowski, 1978; Rabo, 1986; Hinnebusch, 1990.
18 Rabo, 1986.
19 Hinnebusch, 1990, p. 17.
20 Quoted in Harker, 1990, p. 103.
21 Hinnebusch, 1990.
22 See studies referred to in footnote 3.
23 Leveau, 1977.
24 Hinnesbusch, 1990.
25 Khalaf, 1981.

References

Al-Asad, R. (1973). *Economic, Social, and Political Development in Syria Between the Class Revolution and the National Revolution, 1946–1963.* (in Arabic). Damascus: Ad-Dar al Wataniyyah.

Altorki, S., and Cole, D.P. (1989). *Arabian Oasis City. The Transformation of Unayzah.* Austin: University of Texas Press.

Antoun, R., and Harik, I. (eds.) (1972). *Rural Politics and Social Change in the Middle East.* Bloomington: Indiana University Press.

Apter, D. (1963). "Political Religion in the New Nations" in C. Geertz, ed., *Old Societies and New States.* New York: Free Press of Glencoe. Pp. 57–105.

Bourdieu, P. (1977). *Outline of a Theory of Practice.* Cambridge: Cambridge University Press.

Bujra, A. (1971). *The Politics of Stratification.* London: Oxford University Press.

Crystal, J. (1990). *Oil and Politics in the Gulf: Rulers and Merchants in Kuwait and Qatar.* Cambridge, Cambridge University Press.

Fernea, R. (1970). *Shaykh and Effendi: Changing Forms of Authority Among the Al-Shabana of Southern Iraq.* Cambridge, Harvard University Press.

Gerholm, R. (1977). *Market, Mosque, and Mafraj: Social Inequality in a Yemeni Town.* Stockholm, Stockholm U. Press. Studies in Social Anthropology no. 5.

Gilsenan, M. (1977). "Against Patron-Client Relations" in E. Gellner and J. Waterbury (eds.), *Patrons and Clients in Mediterranean Societies.* London: Duckworth. Pp. 167–84.

Gilsenan, M. (1986). *Imagined Cities of the East.* Oxford: Oxford University Press.

Harker, R., Mahar, C., Wilkes, C. (1990). *An Introduction to the Work of Pierre Bourdieu.* London: Macmillan.

Hinnebusch, R. (1977). "Rural Politics in Ba'thist Syria: A Case-Study of the Role of the Countryside in the Political Development of Arab Socialism" in S.E. Ibrahim and N. Hopkins, eds., *Arab Society in Transition.* Cairo: The American University in Cairo Press. Pp. 278–96

Hinnebusch, R., (1989). *Peasant and Bureaucracy in Ba'thist Syria. The Political Economy of Rural Development.* Boulder: Westview Press.

Hinnebusch, R. (1990). *Authoritarian Power and State Formation in Ba'thist Syria. Army, Party and Peasant.* Boulder: Westview Press.

Ismael, J. (1982). *Kuwait: Social Change in Historical Perspective.* Syracuse: Syracuse University Press.

Khalaf, S. (1981). "Family, Village and the Political Party: Articulation of Social Change in Contemporary Rural Syria". Ph.D. thesis, Anthropology, University of California at Los Angeles.

Khalaf, S. (1991). "Land Reform and Class Structure in Rural Syria" in R. Antoun and D. Quataert (eds.), *Syria: Society, Culture, and Polity.* Albany: State University of New York Press. Pp. 63-78.

Khuri, F. (1975). *From Village to Suburb: Order and Change in Greater Beirut.* Chicago: University of Chicago Press.

Khuri, F. (1980). *Tribe and State in Bahrain.* Chicago: University of Chicago Press.

Leveau, R. (1977). "The Rural Elite as an Element in the Social Stratification of Morocco" in C.A.O. van Nieuwenhuijze (ed.), *Commoners, Climbers and Notables.* Leiden: E. J. Brill.

van Nieuwenhuijze, C.A.O. (1977) (ed.), *Commoners, Climbers and Notables.* Leiden: E.J.Brill.

Peters, E.L. (1963). "Aspects of Rank and Status Among Muslims in a Lebanese village" in J. Pitt-Rivers, ed., *Mediterreanean Countrymen.* The Hague: Mouton.

Peters, E.L. (1972). "Shifts in Power in a Lebanese Village" in R. Antoun and I. Harik, eds., *Rural Politics and Social Change in the Middle East.* Bloomington, Indiana University Press. Pp. 165–97.

Rabo, A. (1986). *Change on the Euphrates: Villagers, Townsmen and Employees in Northeast Syria.* Stockholm: Stockholm University Press. Studies in Social Anthropology no. 15.

Sadowski, Y. (1978). "The Knife's Edge: A Study of the Failure of Liberalization in Syria". Unpublished paper, University of California at Los Angeles.

Salame, G. (1987). *Al mujtama' wa ad-dawla fi-l-mashriq al 'arabi.* Beirut: Markaz al-Dirasat al-Wuhida al-'Arabiyyah.

Salzman, P. (1974). "Tribal Chiefs as Middlemen: The Politics of Encapsulation in the Middle East". *Anthropological Quarterly* 47:203–210.

Seale, P. (1965). *The Struggle for Syria.* London: Oxford University Press.

17

The "Bread Revolt" in Rural Tunisia: Notables, Workers, Peasants

Mouldi Lahmar

In January 1984, the price of food products was increased in Tunisia. Tunisia then went through several days of popular revolt which threatened the stability of the regime. The scale of these events in the major urban centers caused observers to overlook their importance in the rural areas. The reaction of the peasantry did not arouse any interest from the media, the political decision-makers, or the analysts.

I would like to examine the way in which two agricultural villages of the Sfax region experienced these events, placing myself within the general debate on the political weight of the peasantry in Tunisia, and, more generally, in the Maghreb. This peasantry, which fought the colonial occupation fiercely, and which determined by its armed resistance the outcome of the Algerian independence movement, sees itself today as without any decisive influence on public life. The Algerian agrarian reform only took place ten years after independence, and without any pressure from the grassroots. In Tunisia, the poorer strata of the peasantry, which expected that independence would help them recover the lands which the colonial system seized, soon found themselves threatened by a massive proletarianization organized by the State itself. Thus, during the Ben Salah period, in the 1960s, the small farmers set up production cooperatives but were unable to manage them themselves. When the farmers became salaried, they were encouraged to resettle in small urban centers. Meanwhile, those who had nothing to bring to such cooperatives but who lived by farming family land also found that they had become proletarianized. The failure of this experiment led to a substantial migration to the cities.

The motivation given for the January 1984 riots was the increase in the price of food. By provoking a general discontent, this price rise highlighted the gap that had opened up between the civil society and the political society. One of the reasons given by the government for raising prices was its desire to "help the farmer" by providing higher prices for farm products. However, although theoretically they were protected from the negative effects of this price rise, the farmers were nonetheless affected.

From *Esprit,* April 1985, pp. 9–19. Translated by Nicholas S. Hopkins. Reprinted by permission. Mouldi Lahmar teaches sociology at the University of Tunis.

First of all, the word *fellah* no longer corresponds to today's social reality. By stressing, in both classical and dialectical Arabic, the peasants who plow and sow (*falaha* = plow the soil), the term contrasts them to the nomadic or semi-nomadic herders called "Bedouins." Having become sedentarized, the herders have today become peasants, fellahs, while the word bedouin has come to mean savage, uncivilized. The changes which the rural areas have gone through in the last century have created a situation where thousands of peasants neither plow nor sow. They are unemployed, but they call themselves and are called by others fellahs. This word thus plays an ideological role by masking the social contradictions found in the countryside, and it has led to errors of judgment with regard to the political situation. The events of 1984 undoubtedly had the effect of demonstrating the scale of these contradictions.[1]

Two Villages in the Sfax Region

I was carrying out fieldwork in the Sfax region when the riots occurred. I was thus able to follow events in two villages, El-Hencha (about 3,500 inhabitants), north of Sfax, and Bir Ali Khalifa (about 3,000 inhabitants), 65 km southwest of the city.

Olives are overwhelmingly important in the first village. El-Hencha is also the site of a textile factory which employs 200 workers, girls from 16 to 25 years of age. On Tuesday, January 3, at 5 p.m., these girls began to demonstrate: leaving the factory, they headed towards the center of the village, chanting slogans against the rise in food prices. They then continued to march in the main street, passing in front of small shops where old merchants and fellahs usually gathered to play cards or to gossip. The crowd continued its march and passed in front of the only café in the village, where young day workers, pupils (school-boys), and some officials had the habit of meeting daily. The girls, with their ululation, encouraged them to join the demonstration. Thus the crowd grew in size and the rhythm of events speeded up. The demonstrators then headed towards the high school where they were joined by pupils, then by other villagers, by children, and by some construction workers who were married with children. Then violence broke out. A car belonging to the high school administration was burned, the seats of the town council and the national guard were attacked, and the police station was sacked. During the confrontation with the police forces, three persons among the demonstrators were shot and killed and several were wounded.[2]

At Bir Ali Ben Khalifa on January 3, the day of the weekly market, people were following closely the news coming from southern Tunisia, which was in revolt, but people were even more worried about a rumor that the Ouled Mahmoud, a local kinship group, wanted to organize an attack on the market. The previous day, the "délégué" (delegate), who is the local representative of the government, had already contacted the omdas or shaikhs, as they were still called, together with the notables and some civil servants who were natives of the village. On January 3, through numerous contacts, the delegate asked them to "calm down" their relatives and their communities. Early in the morning, the high school students, most of whom were boarders, were sent home in pick up trucks. Between 9 and 10 a.m., the market closed without incident and everyone went home.[3]

From these two examples, one can trace the social actors who played a political role during the events, through five variables:

1) Age: At El-Hencha, all the demonstrators were young, less than 30 years old. At Bir Ali, it was the *kbar* [4](the "big men") who played the main role in blocking (defusing) possible demonstrations.

2) Gender: the number of women among the demonstrators at El-Hencha was very large, and they were the ones who started the movement. In Bir Ali, women were absent from public life. In this village, there is only a small training center attached to the National Crafts Office, and the number of girls who work there is small.

3) Social origin: At El-Hencha, the workers, the unemployed, and the students were the main actors. In Bir Ali, the determining role was played by notables and some officials.

4) The form of mobilization. In El-Hencha, it was individual, while in Bir Ali it was collective, since a whole "community" had threatened to sack the market.

5) The type of action. In El-Hencha, the reaction of the discontented actors was violent, while the fellahs, the merchants, and the small landowners were passive. In Bir Ali, the rather mixed population of fellahs, merchants, small landowners, unemployed, day workers, and students was cautious and held back.

This comparison leads to three remarks:

1) The overall passivity of the fellahs: While at El-Hencha the two or three notable families among the fellahs did not intervene at any time in the action, in Bir Ali they helped block any manifestation of a discontent which was nonetheless widespread.

2) The active role played by factory girls, by the unemployed, and by students at El-Hencha: a remarkable mobilization of actors on the basis of their professional and economic status.

3) At Bir Ali, on the other hand, the alleged and feared mobilization was that of a traditional group based on kinship, and the reaction to it was organized by traditional actors: it was the notables who found a way to stop the movement.

To understand the different attitudes which we observed in the two villages, we have to call on history, and in particular the changes introduced into the region during the colonial and post colonial periods. At El-Hencha, the notables lost their material base and were dispossessed during the colonial period. On the other hand, the elite of Bir Ali survived, because the land tenure system prevented the land from being divided and lost. They were living on *waqf* land (inalienable property resulting from a pious foundation), and so they did not lose their land either to the colonial farmers or to urban people. Meanwhile at El-Hencha the fellahs were marginalized and their elite was discredited, and new social actors emerged, freed from traditional constraints: workers, the unemployed, students.

How the Methellith Lost their Land

The people of El-Hencha are the Ouled Mhrah, belonging to the Methellith tribe, who, on the eve of the colonial period, occupied the plain of Sfax. A family of urban notables, the Siala, had been given the control of the land around the city by the central government. These are the famous "Sialine lands." This control took the form of tax collecting and of rights collected for measuring out land brought under cultivation by the urban people. But the sovereign (the Bey of Tunis) could revoke this concession at any time, and he did so in 1871. Ten years later, the colonial government, which wanted to acquire fertile land, opened up the question of the "Sialine lands," and referred to a biased interpretation of Muslim law to challenge the right of the Methellith to occupy the land. The colonial lawyers pointed out that according to Muslim law, the land belonged first to God, then to the sovereign, and then to the Muslim community. Therefore, the sovereign had a right of eminent domain over all the land in the country. Only those lands whose owners held titles or lands cultivated according to the Muslim precept that specified that someone who cultivates land becomes its owner, could be considered as private property. The *waqf* also kept its status as inalienable land. Thus groups like the Methellith, whose land was neither private property nor *waqf*, were the most vulnerable.

The economy of the Methellith was based on extensive herding and a risky cultivation of cereals, depending on the caprices of a semi-arid climate. This extensive economy corresponded to a certain mobility of the people, required by the search for grass, for water, and for cultivable lands. The very nature of this economy made it impossible for the Methellith to claim, based on the law of "land to he who farms it," to be the owners of this land which they held collectively without title and without individual property rights. In order to claim that the land was theirs by right of cultivation, they had either to plant trees or to have paid the *'ashur* tax on farm production for ten consecutive years (according to Islamic law, the producer must pay a tenth of his yield to the state), and semi-nomadic pastoralists could not do that.[5] This legal manipulation—which was not due only to the intentions of the colonial farmers to seize good land, but also to a "cultural slippage"[6] in the understanding of Muslim law and of local customs—led the colonial authorities to consider all the plain around Sfax as state or dominion land belonging to the sovereign. This allowed the Agricultural Directorate to sell the land, which was to the advantage of the colonial farmers and the leading families of Sfax who bought it.

Collective Lands and Dispossession
The collective character of the lands of the Methellith supported a tribal social organization where the lineage and the extended family played an important role. The fate of the individual was linked to that of the group. This structure gave to the dispossession of the Methellith a particularly dangerous aspect, for it meant that the loss of a parcel of land, whether by expropriation or by sale in a time of crisis, dropped the whole lineage below the poverty line. There is a striking example. To the West of Sfax, the colonial authorities left only 12,000 out of a total of 47,000 hectares to the Ouled Nejem branch of the Methellith, who responded: "Formerly we had more land than we needed; today land is short and we have to fight over it, and defend it against the encroachment of neighbors. . . . What will become of us if we are not protected?"[7]

For these sheep herders, wealth was primarily in livestock, which require free access to large areas of pasturage. But the speed with which the colonial and urban landholdings invaded the Methellith lands, and the spread of olive trees—planted first by the colonial farmers and the Sfaxians as a long-term investment, then by the Methellith as the only way to protect themselves against daily encroachments—quickly undercut this form of wealth, before the richer Methellith herders could switch to olives. Also, the Sfaxian tree-growers used the *mgharsa* contract quite effectively to become landowners.[8] The Methellith themselves could not take advantage of this stratagem: on the one hand, they were not used to tree cultivation, and being used to an economy in which money played only a small role, they did not realize until too late how valuable on the market the olives were; on the other hand, the mgharsa contract puts all the responsibility for the success or the failure of the enterprise on the mgharsi who has to clear the land, to plant the trees (mostly olives), and maintain the farm. This task requires a yoke of oxen and steady work for a period of 8 to 10 years, which is a long-term investment. The majority of the Methellith who became *mgharsi* gave up the job before the end or went into debt and had to give up their shares of the land to pay their debts.

According to the agricultural survey of 1962 (six years after independence), in the *shiakha* (the smallest administrative division) of El-Hencha, only 13 landowners out of 785 owned more than 50 hectares while 591 owners, or 75.3 percent of the total number of landowners, held 10 hectares or less. These 13 big owners belonged to four families, of which the richest (then and now) acquired its land during the colonial period. This is a family of former khalifas and shaikhs allied to the colonial government. This political past explains why its ideological influence on the lower ranks of the fellahs declined a great deal after independence. This family remained on the margins of village political life until recent years. Its wealth never seemed legitimate to the people, which forced it into a kind of economic isolation: the family avoided any investments for fear of attracting attention.

The relatively rapid transformation of the agrarian structures deeply shook up the traditional structure of the Methellith and weakened lineage solidarity. One factor in particular played a key role in this weakening of links: the principal authors of this change were not rural people, but urban people and colonial farmers who, by creating large estates, introduced capitalist relations of production independent of the kinship ties which are the foundation of rural society. Since there were practically no rich fellahs in El-Hencha, there were no notables who combined economic power with political and moral authority. Since the whole region (75 percent of the land) is planted in olives, the majority of the small fellahs, who are both small owners and seasonal workers, are obliged— because of mechanization and because olives, once they begin producing, no longer require intensive labor—to become "unemployed." This is why today in El-Hencha there is a mass of poor and illiterate old fellahs, receiving public assistance, who have to buy all their food—precisely these cereals whose price was raised.

The Workers Revolt and Fellahs are Quiet
The children (workers and students) of these fellahs must feed them, and they are the ones who, with the pupils and the unemployed, started the demonstration to protest the rise of the price of food, while the fellahs themselves sat it out—the poor because they are scattered, marginalized, excluded from the sphere of production, and the notables because they are few and because of their weak position in the political arena. Having been compromised during the colonial period, they later had to hold their peace.

The local branch of the Destourian party (the PSD, Parti Socialiste Destouvieu, which had held power in Tunisia since independence in 1956), was established at El-Hencha before the 1950s, and until the 1970s it included petty merchants and small peasants who had lost their land to one or another of the leading families. Its members derived their political legitimacy from their "glorious" participation in the national liberation struggle. Over the years, officials and small contractors had joined the branch. Four years ago, a crisis inside the branch (among the branch members) allowed a family of notables, formerly pro-colonial, to re-enter politics. One of its members succeeded in being elected as the head of the branch. This restoration went over poorly with the old "militants" for it devalued their own past. On the other hand, it represented an economic danger, for [access to] the party cadre could become a tool for strengthening the hold of this family on the local economy. Thus there was a split, which resulted in the creation of two rival party branches, neither one of which had any influence on the fellahs, which explains their powerlessness during the January events.

The Mehedhba and Neffat Communities

It seems that it was the status of the land in Bir Ali which protected the rural communities and allowed certain local notables to consolidate their holdings and to strengthen their political influence over the members of their group.

The Inalienable Lands of the Mehedhba and the Neffat
While the Methellith lands were considered by the colonial authorities as public lands, the lands of the Mehedhba and the Neffat had been for a long time a *waqf* recognized by the central government. Legal texts recorded a donation to the benefit of the Mehedhba. The Neffat were not part of the legal beneficiaries of the *waqf*, which was not in their name, but the Mehedhba considered them as established renters, stable occupants who paid a rent in perpetuity to the *waqf* administration. In this circumstances, the colonial authorities could not easily take over the *waqf*, and its inalienable character and the specificity of the two tribes who lived there were an obstacle to the extension of colonial and urban land ownership in this region.

The Mehedhba were a maraboutic tribe, which claimed to be descended from the holy Sidi Mehedheb. They lived on land which had *waqf* status and were exonerated from taxes until 1885. The exploitation of the *halfa* (esparta grass) beds by European companies based in Skhira transformed some Mehedhba into workers collecting halfa for sale to these companies, but the social implications of this commercial intrusion were limited by the fact that the Mehedhba lands were inalienable, and the indebtedness of some individuals did not lead to loss of land. The religious character of the Mehedhba differentiated them from other tribes, especially their Neffat neighbors, and the *zawiya* (place of prayer) which they maintained, and where each year there were religious ceremonies bringing together many Mehedhba and others, symbolized the continuity of this tribe. During the colonial period, the Mehedhba found that this *zawiya*, which received the rental fees from lands rented to non-Mehedhba, was a legal and financial support against efforts to infiltrate their territory.[9]

As for the Neffat, they were a *makhzen* tribe, that is one allied to the sovereign, the Bey of Tunis. The tribe supplied horsemen to his army during the tax collection season and if necessary participated in crushing the revolts in the Central and Southern parts of Tunisia. The role which it played for the central government required it to maintain its strength. (Many Neffat, and especially the Ouled Hamed of which the *qaid* Ali ben Khali was a member, were freed of taxes.) The Neffat also owned palm trees in the oasis of Chenini, near Gabes, and they had many relationships with the Zlass, to the north around Kairouan city, where they went in search of pasturage and grain. To settle on the *waqf* land of Sidi Mehedheb and on the Mehedhba land, the Neffat had benefited from a certain support by the authorities and were protected by the successive qaids of Mahares, who were generally chosen from among the Neffat, since this *waqf* was under the authority of this qaidate.[10] When the colonialists arrived, this marked the loss of their privileges, and it is no surprise that the Neffat led the resistance to the establishment of colonial power, under their chief, Qaid Ali Ben Khalifa.

The number of Mehedhba and of Neffat compared to the size of the *waqf* is less than that of the Methellith compared to their territory. In 1885–86, there were 700 Mehedhba and 5338 Neffat on the *waqf* territory, while on the Methellith land there were 5,597 Mraya and 5819 Ouled Nejem.[11] The low population of Bir Ali allowed its people to claim holdings that were much larger than those of the Methellith.[12]

Thus we have here two tribes, one maraboutic and the other makhzen, located in a *waqf* territory which foreigners could not penetrate easily. We know that the colonial authorities were able to confiscate 32,000 hectares for the Sfax-Gafsa Phosphate Co., and that a few colonial farmers were able to slip into the region, but the Mehedhba, thanks to the legal act of donation, were able to prevent this loss from becoming massive. The colonial government stirred up a conflict between the Mehedhba and the Neffat (the former considered the latter as squatters who refused to pay rent to the zawiya) in order to encourage the Mehedhba to sell to the colonial farmers the lands occupied by the Neffat, but for this maraboutic tribe, the sale of any land would have undercut the validity of the *waqf* itself. The numerous court cases brought against colonial farmers who tried to seize *waqf* land illegally—the most famous was the one brought against Roderie[13]—testify to the ability of the Mehedhba to defend their territory.

The Mehedhba and the Neffat thus enjoyed the protection of the *waqf*, which, without stopping the expansion of colonial and urban landholding, slowed it down a good deal. But this protection had another result, much more important, on the evolution of the two tribes: it allowed certain local notables—in the absence of any serious external competition—to become rich and influential.

"Traditional" Social Structure and the Emergence of Politically Influential Fellahs

The economy of the Mehedhba and the Neffat, like that of the Methellith, was based on grain cultivation which depended on unpredictable rainfall, and on extensive herding. The land was held collectively, and the livestock belonged to the domestic units. This socioeconomic structure, supported by the inalienable nature of the land, allowed them to avoid colonial and urban land expropriation which would have upset social relationships and brought a brutal change out of the control of the inhabitants. The agrarian evolution of these communities was relatively slow compared to that of the Methellith. The masters of this transformation were the local notables.

Take for example the family Ali H.L. of the Ltaifa (branch of the Mehedhba tribe), near Bir Ali. Ali H.L., the founder of this large family, had four brothers, of whom three founded other and less prestigious families (they are known today by their surnames, while only the family of Ali has kept the name of H.L.) We have no exact information on the wealth of this family before the end of the nineteenth century, but we know that H.L., Ali's father, settled in Sfax with his third wife well before the colonial period. He had a handsome house there. His sons, including Ali, remained in the Ltaifa territory. Ali married only once, and had five children, all boys. Only the youngest, born in 1905, was still alive in 1985. The main activity of the family at the beginning of the twentieth century was to raise sheep and camels and to cultivate cereals. Through the grandfather, H.L., and through merchants who came to buy animals, the family maintained steady relationships with urban people, and very early on it was able to buy olive groves near Sfax. Thanks to the yokes of oxen it owned, it was able to bring in more than 15 workers under the sharecropping contract of *rabaa*[14] in years of good rainfall. A few herdsmen looked after a large flock. The family went through numerous crises: the death of Ali, then that of his eldest son who took the affairs of the family in hand at the death of the father. Eventually, Khalifa became the head of the family and also the head of the zawiya of Sidi Mehedheb.

When the Sfax-Gafsa Co. developed tree cultivation, in the Chaal estate (the 32,000 hectares mentioned above), the Ali H.L. family became aware of the importance of olives. In the middle of First World War, the family sold its olive trees and part of its flock to buy the important olive estate of a Sfaxian[15] located on the edge of the Ltaifa territory. In 1927, it began to plant trees on the land which it had been farming with the help of its many yokes of oxen and its many sharecroppers, and created a major olive grove. This plantation did not prevent cereal cultivation because the family was always able to clear or buy other lands, which it then brought under cultivation.[16] At the end of the 1940s and the beginning of the 1950s, the family had as many as eighteen sharecroppers who harvested the cereals planted on the lands it owned. The pasturing of the flocks was taken care of by renting pasture land, usually outside the Ltaifa territory. Thus we can reconstruct the expansion process of this family's lands: they brought as much land as possible under cultivation; once this sign of effective use was established, the land was planted in trees, which permitted the de facto acquisition of the land. By purchase and by land clearing, the same operation continued. The livestock actually functioned as the bank that financed this enterprise.

Using non-capitalist contracts such as sharecropping or payment in kind for harvesting,[17] the family successfully developed a capitalist enterprise. Before the Second World War, it built an olive press. Thus it multiplied the social and ideological relations it had with the rural people, and especially with the Ltaifa, and it gave those relations a new meaning.

The family H.L. is very religious. Three of the five sons of Ali H.L. and their eldest sons are *hajjs*, having made the pilgrimage to Mecca. They have always paid their alms *(zakat)*, which is one of the five pillars of Islam. Through its religious character, the family of Ali H.L. has strengthened its relations with its community and appears as the most prestigious family of the Ltaifa.

The Neffat did not have the same relationship as the Ltaifa to the zawiya, but their presence on *waqf* lands protected them from the forced land division which some Methellith communities (such as the Ouled Hamad, north of El-Hencha)[18] went through. This situation left the play of land appropriation relatively open to competition among the members of each community.

This is the historical and social framework within which political actors operate at Bir Ali ben Khalifa. The Ltaifa have had their PSD branch since 1957, but in twenty-seven years it only once had a true election of the leaders of the branch: during the serious crisis which shook the PSD at the beginning of the 1970s. With this one exception, the head of the Ltaifa party branch was also locally chosen "with the agreement of all." The head is the grandson of Ali H.L.

Now we can see why the Bir Ali notables could play the role they did during the events of January 1984, by blocking all protest movements. The Bir Ali workers are not only dominated by the social framework which we have described, but they are also physically absent: the village of Bir Ali is a center for the families of migrants pushed out of their community.

We can also see how, at the local level, the profound changes in the economic, social and political domains during the colonial period and since independence, have led sometimes to the disintegration of the traditional society and the appearance of new social actors, and sometimes to reinforcing the old framework and to reactivating them each time there is a crisis in the country.

Political life in the Tunisian countryside, which was for a long time monopolized and covered over by the ruling Destourian Socialist Party, ended up by bursting onto the national stage. But its manifestations were very complex, given the special historical evolution of the rural communities. National politics, shaped until the last few years by the absence of the peasantry, cannot escape in the future the influence of rural interests, even if the fellahs, so often marginalized, keep all their reluctance to get involved. We must avoid any hasty conclusion, since the events of January 1984 are a warning, perhaps a parenthesis whose sociopolitical implications it is hard to measure.

Notes

1 We use the term "peasantry" in the broadest possible sense, but we must distinguish the mass of fellahs (both the small landowners and the unemployed) from the notables who constitute an elite of owner-operators, as they are both farmers and enterpreneurs in commercial or even industrial activities, such as olive presses. These fellahs are notables because of the respect and authority they enjoy in the local community.

2 The factory in El-Hencha where the girls worked was owned by German capital. The girls had been unionized a year or two before these events (1982–83). When things turned violent in El-Hencha, the women were not involved, though one was wounded in the shooting. There were more lycéens than usual in El-Hencha because the schools they attended in nearby towns had closed down and sent them home. The workers in El-Hencha mostly came from parts of local society that did not share in the governance of the community through the party branch and the town council; they were not "local". For these details, see Mouldi Lahmar, *Du mouton à l'olivier: essai sur les mutations de la vie rurale maghrébine.* Tunis, Cérès Editions, "Horizon Maghrébin", 1994, pp. 237–38. *—Ed.*

3 Girls had been recruited for factory work from Bir Ali also, but they were bused away from the community, to a factory near Sfax also financed with German and local capital. More of the local working class in Bir Ali was working outside the community (often in Libya), thus leaving local politics to local notables. See M. Lahmar, op. cit., pp. 245, 247. *—Ed.*

4 The word *kbar* (singular: *kbir*) means "big," but it also brings in other variables, such as relatively advanced age, authority, and sometimes wealth.

5 Given the unpredictability of rainfall, the Methellith did not sow the same land each year, because they were moving with their flocks. The result was that they did not pay the tax every year, or if they did, it was not for the yield of the same land. *—Ed.*

6 B. Etienne, "La paysannerie dans le discours et le pratique" in *Problèmes agraires au Maghreb*, CRESM, CNRS, Paris, 1971, p. 10.

7 G. Rectenwald, "Les terres sialines" in *Revue algérienne, tunisienne, et marocaine*, Algiers, May 1919, p. 18

8 The owner gives his land to a person, the *mgharsi*, to plant trees; when the trees begin to bear fruit, the area planted is equally divided between the two parties. *—Ed.*

9 AGGT (Archives générales du governement tunisien), C.69, dossier "Habous de Sidi Mehedheb."

10 J. Despois, *La Tunisie orientale. Sahel et basses steppes*, Ed. des Belles Lettres, Paris, 1940, p. 499.

11 Archives de Vincenes, Armée de Terre, MR, Dossier 1322, 1323.

12 In 1962 only 6 percent of the Ouled Mahmoud had between 0 and 5 ha, while such smallholders at El-Hencha included 51 percent of the landowners.

13 AGGT, C.69, dossier "Habous de Sidi Mehedheb."

14 In the *rabaa* system, the owner provides the land, the animals, and the seeds, while the worker, *rabaa,* provides his labor force: he plows and harvests, and receives a quarter of the yield. The word *rabaa* comes from *arbaa,* "four." The *rabaa* contract varies from one region to another.

15 This property belonged to a colonial farmer who died during the First World War. Some Sfaxians bought it, and then resold part to the H.L. family for a profit. Is this a case where urban notables exploit rural ones?

16 The *waqf* lands are inalienable, but among Mehedhbas land under cultivation could be bought and sold; this purchase was neither registered nor notarized.

17 Such as the *achara,* which comes from the word *achara,* "ten." The reference is to the harvesters: the worker, *achar,* keeps one out of every ten bundles he reaps.

18 Cf. J. Despois, op. cit., p. 490–91.

Five

Introduction

Political Transformations

The political challenges confronting the Arab world in the closing years of this century remain the same as those of earlier decades: Arab unification, socioeconomic development, a resolution of the Palestinian question, and democratization. The selections which follow deal with some persistent issues in Arab politics, as well as some new ones. Each of the articles stresses the relationship between the socioeconomic structure and the political expression of that structure. Each raises political issues within a national framework.

Reluctant Democratization

When our second edition appeared in 1985, there was hardly a democratic government in the Arab world. Lebanon, which had been the longest-surviving democracy from the 1940s, came to a virtual halt and then disintegrated in the mid-1970s because of a brutal and protracted civil war. Equally, Kuwait which had enjoyed a limited electoral democracy since independence (1961), suspended its parliament twice in the 1980s because of events in the Gulf area— first the Islamic Revolution in Iran (1979), and then the Iran–Iraq War (1980–1988). The Iraqi invasion of Kuwait (August 1990) represented the worsening crisis of Arab regimes—erosion of legitimacy and effectiveness on the one hand, and growing repression and corruption on the other. The Iraqi invasion of Kuwait exposed the so-called radical or populist regimes as greedy, adventurous, and despotic. It exposed the conservative royal regimes, especially of the Gulf, as inept, dependent on the West for protection, and equally despotic. The climax of these events was the Second Gulf War (January–February 1991) in which an International Coalition led by the US declared war to liberate Kuwait from Iraqi occupation. In the process, not only were Iraqi troops defeated and expelled from Kuwait, but Iraq proper was systematically devastated by the far superior air-power of the Coalition. The Arab world was bitterly divided over these events.

However, one of the few positive fall-outs of the Gulf crisis and the Second Gulf War was to expedite a "democratization" process which had already been timidly underway. To be sure, some ten Arab countries have introduced marked elements of political pluralism and electoral politics. Some have allowed, for the first time, multiparty systems—e.g., Mauritania, Algeria, Tunisia, and Yemen.

339

Some have reinstituted multiparty systems or allowed them to work—e.g., Morocco, Egypt, and Jordan. Lebanon and Kuwait resumed their long-suspended electoral politics in the 1990s.

Even the most traditional nondemocratic royal regimes of the Gulf and the Arabian Peninsula began a guarded process of "power-consultation." Oman, the United Arab Emirates (UAE), Qatar, Bahrain, and Saudi Arabia instituted what came to be called "Consultative Councils" *(Majlis al-Shura)*. These are semi-legislative bodies, whose members are not elected but selected by the ruler (king, sultan, or emir) from the "notables" in various walks of life—e.g., merchants, professionals, tribal chiefs, and leaders of major sects. Oman has evolved its Shura to a semi-electoral system, by allowing organized entities (e.g., merchants, professional associations, or clubs) to elect their own representatives to the Shura Council, which in turn has been given more legislative powers.

New national pacts, charters, and/or constitutions have accompanied these moves toward more democratic, pluralistic, or electoral politics. These may seem like modest steps compared to what Samuel Huntington calls the "Third Wave of Democracy" which had swept Southern Europe (1970s), Latin America (1980s), Eastern Europe, East Asia, and even some sub-Saharan African countries (1990s). Nevertheless, they indicate that the Arab world is slowly, albeit reluctantly, joining the "global democratization" process. It is often noted that for such democratization to strike roots and be sustainable, there must be a growing middle class and thriving organizations of civil society. Empirical evidence on the latter seems quite mixed in the late 1990s, and needs to be examined in each Arab country.

Some Western orientalists contend that Arab–Islamic culture does not lend itself to the development of civil society or democracy. Similar assertions were made about Japan and Germany in the 1930s; yet democracy has struck roots in both countries. The compatibility of democracy, Arab culture, and Islam warrant a debate (see the article by Harik in this section).

The Issue of Palestine

The only Arab country whose existence is not internationally recognized is Palestine. The country was placed under British mandate following the First World War. For the following three decades, Britain opened Palestine to European Jewish settlers under the banner of the Zionist movement. Leaders of that movement had obtained, during the First World War, a promise since known as the Balfour Declaration, to establish a "Jewish national home in Palestine." In 1948 Britain suddenly withdrew, leaving behind two communities fighting for the land of Palestine: the original native Palestinian Arabs and the new European Jewish settlers. Israel, a Jewish state, was immediately declared independent in a part of Palestine; and a series of wars resulted with the Palestinians and neighboring Arab states over the next three decades. Israel, with direct and indirect help from the West, won three of four wars in 1948, 1956, and 1967. With every victory, Israel expanded territorially and displaced more Arab refugees. In the 1967 War Israel not only conquered the remainder of Palestine but also occupied all of Egyptian Sinai and the Syrian "Golan Heights."

The Arab regimes joined together in a partially successful war against Israel in October of 1973, and forced Israel to withdraw from some of the Arab territories occupied in 1967, while the Palestinian resistance movement, known as the Palestine Liberation Organization (PLO), waged a military-political struggle against Israel. But other Arab territories, including most of Palestine, have remained under Israeli occupation. After the 1973 War, most Arab regimes opted for a peaceful settlement with the help of the United States. Egypt signed agreements with Israel to this effect: the Camp David accords (1978) and the Egyptian–Israeli peace treaty (1979). Egypt regained Sinai, and in turn established diplomatic relations with Israel. These initiatives by Egypt's President Sadat created much dissension in Arab ranks in the late 1970s and much of the 1980s. Egypt's membership in the Arab League was suspended for having signed those agreements without collective Arab approval. In the 1990s, however, the Arab–Israeli peace process has gained more supporters among Arab regimes. Many of them attended the Madrid Peace conference in the autumn of 1991. Palestinians and Jordanians signed peace agreements in 1993 and 1994, respectively. The Palestinian National Authority (PNA), which came into existence after the Oslo Agreement (September 1993), has taken over from Israel several townships, held legislative and presidential elections (January 1996), and is believed to be the embryonic state of Palestine. But with continuous Israeli settlements in the West Bank and hardliners refusing to budge on East Arab Jerusalem, the anticipated Palestinian state, if it ever materializes, would be a tiny pebble of survival on its own. However, at this writing (1997), Israel still occupies substantial parts of the West Bank and the Gaza Strip as well as the Syrian Golan Heights and parts of southern Lebanon.

Enduring Problems

Other enduring problems include those of failing to come to grips with ethnic or sectarian issues, population explosions, redundant bureaucracy, and socioeconomic development. Ethnic relations have proved to be an especially thorny political problem for Lebanon, Iraq, Sudan, and Bahrain. In these countries, ethnic diversity along religious, linguistic, or national lines has resulted in long bloody conflicts. The rise of Arab national consciousness made it inevitable that minority groups in the Arab world would develop a particularistic ethnic consciousness of their own. Such groups as the Iraqi Kurds, the southern Sudanese, and the Lebanese Maronites felt a real or imaginary threat to their identity and cultural heritage. They sought to protect their interests through secession or the establishment of their own states. Both Iraq and Sudan managed to resolve the issue for a while by granting autonomy and self-rule to their minorities. But in both countries, the ruling elite quickly reneged on these autonomy agreements, leading to new armed eruptions in the 1980s and 1990s. After fifteen years of intermittent warfare (1975–1990), the Lebanese conflict was settled by regional and international mediation, with Syria and Saudi Arabia as the principal brokers. The settlement was formalized in the Ta'if Agreement (1989) which made power sharing among Lebanon's 16 religious sects more equitable, with the Shi'a Muslims as slight net gainers, and the Maronite Christians as slight net losers. However, the situation in Lebanon has remained unstable, especially in the South, where Israel and its Lebanese allies occupy what is known as a "security zone," and a Shi'a-led resistance, known as Hizbullah, keeps fighting Israeli occupation.

The Arab world has only about 6 percent of the world population, but accounts for some 20 percent of the world's armed conflicts since 1945. The following table summarizes these armed conflicts since the first Arab–Israeli war in 1948. Armed conflicts within countries (i.e., civil wars) have claimed more lives and uprooted more people than armed conflicts among the states of the region (see the article by Ahmed in Section Six). Both types of conflict are directly or indirectly linked to the formation of new states, and their mismanagement since independence. One manifestation of mismanagement is autocratic monopoly of power either by traditional elites, or modern, but despotic regimes. A quest for a more equitable power sharing is what "democracy" is all about.

Politics of course is a never-ending process, dominated by partial successes and partial retreats. Many Arabs aspire to a more democratic Arab world, based on a higher level of development and individual well-being and on the resolution of the major disputes which have dominated life for the last generation or two. Whether this will happen, and what the circumstances are under which this general goal can be attained, are questions for the future.

In This Section

Iliya Harik offers an overview of the state of democracy in various Arab countries. He argues that democracy flourishes better in a democratic political culture, which implies a multiplicity of political institutions marked by internal democracy. He uses the concept of "civil society" relatively broadly, to include not only voluntary organizations but also family, kin, and neighborhood structures. Harik points out that these are themselves not necessarily "democratic" internally, but that competition between them, when they are evenly balanced, is the nearest approach to democracy.

Table 1
The Cost of Armed Conflicts in the Arab Middle East and North Africa (AMENA) Region, 1948–1996

Type of conflict	Period	No. of casualties	Estimated cost (billions of US$, 1991 value)	Estimated population displacement
Inter-state conflicts				
Arab–Israeli	1948–90	200,000	300.0	3,000,000
Iraq–Iran	1980–88	600,000	300.0	1,000,000
Gulf War	1990–91	120,000	650.0	1,000,000
Other inter-state conflicts	1945–91	20,000	50.0	1,000,000
Sub-total		940,000	1,300.0	6,000,000
Intra-state conflicts				
Sudan	1956–95	800,000	50.0	4,500,000
Iraq	1960–95	500,000	50.0	2,000,000
Lebanon	1958–95	180,000	50.0	1,250,000
Yemen	1962–72	100,000	10.0	500,000
Algeria	1992–96	60,000	10.0	300,000
Somalia	1989–95	50,000	3.0	250,000
Syria	1975–85	30,000	0.5	150,000
Turkey	1980–96	20,000	2.0	200,000
Morocco (Sahara)	1976–91	20,000	3.0	100,000
S. Yemen	1986–87	10,000	0.2	50,000
Other intra-state conflicts	1945–91	100,000	10.0	400,000
Sub-total		1,870,000	188.7	9,700,000
Grand total (all armed conflicts)		2,810,000	1,488.7	15,700,000

Source: Compiled from the files of the Arab Data Unit (ADU), Ibn Khaldoun Center for Development Studies, 1997.

Kiren Aziz Chaudhry takes on the difficult task of unraveling the political economies of two hermit countries, Iraq and Saudi Arabia, using the tools of the "new institutional economics." Her fundamental theoretical argument is that a free market (liberalization) is more than the absence of state control. It involves a set of institutions, corporate interest groups, and a culture all of which often have to be provided by the state through legal and institutional means. Overall,

Introduction

Chaudhry makes analytical use of such notions as class, primordial or ethnic group, the state, and the market. When states are unable to regulate the market, they are likely to fall back on direct intervention or nationalization. Government regulation of the market reflects not technical but political factors, including the favoring of certain groups or classes over others and the survival of the regime. What Iraq and Saudi Arabia have in common is their reliance on oil exports for state revenue. When that revenue is high, the state has used it to attach people to the state; when it declines, the state attempts to withdraw from such commitments. What distinguishes Iraq from Saudi Arabia is its history.

Another approach to democracy is reflected in Khalil Shikaki's article on the prospects for democracy, the peace process, and reconstruction of the new Palestinian state. It should be noted that Shikaki's article was written before the Palestinian and Israeli elections of 1996. The Palestinian elections confirmed Arafat in power, while the Israeli elections replaced the Labor government with a Likud one, understood to be less favorable to the peace process. Like Harik, Shikaki sees that democracy is linked to various social and cultural factors. He uses the results of public opinion polling in Palestine to assess the strength of these different factors, and therefore the level of commitment of Palestinians to the democratic process. The public opinion results have to be analyzed in the context of the different Palestinian elites.

Anh Nga Longva's article on Kuwaiti women discusses the way in which gender possibilities and identity vary with social class and other forms of status distinction. Longva shows how the strategy of women from the three main categories of the Kuwaiti population varies, and also differs from the migrant worker population. The most likely to be employed are those from the lowest status group, the least likely are from the highest. Women also mark their status by an elaborate dress code. Again in this article we see the intersection of gender, power, and status or class—against a background of the importance of cross-gender relations for society.

18

Pluralism in the Arab World

Iliya Harik

In seven of the Arab world's twenty states—from Yemen on the Indian Ocean to Morocco on the Atlantic—a process of guarded democratization has been taking place. Ordinary citizens are receiving more opportunities to participate freely in politics, while economic privatization and the encouragement of free enterprise are also gathering steam. In both cases, functions once performed by government agencies are being fully or partially delegated to citizens and corporations, making for a more voluntaristic and self-regulated civil society.

In addition to discussing these liberalizing and democratizing trends in Arab countries, this essay also seeks to assess whether the growth of a flourishing "civil society" is a prerequisite for the installation of a democratic government or, alternatively, whether the development of a civil society and a democratic government may be pursued simultaneously.

Democratic governments function poorly, if at all, in the absence of certain explicit and implicit cultural practices and assumptions. A number of attitudes must be first ingrained in the social order, such as a certain degree of individualism, public-spiritedness, respect for and tolerance of others, and acceptance of winning and losing according to "the rules of the game." Indeed, a major reason for the emphasis placed on civil society is the belief that a democratic system of government planted in a hostile and alien culture is not likely to survive, let alone prosper. Can one find in Arab societies attitudes and concepts supportive of democracy?

The first place to look is in the sphere of high culture. Is there a line of thought among the Arabs that can serve as a philosophical bedrock for the establishment of civil society? The Arab political tradition remains to this day tightly intertwined with Islamic doctrines and the historical precedents set by premodern Islamic states, which were typically ruled by authoritarian sultans. Islam itself contains the seeds of individual dignity and group integrity, understood as reflections of the divine spark that all the world's revealed religions confirm and celebrate. In this respect, Islam is similar to the natural rights idea, which also has its deepest roots in convictions about a divine order.

From *Journal of Democracy* 5 (3):43–56 (1994). Copyright © 1994 by The Johns Hopkins University Press. Reprinted by permission. Iliya Harik is Professor of Political Science at Indiana University.

Islamic thought is vast and complex; what concerns us here are those strains that may serve as a basis for the growth of civil society among Islamic peoples.

In Islam, one finds the idea of individual integrity juxtaposed with that of integral membership in the community *(al-jamaa'a)*, a dualism that has served those who preferred a strong civil society as well as those who wanted a strong and authoritarian system of government. Those today who favor civil society—mainly Muslim jurists scandalized by the injustices of autocratic governments—understand *al-jamaa'a* in a sense consistent with the idea of civil society. Their major contribution has been to argue that the implementation of Islamic law is the preserve not of government but of Muslim leaders and councils at all levels of society working closely with their communities. We see this position stressed again now by contemporary Muslim writers such as Muhammad 'Abid al-Jaabiri of Morocco and Sheikh Hassan al-Turabi of Sudan. Arab believers in civil society today, however, are not confined to the religious tradition. Many, like the scholars at the Ibn Khaldun Center in Cairo, are secular and approach the subject from a liberal democratic point of view.

The more dominant line of thought—one widely held by Islamic revivalists—is that a Muslim government is an essential pillar of the Islamic religion. Fundamentalists take as their political cornerstone the belief that the main raison d'etre of government is the implementation of divine law *(shari'a)*. While Muslims of this persuasion are not necessarily less committed to a reduced governmental role in society, in general they tend to leave less space for individuals and organizations and put more emphasis on the Islamic character of government. However, moderate advocates of the Islamic state have recently sought to present themselves as sympathetic to the notion of limited government. Certainly, adherence to the rule of law is cherished in Islam no less than in the West. Also favorable to civil society is the Islamic emphasis upon the economic liberty of individuals and associations. Thus rarely do we see an Islamic government opposing privatization from a doctrinal point of view. Iran remains the most divided on this issue, but leans toward the private sector.

With respect to the other main ideological tributary of modern Arab political culture—Arab nationalism—the story is more troubling. During this century, Arab nationalism has shown itself to be less tolerant and has allowed less room for democracy, both in theory and in practice, than Islam. Concerned mainly with vindicating communal identity and winning freedom from colonialism, Arab nationalism has long stressed political unification and uniform national character, allowing very little room for diversity. Ironically, its founders were not Arab governments, but rather Arab intellectuals. Nationalism thus arose first in civil society, and then spilled over into the making of the authoritarian national state.

The Need for Strong Government

The happy coincidence of democratic civil societies and democratic states in the advanced industrial countries makes it possible for advocates to dwell at length on the virtues of civil society, not the least of which is its role in advancing and consolidating democracy. The case is markedly different in Arab and other less developed countries.

The challenge for those who deal with developing societies is to determine what to do when an authoritarian system of government is a reflection of authoritarian relations in society. In the Arab world, authoritarian relations prevail in the family, the religious community, the workplace, and between social classes. Moreover, in many Arab and other less developed countries, the expansion of governmental roles has been directly related to the large empty space left by society. In countries such as Saudi Arabia and the Gulf states, governments (bolstered by oil revenues) have moved in to take primary responsibility for education, health, housing, and industrial development. Governments became entrepreneurs in such areas as banking, industry, and commerce.

Moreover, the culturally conservative (and decidedly nonsocialist) attitudes of officials in those countries seem to reflect the predilections of the people, who even take initiatives to maintain that conservatism in the forefront of national policy. As a result, these conservative regimes, with the possible exception of Saudi Arabia, do not seem to be experiencing the severe tensions common in some other countries in the Arab world, nor are they as frequently featured on lists of the worst violators of human rights.

One should treat with caution the claim that less developed countries tend to have strong societies and weak states. In terms of social policy effectiveness, it is true, almost all less developed countries have weak governments, but when it comes to internal security, these same states are potent and very effective. This is true of Morocco, Egypt, Tunisia, Iraq, and Syria. Moreover, the apparent failure of so many Third World regimes has had much to do with the ambitious targets they set for themselves; we should take care, therefore, to avoid underestimating their actual achievements.

Scholars agree that the aggrandizement of governments in less developed countries has been a response to societal pressures. The extensive role of government in less developed countries may thus be as much a concession to popular demands and expectations as it is a grab for power. In many of these states, citizens are heavily dependent on government. About 40 percent of the population continued to live below the poverty level in the late 1970s in Egypt, even after strenuous official efforts to redress income inequality and introduce a welfare system. The situation is not much better in most other non-oil-rich Middle Eastern countries. In most such countries, the high birthrates and the dislocation of rural dwellers to squalid cities have aggravated an already difficult situation.

Most workers live below but not outside the market economy. They are either underproductive or underpaid. In either case, they are needy and must have a patron; typically, it is the government. In Arab countries without oil wealth, the dependency ratio—the number of unemployed in a family to those employed—is as high as six to one. Considering that most of the employed earn barely more than subsistence wages, the clamor for government to play the role of provider is understandable.

The high dependency ratio suggests that civil society may itself be the source of government's augmented role. And an expansive government, we must remember, is a much better candidate to turn authoritarian than a limited one. Whether one looks at socialist-oriented countries with regimes based on mass mobilization (such as Iraq, Syria, Egypt, Tunisia, and Algeria) or former-ly poor countries grown rich off petroleum (such as Saudi Arabia, Kuwait, Qatar, Bahrain, Oman, and the United Arab Emirates), society has demanded actively munificent governments. The only difference is that the latter countries have had the wherewithal to manage such extensive responsibilities, while the former have not.

A focus on civil society alone is thus not likely to do much for democrati-zation in Arab societies. A more inclusive approach is far better, because the interdependence between governmental institutions and private, civil associa-tions is quite strong. Moreover, the strengthening of civil society in Arab coun-tries may well depend upon the rise of greater governmental effectiveness. Fortunately, the key to such effectiveness may lie not in expanding government but in reducing its size and scope.

Ambiguities of Democratization

If democracy is the goal, does one start by building civil society as the neces-sary foundation, or is it better first to confront the issue of political power squarely and deal with governmental institutions straightaway? The writing that Arabs have been producing on civil society is not enlightening in this regard, but then neither is the Western literature on civil society.

To begin with, the claim that a democratic society is essential to a democra-tic government, a truism in the developed West, may serve in most less devel-oped countries (including all the Arab states except Lebanon) only to hinder the progress of democracy by allowing those who wish to delay the process of democratization to argue that the building of civil society must precede democ-ratic political change. Any effort to make the path to democracy pass first through a strong civil society will mean the indefinite postponement of democ-racy.

Another problem is that in most Arab countries, traditional solidarities con-stitute the most common social bonds, whether tribal, ethnic, communal, religious, or kinship-based. Yet Arab intellectuals—the biggest promoters of civil society—generally loathe traditional loyalties and attitudes, and offer a vision with no place for associations based on primordial ties. To these intellectuals, only modern associations with voluntary memberships are acceptable.

Yet civil society, let us recall, is supposed to act as an intermediary between the individual and national leaders, and in doing so is also supposed to serve as a check on the power that those leaders can wield. Should Arab intellectuals succeed in marginalizing traditional associations, they would harm the cause of democratic transformation by knocking out precisely those groups that are best able to mediate between citizens and their government, and that have the ability to restrain the latter's power.

Lebanon, whose democratic tradition is based on the acceptance of communal ties as politically relevant, has long drawn severe criticism from liberal Arab intellectuals who consider communalism backward and blame it for the civil war there. Such attacks are misguided, for Lebanon's communal-based democracy is a mechanism for conflict resolution rather than a cause of communal strife. Other democratizing Arab states have strong and diverse communities; is it prudent to portray democratization as a threat to communal identity and a communal role in the polity? Even aside from such practical considerations, Arab intellectuals have yet to offer any theoretical justification for denying traditional associations a role in the democratization process.

Another point of concern is that private groups, whether corporations or traditional associations, often have predatory tendencies, which introduce ambiguity into the relationship between civil society and democratization. Attempts by individuals or private groups to gain advantage at the expense of the public are a problem in all societies. The special favors that some private companies and businessmen enjoy in Saudi Arabia and Kuwait practically amount to the privatization of government. In Egypt, conversely, the rapid growth of the Islamic Investment Funds and their influence in and out of government circles led a fearful government to destroy them. The government's fears, it may be noted, were not entirely unfounded.

Two other arguments further justify rejection of the thesis that civil society should be treated as a precondition for democracy in the Arab world. First, processes of privatization or political liberalization in many Arab countries have begun as government initiatives. Second, many of the Arab countries' most "modern" associations—business groups, labor unions, professional and intellectual societies—show little or no interest in democratization. It was academics and journalists, after all, who in 1992 publicly urged President Mubarak of Egypt to go slow on democratization, for fear of repeating the Algerian example, in which rapid democratization measures taken by the government brought about an Islamist majority.

This raises the question of just who in Arab society has a vested interest in democracy. Among the "modern" groups listed above, each has its reasons for lacking a vigorous concern with democratization. Moreover, authoritarian governments have in many cases succeeded in making clients of such groups. Businessmen have been reduced in power and functions, made to depend on government commissions, and seduced with favors such as licenses, credit, or subcontracts. In the oil-rich countries of the Gulf, businessmen have done very well off of government largesse and see no reason to rock the boat.

Trade unions, on the other hand, have played a more mixed role. In Egypt, Algeria, and Syria, trade unions became partners in single-party regimes, giving up the right to strike in return for special favors. In Egypt, nonetheless, some unions spurned this old bargain and staged wildcat strikes, while in Tunisia unions proved largely unwilling to surrender their activism and went through a costly struggle with the overbearing regime of President Bourguiba. Without much support from other groups, they made very little headway in democratizing the Tunisian political system, and have shown more caution recently under President Ben Ali, who has shown himself to be no less authoritarian than his predecessor. Trade unions in Morocco, like their Tunisian counterparts, have a distinguished record of fighting for freedom and democracy, but have never had to resist attempts to incorporate them into the regime. In the oil-producing countries, transient and foreign work forces plus official opposition have made labor organizing a forlorn hope.

Intellectuals, the third "modern" group, remain an enigma. While they have a considerable stake in democracy and freedom of expression, their record in most Arab countries has not been impressive. While it is true that some intellectuals have been in the forefront of the human rights organizations that have cropped up across the Arab world since the early 1980s, intellectuals as a class have shown few signs of strong commitment, understanding, or leadership in the struggle for democracy. The human rights groups, moreover, remain limited in following and influence.

The ambivalence among intellectuals comes partly from ideology and partly from career considerations. Having been major allies of socialist and nationalist regimes, Arab intellectuals have become bitter and cynical in the wake of socialism's failure. Many cling to the belief that socialism is just, while democracy is not. They fear that liberalization will widen the gap between classes, work against the poor, and favor the rich. Most Arab intellectuals, moreover, remain government employees and do not enjoy the luxury of freely expressing (much less acting upon) views that might run contrary to their employer's interests. Although liberalization and privatization may eventually change the conditions facing Arab society's quiescent "modern" groups, and in so doing spur a change in their attitudes and behavior, for the time being one must describe their role in democratization as quite modest.

In regimes in which some political liberalization has taken place, political parties have done the most to seize the opportunity. Yet these parties tend to be undemocratically run; unless checked, most would act in an authoritarian fashion once in power, just as the National Islamic Front (NIF) has done in Sudan and the Islamic Salvation Front, to judge from its pronouncements, was about to do in Algeria. At any rate, political parties are not, strictly speaking, parts of civil society.

A Dependent Relationship

Another reason to reduce the emphasis usually placed on civil society is its dependent relationship with government. In the Arab world, governments have taken the major initiative in the development of civil society. As far back as the 1940s, the Iraqi government tried to create an entrepreneurial class by building industries that could later be turned over to private entrepreneurs. Most of the entrepreneurs in Tunisia today are former government officials who left, with some official encouragement, to start their own businesses. The Egyptian and Tunisian governments have been actively involved since the 1970s in supporting cottage industries and encouraging the formation of small groups and associations. Agrarian reform in Egypt contributed not only to the welfare of poor peasants but to the emergence of new political leaders amongst them. It was also government-induced agrarian reform that created local institutions such as cooperatives and elected municipal councils.

In the oil-rich Gulf countries, government largesse helped to spawn a middle class of businessmen and professionals. Finding the private sector very small, the Saudi government decided both to expand the public sector and to encourage private entrepreneurs through grants, easy loans, subsidies, and commissions. In the vital area of education, the governments of most Arab states have shouldered responsibility for providing free schooling from the primary grades all the way through university, and have made tremendous progress in the last 30 years. Today, thanks to such governmental efforts, the educated middle class constitutes a major formation in those societies.

Although socialist regimes in the 1960s undermined many well-established entrepreneurs in Egypt, Syria, and Iraq (and to a lesser extent in Libya during the 1970s), the expansionist macroeconomic policies generally pursued by other Arab governments during that era proved quite helpful to private entrepreneurs, who found much demand for their services in the public sector.

If there is a single overriding reason why liberalization and democratization measures have been so slow in making progress in most of the Arab world, it is that they were introduced at the pleasure of governments and for reasons of state, and not because of pressure from civil society. Unable to cope with the business, services, and welfare responsibilities that they had undertaken, Arab governments in the 1980s decided that their survival hinged on shifting part of the burden to private groups. At best, such groups showed no more than a very cautious willingness to respond. In the face of government delays and double-talk, entrepreneurs shied away from confrontation or political activism, resorting instead to subterfuge and to uncivic activities such as smuggling and black marketeering.

Democratization must be seen as an objective in its own right that calls for concentration on the structure and behavior of government, whether or not a country has a democratic civil society. One of the major conditions of democratization lies in active communication and cooperation between governments and social groups, especially in developing countries where the formal structures of government are not sufficiently developed or responsive to popular demands. A cooperative relationship between government and such groups, regardless of their character, is likely to contribute to the viability of democracy and a more successful government.

Important as the democratic character of civil society is, it is not a precondition for political democracy. Democratic government is feasible in a society in which the internal decision making of most groups and organizations is not democratic. Independent groups, whatever their internal decision-making structures, contribute to pluralism, to the division of power, and to the control of government. The dichotomy between government and civil society that is posited in many of the standard scholarly accounts of democratization is more apt to be confusing than helpful when it comes to the Arab countries, where the role of government in the democratization process is so prominent.

Having stressed the role of government, it would be useful to consider the exceptional cases of Morocco and Lebanon, where civil society is strong and its strength is reflected in the active relationship with government. Although Morocco's King Hassan II (r. 1961–) has been willing to take steps in the direction of liberalization and democratization, labor unions and political parties have been instrumental in steering the government down that path. In Morocco, freedom of the press and of association has been the rule since independence in 1956, albeit with some interruptions. While the monarchy's autocratic tendencies were as pronounced there as anywhere else, years of pressure from unions, the press, and the parties (by no means all secular or internally democratic) have produced considerable democratic progress.

In Lebanon, another unusual case, civil society is stronger than the government. The former spawned private militias that fought a 17-year civil war while the government sat on the sidelines. Not only did civil society carry on essential activities such as banking, schooling, and publishing during the war, it also added new ones. The most remarkable was the flourishing of the broadcast media, which had been a public monopoly before the war. Warlords and private entrepreneurs alike took advantage of the government's inability to enforce its regulations and started their own radio and television stations, most of which quickly became profitable and soon surpassed the established public radio and television networks by leaps and bounds, connecting the country to important international media sources. Now the government is trying to restrict the programming on these stations, drawing a chorus of opposition from various sources including the Islamist party, Hezbollah. Many Lebanese newspapers and magazines migrated to European cities and published there during the war, but most have returned by now, and the written press remains free and prosperous.

The Lebanese combination of a vibrant civil society and a democratic system of government is quite rare in the Arab world. Yet Lebanese civil society bears many fundamental similarities to other Arab societies. Political parties and corporations are not run democratically, but are dominated by traditions of familial and sectarian loyalty. Indeed, the national parliament does not revolve around party alignments, for parties control no more than a third of the seats. Most members of parliament are independents, whose ties with their local constituencies are strong enough to elect them without the aid of a political party. Although this is by no means a "modern" system of government, it has worked for half a century.

The main reason why Lebanon's non-Western system of democracy works is the pluralism of competing actors. Competition checks authoritarian tendencies. When five or more hierarchically organized and led associations compete in one arena, they check one another just as much as when five democratically run and led agencies do. To regard such a system as nondemocratic simply because it does not correspond to or mimic Western forms of democracy would be both intellectually indefensible and shortsighted.

Recent Progress and Setbacks

Whereas in 1970 Lebanon had the only democratic government in the Arab world, by 1994 seven states—Egypt, Kuwait, Jordan, Yemen, Tunisia, Morocco, and Mauritania—had moved in the direction of democratization. With the exception of Egypt, where halting democratization began in the late 1970s, all have made their moves since 1990. In all these states, a parliament has been more freely elected, either for the first time or with increased powers. In Yemen however, democratization is currently in a precarious situation with the outbreak of renewed conflict between the northern and southern halves of the country, unified only since 1990.

Sudan and Lebanon are special cases. In the former, the head of state is an army officer; opposition parties are banned, and some of their leaders are imprisoned, under house arrest, or in self-imposed exile. The Sudanese press is muzzled and is limited now solely to government newspapers. (Although the government theoretically permits the establishment of private newspapers, the only one to test this freedom, *The Sudan International,* was suspended and its editor and staff jailed in March 1994.)

Sudan's record on human rights has been under attack from Amnesty International, Middle East Watch, the Arab Organization of Human Rights, the Federation of Arab Lawyers, and the Cairo-based periodical Civil Society. The UN General Assembly in December 1992 indicted the Sudanese government for rights abuses. The setback to civil society resulting from the coming to power of the NIF has been grievous. Among other things, the NIF-military regime has succeeded in abolishing the constitution; imposing a state of emergency; arresting people without warrant; setting up special courts to try political opponents; dissolving the elected councils of trade unions and associations in favor of NIF-appointed special committees; purging members of the opposition from the bureaucracy; and replacing about a thousand officers and 57 judges with NIF loyalists. About 40 daily and weekly publications have been closed and more than a thousand journalists dismissed. Summary executions and torture of prisoners have been common. Islamic law has also been imposed on the country and women forced to wear the veil.

Since it took over in June 1989, the NIF-military government has also expanded Khartoum's war against the largely Christian and animist dissidents of the south, whose main demands are local autonomy and exemption from Islamic law. Apologists for Sheikh Hassan al-Turabi, the NIF's leader, claim that he continues to hold democratic views, but it is very difficult to feel assured about al-Turabi and the Sudan at the present time considering the NIF's known penchant for forming militias and intimidating its political opponents. It is possible that extraordinary measures have been resorted to temporarily in order to establish an Islamic order, but it is difficult to imagine an Islamic or any other order imposed by force continuing to survive without force.

Lebanon, as usual, is complicated and exceptional. It has recently emerged from civil war with a new political arrangement that redistributes power among its various communities in a way that more closely reflects demographic facts. In August 1992, parliamentary elections took place for the first time since 1972, and most militias had laid down their arms. The country is now enjoying peace, and reconstruction is proceeding at a feverish pace. Muslim professional women fill numerous important positions in organizations as varied as banks and schools. Another striking fact is that only in Lebanon has a Muslim fundamentalist party, Hezbollah, been allowed to run for parliament. It has won eight seats in parliament, follows a policy of accommodation with other parties and factions in Lebanese domestic politics, and is quite vociferous in its defense of liberties. In Lebanon the private sector of the economy has always been predominant, and the government is now also proposing to privatize the telephone, electrical, and railway systems, as well as other parts of the country's infrastructure.

Nevertheless, enough problems linger to keep Lebanon from being fully democratic or fully at peace. The once-pre-eminent Maronite community boycotted the parliamentary elections, citing serious objections to the electoral law and to holding elections under the guns of the Syrian army. In some constituencies, voter turnout was 10 percent or less. Some candidates gained office who would have had no chance of winning truly competitive elections. Human rights organizations have expressed serious concerns about isolated incidents of violations, especially of prisoners' rights. Moreover, the government has recently prohibited private radio and television stations from presenting news reports, pending the passing of a new broadcast-regulation law. The written press, long famous as the freest and liveliest in the Arab world, continues to flourish, though not without some government harassment.

Under the pretext of resisting Israeli occupation, Hezbollah is the only group allowed to carry arms, not only in the south but also as far north as Baalbeck. The Syrians continue to maintain an undiminished military presence in the country despite the Taif Agreement, which set a timetable for their withdrawal, and the Syrian government enjoys a transparent hegemony over Lebanese affairs. Moreover, part of southern Lebanon is still under Israeli occupation. Thus it is small wonder that many Lebanese see their country as falling short of total peace or democracy.

If the case of Lebanon offers grounds for guarded hope, Yemen's story is the stuff of tragedy. In the early 1990s, the Yemenis achieved political unity between the north and south, and then introduced constitutional democracy. Today, civil war is threatening to engulf the country in blood as powerful parties square off over regional issues and disputes concerning the power-sharing arrangements that made unification and free elections possible.

Of all the Arab countries, Morocco and Kuwait have perhaps made the most progress in democratization recently. In 1993, Morocco conducted its freest parliamentary elections since the 1960s and undertook extensive privatization of government-owned corporations and properties. When parliamentary elections were first resumed in the 1970s, the legislature was hardly more than a rubber stamp for the king. The elections of 1993, however, were carried out under a new electoral law and a new constitution that increased the powers of parliament. Eleven political parties and a score of independent candidates participated in an election held under judicial supervision. For the first time, the opposition parties gained a plurality, though not an outright majority. Moreover, two women were elected out of a record number of 33 female candidates.

The king still names the prime minister, but the latter now chooses the cabinet himself. For the first time, parliament can hold votes of no-confidence in the government. Under the new constitution, moreover, a third of the MPs are to be indirectly elected from Morocco's local chambers of commerce, its agricultural and professional syndicates, and its popularly elected municipal councils. In just one other Arab country, Egypt, is such corporate representation recognized. Its importance for invigorating civil society should not be underestimated. Finally, it should be noted that even during the repression of 1965–77, Morocco's political parties and its press enjoyed some freedom.

In Kuwait, the monarchy's defeat at the hands of Saddam Hussein's invading army in 1990, at a time when parliament had been dissolved, damaged royal prestige. Kuwait's experience with elected parliaments goes back to 1962 (the year after its independence), but has not been uninterrupted. In 1992, the opposition asserted itself in newly liberated Kuwait and returned to parliament with increased powers. Although the Constitution still forbids the formation of political parties, seven political "formations" took part in the 1992 voting. In addition to the election of a new parliament, the emir agreed to select six cabinet ministers from among the ranks of MPs, a first in Kuwaiti history. The new parliament has proved to be the most assertive ever, especially in fiscal matters. It has forced the government to compromise on the defense budget and the issue of military preparedness, as well as on the paramount question of how to settle the royal family's bank loans. Kuwait has enjoyed a lively and relatively free press since independence, and free debates also occur regularly in small private gatherings called *diwaaniyas*.

Egypt is perhaps the best-known case of liberalization an the Arab world. Reforms began under the late President Anwar al-Sadat in the mid-1970s, but serious progress was made only in the 1980s under President Hosni Mubarak, who succeeded the assasinated Sadat in 1981. Mubarak has pursued a policy of gradual liberalization and democratization, and has followed the same approach in the area of economic reforms and privatization. Eleven political parties now compete; seven of them were licensed by an administrative-court ruling that overturned the government's attempt to deny them legal status. The press remains mostly state run; a private opposition press has emerged and gained in confidence, but now faces a clampdown at the hands of a government made nervous by violent Muslim-extremist groups. The courts remain independent and willing to rule against the government.

Still, Egypt's democracy is marred by three major flaws. First there are the state-of-emergency laws, which have been in effect since 1981 despite strong opposition. Second, presidental elections continue to be plebiscitary rather than competitive. No contender has run against the incumbent since Gamal Abdel Nasser and his Free Officers movement abolished the constitutional monarchy in 1953. As in Mexico, the ruling party continues to maintain uninterrupted dominance. Finally, the fight against the Islamic insurgency has resulted in many human rights violations and a retrenchment in the democratization process.

Small Steps Forward

Democracy remains at the embryonic stage in some Arab states, and is nonexistent in most. It has made respectable progress in countries like Morocco, Kuwait, and Lebanon, and more modest gains in Jordan and Tunisia. In Egypt, on the other hand, it is barely holding its own, while it has suffered outright reverses in Algeria, Yemen, and Sudan. Libya and Iraq are still dictatorships; the Arabian peninsula, dominated by authoritarian monarchies, remains politically conservative.

Both practically and theoretically speaking, the best approach to gauging the status of democracy in the Arab states is to disaggregate the concept and then consider which aspects of it are making progress and where. This approach enables us to acknowledge small steps forward and not become too discouraged over the paucity of achievements. Although what has been achieved falls well short of full democratization, it nonetheless deserves recognition, assistance, and consolidation.

This essay has questioned the notion that civil society in the Arab world can perform an essential role in the democratization process. In examining the Arab states, we have discovered that government and civil society mirror each other in certain ways. Civil society reflects the government in its weakness as well as in its authoritarian attributes; it therefore has limited potential as an engine of democratization—a judgment that can only become firmer when one considers the traditional dependence of civil society on government in the Arab world.

In practice, the best way to assist civil society is to encourage the privatization of cultural and social organizations. Governments have already begun to implement enterprise privatization; they should extend the process to include cultural institutions such as schools, newspapers, journals, publishing houses, movie studios, theaters, radio and television stations, and the like. Privatization should also extend to trade unions, cooperatives, and professional syndicates—institutions which in many countries have long been dominated and manipulated by governments. Governments that manage or manipulate these organizations should give them complete freedom. In other cases, autonomy rather than total independence would be more helpful. Sports clubs, for instance, are rarely self-supporting in less developed countries, and can benefit considerably from government subsidies. In short, privatization in the above-mentioned areas is essential for improving the quality of democracy and consolidating it in Arab countries.

Too much emphasis on the concept of civil society seems to distract one from focusing on democratization. If the government's authoritarian attitudes are shared by civil society, democrats may well view the latter as part of the problem rather than part of the solution. If, on the other hand, civil society tends to be democratic, it will probably already be supporting democratization. In this case, it is more difficult (though probably less important) to know where and how to intervene.

In the long run, of course, a democratic government needs a democratic political culture, and vice versa. A glimmer of hope resides in the decisions that Arab governments have been making, usually for their own reasons, to reduce their own powers and responsibilities and to introduce democratic measures. With the passage of time, democratic practices may become firmly rooted. Second, as we have seen, governments in Arab states have had more to do with creating and promoting civil society than civil society has had to do with democratizing government. Then, too, many traditional organizations not usually included under the rubric of civil society have a contribution to make in establishing limits on governmental powers in Arab states. Finally, the sheer presence of a multiplicity of organizations (whether "democratic" or not) in the political arena serves to create checks and balances. These groups limit one another's power, and all together they tend to limit the state, thus creating a situation favorable to democracy.

19

Economic Liberalization and the Lineages of the Rentier State: Iraq and Saudi Arabia Compared

Kiren Aziz Chaudhry

As the 1980s came to a close, economic liberalism assumed a virtually uncontested position in development economics, signaling the triumph of what Hirschman called the "monoeconomics" claim.[1] The central tenet of development economics—that late developers were vulnerable to severe market failures which presaged a large role for the state in economic planning—was thoroughly discredited. Étatisme, in all its guises, came under attack, and "state shrinking," privatization, and liberalization became the watchwords of a new ascendancy in development policy. In the popular realm, economic liberalization and privatization were increasingly viewed as indicia of a grand historical teleology in which markets and democracy were triumphant.[2] In scholarly discourse, where, beginning with the first critiques of modernization theory, the emphasis had been on explaining discontinuity and diversity, the new orthodoxy reasserted the uniform laws of neoclassical economic theory.[3]

In practice, of course, market reforms have produced widely divergent results which belie neoclassical assumptions about uniform human behavior and economic processes. This essay focuses on the important but neglected issue of explaining the relative success of market reforms in two "most similar cases," Iraq and Saudi Arabia. Iraq and Saudi Arabia initiated economic liberalization programs in the 1980s, when declining oil prices depleted reserves and generated severe fiscal crises. Iraq's massive reform program was implemented quickly and without opposition. In contrast, in "laissez-faire" Saudi Arabia, a much milder liberalization program was stalled almost instantly through opposition by business elites. Identical placement in the international economy accounts for the contemporaneous initiation of reforms in the two oil exporters. The dramatically divergent reform outcomes illustrate the part of domestic political coalitions and institutional structures in determining them.

Explaining the differences between the reform efforts of Saudi Arabia and Iraq highlights the primacy of politics in shaping economic outcomes and emphasizes the centrality of historical contingencies in determining social

From *Comparative Politics* 27 (1):1–25 (1994). Reprinted by permission. Kiren Aziz Chaudhry is Associate Professor of Political Science at the University of California, Berkeley, where she also directs the Mellon Colloquium on the Moral Economy of Islam.

responses to economic liberalization. The two cases show the utility of historical analysis in discovering the relative weight of political coalitions, institutional structures, and policy in determining the outcomes of economic liberalization
programs. They suggest that the nature of initial government involvement in the
economy conditions not only the character, but also the very viability of future
efforts at market reform. I trace differences in reform outcomes to the divergent
patterns of business–government relations upheld by Iraqi and Saudi étatisme,
arguing that the nature of the state's involvement in the economy and different
patterns of business–government relations ultimately determine reform outcomes.

Taken together, the Iraqi and Saudi cases challenge the straightforward
recipes for market liberalization put forth by neoliberal analysts. In explaining
outcomes, neoliberal developmentalists have emphasized the importance of
"speed," "thoroughness," and phasing, usually in a posthoc fashion.[4] These
explanations begin with a reified concept—"the market"—and then proceed to
illustrate the ways in which particular policies either liberated or failed to liberate prices. These explanations do not capture, let alone explain, the texture and
diversity of outcomes in liberalizing late developers. The experiences of Iraq
and Saudi Arabia demonstrate how difficult it is to create and sustain functioning market economies after long periods of étatisme. They illustrate the part of
historically constituted institutional, political, and economic relationships in
forestalling "transitions" to market economies. As such, these cases provide an
opportunity to reflect on the prerequisites for the construction of market
economies and highlight the international and domestic processes through
which the institutional underpinnings necessary for the creation of market
economies can be eroded.

Drawing on the insights of the new institutional economics and on examples
from early modern Europe, this paper outlines some basic prerequisites for the
emergence of functioning market economies in late developers. It then presents
case material on the Saudi and Iraqi reforms of the 1980s. Differences in business–government relations in these two "most similar cases" are traced to the
way that key conflicts in the process of state and market building in the period
between 1930 and 1965 were resolved. Finally, both the historical and contemporary case material is situated in the broader context of economic restructuring
in late developers. I argue that initial state interventions of the 1930s, born of
administrative and political weakness or desperate economic crises, were
expanded in the 1970s and early 1980s, when many developing countries gained
access to large amounts of foreign exchange through borrowing, aid, and oil
revenues. To the extent that these revenues undercut the emergence of the institutions and norms necessary for the construction of market economies, reliance
on external capital inflows created large and perhaps insurmountable barriers to
the creation of national markets in the 1990s.

Some Prerequisites for the Creation
of Market Economies in Late Developers

It is perhaps necessary to begin by restating the most basic tenet of the institutional economists: functioning national markets cannot exist without legal, administrative, and regulatory institutions maintained by the state. Self-regulating labor and commodity markets do not automatically emerge in the absence of state action. Instead, they are conscious institutional constructs rooted in historical trajectories and based on evolving political choices. To create competitive markets, it is not enough to smash the state bureaucracy that owns, controls, or regulates goods and services; rather, the instruments of the state must be redeployed to perform the much more difficult task of indirect regulation and administration. Commonly recognized in the literature on regulation in advanced countries, this point has somehow escaped the notice of current advocates of the free market in the Third World.[5] Furthermore, the absence of state regulation results not in unbridled competition—the uncertainties of such competition are unacceptable even to entrepreneurs—but rather in collaborative agreements among producers that either provide informal rules to govern competition or directly create monopolistic conglomerates. Unregulated markets develop their own form of organization to stem uncertainty and introduce some level of predictability into commercial transactions. In the absence of state regulation, these agreements evolve into pacts that neglect the consumer and reflect only the preferences of investors and entrepreneurs.[6]

More sophisticated defenders of free market economies accept the minimal role of government in protecting collective property,[7] defining the institutional context within which labor and business bargain, protecting consumers,[8] and preventing the emergence of monopolies. The developmentalist literature generally fails to recognize, however, that the pervasiveness of the state in LDCs coexists with regulatory and administrative capacities of a specific, narrow character. Governments in the developing world may directly control large swatches of the national economy through production, distribution, and price fixing, but they rarely possess the qualities associated with Adam Smith's minimalist "watchman state." Indeed, more often than not, state capacities to regulate, define, and enforce property rights, dispense law, and tax are strictly circumscribed. To successfully make the "transition" to a market economy, these capacities become absolutely necessary. Understanding how these capacities evolve, or fail to evolve, is crucial in understanding both initial patterns of government intervention in the economy and the current crisis in the Third World and in the command economies of eastern Europe and the former Soviet Union, where attempts to liberalize the national economy have repeatedly failed. Indeed, the relative success of the Chinese reforms directly contradicts the neoliberal emphasis on speed, comprehensiveness, and the incentive generating powers of private property. Perhaps imagining that institutional capacities to regulate market economies exist in LDCs, economists have paid scant attention to the process by which precapitalist monopolies such as guilds, merchants associations, and agricultural monopolies are eroded or to the particularly difficult process of regulating and undercutting monopolies and monopolies upheld through partnerships between foreign companies and local businessmen. While recognizing that over time national markets tend to generate monopolies and create systematic social inequalities, economists neglect completely the role of state institutions in breaking down precapitalist arrangements that thwart the initial expansion of competitive market forces.

Although "transitions" to market economies were not governed by any grand teleological design, the historical account of early developers suggests several social, political, and institutional prerequisites for the creation of functioning national markets in late developers. Recognizing that there is nothing "natural" or automatic about the rise of market economies pushes us to reexamine the conventional account of the state's role in Third World economies from a different angle, one which stresses the social and political rigidities that governments must overcome to forge national markets. There are at least five basic prerequisites for the creation of national markets: political will, normative choices or political decisions, institutions, corporate interest groups, and market culture. I discuss each in turn.

Political process precedes bureaucratic restructuring and administrative resolve: the first political choice that elites must make about markets is the decision to have them. As the neoliberals recognize, there must be sufficient political will to withstand opposition from shifting coalitions among the bureaucracy, consumers, businessmen, and workers. While contemporary accounts of failed attempts to liberalize because of opposition from consumers and labor abound, the assumptions embraced by development economists kept them from appreciating the interest political and economic elites may have in forestalling the creation of functioning national markets. Creating markets is politically dangerous. Functioning markets provide opportunities for mobility that undercut lineage and traditional rights of privilege, thus threatening the status quo. Markets create inequalities in wealth that may not match existing patterns of income distribution, status, power, and entitlements; they dislocate groups in both the political and economic realms.[9]

In Europe this process was long and drawn out and was manifested in the destruction of the guild system, the erosion of the privileges of the nobility, the termination of barriers to rural–urban migration, and the displacement of rural labor. Substantial variation, reflecting differences in timing and in the organizational characteristics of social classes in the precapitalist era, existed among European cases.[10] For example, one may contrast the relatively smooth transition in eighteenth century England, where guilds were weak, with the enormous barriers to the expansion of domestic markets into the hinterlands of France and Italy, where highly organized urban guilds forestalled this expansion through sanctions and barriers to entry enforced by city administrations.[11]

As in the case of early developers, the decision to create markets was made and unmade repeatedly in late developers. Even revolutionary socialist regimes repeatedly revised the laws governing the private sector. [12] Unlike early developers, where pressures from emerging urban groups coincided with the center's expanding fiscal appetite, market reforms in contemporary LDCs are opposed both by national entrepreneurial classes accustomed to high levels of protection and by labor and consumers. Only in cases where national industrial elites have strong links to multinationals, as in Brazil, Argentina, and Mexico, is there a strong constituency for opening up to international markets.[13] As a result, most governments turn from the reforms early on.[14] Many countries, including Turkey, Egypt, Chile, and Brazil, initiated liberalization programs more than a decade before their most recent efforts only to backtrack.[15] A corollary of the argument that markets are conscious constructs—in the same vein that command economies are deliberate arrangements—is that they are based, by design or default, on political principles (that is, who gets what, why, and how)[16] and on choices about how individual resources, rights, aspirations, and possibilities are reconciled with collective ones. The tensions and convergences between collective and individual utilities have been a major theme of political economics since the discipline was born. While liberal development economists have focused exclusively on efficiency, those familiar with the debate on the role of the welfare state in advanced industrial democracies will recognize the centrality of these issues, which are often cast as conflicts between individual freedom and social good.

Market economies, whether in Bangladesh or Sweden, are based on conscious choices enforced through state regulation. Markets are not politically neutral. In contexts where debate over the shape of the market coincides with questions centered on the territorial boundaries of the state, the composition of political community, and the allocation of initial property rights, neither liberal political theory nor neoclassical economics is a useful starting point. Wrenching social struggles precede and shape the rules that govern the economy. The Hungarian and Polish debates about how to privatize expose this void at the heart of liberal theory, and disclose the persistence of a solid political culture of economic egalitarianism in these countries. It is, indeed, a symptom of the current global climate and a testimony to the depth of corruption in the collapsing socialist regimes that many appear to view the market as an equalizing force.[17] In most developing countries, political values and institutions are ephemeral, the borders of the state, formal markets, and informal markets are vaguely defined, if at all, and connections between the economic and political systems are not imbued with the legitimacy of procedural norms. Thus, the administrative burden of creating markets must be accompanied by explicit political choices, which are, in turn, heavily contested. It is not enough to legislate these "choices" from above. These decisions must, at a minimum, have the support of entrepreneurs and investors, on whose confidence the market system relies.

To call an economic regime a "market" system without reference to existing political, social, and economic relationships is essentially meaningless. The term by itself fails to describe the relative power of labor, producers, importers, and consumers or the constraints under which they interact.[18] The argument becomes clearer when one considers that England, Japan, Taiwan, and the United States have all been described as market economies, even though they have vastly different incentive systems for producers, consumers, and labor and are characterized by divergent patterns of business–government relations.[19] In the United States, the starkness of the political choices embodied in the regulatory regime are often concealed in tradition or hidden in complex tangles of evolving legislation.[20] Where the "free market" and individual freedom are definitive tenets of national ideology, raising questions about systematic biases in the market and the legal system that upholds it is considered unpatriotic, a gross violation of social gag rules. In contrast, in countries trying to make the change from nonmarket to market economies, the politics of the rules that govern the market become the focus of public debate, especially when political liberalization accompanies market reform, as in the cases of eastern Europe and the former Soviet Union. Often explicit statements of how the burdens of the market mechanism are to be allocated are necessary to craft social consensus. These choices embody repeated attempts to generate an acceptable way of dealing with the inherent tensions among individual, group, and collective utilities.[21]

The third prerequisite for the creation of markets is the resuscitation or creation of those particular administrative, extractive, and regulatory institutions that maintain the legal and administrative foundations of the market and embody normative choices of ruling coalitions.[22] These include extraction (taxation, information gathering), administration (law, property rights), regulation (currency, prices, collective goods, weights and measures, banking, buildings, licensing), repression and enforcement (police, surveillance), distribution (subsidies, transfers, gifts from funds not derived from domestic taxation), redistribution (subsidies, transfers, social insurance, welfare programs from domestic tax funds), and production.

These institutional structures cannot be assumed to exist. As I have argued elsewhere, and as the two cases in this study show, institutional development in late developers is conditioned by international economic changes and their interaction with the national political economy.[23] When the construction of basic state institutions coincides with large inflows of external capital, the resulting bureaucracies develop uneven and lopsided extractive, administrative, productive, and distributive capacities. Both the development economics and neoliberal schools view the market as a ready-made alternative to state intervention. For the neoliberals it is enough to smash the étatiste construct for functioning national markets to emerge. Development economists, for their part, view state participation in the economy as the burden of backwardness. Like the neoliberals, they assume that markets exist, with all their legal, regulatory, and administrative characteristics. They differ from the neoliberal school in their prescriptions and in their view that state control is administratively more difficult than the alternative of creating and regulating national markets.

As both the Iraqi and Saudi cases show, it is harder, under conditions of administrative weakness, to create and regulate functioning national markets in goods, labor, and finance than it is for government to manage all production itself. At a practical level, creating and regulating markets requires myriad financial, legal, and civil institutions, with stable and firm long-term commitments to regulate the actions of producers, importers, and labor, enforce contracts, and ensure the free exchange of information among economic groups.[24] In cases where the government becomes the primary employer and producer and assumes the role of setting prices, its task is reduced to monitoring the activities of corporations and agencies that it owns and manages.[25] Direct state participation in the economies of developing countries serves as an administrative shortcut and generates institutional structures entirely inappropriate for creating market economies.[26] At a purely administrative level, the involvement of the state as a producer, direct employer, and lender in countries lacking a regulatory infrastructure is simpler than, and thus preferable to, the much more elusive alternative of creating and regulating a market economy. It is thus not surprising to find that major attempts to reform the private sector in developing countries end with nationalization.[27] Contrary to what Gerschenkron suggested, government ownership is more often a response to the administrative weakness of the state in developing countries than it is a reaction to the private sector's inability to provide the skills and capital necessary for bulky investments.

Fourth, national markets can not function in contexts where primordial sentiments inform behavior in the economic realm or where overlapping ascriptive and occupational cleavages become exceedingly politicized. The complex process through which economic groups supersede ascriptive ones can be a result of state policies and/or structural economic change that undercuts ascriptive identifications, such as kinship and sectarian ties. In bureaucracies or sectoral groups where corporate and primordial identities coincide, effective bargaining is impossible. I am not suggesting that such loyalties and groups completely disappear or that, once gone, they can not reemerge. Rather, unless collective action based on common economic interests supersedes these identities, at least in the economic sphere, the allocation of goods in society can not, at the margin, be determined by the price mechanism.

In many late developers, the promotion of the old bourgeoisie often con-
flicted with the broader and more pressing political goals of state building and
national integration. On the eve of independence in many countries, the private
sector was, for a variety of historical circumstances, dominated by an ethnic,
sectarian, or regional group different from that which controlled political power.
In these cases, the most intrusive policies of the state were aimed, not at supplementing private capital to promote international competitiveness, but rather
at creating a national bourgeoisie which would support the state, if not mirror
the ethnic, religious, sectarian, and tribal characteristics of the new political and
military leadership. In Turkey for example, Ataturk viewed the *haute bourgeoisie* of Jews, Armenians, Greeks, and Europeans that had become entrenched
through the successive capitulations of the declining Ottoman Empire as a threat
to his nationalist mission. Building a "national" economy meant replacing them
with a Turkish bourgeoisie. The Egyptian, Syrian, Iraqi, Yemeni, Lebanese,
Malaysian, and Saudi cases show similar patterns, as do several African countries, including Nigeria, Kenya, and Uganda.[28] These cases suggest that state
intervention in the past had political motivations related to the more pressing
project of national integration. As the Saudi and Iraqi material demonstrates,
these motivations were critical in initial state interventions and resurfaced in a
different form when liberalization was attempted in the 1980s.

The character of the state's initial involvement in the economy conditions
future attempts to reform the system. Once government becomes involved in
governing the economy in direct, intrusive ways, it becomes entwined in mediating economic and social relationships. Stepping out of such a role is both economically disruptive and politically dangerous. Since groups do not emerge
fully grown the moment the government decides to withdraw from its economic role, a regulatory substitute for direct state involvement must be found if relatively stable agreements are to be forged between groups with conflicting interests. These substitutes include alternative institutional mechanisms for resolving conflicts and the revitalization, creation, or legalization of corporate groups
in civil society.

Fifth, and finally, the emergence of corporate groups involves the replacement of precapitalist loyalties with legally defined individual rights and corporate entitlements. This transformation is the centerpiece of what I call, for lack
of a better term, the "culture of the market." One aspect of this cluster of psychological and behavioral transformations is the acceptance and expansion of
the notion of self-interest as a legitimate and dominant motive force for economic behavior.[29] As Stephen Holmes has pointed out, the concept of self-interest, so central to economic analysis, has been progressively simplified by economists, concealing its historical specificity.[30] For market relations to exist, self-
interest must displace other forms of behavioral motivation, such as honor,
altruism, revenge, and racial and sectarian hatred. The acceptance of rational

self-interest in the western tradition was related to the emergence of impersonal market relations and the demographic, political, and social changes that accompanied them. Precapitalist forms of identification and behavior, based on primordial ties built on "nonrational" and in some cases explicitly communitarian notions, are antithetical to market relations because they introduce uncertainty and economically irrational behavior into a system that cannot sustain them.

In the contemporary setting, the "culture of the market" also means the broad acceptance of the rules that uphold this notion of self-interest. For entrepreneurs in late developers who are accustomed to functioning on the margins of the formal market (if not entirely in the black market), or alternatively in an environment dominated by bureaucrats, this acceptance requires internalizing the norms that govern success or failure in a market economy and accepting a system of uniformly applied laws. This change comes hard in countries where ascriptive attributes are a business credential. At a broader level, the often noted distrust of commercial profit and wealth, so common in LDCs, must be replaced with the notion that economic inequality can be legitimate.

Needless to say, these prerequisites are linked so closely that it is possible to identify their emergence only by tracing historical events in all their complexity. All the processes described above have been and will continue to be discontinuous. They are not linear and are, doubtless, in different stages of construction and deconstruction at a given time in any particular case. Historically, these processes evolved fitfully into systems that bear little resemblance to the liberal economists' market ideal, an ideal that has yet to be consigned to its rightful place among other ideal-types. For contemporary LDCs attempting to construct functioning market economies, these prerequisites can rightly be seen as barriers to the creation of market economies.

The Recession and the Reforms in Iraq[31] and Saudi Arabia

In the 1970s, Saudi Arabia and Iraq went through a period of intense statism under the very different labels of "laissez-faire" and "Arab Socialism," respectively. Both governments initiated economic liberalization programs in response to the recession of the 1980s. The case material begins with a summary of the reforms. I then offer a historical-institutional explanation of the two oil exporters' divergent liberalization experiments.

In Iraq, both liberalization and privatization policies were pursued simultaneously. The most far-reaching reforms were in the agricultural sector. While halting attempts to divest state-owned farms and agricultural projects had begun in 1983, privatization began in earnest in 1987 and gained momentum beginning in the fall of 1988 after the cease-fire with Iran was announced.[32] On the eve of the reforms, the government directly owned approximately 50 percent of all agricultural lands; by January 1989, 88 percent of land was privately owned, 11 percent was rented from the state by private companies, and only 1 percent was state managed.[33] Prompted by the steady decline in agricultural yields since the mid-1970s, which generated a soaring import bill and created widespread rural to urban migration, the new agricultural policies reflected a radical shift in emphasis from equity to efficiency. The privatization of agriculture transformed the social organization of rural Iraq, where farmers had previously been forced to join state-sponsored cooperatives and collective farms.[34] The extent to which the socialist and collective farming sector was held together by law alone was reflected in the spontaneous disbanding of agricultural cooperatives in the 1980s after access to government credit was delinked from membership in the cooperatives.[35] To encourage farmers, the government doubled production subsidies for wheat, rice, barley, corn, and tobacco in 1989.[36]

In addition to leasing state farms and distributing previously nationalized land, a variety of large poultry, dairy, and fishing enterprises was sold to the private sector outright. By 1989, nineteen of the state's twenty-nine poultry farms, three of the four large national fisheries, six of the large poultry feed projects, six of the ten large dairy farms and virtually all mills and bakeries were privatized.[37] In industry, the Iraqi government divested itself of seventy large factories involved in construction materials and mineral extraction, food processing, and light manufacturing in a single year.[38] As it privatized, the government removed barriers to private investment that had been in place since the nationalizations of 1964,[39] including ceilings on private investments and the law against cross-sectoral investment, designed to prevent the concentration of private capital. Tax schedules which had directly claimed up to 75 percent of profits and then allocated 25 percent of the remaining profits to workers' social security funds were annulled, and private industry was given tax holidays of ten to fifteen years.[40] Under the new Arab Investment Law, Iraq issued an open invitation to Arab investors and offered a wide range of incentives, including guarantees against nationalization, unrestricted profit repatriation, a fifteen year tax holiday, and free labor import policies.

In the service sector, the government sold small hotels and tourist resorts and leased state-owned gas stations to the private sector. In construction, which had been the preserve of private companies all along, laws that gave preferential treatment to the six large state-owned companies were repealed, forcing state construction companies to compete with private contractors even for government projects. Trade was liberalized, and export promotion policies were promulgated.[41] Imports, which had been completely state-controlled, were liberalized in 1987, with the provision that private sector imports be paid for with foreign exchange held outside the country.

Dramatic changes occurred in social policy as well. Labor unions were dissolved outright, and the minimum wage was abolished.[42] Under the laws of the

Arab Cooperative Council, founded in 1988, Yemen, Egypt, and Jordan were permitted to export labor freely to Iraq, which, along with the demobilization of the army, put further downward pressure on wages. The managerial tier of the bureaucracy was eliminated and politically neutralized when 200 general directorships and their entire staffs were dissolved by decree. The organizational structure of remaining state-owned industries was revised to encourage production through bonuses, incentives, and management autonomy. Most important, the government liberalized prices, with drastic results for the living standard of the average Iraqi consumer. Price controls on all but a handful of basic goods were removed. Previously, the state set prices by selling imported and local goods directly in the market through well-stocked retail outlets. With cuts in government imports, access to state retail outlets was restricted to high-level bureaucrats and the army under a new quota system.

Dramatic as they appear, the reforms did not signal a fundamental change in the absolute balance between public and private shares in industry. Despite a hike in private investments,[43] the government's share in manufacturing grew apace.[44] At no point did the state's share of industrial production fall below 76 percent, and the government's intent to maintain control of the "commanding heights" of the economy was signaled by several new joint ventures with foreign companies in automobile manufacturing, heavy industries, and arms manufacturing.

In terms of pure efficiency, the private sector performed well. Agricultural production doubled in one year, productivity in state-owned factories increased by 27 percent between 1987 and 1988, and labor productivity jumped by 24 percent. In agricultural products, yields doubled in a single year. Industry's performance was more difficult to evaluate because of shortages of raw materials and spare parts. The new owners managed, however, to trim labor costs dramatically, improve production methods, and substitute local inputs for imported ones.

In contrast to the Iraqi case, privatization was a minor part of reforms in Saudi Arabia, where most industrial, agricultural, and service sector businesses were privately owned to begin with. The emphasis, instead, was on taxation and on cutting budgetary outlays by withdrawing consumption and production subsidies. Income and corporate taxes were introduced, and the government announced its intent to begin collecting heretofore unenforced taxes. New labor regulations were introduced to force the private sector to replace cheap foreign labor with Saudis and assume the burden of social security payments previously covered by the government.[45]

The governments of both oil exporters liberalized their economies in response to the decline in oil prices, but the initial results of the reforms differed radically. In Iraq's broad-based reform, all previous entitlements to the regime's constituencies were abrogated without a formal revision of the regime's ideology. The majority of the population, especially the main beneficiaries of Iraqi étatisme, was hard hit: consumers, the bureaucracy, labor, and the army—the core supporters of the regime—suffered high rates of inflation and shortages in basic goods to which they were completely unaccustomed. The demobilization of the army in 1989 injected hundreds of thousands of soldiers into a work force saturated with migrant laborers from the countries of the Arab Cooperative Council, resulting in high levels of unemployment.[46]

Unlike the Iraqi liberalization, the Saudi reforms failed immediately. All those policies which affected the entrepreneurial elite, including corporate and individual taxes, zakat payments (Islamic tithes), progressive fees on the consumption of electricity, water, and gasoline, the new Labor Transfer Law (requiring businessmen to get authorization for the import of foreign labor), the Saudization Law (requiring businesses to hire Saudi labor instead of foreign workers), the new Social Insurance Law (requiring business to pay social insurance payments previously covered directly by the state budget), and the withdrawal of agricultural subsidies were successfully opposed by businessmen and their collaborators in the bureaucracy. Only those changes that affected either low income consumers or foreign workers, including fees on passports, document verification, and revised customs duties, survived.

In fact, the Saudi private sector extracted new concessions from the government in direct opposition to the state's aims of cutting spending and liberalizing prices. For the first time in its short history, the state-sponsored Saudi private sector united in the organizational forum of the Confederation of Saudi Chambers of Commerce to demand broad-based protective measures against foreign competition in commodities and contracts. Protectionist laws that had never been implemented during the boom began to be enforced in the recession,[47] winning Saudi industrialists and importers protection against "unfair dumping and competition from foreigners," more comprehensive protective tariffs, and substantial new indirect subsidies.[48] Efforts to achieve protection under the "buy Saudi" laws led to the creation of a centralized agency composed of bureaucrats and chamber representatives to ensure that all public needs were supplied with locally manufactured products.[49] Some private sector elites even suggested that the government stop announcing tenders and preselect local factories from which to purchase goods.[50] Further, in recognition of massive overcapacity in many industries, Saudi industrialists lobbied for export promotion subsidies so that they might compete in foreign markets. What privatization there was in Saudi Arabia was, unlike in Iraq, risk free, both economically and politically: like previous sales of shares in public utilities and other state industries, the sale of SABIC (Saudi Arabian Basic Industries Corporation) shares and public utility companies in 1987 was, in response to business pressure, made on the basis of a 15 percent guaranteed rate of return.

The concessions won by Saudi business were fantastic, particularly in light of declining state revenues and the high levels of government support already enjoyed by local industry. The government capitulated to business pressure quickly and completely. Strict guidelines were issued requiring contractors for state projects to use only local materials, services, transport, insurance, food, and banking. In response to contractors' demands, as expressed in the March 1985 Business Conference in Riyadh, the existing 30 percent rule stipulating that foreign contractors subcontract at least 30 percent of their projects to local companies was expanded to require all contracts to be split into small enough portions for local contractors.[51] Wide-ranging policing powers were delegated to the Confederation of Saudi Chambers to investigate complaints of local suppliers against government agencies and to link up suppliers and subcontractors with specific government projects.[52] In December 1985 an export promotion agency was set up with the participation of 160 local businessmen to study and distribute export subsidies to local manufacturers.[53] The successes of the Saudi business elite in defining the terms under which the postboom economy would function were extensive and directly challenged the stated objectives of the government.

Despite its initial successes, especially compared with the spectacular failures in Saudi Arabia, Iraq's achievements in liberalization were short-lived. Ironically, the very factors that guaranteed the initial ease with which Iraq's reforms were undertaken sealed their fate in the medium term. First, the immediate aim of the government was to save foreign exchange for rebuilding Iraq's war-ravaged economy and for new industrial and military investments. Shortages in foreign exchange thus precipitated a severe credit crunch for the private sector. By winter 1989 many factories lacked the necessary raw materials and spare parts to produce at full capacity. Declining production, shortages, and inflation emerged as serious problems. Second, the method of privatization in Iraq did not produce competition among local industrialists. Ownership of the newly privatized enterprises was highly concentrated: thirteen of the seventy large factories that were privatized were bought by one family; not counting agricultural projects, this same family owns thirty-six of the very largest industries and over 45 million square meters of land. Wary of each other, the legal system, and the regime's commitment to uphold contracts, entrepreneurs structured their new investments with the exclusive aim of insulating themselves from each other by gaining control of all upstream activities in a particular product group. Thus, as in many other cases, the sale of industries to the private sector in Iraq simply meant the transfer of public monopolies to private monopolies, with the usual consequences for consumers.

The short-term problems of the transition were amplified by the regime's inability to craft a stable set of property rights, which would have created confidence and encouraged Iraqi, Iraqi expatriate, and Arab companies to make fixed capital investments. Part of the problem was simple political insecurity, heightened by the regime's refusal to recast political values to support the eco-

nomic dislocations of the 1980s (and especially the entrepreneurs who benefited from those dislocations). By widely publicizing its withdrawal from the
economy and divesting itself of those industries that catered specifically to the
needs of the average consumer, the government freed itself from direct responsibility for inflation, shortages, and the mushrooming black market in goods,
currencies, and services. Stepping out of its heavy role in mediating the relationship between producers, on one hand, and consumers and labor, on the
other, the government placed the blame for economic hardships squarely on the
shoulders of the newly affluent private industrialists. The resentments of consumers, bureaucrats, and workers, who bore the burden of the reforms, were
perceived by businessmen as a political facility that the state could use with
impunity against the new entrepreneurs at any time. Particularly in light of the
historical acrimony between private capital and the Ba'thist state, the shaky
foundations of the political alliance on which the reforms rested made businessmen reluctant to sink large amounts of capital into any venture that did not
promise a total return on capital within two years; goods were priced with such
profit margins in mind. Partly as a consequence, inflation was rampant. Access
to dollar-denominated oil revenues freed the government from the effects of the
deteriorating value of the dinar, while Iraqi industrialists and importers using the
black market for raw materials, spare parts, and finished products passed inflation on to consumers.

Finally, although extremely efficient in directly managing production and
distribution, the Iraqi bureaucracy lacked the administrative capacity to monitor
the increasingly large private sector. These regulatory problems proved far more
difficult than anticipated, particularly since the remaining fixed-price goods
required new forms of cooperation between the bureaucracy and private enterprises. For example, a formidable reorganization of the bureaucracy became
necessary simply to ensure that bread reached consumers at the fixed prices. The
absence of investor confidence in property rights, the regime's avoidance of the
difficult process of generating support for its reforms, and the weakness of the
Iraqi state's regulatory and extractive bureaucracy plunged the Iraqi economy
into chaos at the turn of the decade and initiated the government's desperate
quest for new sources of foreign exchange.[54]

Explaining Relative Success:
The Bourgeoisie and the Bureaucracy

The differences in the Iraqi and Saudi experiences with liberalization and privatization during the recession of the 1980s can be understood by reviewing key
junctures in the economic histories of the two countries. Variations in the political coalitions which were so critical in the reform period reflected the resolution
of prior conflicts in the two oil producers which defined the contours of Saudi

and Iraqi étatisme. These conflicts cluster around critical junctures in the Saudi and Iraqi governments' initial attempts to create and regulate national markets in the crises of the 1930s, 1940s, and 1950s. In both cases, attempts to regulate the economy at the initial stages of state building generated patterns of state intervention which upheld radically different patterns of business–government relations. In the reform period, these differences came to the fore, conditioning the viability of market reforms and ultimately determining economic policy.

In the initial period of national consolidation both the Saudi and the prerevolutionary Iraqi regimes were faced by organized and monopolistic merchant classes. As in most other late developers, the global economic crises of the 1930s created a pressing need for state regulation. Simply to maintain their incumbency, both governments were pulled into economic regulation, both to provide a modicum of economic stability and to protect consumers, against organized conglomerates of guilds in Saudi Arabia and against foreign companies and their local collaborators in Iraq.

This initial confrontation between business and government differed radically in the two countries. Indeed, the character of the two business classes was very different. Iraq was under colonial rule. There, the domestic merchant class was allied with foreign companies who held legal monopolies and wielded much political power through the British administration. Saudi Arabia, in contrast, had no history of formal colonialism. The Hijazi merchant class was confined to the small enclave of the Haj economy, and the foreign presence there was minimal. The nascent Saudi bureaucracy, staffed by tribal groups from the central province of the Nejd, was too weak to legislate directly against the Hijazi guilds. In the late 1930s and 1940s the guilds and the merchants began to hoard, creating inflation and shortages and openly profiting from scarcity at the expense of consumers. The acute suffering of the general population prompted the government's first attempts to undercut the power of the guilds and protect consumers.[55] These efforts failed, and the government overcame the crisis through foreign borrowing and grants. Eventually, new technologies of coercion, transportation, and regulation tore at the complex relations of the guild system and introduced new realms of conflict that expanded the role of the state in adjudicating legal disputes among the merchants and guilds. As political authority was consolidated, the government began to decide key disputes. This new role gave the government the leverage it needed to undercut monopolistic agreements among the Hijazi business class and initiate the construction of a unified national economy.

In the 1950s, when the Saudis adopted an import substitution regime, the government worked in concert with the traditional Hijazi merchant houses, gradually expanding the domain of the economic activities it regulated. This gradually expanding regulatory role was utterly reversed in the oil boom of the 1970s, when the government used its oil revenues to create a new merchant class which mirrored the tribal and regional characteristics of the bureaucracy. There was never a direct and decisive conflict between the precapitalist guilds and merchants of the Hijaz and the Nejdis that dominated the central state. The power of the old merchant classes was eroded instead through the state's sponsorship of an alternative middle class. It was this state-created business group, which had strong kinship and business links with the bureaucracy and the political leadership, that successfully opposed the government's reforms in the 1980s.

In Iraq, too, the regulatory and administrative capacities of the state were weak. In the Mandate period, and particularly during the economic disruptions caused by the global depression and World War II, British conglomerates and local merchants with monopolies in trade and agricultural produce cooperated to create widespread shortages through hoarding and other speculative (and extremely profitable) activities.[56] During World War II this pattern became commonplace in Iraq as in other places, precipitating riots and fomenting labor unrest among Iraqi employees of the large railway, oil, and port authorities. To uphold commercial interests, the British, by their own unabashed account, frequently gained concessions from the government through political pressure, bribes, and threats.[57]

Parliament, in both the Mandate and post-Mandate periods, was dominated by a landed elite that controlled virtually all the productive farmland and had a keen interest in preserving the monopolies which collected, packaged, and transported Iraq's substantial agricultural exports.[58] Still, so great was the economic hardship caused by the speculation and profiteering of the private sector during this period, and so widespread was the threat to the incumbency of the regime, that the government attempted, albeit unsuccessfully, to legislate against the "neutral" workings of the "market."

Unlike Saudi Arabia, business–government relations during the British Mandate of Iraq, as well as during the post-"independence" period, were marked by dramatic confrontations and devastatingly costly failed attempts to enforce price controls and curtail profiteering.[59] Comprehensive attempts to regulate the economy began early on, first in 1939 with Regulation 58, governing "Life during International Crisis,"[60] and then in 1942 with the "Law Regulating Economic Life of Iraq." The intention of the latter was to prevent monopolies and price manipulation and to maintain required supplies of basic goods. To achieve these aims, the government began to restrict exports, fix prices, and import basic commodities to fill domestic consumption needs.[61]

The Iraqi regulations failed miserably. For a variety of reasons, including weak enforcement capacities, interference from the British authorities, the involvement of powerful foreign companies, and the cohesiveness of the local merchant group, the private sector was able to ignore the law. The results were devastating. Speculation, hoarding, and profiteering abounded, resulting in inflation rates of between 200 and 300 percent in the late 1930s and early 1940s,[62] which continued on and off through the early 1960s.[63] The response of the government to these repeated administrative failures began with direct entry into trade to alleviate shortages and lower prices[64] and reached its zenith with the creation of government monopolies in agricultural goods.[65]

Together, regulatory struggles and the pressing need to create a unified national market were linked up with the problem of regime maintenance and nation building in both countries. Historically, both regimes were dominated by sectarian, regional, and tribal minorities which were different from, and opposed by, the commercial elites. Both the Saudi and Ba'thist regimes assumed political power despite the opposition of traditional commercial classes composed of opposing regional and ascriptive groups; both faced the task of constructing a social base of support while undercutting the economic dominance of their rivals.

Unlike Saudi Arabia, where the divide between the old Hijazi commercial class and the Nejdi state was particularly stark, the social cleavages between business and state elites in Iraq underwent complex changes between 1930 and 1968. The commercial class of Iraq had historically been dominated by the Christian and Jewish minorities. Until 1950, when the British arranged to airlift the vast majority of Iraqi Jews to Israel, commerce and banking were dominated by a small Jewish minority who collaborated with British companies in trade, finance, and service monopolies.[66] Meanwhile, an incipient Shi'i merchant class was growing in the south, largely in response to the Iraqi government's attempts to attract capital: in 1932, in response to the mass migration of Iraqis to Iran during the acute economic depression, the Iraqi government offered Persians immunity from taxation for five years if they became Iraqi citizens.[67] Then, in the early 1950s, when annual migrations of Iraqi laborers to Kuwait reached 35,000 to 50,000, a law designed to attract Kuwaiti capital was passed which granted Kuwaitis the right to own land, commercial establishments, and industrial property in Iraq. Many rich Kuwaitis and Persians settled in Basra,[68] and after 1951 a mix of Persian and Kuwaiti merchant families, the vast majority of whom were Shi'i, replaced the Jewish merchant community.[69] On the eve of independence, both the landed and commercial elites of Iraq were dominated by Shi'is.

In both Iraq and Saudi Arabia, the deep primordial cleavages between the state and business meant that the regulation of business was tightly entwined with pressing issues of national integration and state building. This linkage of economic and political tasks was expressed in a particularly stark form in Iraq, as a consequence of the colonial legacy and the strength of private sector conglomerates. Whether by historical accident or colonial design, the military was composed of a different primordial group than the business class. By 1958, when the Hashemite monarchy was overthrown, Shi'is dominated the ranks of both the landed and merchant elite while the civil service and the army remained under control of the Sunni minority.[70]

After the 1958 coup in Iraq, business leaders feared the populist agendas of the Sunni military leaders who came to dominate politics The most basic threat to the commercial elite was the newly independent government's interest in expanding competition, protecting consumers. and undercutting the long-standing monopolistic pacts that bound domestic commercial elites to the foreign corporations that had thrived under colonial rule.

During Abd al-Karim Qasim's tenure immediately following the 1958 coup, private investors, largely of the Shi'i south, withheld industrial investments and created shortages in basic commodities in an attempt to destabilize a regime which was seen as being too close to the Communist Party. Despite Qasim's apparent support of local industry, his populism was based on economic measures—limits on profits from consumer goods, cuts in prices and rents, and land reforms—that were hardly designed to win the support of the commercial classes.[71] The series of coups that followed Qasim's regime marked the ascendance of the army and the initiation of the purging of Shi'i elements within the Ba'th party. Then, in 1964, under the guise of preparing for economic and political union with Nasser's Egypt, the regime of Abd al-Salam Arif, closely identified with the Sunni north, nationalized all agricultural lands, industry, banking, insurance, and services, which resulted after the consolidation of land reforms in the 1970s in the virtual elimination of the top layer of the largely Shi'i commercial and landed elite.

The triumph of Iraq's "republican moment" was thus not supported by its entrepreneurial elites. While the nationalizations of 1964 are often attributed to the Iraqi government's preparations for economic union with Egypt, more likely reasons for the seizure of private property can be found in the speculation, capital flight, and shortages that racked the economy between the creation of the Joint Presidential Council with Egypt in May and the final nationalizations in mid-July. Having witnessed the fate of Syria's business elites in the short-lived United Arab Republic, Iraq's Shi'i economic elites had both class-based and sectarian reasons to oppose the unity agreement with Egypt. The behavior of the private sector at this juncture added to already high levels of inflation.[72] From incremental and sporadic entry into commodity markets and banking coupled with spates of unsuccessful regulation, the Iraqi state finally began to manage all aspects of the economy from imports and production to distribution and retailing. Subsequent regulation restricted the private sector to the confines of small industry, retailing, and transportation.

In both Saudi Arabia and Iraq, the need to protect consumers from dysfunctioning markets was entwined with the political goal of eliminating the stronghold of commercial elites bent on subverting the political power of governments controlled by opposing "primordial" groups. The divergent paths that the two countries took are explained by differences in the character of the initial and continuing confrontations between the regulatory aims of the government and the interests of the two highly monopolistic and powerful private sectors. The abrupt nationalization in Iraq was the result, not of a stronger and more powerful state (that came later), but rather of the insularity and strength of the domestic private sector and its foreign collaborators who were dedicated, for a variety of reasons, to the destabilization of the populist regime of Qasim and the Sunni-dominated regimes that followed him in 1963 and 1968.

The structure of the two economies and Iraq's colonial experience are critical in explaining the differences in the severity of the confrontations between business and state. Unlike the Hijazi commercial class, whose activities were confined to a small enclave centered around the annual pilgrimage to Mecca, the powerful foreign companies and their collaborators among Iraqi businessmen extended into all aspects of Iraq's economy, and the export business led to substantial investments in infrastructure that generated enclaves of modern working-class activism.

The original confrontations between the governments of the two oil states and their respective private sectors marked a critical juncture that determined the character of state intervention in the economy over the long term. In the 1970s, when enormous inflows of oil revenues expanded the economic role of the state in both cases and empowered both regimes to create new social bases of support in society, the changes conformed to the outcomes of prior struggles between government and business. In Saudi Arabia, state contracts, loans, gifts, and a variety of formal and informal distributive measures were used to create a large new entrepreneurial elite with strong kinship and business ties to the bureaucracy and political elites. In Iraq, oil revenues expanded the government's role in direct ownership and control of industry, trade, agricultural services, and even retailing. Through direct setting of wages and prices, the Iraqi government cultivated a broader level of economic dependency among labor and consumers, who were protected from inflation during the 1970s and the subsequent eight years of war with Iran. The Iraqi state's core supporters were located in the army and the bureaucracy. In contrast to the Saudi case, so acute was the Sunni government's sense of threat from the Shi'i commercial classes and their cosectarians, who form a majority of the Iraqi population, that it took every opportunity to eliminate the Shi'i leadership in both the economic and the socioreligious realms through mass deportations, imprisonment, and violence. Key positions in state institutions increasingly become the preserve of individuals from the village of Takrit and its environs, many of whom were related to Saddam Hussain, chairman of the Revolutionary Command Council. By the 1980s, then, both regimes managed to eliminate, replace, or neutralize the old commercial elites, but through remarkably different processes.

In the recession of the 1980s, as both regimes tried to withdraw the flow of oil wealth from their respective clients in society, the forces of opposition to the liberalization policies were also very different. Variations in the initial outcomes of the reforms were the result of the different sources of social opposition to the new economic policies. In Saudi Arabia, where a large state-sponsored private sector existed, the commission entrepreneurs joined with the bureaucracy, with whom they had strong business, tribal, and financial links, to successfully oppose the state's attempts to liberalize the economy. Unwilling to withstand the disruption that the policies would have created in existing patterns of wealth and privilege, and lacking the requisite political will to override their objections, the government withdrew the austerity measures almost immediately. In Iraq, where no such state-sponsored class existed, the regime overcame social opposition to the reforms by neutralizing key segments of the bureaucracy and labor at the onset and was able to push through a comprehensive reform package. Political will alone, however, was not enough. Despite the Iraqi regime's willingness to use draconian measures, its privatization and liberalization program quickly showed signs of failure. This failure was largely a consequence of the regime's inability to create a system of property rights that was stable enough to attract the level of private investment necessary to sustain the successes of early market reforms.

Forging States and Creating Markets in Late Developers

The Saudi and Iraqi experiences speak volumes about the obstacles to the expansion of domestic markets in late developers. They reveal the process by which national markets are formed and the administrative and social rigidities that must be overcome for them to function. When examined in light of broader processes of state building, national integration, and the creation of a social consensus for radical shifts in economic policy, their programs shed light not only on the conflicting pressures confronting a very special subset of late developers with intimate ties to the global economy, but also on the common experiences of late developers in the twentieth century.

Tracing the differences in the ideologies of the two regimes is of little help in explaining outcomes. Unlike the Soviet and eastern European cases, the reforms in Iraq and Saudi Arabia neither stemmed from nor generated ideological revisions. No attempts were made to redefine the political values embodied in economic relations. Both regimes are authoritarian, but they are formally committed to fundamentally different ideologies. Saudi Arabia professes an ultraconservative version of Hanbali Islam as its political ideology and has always upheld its commitment to a laissez-faire economy. The Ba'thist regime that has dominated Iraq since 1968, in contrast, is a secular socialist regime that has strong similarities to European variants of fascism. The real political economies of both countries embody perplexing ambiguities. Ideologies aside, the role of the state in both economies during the period under consideration was large enough so that the creation of classes and the distribution of wealth on a wide scale were seen as part of the normal range of policy options.

If one accepts the view that the creation of functioning national markets requires basic institutional, social, and political changes rather than the simple withdrawal of state controls on prices and the sale of state property to the private sector, the dirigisme of the Third World becomes more comprehensible. The argument can be stylized as follows.

The regulatory capacities of LDCs were weak to begin with. The governments of many developing countries confronted the task of creating domestic markets in commodities and labor at short notice, immediately following the abrupt withdrawal of colonial powers and with the explicit intent of replacing trade with domestic manufactured goods. Evidence from cases as diverse as India, Pakistan, Iraq, and Egypt suggests that governments in late developers became directly involved in the economy by nationalizing foreign and domestic assets and financial institutions only after long and frustrating failures to tax, redistribute, and regulate the behavior of private actors following decolonization or during the systemic crises of the 1930s and World War II. These exogenous shocks mark the juncture at which the policies most harshly criticized by the economic liberals were initiated. The populist agendas of the Nassers, the Bhuttos, and the Qasims demanded redistribution and regulation of wages and prices which, in theory, could have been effected through a strong regulatory and administrative apparatus by taxing and regulating private industry, commerce, and agriculture without directly taking over productive assets.

In many cases nationalization and direct controls on the private sector can best be explained, not by private sector weakness, but rather by the inordinate strength and cohesion of private elites and their ability to thwart the government's regulatory policies. The import substitution programs adopted by most developing countries in the 1950s and 1960s involved the state in directly planning and controlling domestic investment and prices. Unlike export-led industrialization, import substitution programs do not require governments to hold down domestic wages.[73] Regimes with weak domestic legitimacy often designed elaborate redistributive policies based on directly controlling the means of production and fixing wages. Similarly, prices for basic necessities were often directly controlled through state ownership. Import substitution required highly intrusive regulation that enabled weak administrative apparatuses to directly manipulate the economy but constrained the ability of business to take advantage of new opportunities. The systems of licensing, preferential finance, and price manipulation became perverted over time, as the instruments of economic control were increasingly used to serve the political ends of incumbent regimes.

In the decade between 1973 and 1983, the inflow of wealth to many developing countries in the form of aid, loans, oil revenues, labor remittances, and investment further curtailed the need for market reform and encouraged the expansion of state control of the economy. It is critical to note that the character of this expanded role was uneven: the expansion of productive and credit-giving functions was not matched by advances in regulatory and information-gathering capacities. The bulk of external capital flows accrued directly to the state, but even in countries where the sources of external capital, such as labor remittances, were privately controlled, the institutional response of the state was to shrink regulatory institutions and pursue the most politically convenient regulatory strategies possible. Access to external capital inflows had a profound influence on the institutional, social, and political structures of recipient countries in ways that make market reforms more difficult now than at earlier periods.

Thus, in sharp contrast to the neoliberal position, the evidence presented here suggests that LDCs may be less prepared to undertake genuine market reforms now than at any time in their postindependence history. The role of external capital inflows in retarding and undermining the very institutions, norms, and social changes that are critical to the creation of domestic market economies is nowhere clearer than in major oil exporters, where they influenced the structure and functions of state bureaucracies by undercutting regulatory and extractive institutions and augmenting the role of the state in direct production and distribution.[74] Oil revenues, like state-controlled loans and aid, saved the government from having to tax its population directly and enhanced the ease with which the state could ameliorate political conflict by directly distributing resources through gifts, subsidies, loans, and state contracts. During the 1970s, distribution and direct state control of production became the primary, if not sole, instruments through which oil exporters regulated the economy. Along with extractive and regulatory institutions, capital markets, commercial law, banking, and insurance industries remained underdeveloped; the old bourgeoisie was eliminated or driven into the lower echelons of the business community and replaced by bureaucratic and private elites with strong links to the state.

The inflow of oil revenues to state coffers in the 1970s expanded the role of the state in major oil exporters to such a degree that even in those countries that professed to have market economies it was difficult to distinguish between the public and private sectors. In Kuwait, Saudi Arabia, Libya, the UAE, Iraq, and Iran, oil revenues comprised over 50 percent of the GNP in the 1970s, giving the government ample funds simultaneously to subsidize producers, importers, and consumers. The volume of these subsidies was such that the price mechanism in labor, commodity, and financial markets ceased to function. The key difference between countries like Iraq and Libya on the one hand and Kuwait and Saudi Arabia on the other, was not the extent of state interference in the economy, but rather the size and composition of the state's client groups. The "socialist" oil states entered directly into production themselves, taking over industry, agriculture, trade, and services, and they used their control to uphold the living standards of a broad base of consumers. The "capitalist" oil states, in contrast, distributed oil wealth to create clients in society who had strong primordial links to bureaucrats and decision makers.

Through a variety of means, including state contracts and consumption, interest free lending, and patronage, a class of private sector "commission entrepreneurs" emerged in each country during the boom years. In all but the Kuwaiti case these groups were distinct from the old merchant classes. While the size of the client groups varied a great deal, oil states uniformly practiced corporatism on a grand scale, using distributive policies to create economic groups as a base of social support and to ameliorate conflict among sectoral, occupational, economic, and social groups. Explicitly designed to depoliticize the population, these distributive policies forestalled the emergence of class conflict and public debate about the ends of development and growth. In all cases, governments deliberately destroyed independent civil institutions while generating others designed to facilitate the political aims of the state. In Saudi Arabia, Iraq, and Libya, governments deliberately destroyed the strongholds of the old private sector, although the means employed to this end varied greatly. The new private sector elites emerged in a peculiar economic period where quick profits and low risks were the norm. In the highly insulated business environment of the 1970s, these elites failed to develop the entrepreneurial skills that would enable them to withstand either domestic or international competition. Social relations between business and labor, importers and exporters, and other subgroups of the business community were heavily mediated by the state. As the bureaucracy and the political leadership themselves represented particular sectarian, regional, and tribal groups, even in "capitalist" oil exporters, economic success depended less on skill than on ties with the government. In this context, the cluster of behavioral and psychological developments described above as the "culture of the market" not only failed to emerge, but also was deliberately subverted to prevent the rise of social conflict and political opposition.

In the recession, when oil exporters faced pressure to cut state spending, rationalize prices, and solicit the participation of the private sector in economies suddenly less insulated from risk, none of the social and institutional prerequisites for creating competitive domestic markets existed. These societies and governments were singularly unprepared for the untempered ravages of the international economy which were visited upon them during the recession. Extractive and regulatory institutions had atrophied; accounting procedures in the private sector were primitive; and formal links among members of the commercial-industrial class and labor were weak. In institutional terms, the task facing the Iraqi and Saudi governments in the recession was nothing less than a thorough reform of the public and private sectors. This task entailed forging national regulatory, legal, and extractive institutions and their ancillary information gathering and enforcement agencies and creating legal, accounting, and disclosure requirements for private business elites who had yet to experience the burdens of regulation. The difficulties of these tasks were intensified by the political economy of the prior decade. The oil state's abundant resources in the 1970s and early 1980s had allowed it to postpone the creation of alternative mechanisms for the expression and reconciliation of conflicting economic claims and interests. At the same time, the distributional patterns of government spending intensified primordial and regional divisions. As a result, the confrontation between state and social forces during the mid- and late 1980s was particularly stark, both because of the cumulative effects of political abstinence and because primordial sentiments were enmeshed in the struggle between groups vying to protect their economic interests.

In this context, fiscal crises quickly became political crises. Governments with large client bases were forced to withdraw the distributive policies of the 1970s and confront client social groups that opposed austerity measures. The recession forced the oil states to meet the fiscal requirements of the state in a political context where granting participation in return for taxes was ruled out at the onset. One result of the apolitical years of the 1970s was that, when the recession came, it was unclear who was entitled to bargain on policy issues. The boom years favored individual or primordial group strategies over sector-specific ones, and the awareness of convergent or conflicting economic interests remained dormant. Few legal, organized civil groups existed to aggregate and voice collective interests. The recession forced the government to step out of a direct mediating role and to replace the distributive bureaucracy with institutions that would provide for the aggregation of interests and the resolution of conflicting claims, tasks which were made more difficult by the patterns of state involvement in the economy during the previous decade.

Conclusion

In viewing markets as "natural" constructs that blossom without the pernicious influence of the state, neoliberals skirt the critical question of why late developers failed to create functioning national markets to begin with. The notion that direct state participation in the economy is a special burden for developing countries assumes not only that markets with all their legal, regulatory, and administrative characteristics exist, but also that state control is administratively more difficult than the alternative of creating and regulating national markets. Examination of how the exigencies of national integration, the sacrificing or maintaining of distributional coalitions, and the simple act of staying in power have influenced economic policy is crucial not only in explaining the dirigisme of the developing world, but also in understanding the severe problems confronting contemporary efforts to forge national markets in a finance-poor global economy.

While the immediate cause of the failure of the Saudi attempts and the initial success of the Iraqi government is to be found in the organizational strength of social groups opposed to economic restructuring, both governments failed in achieving even a partial transition to a market economy. To the extent that these cases illustrate the diverse sources of opposition and resistance to "market forces," they might be instructive to the proponents of the new economic liberalism. If nothing else, the Saudi case shows that the private sector is not always in favor of "markets." Indeed, the absence of a large and pampered entrepreneurial elite was critical in Iraq's initial reform successes. The issue of whether the initial process of market reform might be easier in completely state-dominated economies where a protected entrepreneurial class does not exist might be one focus of future inquiry.

On the other hand, the barriers to sustained investment necessary for competitive, functioning markets are likely to be high in cases where potential investors fail to gain confidence in the regime's commitment to free enterprise. The Iraqi case demonstrates the importance of confidence and clearly defined property rights in enabling initial successes to be transformed into lasting changes. In the economic crisis that followed the transfer of public monopolies to private monopolies, the resentment of labor and consumers against the new private sector elite in Iraq grew. Having distanced itself from the shortages and inflation that accompanied the privatization measures, the regime would certainly have won wide support if it had decided to renationalize, repeating the pattern of profiteering, failed regulation, and nationalization that unfolded between 1958 and 1964.

While major oil exporters are unique in a variety of ways, they share certain experiences with other late developers. Although the particular contours of the liberalization process and the conflicts it evokes vary according to national circumstances, these cases demonstrate how heavy reliance on external capital inflows can undercut the institutional and social changes necessary for successful economic liberalization. Entrepreneurial elites in all countries with import substitution regimes are accustomed to levels of protection and privilege that are inconsistent with market reform. As in the Saudi pattern, it would not be surprising to find that resistance to economic liberalization is located precisely in the upper echelons of the private sector in developing countries. In contrast, in cases where the dominance of the state has been almost complete, as in Iraq, the initial barriers to reform may be easily surmounted with the requisite political will. To last, however, initial successes require complex institutional and social changes that are as likely to create the conditions for renationalization as to lay the foundations for a market economy. Even in these "most similar cases," the social barriers to reform differ. Focusing on key junctures in the economic his-

tories of Iraq and Saudi Arabia illuminates the ways that very different economic regimes emerged in major oil exporters. Thus, despite the deep similarities in their economic structures, government attempts to craft and to implement
radical changes in economic policy can be expected to yield very different
results. Policies may have their genesis in a uniform set of economic crises, but
outcomes can be understood only through historically grounded comparative
analyses in the classical tradition of political economy.

Notes

I am grateful for Ken Dubin's comments on earlier drafts of this paper. The research
for this paper was conducted under the auspices of the Harvard Academy for
International and Area Studies, with the Support of the Kukin Fellowship. Field work
in Iraq was funded by the Social Science Research Council. Field work in Saudi
Arabia was funded by the Fulbright-Hays Commission and the Social Science
Research Council. The views presented here do not represent the opinions of any
funding organization.

1   Albert Hirschman, "Rise and Decline of Development Economics," in Albert
    Hirschman, *Essays in Trespassing* (New York: Cambridge University Press), pp.
    1–24.
2   Francis Fukuyama, *The End of History and the Last Man* (New York: Free Press,
    1991). See also Ian S. Prybyla, "The Road from Socialism: Why, Where, What and
    How," *Problems of Communism* 40 (January–April 1991), pp. 1–17.
3   See, for example, Hernando De Soto, *The Other Path: The Invisible Revolution in
    the Third World* (New York: Harper and Row, 1989); P. T. Bauer, *Dissent on
    Development: Studies on the Debate in Development Economics* (Cambridge, Mass.:
    Harvard University Press, 1972); Robert Bates, *Markets and States in Tropical Africa*
    (Berkeley: University of California Press, 1981); Robert Bates, "Governments and
    Agricultural Markets in Africa," in Robert Bates, ed., *Toward a Political Economy of
    Development: A Rational Choice Perspective* (Berkeley: University of California
    Press, 1988), pp. 331–58; Deepak Lal, *The Poverty of Development Economics;* Bela
    Balassa et al., "Toward Renewed Growth in Latin America" (Washington, D.C.:
    Institute for International Economics, 1986).
4   Bela Balassa, "Policy Choices in the Newly Industrializing Countries," and Jeffrey
    Sachs, "Poland and Eastern Europe: What Is to Be Done?" in Andras Koves and Paul
    Marer, eds., *Foreign Economic Liberalization: Transformations in Socialist and
    Market Economies* (Boulder: Westview Press, 1991), pp. 71–80 and 235–46, respec-
    tively: Armeane Choksi, et al. "The Design of Successful Trade Liberalization
    Policies," in Koves and Marer, eds., p. 55; Thorvaldur Gylfason and Marian
    Radetzki, "Does Devaluation Make Sense in the Least Developed Countries?"
    Economies Development and Cultural Change 40 (October 1991), 1–25; Bela
    Balassa, *New Directions in the World Economy* (New York: New York University

Press, 1989), p. 27.

5 See essays in Roger Noll, ed., *Regulatory Policy and the Social Sciences* (Berkeley: University of California Press, 1985). For a critique of the British neoliberals, see Dieter Helm, "The Economic Borders of the State." Alan Ryan, "Value-Judgments and Welfare," Amartya Sen, "The Moral Standing of the Market," and Christopher Allsopp. "The Macro-economic Role of the State," all in Dieter Helm, ed., *The Economic Borders of the State* (London: Oxford University Press, 1989).

6 Yair Aharoni, *The Evolution and Management of State Owned Enterprises* (Cambridge, Mass.: Ballinger Publishing Company, 1986), pp. 69 and 105; and Mitchel Abolafia, "Self-Regulation as Market Maintenance: An Organization Perspective," in Noll. ed., pp. 312–43.

7 Fred Hirsch, *The Social Limits to Growth* (Cambridge, Mass.: Harvard University Press, 1976).

8 See Laura Nader and Claire Nader, "A Wide Angle on Regulation: An Anthropological Perspective," and Carol MacLennan, "Comment," in Noll, ed., pp. 146–48.

9 Ivan Szelenyi, "Eastern Europe in an Epoch of Transition: Toward a Socialist Mixed Economy?" in Victor Nee and David Stark, eds., *Remaking the Economic Institutions of Socialism: China and Eastern Europe* (Stanford: Stanford University Press, 1989), pp. 208–32.

10 For different views. compare Barrington Moore, *Social Origins of Dictatorship and Democracy* (Boston: Beacon Press, 1966), pp. 413–32: Gregory M. Luebbert, *Liberalism, Fascism, or Social Democracy: Social Classes and the Political Origins of Regimes in Interwar Europe* (New York: Oxford University Press, 1991); and Alexander Gerschenkron, *Economic Backwardness in Historical Perspective* (Cambridge, Mass.: Belknap Press of Harvard University Press, 1962).

11 David Landes, *The Unbound Prometheus: Technological Change and the Industrial Revolution in Western Europe from 1750 to the Present* (Cambridge: Cambridge University Press, 1987), p. 134.

12 See Benjamin Cohen and Gustav Ranis, "The Second Postwar Restructuring," in Gustav Ranis, ed., *Government and Economic Development* (New Haven: Yale University Press, 1971), pp. 231–468, for a discussion of the first such "liberal" shift in LDCs.

13 Pierre Ostiguy, "Privatization Processes: The Latin American Experience in Perspective," unpublished paper, University of California, Berkeley, May 1991.

14 The experiences of African, Turkish, Indian, Egyptian, Algerian, Tunisian, Libyan, and Latin American countries have been far from encouraging. See Atul Kohli, "Politics of Economic Liberalization in India," John Staatz et al., "Cereals Market Liberalization in Mali," Pan Yotopoulos, "The (Rip) Tide of Privatization: Lessons from Chile," Henry Bienen and John Waterbury, "The Political Economy of Privatization in Developing Countries," Peter Heller and Christian Schiller, "The Fiscal Impact of Privatization, with Some Examples from Arab Countries," and William Glade, "Privatization in Rent-Seeking Societies," all in *World Development*

(1989): Jon Marks, "Algeria Breaks with the Past," *Middle East Economic Development (MEED)*, Apr. 14, 1989, "Infighting Leads to PM's Dismissal," *MEED*, Sept. 22, 1989, "Setting the Course for Reform," *MEED*, Sept. 29, 1989, "Reform Gets Only Qualified Support," *MEED*, Dec. 15, 1989: Angus Hindley, "Gaddafi Keeps a Check on Reform," *MEED*, Nov. 17, 1989: Roger Leeds, "Malaysia: Genesis of a Privatization Transaction," and Elliot Berg, "The Liberalization of Rice Marketing in Madagascar," both in *World Development* (1989).

15 Joseph Ramos, "Stabilization and Adjustment Policies in the Southern Cone, 1974–1983," *CEPAL Review* (April 1985), 85–109: and Victor Tokman, "Global Monetarism and Destruction of Industry," *CEPAL Review* (August 1984), 107–121.

16 Cf. John Zysman, *Governments, Markets and Growth: Financial Systems and the Politics of Industrial Change* (Ithaca: Cornell University Press, 1983), pp. 11–80.

17 David Stark, "Privatization in Hungary: From Plan to Market or from Plan to Clan?" *East European Politics and Societies* 4 (Fall 1990), 351–92.

18 Studies of the Japanese economic system and successful cases of intervention in Korea, Taiwan, Singapore, and Hong Kong have been at the forefront in reexamining the various forms of state intervention within a market system. See Roben Wade, "East Asia's Economic Success: Conflicting Perspectives, Partial Insights, Shaky Evidence," *World Politics* 44 (January 1992), 270–320.

19 Peter Hall, *Governing the Economy: The Politics of State Intervention in Britain and France* (New York: Oxford University Press, 1986), pp. 34–37, 229–83.

20 See MacLennan, "Comment," in Noll. ed., esp. pp. 168–69.

21 John Zysman and Gabriel Eichler, "L'apres Communisme: Une troisieme voie?" *Le Débat* 59 March April 1990).

22 The list deliberately excludes representative institutions. While it is clear that market economies require access to information, they do not require mass democracies. Issues of political control and the substance of the property regimes upheld by and embodied in state institutions are addressed in the case material.

23 Kiren Aziz Chaudhry, "The Myths of the Market and the Common History of Late Developers," *Politics and Society* 21 (September 1993).

24 Mustapha Nabli and Jeffrey Nugent, "The New Institutional Economics and Its Applicability to Development," and Douglass North, "Institutions and Economic Growth: An Historical Introduction," both in *World Development* 17 (1989), 1333–47, 1319–32.

25 In particular, as Nicholas van de Walle has noted, information costs are higher for state regulation than for state ownership. Nicholas van de Walle, "Privatization in Developing Countries: A Review of the Issues," *World Development* 17 (1989), 607.

26 Recent work on taxation presents powerful evidence for this claim. See Athar Hussain and Nicholas Stern, "Economic Reforms and Public Finance in China," Gur Ofer, "Fiscal Development and Economic Reforms in the Soviet Union, 1991: Can a Gradual Reform Work?," Robert Holzmann, "Tax Reform in Countries in Transition: Central Policy Issues," and Berry W. Ickes and Joel Slemrod, "Tax Implementation Issues in the

Transition from a Planned Economy," all in Pierre Pesticau, ed., *Public Finance in a World of Transition,* supplement to *Public Finances/Finances Publiques* 47 (1992).

27 Van de Walle, pp. 602–603.

28 Paul Kennedy, *African Capitalism: The Struggle for Ascendancy* (London: Cambridge University Press, 1990), esp. chs. 1–4.

29 Albert Hirschman, *The Passions and the Interests: Political Arguments for Capitalism before its Triumph* (Princeton: Princeton University Press, 1977).

30 Stephen Holmes, "The Secret History of Self-Interest," in Jane Mansbridge, ed., *Beyond Self-Interest* (Chicago: University of Chicago Press, 1990), pp. 267–86.

31 The case material presented here draws heavily on material collected in Iraq and on interviews of businessmen, bureaucrats, policymakers and labor leaders in Baghdad in October–December 1989.

32 See Robert Springborg, "Infitah, Agrarian Transformation and Elite Consolidation in Contemporary Iraq," *Middle East Journal* 50 (1986).

33 Government of Iraq, 1988 Statistical Yearbook, p. 130. Government-owned grain farms were huge: two of these, for example, were 29,000 and 25,300 donums each.

34 Government of Iran, *Statistical Yearbook,* 1988, p. 128.

35 From 1,635 cooperatives with 23,109 members in 1975, the number of cooperatives plummeted to 713 by the end of 1988. Collective farms declined from seventy-nine to seven: and specialized cooperatives shrank from 173 in 1975 to fifty-two in 1988. See Robin Theobald and Sa'ad Jawad, "Problems of Rural Development in an Oil-Rich Economy: Iraq 1958–1975," in Tim Niblock, ed., *Iraq: The Contemporary State* (London: Croom Helm, 1982), p. 204: and Government of Iraq, Statistical Yearbook, 1988, p. 125.

36 Total subsidies for grains were over ID 300 million in 1988. The subsidized grain purchase prices were raised in September 1988 as follows (all figures in Iraqi dinars per ton): wheat, 270 (from 170); rice, 500 (from 400); barley, 180 (from 120): corn, 550 (from 450). Whether or not these subsidies raised the domestic price of these products above their international prices depends on whether the dinar is valued at the official or black market rates. For example, the international price of wheat is about $170/ton. Using the official and black market exchange rates, the domestic purchase price of wheat in 1989 would have been $891 and $90, respectively. Even if calculated at the black market rate, at which prices were well below international prices, the difference between the price at which wheat was bought and the price at which the government provided it to the private bakeries, $80 per ton, represented a subsidy to consumers .

37 All of these enterprises were very large. For example, the capacity of each poultry farm was between 100 and 270 million eggs. The capacity of the dairy farms was at least 800 milk cows each. In at least three cases, the dairy farms were in mint condition. At the end of 1989 the government still owned two of the twelve mills and fourteen of the twenty bakeries.

38 Sixty-six factories were sold by auction, and four were transferred to the "mixed sec-

tor," in which the Industrial Bank, individuals, and other mixed sector companies hold shares.

39 By 1983 the investment ceilings had already been raised to ID 2 million and ID 5 million for solely owned and limited share companies, respectively.

40 In 1987 the maximum tax on industrial profits was lowered to 35 percent, then in 1989 all industries were given a ten-year tax holiday.

41 Export promotion took the form of preferential access to foreign currency from the state at a one to one ratio (compared with the official rate of ID/3.3$ and the black market rate of 3.3ID/$), provided that export earnings covered the import credit by 120 percent within two years.

42 The right to form new unions applies only to private sector establishments with over fifty workers, a category which covers only 8 percent of the total industrial work force. Prior to its dissolution, the General Union of Iraqi Labor had a membership of 1.75 million.

43 Licenses granted for private factories to be set up with the use of foreign exchange held abroad increased from seven in 1987 to sixty-three in 1988 to 117 in 1989. However, total investments in these factories was small, comprising only ID 17 m in 1988 and ID 33 m in 1989. At the official exchange rate, the 1989 figure comes to about $99 million. Most of the planned private investment is in plastics (60 percent), the rest in textiles and construction (15 percent), food processing (15 percent), and metal industries (10 percent).

44 Government investment in downstream petrochemical projects in 1989 alone was $3 billion.

45 Kiren Aziz Chaudhry, "The Price Of Wealth: Business and State in Labor Remittance and Oil Economies" (Ph.D. diss., Harvard University, 1990).

46 The Arab Cooperative Council (ACC) with Egypt, Jordan, and Yemen as members was formed in late 1988 under Iraqi leadership as a counterpart to the Gulf Cooperative Council, an economic and military alliance of the United Arab Emirates, Kuwait, Saudi Arabia, Bahrain, and Qatar.

47 Kingdom of Saudi Arabia, Royal Decree M/14, 7/411397 (1979).

48 The Center for Finance and Investment, *The Present Condition and Future of the Saudi Private Sector,* Report Prepared for Riyadh Chamber of Commerce, 1986, p. 183.

49 Ibid., pp. 173–74, 176.

50 Interview, Muhammad Al Muammar, Chairman, Committee on Industry, Riyadh Chamber of Commerce, Riyadh, December 20, 1985.

51 Economist Intelligence Unit, *Annual Supplement: Saudi Arabia* (London: Economic Intelligence Unit, 1985). The old 30 percent rule, in place since 1974, forced foreign contractors to subcontract 30 percent of government projects to Saudi firms.

52 Standard forms for public sector contracting, consulting, and supplies were issued in *Al Riyadh,* (Daily), Nov. 6, 1984, p. 7. The implementing rules for revised "buy Saudi" regulations and subcontracting were issued in Ministry of Finance Circular, No. 5767/404, August 6, 1984, and supplemented the Council of Ministers Decree

124, 29/5/1403 (1983).

53 *Arab News,* Dec. 10, 1985. The Export Promotion Committee worked with a newly created Exporters' Association created in 1985 in the Riyadh Chamber of Commerce. Interview, Abdulrehman al Jeraisy. Chairman, Committee for Trade. Riyadh Chamber of Commerce, Riyadh, December 16, 1985.

54 Kiren Aziz Chaudhry, "On the Way to the Market: Economic Liberalization and Iraq's Invasion of Kuwait," *Middle East Report* (May–June 1991).

55 By the mid 1950s, the government regulated profit margins on basic foodstuffs and other commonly used merchandise. See Amr Malaki, 1281/4112, 1377/4/12 (1956).

56 Often merchants would create shortages by getting licenses but not using them, thereby creating ideal conditions for the earning of windfall profits. *Economic Report,* July 1951, PRO EQ 1013/8, v. 91644. After the departure of the Jewish merchants, their Basrawi replacements prevented confiscated Jewish merchandise from being unloaded onto the market to maintain scarcities which were the source of their profits. *Basra Report,* May 1951, PRO EQ 1013/6, v. 91644.

57 For evidence of official collaboration in British commercial interests' bribery of Iraqi officials, see PRO VQ 1154/1–9,v. 111019. Pressure for help in getting contracts is cited frequently. See, for example, PROEQ 1156/1–3, v. 104702. In 1940 laws were passed restricting trades to Iraqis, but Britain forced the government to exempt British Indian subjects. E 2428/93 and 257512428193, 15 and 30 August, 1940, respectively, both in v. 24562. The weak bargaining power of the government is reflected in repeated attempts to nationalize power companies even after the general fear of nationalization resulted in the foreign company's refusal to make adequate investments to meet future projected needs. "Nationalization of Power Companies," PRO VQ 1533/1–15, v. 111036, 1954.

58 For a detailed analysis of the composition of the parliament, see Hanna Batatu, *The Old Social Classes and the Revolutionary Movements of Iraq* (Princeton: Princeton University Press, 1978), pp. 178–79: compare Table 5-3, pp. 58–61, with Table 9-14, p. 313.

59 See, for example, the account of the merchants' resistance to the ministry of agriculture's announcement of fixed commissions on agricultural machinery, *Middle East Report,* February, 1954, PRO VQ I 101/4, No. 2, v. 11 1005. The powerful Jewish community opposed the Banking Control Ordinance of 1950. Of their opposition, the British wrote, "it is generally believed that it was in order to prevent them from trying to block it in parliament that the Minister of Finance decided to put it into force by special ordinance." The law placed a minimal capital requirement on money lenders and required licensing. See *Control of Banking Ordinance,* Law No. 34 of 1950, PRO EQ 1117/1, v. 82434, 1950. After the legislation went through, there was a run on the banks. "Report from Sir Henry Mack," Baghdad, 23 March, 1950, PRO EQ 1103/1, PRO EQ 1103/1, v. 82422.

60 This law created a central supplies committee, restricted exports, and is expanded in Ordinance 63 of 1939 to prevent reexportof local or imported products. See PRO E

6579178193, vol. 23203, 1939.

61 The April 1942 Law Regulating the Economic Life of Iraq is reproduced in PRO FO vol. 31360, E 3292. Regulations for the Occupation of Immovable Property allowed the government to occupy any property necessary during the war and authorized it to take possession of commodities and sell them at fixed prices, use compulsory labor service on fixed wages, and take over and operate mills, factories, and transportation facilities. See Law 27 of 1942. PRO FO v. 31360, E 4250117193.

62 Economic Report, 22 October 1942, PRO FO E 6607131193, vol. 31361.

63 Batatu, pp. 470–71.

64 For a detailed discussion of government policy, see "Review of Commercial Conditions in Iraq," 22 December, 1944, PRO E 788817888193, v. 40109: *Basra Report,* December 1952. PRO Q 1015/1. v. 104664: and *Economic Monthly Report,* January 1951, v. 91644,

65 See *Basra Report,* January 1953, PRO Q 1015/2, v. 104664.

66 The total Jewish population was estimated to be 90,000 in 1938, or slightly more than 3 percent of the population. "Report from Sir Henry Mack," Baghdad, 23 March, 1950. PRO EQ 1103/1 v. 82422. According to the British records, as many of 75 percent of importers, exporters, and commission agents were Jewish, as were many retailers. All of the money changing and informal lending to retailers and wholesalers was controlled by Jewish community. *Baghdad Report,* 21 March, 1950, PRO EQ 1103/2, v. 82422. The three British banks, Eastern, Imperial Bank of Iran, and Ottoman Bank, were used mainly by foreign companies and by the money changers themselves. In 1938–1939, of the 498 members of the Baghdad Chamber of Commerce, 212 were Jewish, 87 were Shi'i, 43 were Christian, and 156 were Sunni. Figures are drawn from Hanna Batatu, *The Old Social Classes and the Revolutionary Movements of Iraq* (Princeton: Princeton University Press. 1978), p. 245.

67 "Economic Situation in Amarah Liwa," 1932, PRO E 362713627193. v. 16049.

68 This policy was described by the British as "rather a first step in trying to get the Kuwaitis to invest some of their embarrassingly large oil wealth in Southern Iraq and leaving the Iraqi government presumably to spend its new oil riches in Baghdad and Northern Iraq." *Basra Report,* March 1953. PRO EQ 1015/4. v. 104664, p. 3.

69 *Basra Report,* February, 1950, PRO EQ 1013/3, v. 91630.

70 Batatu, pp. 49, 271–72.

71 See Fran Hazelton, "Iraq to 1963," in *Saddam's Iraq: Revolution or Reaction?* (London: Committee against Repression and for Democratic Rights in Iraq, 1986), pp. 1–29.

72 See U. Zaher, "Political Developments in Iraq, 1963–1980," in ibid., pp. 30–53.

73 For a broad comparison of import substitution regimes, see David Felix, "Import Substitution and Late Industrialization: Latin America and Asia Compared," *World Development* 17 (1989), 1455–69.

74 Kiren Aziz Chaudhry, "The Price of Wealth: Business and State in Labor Remittance and Oil Economies," *International Organization* 43 (Winter 1989).

20

The Peace Process, National Reconstruction, and the Transition to Democracy in Palestine

Khalil Shikaki

With the signing of the September 1993 Israeli–Palestinian Declaration of Principles (DOP), the West Bank and the Gaza Strip have witnessed the acceleration of the development and interaction of three processes—the peace process, the national reconstruction and nation-building process, and the transition to democracy. This paper seeks to describe the three processes and to examine their interaction, with special focus on democratization and the impact of the first two processes on its pace, dynamic, and prospects.

The Peace Process

Peace, national reconstruction, and democracy are the three most important issues shaping the Palestinian future today. Of the three, the peace process has been the most effective. The DOP, which provided a basis for ending decades of conflict between the Israelis and Palestinians, was followed by the Gaza–Jericho agreement of May 1994 which ended the Israeli occupation of most of Gaza and a small part of the West Bank. The interim agreement (Oslo II) signed in Taba in September 1995 calls for Israeli redeployment from about 31 percent of the West Bank in a first stage, to be followed by three further redeployments that should take Israel out of most of the West Bank by the end of 1997. Negotiations for the final status of the West Bank and Gaza, including the most difficult issues of settlements, Jerusalem, refugees, and borders, are scheduled to begin in May 1996. Despite continued violence from both sides, but especially from the Islamist groups, the Palestinian Authority (PA) has gradually been able to maintain security in areas under its jurisdiction.

Palestinian public opinion has been very supportive of the peace process and has gradually shifted from supporting armed attacks against Israelis to opposing them. Data from regular polls conducted by the Center for Palestine Research and Studies (CPRS)[1] in Nablus have shown consistent support for the ongoing Palestinian–Israeli negotiations. Even at a time of widespread disappointment

From *Journal of Palestine Studies* 25 (2):5–20 (1996). Copyright © 1996 by the Institute for Palestine Studies. Reprinted by permission. Khalil Shikaki is Director of the Center for Palestine Research and Studies, Nablus, Palestine.

on the Palestinian street due to the Israeli failure to keep deadlines, 51 percent in January 1994 supported the negotiations; support increased to over 65 percent in March and May 1995, when progress in the negotiations created a measured degree of optimism. In an August–September 1995 poll, in the wake of leaks of an impending agreement, support for the peace process reached 71 percent. Even among students, the most hardline group in the Palestinian community, support for negotiations increased from 44 percent in January 1994 to 62 percent in August–September 1995, with opposition to the talks dropping from 47 percent to 24 percent over the same period.

Support for the specific agreements has been less stable, fluctuating in response to major events and the pace of negotiations. The DOP received 65 percent support in September 1993, but that support dropped to 40 percent in February 1994 due to continued deadlock in the negotiations. Support for the Gaza–Jericho agreement shortly after its signing in May 1994 reached 57 percent, while Oslo II received 72 percent support in October 1995, the highest level of support for the peace process ever registered. On the other hand, while about 57 percent were willing to amend the Palestinian charter in order to gain Israeli recognition of the PLO in September 1993, by October 1995 only 50 percent were willing to do so as required by the interim agreement.

The success of the peace process can also be seen in the level of support received by the factions that embraced it. Political forces in the West Bank and Gaza can be divided into three main groups according to their positions on the peace process: the "peace" or "support" camp consists of Fatah, FIDA (the DFLP faction headed by Yasir 'Abid Rabbu), and Hizb al-Sha'b (the Palestinian People's Party); the national opposition consists of the Syrian-based PFLP and DFLP; and the Islamist opposition consists of Hamas, Islamic Jihad, and other Islamist parties and independent Islamists. Monthly CPRS polls show an increase in general public support for the "peace camp," from 39 percent in January 1994 to 55 percent in October 1995. Meanwhile, the level of support for Yasir Arafat rose from 44 percent in November 1994, when performance of the PA was poor, to 58 percent in October 1995, after the signing of Oslo II. During the same period, support for Ahmad Yasin, the leader of Hamas, dropped from 20 percent to 14 percent, and support for PFLP head George Habash dropped from 7 percent to 3 percent. Among the young and educated, especially students, support for the opposition is higher than among the general public, yet among students, too, support for the opposition dropped from 41 percent in January 1994 to 25 percent in October 1995.

As the peace process progressed, Palestinian support for armed attacks against Israeli targets declined from 57 percent in November 1994 to 46 percent in February 1995 and to 33 percent a month later. These polls were conducted in the aftermath of major suicide attacks carried out by members of Hamas or Islamic Jihad. In August–September 1995, only 18 percent of the Palestinians surveyed supported attacks on Israeli civilian targets, although 70 percent supported attacks against settlers and military targets (this indicating not opposition to the peace process but Palestinian insistence that the process entail an end to occupation and the settlements). Even among students, support for suicide and civilian attacks dropped from 72 percent in November 1994 to 30 percent in August–September 1995.

Support for the peace process, however, does not necessarily mean optimism concerning the desired outcomes of Palestinian statehood or a lasting peace. In September 1993, only 45 percent believed that the Oslo agreement would lead to the establishment of a Palestinian state; some 34 percent believed it would not. These figures reached 55 percent and 33 percent respectively, in February 1994. By August 1995, almost 60 percent did not expect a lasting peace. Skepticism increased with the level of education: in the August 1995 poll, 69 percent of those with university degrees believed the peace process would not lead to lasting peace. Part of the explanation for such pessimism lies in Palestinian perceptions of Israeli intentions: in response to another question in the August 1995 poll, only 7 percent said they trusted Israeli intentions concerning the peace process, while 81 percent said they did not. On the other hand, some of those who answered pessimistically may not want a "lasting peace" if it is considered to be "dictated" and not reflecting their vision of what peace should be. Despite the lack of trust, the process of "normalization" has been more extensive between Palestinians and Israelis than between Israelis and Egyptians or Jordanians, even though Palestinians have sometimes called upon the Arabs to slow down normalization. The Palestinians and Israelis have been forced to "live" together for over twenty-eight years. The Palestinian economy has been totally dependent on Israel. Palestinian workers seek employment in Israel by the tens of thousands; most of what Palestinians consume is either produced in Israel or imported by Israelis; Palestinians see in Israel their most profitable market. Extensive links in many social and technical spheres have resulted in daily contacts between thousands of average Israelis and Palestinians.

National Reconstruction

The peace process, by giving rise to the establishment of the PA that will soon have jurisdiction over all Palestinians, has given strong impetus to the state-building process and in so doing has greatly strengthened the Palestinian sense of identity and independence after decades of life under occupation and in exile.

At the same time, however, the peace process has had a negative impact on national reconstruction by leaving unresolved the major issues of the conflict, including the future of Arab Jerusalem, Jewish settlements, and Palestinian refugees, to say nothing of the question of sovereignty over the land and the nature of the Palestinian political entity. Deferral of these issues to future negotiations has created serious defects in the state-building process and deepened Palestinian divisions regarding the Palestinian political order and the consensus on which it was built.

At the core of the Palestinian political system was the PLO, which emerged under difficult circumstances in the diaspora and under occupation.[2] Its legitimacy derived from a Palestinian consensus on "national liberation" as the goal and "armed struggle" as the means to achieve it—core values expressed in the Palestinian national charter as amended in 1968. Cracks in the structure began to appear in the mid-1970s when the PLO embarked upon the path that eventually led to its formal embrace of the two-state solution at the Palestine National Council (PNC) of November 1988. The internal erosion of legitimacy that accompanied this evolution was compounded by the Gulf War of 1990–91, which not only ended the PLO's funding sources but tremendously weakened its status and legitimacy at the regional and international levels.

The peace process came at a time when many were expecting the demise of the existing Palestinian political center. The emergence with the peace process of a new political order, based on independence and state building as the goal and negotiations as the means to attain it, has not achieved consensus. Indeed, even as the PA and its institutions were being established, many Palestinian political factions, both inside and outside the PLO, saw the emerging body as illegitimate. The bloody confrontation in Gaza in November 1994 between the PA security forces and supporters of Hamas exemplified the size of the gulf between an order claiming legitimacy and contending forces refusing to acknowledge its legitimacy. Still, even while the peace process dealt the final blow to the old consensus, it provided the basis for a new source of legitimacy—the popular will and the elections through which that will could manifest itself.

The Transition to Democracy

While the most successful of the three interacting processes has been the peace process, the least successful has been the transition to democracy. Indeed, this last has seen some reversal. The very early stages of the process in the early 1990s brought a gradual loosening of Israel's grip on Palestinian life, entailing for the Palestinians greater freedom of the press, a freer rein for nongovernmental organizations (NGOs), party and factional activities, and political mobilization. The result was a revitalization of democratic life and "resurrection" of civil society.

But the peace process and the PA it engendered also had negative repercussions on the transition to democracy. Holding to the view that the requirements of democracy may contradict those of national reconstruction,[3] and that in the early stages of state building it is more important to assert the state's right to monopolize power and eliminate competitors for the people's loyalty than to democratize the political system, the PA adopted undemocratic policies aimed at "protecting" the peace process and the process of national reconstruction. Meanwhile, the donor community's emphasis on building the capacity of the PA, rather than supporting institutions of civil society, reveals a similar belief that the success of the peace process requires political stability achievable only through the creation of a strong central authority.[4]

The setback to the democratization process can be seen particularly in two areas: civil institutions and NGOs, and the authority's practice of the rule of law.

Concerning the first, the Palestinians during the 1980s succeeded in creating social, political, professional, and popular civil institutions and NGOs that fulfilled many functions, including those performed in normal circumstances by the state. Most of these institutions received the full support of the PLO, which saw in their creation preliminary steps toward a future Palestinian state. With the establishment of the PA, some of these institutions became redundant. Some had already been weakened by the financial difficulties brought on by the Gulf War. Others were absorbed by PA institutions and ministries established in 1994 and 1995; still others lost their top men to the PA.

After the DOP and especially the Gaza–Jericho accord, many of these Palestinian NGOs found themselves without the foreign financial sources they had counted on to fund their projects. With the delays in the peace process and weakening of the PA under the impact of rising unemployment, economic stagnation, political violence, and Israeli closures, donor focus shifted from strengthening Palestinian civil society to building the capacity of the central government. More resources went directly to PA institutions, bureaucracy, and security services.[5] The shift in priorities not only weakened the institutions of civil society, but also served to strengthen the ability of the PA to contain and, if necessary, emasculate these institutions.

As for civil liberties and democratic practice, these have been seriously undermined by PA policies aimed at strengthening central control, "protecting" the peace, and asserting national agendas. The military security courts, established in February 1995 to deter Hamas and Islamic Jihad from attacking Israeli targets and to demonstrate to the Israeli government the PA's seriousness about combating terrorism, were based on the hated 1945 Emergency Regulations under which Palestinians were subjugated by the Israeli military occupation for over twenty-eight years.[6] Several people, including opposition figures not directly involved in attacks against Israelis, were convicted by these courts, sometimes in the absence of lawyers. Mass arrests of opposition leaders and activists, without charge or trial, became routine after every major attack on Israeli targets. Many people complained of torture, and several suspects died in jail during interrogations.

The PA also took repressive measures against the press, including temporarily closing opposition papers and banning the distribution of the mainstream *Al-Quds* for publishing anti-Oslo views. *Al-Nahar* was temporarily banned in July 1994, for its pro-Jordanian tendencies, and was allowed to reopen only after insuring a change in editorial direction. Another pro-Jordanian paper banned at the same time, *Akhbar al-Balad*, never reopened. Newspaper editors got the message and began to exercise self-censorship. *Al-Quds* has refrained from publishing stories about torture in Palestinian jails, reports by human rights organizations on press freedom, and opinion polls showing widespread opposition to PA restrictions. Threats have also been made against several academic and political figures opposed to the peace process and to Arafat's leadership. At least one human rights organization and some NGOs have come under similar pressure.[7]

Meanwhile, proposed legislation along these lines will soon provide the PA with legal means of coercion. A press law requires research institutions, publishing houses, printing shops, and polling organizations to obtain permits for their activities and to submit copies of their publications to the information ministry. Under pending legislation, NGOs are required to seek permission before they can accept funding from foreign sources; political parties must make their files and mail available for government inspection on a routine basis.[8]

Needless to say, the PA's antidemocratic trend goes beyond the constraints of the peace process and the requirements of national reconstruction. Deeper dynamics, such as socioeconomic development and political culture, are clearly also at work. Public opinion, the nature of the emerging ruling elite, and the structure of the new electoral system also play a significant role in the transition process.

Prerequisites to Democracy

Does the Palestinian case, as an Arab and Islamic case, represent an exception to the universal trend toward democracy? Conceptually, modernization theory postulates as preconditions for democracy the development of a socioeconomic structure and a certain political culture.[9] It has been argued that such socioeconomic development—entailing the emergence of a strong middle class, redistribution of wealth, urbanization, and a high level of literacy—is a precondition for democracy insofar as it contributes to breaking old authority structures and the emergence of new political forces and pressure groups. A market economy is also seen as a contributing factor since, by weakening state control over the means of production, it facilitates the emergence of new economic power bases and strengthens the institutions of civil society. Still, it is possible to make the transition to democracy without such prerequisites. In any case, the Palestinian level of socioeconomic development, its urbanization, GNP, and literacy rate, particularly in the West Bank, are not far behind (and may even exceed) that of some of the southern European and Latin American countries that have recently made that transition.[10]

Some see in Arab and Islamic political and social culture obstacles to the democratization process. Islam, it is argued, emphasizes sacred as opposed to secular sources of authority, and divine as opposed to popular sovereignty. It is also claimed that Islam stresses values of law and order rather than those of rebellion against tyranny, that it institutionalizes inequality with regard to religious minorities and women, and that it does not embrace the principle of freedom of expression and belief. Others see as an obstacle to democratization Arab culture's traditional emphasis on narrow loyalties to family, tribe, and ethnic community, or postulate Arab and Islamic lack of tolerance for opposition and defectors. The debate on Islam and democracy is a rich one,[11] but this is not the place for it. The characterization of Islam as nondemocratic can be argued, and, judging from recent democratization experiences in southern Europe and Latin America, what can be seen as deeply rooted cultural attitudes might be nothing more than products of political and social coercion. When regimes change, attitudes and behaviors change; cultures become adaptable to democracy.

Public Opinion and Democracy

To the extent that public attitudes reveal a deeper culture and value system, survey research on Palestinians appears to show a political culture hospitable to democratic values and practices. Palestinians overwhelmingly support a democratic political system and show readiness to participate in the political process. They support freedom of the press, the rights of the opposition, and the right of women to political participation.

As shown in a November 1993 CPRS poll,[12] 74 percent supported a democratic political system or a system similar to that of Israel. Support for a democratic/parliamentary system is widest among supporters of nationalist and secular forces such as those who support Fatah and PFLP. The same poll showed 72 percent supporting guarantees for the right of opposition groups to exist and freely express their views, though the data show more West Bankers (80 percent) supporting these values than Gazans (59 percent; 54 percent for Gazan refugees) and more Fatah sympathizers (79 percent) than Hamas sympathizers (65 percent). Gazans are also more supportive of the opposition's right to violent expression, with a September 1993 poll[13] showing 28 percent of Gazans (40 percent for Gazan refugees) approving the use of "violence if necessary," compared to only 6 percent of West Bankers holding this view.

Elections have been supported since September 1993 by an average of 77 percent in both the West Bank and Gaza: even among Hamas sympathizers, such support reached an average of 75 percent. Since September 1993, an average of 71 percent of all Palestinians questioned have said that they will participate in the elections for the Palestinian Council. In October 1995, 68 percent said they would participate even if the opposition called for a boycott. Support for elections is strongest among the most educated and weakest among the least educated.

Concerning freedom of the press, an August 1994 poll showed some 66 percent opposing a decision by the PA to ban the distribution of two Palestinian newspapers with pro-Jordanian tendencies, *Al-Nahar* and *Akhbar al-Balad*. Only 16 percent supported the ban, and only 13 percent favored a Palestinian press that expressed only the official PA line.

From Table 1 below, it is clear that most Palestinians consider democratic values to be "very important" or "important." This table[14] shows the extent of support for the following values: a free press, a multiparty system, the right to criticize government without fear, fair and periodic elections, equality for all under the law, control of police and security forces by civilian government, minority rights, and the establishment of an elected parliament.

Concerning women's rights, a majority of about 80 percent in April 1994 supported women's right to vote and 63 percent said they would vote for a competent woman candidate. Only 11 percent opposed women's right to run for election. In May 1995, 71 percent said they would vote for a woman candidate.

Table 1
Importance of democratic values, August–September 1995 (%)

	Free press	Multiparty system	Right to criticize	Fair elections
a) Very important	40.6	32.3	49.6	50.7
b) Important	42.0	39.1	38.6	41.0
c) Somewhat important	6.8	6.8	5.6	4.3
d) Unimportant	7.8	15.5	4.5	2.8
e) Very unimportant	1.4	3.3	0.6	0.3
f) Don't know	1.4	3.0	1.1	0.9

	Equality	Civilian control	Minority rights	Elected parliament
a) Very important	63.9	35.3	32.3	46.7
b) Important	34.0	44.3	47.1	42.5
c) Somewhat important	1.4	6.5	9.5	4.2
d) Unimportant	0.4	8.6	8.7	3.4
e) Very unimportant	0.3	0.8	1.1	1.0
f) Don't know	0.1	4.5	1.2	2.2

In August–September 1995, 74 percent agreed, or agreed strongly, that women should be represented in parliament; 81 percent agreed, or agreed strongly, that women should have equal job opportunities and wages to men. West Bankers are slightly more liberal than Gazans in this regard. Also, the young and educated are more supportive of women's rights. Islamists tend to be less liberal: in May 1995, 48 percent of Hamas supporters, compared with 78 percent of Fatah supporters, said they would vote for a woman candidate.

Nonetheless, while data from public opinion research show wide support for democratic values, they also show a large degree of public opinion vulnerability to manipulation by political authorities, perhaps an effect of the kind of political socialization prevalent in neighboring authoritarian Arab countries. As can be seen from Table 2[15] below, a majority of respondents in the West Bank and Gaza agree or strongly agree that leaders must be obeyed because they are more knowledgeable of the public interest; that improving economic conditions is more important than democracy; and that the president of the Palestinian state must have a wide-ranging authority. These attitudes reveal the extent of fragility of Palestinian public opinion support for democratic values.

Table 2
Fragility of public support for democratic values, August–September 1995 (%)

	Leaders should be obeyed	Economy more important than democracy	President should have wide authority
a) Strongly agree	16.7	38.0	19.5
b) Agree	47.1	37.6	42.0
c) Disagree	23.0	16.4	24.3
d) Strongly disagree	9.9	5.2	10.5
e) Don't know	3.3	2.9	3.7

The Emerging Ruling Elite

The prospects of democratization in Palestine and the emerging power structure under the PA cannot be understood without a brief survey of the successive political elites that held sway in the West Bank over the last decades. There are three such elites: (1) the traditional commercial class and big clans, (2) the national bourgeoisie, and (3) the grass-roots and popularly supported leadership of the factions and resistance movements.[16]

In the aftermath of the 1948 defeat and during the years of Jordanian rule, the traditional commercial class and landowners predominated. The Israeli occupation in the West Bank in 1967 unintentionally led to the gradual weakening of this class. Israel's land confiscation, water, and labor policies, by hastening the process of the proletarianization of the Palestinian peasantry and its movement to the cities, weakened the hold of this class over Palestinian rural society. At the same time, the rise of Palestinian nationalism in opposition to the Israeli occupation forces weakened this class's hold over the cities and towns: its traditional support of the Hashimites and continuing pro-Jordanian tendencies made its loyalty to the national agenda suspect in the eyes of the PLO and its supporters.

The late 1960s and early 1970s witnessed the emergence of the Palestinian national bourgeoisie, whose nationalist agenda and opposition to the occupation gradually gave it popular legitimacy. The members of this new elite came from families belonging economically to the commercial class and from urban middle-class intellectuals and professionals. This elite was the first to articulate the demand for an independent Palestinian state and certainly contributed to the PLO's adoption in the mid-1970s of statehood as a national goal. But before it succeeded in organizing grass-roots support, the new elite was decapitated by the policies of then Defense Minister Ariel Sharon, who preferred to revive a traditional rural class of landowners and elite families. By the early 1980s, then, West Bankers were without a dominant elite.

A popular leadership of national activists emerged to fill the vacuum. Many grass-roots, student, and professional organizations flourished in the 1980s, a period that saw the politicization of the poor and the middle class and their mobilization in the service of organized political and paramilitary factions. During the same period, the Israelis, in an attempt to weaken the nationalists, contributed to politicizing the traditional Palestinian Islamists. It was the new popular leadership, mostly poor and lower middle class, that led the intifada that broke out in 1987.

The peace process in the early 1990s led to the creation of a coalition between the grass-roots leadership that effectively controlled the street and the national bourgeoisie that received the media attention. While the former's legitimacy derived from popular support, the latter had to rely on PLO backing for legitimacy. With the formation of the PA and the return to Palestine of Yasir Arafat with some 5,000 Palestine Liberation Army (PLA) men and several hundred members of the PLO bureaucracy, a new coalition began to take shape.

In the first months of his arrival, Arafat sought to base his authoritarian rule on three main groups: (1) PLO senior officials, professionals, and bureaucrats from the national bourgeoisie, (2) business leaders from the commercial class and the big families, and (3) the leadership echelons of the PLA.

The first group, primarily returning PLO cadres and Fatah leaders who belonged to the middle and upper middle class, owed their positions to Arafat rather than to their own power within the community. This political elite, socialized in Arab countries, had been raised with an emphasis on national as opposed to democratic agendas: a quota system such as prevails within the PNC was the closest they had come to democratic practice.

The second group, the commercial class needed in the reconstruction effort, posed no immediate threat to Arafat's hold on power. Commanding little loyalty in the street and having been effectively eliminated from power positions during or just before the intifada, most of the leaders of this class had only recently returned to the West Bank. One might remark that the economic interests of the commercial class do not necessarily invite public participation in the political process.

The third partner in Arafat's original coalition was the Palestinian military. Initially, in his attempt to present himself as the leader of all Palestinians, Arafat had sought to marginalize Fatah, whose effective participation in the ruling elite could be seen to weaken his hold on power. In contrast, the PLA, an essentially apolitical body, posed no threat to Arafat's rule, having been deployed in several Arab countries and never having had any effective unified command and control. The fact that the PLA came from the outside meant that they had no local constituencies, and the man Arafat appointed to head the national security forces had little political ambition or following. Arafat believed that a nonpartisan PLA would be more successful in maintaining security, the most essential element in the Israeli–Palestinian peace process.

The failure of Arafat's policy of relying on the PLA to shield him and the peace process from the Islamist opposition became apparent with the bloody confrontation between the Islamists and the Palestinian security forces in November 1994. The Gaza clash led Arafat to introduce changes in his ruling coalition. Fatah now was invited to become a true partner in order to confront and neutralize Hamas. Palestinian security forces were opened to thousands of Fatah activists. The number of armed Palestinian policemen increased from 8,000 to about 18,000. Most of the Fatah men had spent years in Israeli jails and had been repeatedly subjected to Israeli interrogation techniques.

Palestinian Elections and the Three Processes

Palestinian elections—both for the eighty-eight-member council empowered under Oslo II to enact "primary and secondary legislation, including basic laws, regulations, and other legislative acts" and for the president of the executive authority (who will form a cabinet from among the council's elected members)—are likely to be one of the most critical developments in modern Palestinian politics. Elections will have a significant impact on all three processes of peace, national reconstruction, and democratization.

With regard to the peace process, three highly significant developments are awaiting the holding of elections: the formation of the council and transfer of powers, further Israeli redeployments and the extension of Palestinian jurisdiction, and the amending of the Palestinian charter. Under Oslo II, it is the elected Palestinian Council that is to exercise the powers and responsibilities being transferred by the Israeli military government and civil administration; the PA created by the Gaza–Jericho agreement is carrying out these powers only temporarily, pending the inauguration of the elected council. The elections are also the event signaling further Israeli redeployments, which are to commence six months afterward, and the consequent extension of Palestinian jurisdiction to the areas from which the Israeli military pulls back—in effect all the West Bank and Gaza except for the areas subject to final status negotiations. Finally, it is after the elections that the PNC is to be convened to amend the Palestinian charter by removing articles which deny Israel's right to exist and other references which violate the Palestinian commitment to renounce violence. By consecrating the new political order, elections deny legitimacy to the use of violent and nondemocratic means, hitherto deemed legitimate under the Palestinian charter.

Concerning the impact of elections on national reconstruction, the legitimacy conferred on the emerging Palestinian political system by democratic elections will give a powerful boost to the creation of strong political institutions and help institutionalize a new consensus based on modern political practices. Elections are also a useful means of unifying Palestinians in the two geographically separate areas of the West Bank and the Gaza Strip, and of integrating the Palestinians of Arab Jerusalem into the political process of national reconstruction. Given that Oslo II describes elections as "a significant interim preparatory step toward the realization of the legitimate rights of the Palestinian people," many Palestinians (and non-Palestinians) see them as an expression of popular sovereignty and a prelude to self-determination and statehood.

On the other hand, elections in the "inside" (i.e., the West Bank and Gaza) may lead to the marginalization of the concerns and institutions of the Palestinian diaspora, a process exacerbated by Oslo II. It is worth recalling that elections in every Israeli self-rule proposal since Menachem Begin's Camp David proposals in 1977 have aimed at creating a local Palestinian leadership that would replace, or rival, the PLO. While replacing the PLO is no longer an issue, elections still serve a related Israeli goal: to focus Palestinian energies on the internal agenda, that is, independence, thus marginalizing the Palestinian diaspora and its agenda, including the right of return. The election of a council for the "inside" accelerates the marginalization of the "outside" insofar as the new elected council could be seen as having more legitimacy than the appointed PNC in Tunis, whose mandate might now be questioned. Other PLO institutions are likely to be weakened as their functions are gradually assumed by the new institutions in the "inside" and as they lose their financial resources.

But it is for the transition to democracy that elections are most important. In such a participatory process, individuals, factions, and political parties have the opportunity to exert influence, mobilize forces, and aggregate interests, thus enhancing respect for political and civil rights. Palestinians committed themselves in Oslo II to "open government," accountability, and the separation of powers as the democratic basis for the establishment of Palestinian political institutions.

But elections could also become the means to regulate and institutionalize dissent or, even worse, legitimize repression. The ruling Palestinian elite could use them to obtain legitimacy and consolidate power. An examination of the nature of the election law that will regulate the Palestinian electoral system may provide some understanding of the potential role of elections in Palestinian politics.

The election law, as designed by an officially appointed election commission headed by the minister of local government, Saeb Erakat, calls for a simple majority system with open lists.[17] Under this system, the West Bank and Gaza Strip are divided into sixteen districts of unequal size, each with a number of seats proportionate to the number of eligible registered voters. Political parties, factions, and groups of individuals in each district can present their candidates in "party lists," the number of candidates on each list not to exceed the number of seats allocated to that district. Ballot splitting is permitted, though voters cannot vote for more candidates than there are seats in that district. Thus, voters in the largest district, Gaza City, can vote for twelve candidates, while voters in Tubas district, near Nablus, can vote for only one. The candidates with the largest number of votes win in their districts.

The majority system has been severely criticized by the opposition factions, the Independent Palestinian Election Group, and large numbers of academics and intellectuals.[18] Their argument is that the majority system and the districting scheme give Fatah, the "ruling party," a major advantage; indeed, Fatah, which has a plurality if not majority in all districts, may actually win all eighty-eight seats. A majority system could therefore help consolidate the hegemony of the emerging ruling elite and the largest political faction, raising questions about the legitimacy of the new political system. Moreover, it is argued, a majority system in these circumstances would not promote compromise in the manner of coalition-formation politics. While a majority system might be suitable for stable democracies, it might not be appropriate for societies with deep political divisions and in which fundamental questions about national identity and territorial boundaries remain unresolved.

Many of those opposing the majority system, including the Independent Palestinian Election Group and prominent political figures such as Faisal Husseini, had advocated a proportional representation system of countrywide voting that would allow all political factions to be represented in the Palestinian Council. This system, it was felt, would not only have encouraged the participation of all factions, but could also have helped moderate Palestinian political discourse. Through coalition-formation politics, it would also have encouraged the creation of a participatory political culture.

When it became apparent by late 1994 that a majority system was being designed, two trends emerged among those objecting to the system. One was to back the opposition forces that had been calling for an election boycott on other grounds. The other was to try to form a "third bloc" from the scattered and fragmented leftist, secularist, and democratic political forces critical of Arafat and the management of Palestinian–Israeli negotiations. This "third bloc," it was hoped, could situate itself between the "ruling party" (Fatah and its allies in the commercial class and the "peace" camp) and its Islamist opposition,[19] and hopefully be reinforced by other marginal groups, some seventeen of which have already been established.[20] Under the "three bloc" scenario, the election campaign would probably focus on ideologies and serious political issues such as the peace process, democratization, and secular versus religious values and political identities.

Today, however, one month away from the elections, this scenario appears unlikely. The Islamist and national opposition seem determined not to run even though they appear willing to allow supporters to participate in the voting (and a few "independent" Islamist and national opposition figures may run separately or in conjunction with other independents in an effort to capture such votes). If the opposition maintains its decision to boycott, the main competing forces could be clans and special interest groups. Moreover, in the absence of a threat from the opposition, Fatah might not even be needed by the emerging ruling elite to block threats to its dominance. The debated issues will change to socioeconomic interests and localized issues, and old family and clan rivalries could return to haunt Palestinian society in the major cities.

Conclusion

The process of transition to democracy in the West Bank and Gaza faces severe challenges. The peace process will probably continue to affect it negatively, particularly as popular frustration mounts when final status negotiations are deadlocked. The resolution of the conflict between national and democratic agendas will depend on how decision makers order the hierarchy of their priorities. Will the security-related agenda, political independence, and economic well-being continue to take precedence over political participation, accountability, and freedom of expression? Will the elected council play a prominent role in Palestinian politics? Or will it become subordinate to the executive authority? The preceding discussion may have already provided some answers to these questions, but the next few months will provide more needed and critical clues.

Editor's Note

Over 75 percent of registered voters participated in the election on January 20, 1996. Fatah won 30 percent of the vote, and 57 percent of the seats in the Assembly. Independents received 60 percent of the vote, and won 40 percent of the seats, while the opposition parties that participated received 10 percent of the vote and 3 percent of the seats. Yasir Arafat was elected president of the Palestinian National Authority with 87 percent of the vote over Samiha Khalil,
See As'ad Ghanem, "Founding elections in a transitional period: the first Palestinian general election" in *Middle East Journal* 50 (4):513–28 (1996).

Notes

1   Public opinion survey research in the West Bank and Gaza is a recent development. In the past, attempts to conduct such research met political and social constraints, and those which succeeded suffered from lack of political credibility and/or scientific reliability. Since the beginning of the peace process in 1991, however, survey research gained momentum. Today there are at least three Palestinian media and research institutions conducting public opinion polls. The Center for Palestine Research and Studies (CPRS) in Nablus has been conducting regular polls since September 1993. All data used in this article are based on CPRS regular polls.

2   For more information on the PLO and the Palestinian political system, see Cheryl Rubenberg, *The Palestine Liberation Organization: Its Institutional Structure* (Belmont MA Institute of Arab Studies 1983); and Helena Cobban, *The Palestine Liberation Organization: People, Power and Politics* (London: Cambridge University Press, 1984).

3   Briefings and interviews at CPRS with Palestinian officials.

4   Briefings and interviews at CPRS with officials from donor countries.

5   Briefings at CPRS with officials from donor countries.

6   For the full text of the PA order to establish the security courts, see "Document," *Al-Siyasa Al-Filastiniyya* 5 (Winter 1995), pp. 183–86.

7   See reports by human rights organizations such as Human Rights Watch, B'Tselem, Al-Haq, and Gaza Center for Rights and Law. A summary of such reports is in "Reports by Human Rights Organizations," *Al-Siyasa Al-Filastiniyya* 5 (Winter 1995) pp. 104–32.

8   Draft laws have been published in the local Palestinian newspapers. They have also been reprinted in issues of *Al-Siyasa Al-Filastiniyya*, issued by CPRS.

9   See, for example, Dankwart Rustow, "Transition to Democracy: Toward a Dynamic Model," *Comparative Politics* 2, no. 3 (April 1970), pp. 337–63.

10 For information on the Palestinian economy, see *Israeli Statistical Yearbook*. For information on countries of Latin America and Southern Europe see Tatu Vanhanen, *The Process of Democratization* (New York: Crane Russak, 1990).

11 See in particular, Ghassan Salame (ed.), *Democracy Without Democrats? The Renewal of Politics in the Muslim World* (London: I.B. Tauris, 1994) and Yahya Sadowski, "The New Orientalism and the Democracy Debate," *Middle East Report*, no. 183 (July–August 1994) pp. 14–26.

12 CPRS, Poll no. 3, November 1993.

13 CPRS, Poll no. 1, September 1993.

14 CPRS, Poll no. 19, August–September 1995.

15 Ibid.

16 On West Bank leadership, see Emile Sahliyeh, *In Search of Leadership: West Bank Politics Since 1967* (Washington: Brookings Institution, 1987).

17 The proposed election law has been published in series by *Al-Quds* newspaper during the first week of February 1995. It has also been published in a booklet format by the Palestinian Election Commission.

18 See for example The Independent Palestinian Election Group, *Al-Intikhabat Al-Filastiniyya* (Jerusalem: Author, October 1994).

19 Attempts to form a "third bloc" are led by the Palestinian People's Party. Several political meetings and academic conferences had been organized in Ramallah during the past few months in order to create interest and promote the idea.

20 CPRS has compiled information on all seventeen groups as part of a project on Palestinian opposition.

21

Kuwaiti Women at a Crossroads: Privileged Development and the Constraints of Ethnic Stratification

Anh Nga Longva

As elsewhere in the developing world, the Arabian peninsula has undergone sweeping changes since World War II, with the important difference that the process here has been blessed with unprecedented prosperity and not marred by economic difficulties. To say that the effects of modernization upon the local societies differ as a result from what can be observed in other countries would be to state the obvious. Yet, when it comes to understanding the position and status of contemporary women in the Arabian oil producing countries, prosperity and the particular circumstances around it are rarely considered as crucial variables. The women's situation often is evaluated, mainly if not exclusively, in light of the religious injunctions and traditional norms that govern the female condition in a Middle East that, by the same token, appears curiously monolithic and timeless. There seems to be an assumption that Arabian women are not part of the societies in which they live, and that, by virtue of some unique cultural principle, their condition remains unaffected by the vectors of change that have turned upside down all the other areas of life around them. Hence the general tendency to assess women's opportunities and constraints in terms of what the Qur'an and Islamic tradition dictate, not in terms of secular and more immediate concerns they may share with the rest of the society.[1] Aside from assuming a spurious dichotomy between the women and their societies, such an approach disregards the historical and material specificity of particular areas in the Muslim world. It also arbitrarily and a priori defines the character of the meeting between "Islamic tradition" and "modernity," instead of leaving it open to empirical investigation.

In this article, I will focus on the interplay between the socioeconomic context peculiar to Kuwait and the predicament of Kuwaiti women. My central thesis is that their status must be understood within the ethnic composition of the population and in the context of the relations between the large expatriate community and the Kuwaitis. I will argue that, in order to preserve Kuwaiti identi-

From *International Journal of Middle East Studies* 25 (3):443–56 (1993). Copyright © 1993 Cambridge University Press. Reprinted with the permission of Cambridge University Press. Anh Nga Longva is associate professor of social anthropology at the University of Bergen, Norway.

ty in a country where the majority are foreign migrants, certain rules of self-presentation and conduct are adopted by the nationals to emphasize their distance
from the expatriates and maintain their "honor" and "dignity"—concepts that
increasingly are understood by the actors with reference to the multiethnic reality in which they live. Two related instances discussed here are the dress code
and the attitude toward work among Kuwaiti women.

My analysis is based on anthropological fieldwork carried out between 1987
and 1990. Although many features described here can be seen in today's postwar Kuwaiti society, my observations refer to the situation before the August
1990 invasion by Iraq. At the end of the article, I will offer a few reflections concerning the later developments.

Until the 1950s, Kuwaiti women lived under constraining physical and
social conditions often associated with orthodox Muslim female conditions of
the past: secluded, veiled, and overwhelmingly illiterate, they were married at
puberty to a male relative, and their social horizon was limited to the immediate neighborhood of their homes.[2] At the end of the 1960s, two decades after the
start of modernization financed by oil revenues, and with 43 percent of all
school students being women, the rate of female illiteracy was still around 65
percent.[3]

By 1989, however, change had become notable: the number of Kuwaiti
women at Kuwait University was more than double that of men (many of whom
went abroad to study) and women were found among deans, undersecretaries in
the civil service, lawyers, and doctors. In the private sector, women invested
money, managed companies, and were on boards of directors of corporations.
Kuwaiti women were known throughout the Gulf for their active participation
in social life compared to their Arab sisters. They could be seen everywhere, not
walking meekly behind their male chaperons but at the wheels of their own cars.
Primary and intermediate education were by now compulsory for both sexes,
and the university was coeducational. With the exception of cabinet and ambas-
sadorial positions, there were, in principle, no secular jobs that were out of their
reach.

Official statistics indicate that there was an increase in the Kuwaiti female
participation in the labor force from 2 percent in 1970 to 14 percent in 1985.[4]
On the basis of this computation, the total Kuwaiti participation in the labor
force was 36 percent in 1985.[5] In April 1989, the assistant undersecretary of the
Ministry of Planning personally refuted these statistics and announced at a press
conference that the Kuwaitis represented only 14 percent of the labor force.[6] He
did not give any breakdown by sex, but, without denying that an increase had
indeed occurred since the early 1970s, one must assume that the percentage of
national female workers was probably much lower than the 14 percent previously announced. The official, Dr. 'Abd al-Wahhab al-'Awadi, explained that
the difference between his figures and the previous statistics was due to the

inclusion of the stateless bedouin[7] (*bidoun jinsiyya*) among the Kuwaiti category. This official rectification complicates the task of assessing the national participation in the labor force and calls for a reconsideration of some conclusions about the economic activity of Kuwaiti women by social scientists.

One instance is the excellent 1990 study by Shah and al-Qudsi of female work roles in Kuwait.[8] Based on official statistics collected before 1986 when the policy concerning the *bidoun* tightened up (see n. 7), the authors quote, among other things, a finding according to which in 1983, the largest female Kuwaiti participation in the work force originated from the lowest-income level (24.5 percent), while the equivalent participation in the upper-income level was only 5 percent (Table 1).

In light of Dr. al-'Awadi's rectification, how large was the actual percentage of the Kuwaiti workers and in which income levels did they belong? It may not be incorrect to assume that the largest slice—the lowest-income level—consisted mainly of *bidoun* women rather than national women. This claim cannot be formally substantiated since no official information is available concerning the socioeconomic situation of the *bidoun* as compared with the nationals.[9] However, it is built on the following observations.

As a category, the *bidoun* did not have access to the same amount of financial and social support granted by the state to its citizens, nor were they involved in the major trade and business activities that were the real source of wealth in Kuwait and were the preserves of the citizens. Although these privileges were often retained by the male heads of Kuwaiti families rather than by the female citizens, the cumulative result throughout the years was the enrichment of the national families, which represented a definite economic guarantee for their daughters. According to the law, women can inherit and administer their own fortunes independently of their husbands. Therefore, when a woman issues from a rich family, she often enjoys considerable material independence and security, also in case of divorce. For women issuing from ordinary families, on the

Table 1
Proportion of women in the labor force by the distribution of household income (private households only)

Households	Kuwaitis	Arabs	Asians
Bottom 40%	24.5	26.1	78.6
Middle 40%	16.3	19.2	39.2
Upper 20%	5.2	4.8	10.8
Average	19.3	19.1	49.3

Source: Central Statistical Office, 1983, quoted in Shah and al-Qudsi, page 232 (see note 8).

other hand, such a security is often lacking, and divorce threatens to leave them economically stranded. Compared with the citizens, the *bidoun* tended to aggregate towards this end of the economic continuum. Insofar as there were nonexpatriate women who were engaged in the labor force for economic reasons, they were likely to be recruited from among this group rather than among the nationals, many of whom did not strictly depend on a salary for a living. Besides, until the mid-1980s, not only was education open to the stateless, but they also seem to have had fairly easy access to the lower-level jobs in the public sector.[10]

As far as occupational distribution is concerned, this approach to the data would elucidate a finding quoted by Shah and al-Qudsi, and which the authors themselves have described as "unorthodox": the concentration of Kuwaiti women in clerical work, which, they say, ran counter to "the traditional values concerning the segregation of the sexes" (p. 218). While I would qualify Shah and al-Qudsi's remark by adding that the Kuwaitis are worried about segregation only under certain conditions, I fully agree that the custom of segregating the sexes is deep-seated enough to lead women to try to observe it insofar as their economic situations allowed them to do so. Here, as elsewhere, people who choose "unorthodox" occupations are often those faced with restricted options. Skilled *bidoun* women were more likely to settle for clerical work than skilled national women who could aim at higher positions.

Even more striking, I would suggest, is another finding pointed out by the authors, namely that the "Kuwaiti" service workers "were overrepresented in cooking and housekeeping jobs."[11] Anyone who has lived in the emirate is bound to feel puzzled: this finding contradicts the common knowledge that Kuwaiti nationals never opted for the low-status jobs that were exclusively associated with non-Kuwaitis, in particular Asian women, and possibly with unskilled stateless women.

These peculiar features of the "national" female labor force become more consistent with empirical observations if the distinction between the *bidoun* and the Kuwaiti components in it is made and assuming (in the absence of official confirmation) that the majority—or at least half—of the nonexpatriate female workers consisted of *bidoun*, for whom salaried work was a necessity. It was a common, unofficial assumption before the Iraqi invasion that the actual Kuwaiti female rate of labor participation was at most 6 percent.[12]

The Kuwaitis' conspicuous absence from the labor force is an interesting phenomenon. Although it might not be unexpected in a country where the per capita income had been, for the past decades, among the world's highest, this absence cannot be entirely explained in terms of economic prosperity. As far as Kuwaiti women were concerned, lack of involvement in working life was all the more striking when considered against their usually excellent educational performance (compared with the men's), their declared view of work as a positive human experience,[13] and the relatively tolerant social atmosphere in Kuwait.

Among foreign observers and social scientists, Kuwaiti women's reluctance about working and their occupational concentration overwhelmingly in the field of teaching[14] are generally assumed to be the result of tradition and practically no attempts have been made to probe deeper. Considering that modernization came to Kuwait less than fifty years ago, it is impossible to ignore the role played by tradition in this matter. The question is, when was tradition invoked to justify that a "modern" activity was "unsuitable" for a Kuwaiti woman? Why, for example, did Kuwaiti women not fear social stigma when they drove a car, attended desegregated lectures at the university, or held high positions in government offices? And why were some types of work by women more alarming than others? If one argues from the traditionalist point of view that this is because indiscriminate interaction between women and men at the work place is frowned upon by Islam, we have to ask why this interaction was acceptable when it took place between high-ranking officials in a ministry and not, for example, when it took place between a female Kuwaiti nurse and an expatriate patient. To explain this situation by referring to tradition alone is clearly inadequate and begs the question. Instead of adopting the conventional "modernization-hampered-by-religious-norms" approach, I suggest that we assess the situation against the sociomaterial circumstances (demography and resource and power distribution) under which work and other activities took place in this society. Tradition did indeed play a role here, though not as the "dead-weight of an ossified past,"[15] but as an active element in the Kuwaiti politics of ethnic stratification.[16]

In 1989, there were roughly 650,000 Kuwaitis compared with 1.3 million migrant workers,[17] and approximately 250,000 *bidoun*.[18] All people residing in Kuwait benefited from the state's health care, subsidized water, electricity, and gasoline, and paid no income tax. Kuwaiti citizens enjoyed, in addition, free education and practically free housing. They were also guaranteed a job in the government sector if they wished to work there, and were entitled to a series of state financial supports, from living allowances to bride-price grants for first marriages and subsidies for the wedding celebrations. Some categories of expatriates had access to free or subsidized education,[19] but only the highly skilled expatriate employees in the public sector were entitled to free housing. All foreigners were subject to residence and labor laws aimed at preventing them from settling down permanently in Kuwait and at curbing their influence in Kuwaiti society. Non-Kuwaitis were not allowed to own real estate and other permanent assets in Kuwait; nor did they have access to active membership in trade unions.[20] They could enter the country only by being sponsored by a Kuwaiti citizen or institution, or by a foreign resident who was himself Kuwaiti-sponsored. The *kafil* or sponsor was by law also the employer.

The government sector had the highest number of Kuwaiti employees (44 percent), whereas the private sector was almost entirely staffed by non-Kuwaitis

(97 percent).[21] Salary structure was usually based on the nationality of the employee: non-Kuwaitis worked longer hours and earned less than Kuwaitis. Among non-Kuwaitis, Asian expatriates worked longest and earned least, while Palestinians were the most privileged in terms of position, salary, and working hours.[22]

Asian workers increased from 18.7 percent of the expatriate population in 1975 to 35 percent in 1985, and the number of women among this group increased from 20,000 in 1980 to nearly 73,000 in 1985.[23] Before the war, they were found in professional, technical, and clerical work, but the majority were concentrated in service work, with as many as 84 percent employed as domestic servants in private homes.[24] These women were mainly non-Muslims from India, Sri Lanka, and the Philippines.

Practically all foreigners in Kuwait were contract workers. The *kafil* held vast powers over them since it was his/her sponsorship that allowed the worker to obtain an entry visa, a residence, and a work permit. All expatriates had to surrender their passports to their sponsors when they arrived, and thus were not free to leave the country without the sponsor's consent. Sponsors were responsible for their employees complying with Kuwaiti law, especially seeing to it that, upon termination of the contract, the employees left the country and did not go on to another job.

Kuwait had developed a system of labor courts to deal with labor conflicts. In these, expatriates could sue their employers for breach of contracts and other infractions. Throughout the years, Arab white-collar workers had resorted to these courts to settle their differences with their employers, but this was not a course of action easily available to unskilled laborers—in particular, non-Arabs—who were also the frequent victims of gross labor exploitation. Although the state provided needy laborers with free legal assistance, many factors, especially unfamiliarity with the system and insufficient resources to last out a trial, discouraged them from approaching the court. Even for white-collar workers, it remained a last resort. Expatriates nearly always opted for conciliation, placating their *kafils* as best they could, often by adopting a docile and subservient attitude, which only heightened the Kuwaitis' feelings of superiority. The result was a simultaneous elevation of the status of the Kuwaiti employers and a debasement of the non-Kuwaiti employees.

This attitude extended beyond work to cover practically every encounter between the two populations. For example, in a queue, a Kuwaiti seldom expected, or was expected, to stand behind an expatriate; people would find it normal for him or her to go to the head of the line. Likewise, at a crossroads or a roundabout, many expatriate drivers yielded instinctively to a Kuwaiti driver. Such reactions were triggered almost automatically in foreigners at the sight of anyone wearing the distinctive Kuwaiti national costume. A Kuwaiti friend told me of being stopped once in the street for identity control. When he showed his

Kuwaiti identity card, the police officer explained that he had mistaken him for an expatriate because he was wearing jeans. "Next time, wear the *dishdasha*," the policeman advised him. People were also clearly less polite to him whenever he dressed in non-Kuwaiti clothes. Wearing the *dishdasha* obviously made life easier for the citizens.

The women's *abaya* conveyed the same sense of "Kuwaitiness" in native–expatriate interaction. But, whereas the *dishdasha* was commonly accepted as a symbol of social power and privilege, the symbolism attached to the *abaya* tended to be diverted to the domains of religion and tradition. In itself, the differentiation between the imputed meaning of male and female clothing is interesting. The books of *fiqh* devote the same amount of attention to men's and women's dress codes.[25] Yet it was the use of the *abaya* which we interpret as a sign of religiosity, not the use of the *dishdasha*, and we seldom pause to reflect over the possibility that the *abaya* might also be of crucial relevance in the politics of ethnic stratification. It is my contention that the religious message of the *abaya* in Kuwait has been much exaggerated. In the collection of Bukhari's hadith, commonly regarded as the most detailed book on canonical clothing, it is said that Muslim women should be modest, "lower her eyes and conceal her private parts."[26] In other words, the correct dress for Muslim women consists of a head scarf and a full-length, long sleeved, non-form-fitting dress. The *abaya* is nowhere mentioned as a prescribed garment.

In the capital, the *abaya* was worn exclusively by Kuwaiti women and women of the Gulf region. Arab expatriates from the Levant, Egypt, Sudan, and the Maghrib were usually never seen with the *abaya*, even those who wore the head scarf. Even among Kuwaiti women, wearing the *abaya* was a sign of religiosity and sexual modesty only when it was worn from the head down, over a head scarf, and was held tightly closed under the chin. But there were various ways the *abaya* could be worn, for example, from the shoulder down, with its front open (so that the dress beneath became visible), and without the head scarf. Used that way it could hardly be interpreted in terms of religion; rather it was a signal of "Kuwaitiness." The *abaya* was indeed a symbol much less of Islamic fervor than of ethnic identity, the purpose of which was to illuminate the expatriates, not least the men, on the attitude to adopt when interacting with Kuwaiti women.

A substantial proportion of the foreign-worker population were adult men, administratively referred to as "bachelors" because, whether or not they were married, they migrated alone to Kuwait. The local authorities were wary of these bachelors and saw them as a threat to the female population. For that reason, the number and location of the areas where bachelors were allowed to rent accommodations was severely restricted. The poorest among them, mostly Asian and Middle Eastern laborers, were confined to "bachelor cities" on the outskirts of the capital. Middle-class professionals and Westerners lived in ethnically mixed residential areas. Bachelors could not live in the areas reserved for Kuwaitis only.

For these men, opportunities for contacts with women were restricted as well. Before the war, the local press used to carry almost daily reports of sexual offenses committed by expatriates. Although the crimes seldom involved native victims their reporting made the Kuwaiti population uneasy and encouraged Kuwaiti women to advertise their privileged identity by wearing the *abaya*.

The use of the *abaya* increased in the 1980s, in tandem with the growing demographic imbalance. Between the mid-1950s and the mid-1970s, Kuwaiti women had begun to shed their cloaks, wear Western clothes, and demand political rights.[27] By the mid-1980s, many of these same women were never seen outside their homes without the *abaya*. Although the timing corresponded with the growing political unrest elsewhere in the Muslim world, I suggest that the trend in Kuwait was triggered by ethnic circumstances within the country itself. In Kuwait, the Islamic movements, after peaking between 1981 and 1984, suffered a setback in the parliamentary elections,[28] but the conservative dress code remained unchanged. At least until the war, resort to Islamic symbolism seemed to be mainly an expression of the malaise that resulted from the ethnic imbalance in the community and of the need for Kuwaitis to control the situation and reaffirm their identity. The speech forms, the dress code, the careful choice of children's names, the strict observance of marriage rules, were some of the mechanisms used to reproduce what was, at any particular moment, consensually defined as Kuwaiti identity.

Like all ethnically defined identities, this one acquired its full significance only within a context where it was meant to make a difference for those who espoused it. The *abaya* was a discourse by the Kuwaiti women that was aimed principally at the non-Kuwaiti audience. Its message was mostly about the female citizens' dignity and status, and the social deference they expected from non-Kuwaitis, especially the males. The use of the head scarf by non-Kuwaiti Arab women served the same purpose. It was a signal not so much of the wearer's religiosity as of her ethnic origin and social circumstances: it was common knowledge in this society that Arab female expatriates in Kuwait most commonly lived surrounded by family and kin who provided their best guarantee against sexual harassment.

In Kuwait, it was the Asian female workers who were the most frequent victims of sexual aggression. These women wore neither the *abaya* nor the head scarf, but saris, jeans, or Western dresses. This was often interpreted as a sign of un-Islamic moral predispositions, especially when combined with free interaction with men, as, for example, in the case of the Filipinas. Among the Kuwaitis, there was little doubt that most Asian female expatriates were responsible for their own miseries. One can claim, however, that the stereotype of the "sexually lax Asian woman" arose neither from the way she dressed nor from the way she interacted with men, but rather from her being positioned at the bottom rungs of the labor hierarchy and her lacking any protection derived from family or middle-class ties.

The fact that a large majority of the Asian women worked in low-skilled, service related jobs, where they were entirely subordinated to a male sponsor or came into indiscriminate contact with male customers, was a key element in the society's elaboration of their negative image. In a context where female leisure was associated with ethnic privilege, and sexual morality was closely related to the status of those with whom a woman associated, there seemed to be a tendency to confuse indiscriminate social accessibility with indiscriminate sexual accessibility.

That lack of family and middle-class status protection also played a role was borne out by the difference in the treatment given Asian female workers and Western women, with whom they can be compared as far as dress code and cross-gender relations were concerned. Unlike the Asians, Western women in Kuwait were not systematically stigmatized and harassed, due to their status as nonworking wives or skilled and well-paid workers.

In prewar Kuwait, a powerful ethnic distinction was made in the contrast between the image of the native woman—aloof, covered, and sexually modest—and the expatriate woman—conspicuously accessible and uncovered. This stereotyping has had an important bearing on the Kuwaitis' attitudes towards work.

In the early days of modernization, the expatriate women who worked in Kuwait were usually educated Palestinians, most of whom taught in the newly established girls' schools.[29] Teaching was then a highly regarded occupation, and the working Palestinian women served as models for a whole generation of young Kuwaiti girls. From the mid-1970s onwards, however, migrant women were found in a variety of jobs, but most of these did not enjoy the prestige of teaching. The respect formerly granted working expatriate women was thereby dealt a blow, and it further decreased as the ethnic composition of the non-Kuwaiti population grew ever more diversified. Whereas the typical migrant woman was at first an educated Muslim Arab in a "respectable" job, she was now more likely to be a poorly educated Asian woman, employed in a menial job, ignorant of Islamic rules of conduct, and easy sexual prey to men.

At the same time, the image of the Kuwaiti woman had evolved in the opposite direction: it no longer was that of an illiterate and secluded person, unable to work because she lacked the necessary skills, but that of a rich and sophisticated woman who could afford to remain idle and who, as a citizen, held the formidable power of sponsorship over migrant workers. Kuwaiti wealth, leisure, and power now stood in stark contrast with expatriate poverty, dependence, and labor. The dichotomy between Kuwaiti leisure and non-Kuwaiti labor became a central theme around which both components of the emirate's population, but in particular the Kuwaitis, spun their ethnic stereotypes and built their social identities. The embracing of these identities meant the embracing of related values, norms, and expectations that inevitably influenced the role repertoire of the actors and determined their choices. As a direct result of these developments, work—which had seemed to many Kuwaiti women an exciting and liberating activity in the 1960s, because it was then the symbol of education and modernity—became more ambivalent in the 1980s, and the criteria for a "good" job were now defined in terms of ethnically situated status and morality, as well as economic gains and personal achievement. Thus, it became crucial for working Kuwaiti women to dissociate their type of work from the kind carried out by expatriate women. Hence the precautions with which Kuwaiti female work was framed: most importantly, it had to take place in a "protected" environment (e.g., a school, a government agency) and among socially acceptable people (preferably Kuwaitis). In cases where such precautions are not possible (ethnically mixed occupations, or low-level positions), extra care is taken by native women to use the *abaya* and the *hijab* (head scarf) to mark themselves off from their expatriate colleagues.

Prosperity, the abundance of cheap expatriate manpower, and the lack of familiarity with salaried work made it easy for Kuwaiti women to stay home. While conservative Kuwaitis applauded that decision, they were less pleased when women began instead to move around freely and no longer busied themselves exclusively with housework and child rearing. Kuwaiti women had at their service on average two servants[30] who relieved them from practically all housework, including the care of their children. They were left to make social calls, shop, or engage in activities that took them out of their homes (e.g., charity and community work). A major task became to reconcile the traditional definition of female morality—associated with a theory of protected space—with their newly gained freedom of movement most appropriately symbolized by the car, commonly described as "the Kuwaiti woman's best friend." Driving made her comings and goings, as well as her acquaintances, a lot more difficult for her husband and family to control, and also increased her propensity for being absent from home.[31]

Many viewed the demise of the traditional housewife with concern, as it appeared to be linked to various problems faced by the modern Kuwaiti nuclear family. According to statistics compiled by the Ministry of Justice, divorces among Kuwaitis increased by 100 percent within ten years, from a mere 616 in 1978 to 1,284 in 1988.[32] Juvenile delinquency, drug addiction, poor school attendance, and a general sense of aimlessness among the youth grew as well. Although the crisis of modernization involved the whole of Kuwaiti society, it was usually the women who got most of the blame for it. They were criticized for neglecting their duties as child rearers and surrendering the care and upbringing of their children to foreign maids. In comparison, husbands and fathers were seldom blamed for the turn taken by conjugal and familial events.

During the past decade, motherhood had grown as a common theme in conversations and in the newspapers, which coincided with the national policy of increasing the native Kuwaiti population. One of the targets of the last preinvasion five-year development plan was the correction of the demographic imbalance between Kuwaitis and non-Kuwaitis, for which an increase of the Kuwaiti birth rate was essential. The citizens' position as a minority emphasized the important function of mothers, not only as human reproducers but also as cultural reproducers. Giving birth to Kuwaiti children was important, but much more so was the task of raising them and making sure that they embraced a rigorously Kuwaiti identity.

Under the circumstances, motherhood seemed the most important way Kuwaiti women could solve their problem of being neither traditional house-wives nor workers. It was a role that was consonant with both traditional expectations and contemporary realities. It gave the modern Kuwaiti woman moral legitimacy in the eyes of her own society as a reproducer of privileged Kuwaiti citizens. The role of mother also involved women more deeply in legal obligations.

Codified in 1961 and modeled on the French-inspired Egyptian legal system, Kuwait's law drew much of its inspiration from Western secular sources, especially in commercial matters. However, in matters related to personal law and family, the shari'a of the Maliki school prevailed.[33] The laws regulating marriage, polygamy, divorce, and child custody remained unaffected by changes in other aspects of social life.[34] Thus, while Kuwaiti women were free, and even officially encouraged, to acquire higher education and seek prominent jobs in public life, they were at the same time still expected to acquiesce to their husbands having other wives or to being repudiated. They had also to put up with a lack of political rights.[35]

In all these respects, the general failure by Kuwaiti women to challenge the status quo seems to require an explanation. We need to know, for instance, why, despite numerous private complaints by female citizens about divorce and polygamy, there had never been public suggestions on the part of any Kuwaiti women's groups that the family law be revised, or that its implementation be more sharply controlled. Nor did any one ever publicly connect problems of the nuclear family with a disregard of women's rights. Scholars have pointed out that practically all over the Middle East, the personal status code has been the least modified of all legal codes.[36] To ascribe this tendency to a uniform and persistent moral code in the area would beg a great deal of questions endemic to each individual state. In the Kuwaiti context of population imbalance and asymmetrical power structure, traditional family law may be said to owe its survival at least in part to the fact that it was an integral element in the

Kuwaiti national agenda of ethnic self-protection in the face of massive work immigration.

In a study on European racial politics in colonies in the early 1900s, Stoler[37] focuses on the ambiguity of the position of European women in Dutch, French, and British colonies in Asia and Africa, an ambiguity that derives from these women being "both subordinate in colonial hierarchies and active agents of imperial culture in their own right."[38] European women played an important role in the methods devised by colonial rulers to safeguard European privilege and power: as bearers of the rulers' legitimate progeny, they reproduced the colonial elite and acted as its symbolic gatekeepers.

A parallel could be drawn between this situation and the one that existed in Kuwait. Although the Kuwaitis, of course, ruled over their own land and not over colonized territory, theirs was still the rule of a small, privileged minority over a majority of administratively and economically dependent expatriates who performed functions crucial to the maintenance of their living standard. Their fear of being overrun was all the greater as the exclusive privileges bestowed upon the citizens were perceived by both Kuwaitis and migrants as being of considerable value. Therefore, not unlike the Europeans in Stoler's study, the Kuwaitis' existence seemed to depend on elaborating and maintaining categories that clearly defined who had access to power and benefits and who did not. And like the Europeans in the colonies, Kuwaiti women were instrumental in this "politics of exclusion"[39] through their role as cultural gatekeepers and reproducers, while at the same time they held considerable power over the population of non-Kuwaiti workers as citizens and through their right to sponsorship.

Citizenship in this society was the ultimate privilege, but it came at a price. Concerned about their prospects of survival as a national group, the Kuwaitis attached great importance to presenting a united front to the external world, whatever their internal divergences and conflicting interests. For Kuwaiti women to challenge openly the domination of their men through organized action was to deal a dangerous blow to this facade. Read in the light of the natives' self-perception as a minority under siege, such a challenge would be interpreted as a betrayal of cherished Kuwaiti traditions and an embracing of alien values, which were all the more unattractive since they were identified with the marginal and powerless expatriates.

How did Iraq's attempt to dismantle Kuwaiti society and wipe out Kuwaiti identity affect this process of national identification and the role of Kuwaiti women in it?

War and occupation have a unique capacity to strengthen a people's national identity. The Kuwaitis emerged at liberation with a national consciousness that seemed to rest on stronger foundations than it had previously. Especially for those who remained under Iraqi occupation, unity was no longer a painstaking construct, but a genuinely experienced feeling crystallized around the sharing of common ordeals. The question is, how deep-seated is this consciousness and how will it fare under peaceful and prosperous circumstances?

It is too early to make any definite statements. I can at most venture some suggestions based on observations made during two postwar field trips, one in March 1991 and the other in November–December of the same year.

The difference between the two visits was striking. In March 1991, Kuwait, as can be expected, still bore all the marks of destruction and occupation. There were few people in the streets, electricity and water were still missing in most areas, but there was, in the wake of liberation, an unmistakable euphoria in the air. People mingled in the streets and greeted one another spontaneously, Kuwaiti employers sat down at meals with their expatriate employees. The graffiti scrawled all over the city spoke eloquently of the people's attachment to their country and to freedom and their gratitude for the allies' assistance. There were very few *dishdasha*s in sight, although for the first time since independence, the Kuwaitis were more numerous than the non-Kuwaitis.

In November 1991, Kuwait had returned to its elegant, tidy, functional self. The graffiti was painted over and replaced by placards with neatly printed, conventionally formulated messages. The euphoria had settled, the expatriates were back at work, though less numerous than before August 1990. With the end of martial law, and the return of the national refugees, the *dishdasha*s were ubiquitous, and the social distance between natives and expatriates prevailed once more.

As far as the female dress code is concerned, two opposite trends exist in postwar Kuwait. While urban women seem to have adopted the Western-style clothing even more wholeheartedly, women with a bedouin background have not only kept the *abaya* but also have started wearing the *niqab* (face veil), even when driving cars, a practice that was unheard of previously (driving with the *niqab* was, and still is, prohibited by law). In December 1991, the threat of exclusion issued by the dean of the faculty of medicine against female students who wear the *niqab* when attending classes, triggered heated public debates in which "modernists" and "traditionalists" hurled accusations at each other.

A discussion of these developments will have to be carried out elsewhere. I would like to suggest here that the two differing dress codes adopted by Kuwaiti women after the war are discourses meant for internal, Kuwaiti audiences, as opposed to the prewar discourse of the *abaya* addressed primarily to a non-Kuwaiti audience. In the present debate, I find the spontaneous expression of two alternative ways of defining "Kuwaitiness," not in contradistinction to a foreign majority, but to each other, and in terms of the historical duality of sea/desert or settled/nomadic cultures.

Since independence, the Kuwaitis have never come to terms with, nor discussed openly, this duality that is perhaps one of the most serious stumbling blocks in their efforts at nation-building. Most of their exertions have gone in the direction of protecting themselves against the alien migrant population. The present internal dialogue is a first step toward breaking up the monolithic facade of Kuwaiti unity—a development that may not be seen favorably by all concerned. A crucial precondition for the expression of such an internal pluralism (as opposed to the Kuwaiti–expatriate pluralism) is the absence, or at least a more subdued presence, of non-Kuwaitis on the social scene.

The demand for female suffrage may also be viewed in this perspective.[40] During occupation, the active role of Kuwaiti women in the resistance had led the government-in-exile to declare that their "role and contribution [would] be even more significant" after liberation.[41] Delivered in conjunction with promises on constitutional democracy, this statement was interpreted by many as a promise of female suffrage. However, the prospects for such an event—which would be another important sign of internal pluralism—have grown dimmer, just as the well-meant resolution taken by Kuwaitis during exile to participate more in the work force has vanished as Kuwait returns to normalcy, that is, as the number of expatriates moving back to the emirate has grown larger. With the old pattern of ethnic and labor stratification being restored, the chances for Kuwaiti women to free themselves from their narrow role are decreasing. Not only are their chances considerably reduced but also their incentives to ask for change, as the women revert to their roles as vessels of traditional morality and cultural gatekeepers for a privileged ethnic minority.

Notes

1   For a cogent critique of the ahistorical, exegetical approach to the study of women and Islam, see Deniz Kandiyoti, ed., *Women, Islam and the State* (1991).

2   Besides referring to Kamla Nath, "Education and Employment among Kuwaiti women," in *Women in the Muslim World,* eds. Lois Beck and Nikki Keddie (1978) and Zahra Freethe, *Kuwait Was My Home* (1956), I am relying here on my own interviews with Kuwaiti women between the ages of fifty and sixty-five.

3   *Annual Statistical Abstract 1989* (Central Statistical Office, Kuwaiti Ministry of Planning, 1989).

4   Ibid.

5   Ibid.

6   *The Arab Times,* 8 April 1989. He also indicated that Kuwaitis made up only 28 percent of the total population not 40 percent, as previously stated in the official statistics. For the analysis of population statistics as an expression of political and nationalist projects, see Benedict Anderson, *Imagined Communities* (1991) and Deniz Kandiyoti, "Identity and its Discontents: Women and the Nation," *Millenium* 20, 3 (1991): 429–43.

7   For more information on the category *bidoun jinsiyya* (without nationality), see the

information published in Kuwait in April 1991 by the Committee for the Support of the Stateless.

8   Nasra Shah and Sulayman al-Qudsi, "Female Work Roles in a Traditional Oil Economy: Kuwait," *Research in Human Capital and Development* 6 (1990): 213–46.

9   The Committee for the Support of the Stateless does not provide systematic comparative data.

10 Interview with the head of the Zakat House in Kuwait, 19 November 1988. In addition, I also refer to the information sheet by the Committee for the Support of the Stateless.

11 Shah and al-Qudsi, "Female Work Roles," 225.

12 Nesta Ramazani, "Islamic Fundamentalism and the Women of Kuwait," *Middle East Insight* 7 (January/February 1988): 21–25.

13 Jamal A. Sanad and Mark Tessler, "The Economic Orientations of Kuwaiti Women," *International Journal of Middle East Studies* 21 (1988): 443–68.

14 Clerical work and social service also were listed in the statistics. But I chose not to include them, since the workers here were more likely to be *bidoun* than Kuwaitis.

15 Frederik Barth, "Problems in Conceptualizing Cultural Pluralism with Illustration from Sohar, Oman," in *The Prospectus for Plural Societies* ed. David M. Lewis (1984).

16 On the relationship between women's conditions and the general problem of resource allocation, see Fatima Mernissi, *Beyond the Veil* (1985).

17 The majority of the non-Kuwaitis were Arabs. According to the last prewar census (taken in 1985) they represented 63 percent of the non-Kuwaiti population, followed by the Asians (35 percent) and the Europeans (1.2 percent).

18 The Committee for the Support of the Stateless.

19 Before the war, these were usually the children of Arab expatriates employed in the public sector.

20 They could join after five years' consecutive residence and employment but without the right to elect or to be elected (Article 72 of the labor law).

21 *Research Studies on Population 1985 Census Analysis,* no. 1 (Central Statistical Office, Kuwaiti Ministry of Planning, 1987).

22 N. Shah and S. al-Qudsi, "The Changing Characteristics of Migrant Workers in Kuwait," *International Journal of Middle East Studies* 21 (1989): 31–55.

23 *Research Studies on Population.*

24 Shah and al-Qudsi, "Female Work Roles"; N. Shah, S. al-Qudsi, and M. Shah, "Asian Women Workers in Kuwait," *International Migration Review* 25, 3 (1991): 464–86; Sharon Stanton Russell, "Policy Dimension of Female Migration to the Arab Gulf" (Paper presented at the United Nations expert group meeting on International Migration Policies and the Status of Female Migrants, San Miniato, 27–30 March 1990).

25 Abdelwahab Bouhdiba, *Sexuality in Islam* (1985).

26 Ibid., 33–36.

27 Mohammed Rumaihi, *Beyond Oil* (1986).

28 Jill Crystal, *Oil and Politics in the Gulf: Rulers and Merchants in Kuwait and Qatar* (1990); Shafiq Ghabra, "Voluntary Associations in Kuwait: The Foundation of a New System," *Middle East Journal* 45, 2 (1991): 199–205.

29 Shafiq Ghabra, *Palestinians in Kuwait: The Family and the Politics of Survival* (1987). Laurie A. Brand, *Palestinians in the Arab World* (1988).

30 Shah, al-Qudsi, and Shah, "Asian Women Workers in Kuwait," 470.

31 It is interesting that female car driving has never been a major social issue in Kuwait.

32 *The Arab Times,* 4 May 1989.

33 W. M. Ballantyne, *Legal Development in Arabia* (1980); S. H. Amin, "The Legal System of Kuwait," *Hannoversche Studien über den Mittleren Osten* (1988); Badria al-Awadi, *The Status of Women in Kuwait* (Kuwait, 1985).

34 B. al-Awadi, *Legal Status of Women in Kuwait;* J. Chamie, "Polygyny among Arabs," *Population Studies* 40 (1986): 55–66.

35 Crystal, *Oil and Politics in the Gulf,* 103.

36 See, for instance, Nadia Hijab, *Womanpower* (1988); Kandiyoti, "Identity and its Discontents"; Mernissi, *Beyond the Veil;* R Patai, *Society, Culture and Change in the Middle East* (1971); Ralph H. Magnus, "Societies and Social Change in the Persian Gulf," in *The Persian Gulf States,* ed. Alvin J. Cotrell (1980).

37 Anne L. Stoler, "Making Empire Respectable: The Politics of Race and Sexual Morality in Twentieth Century Colonial Cultures," *American Ethnologist* 16, 4 (1989): 634–60.

38 Ibid, 634.

39 Ibid.

40 It would be a reductionist approach to claim that ethnic constraints alone account for the various organizational dilemmas faced by the Kuwaitis. I do argue, however, that ethnic constraints are among the most predominant and, so far, the most overlooked factors that could help cast light upon the main forms of social organization in Kuwait.

41 The crown prince's speech at the Kuwaiti People's Conference in Jedda, October 1990.

Six

Introduction

Social Movements: Environment and Human Rights

A social movement is a collective action to bring about desired change, or to resist undesirable change. Social movements appear when conventional wisdom and normal institutional means fail to perform to the satisfaction of certain groups in society.

Social movements are found at either or both ends of the process of social change. A desirable social change may be long overdue; hence a social movement springs and tries to bring it about. On the other hand, change may already be occurring, but at a faster pace or in a more chaotic manner than some people can handle. Hence they feel threatened by it, and band together to resist, slow down, or attempt to regulate that change.

From our ongoing readings and discussions of Arab society in transition, it is possible to cite numerous aspects which warrant social movements—i.e., irregularities, distortions, mismanagement, gaps and lags, inequities and inequalities. This section deals only with social movements bearing on the two broad areas of environment and human rights. Other types of social movement are also important for Arab society, including women's movements, religious movements, and working-class movements.

For example, Islamic movements in several Arab countries—e.g., Egypt, Algeria, Tunisia, Kuwait, Lebanon, Yemen, Sudan, and Jordan—are one type that has been quite prominent in the last two decades. Ethnic and democratic movements have also made themselves felt. In fact, in terms of use of militant means in pursuing their objectives, religious militant movements have been louder and bloodier. For example, Islamic militants of Algeria, under various banners, have engaged the state in violent armed confrontations which claimed the lives of more than 60,000 people in five years (January 1992–January 1997). Likewise, the Southern Sudanese rebels have engaged the state in similar violent confrontations on and off since the country's independence in January 1956—more than 41 years. The result has been more than one million casualties, and more than three million displaced and uprooted Sudanese, not to mention billions of dollars in physical damage and the derailing of the country's development.

Militant social movements use radical means in their attempt to bring about radical change in confrontation with conservative forces of the establishment which want to maintain the status quo. Thus in Algeria, the Front de Libération

Nationale (FLN), after leading the struggle which won independence in 1962, ran a single-party government. Popular protest movements in the 1980s forced the regime to open up the political system: more than 40 political parties were quickly established, a new constitution was approved, and parliamentary elections were held in December 1991. Islamic parties seemed poised to win a majority of the seats. Suddenly, the forces which had been in power for nearly thirty years staged a military coup d'état to maintain the status quo and prevent the Front Islamique de Salut (FIS; "Islamic Salvation Front") from reaping the fruits of its imminent parliamentary victory. FIS and other Islamic militants struck back and a brutal civil war ensued.

The same applies to Sudan. The southern part of the country is populated by tribes which differ from the Arabized Muslim North in several basic ways—religion, language, and ethnic origin. Rightly or wrongly, the southern Sudanese have deep-seated grievances toward the North, and wanted to separate and form their own independent state. The North resisted such separation. Force and counterforce have been used by both sides since 1956. At present, the southern quest is symbolized by the Sudan People's Liberation Army (SPLA), which has modified its objectives from separation to "self-determination," southern self-rule, and in all cases "democracy" for all of Sudan. To bring about such change, the newest phase of fighting has killed or maimed at least half a million people since 1983. There has also been vast population displacement and ecological disruption.

However, not all social movements are radical in their methods. In fact, most social movements are "reform" ones—those seeking partial gradual change, by peaceful means. Among these, we single out two for more specific analyses in this section: the environment and human rights movements. Both are partly triggered by objective factors at home and partly by worldwide concern, thus reflecting a dialectic between the "internal" and the "external."

Concern over environmental deterioration goes back to the beginnings of the Industrial Revolution in the West at the turn of the nineteenth century. But the quest for material progress was too strong to cede to these environmental concerns. Only in the late twentieth century would such concerns be taken seriously by social groups and governments, then reluctantly by industry. The Club of Rome produced a report in the mid-1960s entitled the "Limits to Growth," which forcefully and graphically made the case against the West's obsession with material progress and consumerism. University students in the West have since been instrumental in what came to be generally known as the "ecology," and later the "environment" movement. In the West, it is more of a "post-industrial" movement. In the Arab world, as elsewhere in developing countries, environmental deterioration has been equally serious, but caused by a different set of factors. To be sure, some of these go back to Western colonial pillage of nonrenewable resources. But many such factors have to do with mismanagement during the early industrialization period, overpopulation, and overurbanization, hunger and need for food (see Sections Two and Four). In other words, if environmental degradation in the West has been caused by material greed, in the Arab and developing worlds it has been often caused by dire need.

In 1992, the UN Conference on Environment and Development (UNCED), often referred to as the "Earth Summit," in Rio de Janeiro (Brazil) was attended by more than a hundred heads of states anxious to show the urgency of overall environmental degradation: from air and water pollution to topsoil erosion, and from depletion of the ozone layer to the depletion of ocean fisheries. The old paradigm pitting "development" against "environment" was challenged and rejected in the Earth Summit. A new paradigm of "environmentally sustainable development" was adopted in the final declaration of UNCED, which was titled "Agenda 21"—an action plan for the twenty-first century. The Earth Summit and Agenda 21 gave the embryonic Arab environmentalist movement a push. Some Arab environmental groups and nongovernmental organizations (NGOs) went to Rio, and participated in the NGO Forum of the summit. But more such NGOs sprouted afterwards. Together, they have managed peacefully to persuade Arab governments to take protection measures. Some Arab countries (e.g., Egypt, Jordan, Morocco, Tunisia), have set up state environment agencies or new ministries. But as in all aspects of development, popular awareness, cooperation, and participation are essential. Hence the Arab environmental movement has a long agenda, especially with regard to water management, the encroachment on scarce agricultural land, soil erosion and desertification, coastline management, and wildlife preservation.

One unavoidable long-term limit to growth in much of the Arab world is water. There is dire water scarcity in an arid region with rapid population increase. Only through rational water management and the development of water resources can the Arab world hope to meet its water deficit.

The human rights issue is more problematic in the Arab world at present. While equally peaceful, the Arab human rights movement runs up against more governmental opposition. The irony is that nearly all the Arab governments have signed the UN Universal Declaration of Human Rights (approved by the General Assembly, December 10, 1948). Likewise, Arab governments signed other human rights declarations and covenants—e.g., Civil and Political Rights (December 16, 1996) and Economic, Social and Cultural Rights (December 16, 1996). But it seems that nondemocratic Arab governments often do not implement what they commit themselves to in international forums. Worse still, several Arab countries have witnessed steady deterioration in human rights since the 1960s. By the early 1980s mass violations of such rights by authoritarian despotic regimes became widespread, prompting scores of Arab intellectuals and political activists to establish an Arab Organization for Human Rights (AOHR). Soon, several chapters and branches of the AOHR sprouted in the

Arab world, from Morocco to Bahrain. Some have been established by Arabs living in the West, not only to defend human rights in the Arab world, but also to defend these rights in the face of growing racism in their host countries. In brief, the human rights culture, like that of environmental awareness, has slowly and gradually been growing and striking roots in Arab sociopolitical soil.

The role of the Rio Earth Summit for Arab environmental NGOs was played by several international conferences for the Arab human rights movements. Thus the UN organized an International Human Rights Conference (held in Vienna, Austria, in 1993) in which all the previous declarations were reasserted, with more emphasis on rights of specific groups like women, children, the poor, minorities, indigenous peoples, and migrants. The issue of human rights, which began with concern for mistreatment of prisoners of conscience, has now expanded into other domains. Again, as a result of the Vienna Conference, the Arab human rights NGOs, while still at odds with their own governments, have acquired more popular legitimacy in their respective countries. Being part of a worldwide network of human rights movements has given them more protection to fight for their respective causes. Like some Asian and African governments, Arab governments often claim that some of the human rights enshrined in the West "offend" or "contradict" deep-seated beliefs or cultural patterns in their non-Western countries. While it may be partly true, the fact that the issue of cultural specificity is often raised by the most oppressive regimes casts substantial doubt on the authenticity or sincerity of the claim.

The issues of development vs. environmental protection, and of human rights universality vs. cultural specificity claims, merit further elucidation and debate.

In This Section

Khaled Kamel, a medical doctor, focuses on a social movement aimed at closing a lead factory in an inhabited area in Cairo, and shows the various stages of the process that led to closing the factory. The process involved legal and medical expertise as well as the mobilization of local residents. Contacting officials and seeking exposure in the media were among the strategies used, and the process shows the need for greater transparency in public affairs.

The geographer Marc Lavergne reviews the various environmental problems of Jordan and Syria—deforestation and desertification, clean water, coastline management, industrial pollution, disposal of human waste, etc. The physical similarities of the two countries make for an interesting contrast; Lavergne attributes the differences in approach to different styles of governing.

Abdel Ghaffar Ahmed uses his long experience in rural Sudan to describe the ravages that war has brought on the environment. Disruption of the environment has destroyed the way of life for many people throughout Sudan, causing them to flee to neighboring countries or to the cities. Even the major development projects, like the Jonglei Canal, have been halted before completion with the result that they are doing more harm than good. There is also the question of identifying the elites who are responsible for the continuation of this long civil war, and so, perhaps, to find a solution.

Rachad Antonius raises the interesting and important question of knowing whether human rights are truly human, i.e., universal, or whether they are culturally specific. Can each society define certain rights which it calls human, but which are only valid for it? What happens when outsiders want to impose a certain definition of rights on a particular society? Antonius distinguishes between liberty rights (such as freedom of speech), claim rights (a right to healthy surroundings), and nondiscrimination (rules are applied equally to all), and argues that in practice rights are best understood through what are considered violations.

Kevin Dwyer's book, *Arab Voices: The Human Rights Debate in the Middle East,* from which our selection comes, covers various aspects of the human rights debate in Egypt, Tunisia, and Morocco. He deals with the human rights movement itself and also with its links with the Islamic movements and with feminism. Dwyer's technique in this book is to let people speak for themselves as much as possible. Clearly, of course, the transcripts have been edited and organized to tell a story; still, as much as possible of that story is in the words of the participants. Here the story involves the creation and troubled history of a monthly magazine for women in Tunisia. This selection includes interviews with some of the main participants in creating Tunisia's first feminist journal, and illustrates the ways in which their concerns fit into the feminist and social movements in Tunisia in the 1980s. These concerns and movements are the outgrowth of middle-class, urban Tunisia, as indeed are similar concerns in other Arab countries. Dwyer illustrates the challenges and the obstacles to effective organization for social goals in this situation.

22

A Tale of Two Factories

Khaled Kamel

In the continuing struggle to promote environmental and health awareness, grassroots activism has been a crucial force in many parts of the world. In Egypt, the impulse for the activism necessary to mobilize the population and promote widespread societal change is present within its communities. However, for various reasons, the impulse is often thwarted or never fully realized.

What follows is an account of a successful grassroots campaign in Egypt. It involves a group of doctors, medical students, and residents of Cairo's poor el-Waily district and their fight to close two factories that were emitting lead into a densely populated area. The closing of the factories, which were proven to cause serious respiratory ailments and possibly other ailments associated with lead poisoning, was a coup for those seeking to stop air pollution in Egypt. Community involvement was central to that success.

None of the participants, myself included, had any previous experience in such activism and the lessons learned along the way are beneficial to all future grassroots campaigns. From the experiences of the el-Waily group, it becomes clear that the potential for community mobilization is present, as well as the potential for great achievements. But there are hindrances to the realization of widespread activism that must be addressed if Egypt hopes to make peaceful advances towards the improvement of its environment and the health of its people.

The Emergence of the Primary Health Care Center

The deterioration of Egypt's public services after the October War in 1973 prompted many Egyptian university students and intellectuals to organize in the search for ways to improve the system. Many medical students and doctors were particularly concerned with health care services which suffered considerably from government cuts in funding. Clinics and other health facilities were deteriorating rapidly and often lacked supplies. Salaries for health care workers were extremely low and many care givers lacked sufficient experience or knowledge.

From *Cairo Papers in Social Science* 17 (4):29–39 (1994/5). Copyright © 1995 by The American University in Cairo Press. Reprinted by permission. Khaled Kamel is director of the Primary Health Care Center, el-Waily, Cairo.

Many people, the poor in particular, were unable to gain access to proper health care and felt abandoned by a system that they relied on for basic needs

Numerous concerned people began to discuss different ways of improving the health care system while making it more accessible to the larger population. Some preferred to seek improvements by lobbying the doctors' syndicate against such things as privatized health care. Others, particularly those already working in the public service system, preferred to organize from within to generate change.

Several of these individuals, myself included, joined together to form the Association of Health and Environmental Development (AHED) in 1980. The group has since sought to establish alternative systems of health care based on the idea that curative medical services are only part of a greater package. AHED asserts that it is also necessary to tackle the social and environmental causes of poor health. Such an approach necessitates the transformation of society, a process that, with the help of community participation and education, must occur in such areas as sanitation, personal hygiene and child care.

In 1988, a group within AHED decided to establish a Primary Health Care (PHC) center in el-Waily, a financially deprived area of Cairo. Of the many poor areas of Cairo, el-Waily was chosen because one member of the PHC group had worked with the community there previously. He had gained the trust of el-Waily residents, which helped the organization to establish itself in the district. The group decided that the center would focus on preventative medicine through the establishment of a mother and child care unit, a patient screening system, and health education classes. We also sought to tackle environmental hazards in the area with the help of el-Waily residents.

The Conditions of Cairo's el-Waily District

El-Waily is just one of the many low-income areas in Cairo. There are 26 fully functioning factories in the area including fourteen metal-smelting operations, four textile factories, three dye factories, two rubber factories, and two factories that process chemicals and perfumes. Most buildings in the area are over three stories high, and most flats do not exceed areas of 60–70 meters square. Most of the living quarters are supplied with clean water, electricity, and sewage disposal. There are about five main streets that are 10 meters wide, but the majority of streets are no more than 4 meters wide.

The average family size is six people and there are schools of all levels in the area. There are no public hospitals in el-Waily, though there are several volunteer clinics, some private clinics, and a relatively expensive private hospital. There is one public mother and childcare center which provides immunization, registration of births and deaths, and, theoretically, health education.

Many residents of el-Waily have suffered significantly from the effects of changing economic policies, particularly structural adjustment and privatization. Unemployment is extremely high. Many workers have lost jobs or suffered severe cuts in pay. Families are struggling to make ends meet. This economic situation combined with the deterioration of social service facilities has led to a growing feeling of alienation among el-Waily residents. This has created an angry climate in the district.

The Threat Posed by Lead Factories in el-Waily

The PHC center immediately identified the numerous factories in the area as possible health risks to the el-Waily community. Two lead factories were singled out as posing the greatest threat to public health. Both were using primitive techniques to transform lead plates of old car batteries into sewage collecting equipment, a process that also produced lead oxides and sulfur oxides that were emitted into the air.

The dangers of lead poisoning are widely known. In children, low-level lead poisoning can slow physical and mental development, damage red blood cell production, and cause behavioral or learning difficulties such as hyperactivity and attention deficit disorders. At higher levels, damage may occur to the nervous system, kidneys, and/or reproductive system. Symptoms of lead poisoning are often not obvious or they are mistaken for signs of flu or other minor illnesses. Such symptoms include irritability, fatigue, frequent vomiting, constipation, headaches, sleep disorders, and loss of appetite. As more and more lead accumulates in the system one can experience a loss of coordination and the loss of recently acquired skills. In addition to smog from lead smelters, high levels of lead are also found in the exhaust fumes of cars fueled by leaded gasoline, lead-based exterior paints, and food stored in open cans with lead seams.

Everything about el-Waily increased the chances of lead entering the systems of residents at relatively high levels on a constant basis. The smoke stacks of both lead smelters were only about three stories high. The majority of buildings around the factories were five stories or more. The street dust, accumulating lead from both the factories and car exhaust, threatened the health of children in particular, since they often play in the street and eat sticky candy with dust-covered hands. The number of food handlers working in unsanitary conditions throughout the district, as well as the large Pepsi Cola factory just five meters from one of the smelters, added to the health risk. Residents of el-Waily may not just have been inhaling lead oxides but also ingesting them.

Assessing Community Awareness

Although the center was concerned with possible risks in all 26 factories in the area, financial constraints and a lack of manpower forced the group to focus its efforts on the two lead factories alone. PHC volunteers talked to members of the community, many of whom were well aware of the dangers they faced. Often, they shared their own experiences and fears. One 35-year-old driver said, "I suffer from severe asthma because I have been inhaling smog day and night. I spend at least LE80 per month for medicines. I am very tired and I can't work anymore." A 49-year-old mother complained, "I live in fear that smog will choke my children. My youngest son is suffering from a chronic cough and bronchial asthma. He spends most of his time in bed ill." One man, who lived in a house near one of the factories, blamed the lead smelters for the death of his wife from a severe chest disease. "My wife had been suffering for six years. She left me three kids," he said. "All that I hope now is to have my children breathe clean air. You can't keep any clothes clean for more than five minutes." A manager of the Pepsi Cola factory near a lead factory also showed concern. "It is a crime for a lead smelter to operate in such a densely populated area with so many food shops and food factories nearby. The emitted smog probably contains toxic gasses, polluting the air as well as our products," he said. "We are trying hard to keep the products in stores clean. We wash the Pepsi Cola bottles several times with chemicals to remove any trace of the smog. Factory workers suffer because of the smog they are exposed to day and night."

The organization also met with several community activists who had raised the lead factory issue years before. They told stories of thwarted efforts and great frustration. "I began working on this problem eight years ago," said one activist. "I sent complaints to local authorities as well as to each of the successive governors of Cairo and officials in the Ministry of Health. They were all filed in vain." Another activist added, "I met the governor of Cairo, Mahmoud el-Sherif, when he opened the child care center only 10 meters away from a lead smelter. He asked the head of the Zaytun district, Raafat el-Tawil to shut down both smelters. This was two years ago and nothing has changed."

Discussions with activists and residents revealed that there was a widely held suspicion of factory owners and local officials throughout the community. Many suggested that the factory owners might have avoided closure even after decrees were issued by successive governors of Cairo in 1989, 1990, and 1991, by bribing district officials and the local police officers responsible for executing the decrees. The decrees were issued on the grounds that the factories violated Egyptian Law 453 of 1954 which prohibits the operation of facilities deemed threatening to public health. Residents claimed that the owners, on several occasions, boasted that no matter how many times they were ordered to close, they could bribe as many people as necessary to prevent them from shutting down the factories. There was also the feeling among residents that the government did not take the issue very seriously and failed to make all the efforts it could have to ensure the closing of the factories. Residents felt powerless. Some believed that the only solution would be to have the factories burned or destroyed.

Mobilizing Community Volunteers

By 1992, the PHC center and its team of organizers had become the nucleus for a group of volunteers fighting to close the illegal lead smelters. The group believed that solidarity and organized action within the community was a tool that could counter the wealthy and corrupt factory owners. All of the group's activities were to be legal and peaceful to avoid turning the victim into the criminal.

As it began the fight to close the factories, the PHC team had a number of very strong fears. The degree to which a health center should be involved in the fight was debated, particularly when the anger of the residents had the potential to manifest itself in actions that the center could not support. There was also concern over the group's ability to recruit from the community. The greatest fear of all, however, was of government action against the group.

Egyptian Law 32 of 1964, which limits the degree to which non-governmental organizations (NGOs) can work among people at the grassroots level, had recently been used by the Ministry of Social Affairs to shut down at least six effective organizations. Among the organizations closed was writer Nawal Saadawy's feminist group, Arab Women's Solidarity Union, which the ministry forced to merge with another group with an opposing viewpoint after it confiscated materials from its headquarters.

In spite of the very real and intense fear of government intervention, the PHC team and the administrative board of AHED, decided that the fight against polluting factories was essential to the group's overall objective: to influence detrimental health and environmental policies. It was necessary that the group take certain "risks."

Its mission established, the PHC team began its work. It approached the el-Waily community through a series of newsletters about the dangers and sources of lead pollution, methods of protection against pollution, and the symptoms and signs of lead poisoning. Volunteers then distributed the newsletter by hand and launched a campaign to recruit more volunteers. Discussions were initiated between the residents and the volunteers about uniting to lobby the government for action against the factories and the need for nonviolent action.

Many residents were eager to fight against the lead smelters but expressed fear of arbitrary arrest or some other action by the government for participating in the group's activities. For some, this feeling of powerlessness was expressed by calls for violent action. One resident made a statement that echoed the feelings of many: "If we were in a war against the factory owners, they would be considered war criminals for using chemical weapons against women and children. The only solution is to destroy the factory by planting a bomb."

The fear and reticence of many residents was somewhat discouraging, but the PHC team continued to reach out to the people of el-Waily. It prepared health education sessions in public places, such as coffee houses and the local community development association. Some residents did join the fight, young university graduates in particular.

The Search for Information

The PHC team also began extensive research into the laws governing the operation of factories and the legal status of the two factories in question. As members tried to obtain information, however, they experienced a great deal of difficulty. Clerks in the Zaytun district allegedly told members that they did not have the right to photocopies of the decrees ordering closure of the factories. Information about a legal case raised by the factory owners against the governor of Cairo for issuing the decree of 1991 was also withheld. Some sympathetic officials were able to provide the team with some information, including an opposition party member who is the el-Waily representative in the People's Assembly. He was able to obtain copies of the decrees. Our informant also discovered that the factory owners had a certificate issued by the Institute of Metal Studies in 1991, which said that filters had been installed in the smelters that reduced lead pollution by 80 percent, a certificate the PHC team found highly suspicious.

The team also learned that the factory owners had tried to open other lead smelters in Tenth of Ramadan City, but were thwarted by influential entrepreneurs who were afraid that the smelters would negatively affect their businesses. It also discovered that the local police justified their refusal to execute the decrees for closure on the grounds that the firing of 400 workers posed a great threat to security. The total number of workers in both factories did not exceed twenty.

In spite of all the information it was able to obtain, information about the legal case, in particular the case number, continued to elude the team. Several lawyers joined the group and volunteered to track down the case number. They also emphasized the need for solid evidence proving that the factories posed a threat to public health. Such evidence, they suggested, would also help residents sue for financial compensation.

Obtaining Scientific Proof

The need for concrete proof that the factories directly compromised the health of the people of el-Waily, made it clear that scientific research was critical for the advancement of the PHC team's campaign. It was assumed that universities or national research institutes would have the expertise and facilities necessary to conduct a thorough and reliable study. When such institutions were approached, it became clear that there was a huge gap between the institutions and the community, between science and the people who need its help. The PHC team found that universities and national research institutes have their own plans and agendas, but it is not clear how or why certain research projects are chosen. For example, are community needs considered when study plans are made, and do the results of studies of environmental health risks benefit anyone but the researchers themselves?

It was apparent that the only way to get universities or national research institutes involved in a community issue was to pay the costs for that research. In this case, the sum was beyond the PHC center's means. Fortunately, one person volunteered to conduct the study out of her own personal interest in the subject.

The PHC team now had to collect blood samples from residents to assist the researcher in her study. Many residents were extremely cooperative and showed a tremendous amount of trust in the team. Many even allowed the team to take blood from their very young children. A sympathetic local official warned us that some residents signed a complaint against our activities which said that we were disseminating panic among the residents by taking blood samples. The complaint appeared to be prompted by the factory owners. To protect ourselves from further complaints, we took all blood samples within the PHC center itself. We also learned that the factory owners had approached the head of the department in which our researcher worked, warning the supervisor against the continuation of the study. Fortunately, all of the samples had been collected and analyzed by the time the complaint was made.

After all the exhausting work the team went through to obtain a researcher and assist in the study, the researcher refused to release the completed study to the group. The reason she gave was that she planned to publish her research and was afraid that use in court would violate copyright laws. Some members, however, felt that she had bowed to the factory owners' threats to her supervisor. Whatever the reason, the PHC team faced a crisis because of her reluctance. Many residents were eager to find out the results of the tests and the inability of the team to provide answers was difficult for many members. Were it not for the support of other NGOs and other residents, the team's fight may have ended then. After several months of persistence, however, the team was able to convince the researcher to photocopy the study for our purposes. The results of the study were startling.

The Results of the el-Waily Study

In this study, the researcher tried to evaluate the role of lead smelters in polluting the surrounding atmosphere and the effects of high concentrations of atmospheric lead on the level of lead in the blood of the general population, and particularly children living near the smelters. Suspended particles were collected from the ambient atmosphere at a height of 10 meters above the ground. Air samples were taken for 24 hours twice a week over a three-month period (May through July 1992). Samples of street dust were collected from both el-Waily and el-Maadi residential areas for comparison. Lead concentrations were measured in the blood of thirty subjects, 70 percent of whom were children between the ages of three and fifteen years old. Fifteen control samples were taken from subjects living outside of el-Waily.

The concentration of suspended lead particles in the air of el-Waily was unexpectedly high (Table 1). Comparisons between measures of total suspended particulate (TSP) in el-Waily to TSP in Cairo's City Center and residential areas such as el-Maadi and el-Dokki, suggest that industrial emission is responsible for the extremely high levels of TSP found in el-Waily. El-Waily showed TSP levels nearly three times higher than those of el-Dokki and el-Maadi. Suspended particulates are particularly dangerous because the fine particles remain suspended in the air for long periods of time, affecting the respiratory system, corroding buildings, and affecting climate. The level of atmospheric lead was also much higher than other areas of Cairo—nearly thirty-five times the levels measured in Cairo's city center and el-Maadi (Table 2). The levels are also nearly fifty times greater than the air quality standard for lead in the United States. The mean lead concentration in the blood of both children and adults in the el-Waily area was more than twice as high as that of the control group (Table 3). The mean concentration of lead in street dust was eight times that of el-Maadi (Table 4).

Table 1
Mean concentration of total suspended particulate in the atmosphere of the investigated area and other residential sectors ($\mu g/m3$)

Location	Concentration	Source
Cairo center		
City center	641.00	Shakour, 1993
el-Dokki	316.00	Hindy et al., 1990
el-Maadi	.331.06	Shakour, 1992
Present study		
el-Waily	911.06	
Baghdad	340.00	Kahbour, 1985
Chicago	115.90	Butler, 1979
London	96.00	Butler, 1979
Japan	88.80	Butler, 1979
Brazil	100.00	Helen et al., 1981
Air quality standard	75.00	Geometric mean

Table 2
Mean concentration of daily measurements of atmospheric lead

	Pb level	
	$\mu g/m^3$	%
Range	220–14.6	28–1.1
Mean	86.9	9.5
SD	± 51.6	
Air quality standard	1.5	
Cairo center	2.8 (Shakour, 1982)	
el-Maadi	0.15 (Shakour and Hindy, 1992)	

Table 3
Mean blood lead concentration in the exposed and control group ($\mu g/dl$)

	Exposed Group		Control Group
	Children	Adult	Children
Range	80–22	90–25	28–12
Mean	55.18	49.11	20.70
SD	± 17.20	± 24.66	± 5.20
Normal Concentration	30	40	

Table 4
Mean concentration of lead in street dust ($\mu g/g$)

Site	el-Waily	el-Maadi
Mean	1965.7	239.5
SD	± 760.7	90.5

The Culmination of the Campaign

By the time the study was released, local elections had started and all of the candidates put the closure of the two factories at the top of their election platform. Several NGOs were also supportive of our efforts. The director of the Center for Egyptian Civilization Studies and the Association for the Urban Development of Islamic Cairo published an article joining us in the demand for free access to information and the abolishment of Law 32 of 1964. This attention boosted the PHC team's confidence. The group's efforts were finally being recognized.

The group then decided to take all of its information to the Egyptian Environmental Affairs Agency (EEAA) for support. After the severity of the situation was explained, the agency failed to react. They merely said that a case was pending surrounding this issue. What the group finally obtained, however, was information about the case against the governor, including the elusive case number. PHC lawyers obtained documents showing that the judge in the case ruled the 1991 order to close the factories null and void because there was insufficient evidence that the factories presented a real hazard to public health. The owners had then demanded LE5 million in damages.

The PHC team disseminated the results of the el-Waily study extensively. We felt that it was our moral obligation to tell the residents of el-Waily about the risks they faced, even if we could not provide solutions. Our activities inspired a member of the People's Assembly to raise the issue with the Assembly's Committee of Health. We sent our information to the media which led to thorough coverage of the el-Waily situation by newspapers, magazines, and radio throughout 1993. The governor of Cairo issued a new decree calling for the closure of both factories and insisted that the decree be implemented. In July 1993, the factories were closed for the first time since they had opened in 1972.

Once again the factory owners decided to sue the governor for issuing the decree against the factories. The hearing was set for January 1994 and the PHC team planned to be there. The date of the hearing was changed mysteriously and neither the group nor the government representative was notified. By the end of October 1993, one of the factories had reopened. The other factory closed down the smelters and sold the pipes. The owner of the closed factory owned other lead smelters in Shubra el-Khema.

On 10 November, 1993, a decision was taken to shut off all water and electricity to the remaining factory. This order was not carried out. In mid-February 1994, a petition was circulated among the residents of el-Waily. The area representative and some residents took the petition to the governor, only to be informed that the local council representatives were going to the factory to confront the owner. To their surprise, the owner had removed the doors of the factory to prevent closure. The representatives placed a ladder in the doorway with a red wax seal, which workers walked around the next morning to enter the factory. Residents kept up the pressure on the governor, who was finally able to shut down the lead factory. It remains closed.

Conclusion

The experiences of the PHC team in its campaign against the el-Waily lead factories show that peaceful social change is possible in Egypt. However, certain things are essential for that success: community involvement and the freedom to organize. The people of el-Waily were eager to change the hazardous conditions that affected their lives, but many felt powerless to do so. The PHC team wanted to take action against the factories, but it was afraid of governmental action against it. Had the community and the team not gotten over their fears, the factories might still be poisoning the air or anger might have erupted into a violent attempt at change.

The people of el-Waily, like those in many of the poor communities throughout Egypt, feel alienated from their government and their society. As the government implements policies such as structural adjustment and privatization, the lives of large segments of its population are being hurt. What results is a malignant process of continuous marginalization of much of the community. It is in this margin, the space that houses the powerless, that anger flourishes, and it is anger that groups who seek to use violence to change this country into another thrive upon.

In el-Waily, the PHC center was not just a catalyst for community mobilization. It was also a peaceful outlet for the frustrations of el-Waily's community and bridged the gap between the "haves" and "have nots." Legal restrictions, such as Egyptian Law 32 limiting the interaction between NGOs and the larger population, may hinder the effectiveness of groups like the PHC team. Restrictions on access to information also impede the efforts of activists attempting positive change. Such policies only hinder the very organizations that may help maintain peace in Egypt as the country lurches through these difficult times. The freedom to organize, be it as syndicates, NGOs, or community groups, will help Egypt to remain a peaceful society. Such associations should be encouraged to organize for the betterment of all Egypt, rather than be continually thwarted.

23

Environmental Threats in Jordan and Syria

Marc Lavergne

"Do not corruption in the land, after it has been set right"
—*The Koran Interpreted,* translated by A. J. Arberry, "The Battlements," v. 54.

The Near Eastern ecosystem is fragile, perhaps nowhere more so than on the shores of the eastern Mediterranean, where the transition between the conditions on the coast and the desert milieu of the interior is sharper than elsewhere: only in the north is the strip of inhabited land, parallel to the shore, and which is the western segment of the Fertile Crescent, more than 100 km wide.

Fragility is thus first of all caused by aridity: the rainfall, which comes between October and March, is low in the shadow of the coastal mountains. Its annual range is from 300 to 450 mm at Amman, while at Damascus it averages 200 mm. Rainfall also varies a good deal from one year to the next. This aridity is accentuated by the nature of the soils, which are mostly thick and very permeable limestone soils, with large areas in the Hauran and the Jebel Druz where equally porous basaltic lava has spread. Rainwater thus sinks in quickly, and the countryside appears, as soon as the summer heat hits, to be sterile and desolate. This impression is often misleading, because, while the summers are hot and dry, the rainy season is cold and humid; snow is frequent and can remain several weeks in the plains, and several months in the mountains. Spring and autumn are only two brief interseasons, spring in particular being splendid, but they do not have much influence on the climate.

These conditions are not hostile to agriculture; on the contrary, the lightness of the soils and the ease of clearing the vegetative cover explain how it is that in the Neolithic period one of the earliest centers of sedentary life and of agriculture appeared here.

But to correct for the excesses of the climate and the defects of the skeletal soils, people early had to invent a technology, such as terracing on the hillsides, to retain the water and the precious soil. Thus during times of peace there developed here a prosperous rural life, based on the triad of wheat, grapes, and olives, and on the raising of small livestock (sheep and goats). But these corridors of

From *Peuples Méditerranéens* 62/63:115–32 (1993). Translated by Nicholas S. Hopkins. Reprinted by permission. Marc Lavergne is a geographer at URBAMA, University of Tours, France.

fertility, open to all the conquerors in history, rarely knew such periods of peace. The Roman peace was one of the longest, and regions like the Hauran were one of the wheat granaries of Rome.

Next to this permanent cause of the fragility of the ecosystem, there was a second, as a kind of counterpoint. The periods of peace led inevitably to population growth, and to the concomitant risk of a breakdown in the equilibrium between humans and the environment. There is a striking historic example in the fate of the limestone hills of North Syria, which were densely populated and prosperous until the fifth century after Christ.[1] One can still visit intact Byzantine villages with richly decorated basilicas in a landscape that is now naked and deserted. This hill zone was overused, and then had to be abandoned when the soils were exhausted, even though other factors such as wars, or on the other hand the pacification of the plains, epidemics, earthquakes, and deterioration of the climate also probably played a role.

Today the same threat appears, in other forms. There are 3.3 million people in Jordan (60 percent of them being refugees from Palestine who arrived in the last half-century) and 12 million in Syria, and the pressure on space and on water resources is worrying. The rural regions, which until recently were left to scattered bands of pastoral nomads, now have population densities of 400 people to the square km in North Jordan,[2] and 350 in North Syria.[3] Urbanization increases (70 percent of the population in Jordan, and 50 percent in Syria, is urban) and industrialization are the engines of economic development, to meet the constantly increasing needs of a population whose growth rate is very high (3.4 percent annually in Jordan, and 3.5 percent in Syria).

Thus the degradation of the environment may appear unavoidable. In fact, these interior border lands of the Fertile Crescent have historically known major upheavals. At the end of the Ommayad Empire, in the eighth century, sedentary life shrank rapidly. The steppe was given over to camel-raising Bedouin, who raided caravans and obliged the few remaining villages hidden in the hills to pay the "brotherhood tax," the *khuwa*. This Bedouinization was certainly one of the reasons for the almost complete deforestation of this region, which in the Roman period had beautiful forested mountains.

It was only in the middle of the nineteenth century that the Ottoman sultans encouraged the settlement of farmers (Circassians who came as refugees from the Caucasus mountains), and gradually succeeded in getting some of the major Bedouin confederations (such as the Beni Sakhr in Jordan) to settle and to transform the steppe pasture lands into cereal cultivation.[4]

But the impact of Bedouinization is still perceptible, in that the attachment to the land is weak, apart from the patches of old settlement in the mountains. Agricultural development has thus not included heavy investment in soil conservation or in tree planting, especially since much of the land use remained collective and subject to rotation under the *musha'* system until the 1930s.[5]

An awareness of the consequences of urbanization and industrialization for the environment has been lacking.

This takes us back, in the perception both of the public and the leaders, to the relationship which society has with the state and with nature: the state form which this region had could best be characterized as an "oriental despotism," not in the sense of Karl Wittfogel,[6] which led to the major hydraulic engineering works of the Nile Delta or the Far East, but in the sense of the more recent Ottoman Empire, which like its immediate predecessors the Mamluks, was only interested in the countryside as a source of tax revenue. This was an outsider, predatory state which pushed people to retreat into their own lives, concerned above all with survival.[7]

Modern states, and especially Syria, which base their legitimacy on various forms of Arab nationalism, tried to create a sense of citizenship through the education of the youth and the militarization/structuring of society. But power was held by privileged minorities, concerned to realize rapid profits, and society was little inclined to develop a sense of the common patrimony, or to stress the preservation of the interests of future generations.

The ecological equilibrium of Jordan and Syria is thus worrisome, but the situation is not catastrophic. One should note that the air is clean and dry, so far spared atmospheric pollution, away from the major industrial centers at any rate. There are also the advantages that come from a hilly environment that allows for good drainage.

Three ecological zones seem to be the most threatened, in the most populated areas of these two countries.[8]

1) The closed basins, which receive the streams of water separated from the ocean by the mountain chains of Palestine, of Lebanon, and of the Alawites. On the banks of these river basins major cities have developed. On the one hand, there is the Jordan valley system, including its tributaries such as Wadi Zarqa which rises in Amman, the capital of Jordan, and passes through industrial zones before flowing into the Jordan. On the other hand, there is the Barada river, which passes through Damascus before irrigating its oasis, the Ghouta, and then empties itself out in the steppe. And there is also the modest river of Aleppo, the Quweiq, whose banks are lined with orchards.

2) The mountains, which were deforested during the Bedouinization phase, and by the need for firewood and for construction wood in the cities and for the Hejaz railroad (built from 1900 to 1908, and which continued to work until it was destroyed by Lawrence of Arabia in 1918). Today, there are many reforestation efforts, to halt erosion and develop tree cultivation, but these efforts also have their negative effects as we will see.

3) The coasts, narrow maritime windows on the Gulf of Aqaba and the Mediterranean, both of which have warm water and are not turbulent, and are thus poor in plankton and very fragile. The coastal areas also have numerous

activities, notably the ports, industries, tourist zones, and even farmlands on the Syrian coast.

This quick review allows us to examine the environmental policies followed by the two countries. The natural conditions are similar, and the people have the same way of life, culture, and civilization, but the political authorities have chosen contrasting development models: "Arab socialist" in Syria, and Western-oriented liberal in Jordan.

Urban Growth, Industrialization, and Water Pollution

Interior drainage is almost always the case for the regions located east of the mountain chains along the Mediterranean shore. Only the Orontes ['Asi] river manages to find its way through a narrow pass in the northern hills, and to flow into the ocean through Turkey. The streams thus mostly flow away from the mountains towards the steppe, or into the Jordan river system, which in some ways mirrors the Orontes to the north, but without reaching the sea.

The discharge of these rivers is rather low. Many are intermittent, and the flow of the few permanent rivers is reduced to a trickle in summer. This makes them all the more vulnerable to pollution.

These small streams with precious water[9] were the origin of the growth and the splendor of such ancient cities as Damascus, Aleppo, Hama, Homs, and Philadelphia (Amman). People still enjoy their fresh streams on summer evenings by sitting on the terraces of the cafés and restaurants of the Barada gorges, above Damascus. But these cities have now become large metropolises (Damascus has 1.2 million people, Aleppo has 1.1 million, and Amman has 1 million), which produce a great deal of wastewater, of solid matter, and of industrial waste.

The River Basins

All three rivers, the Quweiq in Aleppo, the Barada in Damascus, and the "Seil" tributary of the Zarqa in Amman, were covered over in this century by slabs of cement or marble, and transformed into streets and pathways in Amman, and into the site of the International Fair in Damascus. Underneath this covering, they now flow as disgusting sewers, which are sometimes visible when they appear in the open, as in the area north of the Citadel in Damascus, where they carry waste matter through the old working-class neighborhoods and the aging factories which will soon be demolished. Leaving the city, the central branch of the Barada flows into the orchards which it irrigates, but only after having crossed the industrial zone occupied by potters and makers of construction material. At this point its waters are no more than a heavy gray mud, with an unbearable smell.

Jordan has the same problems with the Zarqa river.[10] The Zarqa, having crossed the industrial suburbs of the capital, flows through a canyon which winds between the hills of the Beni Hassan country. Its waters are used to irrigate the vegetable gardens on its banks, before they are stored in the King Talal Reservoir,[11] brought into service in 1977. From the reservoir, water is released in summer into the East Ghor Canal, which irrigates the lower Jordan valley. This valley is the principal agricultural region of Jordan. Thanks to its year-round warm climate (since it is 300 to 400 m below sea level), and to perennial irrigation with the damming of the tributaries of the Jordan river, it provides the domestic market and the Gulf countries with early vegetables and both temperate zone and tropical fruits.

The pollution of the Zarqa river has nevertheless reached alarming levels in recent years. The waters carry a foam and toxic industrial waste, which the purification plant at Khirbet al-Samra is unable to deal with. On the contrary, this plant is too small and badly designed, and it worsens the pollution by letting its waste enter into the water table, from where it flows back into the river.

This situation led, during the dry years of 1988–90, to a prohibition on the use of the Talal Dam waters for irrigation. The government then had to confront public opinion angry about industrial waste, and people refused to consume the produce from the valley. A purification program was launched, but the present, unchanged, state of the river makes one wonder how effective it was. The problem seems to be the corruption found in the upper levels of the Jordanian administration, whose interests are linked to those of the foreign consultancy companies called in to improve the situation. An environmental political party was even started up in 1989, after two people died from exposure to pollution.

The problem could be solved by rebuilding the whole system of wastewater disposal and by adding new and better purification stations. But until now, the managers of the existing stations, which were costly to build, stubbornly claim that the stations are doing their job.

In 1987–89 the SOGREAH carried out a study for Amman City Council which showed that there were losses of the order of 40 percent in the network collecting the wastewater. Amman had 246,000 inhabitants in 1961, 649,000 in 1979, and 1,009,000 in 1987. The sewage network did not grow as rapidly, and when in winter there is heavy rain in this city with steep slopes that converge on the Seil valley, the network overflows, and the rainwater is mixed with sewage and with fecal matter.

In Syria, public opinion does not play a role, but the situation in the Ghouta of Damascus is even more catastrophic. The Ghouta is dying, both because of urban growth and anarchic industrialization and because the waters are not treated at all.

In the partly closed basin of the Orontes, where the river water is used to irrigate the Ghab depression brought under cultivation in the 1960s, the situation could begin to resemble that of the Jordan valley, with the growth in the headwaters of Homs, a major industrial center with nearly 600,000 people, and of Hama, with 300,000 people.

The Seasonal Lakes

At the end of their flow, the residual water of these rivers accumulates in marshy depressions, wetlands in the middle of the steppe. The Dead Sea, which receives the Jordan's waters, is distinct, being an extreme case of a lifeless area in a desert climate.

These plains where the waters spread out in huge basins are a key part of the steppe's ecosystem. In winter they become lakes where the rainwater accumulates, and are surrounded by meadows and by brushland; they then shrink in summer and offer a refuge for game and for migratory birds.

Today, there is a threat that these lakes will dry up altogether because of urban extraction of water from their catchment areas. For instance, there is the case of the Awaj river, which runs down from the escarpments of Mount Hermon and is lost south of Damascus, and of the Barada itself. In Jordan, the Azraq oasis is a special case. The water here comes from underground flow from the basaltic areas of the Jebel Druz, but now the water from this huge zone of lakes and swamps is being overpumped to supply the urban centers of Amman and Irbid.[12] In spite of the establishment of the Shomari nature reserve where near-extinct species of animals from the Arabian desert, such as the oryx, are being reintroduced,[13] the future of the oasis is very much in doubt.

With respect to the question of urban and industrial pollution, water is the center of the problem. This resource is valuable and limited, however much breathing space might be found through political solutions (such as a settlement of the Arab–Israeli dispute) or through technical ones (bringing Euphrates water to Jordan, for instance). It thus seems necessary to strictly limit the agricultural use of water, and to save it for high value crops only.[14]

The accelerating urbanization must include the installation of efficient networks for supplying and removing water, with effective treatment systems for used water. People must be made aware of the vital character of the issue, and persuaded, for instance, that water can be reused without harm.

Finally industry (especially the refineries of Homs in Syria and Zarqa in Jordan) must treat its toxic waste, which is dangerous for the surrounding populations and for the river basins and the agricultural zones further downstream. The controlled storage of these wastes should be made easier by the proximity of the desert.

The Advance of Tree Cover

We have seen that the forests suffered greatly from the Bedouinization of earlier centuries and from the demand for wood linked to the urban and technological developments of the twentieth century. Fifty years ago, the fauna was also more dense and more varied in the steppe and in the mountains, where it was not rare to meet carnivorous animals such as lions, leopards, or lynx.

Today, forests only remain as relics, in the most inaccessible regions: for example, the beautiful forests of firs in the plateau of green rocks (serpentine and gabbro) of the Bassit[15] on the Syria–Turkey border, or those of oak (*quercus ilex*) and pines (*pinus pinea*) which cover 18 percent of the area of the northern Alawite mountains, or the sacred groves that surround their whitewashed sanctuaries on the peaks, testifying to ancient nature cults.[16] The other Syrian mountains such as the Anti-Liban and Mount Hermon are completely deforested.

In Jordan, the mountains of Ajlun and of Balqa[17] still have a few woody areas of green oaks and of pines, especially in areas unreachable by flocks of goats. These forests, which were used by the villagers on the western slope to protect themselves against Bedouin raids, also provided refuge for a long time to highwaymen and outlaws—from the first Palestinian fighters of the anti-British revolt of 1936–1939, pursued by the Arab Legion, to the *fedayin* scattering after the Black September confrontation in 1970–71. Today, they also play a role in recreation, with the establishment of national parks at Zay and Dibbin, where hikers and picnickers go on weekends from Amman.

The perception of nature, and certainly of trees, has changed a great deal in the last twenty years, especially in Jordan, where urbanization has been rapid. This translates into a new spread of agriculture and forests, and thus the countryside is changed again.

The Greening of the Countryside
Until recently, the countryside of Jordan and Syria was still largely given over to open field agriculture, but today there is a shift, wherever natural conditions allow it, to more profitable crops. The money earned by the migrants to the Gulf has allowed new technology: deep wells, terracing equipment, water-saving irrigation technology suited to local needs, plastic greenhouses.

Agriculture has become a passion and a favorite investment, which attracts even city people. The Jordanian countryside is being covered with young olive groves geometrically laid out and carefully fenced with barbed wire. The higher areas of the Syrian mountains (Jebel Druz, Jebel Alawi) are being planted in apple trees, while the well-irrigated lowlands are planted in a range of temperate zone and Mediterranean fruits—the traditional apricots, but also oranges and lemons, with cherries near Aleppo, and everywhere grapes grown on cement trellises.

This private-sector and market-oriented agriculture is radically different than the traditional rural civilization: this is an agriculture without peasants, where the work is carried out by day labor, often from abroad (in Jordan, there are workers from Egypt, Syria, and Pakistan).

This agriculture gives rise to a proliferation of personal villas, which breaks up the rural land use pattern and upsets the working of the traditional agro-pastoral structures, by paying no attention to pasturage, to the needs of flocks, or to the fallow rotation system.

It is true that these new orchards require the terracing of the rocky slopes and the trenching of the chalky soils, both of which diminish water erosion, but on the other hand, they leave the improved soil unprotected.

These green spots which remain in the height of the summer heat are thus the sign of a new way of life, linked to growing prosperity and security, which explains this new attitude towards nature. But the opposite side of the coin is the fragility of the system, which is based narrowly on present-day conditions of profitability, and on the availability of irrigation water from deep wells or from streams. Another consequence is the privatization and the division of the land, marked by the careful fencing of the farms, in an area which had been characterized by open fields since high antiquity.

The interference with rights to common pasturage is a deadly menace to a civilization based on symbiosis between herder and farmer, the nomad and the sedentary. But perhaps one should see in the disappearance of the black tents and the flocks of goats in the hilly areas only an outcome of a socioeconomic evolution on a much larger scale, where in a single generation some were able to become rich and to cause their land to bloom, while others, unable to subsist with a small flock on their arid land, were forced to leave the village or the campsite to try their luck in the city.

Reforestation

Reforestation has become a national goal, especially in Jordan, where Queen Nour has headed a movement for a "Green Jordan." This enterprise, begun during the recent period of dry years, set as its goals the struggle against erosion, the creation of awareness among the young of the significance of the collective patrimony, making recreational space available to urban crowds, and last but not least the beautification of urban space.

The spirit of this movement is influenced by fashion coming from America, which the high society of Amman follows closely. Thus every year there is a Day of the Tree, under the patronage of the Queen: every school child plants a tree, but this is not always very effective.

Furthermore, the state, both in Syria and in Jordan, has undertaken to reforest, especially on the slopes of the Jordan valley, the wadi Zarqa, the hills of Balqa province, and the mountains of the south (Tafila, Shaubak). This reforestation unfortunately involves primarily conifers, which, while they hold the soil, also make it acid and do not allow the growth of undergrowth with a diversified flora and fauna. There is a danger of creating "green deserts" if nothing is done to regenerate the forests of old green oaks. In the north (Koura district, near Dair Abi Said) there are of course protected forest preserves full of leafy trees, but in the south (in the Shara mountains, between Shaubak and Petra), the last majestic specimens scattered in the rocks indicate that it would be possible to replant this useful and nourishing tree.

The national parks of Zay and of Dibbin (whose highest peaks are at 1,081 meters and at 1,247 meters respectively) preserve some fine species, especially Dibbin, where there are many Aleppo pines and where the undergrowth is varied. But they are under stress because of the crowds of Friday visitors. They are filled with discarded trash, and sometimes are even used to dump domestic garbage. There is room for a lot more awareness campaigns, and the youth, or even the army draftees, could be mobilized to keep the parks clean and to protect the trees.

On the whole there has been a movement in the right direction, since there is greater awareness, together with the urbanization of the society. Relations to nature change. Nature is now perceived as a place for necessary and helpful relaxation, and therefore worth protecting.

For its part, the state has established an administration and the means that allow it to act. It manages the water, the forests, and the natural resources, it creates new green spaces in the city, and plants trees along the major roads, for instance between Amman and its airport in Jordan, and between Damascus and Homs in Syria.

The Coast in Danger

These zones are quite small (30 km of coastline in Jordan, 183 km in Syria) but they are vital for the national economy. Much in demand for a variety of uses, sometimes contradictory ones, they are threatened with degradation, perhaps even ecological disaster.

The Aqaba Gamble
Jordan is an extreme case: at the end of the Gulf of Aqaba, where the water is warm and very pure, in a zone encircled by desert mountains, Jordan acquired in 1925 from what was then the kingdom of the Hejaz, a coastline of about 10 km. In 1965, anxious to enlarge this window so as to create heavy industry, Jordan obtained the cession of another 20 km of coastline from Saudi Arabia, in exchange for large desert zones in the interior.

The port of Aqaba (50,000 inhabitants) is first of all Jordan's only port. It also serves Syria and the occupied West Bank for their liaisons with countries to the east of the Suez Canal. But above all it became the great rear port of Iraq during the Iran–Iraq war (1980–1988), replacing Basra on the Shatt al-Arab.

The city has developed into an important sea resort, like Eilat, its Israeli twin. It is possible to swim in the sea in the heart of winter, and divers can find untouched underwater zones, including coral reefs. This resort is much appreciated by both local and foreign tourists. An underwater nature park has been created just south of the city, with a research station linked to the University of Jordan. Even more than the pollution and other problems brought about by urban growth and the movement of ships, the real danger for this shoreline comes from the creation, on the Saudi frontier, of a factory to process and load phosphates, and of a potassium loading terminal. These two minerals are the main national sources of mineral wealth in Jordan, and these factories are likely to grow regularly in the coming years.

The phosphate processing plant handled 968,000 tons of phosphates in 1990 (some 6.08 million tons of phosphate was sent by rail from the mines to Aqaba; most is exported raw). This was used, together with 280,000 tons of sulfur and 136,000 tons of ammoniac to produce 596,000 tons of biammonium phosphate fertilizer, 18,000 tons of phosphoric acid and 148,000 tons of aluminum fluoride.

The production of potassium, brought to Aqaba by truck from the mine south of the Dead Sea, amounted to 1.4 million tons.

The air pollution produced by the phosphate fertilizer factory is carried into the desert mountains of the interior by the prevailing winds. But the handling and the processing of so many chemical products present a certain danger for the sea. The state, which owns these factories, keeps an eye on their security; its reputation depends on it, as does the continuation of tourist activity.

Until now, the gamble has been won: Aqaba is a clean town, its urban growth under control. The air is pure and the water is limpid, despite the continuous activity in the area.

State Negligence in Syria
The Syrian coast is a classic Mediterranean coastline: low shoreline, bordered by a marshy plain, and closed off on the landward side by the continuous barrier of the Jebel Alawi (whose high point is 1,563 m, in the north). There are only a few rocky promontories which have allowed commercial ports to flourish since high antiquity.

The first industrial installations on the coast, built after World War II, were the oil terminals of Baniyas and Tartous, where the oil from Iraq and Saudi Arabia was loaded, thus bypassing the Suez Canal. An oil refinery was also built at Baniyas.

Beginning in the 1970s, the coastal plain then went through a period of sustained economic development. The ports of Latakia (197,000 inhabitants in 1981), Baniyas (25,000 inhabitants), and Tartous (53,000 inhabitants) are the main poles for industrial development. Among the principal factors of industrial pollution, there are two cement plants, one 15 km north of Latakia at Borj Islam, the other at Baniyas, a phosphate terminal loading dock at Tartous, and thermal electricity generation plants using relatively polluting heavy fuel oil.

This coastal zone is also the site of intensive agricultural development, through the reclamation of the coastal plain, and the locale of a major seaside tourist development. In the absence, so far, of protection and development measures, the environment is deteriorating rapidly. In 1988–89, the United Nations Development Program presented a report on this situation as part of the Mediterranean "Blue Plan."[18]

According to this report, so great a concentration of urban and industrial activities along the coast has led to pollution of fresh water, of air, of the sea, and of the soil, as well as a noticeable degradation of the countryside. A few examples give an idea of the extent of the damage.[19]

(1) The main spring on the coast, Al-Sin (producing 12 cubic meters per second), which supplies Latakia with drinking water, is contaminated by pathogenic bacteria coming from human waste, by nitrates and by phosphates of agricultural origin, and even by petroleum residues from the Baniyas refinery.

(2) The sea is the most affected milieu. No coastal city has any facility to treat sewage, and the exit points of the sewers are the source of the heavy concentrations of streptococcus and of staphylococcus recorded on the beaches of Latakia, Baniyas, and Tartous. Many beaches do not meet the health standards set down by the Barcelona convention. To this organic pollution is then added industrial waste (hydrocarbons, pesticides) which is harmful to the marine fauna and flora.

(3) Air pollution caused by industrial waste is spreading, pushed inland by the southwest winds, where it is blocked by the mountain barrier.

(4) The soil is heavily eroded, thanks to deforestation and acid rain. The opening up of new farm land, and forest fires, push the forest back, while the oaks and the cedars around the summer resort of Slenfé are dying with no apparent explanation.

The fragile ecosystem of the beaches and the dunes is also under attack. South of Latakia, a sand quarry destroyed one of the few dunes on the Syrian coast, and the beaches no longer receive new sand since the river banks have been diked.

Tourism itself is an important cause of pollution. Cement buildings are often located in unspoiled sites, such as Ras Ibn Hani or Ras el-Bassit. In the latter case, the forest reached the shore, until illegal building and unauthorized camping pushed it back.[20] To the ugliness of these built-up seashores there is then added an aggressive architecture (apartment buildings at Ras el-Bassit, Meridien and Cote d'Azur hotels at Ras Ibn Hani) which also damages the landscape. "Apartment complexes, built on the tops of the mountains, which can be seen on the Kassab road, or the Cham Palace of Safita, are absurd. They are the proof of a mad conception of architecture, completely out of line with the present urban and cultural environment," notes the Blue Plan report.

Tourism is also responsible for a high consumption of fresh water: 150 liters per person per day for local tourism, and 250 liters for international tourism in 1984 (even up to 600 liters per person per day in the international hotels).

Farmers unhappy after three straight dry years (1988–1990) diverted the drinking water pipelines from the Al-Sin spring to Latakia in order to irrigate their orange groves.

Bringing together tens of thousands of extra inhabitants on a few kilometers of beaches in the summer heightens the pressure on the environment,[21] especially in the case of unorganized camping, where there is no sanitary facility, no supply of drinking water, no collection of refuse. The beautiful northern beaches, dominated by the forest-covered al-Bassit mountains, are now filthy.

The Blue Plan suggests, for this situation, installing new facilities in controlled environments, and not in vulnerable ecosystems such as dunes, cliffs, or in remarkable sites such as peaks and promontories. It suggests protecting the sites of Um al-Touyour, Slayeb Turkman, the dunes south of Latakia, the wetlands of al-Laha, and the Slenfé forests, even though the first three are coveted by developers.

Coastal tourism, like other human activities, can perturb the environment if it is carried out with only a short time horizon, and in a predatory manner. But tourism is a mass activity which requires a protected environment.

In Syria, a "socialist" state, public goods are appropriated by private groups and a civil and military nomenklatura which competes for access to the best sites, which paves over the coast and destroys the coastal forests without concern for the future, or for the fate of the greater part of the population which crowds onto nauseating and polluted beaches.

The development of the Syrian coast must be completely rethought, with an eye toward respecting the environment and the well-being of the population, through a carefully balanced analysis of the needs of the different sectors of the economy (agriculture, industry, tourism) as well as of human consumption needs in urban areas.

This summary of the main threats to the environment in Jordan and Syria shows a mixed situation. While the fresh water supply, for domestic use or for agriculture, is threatened by urban and industrial growth, there are means to correct this.

Atmospheric pollution is low, and the air is generally among the purest on earth, but the hearts of the major cities are more problematic, for there people are choked by dust and automobile exhaust.

Vegetation is spreading, after having suffered during centuries of pasturage, and trees are recovering their ability to restrain erosion, to regulate the climate, and to fix the soil, all of which this semiarid zone needs greatly.

However, one cannot help but be worried by the idea that these countries, where urban civilization was born, will fall into the same mistakes as the Western countries: on the one hand, the pleasant orchards of their suburbs, havens of peace and rest for the urbanites, will be inexorably devoured by urban growth and its diseases; on the other, the beaches and the mountains will be paved over by hideous tourist complexes, whose modernity is no guarantee of healthfulness.

Fortunately, public opinion, whether or not it can express itself, is more and more concerned by environmental protection. Local initiatives to protect a place, a forest, an ancient site, are no longer rare. Schools play their role in awakening children to these concerns, and the state, especially in Jordan, which is quite a bit ahead of other Middle Eastern countries in this respect,[22] is increasingly concerned to include environmental protection in its development policy. But, in order not to be the object of the jokes of the singers and the public, these declarations of good intentions must be carried out in reality more than they have been so far.

Notes

1   Georges Tate, *Les campagnes de la Syrie du Nord du IIème au VIIème siècle,* tome 1 (Paris: Geuthner, 1992).

2   Marc Lavergne, "Aménagement du territoire et croissance urbaine en Jordanie: Amman et le 'désert jordanien,'" in *Monde Arabe/Maghreb-Machrek,* #140, 1993, pp. 35–58.

3   Marc Lavergne, "L'urbanisation contemporaine de la Syrie du Nord" in *Revue du Monde Musulman et de la Méditerranée,* 62, 1991/4, pp. 195–208.

4   Norman Lewis, *Nomads and Settlers in Syria and Jordan, 1800–1980* (London: Cambridge University Press, 1987); Rauf Abu Jaber, *Pioneers over Jordan: The Frontiers of Settlement in Transjordan, 1850–1914* (London: I.B.Tauris, 1989).

5   Jacques Weulersse, *Paysans de Syrie et du Proche-Orient* (Tours, 1946); Lars Wählin, "Occurrence of musha' in Transjordan" in *Geografiska Annaler,* 70B, 1988 (3), pp. 375–79.

6   Karl Wittfogel, *Oriental Despotism* (New York: Random House-Vintage, 1981).

7   Volney (Cte. de), *Voyage en Egypte et en Syrie* (Paris-La Haye: Mouton, 1959).

8   We exclude from this study the serious problem of the development of the Euphrates valley downstream from the Tabqa dam. This subject relates more to the general question of major dams in arid areas than to a regional study of the environmental problems of the Mediterranean basin. For further information, see: André Bourgey, "Le barrage de Tabqa et l'aménagement du bassin de l'Euphrate en Syrie" in *Revue de Géographie de Lyon* (+49 (4):343–54, 1974); Günter Meyer, "Umsiedlungsprobleme des syrischen Euphrat-Projektes" in *Geographische Rundschau* (+34(12):553–56 and 565–67, 1982; Jean Hannoyer, "Grands projets hydrauliques en Syrie" in *Maghreb–Machrek* #109 (1985), pp. 24–42; John F. Kolar and William A. Mitchell, *The Euphrates River and the Southeast Anatolia Development Project* (Carbondale: Southern Illinois University Press, 1991).

9   Their names show how precious the water is: Zarqa (blue), Barada (cold), etc.

10 See the collective work published under the auspices of the Friedrich Ebert Foundation, "Water pollution in Jordan, causes and effects" (Amman, 1991). On the ecological problems of the Zarqa river basin, see the study carried out by the Jordanian Ministry of Agriculture with the German Technical Cooperation Agency (GTZ): "Zarqa River Basin Project, Feasibility Study (Lower Zarqa Catchment Area), Interim Investment and Implementation Plan", vol. 1, Main Report, 1983.

11 The erosion of the slopes of the basin, which led to a rapid silting up of the reservoir, was the starting point of the Jordanian-German rehabilitation project: reforestation, levelling, introduction of improved agricultural practices. But the 1988 pollution crisis led to a reorientation of priorities towards cleaning up the bed of the river.

12 Alison Burrel (ed.), *Agricultural Policy in Jordan* (London: Ithaca Press, 1986).

13 The slaughter carried out by Saudi hunters in four-wheel-drive vehicles, with the knowing complicity of the authorities, had in Jordan, as in many other countries in the region, the result that the wildlife almost completely disappeared.

14 For a detailed study of the question, see the papers from a Colloquium organized in October 1991 by the Friedrich Ebert Foundation and the Center for Water Studies and Research of the University of Jordan. They were collected and published by Andrä Gärber and Elias Salameh under the title *Jordan's Water Resources and their Future Potential* (Amman, 1992).

15 This is the ancient Mount Cassius, whose peak is 1,759 m.

16 See Jacques Weulersse, *Le pays des Alaouites*, Tours, 1940, 2 vol.

17 The name "Salt," capital of the province of Balwa, comes from the Latin *saltus*, meaning forest or wooded pass, at the edge of the wadi Shuaiyb.

18 United Nations Development Program, "Preliminary Study of the Integrated Plan for the Syrian Coastal Region, Mediterranean Action Plan (Plan Bleu)," CCP 1988–89, SY-PS Split, February 1990.

19 Data taken from Thaddée de Slizewicz, "Le tourisme sur la côte syrien", Master's thesis in geography, University of Montpellier III, 1991.

20 ENSYC-Groupe Huit-SCAU, "Project de centre touristique à Ras el-Bassit. Rapport d'Etude" (Syrian Ministry of Tourism, 1979).

21 There were 20,000 tourist beds in 1990, plus extensive lodging possibilities in private homes. See Thaddée de Slizewicz, op. cit.

22 At least if one accepts the official discourse. King Hussein gave a speech from the Throne on December 1, 1992, in which he summarized the activities of the government in this area: definition of a National Environmental Strategy, which was to be included in a framework law then being prepared; agreement with the International Union for the Protection of Nature to protect the sites of Dana and Azraq; signing of the Hague declaration, participation in the Geneva conference and at the 1992 Earth Summit in Rio de Janeiro; signing of the agreement on "climate change and biodiversity" and of the Basel agreement on "the elimination of toxic waste and the control of their international transport"; signing of the Ramsar Convention to protect wetlands, as well as the 1987 Montréal protocol on the "Protection of the ozone layer."

24

The Human and Ecological Impact of the Civil War in Sudan

Abdel Ghaffar M. Ahmed

The present crisis of Sudan has to be viewed in the context of the interplay of multiple factors. These are the drought, agrarian policies, civil strife in at least three regions, and the influx of displaced people from neighboring countries. The fact that Sudan also sends refugees to some of its neighbors should not be overlooked: on balance, however, it receives more than it sends. The impact of these factors on the region, which is also considered a war zone, is evident (Doornbos et al., 1992). However, without minimizing the impact of other factors, this paper shall emphasize the impact of civil strife on the human and natural ecology of the region.

The argument here rests on the assumption that, in Sudan, the causal links between environmental deterioration and political and military instability are evident upon closer examination. The paper briefly explores the impact of war on high potential rural areas in order to show the magnitude of devastation that befell the resource base, and the impact of war-related devastation on production systems, lifestyles and social organization. It also considers the consequences of the process of displacement. The political aims of the government and the fighting movements shall be briefly touched upon to pave the ground for addressing the question of how much human and ecological cost should be paid in order to fulfill political aims. Finally, some conclusions will be drawn regarding halting the degradation and working towards sustainable development under peaceful conditions.

The General Context in Sudan

The malfunctioning of the production systems in Sudan is evident in the fact that there are critical food shortages in certain regions. This situation has been brought about by drought, desertification, and civil strife. Food shortage is by

From *Conflicts in the Horn of Africa: Human and Ecological Consequences of Warfare,* ed. Terje Tvedt, EPOS, Department of Social and Economic Geography, Uppsala University, 1993, pp. 114–24. Reprinted by permission. Abdel Ghaffar M. Ahmed is a Sudanese anthropologist and currently the director of the Organization for Social Science Research in East Africa, Addis Ababa, Ethiopia.

far the most common and immediate crisis in the country. However, other features in the economic and political spheres should also be noted in order to elucidate the context. Foremost among these are regional food imbalances that distinguish Sudan from most of its neighbors. Characteristically, many areas are habitually food-deficit, relying on imports from a few surplus areas in the country itself. These surplus areas also feed parts of neighboring countries such as Eritrea and Ethiopia. Although on the national level Sudan is a food-surplus country, the lack of a proper communications system that facilitates the process of distribution, and the lack of application of more equitable policies in directing production, are the major causes of food imbalances. Policy-making is a prerogative of a small group of centrally based military and merchant elites.

A significant number of the population depends on animal husbandry rather than crop production. However, with the present drought, which has affected both pastoralists and agriculturalists, the state of complementarity that used to exist between these two systems of production no longer prevails. The terms of trade in the process of exchanging livestock for grain, which is common practice in relations between farmers and pastoralists, have been working against pastoralists when commodities are available to be exchanged.

Sustainable modes of livelihood are thus becoming difficult, and a process of marginalization of rural people is a pattern that has been in existence for a long time (Ahmed, 1973; 1976; 1987). In addition to those displaced by the civil strife in the country, or who are refugees from civil war in neighboring countries, drought-and-famine-refugees are to be seen moving toward urban areas, or

Table 1
Net cereal production and food demand, 1986/87 (thousands of metric tons)

Region	1987 population	1986/87 production	1987 food demand	Balance
Kassala (Eastern Region) White Nile and Blue Nile (Central Region)	4,286	2614.6	626	+1988.6
Rest of Sudan	20,051	1322.1	2590	-1267.9
Total	24,337	3936.5	3216.0	+720.7

Source: FAO, Memo, Rome 1986.

crossing the borders to what they imagine will be more hospitable areas in neighboring countries.

The causes of the present crisis are not drought and desertification alone, however, nor can the crisis be blamed only on the lack of stability due to civil conflict. Instead it is a combination of these factors, in addition to the misguided agricultural policies adopted by the country over the past three decades, that have led to the crisis (Ahmed, 1987; 1989). This complex web of circumstances, particularly in the context of the expansion of the areas of civil war, has led to certain irreversible trends. These include land degradation, loss of livestock, loss of wildlife and changes in their migratory habits, continuous mobility, and excessive marginalization of rural communities.

The Impact of the Civil War on Different Regions

The most important aspects of the civil war in Sudan are its multidimensional nature, and the fact that its continuity is a result of both internal and external factors (Mohamed Salih et al., 1990). Further, the conflict is no longer confined to one region or one category of the population. It cuts across ethnic and social interest groups as well as across regions. For example, in terms of the composition of fighting groups, there are southerners in the government forces, while there are northerners among the Sudan People's Liberation Army (SPLA). The impact has gone beyond economic, political, and cultural structures. In many instances it has had irreversible effects on the environmental setting, leading to changes in some aspects of the physical habitat that used to accommodate human and animal life in what became known as "the war zone."

The ugly face of war is that of death, injury and material destruction, as well as the destruction of people's sense of communal identity. The fauna and flora of the war zone have been subject to indiscriminate use of weapons of destruction. Social and cultural traditions, built up over generations around a particular region, have begun to lose their meaning. Pastoralists, for example, can no longer live by herding, and thus may become socially alienated as well as materially destitute. This can be seen from the cases of the Dinka, the Nuer, and the Mundari, to name only a few of those in the war zone. Farming communities who used to help each other in times of need may find, as conditions worsen, that family and village solidarity breaks down. This can be seen in the case of the Uduk people of the southern part of the Blue Nile, and the Nuba of southern Kordofan, to whose areas the civil war has recently expanded. Also, the relation between Arab nomads and the Dinka, the Nuer, and the Shilluk, who have come together in grazing areas on the northern borders of the southern region, has been adversely affected.

The complementarity and symbiotic relationships between such groups have given way to military raids, looting, and the taking of hostages. The militarization of these communities became evident in the continuous presence of tribal militias, supported by both the government and the rebel forces. The traditional system of utilization of the grazing areas through well-defined migration routes and conservation of grass and woodlands is no longer attended to. The cultivation of small plots of land by southern groups for purposes of supplementing their diet can no longer be practiced. Fishing and hunting, which used to be daily activities of the youth of these groups during the dry season, are now hazardous. Some pastoral groups inside the war zone itself, such as the Mundari, have had to flee their areas while their herds were either looted or destroyed by disease, and large numbers of people have died (Zeid, 1988). The ethnic rivalry between warring parties in the Bor area in 1991 is but one example that witnesses have given of the type and magnitude of destruction of human life and its resource base.

In eastern Sudan the impact of war has to be seen in the context of the multidimensional pressure facing pastoralists. Though part of this region—Kassala area—is one of the high-potential areas of the country in terms of agricultural production, the rate of degradation as a result of the wars in neighboring Ethiopia and Eritrea has had a negative impact on this potential. Pastoralists in this region have faced difficulties from at least three sides: (a) from the expansion of mechanized farming, (b) from the influx of refugees from Ethiopia and Eritrea, and (c) from thousands of "bandit" groups emerging as a result of the Eritrean–Ethiopian war. Thousands of Sudanese herders, unable to take their usual route to survival by moving south, have had to accept a sedentary lifestyle. They became wage-earning laborers for the very merchant-farmers whose activities and political strength have contributed to their situation. The war has blocked any outlet to the east and has even brought them new competitors for the limited resource base they have. Some of the practices and survival strategies of the refugees, such as wood-collecting and charcoal-making for the urban market, have led to deforestation.

Table 2
Charcoal and wood consumption in northern Sudan, per annum

consumption for all regions of the north	50–60 million 30-kg sacks
Khartoum alone	14 million
Wood consumption per annum	
northern Sudan	15 million m^3
charcoal	44 percent
fuel wood	48 percent
building material	8 percent

Source: National Energy Administration, Sudan, 1991.

Pastoralists, however, are contributing to this process by cutting branches off trees to feed their animals. The environmental pressure on land in western Sudan has worsened as a result of the Chadian war. The influx of Chadian refugees has increased the human and animal population beyond the carrying capacity of the land, and has meant that the traditional migration of some pastoral groups, such as the Kababish, from Kordofan to this region has stopped. The pressure created by land degradation has forced many groups to move south to higher-potential areas, increasing the pressure in such areas and leading to armed confrontation between traditional land users and newcomers. This in turn has led to the rise of organized and armed bandit groups. The recent (1990s) expansion of Sudanese rebel activities in the south and southwestern part of this region has no doubt complicated the situation.

In addition, the increasing pressure on land, with its consequent environmental degradation and loss of the resource base for a large proportion of the people, has led to high mobility and displacement. A high percentage of the population of the southern region has either become refugees in neighboring countries, or moved to central Sudan to seek means of survival in the shanty areas around large towns such as Khartoum. The conditions under which such people live are extremely poor. They lack all basic necessities for survival. Further, such conditions subject the displaced and their host towns to environmental hazards. The government attempts to handle their case in Khartoum, to take one example, have been unfortunate. The possibilities for survival and sustainability have not been investigated prior to resettling the displaced people. This has,

Table 3
People displaced by the civil war, by destination

Khartoum*	3,000,000
Other parts of the country	
(including those from the Blue Nile)	850,000
Total	3,850,000
Refugees to neighboring countries	
Ethiopia	330,244
Uganda	23,000
Kenya	1,300
Total	354,544

*The rate of influx of displaced to the capital (Khartoum) from the southern region and southern Kordofan, during Oct. 1986 and Feb. 1987 was 12,125 persons per month.
Source: Final Report of the National Dialogue Conference on Peace, Sudan Government, Khartoum, 1989.

in certain cases, led to confrontations between government forces and members of the displaced communities. Loss of life has been reported in some of the attempts to resettle people against their will.

In addition to the pressure that displaced communities have placed on the resources of urban areas, their movements from traditional areas have led to the total neglect of what is left of resources there. These traditional areas are now out of production, nonutilized and not conserved. Their development has been halted, and any attempt to start again is going to be demanding.

It is important to note that marginalization in relation to resource utilization, in a multiethnic, multicultural country like Sudan, with a population practicing different systems of livelihood, can provide groups with a ready cause for joining revolts against the ruling elite. It is not, therefore, surprising that most of the armed groups in southern and western Sudan have been formed primarily from pastoral people, although this stems from their independence from the administration and their tradition of armed resistance, in addition to their economic marginalization (Asad, 1973; de Waal, 1990).

However, processes of marginalization have recently had a similar impact on small-scale sedentary cultivators in southern Kordofan and the Blue Nile, and have forced them to resort to arms. In particular, they have been marginalized by the capital-intensive commercial farming sector, which owes its existence and profitability to state intervention and subsidies. As their resource base has been devastated by the new tactic of landmining,[1] these groups have had no choice but to join the armed struggle against the system.

The Decline of Production Systems in the Civil War Zone

In addition to the argument above regarding drought and state policies, it should be noted that the civil war in southern Sudan is a major cause of declining production. The annual rate of growth has remained mostly negative since the renewal of the civil war in 1983. The causes of this negative growth rate in all sectors can be found in the disruption of productive activities due to displacement, lack of security, and lack of inputs. Almost all the large-scale production schemes in the war zone, whether under government or SPLA control, have ceased to function. This situation has led to the total collapse of the economy in the war zone, and made it entirely dependent on commodities moved from other parts of the country or from abroad through relief organizations.

Traditional production systems, mostly in the agriculture and livestock sector, have virtually ceased to operate due to the fact that the land on which these activities used to be practiced is no longer accessible. Landmines planted by the SPLA seem, in many areas, to stop people from attempting to move out of the villages or garrisoned towns to which they have been displaced. This mining operation has also led to a total paralysis of the transport system, and hence no agricultural input can be advanced to those who need them in the war zone. Some villagers claim to have stopped their production activities because of the fear of having their crops taken by rebels active in the area.

Grazing of animals has also become problematic, since there is the risk of coming across land mines. In areas where nomads from other regions such as the Blue Nile, Kordofan and Dar Fur used to move for part of the year and practice some symbiotic relation with the local population, such activities have disappeared. In fact, if they want to move in these areas, nomads have to do without these symbiotic relations. They also have to depend on the protection of their own militia and the government army, or strike some form of agreement with SPLA troops, whereby they provide these troops with food in exchange for freedom of grazing in areas under their control. Although none of the warring parties admits that such agreements exist, the nomads themselves acknowledge their existence and explain that it is the only way they can sustain their animal wealth.

As a result of the civil war, most of the resources in rural areas have been subject to neglect and destruction. The rural environment can no longer support populations, and has thus been gradually marginalized. The traditional sector that characterizes these areas used to support small and large urban centers in the region. This is no longer the case, since small-scale cultivation cannot be steadily practiced, nor can cattle herding be maintained due to the lack of security. The rural population, who used to maintain a reasonable subsistence level and even produce some surplus for urban dwellers in the region, has seen most of what used to be agriculturally productive or high-potential grazing areas in the southern region turn into a no man's land only frequented by the SPLA, government soldiers, or armed militia. Ordinary citizens have been forced toward centers held by the SPLA, or to government-held towns; or they have fled the region altogether.

Indirectly related to the civil war in the south, but with a similar impact, is the growing rural insecurity in parts of western Sudan (Kordofan and Dar Fur), where rural life has been undermined by banditry and interethnic conflicts. In certain parts of this area, for example, cattle rustling has reached such an extent that rural people are selling animals and moving out of the livestock economy. Cattle rustling also seems to be going on in SPLA-held areas in Equatoria, Bahr el-Ghazal, and the Upper Nile, as well as areas where relations between ethnic groups remain extremely tense.

In view of the lack of reliable information on the war zone, one can point to the impact of the war on production by glancing at the position of some economic projects that used to operate in the southern region prior to the renewal of the civil war in 1983. These projects cover the primary and secondary sectors and the service sector, and are executed by public institutions, and private or donor organizations. The performance of such projects during peace time may not have been adequate in relation to the objectives that led to their initiation, but they at least started the process of development. When these projects are prevented from operating, development in the region is retarded and the margin of inequality between the southern region and the rest of the country is increased.

The magnitude of destruction of the economic resources can be seen from the number of projects that ceased to function in the primary sector. According to the final report of the National Dialogue Conference on Peace held in Khartoum during September–October 1989 (which represents to some extent an up-to-date document on the issue), a large number of projects in the agricultural sector had to be suspended with a loss of substantial sums of money or inputs to both the region and the country as a whole. Reference here is made particularly to the large-scale projects run by regional governments and donor organizations. Among these are the Aweil Rice project, the coffee project in Equatoria, and the milk production scheme in Bhar el-Ghazal, to name only a few.

Other schemes to be financed by the UNDP or the World Bank in the area of rural development had to be abandoned together with accompanying agricultural training institutes, such as the ones in Yei and Rumbek. The Norwegian Rural Development Project in eastern Equatoria was also closed and work on the Juba–Nairobi road had to stop.

A major project which could have had a significant impact on agricultural development in the south, the north and Egypt is the Jonglei canal. Construction started in 1977 and was due for completion in 1985. The objective was to secure a flow of 4.7 billion cubic meters of water that would be shared equally between Egypt and Sudan. The immediate benefits for the region were to be the creation of an earth compact road on the eastern side of the canal, linking Malakal with Juba, and that the canal itself was to be navigable and reduce the distance between Malakal and Juba by 350 kilometers. The local population should have been able to use off-take water points for small irrigation projects and watering of their animals. The work of excavation of the canal was brought to a standstill by the civil war, after a length of 260 kilometers out of the total of 360 kilometers had been dug. In 1986, the bucket wheel machine used for the excavation "was reported damaged by aerial bombing, the action of an unidentified enemy, certainly neither the Sudan government nor the SPLA, and not, for that matter Egypt. The Sudan army was guarding the wheel until it was forced by [the] SPLA to abandon it early in 1986. The SPLA was guarding the machine when it was bombed." (Alier, 1990:211). By the time the construction stopped in February 1983 the expenditure on the project was approximately $150 million. The compensation paid to the international companies involved was $17.1 million. In addition, large sums of money given by donors were lost due to the delay of activities.

Halting the excavation and damaging the machine represented the death of a dream for the region and the country as well as for Egypt. The development of a modern drainage and irrigation works, it was hoped, would remove the physical disincentive to farming caused by the frequent danger to crops from floods and droughts (see recommendations by de Mabior, 1981:227). The result has been the existence of a physical barrier to human, animal and wildlife movement, and a new banking system[2] which increases the magnitude of flooding of the eastern plains.

As a result of events in the Jonglei area and the other grazing areas of the southern region the livestock sector has suffered tremendously. The Dinka, the Nuer, and other cattle-owning groups of the region have had severe losses of herds. It is very difficult to give realistic estimates of such losses, but the report of the National Dialogue Conference for Peace (1989) suggests that the figure is in the proximity of 6.6 million head of cattle. It is fair to suggest, given the trend of events in the war, that this figure has increased since 1989.

With regard to the position of wildlife in the war zone, and taking as an example the Boma Plateau and Jonglei area, the situation is alarming. The fighting parties have been indiscriminate in shooting animals, due to the need for food and sometimes for commercial purposes. This has led to almost total destruction of this national resource, and a complete disappearance of some rare species. The existence of the Jonglei canal in its present incomplete shape has also disturbed the movement of these animals to their dry-season grazing areas, and has led to a high percentage of loss in their numbers. As early as 1981, the negative impact of the canal on these animals had been noted, and suggestions to speed the implementation of the semi-natural crossing routes and provision of watering points on the eastern side of the canal were made (Associated Consultants, 1981). The start of the war and its continuance in the area have worsened the situation.

Beyond the Physical Destruction: The Social Environment

In the above sections, attempts have been made to illustrate the destructive nature of the civil war in relation to the physical environment and the spatial context accommodating both human and animal communities. It is perhaps easier to deal with these aspects than with issues related to the social environment.

As a consequence of war, the traditions, values, and lifestyle of societies have totally changed in certain communities. The shift in lifestyle from pastoralists to settled farmers and wage-earners has already been mentioned. This is related to marginalization and loss of control over the resource base. The inability of people to manage non-traditionally owned resources in an adequate manner led to a high rate of mobility, where the majority became destitute.

The war has also led to a disruption of social organization, in situations where people have to abandon their indigenous areas due to lack of security.

From cases reported in refugee camps inside and outside the war zone, it appears the most basic social unit—the family—has been broken during attempts to flee for survival. Women, children, and old people can be found distributed in different camps, unable to locate their close relatives. Merging with other groups also leads to identity crises, lack of leadership, and the inability to utilize traditional systems of cooperation.

The sociocultural dimension of civil strife has meant: (a) the cessation of development, and the creation of gaps in indigenous knowledge, (b) the interruption of known space boundaries as a result of the destruction of physical means of livelihood and displacement, (c) the disorganization and distortion of ethnicity relations, leading sometimes to a total disruption of the social system, and (d) the creation of psychological barriers through the promotion of a sense of superiority and inferiority between those belonging to the winning and losing fighting groups. Though it might be difficult to quantify these aspects, it is possible to suggest that they are easy to observe. Any study of the demographic structure of refugee camps and displaced groups in Sudan shows emerging relations and organizational structures that are totally different from what used to exist in the traditional areas of the involved groups of people. The dynamics of recruitment to the armed forces in the war zone itself also serve as an example. The case of having children in training camps without the knowledge of their families serves to illustrate this point. The rise of new leadership with alliances cutting across ethnic boundaries is another case. The emergence of customs, traditions, and values which are far removed from previous forms in local communities is also an indicator.

It is also fair to suggest that as far as the human environment is concerned, the civil war is leading to an irreversible transformation of local communities. New systems of organization, customs, values, and aspects of social life are leading to the creation of a new social reality. This is a social reality which is closely related to the new physical reality, and is based on the utilization of a new resource base, no matter how inadequate it may be.

Political Aims Versus Human and Ecological Costs

The civil war in the southern Sudan and the armed bandit activities in the western part of the country can be ascribed to several causes. Major among these are ethnic rivalry, religious differences, unequal development, and the domination of state power by a minority ruling elite. While the central government acknowledges some of the grievances of the fighting groups, it suggests its own measures for sharing power and wealth among various regions. The rebels, especially the SPLA, are calling for the creation of a new Sudan, where equality in power and wealth as well as political and religious freedom are ensured. However, the SPLA's program for developing the Sudanese economy and society after having gained a share of power remains less clear, but is mainly based on shifting power from the center to the regions. The question that faces all parties to the conflict is how much human and ecological cost should be paid before any of these aims can be fulfilled. Some of the aspects of the ecological costs of the war have already been mentioned. Although they are difficult to quantify while the war is still in progress, general observations support the claim that the devastation is extensive and irreversible. As far as the human cost is concerned some (back-dated) estimates can be seen in the

Table 4
Losses of government forces, tribal militia, and the SPLA, 1984–89

Year	Gov't forces	Tribal militia	SPLA	Total
1984	89	11	856	956
1985	316	561	5,220	6,097
1986	224	492	5,969	6,685
1987	398	574	6,349	7,321
1988	750	73	7,949	8,772
1989	2,816	834	1,390	4,203
Total	4,593	2,545	27,733	34,034

Source: Final Report of the National Dialogue; based on figures from the Sudan Relief and Rehabilitation Commission.

Table 5
Reported deaths due to disease and famine in 1988, by location

Location	Deaths
Areas bordering Uganda	250,000
El-Mairam	1,000
Awel	8,000

Source: Final Report of the National Dialogue; based on figures from the Sudan Relief and Rehabilitation Commission.

Table 6
Number of people who received aid between 1986 and the end of 1988

Year	Number of people
1986	182,400
1987	518,000
1988	2,500,000

Source: Final Report of the National Dialogue; based on figures from the Sudan Relief and Rehabilitation Commission.

preceding tables. The assumption is that the situation has been going from bad to worse, and the figures on all sides have increased. The internal conflict within the SPLA has added even greater numbers to recent human losses.

Conclusions

Although war-related devastation is increasing, due to offensives by the government forces on SPLA strongholds, and as a result of fighting between the two factions of the SPLA itself, hopes for a negotiated settlement are nevertheless still alive. Mediation by the Organization of African Unity (OAU) chairman, and the efforts of other external forces, may bear fruit in the near future. The conflicting parties are continually insisting that they are in favor of a peaceful settlement, even though their actions do not give support to their claims. However, the fact that conflicts in neighboring countries have been settled, and the process of repatriation of refugees from these countries has started, may reduce pressure on the resource base.

At the same time, Sudan still remains a country with great potential in agricultural and mineral resources. Under peaceful conditions, such resources can be directed to the promotion of sustainable development. In addition to the agricultural potential of the central region, the development of areas around the Jonglei canal and the utilization of the Unity Oilfield can become driving forces behind the country's recovery.

Under peaceful conditions, rehabilitation of devastated areas, reconstruction of services and other facilities, and conservation of what is left of natural resources becomes possible. If the funds spent on arms are directed towards rehabilitation, the repatriation of the refugees and the displaced becomes possible. Once back in their home areas, facilities should be provided to enable them to resume a new life.

Notes

1   The extraction of fertility from the soil for a brief period followed by abandonment. —*Ed.*
2   System of managing the flow of water. —*Ed.*

References

Ahmed, Abdel Ghaffar M. 1973. "Nomadic Competition in the Fung Area," *Sudan Notes and Records*, 54.
———. 1976. Some Aspects of Pastoral Nomadism. Khartoum.
———. 1987. "National Ambivalence and External Hegemony: The negligence of pastoral nomads in the Sudan," in M.A. Mohamed Salih (ed.), *Agrarian Change in the*

Central Rainlands: Sudan. Uppsala: Scandinavian Institute of African Studies.

———. 1989. "Ecological Degradation in the Sahel: the political dimension," in A. Hjort af Ornas and M.A. Mohamed Salih (eds.), *Ecology and politics.* Uppsala: Scandinavian Institute of African Studies.

Alier, A. 1990. *Southern Sudan: Too Many Agreements Dishonoured.* Exeter: Ithica Press.

Asad, T. 1973. "The Bedouin as a Military Force," in C. Nelson (ed.), *The Desert and the Sown.* University of California.

Associated Consultants 1981. "Small-scale Abstraction of Water from the Jonglei Canal," report presented to the National Council for the Development of Jonglei Canal Area Executive Organ.

Doornbos, M. et. al. 1992. *Beyond Conflict in the Horn.* London: James Curry.

Mabior, J. G. de 1981. "Identifying, Selecting, and Implementing Rural Development Strategies for Socioeconomic Development in the Jonglei Project Area, Southern Region, Sudan." Ph.D. dissertation, Iowa State University.

Mohamed Salih M. et al. 1990. "The Impact of War on the Sudan." Report submitted to UNICEF, Nairobi, Sept. 1990.

Sudan Government 1989, Final Report of the National Dialogue Conference on Peace, Khartoum.

de Waal, A. 1990. *War in the Sudan.* London: Peace in Sudan Group.

Zeid, Abu et al. 1988. *War Wounds: Sudanese People Report on their War.* London: Panos Institute.

25

Human Rights and Cultural Specificity: Some Reflections

Rashad Antonius

A brief illustration. Imagine a peasant community in rural Egypt. In many such communities, girls are married at the age of 13 or 14, sometimes without their consent. If you tried using the language of rights, you could say that marrying a girl at the age of 14 without her consent is a violation of her basic human rights. Her father could easily answer that in the local culture of the village this is the norm. Not only is it accepted by the local population (including the girl herself, who may blame her fate for it rather than her father), it is also good for the girl because it protects her from the potential dangers and shame that may result from her being single after puberty. In other words, the specific culture of the village authorizes such violations. Efforts to outlaw such a practice can be denounced, from the point of view of the local culture of the village, as a form of cultural imperialism.

During the 1960s, when the idea of Arab socialism was at its peak, I remember that in our school a student asked the teacher of Social Education *(tarbiya ijtimaiyya):* how about freedom of thought? He answered: you are free, you are totally free, but within the bounds set by socialism and by the National Charter (the *mithaq*). Every freedom has bounds, he said, and is accompanied by responsibilities. He drew a rectangle on the board; a big rectangle, but without any openings. It looks now a little too narrow, as do all similar bounds on basic freedoms, especially when they are justified by very noble ideals for building a better society. These noble and virtuous justifications for bounds on essential rights, used today by the proponents of political Islam, often hide less noble aims, as they did in the 1960s.

These two examples came to my mind when I started thinking about cultural specificity. I think they illustrate two different contexts in which the notion is used. In the 1960s, the language of human rights was not yet fashionable, and the idea of universal human rights was not yet opposed by the idea of cultural specificity. But basically, it was a phenomenon of that order: some people were claim-

From "Human Rights: Egypt and the Arab World," *Cairo Papers in Social Science,* 17 (4):15–23 (1994). Copyright © 1994 by The American University in Cairo Press. Reprinted by permission. Rashad Antonius is a sociologist and mathematician currently teaching in Montreal, Canada.

ing certain rights, in particular the right to express dissident opinions, and these rights were opposed and severely restricted on the grounds that they threatened the legitimate social order. One form of the use of cultural specificity was to prevent people from claiming the right to think differently.

The question of cultural specificity is not invoked only by old fashioned *omdas* (village chiefs) in remote villages. It is also being raised by governments, who use it as an excuse to justify rather repressive policies. One can cite, for instance, the events that led Saudi authorities to issue a statement entitled: *I'raf 'adouika: Asma al-saqitat al-daiyat il al-razilati wa-l-fassadi 'al-al-ard* (Know your enemy: the names of the morally fallen women who want to spread vice and corruption on earth). This list, distributed publicly, did not give names of prostitutes, or of carriers of the AIDS virus, but of respectable women whose crime was that they decided to drive their cars themselves. Their behavior certainly went against dominant cultural practice in Saudi society. It was therefore seen as "deviant" with respect to the norms that are prevalent in Saudi society. However, I believe that the fundamental right of freedom of movement of Saudi women is violated by the dominant social order, and therefore that, at least in this instance, the notion of cultural specificity has been used to reproduce a repressive social order.

The notion of cultural specificity has also been raised by intellectuals, mainly (but not only) associated with the Islamic current, who want to see the Shari'a applied, and who claim that some of the rights recognized by the International Declaration on Human Rights run counter to Arab/Islamic values. Therefore, they claim, not only do they not themselves want to exercise these rights (which I recognize is perfectly within their rights), but they also want to make sure others do not obtain the right to exercise them. Of course, this stand does not prevent them from claiming to believe in human rights. A defender of cultural specificity, criticizing the Universal Declaration on Human Rights, said on this issue, for example: "For us, women and men are equal in law, but they [women] are not the same as men, and they can't be allowed to wander around freely in the streets like some kind of animal."[1]

This kind of discourse is not an exception. For instance, one often finds Egyptian professors writing articles in *Al-Ahram* whose titles appear to uphold equality between the sexes but whose contents argue at length that men and women should not be treated equally.

Given that this outlook is dominant but not hegemonic in Egypt, it is important to discuss the question and to clarify the concept of cultural specificity, its various uses, and the consequences of such uses. It must be noted that governments that claim that the international human rights instruments (such as the Universal Declaration) are alien to Arab/Islamic culture never hesitate to import "alien" military instruments to repress human rights. In a way, the *repression* of human rights is certainly a universal concept, and I have heard nobody invoke cultural specificity to prevent the importation of weapons used against citizens. Nonetheless, I believe the question of cultural specificity is indeed of fundamental importance, and that it should be addressed very seriously. But I would like to propose a perspective that is somewhat different from the dominant one.

The difficult question I would like to address is the following: Can we come up with a definition of human rights that takes into account the cultural specificity of a given society, without sacrificing the fundamental aspects of the idea of human rights?

The answer I would like to propose goes along the following lines: I believe in a universal definition of what fundamental human rights are. However, violations of these rights, and the interests that are protected by such violations, take forms that are specific to a given culture. Therefore, any work on the human rights issue, whether conceptual or practical, must take into account the culturally specific violations of rights as a starting point to determine strategies and priorities of action. My approach to rights will therefore be through an analysis of their negation; examining what I consider to be violations of these rights in order to determine the extent to which the dominant culture, or a given subculture, also considers them to be violations. I will then take as priorities for action the rights that are considered to be violated. Therefore, even if the basic human rights I believe in are universal, the particular instruments used to protect them, the priorities in the demands for guarantees, and the particular forms these guarantees will take, are culturally specific. More importantly, the social movements that are the carriers of these notions of rights and their defenders must be deeply embedded in the culture.

Believing in a universal definition of human rights does not necessarily imply a belief in the internationalization of the issue. I do not believe that any international body or foreign power is sufficiently credible to act in the name of universal moral imperatives. Those who may tend to believe so have just to look at the shameful stand of the US government on the question of Palestine, where a system of official apartheid is being put into place now, with full American support. To me, then, the notion of *universal* human rights is a moral instrument in my hand as a citizen, not an excuse for foreign intervention. It is for local consumption. And it can be useful to me only if it is incorporated in my local culture, this incorporation being a slow, and long-term process that necessitates a thorough discussion of the notion of cultural specificity.

I also reject the notion that a universal definition of human rights is a Western concept. On this issue, after conceding that the notion of human rights as a concept developed as part of Western history, Sami Zubeida states:

> A cursory examination of Western European history will show, however, that far from being inherent, the props of liberal democracy were established in a series of struggles and revolutions. . . . It is true the *concepts* and

doctrines of rights have a long ancestry in European political thought, but the existence of concepts is no guarantee of their application.[2]

He adds:

> The ultimate institutionalization of human rights in the West was not the outcome only of the struggles against Absolutism, but also of the attempt to establish social peace. . . . It was a pragmatic response, trying to put an end to the devastation of rival religious righteousness. Human rights, seen in this perspective, are not culturally specific, not inherent in any one culture, but a pragmatic imperative in relation to felt needs for social peace and stability.[3]

The language of universal human rights is certainly part of the dominant discourse of the industrialized countries. But it is also part of the discourse of many Third World repressive regimes, and of some Third World intellectuals, who use it very selectively. I do not have to believe any of them, if their behavior does not conform to their discourse.

On the Notion of Rights

I claim that the notion of rights is first of all a *moral* notion, before being a legal one. When a right is recognized as such, it can then be made into a law that asserts that individuals or groups can exercise it without being punished by the collectivity, and even with the protection of the collectivity. But the starting point of a right is a moral norm, and that is in essence a component of culture. Therefore, my discussion will be entirely situated in the realm of culture.

Let me start with a question: What if a collectivity does not recognize that something is a right? To go back to my original example, what if the peasant community does not recognize that the peasant girl can say no to a marriage and believes she would be immoral should she oppose her father's will? It certainly means she cannot enjoy her right to say no. If the collectivity you belong to does not recognize that something is your right, it means you cannot enjoy it; or at least you cannot enjoy it openly. But does it mean it is not a right? Imagine, for instance, that in some country the authorities say that Muslims do not have the right to build mosques in the country, or that building mosques requires a presidential decree that is rarely given. Would this mean that Muslims do not have that right, or that they have it but that it is not recognized (and therefore violated)?

These examples illustrate that *asserting that something is a right says more about the person (or group) who makes the statement and about their culture than about the beneficiary of the right or about the right itself.*

Thus, we can identify two different contexts in which rights are not recognized. In the first context, a certain right can be granted by a given culture but not respected by the authorities. Every culture recognizes certain rights, and the set of these rights characterize the dominant social order. In this context, violations are seen as an abuse of power, as an injustice. Criticizing a government from this perspective has nothing to do with a belief in human rights; it has to do with respect for and reproduction of the dominant social order.

In the second context, a certain right is not granted by a *dominant* culture, and is claimed as a right only by some people, who must refer to a subculture, or even to a different culture, to think of this right as *a right*. In this second context, violations of the right are not seen by the dominant culture as violations but as necessary measures of social control. This distinction has tremendous implications on the way human rights activists can conceive of their action.

On the Notion of Human Rights

The same is true about *human* rights: asserting that something is a *human* right says more about the person (or group) who makes the statement than about the beneficiary of the right or about the right itself. But the addition of the adjective "human" indicates that the user of the notion recognizes that the mere fact of being a human being confers certain rights. In this sense, the notion of *universal* human rights is redundant; it is a pleonasm. If a right is not universal it is not a *human* right: it becomes specific to a given culture: it becomes the right of Eskimos, or French citizens, or of Egyptians, or members of a subgroup. To formulate a notion of human rights is to assert that the speaker believes that every human being has a fundamental right to a decent life, to dignity, and to certain freedoms that must be specified and *that they are the same for all human beings*. Implicit in this notion is the idea of *symmetry* of rights between various groups, a notion which I believe is absolutely fundamental and to which I will return.

Three Dimensions of a Right
In order to pursue my analysis I would like to use the distinction proposed by Hohfeld between "liberty rights" and "claim rights." I would like to consider these two kinds of right as dimensions (of varying importance) of any given right. To these two dimensions of right I would also like to add a third one, that of non-discrimination, to end up with three fundamental dimensions in the notion of rights.

Liberty rights. These are the rights to do certain things without being stopped by other actors in the society. For instance, the freedom of movement, or the right to express opinions openly and to debate them are liberty rights.

Claim rights. These are the rights to receive some service from the collectivity. The right to education or to health care are examples of claim rights. Often, a liberty right is accompanied by a claim right. The right to freedom of movement for individuals, which is a liberty right, implies a claim right: if my neighbor threatens me in the exercise of any liberty right recognized as such by the collectivity, I expect the collectivity, or the state, to protect me; and that is a claim right. This is why every right, such as the right to freedom of movement, has these dimensions: part of it is a liberty, and part of it is claim, as we expect the authorities to do something to guarantee such liberty. Here is an illustration: some university campuses in North America offer an escort service to the bus stop or to the parking lot to any student or employee who is afraid to walk alone, especially after dark. Thus the freedom of movement, which is basically a liberty right, is backed up by a claim right: a service provided by the collectivity allows individuals to actually enjoy that liberty right in order to study or to work at the university.

Non-discrimination is a third dimension in a given human right. The idea here is that whatever rights are recognized by a collectivity as pertaining to individuals, institutions, and groups, would have to be given to all individuals or groups, without discrimination based on ascriptive characteristics, i.e., characteristics they were born with: skin color, sex, origin, religion, language, etc. The underlying belief is that there is a fundamental *symmetry* of rights among various social groups that are defined on ascriptive characteristics. Indeed, this is a fundamental reason to call such rights *human* rights. Rights that do not conform to this are not human rights, but more specific rights. The notion of symmetry of rights has important consequences that we will explore later on.

On Domination, Power, and Rights

Historically, the discourse on rights was developed as a way to put limits on the arbitrary exercise of power. The moral and the legal discourses on rights were thus direct or indirect responses to relationships of power and domination. That was for example the case of the Magna Carta. What permitted such a discourse to develop was that the exercise of power was seen as arbitrary. And this arbitrariness resulted from the fact that the social order that legitimized domination had not yet crystallized. The notion of rights was developed in order to set the rules by which power had to be exercised.

Every society functions on the basis of a social order that involves some degree of inequality, and some domination by some over others. The existence of widespread poverty in the midst of extreme wealth of a few, for instance, is an indication of such a domination. But domination does not necessarily mean constant violence. On the contrary, the most stable and the deepest forms of domination are built on the cultural hegemony of those who dominate. This means that the values that justify their domination are internalized by the dominated, who see the social order as essentially "just." And here culture plays a fundamental role. It is in the realm of culture that the social order is justified. Why does the peasant girl who is married against her will accept marriage? Because she feels that others would consider her deviant, i.e., "a bad girl," if she told the *ma'zun* that she refuses to get married. If she has internalized these values, she would consider herself to be deviant if she said no. Such are the processes by which the social order is reproduced without constant recourse to physical violence.

The domination of some over others is sometimes justified by reference to nature (as in the case of apartheid, which rested on and promoted the idea that whites are naturally superior to blacks and should therefore rule) or by reference to some divine order that gives some people, by birth, power over others (as in the case of the caste system in India). Sometimes the reference to divine order is used by some to give themselves power over others, by virtue of the fact that they believe in such a divine order and that they set themselves as the supreme interpreters of what the divine order means. Of course, they would insist that the divine order they believe in is the best guarantee of human rights; on that basis, any person who contests that claim must certainly be inspired by the devil, and therefore should be deprived of the right to speak, and sometimes of the right to live.

Every culture incorporates a set of beliefs and norms that legitimizes the domination of some individuals over others. To the extent that these beliefs are internalized by the dominated groups domination is achieved without coercion. From that perspective, we can understand the vigorous attempt, by those in power, or by those who are on their way to being in power, to discredit the notion of universal human rights, and to substitute that of the cultural specificity of rights, a notion that legitimizes culturally specific patterns of domination.

The way to reject domination is to develop alternative sets of beliefs, alternative visions of the world and of society, that allow the dominated, whether as individuals or as groups, to challenge the justifications of their domination. Those who benefit from the dominant culture (or plan to benefit from it in the near future), try to prevent the dominated culture from expressing itself, and try to portray its efforts to do so as imported, foreign, and therefore not legitimate. For instance, a woman who tries to encourage peasant girls to say no to forced marriages might be accused of being immoral and be expelled from the village. If she finds ways to justify her stand on early marriage with reference to the accepted culture and to religion, she will be able to get away with it. Regarding other kinds of violations of women's rights, she may not find justifications in the local culture.

Violations of Rights

A right that is recognized as such by the collectivity can be violated by a politically dominant group: this is usually done to protect specific interests. Such violations are *seen* as violations and as a breach of justice. For instance, when political prisoners are tortured, this is seen as a violation of their human rights. Governments' lies on this issue are easily discovered.

On the other hand, a right which is claimed by an individual or a group, but which is not recognized as such by the collectivity they belong to, is seen as a violation only by the victims and by those who share their values. This is where cultural specificity is invoked and this is where it really deprives people of their rights. Violations that are embedded in culture are much more difficult to deal with, because they are not seen as violations by the dominant groups. This is why the question is essentially cultural. Put yourself in the shoes of the father who wants to marry off his girl, let's even say an adult girl, against her will. He will justify this in the name of morality, and maybe even in the name of religion. He may even be able to get the official approval of the religious authority in the village, depriving his daughter's protest of any legitimacy.

But if the girl believes that it is her right to choose, she may insist on obtaining this right, and she may indeed obtain it. But if she does not question the dominant values, she will not fight for her right. Thus, it is at the level of culture that people develop their conceptions of rights. In a complex society like Egypt's, it is also at the level of culture that dominant groups propose, and try to impose, their visions of the rights that are accepted as legitimate.

The attempts by adherents of some intellectual trends to accuse those who promote a universal definition of rights of importing foreign values can be read in this context as attempts to suppress more liberal views of rights. I would like to comment on this type of accusation. There are thousands of militants in the cause of human rights across the Arab world, people who subscribe to the notion of universal human rights. Who has the authority to decree that their belief in the ideal of universal human rights is a betrayal of their culture? They have achieved a synthesis of the culture they were raised in on the one hand, and of values that promote equality and non-discrimination among all citizens on the other hand. The fact that there are thousands of them, in many areas of the Arab world, shows that this synthesis is not alien to our most fundamental values, those that are embedded in the traditional culture. Who has the right to declare them to be "cultural apostates"?

Toward a Culturally Specific View of Rights

The way to take into account the specificity of the culture is not to reject the notion of universal human rights, but to try to identify the specific forms of violations that are prevalent in a given society, and to develop actions that aim at limiting these violations, starting with the violations that are seen as such from within the dominant culture, then raising the issues of violations seen as such only by some groups in the society.

The patterns of violations that are prevalent in a given society are not obvious, and identifying them can be a tricky exercise. I would suggest the following approach: for every kind of right (non-discrimination, liberty rights and claim rights), we could try to identify the potential violators. There are several candidates: the family, the collectivity at large, political groups that either are or are not in power, the state, and the international system.

Let us take for example the right of non-discrimination on the basis of sex. Here, almost all actors are violators, the family and the collectivity being so on the basis of the dominant culture. Some of these violations can be limited by referring to other elements within the dominant culture. For instance, it is possible to argue, from within the dominant culture, that a women has the right to refuse a husband she does not like, or that she can include in her marriage contract her right to obtain divorce if she wishes so. But other rights of non-discrimination are less easily arguable from within the dominant culture.

Similarly, non-discrimination on the basis of religion is not easily accepted by the dominant culture, and the *dominant* trend in the Islamic world today is to consider that non-Muslims do not have quite the same rights as Muslims (for example, in matters of testimony in court, in matters of building religious sanctuaries or churches, or in matters of marriage, divorce, and custody of children). Such discrimination is enshrined in the laws of most Arab countries.

A "map" of violations can then be drawn, with an explicit indication of whether these are within-the-dominant-culture violations, or violations from the point of view of a subculture.

Conclusion

I claim that such a global picture, with the explicit distinction made between the two kinds of violation, would be a useful conceptual tool for setting priorities and strategies for the human rights movement in a given culture. These strategies and priorities would thus become culturally specific. The underlying notions of rights that animate such a movement should, however, remain universal. Restricting basic rights in the name of cultural specificity is just a tool used to perpetuate domination.

Most important among rights is that of not being discriminated against on the basis of ascriptive characteristics. Those who believe in human rights should insist on them, without compromise, because non-discrimination results from the notion of symmetry of rights between people. And if rights are not defined in a symmetric way, they are not *human* rights any more, notwithstanding the demagogic posturing of those who advocate discrimination in the name of cultural specificity.

Notes

1 Mohammed Naciri, member of Morocco's Council of Religious Scholars, quoted by Kevin Dwyer in *Arab Voices: The Human Rights Debate in the Middle East* (London: Routledge, 1991), p. 38.
2 Sami Zubeida, "Human Rights and Cultural Difference," in *Peuples Méditerranéens*, no 64–65, Jul.–Dec. 1993, p. 281.
3 Ibid, p. 282.

26

Organizing for the Rights of Women: Tunisian Voices

Kevin Dwyer

"We wanted a different kind of order . . .
But we just didn't have the consciousness it required."

In the period from the 1930s to Tunisian independence in 1956, Tunisian women succeeded in founding a number of major organizations, including the Muslim Women's Union of Tunisia (of a reformist, modernist Islamic orientation), the Union of Tunisian Women (socialist-communist) and the Group of Destourian Women (affiliated to Bourguiba's Destourian movement). Other women's groups were influenced by or affiliated to the Egyptian Muslim Brothers and the Scout movement; still others were involved in running the School for the Young Muslim Girl, kindergartens, and other educational and social institutions.

Their activities spanned both the national and international arenas and the women's organizations encouraged advances in women's education, carried out welfare works among the poor, raised the political consciousness of women in the nationalist struggle, organized assistance and care for those wounded fighting the colonial occupation, supported Algerian independence by providing aid for fighters as well as for Algerian women and children, wrote in newspapers, printed tracts (sometimes clandestinely), fought to improve the status of women within Muslim society, and campaigned for the right to have abortions and contraception.

At independence in 1956, Bourguiba sought to dominate the women's movements, just as he sought to dominate other aspects of Tunisian national life. Those movements that upon independence tried to gain formal recognition as legal associations found their applications systematically rejected, and when Bourguiba promulgated the Personal Status Code, he awarded no recognition to the women's movement nor to its leadership, both of which had been powerful elements in the nationalist struggle.

In addition, he exercised his control over the one official women's organization he did permit to exist, the National Union of Tunisian Women (l'Union

From *Arab Voices: The Human Rights Debate in the Middle East* (London: Routledge, 1991), pp. 192–207. Reprinted by permission. Kevin Dwyer is an American anthropologist and independent consultant living in Tunis, Tunisia.

national des femmes tunisiennes—the UNFT) by appointing to its presidency in
1958 a newcomer to the women's movement.[1] As a result, the women's movement was unable to regain its pre-independence élan, and the UNFT languished
throughout the 1970s under the leadership of Fethia Mzali (wife of the future
prime minister Mohammed Mzali).

But in the late 1970s and early 1980s women again began to struggle to
assert themselves in the public arena, and the effort to launch *Nissa* in 1985 was
the product of several years' prior activity.

Among the women I met who were involved with *Nissa* were Nadia Hakimi
and 'Azza Ghanmi. Both are in their mid- to late thirties; Nadia now works in
publishing design after having earned a geography diploma in France; 'Azza
studied medicine in Tunis and now teaches in secondary schools where she
helps train paramedicals. Both women had signed the letter of 'disillusion' that
appeared in *Nissa's* fourth issue and had withdrawn from the magazine. Before
we began to talk about *Nissa*, 'Azza and Nadia looked back over the rebirth of
the women's movement in Tunisia in the late 1970s.

During our conversation 'Azza did most of the talking but Nadia came in
wherever she thought amplification or correction was needed. They began by
mentioning how difficult it was in the late 1970s for women to come together
and discuss their own problems freely. 'Azza started,

> We began to meet as women in 1979, forming a women's club within the
> Tahar al-Haddad Cultural Center, in Tunis.[2] This was the only cultural
> center in all of Tunisia run by a woman. Around this time Nawal Saadawi
> of Egypt came here to give some lectures, and that generated a lot of dis-
> cussion and interest. We were very politicized at the outset, not in
> Nawal's direction which is close to that of the Communist party, but we
> were sympathetic to the extreme left. This was, after all, the dominant
> current among the student intellectuals of the time.
>
>   Within the women's club, our first big debate was whether or not to
> have a political platform—this was a debate taking place throughout
> Tunisia at that time, in all cultural arenas. I remember that the club's plat-
> form at that time said that the women's struggle was tied to the struggle
> against imperialism, to the Arab world's and the Third World's struggle
> for liberation. At that time you couldn't get into a cultural club of any sort
> without agreeing to the platform.

Why were platforms such a necessary part of activity?

> You have to understand that with all the repression that existed then—
> the lack of freedom of expression, the lack of freedom of the press—
> the left could not speak publicly in Tunisia. So naturally, politicized
> groups on the extreme left tried to work instead in the cultural arena.
> As a result, you couldn't really be in a cultural club unless you were

politicized. Of course, the problem with a platform is that it stifles originality.

At the same time, as women, we were already having some problems with our local and national authorities. In the summer of 1979, there was an international colloquium on family planning run by the Summer University of Tabarka—you may remember the slogan 'at Tabarka, you don't get sunburned like a fool.' The Tunisian government sent only one Tunisian woman delegate—and she actually was an Algerian lawyer, married to a Tunisian and living here. Other Tunisian women—feminists who had studied in France—weren't allowed to participate because they were prepared to say, in effect, 'The problem of family planning isn't simply a question of state programs but is a problem of how women are treated, whether women have choice in their lives.'

During this colloquium the local authorities started to accuse some of the Tunisian women of being whores! They wanted to bring charges against the women for having talked to a Frenchman on the beach or for having had a drink in a café with a foreigner. And they'd plaster the name of the girl all over the newspapers. All this had the effect of motivating many more Tunisian women to pursue these issues.

As a result, in the fall, many more women joined the Tahar al-Haddad club and the debates became much more lively. We'd have eighty or ninety women there sometimes and not enough chairs to go around. You know, everyone was there because it was almost the only place where there was a real debate, where there was a real stake, and every group wanted to get a piece of the cake. So the extreme leftist groups were there, the Communists were there, the independents were there.

Out of all these debates, some fundamental issues emerged that are still with us today: do we as women take a position on all political issues, or should we limit ourselves to women's questions? What is the nature of cultural activity—is it also political? What is the role of ideology? What is a women's movement? Does the women's struggle come first, or must we subordinate it to the struggle for national liberation? What is our relationship to the West?

And what, in fact, was feminism? You know, I remember saying to myself at that time, 'Me, I'm not a feminist, at least not a Western-style feminist'. But in fact, I'd never read even one feminist text, I had no idea what feminism had become after 1968 in Europe. It was kind of a defense mechanism: 'We're feminists, but we haven't sold out to the West.'

Finally, after months of talking and talking, we were all sick and tired of it, and what we really wanted was to get down to work. We adopted an identity card for the club, one that simply said that we were a women's club, that only women could join, we would hold public debates to which men could be invited, we were a club for reflection and study of the condition of women in Tunisia. And we would do all this democratically.

In fact, everything turned on the notion of democracy: the question
of what language to use was based on our idea of democracy, our rules
of order were based on democracy, the fact that we rejected all kinds of
hierarchy was based on democracy.[3] You know, given the domination by
the PSD over public institutions and the domination by the extreme left
in other arenas, the women's club Tahar al-Haddad was really the only
democratic place in all of Tunisia, the only place where people could
actually get up and express different ideas, and still meet the following
week to continue the discussion. It was something truly exceptional in
this country.

How did they actually proceed internally if they rejected all kinds of hierarchy?

Our procedure was quite original, at least as far as we knew in Tunisia:
when an essay or position paper was ready, we would present it to the full
membership signed by its authors. This meant that if there were two or
three different positions, each would be signed by its authors. Unlike
every other institution in Tunisian society, we weren't looking for una-
nimity: for what seemed like the first time in Tunisia, we were respecting the right to be different. In fact, it became a kind of standing joke
among some men, who'd say, 'Oh, feminism, you mean the right to be
different.'

'Azza returned to the chronology:

After those four or five months of intense debating in 1979–80, we wanted to begin to do real work, to study the condition of women. We divided up into commissions. Of course, then we needed a coordinating group
to oversee this work; but at the same time we didn't want any hierarchy.
Well, we set up a coordinating group but because of this dilemma, they
were unable to function effectively.

But behind this was also another question that plagued us from the
beginning and plagues us even now: what is our relationship to the public at large? Over this issue—whether we should confront or be soft with
the public—a number of women left the club.

'Azza went on to say that this was a particularly bad time for the Tahar al-
Haddad women's club. In addition to the above problems,

The attitude in the public at large began to get more hostile—the public
began to develop a sort of Tahar al-Haddad-itis, you know, a kind of disease. Among the men in the cafés, the club became a big item of conversation. Every Saturday the club would meet for three, four, or five hours,
and then we'd all break up and go to the café at the Hotel International.
And as we'd get there, the men would start to say, 'OK, are they already

over, your women's meetings? Are you finished already?' And then some of the men, even men of the left, supposedly enlightened men, began to forbid their wives to go to the meetings.

And, of course, some of the women gave in to this pressure. Some would come to the meetings but then refuse to come to the café with us, refuse to be seen in public with us. Some of them would start to gossip about others, 'Oh, you know who I saw with so-and-so the other day?' They'd say these things to their husbands, or among their circle of friends. You know, these women were perhaps feeling guilty about their own desire for autonomy and were compensating by accusing other women.

Also, you have to understand that many of the men on the left saw the Tahar al-Haddad club as a sign of their own personal failure. First of all, divorces among us were falling like raindrops. Also, this was a period when the left was at sea ideologically, when it seemed unable to respond ideologically to society's problems. The left was beginning to lean towards populism, trying to identify with the masses and afraid of appearing alienated from them. As a result, they began to argue more and more that certain questions, like women's questions, shouldn't be raised because that would upset and disturb the population. Again, this big question of our relationship to the population, and of the intellectual's relationship to the population, was behind much of the debate.

You know, you can call that first period, up to 1981, a period of methodology. This second period was when we tried to apply feminist practice, when we tried to pose and answer fundamental problems. And that is when the real conflicts, the real breakdown started to occur.

I asked 'Azza how they began to pose these fundamental problems and what kinds of difficulties this led to.

First we started putting ourselves into small study groups. I was in 'Women and the Family' and right away the question of sexuality was raised. One of us who was a bit more up on feminism than the rest said, 'Sexuality isn't only heterosexuality, it may also be homosexuality.' 'Ah, yes, that's true,' we said, nodding our heads, and we began to talk about that. But we knew nothing at all about these things. It was really a revolution for us to start thinking about these things.

Up until then we'd been thinking that homosexuality was something physiologically abnormal, socially abnormal. But now, we weren't supposed to allow ourselves to think in that way. On the other hand, we couldn't say that homosexuality was normal either. So the whole question was suspended. And then, what about procreation, what role did it play for women? It was really disorienting us, making us crazy. You know, we'd end up saying, 'What am I anyway? Did I choose to be what I am, or am I here where other people decided to put me?' These really became existential problems for us.

At this point, a couple of women began to say, 'We should really start from our own daily experience if we're going to look at the woman's condition.' Already this was a big step forward: the 'woman' now wasn't the other, the peasant woman, the working woman, the woman in the household, the woman in the shanty town. The 'woman' was also 'me' and my particular experience became just as important as anyone else's, and could give just as good an insight into the woman's condition.

'Azza explained that throughout this period, well into 1982, the women continued to work in small groups, exploring various themes in the respective committees, and coming together in a full group every three or four weeks. She continued,

> The question of feminism kept coming up again and again. Whatever we'd be discussing, the same questions would come up: what is feminism after all? What is the difference between emancipation and liberation? What is the relationship between liberation and feminism? Is feminism a new approach, free of the old ideologies? And so on. Whenever the question of the relationship of women to culture was raised, or any such kind of question, it was always, 'Are we looking at this from a feminist perspective?' At that time, there were some women who already called themselves feminists, others who'd say, 'I don't know what feminism is, I don't know whether I'm a feminist or not.'
>
> You have to understand that, at that time, the word 'feminist' was an insult, it was the main insult. Now of course things are different—it's amazing how in a few months words that were so charged can become so banal. But then it was really an insult, the word 'feminist' meant you'd sold out to the West, and it also meant that you might believe anything at all about sexuality, and that you had no morals.
>
> Anyway, within the club at that time, there emerged a group with similar sensibilities, the group that Nadia and I were in, that was perhaps a bit more marginal than the others. We continued to raise these questions: what is sexuality? What is homosexuality, heterosexuality? We believed that the crux of the problem was, in fact, the woman's body, the vagina, the uterus. We raised questions like, what is marriage? What is it to live with a man without marrying him? What is it to be a feminist writer? I know that over those two years, I experienced unbelievable upheaval on the level of my own self. From the moment you began to raise these questions you didn't know who you were anymore. These questions that people had always refused to raise—well, when you raise them about yourself and your own life, it is very destabilizing, very unbalancing.
>
> But there were also some aspects that helped us through this period. First of all, there was some comfort in knowing that at least we were willing to raise these questions, however difficult they might be. Also this

group—'the single women' as we sometimes called ourselves—ran fewer risks in a way: we didn't have husbands and children who'd be there to remind us every minute, 'Careful, you're forgetting your duties.' There were a few married women with us, too, women who, perhaps because of their strong personalities or their somewhat different upbringing, had somehow succeeded in their married lives and were able to share these questions with their husbands. All in all, we were five or six in this group. The others called us 'the marginals,' or 'the sexuals.'

But tensions within the club as a whole were becoming more acute. Nadia explained,

> We just weren't able to agree on how to approach the whole feminism question, and a number of women had left the club just because of this. So, we thought maybe the best thing would be to do a questionnaire and try to take stock. Also, this was a time when a lot of aggressive things, nasty stories, were circulating about us in the cafés, from house to house, from dinner to dinner. It all poisoned the air. So we really *had* to take stock. With the questionnaire we were hoping to figure things out in a less excitable, less impassioned way. But it really led to nothing, it didn't help at all.

The women of the club then tried to reach out, to organize colloquia to which they invited Moroccan and Algerian women. 'Azza took up the story:

> We planned three colloquia. The first, in 1983, was to be on 'Sexuality, contraception: choice or constraint.' In 1984 it was to be 'Women and power,' and in 1985 'Women and feminism.' In the course of these colloquia things began to explode.
>
> In fact, the first one worked out very well, the first day was really extraordinary, it was like a dream. There was even one moment that was so good it was frightening. I started to notice that there were a couple of women who seemed about to lose control of themselves: they were beginning to break down in tears. There was one who was crying—she never spoke during the whole session, but just cried. On the other hand, there were some women who were stiff as boards, and others who would laugh and joke at their own problems. That discussion went very deep, and I'm sure I wasn't the only one who was a bit afraid that some of the women wouldn't recover from it easily.

The remaining discussions were much less successful and tensions among the women in the club were increasing all the time. Relations became even more strained when a number of women became incensed at the work of one newspaper cartoonist. 'Azza explained,

I can't remember any cartoons offhand now, but they were of the type: two women are standing in a bus, and one of them gets pinched by a man standing behind her. She says to her friend, 'Tell me if the guy is good looking. If he is, I won't say anything.' Wait, I do remember one—it practically encouraged men to attack women. A guy is sleeping and dreams of killing his wife for some reason or other; and then he wakes up smiling, saying, 'Night brings good advice.'

Well, week after week of this—some of us just got sick of it. We decided to launch a campaign to get the newspaper to stop publishing the cartoon. We didn't even realize that there was a big debate in France just then over a Ministry of Women proposal to introduce an antisexist law that would prohibit expression that defamed women.

We called upon the LTDH to support us. Most of them were on our side, but there were a number who said, 'Careful, don't pull the cord too hard on this issue or it will break.' We told them that we couldn't break the cord because, as far as we were concerned, there was no cord. What we were concerned with was our fundamental right to walk unmolested in the streets. The LTDH did give us its support, and we mounted quite a campaign. But we were attacked a lot for this and a number of club members were against the campaign. Everyone was saying to us, 'Why are you taking this so seriously? These are only jokes, only cartoons.' But we couldn't let these kinds of pictures, these debasing words about women, go on circulating.

The controversy went on for a long time and it was only about a year later that Prime Minister Mzali's wife went before the National Assembly and said that such things in the national press were unacceptable. After that, finally, the paper stopped publishing the cartoons.

The club had by then lost much of its momentum—'Azza and Nadia, for example, had both stopped going to meetings for several months. But a number of women had begun working in other arenas to draw attention to women's issues. It was at this time that a women's section was created within the research office of the UGTT, something women had been trying to obtain for years.

'Azza continued, 'So, after a while, there were two main, overlapping groups of women—the Tahar al-Haddad club, and the one within the UGTT.' Nadia interjected, 'But a real need for joint activity arose after the Israeli invasion of the Lebanon, in June 1982. In fact, it was this that led, eventually, to the founding of *Nissa*.' 'Azza went on,

After the Israeli invasion there were a lot of women who were looking for some way to express their outrage. All the other demonstrations were so mild, it was a joke: it was towards the end of summer, the students were still away, and the opposition groups were so divided that they couldn't mount a big demonstration. Well, about fifty to sixty women managed to get together for a demonstration in front of the Arab League. We would have had more people there but for many of us it was a bit of a problem to stand there shouting, 'Arab Palestine, Arab Palestine,' at a time when the wave of Arab nationalism and their reactionary position on women was becoming a problem in itself.

Nadia added, 'You know, for me, there was another problem. I was uncomfortable demonstrating with women, only with women, on an issue where we could be demonstrating as a mixed group. That whole idea bothered me.'

'Azza continued,

In any case, our women's demonstration was quickly dispersed. But we felt the need to take stock of this initiative as well as whatever else we were involved in. And also, there were a number of women involved in the demonstration who had never been in a group of women like this, and who had never been in the Tahar al-Haddad club. We wanted to do something, but we didn't know what.

Then came the Sabra and Chatila massacres of Palestinians in Lebanon and we mounted another demonstration, this time in front of the UN offices. Again this demonstration was dispersed, but with a little more violence this time. By now we had been meeting for some time, asking ourselves, 'What should we do now?' We couldn't really go back to the Tahar al-Haddad club, because that had become purely cultural.

Meanwhile, we were working on the issue of the Israeli invasion. After Sabra and Chatila, we wanted to put out a signed text, but we didn't know what to call ourselves. So we decided on 'The Democratic Women'— 'democratic,' you know, to distinguish ourselves from the National Union of Tunisian Women, which is one of the organs of the PSD. And this was when all our discussion started about whether we should form a women's group, whether a women's group should take a position on all matters in public life or only on what you might narrowly call women's questions. Already, there were marked differences in our points of view.

So we started to say that with all these differences, maybe we should look for something minimal that would bring us together, but would also allow those women who wanted to do more to do it within the framework of this new association. We didn't meet regularly and these discussions dragged on for a year or more. This now had nothing any longer to do with the Tahar al-Haddad club, although many of our women were also members of the club. There were about thirty of us, thirty women, in all.

So here we were, thinking of forming some kind of association, but we couldn't really agree on what to do. This was a time when there was a sort of liberalization of the political system in the air. We figured we should take advantage of that and try to form the association as soon as possible. So, as we began to draft our bylaws and in order to make the

formal application, we had to ask two important questions: 'What distinguishes us from other similar organizations?' and 'How do we avoid
being infiltrated and undermined by groups with other interests?'

For example, to protect ourselves from the Islamists we wanted to
put the idea of secularism in our statute. But some women said, 'No. We
agree with the principle but it is no good to say it explicitly because for
most people secularism means atheism.' And then some others began to
say, 'Why do we have to go through this whole debate again? We know
that for women the question of secularism is crucial, because we have to
have separation of the state and religion, and we have to have statutory
law in order to protect and promote women's rights.'

How did they manage to resolve these differences?

Well, we never did, really. We were completely blocked on these kinds
of questions. And then, all of a sudden, we hit on the idea of the journal.
For a while we had parallel meetings, one group pursuing the idea of the
journal, the other concerned with forming the association.

But the journal moved forward much more quickly than the association, which lost momentum. For the journal, we had some discussion
over who the directrice would be—to fulfill the legal requirements you
have to have a directrice—and we wanted someone who wasn't too identified with one tendency or another within our group. We finally agreed
on Emna bel-Hajj Yahya and we all agreed that we would each have an
equal say in producing the journal. This was towards the end of 1984. We
had put in our application during the month of Ramadan that year, in
July, and we were accepted in November.

It was as we began to produce *Nissa* that the problems really started.

We had now reached the moment when the history of *Nissa* proper could be
said to begin. Some of the problems *Nissa* faced were certainly related to the general problem of launching any publication in Tunisia, and I recalled that
Abdelaziz Krichen had had to abandon hope of continuing beyond the fourth
issue of his promising journal, *Mensuel*. But some of *Nissa*'s difficulties were
related directly to the fact that this was a magazine run by and for women, within a society in which women faced particular problems.

As 'Azza and Nadia began to discuss the problems that arose during the first
three issues of *Nissa*, leading to the letter of 'disillusion' that they both and two
other women had signed in the fourth issue, it became clear that these problems
still touched them deeply. Their anger and pain, as well as the passion that they
had already displayed in their account of the recent history of the women's movement in Tunisia, were apparent in their tone of voice and their facial expressions.

I asked them what they thought were the central problems and how these
were handled. 'Azza responded,

The problems began right in our first issue, on the Personal Status Code. First of all, how would we decide what kind of article would be acceptable? The Personal Status Code was then being attacked by the Islamists, but at the same time it was strongly defended by the government. There was no question, of course, of allying ourselves with the Islamists, but we didn't want to sound like a mouthpiece for the government either. Yet, if we argued too strongly for progressive changes in the PSC, the journal might be confiscated by the authorities and the directrice could be held legally responsible in any judicial procedures brought against us.

So we wanted the directrice to take a stand, to say what she would be willing to assume responsibility for. But she wouldn't do that, she said she'd judge each specific text on its merits.

I thought the directrice's position was defensible, given the legal problems she might face and given the difficulties in elaborating an abstract position independent of specific articles. I asked 'Azza and Nadia what position they thought the directrice should take. Nadia answered,

Someone who is an activist—and she was chosen directrice because this was to be her role—has to be a person who, along with the rest of us, is willing to take upon herself the difficulties of confronting authority. She has to be willing to stand up to those in power, with all the risks involved.

Nadia hadn't really answered my question, but 'Azza broke in,

Another problem in the first issue was also symptomatic of a larger problem. One article generated a lot of disagreement and some people wanted it not to be published. But we said, 'Wait a minute, remember "democracy." Don t tamper with the texts. If it might get the journal prohibited, we can discuss that. But we can't suppress an article just because we don't agree with it.' The text finally did appear, but only after quite a fight.

And then there was another argument over an article Nadia wrote criticizing government statements that women should be elected to a certain quota of municipal positions in the approaching municipal elections. Under the title 'Equal competence,' Nadia argued that women were just as competent as men for these positions and ought to be elected in appropriate numbers. She wrote something like, 'The question isn't whether a man or woman should be elected, it is a question of competence: we have to demand that competence, not incompetence, rules.' After a lot of argument it was finally not published because the coordinating committee never met to discuss it!

' Azza went on to talk about the second issue.

So, none of these problems was resolved in the first issue and, what was worse, a lot of mistrust was created. For the second issue, problems again arose over the subjects—we had decided to treat racism, abandoned children, and the story of a Lebanese girl martyred when she was killed planting explosives.

Nadia explained, 'Most conflict arose over the question of abandoned children. First of all, again we heard, "But why raise this question now, people aren't ready to read about this."' 'Azza interrupted,

> That was the main battle—the question of abandoned children who have no patronymic and who are therefore without papers and who suffer many disadvantages under our civil law. The battle to give them the right to a patronymic had been going on for years, but the government was running scared before the Islamists who argued that to give these rights to abandoned children would be an assault on the integrity of the family. But these children are really in a terrible situation: they are housed separately from other children and many of them become autistic, schizophrenic, and grow up totally isolated from society with hardly any rights whatever. And we also had some controversy over how to deal with racism because of the Serge Adda incident at the LTDH.[4] It was a real struggle, day and night, to get the articles on racism and abandoned children approved, and we had to fight over every word—putting out the second issue was a disastrous experience.

Beyond these disputes over subject matter and content, I wondered how successful the women had been in their effort to avoid the usual hierarchical structures. 'Azza answered,

> Actually, through all this the main argument was over how the journal should be run: what responsibilities the directrice would assume, whether we would publish articles we didn't agree with, and how we should reach decisions on these matters.
>
> The third issue can only be called a 'crisis' issue: we were unable to come up with any solutions on how to settle our differences. This issue came out during the summer, when a lot of us weren't around to follow things through. Then, after we came back to spend a month working on the production side, the journal was thrown back in our faces with the words, 'This is a load of crap.' But it was full of *their* articles! Through all this, Nadia was being exploited shamelessly, and was working day and night to try and get all the production and publicity aspects worked out.

'Azza's voice had risen during her last few sentences, and anyone could have heard her anger and resentment, even her rancor. Obviously many of the people at *Nissa*, at the time, were feeling terribly disappointed and frustrated, although certainly not all for the same reasons. 'Azza went on,

Finally, at the end of the summer, we all realized that things couldn't go on like that. We decided we'd all go to a hotel for two days, pay for the accommodation, and hash things out. The first day we'd discuss the orientation of the journal, and the second day how it would function.

Some of us had already come to the conclusion that, as much as this went against our original objectives and our aim to keep an egalitarian and democratic structure, some sort of centralization was necessary—at the very least we needed an editorial committee. You know, someone, somewhere had to be able to decide things.

Well, to cut a very long story short, although we arrived very relaxed and prepared to discuss everything, it soon became apparent that things had been manipulated beforehand. All of a sudden, just at the end of the meeting, a vote was called for—and we never used to handle things by voting. Well, some of us refused to vote. But we were outnumbered and the votes were pushed through. The whole thing was rigged from the outset. I was really crushed by it all, and was on the verge of tears. One of them saw me in that state and said, 'OK, get the psychodrama out of here.' They were really pushing things to the limit.

It was after all this that we decided to quit the journal. A couple of women came to us later saying, 'You can't leave, you've got no right to leave, this is a collective project, you've got to stick it out.' Well, we went to a couple of meetings more, to see if things could be sorted out. But we kept facing accusations like, 'You're trying to marginalize us' and 'We don't need an avant-garde,' and so on.

Finally, one of the women said, 'As for me, I don't want to hear another word about feminism, we're not a feminist group here.' I answered, 'Look, this journal was started by a group of feminist women, not by just anybody. But when women who weren't feminists wanted to come and work with us, we said, "Fine." And we didn't say it had to be a feminist journal, we all just agreed that we wanted to start a journal. But you can't start now and say that anything that has to do with feminism is off-limits!'

They came back with, 'No, what we need are more academic studies.' And, 'We want to reconsider the question of mixed participation, we think we should have both men and women on the journal.' And finally the directrice said, 'In fact, I don't even see why we did a women's journal in the first place, or why we should restrict it to a women's journal now.'

As 'Azza and Nadia saw things, this was now a betrayal of *Nissa*'s original purpose. I had already been once to see the directrice, Emna bel-Hajj Yahya, before *Nissa*'s fourth issue and the 'disillusion' article had been published but after the disputing between *Nissa*'s various factions had already taken a serious turn. On that occasion, sitting with Emna in her office at the National Library, I sensed that she too felt pain at the dissension within the *Nissa* group and that she would

be reluctant to talk about it. Rather than discuss the dispute directly I had asked
her to describe *Nissa*'s aims, whether she thought the journal was primarily a
cultural or a political one, and what its relationship to feminism was. She
responded,

> The aims of *Nissa*, as I see them, are to focus on the situation of women,
> to study it, analyze it, transform it for the better, in the direction of eman-
> cipating women. As far as feminism goes, we have a serious debate on
> this, and there are many different opinions within the team running the
> journal. I guess you have to say that the journal is political in the sense
> that it seeks to change the situation of women, but I see it as a cultural
> journal, because 'cultural' is a more encompassing term.

When I went to see Emna a second time, after the fourth issue of *Nissa* and the
letter of 'disillusion' had been published, I asked her for her view of the dispute.
Understandably she was reluctant to talk about personalities, and that wasn't my
particular interest either. But she did say,

> The women who wrote the letter of disillusion think that they are the
> more radical ones, and that the rest are timid. But in fact that's not true,
> and that's not the issue at all. Whether there is hierarchy or not there is
> always some form of domination—it is just that some people and groups
> dominate better when the mechanisms are formal ones, others dominate
> better through informal structures. Those who resigned did so really
> because their perspective wasn't the dominant one, and they couldn't
> accept the fact that their point of view didn't dominate.

Emna then turned to what she saw as the larger issues:

> In any case, I think the roots go deeper than that. The problems run-
> ning through *Nissa* are very complicated. First of all, there are finan-
> cial problems, and on this level alone our future is very problematic.
> We just haven't been able to sell enough copies. And then, we've never
> benefited from the normal financial assistance that the Ministry of
> Cultural Affairs routinely provides: they offered to buy only ten sub-
> scriptions whereas they usually buy a thousand from other cultural
> journals; and we didn't benefit from the government subsidy for paper,
> although this may have been our own fault. And then, those of us run-
> ning the magazine, we all also have to work for a living, and most of
> us also have to run a household. We just don't have enough time for all
> these things.

Did she believe there were other problems related to the fact that they were
women? "Well," she went on,

this is hard to say. Perhaps we had expectations that we could get more fulfillment from this kind of situation, perhaps our expectations were higher than a man's would be in similar situations because it is so difficult for us to feel normal in society. Perhaps some of us expected that our relationships with one another would be good, and always good. But that's not possible. In groups there are always difficulties, whether they are composed of men or of women.

Finally, I asked her whether the journal had met official hostility because it expressed political views that were opposed to the government. "In my view," she said,

> it isn't the job of the journal to raise the question of democracy or other political questions. Its only job is to raise women's questions. And I think the regime as it now is believes that in the woman's domain it is all right to allow free expression. But if we decide to discuss political issues, they may begin to think otherwise and they might then close us down.

I spoke to Emna again towards the end of 1986 when the seventh issue had appeared (dated April 1986) but not the eighth. She seemed discouraged by the persisting difficulties at the journal: deep divisions within the staff continued, as did the serious financial problems. Emna was not sure that the next issue would ever see the light of day.

As it turned out, an eighth issue did finally appear, but in a less attractive, less expensive format, and almost a year had elapsed since the seventh. It was to be *Nissa*'s final issue.

When I returned to Tunisia in the early summer of 1989, more than two years had elapsed since *Nissa*'s last issue. None of the women I spoke to at that time, including Emna, had any intention of trying to bring *Nissa* back to life. But, at the same time, several remarked that many of the women involved with *Nissa* were still very active in organizing women in public life, some had become significant journalists on the Tunisian scene, and women's issues were in general thought to be better treated in the popular press than they had been a few years earlier. But one could also hear in their voices the hurt, frustration, and disappointment that continued to color their memories of this experience.

One woman who had been closely involved with *Nissa* but had managed to stay somewhat distant from the clashes between its various factions summed up her feelings:

> We were, throughout the whole experience of *Nissa*, unable to resolve our different points of view about the relationship between the political and the cultural, about our distinct political perspectives, about the relationship between women's issues and broader issues. We also had unre-

solved differences between women who saw themselves as radical feminists, who insisted on directly attacking taboo subjects like sexuality, the body, religion, and who wanted to focus on their own experience and not worry what other people thought, and more moderate feminists who sought to look at all women in Tunisia rather than just at themselves, who sought deliberately to shorten the distance between ourselves—a female elite—and the mass of Tunisian women.

The problem, in fact, wasn't so much that we couldn't resolve these difficulties, because in fact such differences probably can't be resolved, but that we couldn't work with these differences to create a pluralistic magazine. We, and I speak about all of us, just didn't have the minimum tolerance necessary for other points of view. We just couldn't carry this effort off. And don't get me wrong—all this isn't at all because women are less tolerant than men, but basically because we live in an intolerant society.

Much of our inability to work together had its corresponding organizational correlate in our inability to solve the problem of hierarchy, a problem that haunted us from beginning to end. We wanted a different kind of order, we expected to be able to create one, but we just didn't have the consciousness it required, nor were we aware of the kinds of changes and discipline in personal behavior that such a new order would require.

At the end of our talk I asked her to sum up what she thought of the contribution of *Nissa* and the Tahar al-Haddad club.

If I had to sum up the contribution of both, I think I would say that, above and beyond the work of the Tunisian women's movement of the 1930s, 1940s, and 1950s, their merit was their feminist perspective, their focus on patriarchal power, and their arguing that all this constituted a block inside us, inside women. This made it clear to us that the war was not with men but with ourselves, with the way in which we allowed this patriarchal power to block our own expansion as people.

This awareness has given tremendous energy to women in all areas—in the labor movement, in the teaching profession, in journalism, in all kinds of creative areas. All of this has enabled women to confront much more successfully the external violence they experience every day in their lives.

Notes

1   His appointee, Ra[dh]ia Haddad, showed growing independence from Bourguiba over the years, particularly in the late 1960s, when she argued, in the context of Bourguiba's denunciation of Ben Salah, that blame should not be pinned on one man. Bourguiba had her tried and convicted for bad management and diverting funds, a

conviction she successfully appealed against after Ben Ali deposed Bourguiba in 1967.

2 Tahar al-Haddad (1899–1935) was involved early on in the nationalist struggle in Tunisia. With the publication of two books, one on the Tunisian workers' movement and written from a socialist perspective, and particularly a second, *Our Women in Society and Law*, in which he strongly argued against the subordinate position of women in Tunisia, he attracted the hostility of the Tunisian establishment and was attacked from all sides. Today, he remains a key figure in the development of 'progressive' Tunisian thought, particularly on the issue of women's rights.

3 Discussions at the women's club at that time took place in French. I did not directly address the question of why this should be the case in a country where the national language is Arabic but which also experienced 75 years of French colonial rule and in which the use of French was still favored by a self-styled 'modernizing' intellectual elite. Very probably, the use of French at the club at that time reflected both the colonial legacy and the view of many women in the club that they were an avant-garde and were at odds with the 'patriarchal' values of the society around them. Similar discussions taking place today are much more likely to be in Arabic. For example, the 'Democratic Women' now put out their statements and publications primarily in Arabic, although they began by using French.

4 In March 1985, there was an uproar over the election of Serge Adda, a staunch human rights activist and a Tunisian Jew, to the executive committee of the CTDH. In the end his election was upheld.

Seven

Introduction

Religion and Value Systems in a Changing World

Religion is a way of understanding the world, and the place of human beings in it. Muslims share a set of beliefs about the nature of the divine and the human, and about the roles and responsibilities of humans in this world. At the most general level, Arab Christians share essentially the same beliefs. These beliefs lead to, or are identical with, value systems. The beliefs are also consistent with two further dimensions, the practices or rituals on the one hand, and the social organization of religious activity on the other. Despite the unchanging core of belief and practice, there is still considerable variety as Islam and Christianity adapt to different local social circumstances and accommodate different personalities.

Overall, Sunni Muslims are about 90 percent of the population of the Arab world, with the remainder divided between Shi'a Muslims and various forms of Christianity and tiny remnants of the historical Jewish population (see Table 5 in the Statistical Abstract). Sunni Muslims are the majority in every Arab country with the exception of Iraq and Bahrain, where Shi'a Muslims are the numerical majority, and Lebanon, where Shi'a Muslims are the largest single group but are not a majority.

Among Muslims, there is a range from saint cult to Sufi groups to mainstream believers and practitioners to "fundamentalists." These differences reflect historical factors, such as the historically attested conversion of the people of southern Iraq to Shi'i Islam in the eighteenth century, or the role of militant sufis in resisting colonialism in nineteenth-century Algeria and Sudan. But the differences also reflect variation from one social context to another—even in the same society at one time there are class differences, urban-rural variation, gender distinctions, and so on—and they also reflect the range of personality types with different orientations and needs. Within this framework of difference it is important to keep in mind that Muslims feel that Islam is uniform and enduring. This sentiment is a powerful force for conformity.

What it means to be a Muslim (or a Christian), what role religious belief plays in everyday lives, clearly varies. We have seen in our discussion of the family how religiously given rules play a role in organizing family life. Similar demonstrations could be made in other areas. The dominant debate in recent years has centered on the political role of Islam, and in particular on the role played by religiously inspired groups which challenge the government in place

497

(see for instance the discussions by Hermassi in Section One and by Harik in Section Four).

One of the great continuing debates among Arab intellectuals for the last two centuries has been between "authenticity" and "modernity"—i.e., could the Arabs "modernize" along Western lines but still preserve what makes them (their society and culture) unique? The debate has taken different forms with every generation in the last two centuries. One amusing variation on this came in the 1920s, after the collapse of the Ottoman Empire and the abolition of the caliphate, when Arab intellectuals debated whether to continue to wear the "authentic" fez *(tarbush)* or to shift to the "modern" hat. Interestingly enough, thirty years later (i.e., by the 1950s), Arab intellectuals wore neither the fez nor the hat. But the debate over dressing styles and other cultural symbols continues. Blue jeans, rock music, pizza, and colas are believed by some contemporaries to be equally threatening to authentic "Arab ways of life."

In the 1990s, different variations on the same thematic debates have been in full swing. One of the latest has been over what "globalization," the Internet, and other electronic media may do to Arab culture—values, norms, practices, and identity. In the name of cultural authenticity and protecting Arab values, some are advocating blocking out such media, or at least censoring them very closely. But how should we understand the issues involved, and upgrade debate over them? What is the meaning of "values"? Where do they come from? How do they relate to "identity," "norms," and behavior?

Values in the sociological sense are conceptions of the desirable that give people a basis on which to choose between alternative courses of behavior. As such they fit into the general picture of the nature and order of the universe which a particular culture defines as most real. This general picture of the universe is often phrased in religious terms and through religious symbols which are often themselves endowed with great value by people living within a given cultural system. In the Arab world, as there have been political, economic, and social transformations, so there have also been transformations in values and in world view. A number of questions can be raised here: (1) How have the value systems of Arab society changed? (2) How have Arabs used the explanatory possibilities of religion to make sense of the situations in which they find themselves? (3) What are the major currents of ideas which are competing for preeminence in the Arab world today? (4) What social groups or movements form around adherence to particular bodies of ideas and values? (5) What is the role of social science in developing a world view appropriate to a changing society?

One of the functions of religion is to provide people with a set of explanations of the world around them, to assert at a very minimum that the world in all of its apparent inconsistencies can be understood according to a relatively simple framework that "accounts for" everything. People have always invested substantial thought in elaborating religious doctrine as a way of understanding and coming to grips with what is not immediately obvious. Thus religion provides a "model *of* reality." It also provides a "model *for* behavior," a guide to appropriate and valued action. The two are linked in that one's interpretation of the nature of reality is clearly the basis for action within that perceived reality. One of the great attractions of Islam is that it provides a simple and elegant schema for interpreting the world and acting within it.

But Islam, as a religion and a way of life, did not come to people and societies devoid of previous value systems. When it came and spread to become the religion of the majority, "Islamic values" were transplanted, and they submerged, modified, or coexisted with some of the previously held values. For example, in Egypt there have been persistent symbols, values, and norms which are traceable to its hydraulic nature and ancient Egyptian beliefs. By the same token, some pre-Islamic *Jahiliyya* values and norms, while subdued or moderated by Islam, have also persisted. Similar observations can be made in other Arab countries.

Nor has Islam been the only source of post-Islamic values and norms. Many of the present-day values in Arab society were generated during the periods of Mamluk-Ottoman rule (thirteenth to nineteenth centuries) and of Western colonial domination (nineteenth and twentieth centuries). In other words, while Islam constitutes the backbone of the Arab value system, there are several subsystems of values, some preceding and others subsequent to Islam. The mix among all these has produced varying configurations of values, norms, and behavioral patterns in different Arab countries and in different subcommunities within the same country.

From this point of view, as the social reality itself changes, then the comfortable interpretation one had of that reality is no longer adequate. It, too, must be modified, or it will no longer be a suitable guide to action. The tremendous changes in the Arab world over the last century have created this sort of dilemma. The inherited values which were adequate for centuries are no longer adequate. The search for new values, and for a new world view that makes sense of the new world, has begun. The drama of the Arab world is that of people's search for a reasonable and acceptable model of the new and still changing reality that will also serve as a guide for the most appropriate kind of behavior. How can people make sense of their world, and act within it? Depending on their social situation, individuals across the Arab world have made a wide variety of different choices. Some rely on Islam, others on some secular or nonreligious world view, still others on religious practices that are distinct from Islam. But all are striving to come to intellectual and emotional grips with their changing surroundings.

Thus it should not be surprising that the way in which Islam is perceived and put to use will be different in a village or other traditional rural setting from a shantytown or working-class quarter in a large city. Either will be different from the understanding of Islam to be found among the urban middle and upper class. The formal texts and beliefs of Islam are, of course, immutable, but the contexts, social use, and function of religion will vary. So also do the practices and the social organization of religious specialists. In this sense, "Islam observed" differs tremendously from Iraq to Mauritania. There is one formal "Islam" but many informal "islams." The distinction between a textual Islam and contextual "islams" equally applies to Christianity and Judaism.

In this section, the selected articles demonstrate the various value configurations in which Islam has played different roles in different Arab communities—e.g., urban, tribal, and rural. In other words, the same formal religion seems to take different meanings and practices to serve or satisfy various, but legitimate, needs. In all cases, social interpretations of what is "Islamic" seem to intermingle with other non-Islamic elements in their respective subcultures.

In This Section

This quartet of articles explores the link between particular practices of religion and the social contexts or social situations that give rise to them. We use the word "religion" here as a sociological category, not as a reference to any particular religion, such as Islam. Each of the articles examines contrasts in religious practice reflecting gender, class, or other factors. One text analyzes a practice that is marginal to Islam, while the second contrasts two discourses, one of which is considered more Islamic than the other; the third discusses the practice of a mosque-centered and scripturalist Islam, and the fourth raises the question of the social origin of beliefs that threaten to turn into fanaticism or extremism.

Susan Kenyon analyzes the contemporary practice of the *zar* in a Sudanese city, Sennar, and argues that it satisfies certain psychological needs, or corresponds to the social situation of some people in this city. She analyzes the current economic and social situation of Sudan to show the tensions that might correspond to certain forms of religious expression. She presents the *zar* as essentially a healing cult, and raises the question of whether it is what some call a "religion of the oppressed" or whether it reflects the society as a whole. What is clear is the gender difference between a largely female *zar* and a male *zikr* linked to Sufi brotherhoods.

Lila Abu-Lughod compares two different discourses for coping with death in a community of Awlad 'Ali Bedouin in the Western Desert of Egypt. One stresses the conventionalized expression of sadness at loss through explicit forms of grieving, while the other underlines the need to accept the role of the divine will when a loved one dies, and the superiority of faith in God over personal attachments. Her article shows the dialectics of the relationship between these two discourses, and draws implications for gender relations from them. An underlying theme is the cultural construction of such emotions as grief.

Patrick Gaffney analyzes the roles of preachers in two contrasting mosques in the Upper Egyptian city of Minya. He stresses the relatively recent evolution of the importance of the mosque and of preaching in Egyptian Islam, after a period of eclipse, and contrasts the mosque-centered practice of Islam with the Sufi groups and the cult of veneration of saints. The two preachers analyzed reflect different styles, but both within contemporary mainstream Egyptian Islam. Gaffney analyzes their role in terms of what the preacher symbolizes and what he encourages people to do. Collective prayer, especially the Friday noon prayer, is one of the main events of Islam, and Gaffney has provided us with a basic understanding of the meaning of that event.

Galal Amin takes up the question of the change in religious practice and belief in the last generation in Egypt (he could have also invoked similar changes in other Arab countries). The change he has in mind is the strengthening of a text-oriented belief and practice, a form of scripturalism, to use Geertz's word,[1] which in some cases has led to political conflict and violence, in other cases simply to "extreme" opinions, hence his use of the word "fanaticism." Amin offers the suggestion that this is due to frustrated upward mobility in some cases, and to the lack of self-esteem that comes from earning money without work in others. He thus points squarely to the importance of discerning the link between the economic and social system on the one hand and the forms that religious belief and practice take on the other. We are, in a sense, back where we started: a consideration of the role of social class, differentiation, and mobility in Arab society.

Notes

1 Clifford Geertz, *Islam Observed*. New Haven: Yale University Press, 1968.

27

Zar as Modernization in Contemporary Sudan

Susan M. Kenyon

Late one afternoon in August, 1981, I was sitting in a neighbor's courtyard in the town of Sennar, Republic of the Sudan, waiting for a *zar-burei* ceremony to start. It was slow in getting underway and we were growing restless. At last the main gate was pushed open and a woman peered round. Seeing me, she beckoned and hastily withdrew. I followed her out into the street and found the *umiya*, the formal leader of a local *zar* group, waiting with her ceremonial bags and another very agitated middle-aged woman, Khadiga. They urgently wanted me to drive them to the hospital where Khadiga's sister-in-law, Fatima, was a patient, needing immediate attention. The umiya also happened to be related, through her mother's family, to the sick woman.

I had been to the hospital many times before but always had to leave my vehicle outside the gate to the outpatient departments and join the queue of visitors waiting to pay the admission of ten piastres [about 10 US cents at that time —*Ed.*]. Today, we drove right up to the main gate through which only medical personnel are allowed to pass, and Khadiga called to the doorman that it was the umiya on urgent business. The doors opened. Under the umiya's direction we headed for some buildings on the edge of the compound, which I later learned belonged to the isolation wing of the hospital. Parking in front of the room where the sick woman lay, we hurried in, clutching two large plastic bags of equipment. A couple of nurses and Fatima's three daughters were waiting for us and had obviously been comforting her with news of our imminent arrival .

Fatima was weak and distraught. In a corner of the room the umiya quietly unpacked her bags and told me that the patient had been bleeding internally for fifteen days and doctors were unable to stop the hemorrhaging. There was cause for alarm as she was beginning to lose strength fast and her family was told that surgery was planned within a few days. In desperation they had asked the zar to find out what was causing the problem.

The umiya needed only a few minutes to unpack her paraphernalia and take charge. A laborer found idling outside was sent to find some charcoal, returning quickly with an enamel bowl of burning coals which were then placed in the

From *Anthropological Quarterly* 68 (2):107–119 (1995). Reprinted by permission of The Catholic University of America Press. Susan M. Kenyon is Associate Professor of Anthropology at Butler University.

umiya's special incense pot. At the bedside she laid several small tins on the table which had been cleared for her, and extracted from them pinches of various incenses which were dropped slowly and carefully into the incense pot. Inhaling deeply from this, she then passed it thoroughly about the sick woman's clothes. As the smoke suffused Fatima's clothing and body, the umiya, with closed eyes, began chanting almost inaudibly. The other women clung to each other, whispering anxiously, "What do you want?" as they waited for some response from the patient. Fatima wearily lifted her head and began to sob. "Don't cry," the umiya was muttering as she continued to wave the incense in front of the patient.

The umiya seemed to have an inspiration. Putting aside the incense she pulled a small metal cross from one of her large bags. Fatima seized this eagerly and, now oblivious to the rest of us, began to respond positively. The umiya had diagnosed correctly. Fatima did indeed have the sickness of zar, and, furthermore, it was the zar of the cross. Possession by a Christian Ethiopian spirit named Bashir was causing her distress.

We were all relieved. Despite the frightening symptoms, here was a familiar and reassuring diagnosis which made sense to all the women present. Fatima was left alone in a trance-like state for a few minutes and then a bright, cheerful expression came over her face. We knew that she had now entered the stage of active spirit possession, and one by one we went up and shook hands with the newly arrived Bashir. We exchanged the usual polite greetings, Fatima responding in harsher tones than usual, tones which we could recognize as Bashir's. Her daughters wanted to know from him what was the matter. Why was he angry with Fatima? What did he want? "I don't want an operation," Bashir announced firmly through Fatima. "We're sorry . . . never mind . . . don't worry," we chorused, relieved that the problem was so straightforward.

We withdrew to the side of the room, grateful to the spirit for his communication but anxious not to upset him further. Fatima lay stiffly on the bed, for a short while left alone with her spirit. Then she relaxed and peacefully turned over. Bashir had departed, but the solution was at hand.

The umiya repacked her bags quickly and efficiently, shook hands with Fatima's family and hugged her patient tightly. "Don't worry," she murmured, "everything will be all right now," as she and I hurried away. She had remembered that another ceremony was waiting for her.

A few weeks later I asked the umiya about Fatima. "Much better, praise be to God" was the reply. She had stopped bleeding within twenty-four hours of our session in the hospital and it was decided that there was no need for surgery after all. A few days later she was discharged from the hospital and she had since made a complete recovery. I saw her several times after that and she always greeted me most warmly. She said she did not have any recurrence of her problem and generally seemed to enjoy excellent health. I never did learn exactly what had caused her problem in the first place, but she apparently paid her dues to the offended spirit who in turn facilitated her recovery.

Historical Antecedents: Zar and Social Change in Central Sudan

This incident is not only dramatic to relate. It also illustrates some significant trends which have occurred in the form of spirit possession known as zar, as it is found in the Republic of the Sudan. Zar, which refers to both the beliefs and the practices associated with a certain type of spirit (also known as *zar*, pl. *zairan*), is now a well-known phenomenon found throughout northern Africa and parts of the Middle East (the most recent general coverage is found in Lewis et al. 1991). It has been particularly well described for the Sudan (Barclay 1964; Bedri 1987; Boddy 1988, 1989; Cloudsley 1983; Constantinides 1972, 1977, 1991; James 1980; Kenyon 1991a, 1991b; Makris and Al-Safi 1991; El-Nagar 1975, 1980, 1987; Seligman 1914; Trimingham 1949; Zenkovsky 1950), though until recently most description has been drawn from the Three Towns area of Khartoum, Khartoum North, and Omdurman. Boddy's ethnographic contributions from a village in northern Sudan have shown that zar beliefs are also widespread in rural areas, and in my own research I found that they are common in western and southern Sudan, among non-Muslims as well as Muslims. Moreover, zar practices appear to have spread dramatically within the last half century. Not only are they now found in areas, such as western Sudan, where until recently there were no organized activities; but even where they have a longer history, such as those urban areas along the Nile, these activities have intensified.

Zar seems to have been well established in the Sudan in the 1820s (Constantinides 1972, 1991) and probably was rooted in much older, widespread beliefs and practices (Lewis 1991: 10–12; also Ranger 1993: 72ff.; Janzen 1978). Much of the debate until recently has focused on the origins of zar, on whether it was derived from an African (variously Ethiopian, West African, or Central African) or Middle Eastern source (for example, Cerulli 1934; Constantinides 1991; Frobenius 1913; Natvig 1987; Seligman 1914). Zar, in the context of possession cults generally, has also been analyzed from a variety of orientations: cultural and symbolic, social, gender, psychological, medical, and even nutritional (for example, Kehoe and Giletti 1981).

Zar is still best known as a type of healing cult, though this represents only one aspect of a very complex phenomenon. Earlier interpretations of zar saw it as an expression of psychological disorder (see Rahim 1991 for a recent statement of this approach) or as a therapeutic outlet for marginal (peripheral) members of society, especially women (see Lewis 1991 for the latest discussion of his "deprivation theory"). In contrast, recent discussion has focused on zar as a distinct system of communication, of knowledge (after Lambek 1981, 1993), even a metalanguage, a type of counter-hegemony within the larger patriarchal society (Boddy 1988, 1989). The richness and complexity in zar ritual and beliefs reinforce the arguments that this is indeed a very old phenomenon, and one, furthermore, which tells us a great deal about "the whole spectacle of life with all its contradictions and problems" (after Kramer 1993: 115), rather than simply expressing the voice(s) of marginal or powerless groups.

Most writers have noted the importance of gender distinctions in zar. It is striking that the majority of the possessing spirits are male, while many of those actively possessed are women. In fact, zar *beliefs* are found among both men and women, and in both rural and urban areas, but *practices* associated with zar as an organized possession cult[1] are firmly in the hands of women, mainly in urban and semiurban areas. In this article I focus on changes within those beliefs and practices; in addition I consider some aspects of recent gender dynamics in zar, drawing on data largely from the town of Sennar. How far these are related to wider political and economic transformations occurring in the region is a significant issue which underlies much of this discussion.

During the period extending from 1979 to 1988 I carried out fieldwork in Sennar, Central Sudan, a town of 60,000 inhabitants about 200 miles south of Khartoum.[2] Dating back only to the early twentieth century, modern Sennar is a relatively prosperous market town. Located a few miles downstream from the site of the former Funj capital, it originated as a colony for ex-soldiers (known as *Malakiya*) in the early Anglo-Egyptian Condominium period (1898–1956). The original settlement, known as Moqwa, gained enormous impetus with the construction of a dam on the Blue Nile at this point, which was opened with great ceremony in 1925. This made Sennar a focus of the Gezira Agricultural Scheme, a vàst area of irrigated cultivation designed to provide Lancashire mills with a cheap source of cotton, which continues (despite serious problems in recent years) to be the mainstay of the Sudanese national economy (Barnett 1977). The town became the center of an administrative and jurisdictional district, a position it has held (with some variation) ever since. The first hospital, as well as the first (separate) elementary schools for boys and for girls, were opened in the 1930s. By the time the Sudan became independent in 1956 Sennar had a population of 8,000 people drawn from all over the country (Kenyon 1991a: 12–13).

Today the Sudan, like several of its neighbors, is undergoing enormous upheavals which result from a complex combination of political, economic, ecological, religious, and social factors. These upheavals continue to escalate and present real problems of survival for ordinary people. The establishment of a right-wing, fundamentalist Muslim, military regime (the National Islamic Front, NIF), which took power in a 1989 coup, has exacerbated an already dire situation and led to a highly disrupted economy as well as a tense political climate.

A range of strategies have emerged to deal with the problems of daily survival. In turn these solutions may present new difficulties or lead to other drastic changes in peoples' lives. Increasing unemployment and rapid devaluation of the Sudanese pound, as well as tempting opportunities elsewhere in the oil-rich countries of the Middle East, have led people (mainly men) in ever greater numbers to look for work outside the Sudan. This trend, which began in the 1970s, gained great momentum in the 1980s, and has probably slowed down in the 1990s as the country has become more politically isolated. However, it has had far reaching effects on Sudanese society. The remittances of these workers (at all social levels) often provide the only real security for family members left behind, and may lead to rapid social mobility as well as much-enlarged horizons. Those who fail to receive financial assistance from absent relatives, however, are doubly penalized: they lack both the important male support figure and any significant source of income. Thus sudden social changes are added to rapid economic fluctuations. In addition, women at all levels of society have become de facto heads of households, often forced by circumstance to earn a living and to raise their families without the close support of husbands or senior male relatives.

Urban migration has also intensified drastically in the last few decades. Political instability and civil war, drought, environmental deterioration, inappropriate technology, and problematic land management are all factors in the rapid decline of usable land in the countryside. Correspondingly, migration to the towns, particularly along the Nile, has increased rapidly. People come to Sennar, for example, from a wide area of hinterland: southerners such as Dinka or Bari rub shoulders with Shaigiya and Jaaliyin migrants from the riverain north, and people from the Nuba Mountains become neighbors of Beja families originating in the east. In addition, refugees, pilgrims, and immigrants from as far afield as Egypt, Mali, Nigeria, and, most recently, Ethiopia have settled in the town.

Sudanese women on the whole feel positive about life in towns such as Sennar. Many I spoke with were explicit that they moved willingly from their rural villages for the better facilities found in urban areas, including improved employment and educational facilities for themselves and their families, and for access to a wider range of medical services, including zar (Kenyon 1991a). Within the towns, however, pressure for housing, employment, and schooling has led to serious ethnic and intraethnic tensions. At the same time the development of new, mixed ethnic neighborhoods has had significant effects on the cultural and social life in these towns and led to vital exchanges of ideas and customs.

As political and social pressures are felt more keenly at the local level, so dependence on familiar, well-tried resources increases in sometimes unexpected fashion. After Shari'a law was introduced into the Sudan in 1983, for example, I anticipated a decline in attendance at zar ceremonies as people generally feared reactions from the religious and civil authorities to activities which are sometimes regarded as anti-Islamic by its opponents. The reverse happened. Zar activities increased in frequency. This may be because zar provides a well-established outlet from the stress the stricter laws brought, especially to women. Even more likely is the fact that zar provides a forum for women to voice indirect opposition to developments which do not bode well for them, or at least to express discourses other than that which is politically correct. In turn, however, the zar cult was protected by influential supporters, or at least by the wives of influential men. Officially, zar has been banned since 1992 (Gruenbaum 1992), but unofficially, the drums are still beating loudly.[3]

Development, in the sense of directed, rapid change through modernization by government or international organizations, has proceeded unevenly and unequally in this part of the world. Roads remain half-finished, schools are understaffed and oversubscribed, pharmacies are abundant but empty, and factories lack power for production even along the Nile, which is the most industrialized part of the country. As a result, significant syncretic adaptations of outside innovation to local practices are commonplace.

Medicine is a prime example. The Sudan has long had a pluralist medical system, in which the traditional *faqi* (pl. *fuqara*) or holy man, specialists such as the bonesetter or barber, the practices of zar, and a range of home remedies, continue to provide a variety of curing options. The introduction of the Western biomedical tradition in the 1930s added another alternative for those who could afford it. For problems such as malaria, serious injuries, or burns, it offers the best option. However, it also brings added concerns. A new surgical ward had opened in Sennar hospital shortly before the incident related above, and although this provided exciting medical possibilities (which were perhaps most apparent to the doctors who were anxious to take advantage of them), serious problems were still to be surmounted. There are few service workers within the hospital system; doctors may be first-rate and relatively plentiful but there are not many nurses, no social workers, few janitors, no caterers. Equally significantly, resources and infrastructure (such as basic drugs, electricity, even clean sheets) are in short supply. Consequently, the success rate of local "hospital medicine" is not highly regarded. It is certainly felt to be no greater than that of the indigenous healers, including leaders in zar, who continue to provide important services to the country at large, even within the hospital itself.

Possession and Change: The Case of Sennar

At the turn of the twentieth century there were at least three distinct types of zar activities practiced in the Blue Nile Province.[4] Today only two are found, referred to locally as *zar-burei* and *zar-tumbura*. Both are widespread throughout the country, although the former (henceforth called burei) is more popular, while the latter (tumbura) is mainly confined to urban areas and is regarded as being more difficult, strenuous, demanding.[5] Groups of zar-based activities, both burei and tumbura, have been organized in Sennar throughout its relatively short history around the idiom of "the Box," *al-ilba* (Kenyon 1991b), which refers literally to the large metal trunk or container in which the leader of each group keeps her zar paraphernalia and symbols of her knowledge. This is opened whenever she wishes to communicate with the spirits. No two Boxes are the same, as every leader inherits her original Box (metaphorically speaking) from the person with whom she trained, and at the same time acquires equipment, knowledge, and ritual from her own spiritual experiences in zar. Elsewhere (Kenyon 1991b) I have shown that a major mechanism for flexibility in Sudanese zar is this idiom of the Box, which means that changes and variety in ritual, belief, and practice can be incorporated into the local level of zar without any serious dissonance on the wider level.[6]

The leader with whom I worked most closely was the granddaughter of one of the first known leaders of zar in Sennar, who is said to have brought the present Box of burei to this area from Upper Egypt in the early years of this century. She later married a leader (*sanjak*) of tumbura who had brought his Box up from the south, and her ritual descendants, her son and granddaughter (one of the present umiya in Sennar), claim to have the expertise in both groups (Kenyon 1991b), although they practiced only burei. By 1985 there were at least three other, unrelated, leaders of burei and two of tumbura in Sennar. The practices of burei and tumbura remain distinct, but while there are differences in detail of belief and ritual, basically they are part of the same phenomenon.

The Assembly of Spirits *(al-Jum'a)*: Continuity and Change

Zar spirits are distinctive from other spiritual beings which share the human domain. They are largely benevolent and this positive image is reinforced by the euphemism "red wind," *al-rih al-ahmar*, by which they are often referred to.[7] Zar spirits are also presentations or articulations of "otherness," of outsiders or foreigners who have been historically significant. As such, the performances of zar can be read as texts of social and cultural relevance in which the perspective may well contrast with that of the dominant political and patriarchal hegemonies.

Zar spirits are usually described in terms of "seven boats," *sabaa marakab*, which refer to the ways in which foreigners are typically classified in the Sudan. Three boats represent non-African groups. Derewish, for example, are spirits of such Sufi holy men as Sheikh Abdel Qadr al-Jeilani, who first brought the word of Islam to this part of the world from the Middle East. They are always summoned first to any formal ceremony, but I have never seen anyone possessed by them. Theirs is largely an honorific role in Sennar zar. Pashawat are spirits of Egyptians and Turks, those officials who were responsible for the administration of the country through the Ottoman (1821–1881) and Anglo-Egyptian (1898–1956) periods. Khawajat is the generic term for light-skinned, European "officials" or traders, who have also been active in this part of Africa for most of the last 200 years. The term is widely used for both humans and spirits from a range of different ethnic backgrounds and, like Pashawat and Derewish, implies a certain social status as well as place of origin.

A further three boats represent African spirits. The Habbashi (Abbyssinians/ Ethiopians) is probably the best defined group of all zar in Sennar, having a formal genealogy or pedigree of spirits which apparently goes back many generations.[8] It is also a collective term for all peoples of contemporary Eritrea and Ethiopia. The Ziruq, Blacks, the generic term for tribal peoples to the west and south, are much less elaborated in zar than in local human terms. One spirit of this group, however, is regarded as the most powerful zar in the Box of at least one Sennar leader and causes those possessed to behave in a violent and aggressive manner. Zar of the Arabs, the generic term for Muslim pastoral nomads, spirits and humans, are least well defined and appear infrequently in Sennar.

Spirits of all these groups are male, but the seventh boat is that of al-Sittat, "the Ladies," and is said to include female spirits from each of the other groups. Within each boat, however, there are very fluid movements as new spirits enter and old gradually disappear. The boundaries between the boats are not always rigidly defined, and may well vary from Box to Box. However, it should be stressed that, unlike in Madagascar (Sharp 1993, 1995) there are no zar spirits of dead ancestors or famous forebears. There are also no zar spirits of close friends or tribal relatives, as Giles (personal communication) found in East Africa. Zar spirits are always foreigners and as noted above represent only what is alien.

Zar, in the sense of possession, is usually (though not exclusively) inherited. It is frequently passed on from mother to daughter, or to a close relative who in this sense "adopts" or is adopted by the spirit of their relative. This process may result in certain physical symptoms or disorders reappearing in successive generations. Zar is also contagious and may strike at any time. A woman who had no history of zar possession in her family, and had never before visited any zar ritual, described how she attended a zar ceremony of a close friend out of social duty. In amazement she asked, "What's that?" as she watched the appearance of Chinese (khawajat) spirits. At that very moment she felt herself being struck by zar: the spirit of a khawaja.

Possession in itself is not regarded as a pathological condition and zar is not necessarily problematic or debilitating. Many people, possibly everyone, have one or more zar spirits which do not bother them. It is only when that spirit is upset that it begins to cause difficulties, either through sickness, or through causing unusual behavior, or through attracting a series of misfortunes to the host. Zar possession is then confirmed by eliminating all other possibilities through consultations with hospital doctors and holy men ('Abdalla 1991: 44; Boddy 1988: 14; El-Nagar 1987; Kenyon 1991b). It is often a last resort, one which people are loath to accept, mainly because they recognize that this brings a permanent commitment. Zar spirits are never exorcised, simply pacified.

On the other hand, zar can also bring positive benefits. One woman described how she reluctantly accepted her relationship with the zar spirits, and at the outset laid down certain conditions if she were to meet their demands. These largely concerned her children: that they should not be involved with zar themselves and that they should prosper. On the whole she felt that these were fulfilled. Each of her sons and daughters achieved professional success, although neither she nor her husband had had much formal schooling. The premature death of her oldest son, however, was causing her to question seriously the whole basis of trust on which her relationship with the zar depended.

Zar spirits are not particularly spontaneous, in that they only "come down" *(nazal)* to actively possess someone when they are summoned through ritual activity (special incense or drum-beating are the most common means). A person may be possessed and find themselves driven by their zar "guest" to do something unconventional while never actually entering a trance state. Trance, or "manifest possession" (after Lambek 1993: 313), occurs only in highly structured ritualized situations and is controlled by a person who has special powers in zar, usually the umiya. The person in trance may dance, or enact some activity (grinding wheat, or examining a patient with a stethoscope, or strutting around in arrogant fashion) in character with the possessing spirit, but rarely speaks. The possessing spirit communicates through an intermediary, usually the leader, who interprets the message for the person possessed (cf. Lambek 1980, 1981; Sharp 1995; Kenyon 1994).

Detailed unbiased information about zar spirits is scarce in the historical record. From oral accounts of contemporary informants, it is possible to see shifts in the panoply of spirits which at least partly reflect contemporary social events and processes. In the Sennar Box with which I worked most closely, for example, the Ethiopian spirits and the Black African spirits have become increasingly significant, at the same time as the neighborhoods of the town are becoming ethnically more diverse. Khawajat and Pashawat zar, spiritual reflections of an earlier colonial period, now possess people less frequently than informants recall from their youth, although on formal ritual occasions the whole assembly (al-Jum'a) of spirits is said to "come down," at least in the opening ceremony.

Sometimes the older spirits are able to deal with new concerns. Those in the category known as Pashawat, for example, have been around for a long time in Sennar and continue to be active, if less so than certain other spirits today. In a formal ceremony people possessed by Hakinbasha, the "doctor-in-chief" and one of the best-known Pashawat spirits, wear a white coat, carry a stethoscope, and are imbued with a mysterious manner and assumption of special medical knowledge. They do not talk but communicate through a third person with special powers in zar, usually the leader. In recent years, however, new spirits have appeared in Sennar zar, typified by the Ethiopian spirit Bashir with whom our account began. They are described as lowly servants of the other zar, who carry messages back and forth to the broader panoply of zar spirits, and do this through direct conversation with human clients. Bashir (and to a much lesser extent, other Ethiopian spirits such as his relatives Josay and Dashollay) is the only spirit who likes to talk, who comes down and chats with unpossessed onlookers as well as the spirits of other people in a state of manifest possession. Though people possessed by Bashir are often very entertaining, their conversations are always ritually controlled, either as part of the larger ceremony or during an informal ritual held for this purpose.

Bashir and his relatives are sometimes described as "the Children of the Habbash" (the Ethiopian spirits). One woman told me that they came to Sennar "at the time of the Ethiopian massacre," when the Sultan of Ethiopia came to the Sudan. This could refer to Haile Selassie and the political events in 1936 (cf. Constantinides 1972: 90) or it could equally well refer to more recent happenings. In zar terms they are regarded as a new generation, different and less respectable than "older" Habbashi spirits such as Sultan al-Habbash, one of the grander zar of this boat (a situation paralleled in the Swahili case described by Giles, 1995).

Women claim that they like to be possessed by Bashir. He can be fun, if unpredictable; but more importantly he earns money for the messages he takes back and forth. On ritual occasions verbal or written messages are brought to him to be conveyed to the different zar spirits. They may be delivered to Bashir by the person needing help, or by an intermediary, but are always submitted with a small sum of cash.

Bashir has a sister, named Luliya (Sharp, 1993: 173; 1995), describes a similar brother–sister relationship in Madagascar). She too visits regularly and can relay messages to other zar, though concerned only with distinctly "female" topics. Women who are suffering from problems associated with infertility, sexuality, and reproduction seek out Luliya for advice. Many in fact find themselves possessed by her and she is often the first zar spirit to be diagnosed as troubling a person. Significantly she seems to be the zar who first attacks young women, even unmarried girls. One of the unwanted changes that older women commented on was the increasing number of adolescents who are getting involved in zar, through both latent and manifest possession. Young people start behaving in unacceptable ways, with girls spending too much time outside with their friends or wearing unsuitable dress (and not covering their heads) and boys not working hard in school to pass their examinations. Such behavior is said to be caused by a zar expressing displeasure, though it may not lead to their active possession. In addition, at formal ceremonies increasing numbers of young women are being actively possessed and joining in the dancing. Older women view the latter trend particularly with disapproval. "What does a young girl need with zar? She has dresses, beauty, friends to enjoy herself with," one commented sourly.

I was told several stories about the stormy relationship between Luliya and Bashir. Luliya is often described as a prostitute, and when Bashir realized this, he tried to kill her.[9] Now even though she is usually well-behaved (in that for many women who are possessed by her, her demands are restrained) brother and sister spirits never appear together for fear he will harm her. In fact, no two spirits ever come down together at the same time but only the separation of Bashir and Luliya is justified in this way.[10]

It should be stressed that beliefs concerning zar are essentially pragmatic, rather than metaphysical. As Holy (1988: 473, after Keesing) noted for the Berti, there is a greater concern "with means than with meanings, with results than with reasons, with controlling than with explaining." Inconsistencies in knowledge about the nature of zar, collectively and individually, do not pose problems. The existence of zar is not questioned; nor is it often a source of inquiry. Knowledge about the nature of the spirits comes primarily from the spirits themselves, usually mediated by the umiya according to the knowledge framed by her Box, but not otherwise subject to human scrutiny. Categories, boundaries, explanations in human terms may be individually offered but there is no absolute source of understanding against which to measure those boundaries as "right" or "wrong." The efficacy of the knowledge provided by the zar themselves is what counts.

Sudanese Coffee Parties and Spiritual Chit-chat: Changes in Zar Activities

Beliefs about zar spirits, therefore, are constantly changing and responding to new situations, but a certain common structure is provided through both the organization of the Box, and the chains of inheritance to which this leads. Changes in zar activities are also significant, and equally within well-defined limits. Most striking of the developments within zar in recent years is the increasing number of women who participate in each type of activity. Attendance at the formal annual thanksgiving ceremonies (known as *rajabiya* and discussed below), for example, increased dramatically from 1980 to 1985. My rough estimates suggest numbers doubled during this period, a figure certainly not paralleled by the expansion of the town. This group of devotees represents the ongoing active participants associated with a particular zar Box.

People are active in formal activities either when they have a problem which they have taken to a zar leader and are waiting for it to be resolved, or when they have made a major commitment to a zar group and are involved with the organizational side of it. Once a problem has been resolved, most people retain only a loose interest in the group, at least until something else goes wrong. Active involvement in zar is costly both in time and money and few people are prepared to commit themselves in this way.

Different levels of complexity can be distinguished in zar activities. Basic or routine activities occur daily at the house of each umiya, as she is consulted about various zar-related disorders. She is available for help at any time of day or night but normally is not possessed on these occasions. She simply "opens the Box" in which are stored all her ritual paraphernalia, fumigates her client with specific types of incense and variously offers diagnosis, advice, and help of some sort. The client may or may not become possessed as part of this process. Only on extraordinary occasions does the umiya make house calls, such as in the episode at the hospital described above. This is a far from typical example of the umiya's routine work, which is more commonly performed in her home, or at least in her special "house of zar." Generally, she tends to zar business in between seeing to household chores, although the space allocated to zar work is separated in some way from that of the rest of the household. In the case of the four umiyat with whom I worked, one rented a separate house a few blocks away from her home;[11] the others simply set aside one room in their household and referred to this as the "house of zar" and it was used solely for that purpose.[12]

Formal ceremonies, in which the whole assembly (al-Jum'a) of spirits is summoned, are significant public performances which may last for several days, and include special elaborate feasting (for both spiritual and human guests) and dramatic   performances with music, costume, and dance. Those ceremonies which are for curing are sponsored by a needy individual and her ritual support group[13] and are to honor or propitiate the zar spirits which are causing the trouble. The individual host is referred to as either the "bride" or the "woman of zar." Other formal ceremonies are hosted by the leader of a Box and she calls on all those she has helped in the past to support her. They celebrate a specific calendar event, the most important of which is in Rajab, the seventh month of the Islamic calendar.[14] *Rajabiya* represents the major annual ceremony for each individual house or group of zar, when all clients of a particular umiya are expected to show their support for her. They are essentially occasions on which relations with the zar spirits are reaffirmed, both individually and collectively.

More frequent than the formal ceremonies today are informal zar rituals[15] which the umiya, and also other women who have strong powers in zar, hold several times a week in their homes. The most notable of these is the coffee party (*al-Jabana*). By 1988, when I last visited Sennar, this was being held far more frequently, in more private homes, than was the case when I first went to live in Sennar in 1979. On certain days, individuals claiming "strong" zar possession but who may not be umiyat or even training to be leaders, hold a small coffee party for a particular Habbashi spirit at which they become possessed by that spirit.[16] The umiya simply holds this ritual with greater regularity and usually in a rather more formidable (and often expensive) version. For a small sum, neighbors, friends, as well as seasoned zar devotees, can bring requests or problems directly to the zar spirits, with whom they share refreshments.[17] The Jabana is a cheaper and less formal method of consultation than going to the house of zar for a fuller ritual. When one attends, it is invariably to ask for help or advice, given informally by other human guests as well as more privately by petitioning the visiting spirit who may possess only the hostess or several other guests as well. These petitions range from simple requests for diagnosis or material help to more complex pleas for intervention, such as occurred in the hospital. My neighbors were confused about why I should so frequently attend zar ritual and never ask for anything for myself or my family; and when I talked with possessed women, I was very aware that their spirit was wanting to know what I wanted.

The Jabana is associated particularly with the younger generation of Habbashi spirits, those described above as servants, who are able to relay messages and/or requests from humans to all the other zar, collectively or individually. These spirits are expected ahead of time and come with great regularity: in Sennar, for example, Sunday is the day on which the Christian spirit Bashir comes down to those women who want to host a Jabana while Luliya may come down on a Tuesday, though she is not summoned so regularly.[18] Women in Sennar regarded the Jabana as a fairly recent innovation in the town and by 1985, it was also being held in some of the surrounding villages on an irregular basis. During the period from 1985 to 1988 at least two zar leaders in Sennar increased this routine coffee ritual from three to four days a week, because of local demand.

Zar as Modernization

So why do more people seem to be turning to zar? What explanation can be found for the apparent spread of zar beliefs and increase in zar practices in the last few decades? The above developments suggest that a primary explanation lies in the fact that zar is becoming both more popular and more acceptable. Several writers (Constantinides 1972; Hurreiz 1991; Kenyon 1991b) have commented on the club-like resemblance of zar. This, el-Nagar (1975: 296) has suggested, is "a social and religious association of women parallel to the *zikr*[19] . . . and other associations of men." In recent years this social aspect of zar has become more important. As former practices have been abandoned which were abhorrent in Islam (such as drinking the blood of the sacrificed animals),[20] so the dramatic and entertainment elements in zar ceremonialism have attracted a wider audience and range of participants. By the early 1980s zar was becoming publicly identified with traditional Sudanese culture. During the period of my research this process was actively facilitated through media events, popular newspaper articles, and even through academic research. The latter may be infrequent and localized, but it was seen as giving public credibility and authenticity to zar. Performances were televised and widely enjoyed; they were also discussed on radio, as both entertainment and an indigenous form of psychotherapy. While many orthodox Muslims continue to reject zar beliefs for themselves and their families, and some may denounce it as evil and against Islam, others attend its ritual for entertainment, or simply to be sociable when a neighbor or relative is the host.

From oral accounts of older women, it is clear that many of the problems taken to the zar are the same as was true in their youth: physical problems, social and family problems, stress. These are not zar-specific but are shared with the other available curing systems. However, these problems also reflect the wider contemporary political economy. At the time of this fieldwork, difficulties abounded with school examinations or job supervisors or mothers-in-law; there were complications because absent husbands or brothers had not been heard from since they went to work in Saudi Arabia or Libya. All these contributing conditions are of course part of much larger political and economic issues (Morsy 1991). The most pressing problem for most people in recent years has been simple material need. Inflation, unemployment, the failure of traditional sources of subsistence and income, political instability, and breakdown of the traditional kinship system as men move away to towns or overseas and keep up only sporadic contact, all leave many people (particularly women) badly off if not completely destitute. On an individual level, such difficulties may cause physical problems which are variously translated as headaches, strange heartbeats, dizziness, or loss of appetite. The spirits of zar, however, soon get to the heart of the matter and are responding to these needs in various ways.

The spirits are generous when they come down. It is said that the possessing zar spirits (rather than the hosts themselves) give gifts to the drummers, the woman who prepares the coffee, or simply to anyone who impresses them in performance or appearance, as an expression of their largesse. In turn, zar adherents are also expected to give ongoing financial support to the leader who first helped them in zar, to enable her to hold the necessary Rajabiya ceremonies in appropriate style, and simply to continue her work. On the other hand, until recently leaders in zar, whether possessed or not, were not expected to give economic assistance to their followers. Traditionally their help was of the spiritual variety. The new servants in zar, however, offer more practical assistance. Bashir and Luliya, those burei spirits whom we have seen are most associated with recent changes in zar, are renowned for their generosity to those in need. Not only do they, through possession, come and socialize and chat with followers, thus providing a real source of support and diversion. They also earn some income for their hostess and this enables her to give gifts of money and clothes to those who are in greatest need. Furthermore, they do so in ways that are totally consistent with Sudanese ideals of mutual help and reciprocity. One woman told me that she had been helped in this way since before she was married. When she first went to the zar, in dire distress, the possessed umiya gave her three dresses, five Sudanese pounds (about $5 at that time) for the tailor, and some shoes, to help with her marriage plans. Neither she nor I were in any doubt that this was an investment or "duty" (*wajib*), to be returned with interest in due course (Kenyon 1991a: 51–52).[21]

Zar, as a form of knowledge or understanding, is very much a part of everyday life. It is a frequent explanation when things go wrong, a solution to difficulties created by rapid change, as well as a way of dealing with social or physical problems. In the poorer part of town where I lived zar was talked of routinely by women to justify such little foibles as occasional cigarette smoking, regarded as inappropriate behavior for women. It was their zar spirit(s) making them do this, even though they may have no other evidence of zar possession. Similarly zar was offered as an explanation for issues ranging from barrenness to failure in school to stomach disorders, and such a diagnosis is easily followed up with a history and discussion of similar cases. New problems, or conflict between changing values and expectations, can thus be interpreted in familiar terms, and then dealt with accordingly. In turn, zar practices are responding to new demands, as the incident at the hospital illustrates. Zar may be best known as a healing cult, but it also meets a wide range of other needs. Frequently it simply helps ordinary people to adapt to rapidly changing situations and the confusion this may bring to their lives.

It is in this sense that I argue zar is modernization. For many people in Sennar it facilitates their coping with some of the dramatic changes affecting them as they move from rural community to urban life, with the bewildering array of choices that this presents. Zar is embodied knowledge. It not only provides individual women, removed from their family, with a strong social network (Constantinides 1977); it also enables people to deal with new situations, new groups, new ideas with a wealth of experience and confidence. In possession, one becomes the subject being portrayed.[22] Because of their relationships with zar spirits, women I met at the house of zar greeted me warmly and intimately, even though I had never seen them before. Being a light-skinned European I am classified as a (female) khawaja. Women possessed by khawaja spirits felt a very real sense of kinship with me, as well as assuming themselves to be knowledgeable about my culture, in ways analogous to that of the well-read anthropologist who is embarking on her first phase of fieldwork. Zar is a source of knowledge about new cultures, a way of understanding alternative lifestyles as well as of experiencing them in the controlled context of the zar ritual. In the process, women gain perspective on their own lives. As Boddy (1988: 22) has noted, "Possession, like anthropology, is a reflexive discourse."

Furthermore, in many cases, zar actually processes change (after Constantinides 1972)..Zar is incorporating distinctly "modern" or foreign traits into both beliefs and ritual in this process of adaptation. This again is nothing new, having characterized zar throughout its known history. However, it may now be happening more rapidly and more clearly. We can actually observe new spirits being incorporated and new procedures or rituals being adopted which reflect social events. For example, the importance of Ethiopian spirits in contemporary zar in Sennar is matched by the influx to the town of Ethiopian refugees from the civil war during the period 1972–91 (C. Schaefer, personal communication). The increasing use of conventional biomedical procedures (the use of specific "surgery" or consulting times and the style of patient examinations) by the umiya is paralleled by the mushrooming in the town of private biomedical practices by doctors trained in "Christian" (or at least Eastern European) countries. Bashir, as a Christian spirit, was regarded as well-versed in the routines of this type of modern medicine and therefore quite able to extricate Fatima from the clutches of the hospital.

Holy Women and Male Leaders in Zar: Gender, Spirits, and Social Change

In the Muslim Sudan gender segregation is marked. Male and female activities and social roles are highly differentiated and it is not surprising that males are excluded from women's organized pursuits, such as zar, just as women are more visibly excluded from men's (a point also made by Lambek 1981 and Giles 1987 for different cultural contexts).

However, as the practice of zar broadens its appeal in the Sudan, becomes more socially and culturally acceptable, and enters the realm of successful popular entertainment and economics, what until recently has been a predominantly female organization appears to be in the process of being appropriated by men. When I was last in Khartoum (in 1988), I was taken to the house of zar of Sheikh Muhammad Hullu in the nearby town of Kanakla, and there the trends discussed above are clearly apparent. Sheikh Hullu is a faqi who has felt the call of the zar spirits and incorporated many zar practices into his curing ritual. This was orchestrated by his assistant, a former Sudanese film actress. The resulting ceremonies were colorful, dramatic, and technically very sophisticated. His publicity was much more efficient than the traditional word of mouth, and relied on such worldly techniques as picture postcards and videos. He drew on tourists to reflect his status and provide a substantial income, and also to develop and support his claim that he was the head of all zar activity in the Sudan.[23] While this was laughingly and condescendingly rejected in Sennar, where women accused him of fraud, it may also indicate a very real threat, regardless of whether Sheikh Hullu himself ever sees his claims become a reality. It suggests a tendency, paralleled elsewhere in Africa among traditional healers (Chavunduka 1986; Last 1991), for zar, as a system of healing, to become centralized and professionalized. In the Sudan it is unlikely that this will occur under a woman, for that would imply a very real break with the existing organization and functions of zar.

The process of recognition of Muhammad Hullu's claims was being encouraged and ratified by academic interest. The University of Khartoum's Institute of African and Asian Studies undertook a ten-year study of zar at the house of Muhammad Hullu, who was giving them the fullest cooperation and in return received substantial material benefits from the constant flow of visitors, and from undertakings such as videos of his work. It was not clear if in his house of zar, male authorities (of University and/or political arenas) were contriving some of the changes that are occurring in zar. To some extent it is evident that they were trivializing it.[24] On the other hand, they are certainly expediting the process whereby zar becomes an acceptable part of popular contemporary Sudanese culture.

In Sennar beliefs in zar spirits are shared by men and women but mainly women practice the ritual associated with those beliefs. In contrast, only a man can enter the profession of faqi, in which the convention of possession may also be employed in the curing process. In the early 1980s I worked with a unique and very religious woman, the daughter of Jamil (in Kenyon 1991a), who has had an astonishingly successful career in curing and social welfare, assuming a role very like that of a faqi though she herself rejects any claim to be a "holy woman." She is consulted by large numbers of both men and women, who may travel vast distances to see her. She works only through possession and describes this as a "gift from God," the voice of Allah speaking to her through one of his (male) servants, called, maybe significantly, Bashir. This she distinguishes from zar, which she also participates in, though not as a healer or leader. Such blurring of what were once seen as distinctly engendered activities is a significant trend reflected in contemporary zar. It certainly reflects increasingly important social realities, as in the absence of their significant male relatives, women assume more public responsibility for their families and households. For many women the responsibility itself is not new. Through the discourse of zar, they have long been resolving family problems, and participating in a wide social arena. Now, as this discourse becomes more public, we are able to appreciate clearly that it is not a peripheral voice for marginal members of society, but rather an important, ongoing expression and interpretation of the total Sudanese experience.

Concluding Remarks

Although there does seem to be evidence to suggest that the incidence of possession increases in times of social stress (for example, Colson 1970; also Sharp
1993), it is over-simplifying to regard possession as merely a reflection of
symptoms of tension and distress found in the larger society. Rather possession
beliefs such as zar represent a complex and dynamic set of strategies which continue to make sense of the changing circumstances in which various people find
themselves.

As we stood in the hospital with Fatima, trying to help resolve her problem,
I was aware of the relief with which the arrival of the leader of zar was greeted
by patient, family and bystanders. Here was obviously a person who was felt to
have great knowledge and powers, certainly capable of dealing with such a situation, even though a hospital room was not part of the routine round of zar.
Nobody was surprised by her confirmation that the zar were indeed responsible
for Fatima's condition. The response of Bashir was likewise reassuring, representing as he does a more popular guest than the Pashawat spirit Hakinbasha,
who also deals with medical matters but remains more aloof and distant and, it
has to be admitted, is now somewhat dated in his techniques. Bashir can communicate his demands directly as well as represent the whole assembly of zar.
Paradoxically he can be described as the most "worldly" of the zar spirits, who
understands and is able to deal with the problems of contemporary Sennar while
at the same time he has ready access to the more "prestigious" zar spirits of yes-
teryear. His is a strong and effective voice, a bridge[25] connecting the two worlds:
that of the modern diverse environment in which so many zar participants find
themselves, and that of the larger more conservative world view to which many
people continue to subscribe. In the last resort it is in this sense that he, and the
new spirits like him as well as the rituals associated with them, represent modernization in zar. Through such spirits, forms of possession such as this continue
to meet new and increasingly diverse needs in contemporary society and continue to be a relevant interpretation of the daily experience. However, the "era of
the Ethiopians" may well already be passing, as the civil war in Ethiopia has
ended, and meanwhile religious fundamentalism tightens its hold on the Sudan.
Further field research in Sennar may well reveal new configurations of spirits
and ritual with possibly the reemergence of the Derewish spirits as active spiritual actors. Equally possible, new spirits altogether may be emerging which will
provide us with a vital alternative commentary on contemporary local events.

Notes

Grateful thanks are extended to the many people in Sennar who helped with my
research, and especially to the late Rabha Muhammad, Hajja Fatna Abdel Aziz, Najat

Ahmad, the late Soad al-Khoda, Zeinab Bushra, Zachara al-Diya. Miriam Idris, Halina Ahmad, and Nuresham Ahmad. I also wish to express my appreciation to Myrdene Anderson, Erika Bourguignon, and Carolyn Beck for their insightful contributions for the symposium at which this paper was originally presented; to Myrdene Anderson, Linda Giles, and Lesley Sharp for their helpful comments on earlier versions of this text; to the anonymous reviewers of *Anthropological Quarterly*; and to Dr. Phyllis Chock for her patience and assistance throughout.

1   The term "cult" is problematic in discussing zar since it implies greater centralization and cohesion of beliefs and activities than is actually found. Here I use the term simply to refer to those organized activities associated with zar beliefs.

2   See Kenyon 1991a for details of this fieldwork. Although most of my data are drawn from Sennar, I also conducted research into zar in Nyala (Darfur Province) and in Khartoum during this period.

3   During zar ceremonies (both *burei* and *tumbura*), the various spirits are summoned by their own distinctive drumbeat (or "thread") played on large tambourine drums by the leader and her assistants.

4   See Kenyon 1991a and 1991b for a brief discussion of these. Further discussion is forthcoming in Kenyon, "The Red Wind of Sennar."

5   In sum, it is described as being masculine, while burei is feminine, a good example of engenderment within zar. Sharp (personal communication) notes that this is very like *tromba*, which expects people to be "strong" even though the spirits like women because they are easier and weaker targets than men.

6   Giles (personal communication) has observed a similar phenomenon in field sites in east Africa, where it is referred to as the Bag (*mkoba* in Swahili).

7   Again there are significant parallels with the other cases described in this volume. Sharp, for example, notes that tromba inhabit the wind *(tsioka)*.

8   I am still in process of analyzing this and the referents are not entirely clear. However, it would appear to go back until the mid-nineteenth century at least.

9   Here the parallel with the tromba spirit Mbotimahasaky is striking (Sharp, personal communication, 1993: 173).

10   Many people may be possessed by manifestations of the same spirit at the same ceremony at the same time, but no two individuals are ever possessed by different spirits simultaneously. This differs from other locations, where different people do not become possessed by the same spirit. Giles (personal communication) found in East Africa that individual spirits are associated with a particular person, and although they may visit others occasionally, it would be very strange to have two people possessed by the same individual spirit. Sharp (personal communication) stresses that no two people are possessed simultaneously.

11   This woman remained married to her husband of many years and they were both religious in the orthodox Muslim sense, spending a great deal of time in prayer and at the mosque, and having made the pilgrimage to Mecca several times. She also had children whom she did not involve in zar activities. These were kept quite apart from

her personal life. The other umiyat all worked from their home, but kept at least one room reserved for zar locked when it was not in use. These women were divorced and shared their homes with their children and/or siblings and their families, all of whom were involved in zar.

12 Most important of all, domestic space is separated from the place of sacrifice to the zar, the *mayanga*, which is associated with each house of zar (Kenyon 1991a: 198).

13 Such a group would include her close relatives and friends as well as those senior members of a particular zar Box who act as her mentors and supporters.

14 The month of Rajab is a popular time for celebrations of all sorts, coinciding with sacred events in the life of the Prophet, and coming the month before preparations begin for Ramadan (the fasting month).

15 Constantinides (1977) contrasts public and private ritual but this ignores the fact that anyone can attend all types of rituals (although for parts of the formal ceremonies, only the leader, her patient, and the troubled zar spirit(s) are involved). The big difference between formal and informal ritual is that in the former drums are beaten to bring down all the spirits, and these lead to various dramatic dances/dramas/enactments of historical significance.

16 Coffee is the desired beverage of most Habbashi spirits, a choice paralleled by the local experience that Ethiopia produces the best coffee.

17 Such refreshments are always distinctive and express the demands of the different spirits. Coffee has historically been very important in zar in Ethiopia as well as Sudan (Messing 1958) and in Sennar is served to Ethiopian spirits. It is important that it be served without sugar. Non-Muslim spirits frequently demand alcoholic drinks, while female spirits like Luliya prefer sweet drinks such as Pepsi Cola.

18 In other words, Luliya comes only if there is a need. See Kenyon 1991a for a description of a parallel development in zar tumbura

19 *Zikr* (lit. "remembrance") refers both to the type of ecstatic prayers practiced by Sufi Muslims and, more colloquially, to the groups or brotherhoods associated with those prayers. Such groups are all male.

20 Traces of this can perhaps be seen in the practice zar devotees still adopt of daubing on their brows and cheeks the blood of an animal sacrificed to the zar spirits. However, actual drinking of the blood has not been practised at least since 1960, since the death of the "Grandmother of Sennar Zar."

21 This woman was actually possessed by Shirumbay, the "new" spirit in tumbura zar who has many similarities to Bashir. In tumbura it appears that the trend discussed here is even more pronounced. Certainly much larger sums are given away.

22 This phrase was suggested to me by Sharp.

23 Male leaders in burei zar are not unknown (see, for example, Constantinides 1972; el-Nagar 1980) and as noted above, in tumbura, a male leader is the formal head (*sanjak*) of any Box. However, no one would presume to make the sort of claims of dominance being discussed here. Boxes in burei are autonomous and no larger formal organization or hierarchy is recognized. In tumbura I was told there is a loose

centralized organization based on Khartoum North but no one knew of a single head.
24 As Last (1991) noted happened with *bori* in Hausaland. Here, I would disagree with Last (1990: 366), who appears to be suggesting that the zar cult has continued to thrive in Sudan because of the efforts of Sheik Hullu and the support of the university. This view ignores the very autonomous nature of each Box in zar.
25 Significantly, another term for zar is *dastur*, one meaning of which is a hinge or constitution. It is in this sense that we can see how effectively the zar spirits work to connect the human and nonhuman domains.

References

Abdalla, Ismail H. "Neither friend nor foe: The *malam* practitioner-*yan bori* relationship in Hausaland." In *Women's Medicine: The Zar-Bori Cult in Africa and Beyond*, eds. I.M. Lewis, Ahmed Al-Safi, and Sayyid Hurreiz. Edinburgh: Edinburgh University Press for the International African Institute, 1991.

Barclay, H.B. *Buurri al Lamaab: A Suburban Village in the Sudan*. Ithaca NY: Cornell University Press, 1964.

Barnett, T. *The Gezira Scheme*. London: Frank Cass and Co, 1977.

Bedri, Balghis. "The Sociology of Food in the Fetiehab Area." In *The Sudanese Woman*, ed. S.M. Kenyon. London: Ithaca Press, 1987.

Boddy, Janice. "Spirits and Selves in Northern Sudan: The Cultural Therapeutics of Possession and Trance." *American Ethnologist* 15 (1) (1988): 4–27.

———. *Wombs and Alien Spirits. Women, Men and the Zar Cult in Northern Sudan*. Madison: University of Wisconsin Press, 1989.

Cerulli, E. s.v. "Zar." *The Encyclopaedia of Islam*, Vol. IV. London: Brill, 1935.

Chavunduka, G.L. Zinatha: "The organisation of traditional medicine in Zimbabwe." In *The Professionalisation of African Medicine*, ed. M. Last and G.L. Chavunduka. Manchester: Manchester University Press for the International Africa Institute, 1986.

Cloudsley, Ann. *Women of Omdurman: Life, Love and the Cult of Virginity*. London: Ethnographica, 1983.

Colson, E. "Converts and Tradition: The Impact of Christianity on Valley Tonga Religion." *Southwestern Journal of Anthropology* 26 (2) (1970): 143–56.

Constantinides, P. "Sickness and the Spirits: A Study of the Zaar Spirit Possession Cult in the Northern Sudan." Ph.D. diss., University of London, 1972.

———. "Ill at Ease and Sick at Heart: Symbolic Behavior in a Sudanese Healing Cult." In *Symbols and Sentiments*, eds. P. Caplan and D. Bujra. Bloomington: Indiana University Press, 1977.

———. "The History of Zar in the Sudan: Theories of Origin, Recorded Observation and Oral Tradition." In *Women's Medicine*, op.cit.

Frobenius, L. *The Voice of Africa*. London: Hutchinson and Co., 1913.

Giles, Linda L. "Sociocultural Change and Spirit Possession on the Swahili Coast of East Africa." *Anthropological Quarterly* 68 (2) (1995): 89–106.

———. "Possession Cults on the Swahili Coast: A Reexamination of Theories of Marginality." Africa 57 (2) (1987): 234–58.

Gruenbaum, E. "The Islamist State and Sudanese Women." Middle East Report (Nov.–Dec. 1992): 29–32.

Holy, L. "Gender and Ritual in an Islamic Society: The Berti of Darfur." Man 23 (3) (1988): 469–87.

Hurreiz, Sayyed. "Zar as Ritual Psychodrama: From Cult to Club." In Women's Medicine, op.cit.

James, W. "The shanty towns of Port Sudan." In Urbanization and Urban Life in the Sudan, ed. V. Pons. Khartoum: Development Studies and Research Centre, University of Khartoum, 1980.

Janzen, J. Lemba, 1650–1930: A Drum of Affliction in Africa and the New World. New York: Garland Press, 1978.

Kehoe, A. and H. Gilleti. "Women's Preponderance in Possession Cults: The Calcium Deficiency Hypothesis Extended." American Anthropologist 83 (1981): 549–61.

Kenyon, S.M. Five Women of Sennar: Culture and Change in Central Sudan. Oxford: Clarendon Press, 1991a.

———. "The Story of a Tin Box." In Women's Medicine, op. cit. 1991b.

———. "Urban spirits in central Sudan: Male voices in female bodies." Paper presented at the Central States Anthropological Society annual meeting, Kansas City, April 1994.

———. "The Red Wind of Sennar." In preparation.

Kramer, F. The Red Fez. Art and Spirit Possession in Africa. Trans. M. Green. New York: Verso Press, 1993.

Lambek, M. "Spirits and Spouses: Possession as a System of Communication Among the Malagasy Speakers of Mayotte." American Ethnologist 7 (2) (1980): 318–31.

———. Human Spirits: A Cultural Account of Trance in Mayotte. Cambridge: Cambridge University Press, 1981.

———. Knowledge and Practice in Mayotte. Local Discourses of Islam, Sorcery and Spirit Possession. Toronto: University of Toronto Press, 1993.

Last, M. "Professionalization of Indigenous Healers." In Medical Anthropology Contemporary Theory and Method, ed. T.M. Johnson and C.F. Sargent. New York: Praeger, 1990.

———. "Spirit Possession as Therapy: Bori Among Non-Muslims in Nigeria." In Women's Medicine, op.cit.

Lewis, I. M. "Introduction: Zar in Context: The Past, the Present and Future of an African Healing Cult." In Women's Medicine, op.cit.

Makris, G.P. and A. Al-Safi. "The Tumbura Spirit Possession Cult of the Sudan." In Women's Medicine, op.cit.

Messing, S. "Group Therapy and Social Status in the Zar Cult of Ethiopia." American Anthropologist 60 (6) (1958): 1120–26.

Morsy, Soheir A. Spirit Possession in Egyptian Ethnomedicine: Origins, Comparison and Historical Specificity. In Women's Medicine, op.cit.

el-Nagar, Samia el-Hadi. "Women and Spirit Possession in Omdurman." M.A. Thesis, University of Khartoum, 1975.

———. "Zaar Practitioners and Their Assistants and Followers in Omdurman." In *Urbanization and Urban Life*, op.cit.

———. "Women and Spirit Possession in Omdurman." In *The Sudanese Woman*, ed. S.M. Kenyon. London: Ithaca Press, 1987.

Natvig, R. "Oromos, Slaves and the Zar Spirits: A Contribution to the History of the Zar Cult." *International Journal of African Historical Studies* 20 (4) (1987): 669–89.

Rahim, S. I. 1991. "Zar Among Middle-aged Female Psychiatric Patients in the Sudan." In *Women's Medicine*, op.cit.

Ranger, Terence. "The Local and the Global in Southern African Religious History." In *Conversion to Christianity: Historical and Anthropological Perspectives on a Great Transformation*, ed. R. Hefner. Berkeley: University of California Press, 1993.

Seligman, B. "On the Origin of the Egyptian Zar." *Folklore* 25 (1914): 300–23.

Sharp, L.A. "Playboy Princely Spirits of Madagascar: Possession as Youthful Commentary and Social Critique." *Anthropological Quarterly* 68(2) (1995): 75–88.

———. *The Possessed and the Dispossessed: Spirits, identity, and Power in a Madagascar Migrant Town*. Berkeley: University of California Press, 1993.

Trimingham, J.S. *Islam in the Sudan*. London: Frank Cass and Co., 1949.

Zenkovsky, S. "Zar and Tambura as Practised by the Women of Omdurman." *Sudan Notes and Records* 31 (1950): 65–81.

28

Islam and the Gendered Discourses of Death

Lila Abu-Lughod

On a bright day in January 1987, my host in the Awlad 'Ali Bedouin community in Egypt in which I had been doing research invited me to accompany him on
a condolence call. He knew how enthusiastic I was about visiting people who
still camped in traditional tents in the desert, and this set of families, he assured
me, lived in a beautiful area. The group's patriarch had died twenty days ago,
but my host had been too busy to go so only his younger brothers had paid their
respects. He had just heard, though, that the bereaved family was upset he had
not come himself. So we drove off in his car, with his two co-wives in the back
seat, stopping at the market town nearby to buy a fat sheep to take with us. As
they loaded the beast into his car, my host complained about how expensive
sheep had become. The sound of its bleating in the trunk reminded me of trips
to weddings, when sheep are also obligatory gifts.

We drove on tracks through the desert until we saw their tents in the distance. As we drew near, my host asked his wives if they planned to wail. "No,
no, no!" they exclaimed, adding that the deceased was an old man, and he had
already been dead for twenty days. My host dropped us off at one end of the
camp and drove off to the other where the main men's tent was. As we walked
toward the camp, three women emerged from one of the tents and headed
toward us. Suddenly the three approaching women and the two I was with started wailing and when we met, each woman from the camp hugged one of us and
squatted down with her and began the formulaic heartrending "crying together"
(yatabako) that is their funeral lament.

I felt myself gripped by the back of the neck and pushed down to a squatting
position. The woman's black headcloth smelled of cloves and smoke and I could
feel her tears through the cloth. My discomfort was absolute. Paralyzed and
silent, I waited while she went through her loud and seemingly endless lamenting close to my left ear. Then we stood up, I in embarrassment, and all of us
walked to the tent. We greeted the other women in there, sat down and began a
long afternoon of desultory chatting and gossip until the sheep we had brought

From *International Journal of Middle East Studies* 25 (2):187–205 (1993). Copyright ©
1993 Cambridge University Press. Reprinted with the permission of Cambridge
University Press. Lila Abu-Lughod is Associate Professor of Anthropology at New York
University.

was butchered, cooked, and served to us on a bed of rice. When we returned home, the story of my encounter with the lamenting woman was told and retold. Everyone laughed about the woman who had presumed I wanted to lament with her, but several women angrily suggested that they should never have let me get out of the car until after the woman had cried. When I was sick the next day, people asked me, "Did it give you a shock *(infaja'ti)*?"

This was to be my most intimate experience with these powerful funeral laments during my various stays in this small community of Awlad 'Ali Bedouins in Egypt's western desert. Those with whom I was living usually discouraged me from going to funerals, warning, "It's an ugly sight." Lamentation by women is common across Egypt and other parts of the Arab world but the genre has received little scholarly attention.[2] Because I was discouraged from attending funerals and hesitated to bring up the subject of death, I did not record laments or collect texts that would allow for a study of their poetics. However, I can pursue an analysis of the social and discursive place of laments in the context of a single Muslim community in the hopes of contributing to two central questions in the anthropology of Muslim societies: How to treat the relationship of local practices to "Islam" and what to make of women's greater participation in practices frowned upon as unorthodox or even non-Islamic.[3]

I will pursue these questions by exploring, first, the ways in which laments articulate with other Awlad 'Ali discourses on death, and, second, the social significance of their performance only by women. Awlad 'Ali Bedouin women respond to death with more than laments. Equally as important as the formulaic laments and ritual wailing that greet any death are the songs of loss in which women detail in a soulful and reflective way the sentiments associated with bereavement, the Muslim religious discourse on faith that seems to conflict with these other genres, and the multifaceted narratives told about particular deaths. To isolate one of these discourses for analysis would be to lose sight of the complex way death is lived by those it leaves behind.

The first set of issues to be explored, therefore, is where laments fit in a system of meaning constituted by these various discourses on death. The discourses gain their meaning, I argue, through their juxtaposition, and are distinguished by a series of binary oppositions. I do not seek to establish the structural logic of an Awlad 'Ali cultural system but rather to determine how this configuration gives significance to the practices of individual mourners as they move through the various activities that deaths provoke. I examine how these multiple discourses define each other, mark contexts, and structure individual responses to death as certain sorts of statements.

Perhaps the most interesting question raised by this consideration of the discourses of death is the role played by Islam. It is a truism of functionalist theories of religion that religion helps people cope with death. Yet in this Bedouin society, as I suspect in nearly all communities of Muslims, religiously inspired beliefs about death and appropriate religious responses are not the only ones invoked. Religious discourse may not even be the dominant discourse on death even though Muslim practices such as the recitation of the profession of faith, modes of preparing the corpse for burial, and prayer over the deceased are similar across societies.[4] When one considers the uses of religious talk in Awlad 'Ali conversations and narratives, two things become clear: the religious discourse is always in tension with others, and it accomplishes complex ends in the narratives and conversations into which it is inserted. These ends include, on the most mundane level, dampening speculation about human culpability and, on a more abstract level, establishing or asserting the superiority of faith in God over personal attachments, especially to kin.

Like the self-proclaimed orthodox themselves, scholars of world religions often artificially separate localized practices such as ritual lament from the official religion, and then devalue them.[5] Distinctions are drawn between popular and orthodox religion, local and universal belief and practice, the so-called little tradition and the great tradition, or, in the worst case, between ignorance and knowledge of the true religion. Practices disapproved of by learned religious authorities may be dismissed as superstitious vestiges of the past or corruptions. In more socially grounded analyses, the orthodox and "universal" versions of religion might be recognized as the ideology of certain social groups or the world religions themselves as the impositions of dominant outsiders. Anthropologists have, on the whole, become wary of such distinctions and normative claims and have insisted on examining without judgment the interaction of the complex of practices in any Muslim community.[6]

What has not been sufficiently recognized, however, is that in any community of Muslims, individuals say and do a vast number of things, sometimes drawing on or invoking recognizable Islamic traditions and concepts, sometimes not. What we need to examine is how people deploy the various discourses at their disposal, knowing that it is often the same people who will one moment be talking about God's will and the next be lamenting a loss or angrily accusing a neighbor of causing a death.

After establishing the field of meanings constituted by the multiple discourses on death in this Bedouin community, I turn to a second question: What are the social effects of the way women use them? Any study of how people respond to death must also be a study of how they create their lives. Thus, a study of laments must include an inquiry into how the social practices of bereavement may contribute to maintaining a particular form of social life. As in many societies, the responses to death among the Awlad 'Ali Bedouin are gendered. Lamenting, as in many parts of the world and other parts of Egypt, is strictly a woman's activity.[7] I explore in the final section of the paper how the sexual division of the discourses of death works with a set of principles of moral differentiation to produce and reproduce a hierarchical social order in this society that prides itself on its egalitarian ethos.

Voices of Life and Death

We can begin interpreting the significance of laments by exploring their relationship to the other major emotionally charged and gendered verbal genre in
Bedouin society, namely songs. In some ways, laments are diametrically
opposed to songs (*ghinnawas*) of the sort I have discussed at length elsewhere.[8]
They are chanted at funerals while songs—although recited in everyday life
where they can, as I will discuss later, express loss—are in their sung form especially associated with weddings and circumcision celebrations. This contrast
between funerals and weddings has other verbal expressions. Ritual wailing
(*'ayat*), which either takes the form of a special sort of screaming on first discovery of a death or a high-pitched moaning as women approach other mourners, is the opposite of the ululating (*zagharid*) with which women celebrate
good news and guests announce their arrival at weddings.

The opposition between death and life that structures the relations between
the ritualized verbal genres of funerals and the formulaic genres of celebrations
is also enacted in a range of social practices.[9] Laments, wailing, and a repertoire
of conventional nonverbal practices of grief that include tearing one's clothes,
throwing off all jewelry, scratching one's cheeks, and throwing dirt on one's
head, all belong to the confined time and place of the funeral or mourning ceremonies (*'aza*). The reentry of a mourner into the world of ordinary life is
marked with practices that suggest the dangers of crossing the threshold
between the spaces of death and life. When a woman returns from a funeral she
tries to collect on the way a small live twig or a bit of branch with leaves on it
("something growing, something green") to carry with her into her own community. She is greeted always by those left behind with the phrase, "May no one
come to you with bad tidings."

Death is threatening to fertility. Someone who has just been to a funeral
should not enter the room of a woman who has just given birth; people say that
it will "block" (*kabs*) the new mother, either drying up her milk or preventing
her from conceiving again. Once I saw an old woman returning from a funeral
stand outside the courtyard of the house to wait for her daughter-in-law who had
just had a baby to come out and greet her. Only then did she follow her back
in.[10] The dangers to fertility are also suggested by the refusal to let pregnant
women help wash the corpse and such beliefs as that children who had died
may, if they turn over on their faces in the grave, "block" their mothers from
conceiving.

Life for Awlad 'Ali is also associated with sexuality, with its own close relationship to fertility.[11] This accounts for the strong opposition they draw between
weddings and funerals. Weddings (*afrah*), the word for which in Arabic also
means celebration or happiness, are the epitome of joyous celebrations. What
they celebrate is sexuality and fertility. It is considered an affront to hold wed-

dings within the forty-day mourning period that follows the death even of someone in a neighbor's family.

Red is the color of fertility and sexuality, the color of the henna women and girls put on their hands on the eve of a wedding celebration, the color of the belt every married woman wears, the color of the blanket draped on the old bridal litter or the current bridal Peugeot, the color of the blanket draped on the tent to mark where a circumcision celebration (likened to weddings in a variety of ways) is taking place.[12] It is removed in mourning. When someone in her family dies, a woman replaces her red belt with a white rag. No one near a person in mourning can dye wool red. Women in mourning do not color their hair with henna, the old ones going gradually grayer as the months wear on.

The strict opposition between weddings and funerals is apparent in Bedouin dream interpretations. Many consider dreams to be messages sent by God or the saints about the future. Their meanings are interpreted as the opposite of what they would be in ordinary waking life. For example, when a girl reported that she had dreamed of the government, her father's wife assured her that meant good news. When a woman dreams of a funeral, people likewise say that is good. When she reports, however, that she has dreamed of a wedding, their faces darken and they tell her to be quiet. When she says she dreamed they were eating rice and meat (the traditional wedding feast) they interrupt her with phrases like "God forbid evil" and "[God come] between you and me [and misfortune]." These everyday expressions always mark discussions of bad things.

Songs of Loss

Although on one level, and in the most obvious sense, laments and songs, like death and life, can be treated as mirror opposites, in other important ways they are structural equivalents. Of all the discursive genres in this community, laments and songs sound most similar, even if people rigorously deny the similarity. The closeness is sometimes betrayed, as when a woman mimicking the lamenting of someone she did not like commented, "You'd think she was singing!" The songs of loss that women sing, often to themselves, outside the contexts of funerals or weddings, are especially close to funeral laments in sound and sentiment. Just as funeral laments ritually invoke a relationship of kinship, always beginning with phrases like "O my father," or "O my brother," these songs assert attachment to those who have gone, whether absent or deceased.

A sense of the range of sentiments these songs of loss express emerges from the songs one woman sang as she sat washing clothes, just after having been reminded of the recent death of her brother. He had been shot by a guard as he was trying to steal some machinery from a government store. She sang in a peculiar, deliberately quavering voice as the string of songs flowed from one theme to another. These songs of loss were laments of a different sort, ones that detailed the effects of her loss. The first suggests a wish that she were not so helpless in fighting the loss.

lu kan ya 'aziz il-yas	If only despair were human,
bnadam ndirulu fza'	my beloved, we could frighten it . . .

The second hints at the problems of knowing that her brother brought on his own death. After all, he was the one who was committing a robbery.

lu kan li sabab 'azzet	Had I cause, I would have mourned
khata 'aziz daro bghaytu	but the beloved's error he chose himself.

The third suggests that no one knows what grief she is experiencing.

juwwa l-'agl shatat nar	Within the heart a fire blazed
kalatu wla ban dayha	burning up but giving off no light.

Next she sang a song that expressed something rare—an anger at what God has willed in this case.

'tibi ma 'ale makhlug	I blame no living creature
'al-lmola illi rad hukkidhi	but the Lord who intended this . . .

Then she sang a song about what happens when she remembers him, a song I had heard years earlier from someone else who had recited it about a relative of his who also had been killed.

khtura 'ale ghaflat	Caught by a memory unawares
bakka l-'en fi wan it-tarab	bringing tears in the hour of pleasure . . .

Like the last one, the series of songs that followed described how terrible her sadness was by using one of the most common of the poetic conventions of sorrow, the image of weeping.

nasrani glil id-din	The Christian, for all his lack of faith,
shketlu 'ale hali bka	when told of my condition, cried . . .

khatar 'aziz thani lel	Reminded of her loved one late at night
smurat nin sal wsadha	she lay sleepless until her pillow ran with tears . .

A final song suggests the tension between the quasi-religious virtue of "patience" and what she is going through—a tension that I will argue is important. She sings of the difficulty of accepting this fate.

zluma 'aleh is-sabr	Patience is a tyranny
jarha jdid ma zal khatri	for my heart so freshly wounded . . .

Only a few days later, the same woman sang another series of songs. The themes were similar but the vivid physical language was different.

ya 'aziz kusri fik	O loved one what you've broken in me
sittin alf 'am wma jabar	sixty thousand years will not mend . . .
hattok ben yashum wnar	They shoved you between despair and fire
tammeti hafa ya kbedti	you turned to ash my little heart . . .
showa twarfuk ya 'en	He took away those around you
il-yas fik mo dayra shway	O eyes, despair hasn't been easy on you . . .
tamwih dar mo sa'b 'alaya	I could take distance
lu kan gher yas 'aziz	anything but this final despair of him . . .

Where feelings about death are less complicated, as in the natural deaths of older people, one poignant theme is abandonment, being left with nothing. One woman who asked if she might recite a few songs about her situation included what she called a hymn to her mother and several others that she admitted were also about her mother, who had died a few years earlier. As we talked about the songs she said quietly of her mother, "She died, and I had no one but her. Now I'm all alone." It did not matter that she had a husband and five children and her father often came to stay with them. Her songs were of empty places, black nights, and again, tears.

knisso ga'at l-awlaf	They swept clean the loved one's threshing room
dharroha wshalo tibnha	scattering [the grain], carrying off even the straw . .
khallo l-'agl kef id-dar	The heart was left like the camp
illi rhilha shal wbtal	its nomad moved on, abandoned
lelat frag 'aziz	The night the beloved departed
zalma tlis ma fiha gamar	pitch darkness, no moon . . .
gbi haram dam' il-'en	A pity, the eye's tears
kamal nadih ma dar fayda	spilled to no avail . . .

| tiskibik khafa y'amik | Weeping in secret will blind you |
| bki bsot 'ali kherlik | cry aloud, for your own sake . . . |

Religious Discourse

As expressions of deep attachment, laments and songs of loss share an uneasy relationship to Islamic piety. This is fundamental to understanding the meaning and social effects of Awlad 'Ali discourses on death. Evidence of the tension between these two genres and the ideals of religious faith abounds. For example, people often said that it was wrong *(haram)* for women who had been on the pilgrimage to Mecca to lament. This may be an acknowledgment of hadiths condemning lamentation and extravagant shows of grief.[13] I also heard that it was wrong for such women to sing at weddings, although their silences can be awkward. When one woman I knew refused to sing at her nephew's wedding because she had just returned from the pilgrimage, her cousins and sisters were offended. This religious discipline was taken to show a lack of feeling and an unwillingness to share in celebration. Whether any women who had been on the pilgrimage failed to lament at funerals I do not know. The problem was usually the reverse; such lamenting women would be restrained, by others seeking to calm them, with admonitions that it was wrong.

More generally, religious faith is spoken of as a counterpoint to laments and sometimes even to grieving. For example, a woman who was despondent and mourning "excessively" for her son was told by her sister-in-law to wash up and return to her religion. Her niece also told her to pull herself together and to ask God's forgiveness *(istaghfari)*. Her nephew sat with her and, taking her hand in his, asked her to repeat after him, "In the name of God the merciful and the compassionate" (the opening of any prayer). He then made her recite after him the *tawhid* (the short verse from the Qur'an in which God's uniqueness and power are affirmed). Then he told her to ask God's forgiveness several times and to recite the profession of faith *(shahada)* followed by other verses from the Qur'an.

The closeness to God and commitment to proper Islamic practice that concern the Meccan pilgrim or the pious person go along with a serious devotion to prayer and faith, to which a concern with this world and social ties should become subordinate. Most essential to faith is acceptance of God's will. Since all Muslims, including the Awlad 'Ali Bedouin, hold that a person's time of death is determined in advance by God (some say written on his or her forehead), to wail and lament in grief might be seen as a kind of public defiance or protest against God's will. Bedouin men, who are considered more observant than women, are expected not to lament or sing. Even women must stop lamenting while the men pray over the corpse before burying it.

This opposition is expressed in other ways. There is some suggestion that there even can be a trade-off between lamenting a loved one and having special religious powers. This is illustrated by the story people told about how one particular woman from a saintly lineage became a healer.[14] As her neighbors put it, she had been an ordinary woman, just like them. Then one day when she was away visiting her maternal relatives, her ten-year-old son was hit by a car at dusk while walking with her.

In one version I heard, she was reported to have said that when she wanted to cry out two apparitions came before her, one with a beard (a sign of religiosity). He put his hand over her mouth and sprayed her with water to stop her from crying or lamenting the boy. After that, all she would say about the death was, "His life came from God." A year later she fell ill. They took her to doctors and local healers and finally to a *mrabit* (woman healer) who diagnosed her as having been possessed by a saint. To cure herself, she should begin drumming and trancing to become a healer.

In another version a woman explained that after the woman's son was killed,

> she got sick and started going to doctors and going here and there but she
> didn't get better. Finally she went to a woman healer. And when she went
> to her—this after what? After she had gotten worn out from going to all
> the doctors—she talked about what had possessed her. He [the saint possessing her] said, "I came to her because I was afraid for her. She would
> have gone mad if I had not. I have long forbidden her . . . to cry over her
> son." He said, "She should build me a tomb and make me a place." What
> he said, the woman told her to do. And she did it. Then when she started
> to hold trance sessions, the saint would come to her. Her voice becomes
> the voice of an old man.

In both versions, the saint prevented her from crying over or lamenting her son, and in the end she became a healer through whom God, via the saint, could work.

The lore about funerals among the pious saintly lineages helps clarify the tension between lamenting and Muslim piety as one between human attachments and faith. People said that at the funerals of certain families of those particularly saintly tribes known as the "*mrabtin* with blessings" *(mrabtin bilbruka)*, women are not supposed to lament. They are stopped from doing more than weeping silently, "crying tears," as women put it.

Among the most religious of these families women are actually exhorted, "If you love the Prophet, ululate!" Drums are played, the same drums that put people in trances for curing. It is also said that the corpses of holy men dance as they are being carried toward the grave (in the manner of the saint's followers' trance dancing at ceremonies to honor the saint or to heal people). One of the manifestations of piety and God's grace for the saintly lineages is precisely the special ability and willingness they have to actually celebrate deaths as acts of God's will. Since the saints and holy people of these groups perform miracles mostly after death, it is also as if in death they come to life, but a life close to God.

The tension between the ideals of faith—especially as promulgated by the more educated religious authorities in Egyptian cities (rather than the local saintly lineages)—and traditional Bedouin practices of lamenting and their interpretations is especially clear in talk about corpses. In excited tones one woman explained to her mother-in-law what she had heard in a religious program on the radio. The religious teacher, she said, had argued that it was wrong to mourn for someone who dies. But he also talked about cases in which the corpse makes himself heavy and hard to carry and stubbornly refuses to head toward the grave. She said, "You know how we say he's worried about those he's leaving behind—that he doesn't want to part from them? Well, the radio says not at all!" According to the religious authority on the radio, such a person is actually afraid of his deeds; he sees the angels before him and is afraid to go. He who has lived a good life and only done good deeds is not afraid to go to the grave.[15]

The official language of learned Islam thus speaks of eschatology; the Bedouin discourse on corpses is about the bonds between people, usually close relatives. For example, when an old neighbor, a pitiful man who had been blind half his life and partially paralyzed for the past year, died, I and all the younger members of our large household watched from afar as the men of our community carried his shroud-covered body toward the cemetery. Several people pointed out that his little granddaughter could be seen running underneath the bier. This eleven-year-old had been his most constant companion in the past months, bringing him his cigarettes and food and even holding cups of water to his lips so he could drink. A woman who had been there when the pall bearers had first tried to pick up the corpse later explained what the girl was doing there. She reported that the corpse had at first refused to go forward, circling around and around. The little girl was crying because she was not to be allowed to accompany the men. Only when her father took her hand in his did the corpse let them move forward in the direction of the cemetery. "He [her grandfather] was waiting for her," she commented.

Stories like this work to reaffirm the bonds between the deceased and those close to him or her in life; the laments themselves reinforce the nature of this bond as one of kinship. Though they vary in the wording of the second half, the opening words of a lament are always the same. A woman chants, *yana* (which means something like "Oh me" or "Woe is me"), followed by a possessive kinship term like *ya buya na* ("O my father"), *ya yummi na* ("O my mother"), or *ya wlad khuya na* ("O son of my brother"). In discussing funerals, women report what other women have chanted in their laments, often seeming moved by the very way the relationship is invoked—as, for instance, "O my father's son."

Not everyone who laments, of course, is a relative of the deceased. But even in these cases kinship is stressed because the lamenter instead invokes the closest member of her own immediate family who has died, usually a father. As I have written elsewhere, one woman explained this unusual behavior by saying, "Do you think you cry over the dead person? No, you cry for yourself, for those who have died in your life." This interpretation is corroborated by another incident: commenting on how much I had cried at her brother's funeral, the old matriarch of our community marveled, "And your loved ones are still alive!" I also argued that this invocation of one's own relatives may enable people paying condolences to share grief by reexperiencing, in the company of those currently bereaved, their own grief over the death of a loved one.[16]

No one laments alone. But the community that lamenting, as a practice and a verbal genre, creates and affirms is one of particular relationships between pairs: pairs of mourners and pairs of living and dead. Insofar as these specific attachments may be seen as competing with an individual's attachment to God, and with the wider community feeling that being fellow Muslims should generate, it makes sense that lamenting would be considered religiously wrong.

It seems plausible to suggest that this opposition set up between laments and piety inflects the meaning of lamenting so as to intensify its message. When a woman laments, sings songs of loss, or throws dirt on her head, people must interpret that as an assertion that the massiveness of her grief has overwhelmed her ability or desire to maintain the ideals of faith—to worship God and accept His will—that are so central to definitions of the good person, male or female, in Awlad 'Ali society. Lamenting should not, however, be read only as a personal expression with consequences for evaluating the individual women who lament. As I will discuss later, as a gendered discourse it is powerfully implicated in the reproduction of gender hierarchy in Bedouin society.

Narratives of Death

Women lament and wail during the confined period of the few days, and sometimes weeks, immediately following a death. They occasionally sing to themselves. Much more often, however, they talk about the particular death—at the site of the funeral after they finish lamenting, after they return to their homes and communities, and whenever they see someone who wants to talk about it or find out more. The narratives of death they recount, like most of their narratives, are dramatic. I tape-recorded five discussions among women following the death of a young man of some concern to the community; an analysis of these can provide further insight into the social meaning of lamenting and the place of Muslim discourse in Awlad 'Ali responses to death. The women's narratives were structured by four themes: details of the death; how the narrator and/or the woman most affected by the death first learned of it; how people reacted; and finally, how the death can be explained.

The Details

All deaths are different and few deaths ever welcome. This one was especially tragic because it involved a young man of about twenty who was accidentally killed by a ricocheting bullet from a gun fired by his first cousin at another cousin's wedding. The young man was dancing at the time, just outside the room where the groom had gone in to his bride. Men often fire guns into the air at celebrations, just as women ululate. At weddings this happens at the arrival of the bride from her family's household, at the arrival of the groom, and at the jubilant moment just after the successful defloration. Unfortunately, in this case the wedding was being held in a house and there was a cement pillar in the courtyard. The bullet bounced off it, striking the young man in the neck.

The specifics of the accident formed a central part of the women's narratives. The stories were full of details about what happened, what the young man was doing at the time (dancing with his arm around another young man in front of the bride's room), how the bullet struck him in the neck, how he reacted (like a slaughtered animal he ran toward the men's wedding tent and fell in front of them, leaving a flowing stream of blood behind him), who held him, how they transported him to a doctor in a nearby town who referred them to a hospital in Alexandria but then informed the authorities, how the hospital had probably cut him up and taken his organs, what the reactions in his community were, and so forth. Again and again, women remarked on the terrible reversal of a wedding that had turned into a funeral. One vivid image they called up was that of the wedding tents knocked to the ground.

From Ignorance to Discovery

It is perhaps the way death comes suddenly that makes it so terrible at first. In focusing on the moment of discovery, the narratives capture the way death turns life upside down. Every narrative included some mention of how the person speaking, others whom the speaker and listener knew in common, or those family members most concerned (e.g., the mother, sister, or daughter of the deceased) found out about the death and what they did. This aspect of the narratives can be seen as providing commentary on the meaning of death and reflections on personal attachments.

There is often a lag between the time non-family members know of a death and the moment they break the news to the female relative. When the woman whose songs were discussed above lost her brother (the man killed stealing machinery), the news spread quickly within the community. I heard about it in one household and rushed home to my own to find that the bereaved woman's sister-in-law knew, as did her husband and his brother. Yet the men determined that she should not be told that night. We spent a long, uneasy evening, the adolescent girls worrying that later she would ask them, "How could you sit and laugh with me when you knew my brother had died?"

Early the next morning, her husband hired a car to take her home. Only then did they tell her. Her response was immediate—shrieking and wailing and tearing her headscarf as we all tried to restrain her and calm her down enough to gather together a few things to take with her on the trip. It was a terrible moment and I sensed that everyone in the household was as shaken as I was. When I asked her mother-in-law why they did not inform women right away, she asked, "What could they do at night? They wouldn't be able to take her right away." Often they would tell a woman only that the person was ill. In the narratives of the accidental shooting at the wedding, much of the dramatic tension came from the disparity between what people knew and the sister's ignorance of the death of her brother. The day after the shooting, one of her sisters-in-law recounted:

> I thought she had already gone [to the wedding]—it didn't occur to me that she hadn't. I knew only that the invitations that had come said the wedding was Thursday, today, and that yesterday was the evening celebration. The women had gotten all the stuff to take—syrup drinks and all . . . . Each of them had her stuff and was planning to go to the evening celebration. They were waiting for H., waiting for him to wake up so he could take them.
>
> The women could hardly believe the car was finally going! . . . They came by our house to pick me up. They said to my girl, "Has your mother gone?" She said, "Yes, she left with my uncle." They said to the poor woman, "Hey! She beat you to it. She got to your family's wedding before you did!"

She laughed softly at the irony as she repeated this phrase about the woman's envy. Then she confided that the man driving had informed his mother-in-law and his wife, both riding in the cab of the truck with him, about the death. But the women riding in the back of the pickup truck did not know. She continued,

> When they got close, he headed away from the house of the wedding party. When he went the other way, your Aunt N. said, "What's this, Uncle? Why are you avoiding the wedding?" She turned her head like this and lifted it and then she saw the tents knocked down. She started wailing, "Misfortune! Misfortune! . . . What's the trouble? What's happened to them? What's happened to them?" Someone who saw her from the doorway said, "Your brother is dead! May it only happen to enemies." She jumped down and hit the door and tore her clothes.

The woman's mother-in-law told another version of her discovery of the death. This stressed the drama of reversed fortunes.

> The women were ready to go to the wedding. They were dressed up and wearing their gold. The boy came to H. and told him that there had been

a fight in N.'s family and that one of them had shot another and killed him. H. said to his wife, "Where do you think you women are going—taking candy and fruit drink and cookies? They say that N.'s family have fought amongst themselves but I don't know exactly. You want to go to the wedding? Well, there is no wedding." His wife said to him, "We'll go whether or not there is a wedding." N. was wearing her gold, though, ready for the wedding and when they got there she said "Hey, we've passed the wedding party! They're the ones toward the east. Why have we passed them? Why are you going the other way?" He said to her, "Misfortune." . . . They told her, "Your brother M. is the one who's been killed." Oh black night! What a night!

The woman herself had her own narrative of discovery, more detailed and different from theirs in a key element: she stressed that she had had premonitions of misfortune. What she told her sister-in-law and other women can be read as an affirmation of her closeness to her brother. She was agitated as she told it.

Myself, when I came, may it only happen to enemies, my eyes—I still feel there is a fog over them. I can't see with them and I throw up all the time. When I got there I said, "Hey Uncle! Why aren't we stopping at the family's?" From that moment, I tell you, the torrent that flowed in front of my other brother! . . . "The whole world [knew]?" I asked. "The man was shot at ten o'clock in the morning and no one came to get me? . . . Not a single man comes by?"

In her narrative, the woman explained how others had delayed her from going to her family's to attend the wedding. It was a hot day and after she bathed, her daughter asked her what was the matter—why had she put on a dark dress? She continued:

I said, "Sister—from the day I buried my father I don't really feel them, weddings." I just said this. And I had wrapped an old kerchief around my waist . . . . I wore an old rag! I'd never done it before for a wedding. And my dress, dark and down to here, with a big print . . . From the day I buried my father I haven't worn a red dress. And then S. said to me, "Take off that rag! Take it off! What's the matter with you?" "Take it off," she said, chasing after me. I said, "I won't take it off. I feel, I don't feel well . . . ."

As if to suggest a premonition, she described what happened as she walked to her neighbors' to catch a ride:

Suddenly it was as if there was something in my legs. And I couldn't see. Something carried me. A little later I was sitting at your aunt's and they came to me and looked at me. They asked, "What's the matter with you? Why are you wearing that bit of rag?" I said, "The world is empty. I don't feel well." I hadn't eaten and I hadn't drunk. I just said that, just like that.

Since replacing the red belt with a white or light kerchief is one of the signs of mourning, and wearing less colorful dresses also suggests a refusal to celebrate things, her narrative suggested that she had sensed that something was wrong. The effect of this was to attest to her listeners her closeness to her family, despite the distance marriage created for her and her actual ignorance of what had occurred in her family's midst. Thus, while the other women's narratives of discovery stressed the suddenness of knowledge and the way death turns life horribly upside down, hers stressed the attachment to family and played down the ignorance.

How Much They Did!

A third theme in these narratives is the description and evaluation of what in particular other women did and said at the funeral or the period of mourning immediately following. Even men's reactions were discussed, although in less detail. By approvingly or disapprovingly evaluating reactions, the narratives at once reinforce the conventional practices of grief as appropriate and, even more important, reproduce the bonds between community members that kinship is believed to generate. They do so by differentiating between those who react to the loss and those who do not. One of the people who provoked interest was the young man who had fired the shot at this wedding-turned-funeral. One woman commented that the whole family was in bad shape. Another added that death would be better than knowing you had killed your own cousin. A third confirmed, "He was cutting his face and tearing his hair and his cheeks."

Mostly women discussed the women who were there, what they were wearing, how they addressed their laments, and what else they did to mourn. There was something judgmental in these comments. Those who were discussed disapprovingly were those who showed none of the signs of mourning. For example, one long interchange included the following kinds of remarks: "Didn't you see so-and-so's women? Thieves. Those in-laws—not a headscarf tossled, no eye-makeup (kuhl) removed, and the bangs across their foreheads came down to here!" "Not a tear came out of her, God be praised!" (This is an expression of wonder or surprise.) "She was wearing a gold brooch on her chest, I swear by Saint Dmayn—a huge yellow button, gold, from here to there across her chest. What rot! Her kids are almost as old as we are!" "A thief, she didn't get up to greet anyone, didn't wail, didn't lament, didn't raise her voice." Those mentioned with approval were those about whom they could say, "How much she did!" (*yama darat*). To "do much" includes wailing, lamenting, tearing one's clothing, scratching one's cheeks, and throwing dirt over one's head.

These are the conventional gestures of mourning, the recognizable practices of grief.

The person whose reactions were most often discussed in the narratives I taped was the young woman from our own community who had married the young man's brother. For example, her aunt reported,

> Our little B., she threw off her necklace, she wanted to die. She was trying to bury herself, she wanted to die. And she'd say, "He was kind to my little daughters, he was kind to my little daughters. He was so loving with them." She really lamented.

In another version, a different aunt asked where the young woman had been when they arrived at the funeral. Her cousin answered, "She was putting dirt on her head, putting dirt on her head. I told her 'Enough! Your children are crying.' I put her headscarf back on. I told her, 'There are lots besides you who are throwing dirt.'" Another woman interjected, "She wanted to die herself, poor thing."

Making Sense
The fourth and most elaborate theme of the narratives was how to make sense of the death. What is remarkable about much of what the women discussed amongst themselves and many of the details they chose to report is how inconsistent their explanations were. The women's substories and commentaries implied, on the one hand, that blame for the death could be traced to human decisions or actions, and on the other, that all that happens, especially death, is God's will. In the structure of the narratives, the religious discourse seemed to have the last word, putting a kind of temporary stop to speculations about responsibility in the same way that religious discourse was used, as I described earlier, to put a stop to laments.

In the course of the particular narratives of the death I have analyzed, women criticized a number of participants, thereby implicitly suggesting their responsibility for the death. On the most practical level, the stupidity of firing a gun anywhere near a house was the subject of a couple of heated exchanges. Another small whispered conversation criticized the whole family as a bad family where people were always getting into fights. Most of the critical discussion, however, centered on the wedding at which the boy was shot. The effect was to suggest that the wedding had been ill-fated from the start. Wednesdays, it was remarked, were not auspicious days for weddings. Some women criticized the family for suddenly holding the wedding a day earlier than planned and for not, therefore, having the proper evening of prewedding celebration. This was unheard of, and the deviation from accepted practice was condemned. Two other stories about the wedding were repeated, often in hushed tones of condemnation. The first was the story of the angry fit the old woman, mother of the groom, had thrown when the men setting off to fetch the bride said there was no room for her daughter in the cars. She was reported to have shouted, "She's your aunt, she's your aunt. If she doesn't go I'll shit on the cars. Your aunt!" She started throwing dust and wailing. Finally she fainted, frightening everyone. I sensed they thought it was inauspicious to have such negative goings on at a wedding since some women muttered, "If only she'd been the one to die."

The second story concerned what had happened a couple of weeks earlier when the engagement had been decided. A young man who had hoped to marry the bride, and was actually a cousin, was devastated when her family agreed to give her in marriage to a closer cousin who had claimed her. Women described how he had been throwing dirt on himself since he heard the news. His mother too, it was reported in another conversation, had wailed because she wanted the girl for her son. She wailed, as one woman put it, "until her liver wore out" (the liver is used metaphorically the way we use the heart). A final comment on this, by the woman whose brother had been killed, was, "If only they'd given her to them." Was she implying that none of this would have happened if they had?

The final form of human agency occasionally put forth as an explanation of the tragedy was "the eye"—the eye of envy that falls on those with good fortune or new things. One woman said explicitly about the boy's mother, "She said it was the eye—the eye that shot him. The wedding tents were so beautiful!" Later in the conversation two women interrupted each other with praise for the tents. "Hey, what tents they were!" "Whose tent was the old one? It was beautiful." "She [the boy's mother] had made it herself. I swear by Saint Dmayn an eye fell on it." Another day, the same woman said, as she explained to me what was meant by "the eye," "It's like what happened to those people." As if it were obvious she said, "Didn't a wedding turn into a funeral?"

The various forms of blame, however, were put to rest by another kind of explanation often raised just at the end of one of these narrative episodes. This interpretation invoked God's will and seemed to bring closure to a discussion. Women often ended conversations with comments like, "everyone and his fate (*nasib*)," "his life span was short (*'umru gasir*)," and "when a person's life is up." Sometimes, when women were describing decisions the family made (such as the decision to hold the wedding early), a listener would remark, "They said one thing and He [God] said another." Women reinforced this interpretation by telling stories about others who had scolded the mourners, "Be quiet, be quiet! Everything is by God's will!"

Along the same lines, certain stories seemed to take on significance either as premonitions of what was to come or as evidence that God works in strange ways to bring about what must come to pass. For example, some stories about what the young man had done in the last few days of his life seemed heavy with meaning. He was reported to have gone on several visits where he asked people

to take his photograph. Another story seemed to confirm the belief that fate cannot be escaped. One woman reported on what a cousin had told her about how
the young man had almost missed the wedding. On the morning of the wedding
his older brother had told the young man to wait until he got back from deliv-
ering some people to the airport before going to the wedding. This was the boy's
cousin's story. "The day of the wedding, we were watering the fig trees, he and
I. Suddenly he said, 'Hey it's late, I'm not going to stay here. Hurry, hurry!' He
ran off and left me behind, I was still watering the figs when . . . . " At this point
another woman interrupted to add a detail. The boy had said, "I want to go help
out at the wedding. By God I won't stay here!"

The women's narratives explored the various ways to make sense of a sense-
less death. Why did the people decide to have that particular wedding, why did
they move it a day earlier, what made him go to the wedding when he might easily have missed it? There seemed so many ways that the death might have been
avoided—but the fact was that the young man did attend, they did fire the gun
in the courtyard, and he was killed. That killings can occur unintentionally or by
mistake is recognized; there was no talk of revenge. But that death could be an
accident, a matter of chance, was not part of the discourse. People could act
badly and in the end a person's time of death is God-given or "written." Death's
universe of meaning for the Awlad 'Ali was defined in women's narratives by
these two sorts of explanation.

Conclusion

What is the advantage of approaching Awlad 'Ali laments, as I have, by way of
the multiple genres of talk about death? It could be argued that one obvious
advantage of the method is that in covering the range of responses to death one
is approximating more closely the experiences of the individuals involved.[17]
After all, they move from one context to another and produce a variety of forms
of talk from highly formalized funeral laments and ritual wailing to everyday
discussions. Yet greater inclusiveness does not guarantee insight.

I have argued that what we actually gain through this method is the capacity to grasp the complex ways in which juxtaposed discourses on death in a
Muslim community work to give each other special meaning. In particular, I
have been concerned with the place of explicitly Islamic discourses and practices. Elsewhere I explored why the contradictory Bedouin discourses of poetry
and ordinary language, in which people voice radically different sentiments
about interpersonal relations, had to be understood in terms of each other.[18]
Each discourse marked a particular kind of social context—one public and the
other more intimate (and involving equals). But each discourse also made sense
only in terms of a dialectic between acceptance of the official ideology of honor
and modesty (the basis of the Awlad 'Ali moral system which justifies a partic-

ular configuration of power), and resistance to it by the women and young men least served by it.

I analyzed, in one case of death, the contrast between the family members' vulnerability, as conveyed in songs of loss, and the anger and revenge they expressed in ordinary public discourse.[19] I argued that the anger that was a perfect demonstration of adherence to the ideals of honor (including independence and refusal to be dominated) may have been given even greater weight by being juxtaposed with the sadness expressed in the private poems. The very ability to overcome the vulnerability revealed in poetry in order to achieve the ideals of honor in everyday life enhanced honor by showing it to be voluntarily sought and hard to achieve.

In the material on the discourses of death presented in this article, a similar contradiction was shown to exist: between the laments and other generally sad songs of loss, on the one hand, and the apportionings of blame that were such a regular feature of the narratives about the death, on the other. However, ordinary language conversation, which in my earlier analysis of Awlad 'Ali social life I had treated as relatively undifferentiated, turned out to be quite complex. When I began to look carefully at the ways people talked about death, the crucial role of one new element—religious faith—became apparent. Like the discourse of honor, religious discourse is in tension with laments and songs. Most importantly, it opposes acceptance of God's will to the human attachments, especially between kin, that the laments and songs commemorate. Faith in God for the Muslim Awlad 'Ali had to be seen, for men and women, as another moral register in which to read people's practices.

This construction of Islam's place has two consequences. First, it enables lamenting to become a special sort of statement about the meaning of death. When women lament and wail, knowing all the while that people talk about how the pious accept God's will, how Meccan pilgrims remain silent, and how saintly lineages celebrate at funerals, they suggest to those around them that death is so terrible that it prevents them from maintaining faith. It is interesting that another of the things women do in grief is to tear their clothes and go out unveiled in front of men. This is a transgression of the modesty essential to moral standing. Bereavement, they assert through such practices in a field of meaning defined by the differences between faith, independence, and attachment, makes you forget both God and honor. This is not to say that they do forget God and honor but rather that their actions can serve as a general commentary on the power of death.

Second, this configuration makes people's responses to death significant for their social standing. This is where the gendering of the discourses of death becomes significant. Like the code of honor, religious faith provides for the Awlad 'Ali Bedouins a principle of social differentiation, a standard by which people can be ranked. Some social groups benefit from the ways these principles compete. Among Awlad 'Ali men, for example, there is a widespread recognition that pride and tribal loyalty, the two defining characteristics of the honorable "free tribes," go against Islamic ideals of community and equality. This gives the saintly lineages, who are peaceful and pious, some sort of edge. In enacting their greater religiosity through celebrating deaths, these lineages compel members of the "free tribes" to respect them.[20] Through such enactments of piety they offset some of the negative effects of their inability (because of their economic and political dependence) to enact the ideals of independent action that justify the authority of the honorable.

In gender relations, however, the two systems of moral differentiation seem to be working in tandem. Women, by lamenting, singing songs of loss, and emphasizing in their stories the intensity of their reactions to loss and their personal involvements in mourning, simultaneously assert the weakness of their faith and the greatness of their vulnerability and attachment to others. It is tempting to treat these women's moving discourses on death as counterdiscourses that affirm the positive value of human ties and resist the imposition of either the honorable ideals of autonomy or the pious ideals of acceptance of loss. The problem is that women also invoke the other discourses; expressions of Muslim piety, references to God's will, recitation of the profession of faith, and participation in the preparation of the corpse (when female) are not the monopoly of men.[21] Awlad 'Ali women cannot be considered less committed to being Muslim, more ignorant of Islam, not fully "Islamized," or sheltered preservers of pre-Islamic survivals. They value Muslim identity and piety as much as men do. Precisely because men and women in this community participate in producing for themselves a single, if complex, moral universe, the traditionally gendered rituals of mourning—where women lament the people they have lost and men instead invoke God's will as they tell each other, "Pull yourself together" and pray over the body—become an important means by which women publicly enact their own moral, and ultimately social, inferiority.

These conclusions suggest that those studying Muslim societies who are interested in understanding the place of Islam in the everyday lives of particular communities should proceed by attending to where recognizable and acknowledged Muslim religious discourses fit in the universe of discourses and practices of a given community and by asking how these articulate with the organization of social hierarchies and solidarities.

Notes

Author's note: An early version of this paper was presented at the conference on "Lament" at the University of Texas at Austin, April 1989. I am grateful to Steven Feld, the organizer, and to the other conference participants for questions that helped me reformulate the central arguments of the paper. I also thank the anonymous reviewers for IJMES and Nadia Abu-Zahra for their suggestions. The translations of the songs of loss would have been more wooden without Timothy Mitchell's good suggestions. Transcriptions of these songs as well as all phrases and Arabic words approximate the Awlad 'Ali dialect. A Fulbright Award under the Islamic Civilization Program enabled me to complete in 1987 much of the research in Egypt on which this paper is based.

1   For a description of a funeral, see Lila Abu-Lughod, *Veiled Sentiments: Honor and Poetry in a Bedouin Society* (Berkeley, Calif., 1986), p. 21.

2   For exceptions see Nadia Abu-Zahra, "The Comparative Study of Muslim Societies and Islamic Rituals," *Arab Historical Review for Ottoman Studies* 3–4 (December 1991): 7–38; Edward Lane, *An Account of the Manners and Customs of the Modern Egyptians* (London, 1842), p. 474; Elizabeth Wickett, "'For Our Destinies': The Funerary Laments of Upper Egypt" (Ph.D. diss. in progress, University of Pennsylvania). By contrast, the literature on laments in Greece is substantial, includ- ing the classic by Margaret Alexiou, *The Ritual Lament in Greek Tradition* (Cambridge, 1974) and more recently, Anna Caraveli, "The Bitter Wounding: The Lament as Social Protest in Rural Greece," in *Gender and Power in Rural Greece*, ed. Jill Dubisch (Princeton, N.J., 1986), pp.169–94; Loring Danforth and Alexander Tsiaras, *The Death Rituals of Rural Greece* (Princeton, N.J., 1982); C. Nadia Seremetakis, *The Last Word* (Chicago, 1991).

3   The literature on these issues is vast. For recent discussions, see Nadia Abu-Zahra, "The Comparative Study of Muslim Societies" and "The Rain Rituals as Rites of Spiritual Passage," *International Journal of Middle East Studies*, 20 (1988): 507–29; Richard Antoun, *Muslim Preacher in the Modern World* (Princeton, N.J., 1989); Talal Asad, *The Idea of an Anthropology of Islam,* (Washington, D.C., 1986); Janice Boddy, *Wombs and Alien Spirits* (Madison, Wisc., 1990); Ladislav Holy, "Gender and Ritual in an Islamic Society: The Berti of Darfur," *Man*, n.s., 23 (September 1988): 469–87; Nancy Tapper and Richard Tapper, "The Birth of the Prophet: Ritual and Gender in Turkish Islam," *Man*, n.s., 22 (March 1987): 69–92. For a review of some earlier literature on the anthropology of Islam, see also Lila Abu-Lughod, "Anthropology's Orient," in *Theory, Politics, and the Arab World: Critical Responses*, ed. Hisham Sharabi (New York, 1990), 81–131.

4   See Abu-Zahra, "The Comparative Study of Muslim Societies" for discussion of bur- ial practices in urban Egypt and rural Tunisia.

5   Caraveli, "The Bitter Wounding," 185, notes a similar antagonism between the church and women's lamentation in Greece.

6   Good examples are Michael Gilsenan, *Recognizing Islam* (New York, 1982); William Roff, ed., *Islam and the Political Economy of Meaning* (Berkeley, Calif., 1989). But see Abu-Zahra, "The Comparative Study of Muslim Societies" and "The Rain Rituals," for criticism of anthropologists' lack of familiarity with the Islamic textual traditions that inform many local practices and Asad's, "The Idea of an Anthropology of Islam," for a criticism of anthropologists' tendencies to exaggerate local differ-

ences and to deny any universality to Islam by failing to acknowledge a common discursive tradition involving reference to the founding texts of the Qur'an and sunna.

7 For evidence of the gendered nature of death rituals in an agricultural community in Egypt, see El-Sayed El-Aswad, "Death Rituals in Rural Egyptian Society: A Symbolic Study," *Urban Anthropology and Studies of Cultural Systems and World Economic Development*, 16 (1987): 205–41.

8 Abu-Lughod, cf. *Veiled Sentiments*.

9 For a more complex, subtle, and profoundly evocative reflection on the symbolism of life and death in a Moroccan community, see Stefania Pandolfo, "'The Angel of Death Replied': Absence and Longing in a Moroccan Space" (Ph.D. diss., Princeton University, 1991).

10 See Winifred Blackman, *The Fellahin of Upper Egypt* (London, 1927), 121, for a report of a similar belief in Upper Egypt.

11 See Abu-Lughod, *Veiled Sentiments*, chap. 4, for a discussion of this relationship between sexuality and fertility.

12 On the relationship between weddings and circumcisions, see Abu-Lughod, *Veiled Sentiments*, 136; Vincent Crapanzano, "Rite of Return: Circumcision in Morocco," in *The Psychoanalytic Study of Society*, Vol. 9, ed. W. Muensterberger and L. B. Boyer (New York, 1980).

13 Abu-Zahra has explored the social development (in Cairo and the Sahel of Tunisia) of the hadiths that condemn lamentation as *makruh* (disliked) but not *haram* (forbidden) in her "The Comparative Study of Muslim Societies."

14 The place of saintly lineages, collectively known in the western desert as the *mrabtin* is complex.They are clients (euphemistically called "brothers") of particular Awlad 'Ali tribes; at the same time, many of them are considered religious figures. All of the holy men whose shrines dot the western desert come from these groups. Healers who work by trancing at a *hadra* come only from these tribes. See Abu-Lughod, *Veiled Sentiments;* Michael Meeker, *Literature and Violence in North Arabia* (Cambridge, 1979); Emrys Peters, *The Bedouin of Cyrenaica* (Cambridge, 1990).

15 The refusals of corpses to let themselves be carried to the grave was also reported by Blackman, *The Fellahin of Upper Egypt*, 113, who was given a similar explanation.

16 Abu-Lughod, *Veiled Sentiments*, 67–69.

17 The question of personal experience is especially thorny because of the problems of "authenticity" raised by the conventionality of laments, formulaic songs, and even the structure and content of everyday narratives. I argue in "Shifting Politics in Bedouin Love Poetry," in *Language and the Politics of Emotion*, ed. Catherine Lutz and Lila Abu-Lughod (New York, 1990), 24–45, for a strategy of analyzing discourses of sentiment as they are pragmatically deployed in social interactions rather than as reflections of inner states. Catherine Lutz and I show in "Introduction: Emotion, Discourse, and the Politics of Everyday Life" (ibid., 1–23) how modern western ideologies of emotion as natural and individual make the conventionality of sentiment trigger charges of artifice or inauthenticity.

18 Abu-Lughod, *Veiled Sentiments*, chap. 8.

19 Lila Abu-Lughod, "Honor and the Sentiments of Loss in a Bedouin Society," *American Ethnologist* 12 (1985): 245–61.

20 I show in *Writing Women's Worlds: Bedouin Stories* (Berkeley, Calif., 1993), chap. 5, how their religious status is currently undergoing change due to greater influence of urban Islamists who condemn many of their religious practices.

21 I am grateful to Nadia Abu-Zahra (personal communication) for drawing my attention to women's participation in burial practices.

29

Authority and the Mosque in Upper Egypt: The Islamic Preacher as Image and Actor

Patrick D. Gaffney

The jural and theological tradition of classical Islam contains a considerable literature dealing with mosques as places of public assembly and religious cult. From the beginning of Muhammad's foundation of a community in Medina, where the courtyard of his own house became the first mosque, the inherent authority associated with the place of prayer and weekly muster has been plainly recognized. During his life the Prophet himself supervised all activities carried out there and when he was absent or indisposed he specifically delegated temporary responsibility of such leadership to an assistant, most notably Abu Bakr, who later became his first successor or caliph. Furthermore, the Prophet explicitly regulated the establishment of other sites as mosques, even to the point of ordering the destruction of unauthorized buildings such as the 'mosque of opposition,' al-masjid al-darar discussed in the Qur'an (IX:107 ff.) ('Masdjid', Encyclopaedia of Islam, 1936; Calverly, 1925:ch:IV, V).

Given the great importance attached to mosques in the first centuries of Islam, it is hardly surprising that the theme has reappeared in recent discussions of both practical and theoretical interest. Among those most persistently engaged in this pursuit are reformers who view the mosque as the point of departure for an overall revitalization of Muslim society (Mahmud, 1976).

In modern Egypt, efforts to promote general sociopolitical improvement by reforming the mosque as a center of communal religious practice must be understood within the context of wider historical currents. For one thing, Egypt's colonial experience, although it lasted longer than that of many Arab lands, was never one of direct European rule or even a single country's domination. As a result, the decisive steps in the process which led to the elimination of the traditional economic structure supporting mosques were initiated by the Muslim rulers beginning with the great Muhammad 'Ali (1805–48). Among other means employed by Muhammad 'Ali and his successors to consolidate state power and to centralize its administration, were measures that effectively appropriated

From *Islam and the Political Economy of Meaning: Comparative Studies of Muslim Discourse*, ed. William R. Roff (Berkeley: University of California Press, for the SSRC, 1987), pp. 199–225. Reprinted by permission. Patrick D. Gaffney is Associate Professor of Anthropology at Notre Dame University.

waqf properties and placed the dependent mosques under a civil bureaucracy (Baer, 1969:79–92).

In addition, the development of modern educational, legal, and commercial systems caused the increasing marginalization of the traditional religious elite, the ulama (Crecelius, 1972: 167–210; Marsot, 1972: 149–66). In short, the autonomy and scope of religious institutions in Egypt have steadily shrunk before an expanding state apparatus, a process which reached its climax in the 1960s under President Gamal Abdel Nasser. At that time, not only was Cairo's Azhar University, the last great bastion of conservatism, purged and restructured to assure its dependence on secular power but, in reaction to stirrings from remnants of the Muslim Brotherhood, comprehensive laws were passed for the strict regulation of all religious and social organizations.

As a consequence of this history, no mosque in Egypt can function in any formal sense apart from in a defined relationship to the state. Similarly, no Islamic preacher delivers a Friday sermon without an implied form of political as well as religious authorization.

Another current that has marked the character of mosques in modern Egypt stems from a concern for Islamic orthodoxy in both doctrine and ritual. These motives were certainly prominent among such influential writers and teachers as Muhammad Abduh (1849–1905) and Rashid Rida (1865–1935), whose views are well known, but they were also behind the activities of many less intellectually oriented organizers. One representative of this applied dimension of the *salafiyya* movement (literally, return to the way of the ancestors) was Shaykh Mahmoud Muhammad Khattab al-Sibky (1858–1933). He founded in 1913 what has since become a national network of mosques with related social facilities, whose official title is the Shar'ia Cooperative Society of Followers of the Qur'an and Sunna of Muhammad. Their declared purpose is to support the construction and staffing of mosques where practice conforms to the authentic teachings of Islam as found in the Qur'an and Sunna (Berger, 1970: 119). It bears mentioning, in passing, that the Muslim Brotherhood in its early phase was cast in a similar mold, although the vision of its charismatic founder Hassan al-Banna (1906–49) clearly included more political aspirations (Heyworth Dunne, 1950:31–55; Mitchell, 1969:47).

Within this general climate of reform, a zeal for ritual and moral purity on the part of neotraditionalists coincided with the disapproval of ignorance, superstition, and wasteful enthusiasm by the nationalist and liberal thinkers. Both groups, therefore, supported government policies designed to suppress the dramatic displays associated with popular Sufi devotions and to bring these fraternities under the control of state agencies. This gradual process, together with the breakdown of the guild system and the erosion of clan and village solidarity which had provided the strength of Sufi orders, was virtually complete by the beginning of the twentieth century (Gilsenan, 1967:11–18). A by no means minor effect of this course of events was the reassertion of the mosque as the only approved and legitimate institution for public religious expression. Thus, today in Egypt, one finds that certain heads of Sufi *turuq* are integrated into the state-subsidized religious establishment, some holding positions as preachers. This also means that the characteristic relationship of a Sufi *shaykh* with members of the fraternity has also changed to resemble more closely the rapport of other Islamic preachers to their congregations (de Jong, 1978:111).

In addition to the pressures of secularization and reform upon the character of mosques in contemporary Egypt, there is a regional factor. Broadly speaking, Upper Egypt has always been somewhat isolated, conservative, and xenophobic. Its inhabitants tend to be poorer, less educated, and more closely bound to a tribal ethos than the similar peasant population of the Nile Delta, who have benefited from the proximity of more Europeanized cities and the Suez Canal. In Upper Egypt, therefore, the transformation of mosques began later and has been less thorough, but the preacher has none the less emerged as the principal figure of authority.

Finally, the changing shape of mosque practice in Egypt, and especially Upper Egypt, must be seen in the light of the relationship between religion and nationalism. In brief, the nineteenth-century mercantile economy that caused the direct intrusion of world market factors upon the Egyptian peasantry served also to create new forms of centralization and tighter bonds of dependence of the rural sectors upon exterior power centers. Nationalist leaders who blamed European governments and entrepreneurs for this state of exploitation were quick to play on distinctions of religion. Furthermore, by the time of World War I, when the Nationalist Movement began to win popular rural support, not only had mosques become a rallying point for anticolonial protest, but the appeals that mixed modernization and reform had succeeded in stirring still more primordial sentiments. Marshall Hodgson remarks (1974:285), for instance, on the toning down of the 'more emotional and much of the more collective side of religion' in the village cultural life of this period, with the result that 'as emotions were withdrawn from cult, they were invested in politics.' This observation of a high convertability between the values of religion and politics underlines once more the place of the Islamic preacher. Correspondingly, it signals the reason for the increasing official attempts to regulate the use of this ritual authority.

At the beginning of the modern period, the Islamic sermon or *khut-bah al-juma'*, which forms part of the congregational prayer at the Friday noon ceremony, had become ossified into a fixed formulary recitation. In some rare instances where the preacher or *khatib* was a man of classical learning, this oration might be more elaborate, as Edward Lane indicates (1836:93–5) in his description of preaching in the Azhar district of Cairo in the 1830s. But more normally, and certainly for Upper Egypt, if the sermon was not omitted, it typically consisted of a short text of rhyming prose taken from a medieval source. Often, the same verses were repeated each week, even while their actual meaning would be lost on the illiterate listeners and perhaps on the one preaching as well.[1]

In reaction to this illiteracy among preachers and this fossilization of ritual, Muhammad Abduh and others proposed education and administrative schemes designed to modernize the sermon and to upgrade the quality of mosque leadership. Their efforts resulted in a movement that sought to revitalize the sermon, transforming it into a new idiom that would provide a relevant and informed address, spoken in vernacular Arabic and serving to enlighten and direct Muslim consciences (Rida, 1931:630). Also, from the start, this revival of Islamic preaching merged freely with strains of modern political awareness. This fusion of Islamic and patriotic values continues as Malcolm Kerr neatly summarizes (1975:44):

> The dominant, explicitly political movements of the twentieth century in the Arab world—nationalism and socialism, eventually personified by Nasser—have not been altogether secular phenomena, even when their appeals and discussions leave religious terminology behind. Rather, there has been a transposition of religious symbols into secular ones, concealing an underlying continuity of psychological concerns and cultural issues.

In a similar pattern, the ideological converse of this transposition is also common. Note, for instance, how many militant Muslim groups encode their ardent, if somewhat confusing, political agenda in a strictly religious language. Saad Eddin Ibrahim (1980:433), who interviewed a number of Islamic extremists in prison after their arrest under President Sadat, points out that their socioeconomic views closely resembled a moderate socialism hardly distinguishable from those of the British Labour Party or Nasser,

> but any suggestion to that effect invariably produced an outraged response. Islam is not to be likened to any man-made doctrine or philosophy. It would be more acceptable if we were to say that British socialism resembled Islam. In fact, some of them have attributed Mao Tsetung's success in China to his emulation of Islam, rather than to his adherence to Marxism.

What is revealed here is the familiar phenomenon of a single flexible repertory of symbols invested with meaning at different levels of social and cultural reference. This condensation of the sacred and the secular into one elastic vocabulary is particularly well known in Islam, and it is only intensified by an enduring sense of crisis. Under such conditions of increasing tension, the semantic potency of these abstract symbols mounts and consequently a ritualized setting is required for their effective and creative manipulation. Ritual supplies a circumscribed and diminished frame of reference because it separates ordinary language and gesture from the partial or diffuse contexts of everyday usage. Within the culturally construed setting of the sermon, an exceptional mode of discourse becomes possible that concentrates attention on a unity of the ideal and the real which is normally shattered in day-to-day experience. Moreover, since ritual, if it is effective, refracts societal dynamics, its force is generated only through the action of certain recognized persons. In other words, the right publicly to define the meaning of shared symbols and to interpret intersubjective experience by means of them is not arbitrary. Rather, it is the privilege and the responsibility of a designated role, in this case, the preacher, to conjoin and expound the relationship between categories and values that are at once public and private (or sectional). Thus, rightful access to ritual leadership implies authority of itself as Victor Turner suggests (1977: 146) in pointing out that

> the person or party who controls the assignment of meaning to religious
> or political symbols can also control the mobilization efficiency their
> central position has traditionally assigned to them.

Three Types of Preacher

The variety of Islamic preachers found in the mosques of Upper Egypt reflects the diversity of social forms and cultural preferences among the population. Since preaching is a corporate event, it only occurs in conjunction with the appearance of a certain kind of association which might be called a mosque congregation. Mosques too acquire proper identities due to their location in certain quarters or neighborhoods, historical associations and an assortment of physical factors such as size, style, and decor. But most important of all in the identity of a mosque is the question of how it was established, and, usually closely linked to this, by what resources it continues to function. Here, then, a triangular interaction is involved, with the mosque itself providing a symbolic focus, while the preacher serves as a ritual specialist, and spokesman for the congregation of participating worshippers. All these elements combine to form the context for what is pronounced as the text of the preachment. The raw verbal content of a sermon cannot be properly understood apart from its setting, its speaker, and its hearers, which together constitute a system of reference.

In Upper Egypt, we can distinguish between three types of preachers that have crystallized historically into separate though not exclusive images of ideal types, representing compatible aspects of Islamic authority. Such a typology, following Weberian usage, exists as a conceptual abstraction that perceives a this-worldly rationalization of other-worldly sacred values. Each type derives its legitimacy from the particular way it qualifies 'pure' charisma, or, in Weber's terms, from the way it 'proves itself,' which indicates that each corresponds to a certain form of social organization.

The first type is the 'saint' or *wali* whose authenticity is expressed as personal *baraka*, which is not seen as a talent or skill but rather as a 'mode in which the divine reaches into the world'(Geertz, 1971:44). Living, or more normally dead, he is conceptualized as an intercessor and wonder worker, a familiar conduit for divine force and blessing. Classically, the *wali* complex is most fully realized in the localized Sufi order, where the moral bonds of kinship or community and the saint's spiritual favor essentially coincide. Often, the wali is honored as a special patron, and devotion can include practices characteristic of magic and fetishism.

The second type is the 'scholar' or *'alim* whose authority derives from his knowledge or even his personification of the Law, *Shari'a*, which he preserves and applies. Traditionally, the 'alim embodies the prestige of the classical Muslim civilization, particularly in its jurisprudential aspect, and it was his function to legitimate the exercise of political power. The ulama were teachers, judges, managers of charitable endowments, and counselors in public and moral affairs. More recently, since secularization has deprived this clerical class of their monopolies of legal and educational institutions, the 'alim survives as a remnant in only a few places, most prominently as the shaykh of a mosque, where certain residual attributes of the former elite are still honored, notably the Azhari education.

The third type is the reformer or inspired activist who has figured historically as a 'holy warrior' or *mujahid*. Whereas, classically, this 'knight' assumed his task in conquest, defense, and governance, today the image is more closely associated with the claims of modern lay movements, such as the Muslim Brothers and its successors, who strive to establish *al-nizam al-islami* in the modern world. Until their recent suppression, this ideal was most publicly asserted in Upper Egypt by student groups which called themselves *al-jama'a al-islamiya*. The vision of this 'Islamic Society' included not only claims to superior doctrinal and ritual purity, but also forceful demands for moral conformity extended to all areas of civil life. The basis for this authority does not lie in inspiration or learning, but in the capacity to defend and enforce.

Needless to say, this typology represents an abstraction, for, ethnographically speaking, actual preachers are more complex and malleable than the analytic artifice. None the less, it is worth noting that there is a similar three-part classification that roughly corresponds to this one in the official categories that define the legal structure of religious organizations in Egypt. Two of these types of authority are under the Ministry of Waqfs, while the third area of competence falls under the Ministry of Social Affairs. Within the Ministry of Waqfs, a clear and consistent administrative division separates one bureaucracy which is responsible for all that has to do with the system of government-subsidized mosques from a second bureaucracy charged with the administration of Sufi orders and their public activities. The third class of organizations, which are somewhat more diffuse, are called 'voluntary benevolent societies' *(al-jama'a al-khairiya,* or *al-jama'a al-diniya)* and they are supervised by a special division within the Ministry of Social Affairs (Berger, 1970:92).

Minya

The research I conducted on preachers in the mosques of Upper Egypt was concentrated around the city of Minya or, to give it its proper name, al-Minya al-Fuli. I resided there for eighteen months during 1978–79. Although the site has been inhabited since early antiquity, the city as it stands today, some 250 kilometers south of Cairo on the western bank of the Nile, is largely the result of modern urbanization. At its core, traces of the original village are clearly discernible, now surrounded by various stylistically distinct products of various late nineteenth and twentieth century building booms. Also interesting is the shape of the city, with its roughly 250,000 residents, which runs in a long relatively thin urban sprawl for several kilometers along the river bank and incorporates into its northern and southern expansion other distinct preexisting villages. The city serves as the capital of one of the five governorates of Upper Egypt, which means that regional directorates of civil and military administration are situated in it. Likewise, it provides all the other usual services of a provincial metropolis to the largely rural population of the surrounding hinterland.[2]

There are approximately fifty substantial mosques in the city of Minya as well as scores of smaller places of prayer of various sizes and degrees of permanence. But only at about twenty mosques, and these would be the largest, is there a regular Friday noon prayer which includes the formal sermon. Of these, I shall single out two for discussion, chosen because they are among the most prominent and because they represent what is locally understood as the two contrasting types of religious institutions. One of these two mosques is considered old, although the current building is very recent since it has been completely renovated by the Ministry of Waqfs in a style that conforms to their prescriptions for a 'cathedral' mosque. It is a greatly enlarged and enhanced version of what had been a mosque built around a *zawiyya,* a saint's tomb shrine, which probably dates from the early seventeenth century. The saint here honored is a wali who resided and died in Minya, known as Shaykh al-Fuli, who has since become the patron of the city and the most highly regarded wali in the region, at least as measured in terms of popular devotion and public expenditure. The present mosque also enjoys a magnificent location as it is set off slightly from the surrounding buildings and overlooks the Nile at that juncture of the city where the original premodern village meets the straight streets of the first nine-teenth-century expansion. The second mosque represents a newer form of religious institution, and dates from the late 1960s. It was founded by a retired school teacher on an abandoned lot used as a dumping ground, as part of a voluntary benevolent society which was meant to provide certain social and charitable services. It is situated on the western side of the city on the west side of a large canal which had formerly been a sort of natural boundary, although since the 1950s the area has grown into a large popular quarter. Also, this mosque is strategically located adjacent to the major automobile and pedestrian bridge over the canal, and very close to the major bus terminal.

The people of Minya discriminate in practice between only two categories of mosques, defined in opposition to each other. In the local view, mosques are understood either to belong to the 'government', i.e., *masjid hukumi*, or to be 'popular', i.e., *masjid ahali*. Although this difference is framed historically in terms of their financial dependence, today the most significant distinction is given in organizational terms, as a stated contrast between two types of preachers. A government mosque is one that is headed by a professional *imam* who is an Azhar graduate with all that this implies. He is appointed and paid by the Ministry of Waqfs and is identified with its large local bureaucracy, where scores of administrators, inspectors, clerks, and engineers handle all details related to these mosques and their personnel. A popular mosque, on the other hand, functions as a component of a voluntary benevolent society whose primary purpose is to provide its members with mutual assistance or to dispense specific charitable services according to the terms of its charter. The president of such a society oversees its administrative affairs, and usually, as is the case here, where the society also includes a mosque, he serves as its imam and preaches the Friday sermon.

The voluntary benevolent society in the form described here is a modern phenomenon of a protean character. In 1900, records indicated that there were 65 such societies in Egypt, almost all of them located in Cairo and Alexandria. In 1949, there were 1,401 and by 1960, there were 3,195. By 1978, there were probably double this figure throughout Egypt, and perhaps a hundred in Minya alone. But by no means all of these societies are religiously motivated, for, in fact, most are chartered with straightforward social and philanthropic objectives, such as assisting in different aspects of education, health care, or recreation. The remarkable proliferation of these voluntary benevolent societies can be traced to many causes, but certainly one of the foremost is that such groupings have become, for all practical purposes, the only legitimate basis for any regular formal association in Egypt. Thus, as far as mosques are concerned, the founding of a voluntary benevolent society has evolved as the most available legal mechanism for Muslims to form an enduring congregation where they can be assured that their place of prayer will remain in their own hands and that their preacher will be a man of their own choosing. The policy of the Ministry of Waqfs has long been to expand its network not by original construction so much as by the incorporation of already existing facilities into its operations. It is only the exorbitant expense of providing for the maintenance and personnel of the nation's estimated 40,000 mosques that has forced the Ministry to limit the number it actually regulates to approximately 6,000. When the Ministry does take over mosques, however, as it continually attempts to do depending on budget allotments, it purposefully chooses those that are the best established and most heavily used. Hence, without a recognized legal independence to protect them against such eventual absorption, mosques which have been built by local initiatives can be easily brought into government control by the decision of local administrators of the Ministry of Waqfs.

Despite the array of differences and variants between these two institutions, the preachers in both cases can be described in terms of two sets of functions, a ritual role and a mundane, professional identity. But in neither case can the individual totally separate the two dimensions, for the voice from the *minbar* or 'pulpit' is also heard as that of a functionary, a countryman, a neighbor, who occupies a place in the wider social world. It is this double function that invests the preacher with credibility and gives a sermon its pragmatic context. The sermon is a symbolic representation of that which the preacher and ultimately the congregation seek to realize in the realm of moral action. He serves therefore as an image and an actor. He is at once the point of articulation for fixed and sacred ideals and the focus for conduct in a changing human world where interests are in conflict and intention does not suffice for results. The efficaciousness of a preacher's leadership hinges in large measure on his ability to bring consistency to this image and actor relationship. He must preserve this double focus, for should he abandon the tension, by radically isolating his two-fold functions or by attempting to eliminate one or the other, he would deprive the ritual of its dialectical character. The preacher as pure image would ultimately reduce his performance to empty formalism, whereas the preacher as pure actor would lead to sermons of purposeless fantasy. On the other hand, to collapse the two foci together would confound metaphor with reality and thus undermine the essential distinction between subjective and objective experience, opening the way to the distortions of magic and millenarianism.

Shaykh 'Ali

The Azhari preacher, whom we shall call Shaykh 'Ali, should be treated first because he represents that form of religious authority that is socially and culturally most explicit. Because his role is more institutionalized he embodies a wider range of idealized assumptions. It is largely by contrast with this conventional figure that our second example takes its meaning. Several major attributes of his position have already been indicated, such as the 'cathedral' character of the mosque, its association with the eponymous wali, Shaykh al-Fuli, and its full incorporation into the national system overseen by the Ministry of Waqfs. What must be added, however, is that this superimposition of bureaucracy upon *baraka* has not accomplished the easy integration of these two modes. Rather, it is the preacher who, as chief administrator of the complex and as its ritual specialist, is expected to bring these disparities into harmony.

Shaykh 'Ali is in his late forties and is a native son of the region of Minya. He resides at present in his ancestral village a few kilometers north of the city. This fact of indigenous origin is of extreme importance in Upper Egypt, not only for the general comfort of the person concerned, but as a basis for genuine acceptance by others, for Sa'idis (the slightly tainted term for Upper Egyptians) are proverbially suspicious of outsiders and notoriously stubborn in their dealings with rationalized officialdom and its agents (al-Hakim, 1947).[3] Also, it is exceedingly rare to find senior Azhari preachers here with local origins, for there have been very few of the past generation who completed the Azhar curriculum in Cairo and, of those who did, even fewer returned to employment in the mosques of the provinces. Consequently, numerous government mosques in the district are without regular preachers, for qualified men are not available. And the great majority of Azhari shaykhs who do occupy posts in Minya are very young recent graduates who come from the Delta, where religious education is far more developed and the status of a mosque preacher has traditionally been higher. Virtually all of these migrant preachers regard their appointments as a temporary displacement, an inconvenience to be endured until an opening becomes available near their native town, where some of them have left wives and families living. Others are postponing marriage until a more permanent assignment is offered. The most ambitious, of course, aspire to posts in Cairo itself.

Shaykh 'Ali's age is also of importance, because it marks him as a member of the generation whose early adulthood coincided with the high tide of the Revolutionary era and who now dominate the controlling offices in the public sector. Specifically with regard to his role as preacher, his age also indicates that he is a graduate from the 'old' Azhar, that is, the University Mosque, as it is now romantically conceived in its pristine form, previous to its thorough overhaul and relocation by Nasser. Since that watershed, it is the popular view that its great professors have been dismissed, its curriculum has been altogether diluted, and its standards have been considerably lowered. Now, it is said, this religious training only attracts candidates who are barred entrance to other colleges because of their poor academic performance. The sign of this debasement is that almost none of these new preachers know the Qur'an by heart, which is still considered the prerequisite of all religious learning. Interestingly, the Azhar has recently opened a branch of higher studies in Assiut, 130 kilometers south of Minya, where, according to popular opinion, the quality of education is even more retrograde. In sum, therefore, local perception accords Shaykh 'Ali the distinction of a rare antediluvian 'alim who is furthermore 'one of us,' with its underlying implications of familiarity and influence. It might also be noted that the position as head of al-Fuli went unoccupied for some time before this particular Shaykh was appointed.

All Azharis and *a fortiori* all modern reformers attest that the cult of a wali is heterodox, and most young Azharis in Minya urge its active suppression. Some have gone so far as to keep the doors to shrines locked or to have the cenotaph removed altogether. But Shaykh 'Ali pursues a compromise. He tolerates the popular devotional practices that daily enliven the shrine of Shaykh al-Fuli, but he delegates supervision of the tomb and associated activities to subordinates. He is greatly assisted in this double attitude by a convenient spatial separation of the symbols. For in this particular case the customary saint's tomb is not located inside the mosque proper but apart in a cupola shrine, with a veranda and colonnade connecting the two structures. The shrine has one door leading towards the mosque itself and a second door opening to the street outside, which means that entry and exit can be made without encroaching on the mosque. Thus the large numbers of peasants who constitute most of the wali's devoted following, and, of course, women, who normally never go into mosques, can be accommodated without involving the Shaykh personally. He carries out his functions in the mosque and maintains his small office (which has the only telephone of any mosque in the city) on the opposite side of the shrine complex.

Every Friday and on great feast days excitement around the shrine runs high and the traffic in and out of the tomb chamber reaches mob proportions. On these occasions, social distance and a modicum of order is maintained by the shrine's attendants who are strategically stationed at the doorways. Then, during the actual prayer and sermon, the shrine is closed and, with that, the crowds diminish. There can be no doubt that the central appeal of the mosque for these visiting villagers and the numerous similarly oriented city dwellers is the wali. The weekly ceremony that they share is not the formal prayer and sermon but the miniature *mawlid* festival that springs up around the building for a few hours each Friday, when musicians, dancers, Sufi perfume vendors, hawkers of sweets and other curiosities converge, mix, and soon after quickly disperse. Shaykh 'Ali avoids being seen in the midst of this exuberance, but takes no measures to discourage what he concedes to be the misguided pious enthusiasm of the uneducated. Also, after the Friday service, when most of the congregation have departed, he permits an old-fashioned Sufi dhikr to be held on the veranda between the shrine and the mosque, a concession allowed by no other Azhari preacher in the city.

It should also be noted that Shaykh 'Ali's monthly income is regularly supplemented by a share of the donations that are deposited in the almsbox set
beside the saint's tomb. This cash, along with money from the resale of gifts in
kind, principally jewelry and meat, is counted once a month by a delegation of
eight that includes the top administrative staff of the local Ministry of Waqfs
office. All of them receive a special bonus, graded to their rank, for these book-
keeping tasks. The rest of the proceeds are then divided, with three-fourths
going to the Ministry of Waqfs, and the remaining fourth allotted by a complicated formula to the employees of the al-Fuli mosque. The total monthly intake
varies between LE500 and LE700. The preacher's share is just over 4 percent,
which means that Shaykh 'Ali gets roughly LE25–30 a month in addition to what
is already his considerable monthly salary of LE72. (By comparison, the starting
salary of an Azhari preacher was set at LE30 a month, which is approximately
$9.) Needless to say, the idea of benefiting from practices which are condemned
as unorthodox is roundly criticized even by those Azhari officials who participate in the collection of these donations and accept their share.

In addition to being a cult center for *fellahin,* the al-Fuli mosque attracts
another distinct group which regularly attends the Friday prayer and identifies
with its second, related aspect. This group, smaller in number, is dominated by
the urban gentry, including property holders, merchants, middle to high functionaries and some youth who share similar traditional bourgeois values. They
are drawn to this mosque because of its self-evident status as the local embodi-
ment of historical continuity and a politico-religious synthesis. There are older
and larger mosques in the city, and mosques more richly adorned, but this one
enounces a 'classical' heritage, and its ritual is conducted with the appropriate
marks of amplitude, such as the services of a professional Qur'an chanter. The
ritual grandeur attempted here takes the great centers of Muslim civilization as
its model. It is the same highbrow style displayed in broadcasts of Friday prayer
or in familiar photographs from the Egyptian press. It is the local religious
showplace to which notables can bring their cosmopolitan cousins and colleagues who might be visiting the city. Also, the Ministry of Waqfs use this location for the events they sponsor on religious holidays, or for the occasional guest
speaker. General civic ceremonies, such as congratulatory assemblies for public
officials, are also held here. Finally, it is to this mosque that the governor of the
province comes from time to time, arriving, typically, at the last minute in a
flourish of limousines and jeeps, accompanied by his guards and entourage. And
this same select dignity was affirmed most conspicuously in December 1978,
when President Sadat made a rare visit to Minya, at the end of which he attended the Friday prayer at this mosque, on which occasion the service, including
the sermon, was transmitted live over the national radio.

Shaykh 'Ali's personal manner is formal and reserved, with a cordiality
expressed in the liberal courtesies of traditional hospitality. His social self and

his ritual role are closely bound together, as shown most clearly by the fact that he wears the distinctive Azhari uniform at all times. His sermons are delivered in the florid, classical *fusha* (ampleness) of the trained and well practiced religious orator. Although they are given without any notes, their content is highly structured and correctly punctuated with the prescribed verbal formulae that signal introduction, internal division, and conclusion. These stately homilies are gracefully interlaced with illustrative citations from the Qur'an and the *hadith* and they are of typical Azhari brevity, no longer than 15 or 20 minutes, whereas sermons in popular mosques can often continue for an hour or more. In addition to these tokens of Islamic refinement in the sermon, there are similarly indicative embellishments of the ritual prayer such as a sung response to the imam's rubrical exclamations—a feature known as *al-balagha*.

Thus, Shaykh 'Ali projects the image of a double identity that fuses elements from the traditions of the wali and the 'alim. He unites the two constituencies of his congregation—one by active and the other by passive gestures, into an assembly that is meant to reflect the unified community *(umma)* and the nation. He speaks in this dual capacity as protector of the patron saint and as spokesman for the orthodox religion by raising the level of discourse towards a lofty height of generalization and inclusion. He achieves this elevation by making maximal use of what Victor Turner (1967) calls the 'polysemy' or 'multivocality' of the focal symbols of each complex, which in the abstract greatly overlap. He plays down the judgmental or exclusionary tendencies of the reformist context by avoiding drawing attention to the confusions of modern history and the existential limits imposed by competing structures. He does not appropriate to himself the baraka of the wali, nor does he presume to exercise the jurisprudential prerogatives of an 'alim, but rather he allows his own personality to be absorbed into an image that dramatizes their memory. He incorporates a generalized conception of their historical authority. In other words, he forges a synthesis that emphasizes the force of the ritual role which greatly constrains his relevance as a social actor. What he imparts, as a result, is a vision of common action that is more closely identified with the liminal rather than the ethical dimensions of religion. Participation in the saint's blessing and fulfillment of the Shari'a legalism are presented as concentrated upon ritual action rather than upon specific worldly activity or moral behavior. For Shaykh 'Ali, image and actor meet in his position as a proper civil servant in a society where religion is officially institutionalized and the charge over its practice is entrusted to clerical professionals. The proper task of the mosque and the preacher is to provide for the public exercise of religion within these circumscribed structures. Hence his purpose is properly to complement and not to oppose secular authority located in other functionally specific institutions.

An example from the sermon rhetoric of Shaykh 'Ali that illustrates how he interprets his authority in terms of ritualized religious duty rather than concrete moral action can be seen in his manipulation of the term *amn* or 'security' in the sermon he preached in the presence of President Sadat already noted, which I was able to record from the radio. The preacher first proposes a metaphoric parallel that equates contemporary society with the community of believers of Medina where the Prophet first established his polity. Shaykh 'Ali then cites three promises of security made to those who believe, playing on the common semantic root for belief and security, that is, *amuna*, 'to believe'; *iman*, 'belief'; *amina*, 'to be safe, secure'; *amn*, 'security, peace'. The community is first promised dominion over the earth and all its resources for, he says: 'God made men to love work in agriculture that security of nutrition *(amn al-ghadhi)* might be realized and that every living creature might obtain all its needs.' These remarks are made against a background of political strife and controversy surrounding the heavy subsidies that keep the prices of food staples low, subsidies that Sadat has sought to withdraw. In January of the previous year, the announcement that the subsidies were being lifted brought widespread rioting and the government reversed its policy and reinstated them. But at the end of the same month in which this sermon was preached, the original plans were partially reasserted, by the elimination of support for cigarettes and gas while leaving food prices unchanged. The idiomatic expression rendered here literally as 'security of nutrition' is the Egyptian Arabic equivalent of the complex of ideas and feelings known as the 'green revolution,' which is one of the terms Sadat and his spokesmen use[d] when they [spoke] English. The phrase constitutes a slogan and it is ubiquitous in public political rhetoric.

The sermon continues:

> The second promise is the consolidation of religion. This is realized in the security of nutrition and the security of industry, for any nation (umma) independent in its materials will need no other besides itself as it takes steps to build and construct and promote the progress of work toward welfare in the afterlife as well as welfare in this world . . .

Here appears the explicit religious echo, then substantiated by Qur'anic citations, of Sadat's frequently repeated call for new industries and for more aggressive exploitation of untapped natural resources. The official line at this time was full of rosy anticipation of the imminent prosperity that was guaranteed to result from an eventual peace with Israel, friendship with America, and the recovery of the oil fields in the Sinai. In the next section of the sermon, the logic that condenses 'faith' and 'security' into one analogy is even more explicit:

> The third promise is the establishment of [the nation's] full security in the possession of its religious faith. It shall fear God alone, for how shall it fear a creature when it has with it the power of the almighty Creator who responds to dangers when he is called and who uncovers evil. For

God, exalted be he, entrusted to the Quraysh two blessings, the blessing
of nourishment in hunger and the blessing of security in fear . . .

In essence, the accomplishment of God's promises is assured by man's full
faith in them. This faith, in turn, is explicitly demonstrated in the ritual expressions that are most precisely religious as a collective task and destiny.

Shaykh Hassan

The second preacher under discussion is thoroughly a layman who, in theory,
conducts ritual functions only incidentally by virtue of his position as president
of a voluntary benevolent society which has a mosque as one of its facilities. He
is sometimes but not consistently addressed or referred to with the honorific title
of 'shaykh', so for our purposes we shall call him Shaykh Hassan. He is about
the same age as Shaykh 'Ali and also a native of the immediate vicinity. Shaykh
Hassan was long respected as a school teacher before he was recently promoted to the influential post of Director of Public Relations at the provincial office
of the Ministry of Education. His formal education was entirely secular,
although, like many of that period, he attended a traditional *kuttab* for a time as
a child after school hours. When he speaks of the religious education of his
youth, however, he claims to be an autodidact whose great source of enlighten-
ment was *The Life of Muhammad* by the great liberal intellectual and social
reformer, Muhammad Husayn Haykal. He went on to advanced studies at what
was then the British Teachers' College in Assiut, where he specialized in
English.

Unlike the vast majority of more recently trained language instructors in
Upper Egypt, Shaykh Hassan is quite fluent. This unusual competence, given
his relatively modest class background, has brought him to the attention of the
Provincial Governor's office. He is called upon as a translator on occasion, and
he sometimes hosts English-speaking dignitaries on tourist outings to local
attractions, Pharaonic or technological. Through his office, he is daily involved
with teachers and administrators in schools throughout the region and with officials in other bureaucracies, which provides him with a valuable network for
keeping abreast with affairs in a variety of realms. Not surprisingly, he is sometimes called upon by the police or involved parties to act as an intermediary in
the traditional forum for settling feuds called *majlis al-sulh*.

Shaykh Hassan took over the task as preacher of this mosque only very
recently, although he had long been an occasional preacher in some other popular mosques, notably the small room set aside for religious functions at the
local Teachers' Club. He was elected to the presidency of the benevolent society only in January 1978 upon the death of his father, who had founded the
society and had served as its preacher. Shaykh Hassan's father, who had been

a primary school teacher, was best known for his long involvement with the Muslim Brothers, for which he was imprisoned on several occasions. In 1965, when Nasser carried out the last of several purges directed at the Muslim Brothers, Shaykh Hassan was also arrested, although he was released after a short internment. The obvious link to his father and his own experience of persecution for Islam have provided the preacher with an evident prestige among the younger generation of fundamentalists who have idealized the martyrs of this earlier era and who strive to rekindle their struggle. At times in his sermons, Shaykh Hassan makes discretely oblique allusions to prisons, or oppressors of Truth, the meaning of which is transparent to his hearers.

The approximate coincidence of Shaykh Hassan's promotion in the Ministry of Education and his assumption of ritual and administrative duties at the benevolent society has greatly enlarged his exposure as a lay religious leader. While he had already been active as a speaker at assorted groupings in Minya, he was now being called on by more august forums. A crowning achievement was an invitation to appear on a nationally televised talk show called 'This is Islam,' which was broadcast in April 1979. Here, interestingly, the uneven relationship between the two offices, the secular and the religious, was revealed when the host introduced him most elaborately as a senior regional ministry functionary, and quite secondarily as the head of a benevolent society. In fact, still more telling, the host mistakenly introduced him as the head, that is, the Director, of Minya's office of the Ministry of Education.

The physical character of the setting for the ritual also gives important indications about the effect Shaykh Hassan is attempting to achieve. First, the mosque proper is rather small in scale and simple in its adornment. Its pulpit, for instance, is not the elaborate wooden minbar with stairs leading to an elevated platform, often adorned with five carving and decorous curtains. It is simply a low platform, like a small podium with a primitive railing, painted white. But even so, Shaykh Hassan avoids such a symbolic association, for it is his custom to preach while seated on the floor, which is covered with mats rather than carpets, facing his congregation and using a microphone. The crowd that assembles here on Friday for the prayer and sermon is too large to fit into the mosque, although their number could easily fit into the mosque of al-Fuli. Here the overflow is accommodated on mats set up outside beneath loudspeakers that carry the words of the preacher.

In a technical legal sense, Shaykh Hassan's mosque exists as a modest ancillary aspect of a benevolent society whose primary purpose is charity and mutual aid. This particular benevolent society is named *'ilm wa-iman* ('Science and Faith'), although it is virtually never called that except by the preacher himself in certain formal references. Rather, it is called after its preacher, 'the mosque of Shaykh Hassan' or sometimes, reflecting previous usage, that of his father. The proper name is a familiar slogan featured centrally in the 'October Paper' in which President Sadat, in 1974, outlined the goals of his regime, including his progressive, pluralist change of direction and his 'open door' to capitalist investment.

In theory, this mosque of the Science and Faith Society, like other of this 'popular' type, exists essentially for the use of the members of the society, although nonmembers who desire to join in their prayer would certainly not be excluded. This membership is legally defined in terms of a regular monetary contribution to a common fund which maintains its facilities and supports its various activities. The fact of the matter is, however, that very few of the several hundred who attend the Friday prayer at the mosque with any frequency are members in this strict sense, and in practice membership is an extremely loose category. There are certain specific services supposedly provided for the benefit of members, but these services are conceived as also available to the poor who may need them, or others who may have some less direct reason to be associated with the benevolent society, most probably stemming from family or local bonds rather than ideological commitments. One service offered by the benevolent society, and, in the eyes of many, its most significant one, is a food cooperative, the major feature of which is the sale of meat. The meat in question is that of the *gamousa*, the indigenous water buffalo, whose slaughter was at this time strictly regulated by the government. Meat prices are high and fixed officially, although there is a great deal of manipulation by butchers in order to obtain higher rates in the form of tips for better cuts or for holding some quantity back from the rush which often exhausts the limited stock. The benevolent society has some kind of arrangement, which frequently malfunctions, whereby 'members' can order meat in advance and then purchase it at a discount. Sometimes seasonal produce will also be available. Practically speaking, however, no supplies of anything are dependable at this co-op and quality fluctuates greatly so that, when there is an overabundance of perishable goods, the operators are only too happy to sell to whoever can pay. Consequently, householders tend to rely on regular merchants or the market and the co-op seems to spring to life only on Fridays, when occasionally shipments of fruit or vegetables are brought in to take advantage of the crowd gathered for the prayer. At such times the preacher announces the availability of these items or other special sales at the end of his sermon.

Other facilities associated with the Society include low-cost dormitories for students, a primary medical care clinic, and meeting rooms used for such things as supplementary school lessons near to examination time or as workshops for sewing or doing simple repairs.

Attendance at this mosque is in general more selective than the heterogeneous and frequently nonresident group at the mosque of al-Fuli. Those who attend are males from middle- and lower middle-class backgrounds who share a fairly high degree of formal education. The congregation also includes some students and a good number of young graduates, such as teachers, engineers, and clerks, who have not yet married. It can be assumed, for instance, that the members of the congregation will consider themselves by local standards relatively *au courant* with national opinion and world affairs. Consequently, Shaykh Hassan often makes elliptical allusions to items that have recently appeared in the press, to passing styles or public personalities, always carefully measuring his words to impart recognizable comments upon controversial questions with only indirect inferences. As an 'independent' preacher, he is expected to be provocative and critical, but he must avoid explicitness on matters of high religious (including sectarian) and political sensitivity, lest he compromise his impartial stance, which would not only risk alienating some of his listeners, but perhaps subject him to pressure from disapproving civil authorities.

Disparities in status and socioeconomic origin are strongly played down at this mosque and equality is displayed, as seen, for instance, in the customary simple dress of the congregation and the absence of preferential seating. Shaykh Hassan often expounds on this egalitarian theme and he reproaches other mosques for honoring notables or official dignitaries with special entrances and front-row places at prayer. This stress on brotherhood, however, masks an implicit recognition of the positive value of hierarchy (of which he too is a beneficiary), as is displayed in the ways in which the preacher manipulates the symbols of social rank. On one particularly striking occasion, Shaykh Hassan interrupted the main theme of his sermon to discourse on the need for modesty and economy on the part of the wealthy and high officials who are too often attached to pomp and habits of conspicuous consumption. Then, moving from the abstract to the concrete, he proceeded to compliment in glowing terms a certain district supervisor who was 'anonymously' present. Although he did not name the man, he identified him quite elaborately with references to his post, his residence, and numerous specific achievements of the man's career. He then went on to indicate in a sort of guessing game approximately where within the mosque, in what row and on what side, this 'anonymous' guest was sitting, all the time lauding the man for his lack of ostentation. In this way, Shaykh Hassan obeys the convention that forbids him to single out anyone by name, but calls at least as much attention to the subject as he could have accomplished by a formal introduction. He frequently indulges in such verbal maneuvers.

Shaykh Hassan bases his authority on his commitment to reform and action, which implies his freedom from those influences that have compromised the 'official' preachers and turned them into the mouthpieces of the state. Hence, it is a point of high significance, and therefore much trumpeted abroad, that he performs ritual services without remuneration. With his income from his government post, he is hardly in need of another salary, although he clearly receives a certain sum justified as 'expenses' from sources within the benevolent society. Furthermore, others who contribute time and services to activities of the benevolent society also conceptualize them as 'voluntary' although here too there is manifestly regular material benefit received for these services. Likewise, on an ideological level, all who are associated with the benevolent society, including the preacher, assert their independence from government support. But more accurately, it is a matter of degree, for both money and goods, originating directly or otherwise in several official agencies, including the Ministry of Waqfs, the Ministry of Education, and the Ministry of Social Affairs, are sought after and accepted by the benevolent society.

The mentality which depicts the government mosque and the popular one as an alternative pair has recently been complicated by the appearance of a third point in the compass, namely groups representing the new wave of fundamentalist Islam. As was noted earlier, Shaykh Hassan is considered outspoken in comparison to the Azhari preacher, for he dares to comment with stark relevance and critical judgment on local and national foibles. But in the late 1970s, as the conflict between Sadat and militant Islamic groups, some with open foreign support, began to escalate, the battle of words spread to the pulpit. In Minya, this provocative position was represented by zealots from among the student Islamic Society, who moved from merely preaching in their own assemblies to begin preaching in certain small mosques near the university where no Friday prayer had been customary. One effect, however, was to trigger a version of the competitive process that Michael Hudson (1980: 16) refers to as the 'outbidding' of 'claims to Islamic legitimacy' which pressed Shaykh Hassan either to sharpen his own repudiation of established religion or risk being condemned as part of it.

Amid such a climate of escalating dissent, however, this skillful strategist took a middle course, in which he attempted to respond to their aggressive drive towards extremism by selecting themes in his sermons with a double meaning. First, he would signal broad approval of their intentions and objectives by talking at length on the important role that 'youth'(the code term for members of *al-jama'a al-islamiya*) played in the earliest days of Islam. Long sections of many sermons consisted of accounts from the life of the Prophet, involving incidents in which he entrusted to youth the responsibility for leadership in combat, for mission work (*da'wa*) and for government. Among them are stories that pit the idealistic young converts against the callous and greedy Meccan aristocrats, or narratives of combined expeditions in which the young outshine the veterans. But then, in the running commentaries which this preacher always provides in the midst of the episodes he recounts, he turns these stories into mirrors of behavior at a different level. He avoids altogether the triumphant climaxes and concentrates, often with exaggerated self-consciousness, on what he isolates as the excellent personal manners of the Prophet, on the way that Muhammad not only exhibited in his own behavior the consummate perfection of courtesy, patience, generosity, and kindliness, but how it was precisely these qualities that

he rewarded in others, not their capacity to intimidate or to excel in violent confrontations. His emphasis is on reason, '*aql*, and proper moral conduct, '*adab*,
in tacit opposition to what is locally called '*asabiya*, roughly, 'fanaticism.'
Small groups of these student activists had begun to launch disruptive demonstrations, such as praying the evening prayer on a busy bridge so as to cause
massive traffic jams; or picketing the gates to the campus on the day the Camp
David Accords were signed, so as effectively to close the university; or a break-
in shortly after Khomeini returned to Tehran that attempted to seize and occupy
the City Hall in order to claim Minya also for Islamic governance. So Shaykh
Hassan matched them with sermons that dwelt on the moderation, tolerance, and
meekness of precisely those same early Islamic heroes who are most extolled
for their military achievements, such as Khalid ibn al-Walid and 'Amr ibn al-
'As, or 'Umar ibn al-Khuttab and Mu'awiyah, who also exemplified the perfection of good government, in tacit contrast to the current regime.

At the same time, this lay preacher constantly reiterates the scientific basis
for Islamic ritual practices. He encourages resort to the daily prayer, for
instance, as a method for relieving psychological tension, and he likes to quote
remarks from British doctors who he says have demonstrated this finding. His
sermon rhetoric often touches on the scientific breakthroughs of the day, as
reported in the popular media, such as test-tube babies, space travel, or sophisticated telecommunications, as ways of infusing his remarks with perspectives
of a modern changing world and its compatibility with belief. He demonstrates
a similar modernist outlook by the fact that he avoids all tokens of religious
dress, not even a head covering. He presents himself in nothing more formal
than the standard tunic and trousers combination that are universally worn by
men of his station. Although he has a mustache, he refuses to grow a beard,
which serves locally as the deliberate emblem of affiliation or sympathy for the
cause of Islamic fundamentalism.

Interestingly, this preacher also adapts the diglossia of Arabic in Egypt for
his own purpose in the sermon in an extraordinary way. He does not speak
entirely in the pure classical Arabic of the Azhari, nor does he use the rousing
colloquial speech of the popular actor, as do the militants in their more or less
demagogic addresses. Rather, he employs a masterful mixture, frequently
switching between the two levels, sometimes for quick qualification, extrapola-
tion, or exclamation, sometimes for longer disquisitions, all of which can give
the remarkable effect of two voices and dramatic movement. He manages to
mesh the ponderous authority and eloquence of the idealized idiom, like a talking book, with the familiarity, freshness, and humor of everyday banter. As has
been said, he typically structures his sermons around texts recounting episodes
from the life of the Prophet, but intermingled in them is all manner of academic or gossipy comment, which may seem full of digression, but in retrospect is
plainly part of a sort of jigsaw *Gestalt*. At times, he presents a single long pas-

sage from the *Sira*, at other times, he strings together an assortment of isolated incidents, for he preaches from notes, and the text of the book(s) is before him as he quotes it. All these narrations are designed to infer a contrast with contemporary situations.

In one sermon, for instance, Shaykh Hassan built upon texts that told of the consultations held by early Muslim leaders before deciding on a plan for any attack or campaign. They are depicted as calling in experts and charting all the contingencies, and as having the safety of the soldiers and the welfare of their families as their highest priority. This sermon followed shortly after the incident at the airport in Cyprus in February 1978, when a number of Egyptian commandos lost their lives in a tragic and thoroughly bungled rescue attempt. Hijackers who objected to Sadat's rapprochement with Israel had kidnapped *al-Ahram* editor Yusef al-Siba'i, who was eventually killed in the fracas after the Cypriot National Guard opened fire on the Egyptians. The hijackers surrendered unharmed. But even while the focus of the preacher's remarks was unmistakable, buttressed as it was with pellucid geographical allusions to early Muslim sea battles around islands in the eastern Mediterranean, the shaykh extended his innuendo to include carelessness and wastefulness, neglect and irresponsibility in planning and administration at lower levels, including locally, where he spoke of the 'demon of *rutin*,' meaning the inefficiency and immobility of 'routine' or bureaucratic inertia, wastefulness, and mediocrity.

Another theme with numerous variations draws on stories illustrating the accessibility and frugality of the early Caliphs and their eagerness to see justice served beyond any self-interest. Shaykh Hassan explains, without any need to be explicit, how they declined to spend funds on lavish public ceremonies, they wore no elaborate military uniforms, invested in no colossal monuments, and occupied no great palaces. Such remarks clearly rebound upon the national elite, but he likewise presses the examples into service as critical of more immediate extravagances, such as expensive weddings, costly advertising gimmicks, or the hypocrisy of giving lavishly decorated Qur'ans as ceremonious presentations while leaving their contents unstudied. Nor does he hesitate to condemn what is considered the permissiveness of mixed-sex parties, the unscrupulous hoarding or black-marketeering of shopkeepers, and the lack of public spirit and professional solicitude among professionals such as teachers or doctors. He also makes disapproving comments with regard to traditional religious practices, such as the celebration of the Prophet's Birthday, the belief in a wali's miracles, or the allowing of women in funeral processions. But the tone of these condemnations always maintains an undercurrent of respect and a willingness to pursue discussion. This open attitude is perhaps seen most fully in the Shaykh's practice of inviting anonymous questions in the form of 'letters' which he answers publicly at the end of some sermons.

The image Shaykh Hassan projects as a preacher can be seen as an idiosyncratic combination of a modern lay 'alim and a *mujahid* dedicated to moral reform. But it is a composite of social and religious authority which lacks a certain degree of stability and unity. Shaykh Hassan attempts to overcome this implicit inconsistency with regard to his ritual role by his many measures designed to minimize the emotional potency of the religious symbols involved, and to diffuse their marked sacred connotations into the discourse of a community meeting, an academic lecture, or admonitions regarding social priorities. The fact that Shaykh Hassan concentrates his preaching around biographies of the Prophet and other secondary materials and very seldom even quotes the Qur'anic text, except for some of its most stylized phrases, suggests an apt metaphor for the distance he maintains from the crucial core of the collective spiritual value system. This preference for human history over the sacred word is replicated in an emphasis upon moral and individual action over communal and specifically religious expressions of Islam.

But this insistence that 'aql and 'adab constitute the supreme categories for belief and action is also undermined by his need constantly to redefine them in terms of religious symbols whose meanings in relation to the larger community extend well beyond the boundaries of this balanced middle ground. This preacher's attempt to construct a convincing liberal interpretation requires him to compete with two increasingly polarized and highly publicized extremes, and the opposition between them has caused a decline in the collective appeal of a discriminating center. Shaykh Hassan's reluctance to exploit the liminal and emotional potency of ritual symbols has its benefit in an avoidance of their inflation through unharnessed enthusiasm. His casual and sober tone discourages rash actions and escapism. Yet this movement toward rationalization, and the emphasis on the subjective aspects of ritual, poses certain disadvantages as well.

The essential premise of this preacher's ritual role stems from the presumed mundane and practical character of the benevolent society. But as its religious dimension, evidenced by the mosque itself, has grown to dominate all other activities, to the point where it forms the exclusive attraction for most of its congregation, the symbolic context of the ritual role has also changed. The assumption that the weekly prayer and sermon constitute a ceremonial renewal and consolidation for those engaged in a concrete collective enterprise is no longer valid. Those drawn to this mosque can be more accurately described as largely otherwise uncommitted individuals for whom the qualities Shaykh Hassan displays as a preacher are virtually indistinguishable from the qualities he represents as a social actor apart from this position. As a result, the benevolent society, which has its stated function in the application of concrete religious principles within a bounded face-to-face social organization, has been largely transformed into an institution which has ritual as its major, and for most its only, shared experience.

This subtle transition into a community of ritual rather than a community of action represents a certain impoverishment of the religious symbols, however, for their underlying function is not to unify at the highest levels of cultural inclusion, but to articulate opposition. By resisting the centripetal force of the ritual itself, by asserting his identity as actor upon the image of the interstitial religious mediator, Shaykh Hassan reclaims in the pulpit the weight of his secular prestige, but only at the price of narrowing the breadth and depth of reference carried by the symbols he invokes. His ritual authority is no longer validated by collective achievements of structural change, hence his critical and practical posture with regard to the culture-affirming religion of the establishment is either a fiction or it is substantiated by an ideology of opposition to other centers of religio-political power. What is being generated, in short, is a nascent sect, the stirrings of a separate self-justifying institution that does not aspire to unify the diverse and stratified segments of a whole society, but to create a cohesive new self-understanding of a particular interest group that is recent and restless.

Notes

1   Taha Hussein's masterful memoir of his youth (1948) describes well the customary use of classical Arabic with minimum comprehension.

2   See Hill, 1979: 2–8, for a helpful discussion on the difficulties of distinctions between urban and rural in contemporary Egypt.

3   Al-Hakim's classic of modern Egyptian fiction recounts the experience of a magistrate who is assigned to a post in Upper Egypt. The problems of integrating into the society as a lawyer are reminiscent of the difficulties faced by these preachers on district assignment.

References

Baer, Gabriel. *Studies in the Social History of Modern Egypt*. Chicago: University of Chicago Press, 1969.

Berger, Morroe. *Islam in Egypt Today: Social and Political Aspects of Popular Religion.* Cambridge: At the University Press, 1970.

Calverley, Edwin Elliot. *Worship in Islam: Being a Translation with Commentary and Introduction of al-Ghazzali's Book of the Ihya' on the Worship.* London: Luzac and Company Ltd., 1925.

Crecelius, Daniel. "Nonideological Responses of the Egyptian Ulama to Modernization," in Nikki R. Keddie, (ed.), *Scholars, Saints, and Sufis.* Berkeley: University of California Press, 1972.

Encyclopedia of Islam, (1936), s.v. "Masdjid."

Geertz, Clifford. *Islam Observed: Religious Development in Morocco and Indonesia.* Chicago: University of Chicago Press, 1971.

Gilsenan, Michael D. "Some Factors in the Decline of Sufi Orders in Modern Egypt." *The Muslim World*. 57 (1967): 11–18.

al-Hakim, Tawfiq. *Maze of Justice*, trans. A. Eban. London: Harvill Press, 1947.

Heyworth-Dunne, J. *Religious and Political Trends in Modern Egypt*. Washington D.C.: Privately published, 1950.

Hill, Enid. *Mahkama! Studies in the Legal System*. London: Ithaca Press, 1979.

Hodgson, Marshall, G.S. *The Venture of Islam. Vol III. The Gunpowder Empires and Modern Times*. Chicago: University of Chicago Press, 1974.

Hudson, Michael C. "Islam and Political Development," John L. Esposito (ed.), in *Islam and Development: Religion and Sociopolitical Change*. Syracuse University Press, 1980. 1–24.

Hussein, Taha. *The Stream of Days: A Student at the Azhar*. trans. by H. Wayment. London: Longmans, Green and Co., 1948.

Ibrahim, Saad Eddin. "Anatomy of Egypt's Militant Islamic Groups: Methodological Note and Preliminary Findings," International Journal of Middle Eastern Studies, 12 (1980): 423–53.

de Jong, F. *Turuq and Turuq-linked Institutions in Nineteenth Century Egypt*. Leiden: E.J. Brill, 1978.

Kerr, Malcolm. "The Political Outlook in the Local Area," in Abraham S. Becker (ed.), *The Economics and Politics of the Middle East*. New York: American Elsevier Publishing Co., 1975.

Lane, Edward William. *Manners and Customs of the Modern Egyptians*. The Hague: East–West Publications, 1836, rep. 1978.

Mahmud, 'Ali 'Abdul-Halim. *Al-Masjid wa-Altharahu fi al-Majtama' al-Islami*. Cairo: Dar al-Ma'arif, 1976.

Marsot, Afaf Lutfi Al-Sayyid. "The Ulama of Cairo in the Eighteenth and Nineteenth Centuries," in Nikki R. Keddie (ed.), *Scholars, Saints, and Sufis*. Berkeley: University of California Press, 1972. 149-66.

Mitchell, Richard, P. *The Society of the Muslim Brothers*. London: Oxford University Press, 1969.

Rida, Rashid. *Tarikh al-Ustadh al-Imam al-Shaykh Muhammad 'Abdu*. Vol. 1. Cairo: Matba'a al-Manar, 1931.

Turner, Victor W. *The Forest of Symbols: Aspects of Ndembu Ritual*. Ithaca: Cornell University Press, 1967.

———. "Symbolic Studies," in B. Siegel et al. (eds.), *Annual Review of Anthropology*. Palo Alto: Annual Reviews, Inc., 1977.

30

Economic Change, Social Structure, and Religious Fanaticism

Galal Amin

Side by side with the economic changes that have occurred in Egypt over the last three decades, including the transformation of economic policy, economic structure, external economic relationships, and income distribution, Egypt has witnessed an important transformation of its social structure. This has been manifested mainly in the rapid growth and changing characteristics of the "middle class." Many of the economic and social problems associated with Egypt's development over the last thirty years can be traced to this transformation of social structure, which in turn is closely associated with the changes in economic policy. This chapter will investigate the possible relationship between the change in Egypt's social structure and the widely discussed problem of growing religious fanaticism.

The New Middle Class

In trying to justify his "socialist" measures of the 1960s, the late Egyptian President Gamal Abdel-Nasser was fond of describing Egyptian society on the eve of the 1952 revolution as "the half percent society," meaning that the proportion of the Egyptian population that controlled most of Egypt's resources as well as its political life did not exceed that tiny percentage. This may have been an exaggeration but probably a slight one. The statement also implied a very small middle class and its relatively weak position, economically and politically.

Some idea of the smallness and weakness of the Egyptian middle class in the early 1950s can be obtained from a 1955 estimate contained in a British government report of income distribution in Egypt. According to this estimate, 1 percent of the total Egyptian population had an annual income per family of more than LE1,500, compared with less than LE240 for 80 percent of the population. The remaining 19 percent of the population, constituting the "middle class," had, therefore, an annual income ranging between LE240 and 1,500 per family.[1] Out of the total population of Egypt in 1952, of 21.4 million, about

From *Egypt's Economic Predicament* (Leiden: E. J. Brill, 1995), pp. 131–40. Reprinted by permission. Galal Amin is professor of economics at the American University in Cairo.

200,000 persons could therefore be regarded as constituting the "higher class," 4 million as constituting the "middle class," and more than 17 million as belonging to the "lower class." This is not inconsistent with what we know about the distribution of agricultural landownership in Egypt in 1952, when about 2,000 families owned about one-fifth of all agricultural land and about 2 million families (or about half the Egyptian population) owned less than 2 *feddans* per family.[2]

Social stratification cannot obviously be based on the same criteria forty years after the 1952 revolution. Landownership can no longer be regarded as the decisive factor as it was then, since other sources of large incomes have become more important. Higher education is also no longer a main feature of members of the middle class, since several new sources of high income do not require high educational achievement. With the high degree of social mobility that has characterized the last forty years,[3] affiliation to certain families is no longer a necessary or sufficient condition for belonging to the "higher" social strata. "Westernization" or the ability to adopt western patterns of behavior, has lost much of its importance in distinguishing one social class from another as a result of the spread of these patterns of behavior among the lower classes, as well as the rise in social status of sections of the population that have relatively little contact with the West. While income and wealth continue to be important criteria for classifying the population into the three social classes, the *nature* and the *source* of income and wealth have lost much of their importance in this classification compared with forty years ago.

Making use of a variety of data contained in the 1986 population census, of various estimates of the proportion of the Egyptian population falling under the poverty line, and of indicators of income distribution revealed by recent Family Budget Surveys, one may tentatively suggest a level of income of LE300 per month per family in 1990 as the borderline between the "lower" and "middle" classes, and of LE10,000 as the border line between the "middle" and "higher" classes. According to this classification, about 53 percent (or 30 million people) of the 56 million constituting the Egyptian population in 1990 would belong to the "lower class," about 45 percent (or 25 million people) would constitute the "middle class" and the remaining 2–3 percent (1–2 million persons) would constitute the "higher class."

The two figures below are meant to illustrate the change that has occurred in the relative sizes of the three classes over the last forty years. In Figure 1a, the ratios between the three classes, based on the data for 1952 referred to above, are 1:20:85, while the ratios for 1990 illustrated in Figure 1b are 1:17:20. According to these two classifications, the middle class has grown in size more than six times in the last 40 years while the lower class has grown by only 75 percent, and the higher class five to ten times.

But no less important than the change in relative size has been the change in the characteristics of the three classes. The new higher class does not consist

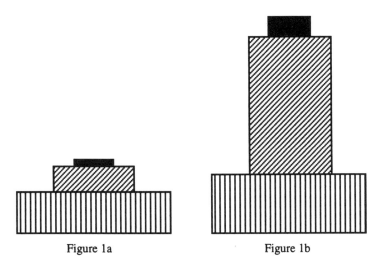

Figure 1a   Figure 1b

mainly of the descendants of the older higher classes, but rather of families of recently acquired wealth, whose fortunes have been accumulated mainly during the 1970s and 1980s, since such an accumulation of wealth would have been possible only rarely before the launching of open-door policies. The main sources of the new wealth were trade, particularly import trade, contractor activities, speculation in land, and commissions of all types. "Intermediary activities" of all kinds were thus the major source of newly acquired wealth and income, in contrast to the main source of income for the older higher class, namely, the ownership of agricultural land. The new middle class includes, like the older middle class, professionals, merchants, the higher and middle echelons of government officials, owners of middle-sized and small manufacturing firms, holders of middle-sized farms and owners of urban property. In addition, the new middle class includes some elements or descendants of the older "higher class" who have fallen in relative status as a result of the various measures taken by the revolution such as confiscation of property, nationalization, sequestration, etc. But most importantly, the new middle class now includes, in contrast to the old middle class, a good proportion of craftsmen and of the higher echelons of employees in private and public sector industry. The lower class now includes, as in the past, landless farmers, small landholders, low-income craftsmen, petty traders and most of agricultural and industrial labor, but it now also comprises a good proportion of the lower echelons of government and public sector employees.

Needless to say, the average income of all three classes is significantly higher than it was forty years ago. The lower class is living, on the whole, much bet-

ter than did the lower class of the pre-1952 years and their conditions of health
and nutrition have definitely improved, while the other two classes are also
enjoying much higher incomes than they did in the early 1950s. This does not
necessarily mean that the lower or middle classes are less frustrated or more satisfied with their lot than the lower or middle classes of the prerevolution days.
In fact, in view of the unprecedented rate of social mobility of the last forty
years, the opposite seems to be the case.

Social Mobility and Economic Frustration

A good proportion of Egypt's "new middle class," no doubt exceeding 50 percent
and maybe as high as 75 percent, consists of what may be classed "lower middle
class," where monthly income per family does not exceed LE600. This lower middle class includes the great majority of the low and middle ranks of employees in
the government and industrial enterprises, the majority of public sector workers
and retail traders as well as a good proportion of those working in private sector
manufacturing firms and small agricultural landholders. There are good reasons to
believe that a high proportion of those belonging to this lower middle class has
been suffering during the last two decades from a growing sense of frustration,
dissatisfaction with their lives, loss of self-respect and a grudge against the society at large. The symptoms are numerous, including the increasing rate of certain
types of crime, which include crimes against close relatives, the rise in the number of emigrants and of applications to emigrate, increasing corruption at various
levels of government, increasing break-ups of families and other symptoms captured more in literary production than in social research. Possible explanations for
this increasing frustration are also numerous but most of them are bound up with
the rising rate of social mobility. The sudden and big increase in opportunities for
increasing income and accumulating new wealth which were associated with the
launching of the open-door policies in the mid-1970s, the opening up of new
remunerative opportunities in the Gulf countries, as well as the sudden rise in the
rate of inflation, have whetted the appetite of a large section of the population but
caused great frustration among those who, for one reason or another, failed to benefit from the new opportunities. When the economy started to slacken in the early
1980s, with the resulting decline in work opportunities in the Gulf countries,
many of the rising aspirations built up in the 1970s were suddenly seen to be unre-
alistic and a strong feeling of frustration followed. The big increase in the rate of
unemployment during the second half of the 1980s, reaching, according to some
estimates, 20 percent of the labor force (an unusually high rate for Egypt) and considerably higher rates among university and intermediate college graduates, must
have intensified the feeling of disappointment among large sections of the population who attached great hopes to educational achievements for themselves or for
their children, as a channel for social advancement.

One may thus be very close to an understanding of the growth of religious fanaticism. A growing tendency towards the stricter observance of religious teachings carried by the rising sections of the population with a very modest social and educational background, can easily turn into religious fanaticism if met with severe disappointment of earlier hopes of social advancement. It is striking how rare it is to find examples of religious fanaticism among either the higher or the very lowest social strata of the Egyptian population. While members of the higher class are obviously exempt from the frustration brought about by a feeling of inferiority, members of the lowest social strata are saved from this frustration by their realization of the near impossibility of changing their relative social status. It is also interesting to note the differences between the expression of religiosity of these social groups and that of the lower middle class, where one finds not only many more examples of fanaticism, but also an obviously greater degree of hypocrisy, which could be the result of the same cause, namely, the frustration of unfulfilled ambitions.

Both recent research and studies of earlier parallel experiences tend to support this conclusion. In his pioneer study of militant religious movements in Egypt, Saad Eddin Ibrahim[4] found that of the thirty-four militants studied who had participated in the attack on the Military Academy in 1974 or belonged to the militant religious group named *al-Takfir wal-Higra*, twenty-one, or about two-thirds, were sons of government employees, mostly in middle grades of the civil service, four were sons of small merchants, three were sons of small farmers (owning between six and eleven acres) and two had working-class fathers. With regard to educational level, nineteen of the fathers had intermediate education and only seven had university degrees. According to Ibrahim, "it is safe to conclude that the class affiliation of these militant Islamic groups is middle and lower class. It is also clear from the results of this study that the educational and occupational attainments of most of the members of these groups were decidedly higher than those of their parents,"[5] which indicates an upwardly mobile social stratum who may easily consider their actual attainments considerably less than what they had originally hoped for or than what they deserved.

Tackling a much earlier period of Egyptian history, Albert Hourani has reached similar conclusions in connection with the growth of the Muslim Brothers' movement in the late 1930s, pointing out that it was "spreading in the urban population—among those in an intermediate position: craftsmen, small tradesmen, teachers, and professional men who stood outside the charmed circle of the dominant elite."[6]

The Rentier Class and Religious Fanaticism

Not only failure, but success could also be a source of religious fanaticism. Just as it could provide an escape from the frustration created by the failure to realize one's material ambitions, it could also provide a useful cover for an accumulation of wealth or income that are either illegal or immoral.

Following the rise in oil prices of 1973–74, Egypt witnessed a period of unprecedented increase in income. Between 1973 and 1984, the average annual rate of growth of Gross Domestic Product was 8.5 percent, which was surpassed by very few countries, and real per capita income almost doubled. But very little of this increase in income was due to the growth of commodity sectors other than oil. Agriculture was growing at a rate well below that of population growth and manufacturing grew at a much slower rate than services and crude petroleum. The major contributors to this rapid growth of income were oil revenues, labor remittances, the Suez Canal, tourism, and foreign aid.

The structure of employment showed a similar imbalance in favor of the service sectors. During the period of most rapid growth (1977 to 1984), employment in agriculture increased by no more than 9 percent, employment in manufacturing and mining by 38 percent, and in all commodity sectors by 20 percent compared with an increase in services by 45 percent.

Egyptian economists have for a long time been warning against the economic dangers of excessive dependence on such unreliable sources of income and employment that are subject to factors largely outside Egypt's control, less amenable to policy manipulation and more sensitive to political changes. But there are also good reasons to believe that there may be a strong relationship between the growth of incomes that have the nature of economic rent and the growth of religious fanaticism.

The growth of unproductive activities, and of some incomes that are largely dissociated from effort, seem to provide fertile ground for the growth of irrational habits of thought. Income and wealth that grew at unprecedented rates are more likely to be explained by "God's blessing" than regular and slow improvements that can be more easily traced to one's own productive effort. Productive activities allow much less leisure for the idle speculation of religious fanatics. Religious fanaticism could also be an alternative source of self-esteem which is no longer provided by the productivity or usefulness of one's work. But most important of all seems to be the use of religiosity as a cover for illegal, immoral, or undeserved income and wealth. Not only may religious pretense create the impression of deservedness of income and wealth but it could also be a very effective smokescreen to hide forbidden or socially unacceptable behavior. The larger the undeserved commission, or the bribe, or the monopoly price charged from the consumer, or the divergence from the safety requirements of building a block of flats, or from the legal requirements of obtaining an import license, or of benefiting from government subsidies, the greater the degree of pretense of being a good Muslim. Some writers have suggested that the fact that so many Egyptians have spent some years during the 1970s and 1980s in the Gulf countries where religious tenets are more strictly observed, may have contributed to the growth of religious fanaticism in Egypt. It seems much more likely that such copying of other people's patterns of behavior cannot become so widespread unless there is sufficiently fertile soil for its proliferation, and what is suggested here is that such a soil was provided by the unproductive, rentier nature of the Egyptian economy during the last two decades. The fact that the decade of the 1960s witnessed much less religious fanaticism but also fewer symptoms of a rentier economy may not be a sheer coincidence.[7]

The relationship between the growth of a "rentier economy" and the growth of religious fanaticism in Egypt may be best illustrated by the emergence and growth of the so-called "Islamic Investment Companies" during the 1980s. These companies managed to mobilize billions of dollars of the savings of Egyptians from their earnings in the oil countries, and competed very successfully with commercial banks in mobilizing labor remittances, by offering considerably higher interest rates (often double that offered by the banking system) through calling it profit rather than interest to comply with the popular interpretation of Islamic principles. Apart from appealing to religious sentiments and offering a higher financial return, this phenomenon could also be seen as a fascinating example of the impact of a high rate of social mobility on economic behavior, of which we have already met other examples. Certain features of these companies and of the way they operated seem curiously to fit with certain features of the savings invested in them and the nature of the activities and aspirations of those who realized those savings. Having made a big jump up the social ladder through migration to the oil-rich countries, or having achieved other windfall increases in income and wealth, and anxious not to lose the newly acquired social status, investors in those companies found the high returns on investment, even though of dubious origin, greatly welcome. When the sources of the newly acquired income and wealth are themselves highly suspect, the secrecy provided by the Islamic Investment Companies was particularly welcome, as was, one may add, the religious cover-up provided by them. When the increase in one's income or wealth is of dubious origin, one may be quite satisfied with an explanation of the profit realized and distributed by these companies, as being "God's blessing," as these companies actually maintained. Investment companies of this type, with their religious pretensions, may therefore be much more understandable in an era of rapid growth of incomes that have the nature of rent, than in more stable times when more incomes are realized from productive activities.

In a book originally published in 1927, the prominent sociologist P. Sorokin presented an interesting thesis which may throw important light on a number of changes in social behavior which emerged in Egypt over the last two decades, including growing religious fanaticism. According to Sorokin,[8] in situations where social structure is relatively stable, the lower classes tend to imitate those patterns of behavior which are associated with the higher classes, but the opposite seems to occur in periods of rapid social mobility when the declining classes are inclined to adopt many of the values and behavior patterns associated with the lower but rising social groups. There are good reasons to believe that this may be true. There is, first, the greater self-confidence acquired by the rising classes resulting from their economic success and allowing them a greater degree of self-assertion. Secondly, there is the sheer spread of their numbers, again resulting from their greater income, making their presence felt to an unprecedented extent in schools, universities, clubs, and other public places which have for long been the protected privileges of the higher classes. Thirdly, there is the increasing infiltration by these rising classes of mass media, resulting from their increased access to education and allowing them to spread their habits of thought and social values to the whole society. Exactly the opposite developments become the fate of the declining classes whose influence gradually recedes with the decline of their self-confidence vis-à-vis their new rivals and their gradual withdrawal from public life. Willingly or unwillingly, but often unconsciously, they come to accept and even adopt the new patterns of behavior and even the moral values of the lower but rising classes, and discard their own.[9]

If our present estimate of the magnitude of growth of the middle class in Egypt is at all close to the truth, the sheer rise of the new middle class, and particularly of the lower ranks of this class, would add strength to the possibility that such influences have been at work in Egypt during the last few decades.

It goes without saying that rapid social mobility, growing frustration among social groups with unfulfilled ambitions, or the growth of a rentier class whose increasing income and wealth are largely divorced from effort, could only be *some* of the factors that contributed to the growth of religious fanaticism. Other factors must be involved and could be important, including possible external influences with or without material support. But it also goes without saying that whatever the role of the external influences, they would be powerless if the domestic economic and social environment did not make such a large section of the population so receptive.

Notes

1   See Issawi, Charles, *Egypt in Revolution* (Oxford: Oxford University Press, 1963), p. 118 and p. 156.
2   See Barakat, A., *Ownership of Agricultural Land between Two Revolutions 1919–1952* (Arabic) (Cairo: Al-Ahram Center for Political and Strategic Studies, 1978), p. 61.
3   See Amin, G., "Migration, Inflation and Social Mobility," in Tripp, Charles and Owen, R., *Egypt under Mubarak* (London: Routledge, 1989).

4   Ibrahim, S. E., "Egypt's Islamic Militants," in Hopkins, N., and Ibrahim, S. E. (eds.), *Arab Society, Social Science Perspectives* (Cairo: The American University in Cairo Press, 1987). Originally published in *MERIP Reports*, no. 103, 1982.

5   Ibid, p. 503

6   Hourani, A., *A History of the Arab Peoples* (London: Faber and Faber, 1991), p. 349.

7   Egyptian social and cultural life has also witnessed the appearance of figures who played a prominent role in the mass media and had wide popular appeal, who were strongly reminiscent of Molière's "Tartuffe," a phenomenon with hardly any parallel in the 1960s. The combination of Tartuffe's false religiosity and materialistic greed seems to flourish more in certain social environments than in others and it is well-known that Molière's "Tartuffe" was a straightforward comment on an important social phenomenon at the time. There is also some evidence to suggest that the "Tartuffes" of late 17th century France were largely to be found among a new, recently enriched "rentier" class. (see, for instance, Lough, L., *An Introduction to 17th Century France* (London: Longman Green Co., 1954), pp. 41–42.)

8   Sorokin, P., *Social and Cultural Mobility (1927)* (Illinois: The Free Press of Glencoe, 1959), pp. 565–68.

9   Amin, op. cit., pp. 117–18.

Afterword

Nicholas S. Hopkins
Saad Eddin Ibrahim
June 2006

Ten years have gone by since we put together this third edition of our reader on *Arab Society* (1997). The Arab world continues to evolve, and so do scholarship and academic attitudes. Soon a new edition, designed with the revised AUC core curriculum in mind, will appear. In the meantime, we can reflect on the changes and trends in the Arab world that affect the selections on offer here.

Of course the main event that has had enormous impact on the Arab world is the attack on the Twin Towers and the Pentagon on September 11, 2001. We will return to the effect of that and related events at the end of this afterword. First we need to review some of the other trends in the Arab world.

Demographically the population of the Arab world continues to grow, overall at a rate of between 2 and 3% a year, and is now over 300 million. At this rate of growth, the population will double in about a generation of thirty years. The distribution of that population continues to shift as more and more Arabs seek a life outside their home country, whether in the rest of the Arab world, or completely outside the Arab world. For a complete study of Arab society, we would now want to include one or two pieces on life in the Arab diaspora and the ways in which that diaspora life interfaces with life at home. Most of the destinations are not new, but the numbers continue to grow—North African populations in Europe, groups of many origins in the United States and elsewhere in the new world. In addition there are continuing migrations to the oil countries, and also political unrest has led to many Arabs living in other Arab countries—for instance, Iraqis fleeing violence to Jordan and elsewhere.

All of the seventeen Arab countries for which we have the Human Development Index scores in both 1995 and 2003 improved their score. (The HDI is based on a combination of personal income, education, and health.) Of course, this is not fully remarkable, because all but fifteen of the 177 countries listed worldwide did likewise. Four Arab countries are in the category of High HD (Qatar, UAE, Bahrain, and Kuwait), while thirteen are in the medium HD category, and three in the low category. (Three Arab countries did not have figures for both dates, and Iraq and Somalia are not listed at all.) (UNDP 2005, pp. 223–26)

Levels of environmental concern have risen in the Arab world. Concern for urban air pollution continues to rise, and cities grow and become more crowded and the number of vehicles increases. In Egypt, a key marker was the so-called 'black cloud' episode of 1999, when air pollution combined with a thermal inversion to produce several days with a perceptible cloud of pollution, a form of smog, in Cairo (Hopkins, Mehanna, and el-Haggar 2001). There continue to be debates about the sources of the pollution (automobile exhaust, factories, burning urban and agricultural waste), but critically this outburst of concern indicated a sharper kind of environmental consciousness. Even though figures now show that the autumn air is not as bad as in 1999, newspapers still mark the anniversary with renewed alarm about air pollution (Government of Egypt 2005). A somewhat different sign of environmental consciousness in Egypt was the elimination of lead in gasoline in 1999, leading to improved air quality and better health (Government of Egypt 2005:21). Unlike the 'black cloud' episode, however, this decision was reached by a small number of people in response to scientific information from abroad. The contrast is instructive for social dynamics.

Fresh water is another issue in the Arab world, which is generally water-short apart from a few favored spots. The amount of renewable water available per capita is less than 20% of the world average (el Ashry [2006] says the Arab world has an average of about 1,200 cubic meters per person compared to a world average of 7,000). Of course, the quantity of available fresh water is affected by water pollution, causing a diminution of the quality. Since the amount of renewable fresh water is more or less constant, an increase in the population means that the amount per capita declines. In some countries in the Gulf, the shortfall is made up by desalinating sea water, and this solution is likely to be more common in the future. Still, desalination is energy-intensive and not suitable everywhere.

Other environmental problems that affect different parts of the Arab world include preservation of forests (e.g., the Lebanese cedars) and other fragile environments including marine environments, solid waste disposal, noise levels, and the penetration of agricultural and other chemicals into the soil, air, and water. Concern for the environment and for the impact of pollution on the individual has not, however, led to any widespread social movement in the Arab world. There is little effective popular pressure on government environmental policy, and such movements as arise are often incorporated into broader political processes rather than able to be self-sufficient (Kingston 2001).

Inspired by the UNDP's Human Development Reports (after 1990), there has recently been a series of three Arab Human Development Reports (2002–05, with a fourth expected) and a series of reports, at least for Egypt, on human development at the national level. These reports have been remarkable for their compilation of data for different countries and administrative subdivisions of countries, and for the accompanying analytical texts. They are also important as they encourage people to examine and reflect on their own society. The Arab Human Development Reports in particular have proven quite controversial, with their identification of the three deficits of freedom, knowledge, and women's empowerment. Although still constrained by the ethos of the UNDP system (for instance, avoidance of criticism of any individual country), these reports have opened up a discussion about these and related issues. They imply an image of a modern society in which freedom of speech, belief, and action would be underpinned by serious and widely shared knowledge and in which women and men could contribute equally. They also imply, of course, that this description does not yet fit the Arab world as a whole and in its parts. Rhetorically they take the position of offering advice to Arab governments on how to achieve the goals which they assume are held in common.

The 2005 Egypt Human Development Report in contrast offers a program for the Egyptian government that was worked out in collaboration with that government, and represents a compromise between members of the research team and government officials. It offers the notion of a new social contract in which the government would invest massively in the health and education of the more underprivileged segments of the population in the expectation that they would then evolve into good citizens, producing value and paying tax.

In some areas of the Arab world the past ten years have not witnessed much change. In areas such as freedom of speech or women's rights, there have been steps forward and backward in the different Arab countries. Human rights have, if anything, regressed partly due to the influence of foreign occupation (the United States in Iraq, Israel in Palestine).

The Arab World still is essentially a producer of raw materials (petroleum and gas) for the more advanced industries outside the Arab world. The Arab world also produces labor, skilled and unskilled, for the rest of the world, as is demonstrated by the importance of the diaspora communities and the amount of remittances, both from the oil countries and from the West. Tourism is another growth area for the Arab world, especially along the coasts and in the deserts. However, parts of the Arab world are difficult for tourists to access.

Most of the development in the Arab world over the last ten years has taken place in the urban areas. Although industrial jobs have stagnated, there are still greater opportunities in the cities, whether for education, health care, or casual employment.

The rural areas have been relatively neglected and have not prospered. Areas in Sudan and Iraq have been disrupted by war. Agriculture has been disrupted by global markets. The growth of rural poverty and confining social structures has encouraged rural people to shift to the cities, where they swell the urban populations. Apart from areas of benign neglect, the most definite step was taken in Egypt, where 1997 saw the implementation of a law passed in 1992 that restructured the relationship between landowners and tenants. By removing the guarantee of perpetual right to rent, and producing much higher costs for agriculture, the law may be pushing many people out of agriculture. For the moment, however, we have only anecdotal evidence focusing on the 'winners' and 'losers' in this process (Saad 2003), and we do not know whether the law has led to the constitution of larger farming units through property concentration.

Pressure from the grass roots to create social development institutions and to adapt government policies has also led to change. The urge to create non-governmental organizations or NGOs is irrepressible and continues apace, where laws and regulations leave any possibility at all. It is important to examine this area because it reflects the ability of individuals to formulate their ideas and to act upon them, as we need to keep in mind that not all initiative lies in the hands of those acting in the name of the state. Initiatives of this kind are hampered by the tendency of Arab states to 'depoliticize' their populations, so that they do not organize or protest.

Already Farsoun in the article reprinted here noted that the class structure of the Arab world is very fragmented, without the clarity of the simple two- or three-part structure of the original theories. Thus insofar as social behavior is an expression of interests tied to class structure, it is also very hard to find that connection. His observation that the class structure of the Mashriq is tied to the petroleum industry and its various offshoots (construction, consumption, etc.) still seems pertinent, as is the implication that the class structure has to be seen on a regional rather than a national scale. Writing of Iraq under Saddam Hussein, the Iraqi political sociologist Isam al-Khafaji (1997:27) also noted that the population was "atomized" and thus found collective action along class lines difficult.

But if class is not an organizing principle in much of the Arab world, what is? al-Khafaji implies in the case of Iraq that the substitute for class is ethnicity. Certainly it could be argued in general that efforts by the political center to demobilize people by discouraging classes and parties leave only the third of Weber's triad, status groups (in this case ethnic groups, tribes, and the like, into which one is born) as a building block of society. This is also not a new trend in the last decade, but it is worth highlighting here. And there is yet another possibility: that society is not composed of broad groupings but of dyadic relations between a higher-level patron and a lowly client. And finally we discuss below yet another notion: that the structure of Arab society can be seen in terms of three broad styles of political action (autocrat, democrat, theocrat).

The position and dilemma of youth are not new phenomena in the Arab world, but awareness of this problem has grown in the past decade. The struggle of the younger generation to find ways to insert themselves into the social structure in acceptable ways continues, and continues to run up against the efforts of their elders to exercise some form of social control over the youth. The younger generation often feels frustrated because the youth are unable to find a place for themselves, either in the world of employment or through marriage and reproduction. Education often does not lead to the jobs it implicitly promises, and so many remain unemployed for long periods, or must accept very different jobs than the ones they were trained for. The restlessness of the youth often leads to a desire to migrate, to graze a different pasture. Even marriage, and with it legitimate sexual activity, is not an easy goal because the cost is often so high (Singerman and Ibrahim 2003).

Certainly another change in the last decade is the increasing density of communications. This is the result of new media, such as cell phones, satellite TV, the internet, and news sources both electronic and print from outside the country. Even old technologies, such as land-line telephones, have been improved. All these open up new horizons and allow for different kinds of interpersonal relations. Cell phones, for instance, allow farmers and other small-scale producers to follow the market in their products, so that they are freed from reliance on their middlemen who formerly were their main source of information. At the same time as the technology advances, Arab governments are likely to want to restrict its use in the name of social control, for instance, by surveillance of the internet. Thus there are both expanded communication and sophisticated ways of limiting that communication. We return to this point in a political context, below.

In the last decade, an enormous amount of attention has been focused on the social role of organized religion, religious beliefs, and religious movements. Shifts in religious practice continue apace, and are reflected in other aspects of behavior, such as dress and patterns of sociability. The change towards a text-based understanding of religion is more than a decade old but it certainly reflects the spread of literacy. The holy books are read and debated by an ever-larger number of people, who are inclined to find in them lessons for life. Meanwhile other forms of religious expression (mysticism, for instance) are stigmatized, go underground, and are less visible. The sociological principle remains, however, that forms of religious practice and belief will also reflect other social patterns.

In the next section we consider the recent political evolution of the Arab World. Political turbulence in some key parts of the Arab World made and make it hard to select reading that will remain relevant for any period of time. Two such key areas are Palestine and Iraq. For such areas we need an analysis that reaches beyond the headlines to identify the basic building blocks of the society, and for different reasons such an analysis is not readily available. The presence of major non-Arab actors also complicates the issue. However, an understanding of these complicated and uncertain cases is critical to an understanding of social processes in the Arab world as a whole. It is a challenge for future scholars.

Political Evolution in the Arab World

Ten years ago, we noted among other persistent features of the Arab world the prevalence of autocracy as a mode of governance. This was confirmed five years later by a much celebrated first UNDP Arab Human Development Report (2002), which identified a "Democracy Deficit." Much of the Arab political landscape has been dominated by three competing forces: entrenched autocrats, challenging theocrats, and timid democrats. The struggle among them, especially the first two, has been lethal, and has boiled over to foreign lands, precipitating military intervention by big outs le powers in Arab affairs. Thus the foreign factor has come back more prominently than ever since Arab countries gained their independence after World War Two. This section is a synopsis of the interplay among the three indigenous forces, and between them and the outside world.

Repeated secular democratic challenges to Arab autocrats largely failed, or at best did not lead to more than cosmetic regime changes. Even military coups d'état for which the region had been so famous in the 1950s and 1960s became rare in the last three decades (1975-2005), and the new rulers were no less autocratic. Nevertheless, there has been a serious challenge to the Arab autocrats by Arab Islamic theocrats. The latter have engaged the former in violent and bloody confrontations. The confluence of many of these would ultimately be the runner-up to the horrific events of September 11, 2001 in the United States. The chain of events here is a classic case of what social scientists have long called the 'unintended consequences of human action.' Curiously in this case the chain of events started in the Arab world, went through non-Arab Afghanistan, the United

States, and came back to haunt the Arab world most ominously in Iraq. In fact much of the regional and global events in the last decade were shaped or tainted by the ascendance of Islamic militancy.

Starting with Egypt in 1974, scores of young Muslim militants attempted to seize power and failed. Others have continued to challenge the regime, culminating in the assassination of President Sadat in 1981, which was followed by assaults on the sensitive tourism industry in the succeeding two decades, such as the Luxor massacre of seventy people in 1997, and dramatic bombings of resort hotels in Sinai (of Taba in 2004, Sharm al-Sheikh in 2005, and Dahab in 2006). Similar confrontations occurred in Saudi Arabia, including a dramatic seizure for several days of the Grand Mosque of Mecca, around the holiest of Muslim shrines, the Ka'aba, in 1979. Sporadic bombings of state or foreign institutions in Saudi Arabia have become more frequent since the Gulf War to liberate Kuwait of a short-lived Iraqi occupation (1990–91). This war entailed the help of non-Muslim American and other foreign troops, which were stationed on Saudi soil. This was considered sacrilege by hard-line Muslim Saudi dissidents. Similar short-lived skirmishes took place in Tunisia involving the Nahdha Islamic Party (NIP) and the avowedly secular government during the late 1970s and 1980s.

A politicized 'Islam' would become a battle-cry for many young disaffected Arabs vis-à-vis autocratic regimes at home or their supporters abroad. These confrontations have varied in their immediate triggering motive, scale, intensity, and duration. Many of these Islamically-coded confrontations were not organically or organizationally linked, but the demonstration effect has definitely been at work, as evidenced by similarities of methods and tactics. Many of the confrontations were short-lived or brutally crushed by the respective autocratic regime—for example, an uprising of Syria's Muslim Brothers in the city of Hama in 1982.

One of the most serious confrontations took place in Algeria in the closing decade of the twentieth century and the opening years of the twenty-first. Following widespread food riots in 1988, the Algerian autocratic regime of Ben Jedid decided to open up the political system. In many ways the unfolding of events represented the unraveling of what social scientists have come to call a 'failed state' in various parts of the Third World. Algeria had been one of the earliest Arab countries to be colonized by a Western European country, France, in 1830. Though the colonial experience was devastating on a human level and socioculturally, Algerians would resist and ultimately rise up and wage a protracted war for independence (1954–62), under the leadership of the Front de Libération Nationale (FLN). After the hard-fought independence was won, the FLN ruled as a one-party populist regime. This was not unusual in those days. Egypt, Syria, and Iraq in the Arab world already had that from of governance. So did such other Third World countries as Indonesia, Yugoslavia, Cuba, and Ghana. It was also typical of the time that such populist one-party systems raised the expectations of their people without the means or capacity to deliver. A 'failed state' has come to mean a country whose government could not control or manage its galloping population growth, over-urbanization, rising unemployment, or inflation, nor provide basic services, curb corruption, or maintain law and order.

Under various names, Islamic activists have taken advantage of the conditions created by the failed state to enhance their own standing with their respective publics. To the poor and needy, they provided basic aid (food, money, and services). To young unemployed graduates, they provided part- or full-time jobs with modest but adequate survival salaries. They matched service provision to the poor with employment provision to fresh college graduates. To the restless and impatient, Islamic activism provided ample opportunities to confront and challenge real or imagined foes at home and abroad.

The bent for pan-Islamism created a 'virtual one world,' in which conventional nation-state borders have become meaningless. Hence young Islamists from many countries converged on Afghanistan in the 1980s and 1990s, ostensibly as 'mujahideen' (holy warriors) to resist Soviet occupation and its Afghan collaborators. Ironically, these expatriate mujahideen were initially encouraged, trained, and supported by either their own governments (possibly to get rid of them) or by the United States (as part of its Cold War rivalry with the Soviets). When they ultimately helped expel the Soviets from Afghanistan, some mujahideen returned home to resume a struggle (jihad) against their own failing and discredited governments—for example in Algeria, Tunisia, Egypt, Yemen, or Jordan. Called the "returnees from Afghanistan" *(al-'a'idun min Afghanistan)*, they have at times engaged government forces in lethal protracted struggle—as happened in Algeria after their electoral success was aborted by a military coup d'état, and in Yemen against President Ali Abdullah Saleh or foreign targets in the country.

However, there were many other Arab mujahideen who stayed on in Afghanistan. Led by a Saudi Islamic dissident, Osama bin Laden, and an Egyptian deputy, Ayman al-Zawahiri, they forged a new organization of their own known as al-Qa'ida ('the base'). In the early 1990s they allied themselves with a like-minded native Afghan Salafi (fundamentalist) group called the Taliban ('students' of religious schools, or madrasas) led by Mullah Omar. By the mid-1990s, the two organizations had fought off other tribally-based warlords and prevailed in much of the country. Afghanistan would soon become again literally and virtually the base, al-Qa'ida, for other Islamic dissidents from all corners of the world. In 1998, a new quest was framed by the three leaders, for an eternal jihad until victory or martyrdom against what were variously called the heathens or "Crusaders.and Zionists."

It was from the ranks of al-Qa'ida that scores of Islamist suicide-bombers wreaked havoc in several sensitive spots around the world. The most shockingly devastating among these was a carefully planned bombing of the twin towers of the World Trade Center in the heart of New York City on September 11, 2001. Four hijacked passenger planes with their human loads were used as rockets to hit strategic targets. Two of them struck the towers within minutes of one another, killing some three thousand people and injuring many more. Two other hijacked planes were supposedly to do the same at the White House and the U.S. Department of Defense (the Pentagon), but one crashed en route over Pennsylvania, and the other succeeded in damaging only part of its target, the Pentagon. The perpetrators involved in those horrific attacks died with many of their secrets. But days later, U.S. investigators revealed that there were at least nineteen of them, most of them Saudis or Egyptians. Many of them had been living in Germany and had trained to fly in the United States, including the leader of the attack, an Egyptian engineering student, Mohamed Atta.

Much has been written on those events that have become simply coded as 9/11, with the often and possibly overstated judgment that America, if not the world, has irreversibly changed as a result of the trauma. For sure, the world shared the feeling of shock, and many sympathized with America. However, in the Arab and Muslim world immediate reactions and feelings were mixed, as some publicly rejoiced (for instance, in Palestinian refugee camps) or were secretly delighted. There were initial denials of responsibility for 9/11; later many Arabs and Muslims challenged America about the perpetrators' nationalities, asking for decisive proof of its allegations. Some entertained counterclaims that it may have been an intelligence stunt (for example, by the American CIA or the Israeli Mossad) to implicate Arabs and Muslims with a conspiratorial intent, providing pretexts to attack one or more of their countries. Some Arab–Muslim commentaries invoked a litany of historical grievances against the United States as if to justify 9/11. As to why the United States would inflict such horror upon itself, some commentaries anticipated American designs to invade Middle Eastern countries with rich oil reserves or to control potential transport routes to high-demand markets to the west (Europe and North America), the east (China and Japan), and the south (India). Again, these commentaries were not unusual in a conspiracy-prone Arab political culture, with the dearth of political participation and public transparency.

For many Arabs, the subsequent invasion of Afghanistan (October–November 2001) and Iraq (March–April 2003) confirmed the conspiracy theory. This was further reinforced by the fact that the primary stated reasons for the two invasions were to destroy the Taliban–al-Qa'ida regime in Afghanistan, and to search out, seize, and destroy Saddam Hussein's weapons of mass destruction (WMD) in Iraq. The argument was that dictators were not to be trusted with the responsible use of WMDs, as such rulers are not accountable or checked by democratically elected parliaments; moreover Saddam had violated UN resolutions, including one stipulating periodic inspection by authorized international teams. Two years after the total occupation of Iraq and the capture of Saddam Hussein, who had managed to escape upon the fall of Baghdad (April 9, 2003), no WMDs were found. The same applies to some extent to the pretext of invading Afghanistan—that is, to get rid of the Taliban and to arrest and try Bin Laden, al-Zawahiri, and Mullah Omar for their alleged roles in 9/11 and other 'crimes.' Again, five years after the fall of the Taliban, and the capital Kabul, the three wanted leaders are still at large.

Conspiracies and false pretexts aside, two outstanding facts remain in accounting for intra-Arab political dynamics as well as for relations between Arab actors and the outside world. First, the Arab state system has for the last five decades been dominated by populist–despotic regimes. In the beginning of that half century, say in the 1950s and 1960s, the emphasis was on quasi-socialist 'populism'—for example, enacting socioeconomic policies such as land reform, universal free education, nationalization of foreign companies, urban rent control, and varieties of industrialization schemes. However, in the following three decades, say 1975–2005, as populism ran out of steam, the emphasis shifted to 'despotism'—for example, massive violation of human rights, personality cults, expansion of internal security services, and hot pursuit of dissidents, incarcerating or killing them at home and abroad. Second, as these autocrats protracted their rule with eroding or no legitimacy, they used emergency law to curtail basic freedoms, including those of assembly, free speech, peaceful marches, or demonstrations, and repressed civil society formations. They have thus unwittingly left the 'mosque' as the only accessible public space where people could gather. Consequently, the mosque expanded its function beyond simple worship and rituals to other sociopolitical activities—from providing services to recruiting and mobilizing dissidents. The slogan that "Islam is the solution" increasingly became a battle-cry for the would-be 'theocrats' to confront and dislodge the entrenched Arab autocrats and their 'foreign backers.' So in a curious way, the enduring Arab autocrats have generated their mirror image, the 'militant theocrats.' It was the latter that hijacked 'Islam' and the 9/11 suicide planes.

The contemporary concept of 'Islam' is a symbol that has been appropriated by many diverse groups for many diverse purposes. Afghan Mujahideen, Lebanese Hizbullah, Palestinian Hamas, and Iraqi insurgents have used it to resist foreign occupation of Muslim lands (Dar al-Islam). But equally, 'Islam' has been used to resist the local autocrats, as we have seen in Egypt, Syria, Algeria, and Yemen. With the inconclusiveness of the confrontations at home, militant theocrats have taken their fights to foreign lands. The American 9/11 was followed by similar bombings a year later in the Indonesian resort of Bali, two years later in a Madrid train station, and three years later in a London subway. The victims in all of these—aptly characterized as terrorist attacks—were civilians. Because the few perpetrators have claimed to be acting in the name of 'Islam,' they implicate all 1.4 billion Muslims in the world today. In search of sensationalism and quick answers, Western media have compounded the confusion by equating Islam and terrorism.

Despite the enduring autocrats of the past fifty years, and the challenging theocrats of the last thirty years, nascent democrats have sprouted in several Arab countries. To start with, thousands of NGOs have been established to provide basic services, to carry out community development, and increasingly to defend human rights. While still under the watchful eye of the autocrats, these NGOs, alternatively subsumed under the concept of 'civil society,' have managed to steadily expand the margins of freedom. Morocco, Jordan, Kuwait, and Bahrain, although all at the periphery of the Arab world, have made significant democratic advances in the last decade. Countries of the Arab center—Egypt, Syria, Saudi Arabia, Tunisia, and Libya—have remained quite autocratic despite gallant efforts by their democrats, often disguised behind civil society organizations (CSOs). Iraq, Sudan, Somalia, Lebanon, and Palestine have remained too mired in civil strife and/or resisting foreign occupation to seriously address the question of governance during much of the last decade (1995–2005).

While resented by many Arabs, the American invasion of Iraq and the accompanying 'democracy promotion' campaign seem to have steadily altered the collective psychic balance among the three indigenous contending forces. The autocrats, though still entrenched and controlling nearly all the state resources, are on the defensive. The democrats, though still vulnerable, are emboldened and more acclaimed abroad than at home. The theocrats are divided—some are still fiercely fighting the autocrats and foreign occupation, and others have opted for playing the democratic electoral game. Thus when an electoral opportunity presented itself former theocrats metamorphosed as would-be 'Muslim democrats.' This was the case with Morocco's Islamists (who appeared as the Parti de la Justice et du Développement [PJD]), Lebanon's Hizbullah, Egypt's Muslim Brothers, and their Palestinian offshoot Hamas. To the surprise of many, all four have done better than expected in recent electoral contests. In fact, 2005 was an unprecedented year in the frequency of Arab elections—three in Palestine, three in Iraq, three in Egypt, one in Lebanon, and the first ever in Saudi Arabia, albeit a municipal one. Despite procedural flaws and allegations of rigging, the voter turn-out was remarkably high (over 65%) in all countries except Egypt, where 75% stayed home, partly in protest. Only time will tell whether this is a fluke or the beginning of a new participatory trend in Arab politics. After all, the Arab region's reluctant democratization has been much discussed in academic and foreign policy circles in recent years. The 2002 UNDP Arab Human Development Report has refueled the debate. Some of the new features of Arab democratic discourse include diminishing fear, growing forms of civil disobedience, public discussions on mushrooming Arab satellite TV channels, the use of the internet, and the spread of blogging. More and more Arabs, especially the youth, have found these new communication outlets empowering and beyond the easy control of autocratic regimes.

Other than their individual and collective empowering effects, the new electronic communication opportunities have significantly contributed simultaneously to a renewed wave of assertion of local identities, pan-Arabism, and disposition to be part of the globalization process. This intricate mix is reflected in the Arab data of the 2002 World Value Survey (WVS) administered by University of Michigan. Clear majorities (over 85%) of the population were in favor of democratic and egalitarian values and practices. The respondents think that religion is still important in their lives and should have a role in public life, but stop short of agreeing to be ruled by clerics *('ulama')* (Inglehart and Norris 2003; see also Moaddel 2006). An interesting survey of a limited number of young Arabs carried out for the 2002 Arab Human Development report found that a majority expressed a strong desire to migrate outside the Arab world in search of work and a future life (UNDP 2002). Meanwhile, cultural and political expressions of ethnic and local identities have emerged, as evidenced recently in Somalia, Sudan, Mauritania, Algeria, Lebanon, Iraq, Bahrain, and Yemen. Quests for autonomy, equitable shares in power and wealth, federalism, and confederalism are becoming part of the Arab public discourse in the early twenty-first century. Related to these is another salient phenomenon of Arabs in the diaspora, especially in Western Europe and North America, whose number is estimated to be around 20 million. Representing at least two generations, benefiting from life opportunities in open and more advanced societies, they have nevertheless felt the negative fallouts of 9/11—guilt by association, stereotyping, varieties of subtle and explicit discrimination. Not only do Arabs and Muslims in the diaspora react or overreact to such developments in the new countries of residence, they also try to mobilize governmental and popular support in their countries of origin to come to their aid. A dramatic example of this was the affair of the Danish cartoons satirizing the Prophet Muhammad, which triggered widespread riots in several Arab and Muslim countries in early 2006. Beyond the immediate feeling of insult for portraying the Prophet as a turbaned terrorist with a machine-gun, the episode is a reflection of a new and growing socioeconomic and cultural interdependence that is yet to find viable management modalities. Again, determining where and how these tendencies are likely to unfold or play out is among the many challenges facing the Arab world in the twenty-first century.

References

El Ashry, Mohamed. "Faltering Ecology in the Arab Region," in *Al-Ahram Weekly*, supplement *Beyond Quarterly*, spring 2006, p. 3.

Government of Egypt. *Egypt State of the Environment Report, 2004*. Cairo: Ministry of State for Environmental Affairs 2005.

Hopkins, Nicholas S., Sohair R. Mehanna, and Salah el-Haggar. *People and Pollution: Cultural Constructions and Social Action in Egypt*. Cairo: The American University in Cairo Press, 2001.

Inglehart, Ronald and Pippa Norris. "The True Clash of Civilizations," in *Foreign Policy* 135 (March–April 2003).

al-Khafaji, Isam. "Repression, Conformity and Legitimacy: Prospects for an Iraqi Social Contract" in John Calabrese, ed., *The Future of Iraq*. Washington: Middle East Institute, 1997, pp. 17–30.

Kingston, Paul. "Patrons, Clients and Civil Society: A Case Study of Environmental Politics in Postwar Lebanon," in *Arab Studies Quarterly* 23(1):55–72 (2001).

Moaddel, Mansour. "The Saudi Public Speaks: Religion, Gender, and Politics," in *IJMES* 38(1):79–108 (2006).

Saad, Reem, "A Moral Order Reversed? Agricultural Land Changes Hands, Again," in Eberhard Kienle, ed., *Politics from Above, Politics from Below: The Middle East in the Age of Economic Reform*. London: Saqi, 2003. pp. 229–41.

Singerman, Diane and Barbara Ibrahim, "The Costs of Marriage in Egypt: A Hidden Dimension in the New Arab Demography," in Nicholas S. Hopkins, ed., *The New Arab Family*, Cairo Papers in Social Science 24(1/2):80–116 (2003).

United Nations Development Programme, *Human Development Report 2005: International Cooperation at a Crossroads*. New York: UNDP, 2005.

United Nations Development Programme. *Arab Human Development Report 2004: Towards Freedom in the Arab World*. New York: UNDP, 2005.

United Nations Development Programme, *Arab Human Development Report 2002: Creating Opportunities for Future Generations*. New York: UNDP, 2002.

United Nations Development Programme, *Arab Human Development Report 2002: Building a Knowledge Society*. New York: UNDP, 2003

United Nations Development Programme and the Institute of National Planning, Egypt. *Egypt Human Development Report: Choosing our Future, Towards a New Social Contract*. Cairo, 2005.